The Concordance to the Peshitta Version

of the Aramaic New Testament

The Concordance to the Peshitta Version

of the Aramaic New Testament

American Christian Press
The Way International
New Knoxville, Ohio 45871

International Standard Book Number 0-910068-61-5
Library of Congress Catalog Card Number 85-051248
American Christian Press
The Way International
New Knoxville, Ohio 45871
 First Edition published 1985
Printed in the United States of America

Dedicated to God the Father of our Lord Jesus Christ
and to the followers of The Way International
whose prayers and loving support
have made this
project possible.

Edited by The Way International
Research Team

Contents

Preface

The concordance to the Peshitta Version of the Aramaic New Testament is a culmination of fifteen years of work by numerous individuals. For centuries, the Greek versions of the New Testament have received their due attention while the Aramaic versions, for the most part, have been neglected. For centuries Greek was treated as the one inveterate language retaining the original Word of God. Discoveries in textual criticism in the last 150 years, however, have shown that the Peshitta text, certain old Latin manuscripts, Coptic (Egyptian), and other versions play as vital a role as the Greek in ascertaining the original New Testament text. These aforementioned versions in particular represent an early role in the text history, so that their interplay with the Greek versions cannot be overlooked.

The Peshitta Version of the New Testament was produced, or more accurately, stabilized, by the fifth century. It became the accepted text of the Eastern church as the Byzantine Greek text became the standard text for the Western church around the same time. Similarly, the Latin Vulgate became the standard text of the Roman church around the sixth century.

The Peshitta Version is written in Eastern Aramaic, called Syriac by Western scholars. It was the language of the Eastern church as Greek was in the early Western church. It is related to, but not identical with, the Palestinian Aramaic spoken by Jesus and the writers of the New Testament. In recent times some scholars have demonstrated that a Palestinian Aramaic original lies behind the Greek versions of New Testament documents. This language, however, is not to be confused with the Peshitta Version written in Eastern Aramaic, or Syriac, centuries later. We have no original Palestinian Aramaic documents. Therefore, to reconstruct the original it is necessary to compare each of the early versions: Eastern Aramaic, Greek, Latin, and others. The research tools of the Peshitta Version are essential to this task.

To determine the original of a passage, one must compare the Greek, Eastern Aramaic, and other texts. At times the Greek clarifies the accurate rendition of the text, while at other times the Eastern Aramaic does. The old Latin, Coptic, and other versions may also contain an original reading lost to other versions. Our task as workmen "that needeth not to be ashamed, rightly dividing the word of truth" (II Timothy 2:15) is to ascertain the perfect, inerrant original through these versions.

The script used in writing the original documents is unknown, since there are no original Palestinian Aramaic documents in existence today. Even first-century inscriptions from the Palestine area are sparse. The oldest known manuscripts of the Peshitta Version were written in the Estrangelo script. The oldest of these manuscripts date from the fifth century and contain no vowel markings. We have selected the older Estrangelo script for our publications as the best representative of the ancient text. The Jacobite and Nestorian scripts of the later centuries do contain the vowel markings, which, in some cases, represent the scribe's interpretation of the text.

This concordance is designed for use by those with either a limited or a thorough knowledge of the Aramaic language. The data base retrieval system that was used to develop the concordance is available to visitors interested in further development of research tools. Using this concordance with an Aramaic or Syriac lexicon and New Testament, along with a Greek concordance, lexicon, and New Testament will make your study of God's Word excitingly valuable.

Introduction

The main body of the concordance is set up alphabetically by root. The roots were assigned according to C. Brockelman's *Lexicon Syriacum* with reference to works by R. Payne Smith, R. Kobert, L. Costaz, and others. The roots are alphabetized according to consonants only. Thus a root spelled ܐܘܫܦܐ , where the ܘ represents a vowel, would be found at ܐܫܦ . A word in parentheses at a root line indicates that the given form does not exist in Syriac but is given in the concordance for alphabetical purposes.

The associated words from each root are located after the root and indented. Each word including the root is assigned a number, a part of speech (or gender, for nouns), and a general English meaning. Each number represents a unique word.

After each word the verses are listed either in a double column or a string format. The string format is used when a word has a large number of verses or for words such as *when* and *then.*

The absolute form of nouns and adjectives at the root level is given when attested. This absolute form functions as the root. The emphatic state form is then given, separated by a comma. Nouns at the associated word level are usually given in the emphatic state.

The only ordinal numbers which have been assigned a number, a part of speech, and an English meaning are the units, tens, teens, and hundreds. All other numbers must be looked up as combinations of these.

Indeclinable words, when not associated with a root, are assigned to be their own root. There are several examples of indeclinable words that are given two forms separated by a comma. These forms represent two common ways of spelling that word.

For regular verbs, the Peal perfect, third person, masculine, singular form has been used as the base form when it exists. When this form is not attested, the probable form is given in parentheses. Verbs with middle weak letters show the weak letter in their base forms. Verbs ending in ܐ are alphabetized with that spelling. Exceptions have notes to refer the user to the proper location in the concordance.

The verses for a given verb are listed under their respective inflected forms. The Semitic verb is inflected by internal vowel changes or by affixes to alter its meaning. The various inflected forms are:

Peal	Ethpeel
Pael	Ethpaal
Aphel	Ettaphal
Saphel	Estaphal
Shaphel	Eshtaphal
P (*designates all quadriliterals*)	Ethp

In simplest terms, the left column expresses the active meaning, while the right column indicates the passive or reflexive meaning. (Sometimes this relationship does not hold.)

Within this format, verses are further separated by their parsing, e.g., Perfect, Imperfect, Participle, etc. At this level there is ambiguity in some forms. For example, in a few verbs, distinguishing between the Peal and Pael perfects with certain suffixes is not available when there is no distinction in meaning. A grammar should be consulted for these ambiguous forms. Some forms of the Ethpeel and Ethpaal for given verbs are also ambiguous. Verses where these forms are found are indicated by an asterisk.

When a verb occurs more than once in a verse, the reference includes a superscripted number. This number gives the order of occurrence for that given reference within the verse.

After the parsings, words associated with the given inflected form are then listed alphabetically. The only exception is when the active or passive participle form is used as an adjective or a substantized noun. When this occurs the form is given its own number, part of speech [(ap), (pp)], and general English meaning. Due to the verbal adjective nature of these words, they are placed at the head of the alphabetical listing. This placement facilitates comparison between the participles and the participles used as adjectives or nouns. Grammars may be consulted for discussion on the difficulty in determining the location of these forms.

Proper nouns have been located after the main body of the concordance. A few proper nouns, however, have been placed in the main

body due to their associated words. Notes are used to guide the user to the proper location.

The English meanings given represent a general definition arrived at by consulting the various lexicons and reviewing the verses where a given word occurs. The definitions were chosen, when possible, to reflect the English of the King James Version. This was done to facilitate comparative work for the beginning student. Of course, a lexicon should be consulted for a further explanation of a word.

Inflected forms of the verb often denote changes in meaning. These changes in meaning are indicated in the definitions by qualifiers (phrases or words in parentheses in the definition). The active meaning of all verbs is given when possible. The meaning of the passive inflections can be determined by the passive or reflexive of the active meaning. When the meaning of a passive form cannot be derived from the active meaning, that definition is provided.

Notes have been included throughout the concordance at points where there may be confusion concerning the location of a given word. Notes are also used to indicate cross-references to related words or idioms.

Every word in the New Testament is included except prepositional phrases with ܒ and ܠ . These inseparable particles have been assigned a number but will not occur in the main body of the concordance. All verses were verified several times, and then a comparison was made against C. Schaaf's *Lexicon Syriacum Concordantiale.* Beginning students should be aware that the verse references in this concordance refer to the Peshitta Version of the New Testament. Discrepancies between verses found in the King James Version and the Peshitta do occur.

The index follows the proper noun section and will be particularly helpful to the beginning student. In contrast to the main concordance, the alphabetical order of the index takes into account the vowels. Hence, ܐܘܡܢܐ is found in the index at ܐܘܡܢܐ . This listing is also in numerical order. Alongside the number and word is given the page number and column of its location in the concordance. Thus the location of any word in the concordance can be determined if its number or spelling is known.

Also included with the word is a guide to pronunciation. Each consonant and vowel of a given word is represented by a standard phonetic symbol. For verbs that do not occur in the Peal inflection, the pronunciation given is identified by the name of its inflection. The pronunciation for the Peal third person, singular, masculine form of the middle weak verbs is given and noted by (pe 3sm). The *linea occultans* (symbol to not pronounce a letter) is indicated by putting the designated letter in parentheses.

How to Use the Concordance

The concordance can be used by looking up the root of any given word. If the root is not known, the user may refer to the index in the back. By locating the word in the index, the user can find the page and column number for the location of the word.

Upon turning to the page number and column in the concordance, the following format is found:

1. A nonverb root

DIAGRAM I

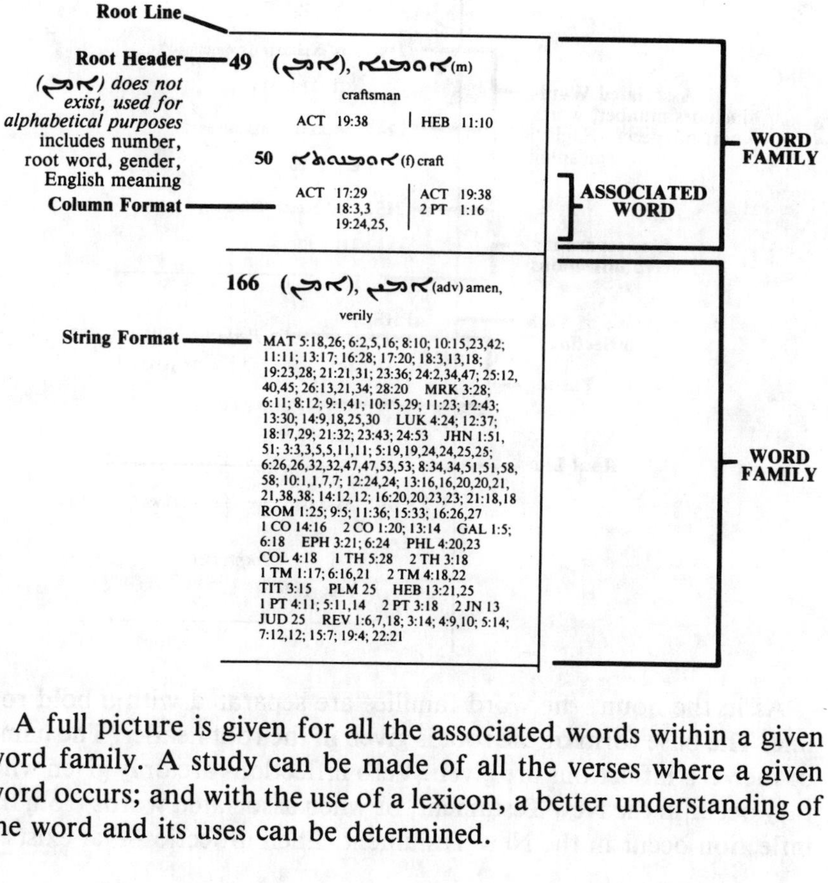

A full picture is given for all the associated words within a given word family. A study can be made of all the verses where a given word occurs; and with the use of a lexicon, a better understanding of the word and its uses can be determined.

2. A verb root

DIAGRAM II

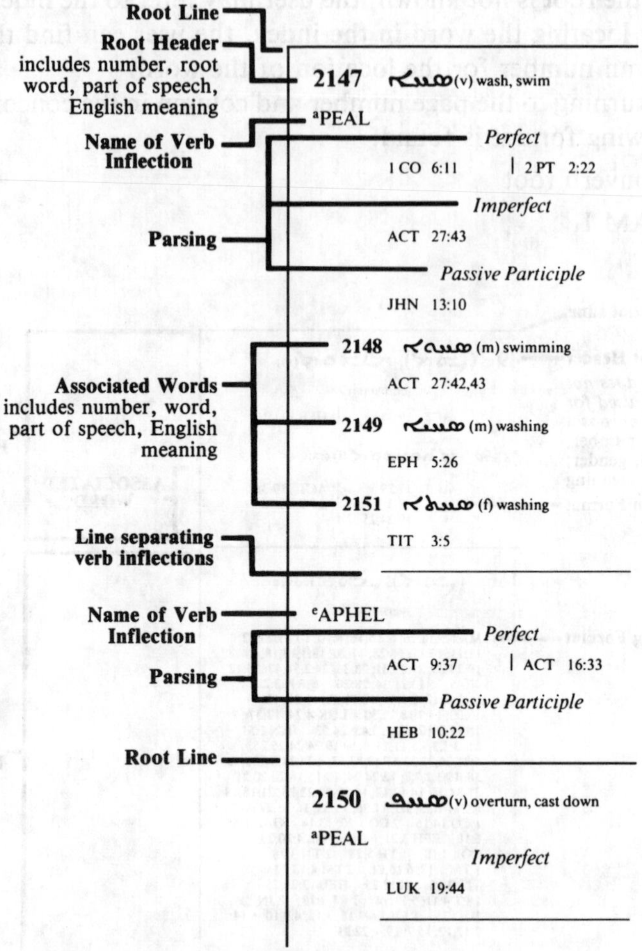

As in the noun, the word families are separated with a bold root line. The base form of the root is given in the root header. The names of the verb inflections are given. Verb inflections are only given when they occur in the New Testament, or when associated words from this inflection occur in the New Testament. Each inflection that exists in

the New Testament is further divided according to its parsing. Associated words of a given verb inflection are indented and listed after the parsings. A light line separates the different verb inflections. Since the inflection of the Semitic verb is often accompanied by a change in meaning, word studies of a given verb should be done within each inflection. The concordance has been designed for this type of study.

DIAGRAM III

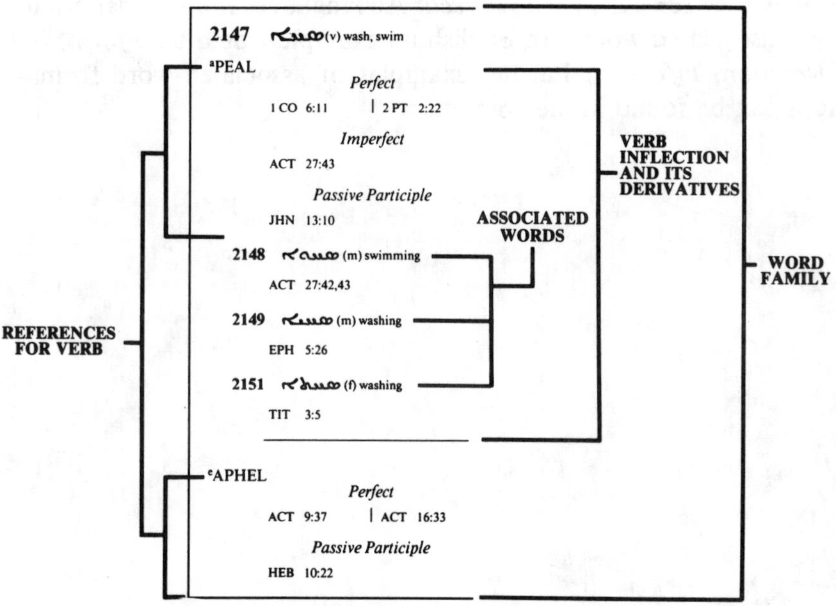

The references for the verb are spread throughout the word family according to each verb inflection. Thus, in the example, notice that some of the verses for the verb are located after the inflection called

PEAL. (The superscript *a* is for easy reference purposes. The number 2147[a] can be used to refer to the Peal of word 2147 in future publications.) The word PEAL is located directly under the number of the verb to indicate that the following verses belong to the Peal inflection of the verb. The word APHEL is also located directly under the number of the verb. The verses following give the occurrences for the Aphel inflection of the verb.

Many words are derived from a particular verb inflection. For example, from the Peal inflection a word with a short vowel or schwa after the first letter and an *ā* after the second letter often stands for the name of the action of the verb, e.g., ܥܒܕ , (ʻəḇaḏ) *to do* is changed to ܥܒܕܐ , (ʻəḇāḏā) *deed.* All languages follow a pattern to form associated words. In English an example would be *inform, information, informer*. Further examples of associated word formations can be found in the grammars.

Pronunciation Guide

As stated in the overview, the index includes a guide to pronunciation for each word. Each consonant and vowel is represented by a standard phonetic symbol. The pronunciation of the letters can only be determined approximately. The letters ܒ, ܓ, ܕ, ܟ, ܦ, ܬ, have two pronunciations. The hard sounds are represented by our English *b, g, d, k, p, and t* respectively and should be sounded the same. The soft sounds are indicated by a horizontal line: *ḇ, ḡ, ḏ, ḵ, p̄, ṯ*. The soft ܒ should be sounded as our English *v*. The soft ܓ cannot easily be distinguished from the hard, and both are pronounced *g* as in *good*. The soft ܕ corresponds to the English *th* in *their* or *other*. The soft ܟ corresponds to the German *ch* in *ach*. The soft ܦ is equal to an *f*. The soft ܬ corresponds to a *th* as in *think*. Rules for determining whether a letter is hard or soft can be found in the grammars. In manuscripts and printed texts a dot is placed above the letter to indicate the hard sound and below for the soft sound.

The ܘ when used as a consonant has the sound of a *w* and the ܝ the sound of a consonantal *y*. The letter ܙ is a soft *s* sound as in *chosen*.

The ܚ is a difficult sound for non-Semitic speakers to pronounce. We have no equivalent Indo-European sound. The closest representative is a gutteral *h* sounded from the throat. The letter ܛ is a *t* sound formed when the tip of the tongue is placed against the palate. The ܩ is similar to the ܚ though its sound is formed further back in the throat. The pronunciation of the ܨ is the standard modern substitution for the original sound which can only be conjectured as the *ts* in *hits*.

The sound of the ܐ and ܥ is another foreign sound to Indo-European languages. These letters represent a glottal stop. The sound of the ܐ can best be illustrated by the glottal stop necessary to make the distinction between the two phrases:

a nice man

an ice man

The ܥ is similar, though it represents a more gutteral sound than

the ܥ . Pronouncing both of these as a glottal stop is a good representative pronunciation. The ܫ is pronounced as *sh* and the ܪ as an *r*. The remaining letters are sounded as their transliteration equivalent.

The length of vowels does not refer to quality as in English (for example: ă, hat; ā, gate) but to quantity. The long ā is similar to the *a* in *father*. The length of time the vowel is sounded in *father* is long compared to the time the vowel is sounded in *hat*. The following chart gives the closest English equivalents to the various vowels and consonants.

Transliteration Chart

Consonants

ܐ	ʼ	ܠ	l
ܒ	b, ḇ	ܡ ܡ	m
ܓ	g, ḡ	ܢ ܢ	n
ܕ	d, ḏ	ܣ	s
ܗ	h	ܥ	ʻ
ܘ	w	ܦ	p, p̄
ܙ	z	ܨ	ṣ
ܚ	ḥ	ܩ	q
ܛ	ṭ	ܪ	r
ܝ	y	ܫ	š
ܟ ܟ	k, ḵ	ܬ	t, ṯ

Vowels

ܰ	a	ܘ ܰ—	au
ܳ	ā	ܘ ܳ—	āu
ܶ	e	ܘ ܶ—	eu
ܺ	ı	ܘ —	u, o
ܐ ܰ—	a	ܝ ܰ—	aı
ܐ ܳ—	ā	ܝ ܳ—	āı
ܐ ܶ—	ē	ܝ ܶ—	eı, ē
ܐ ܺ—	ı	ܝ ܺ—	ī

List of Abbreviations

adj	adjective
adv	adverb
alw	always
ap	active participle
aph	aphel
c	common *(used for both m and f)*
cf	compare
comp	compound
conj	conjunction
denom	denominative
deriv	derivative
eg	for example
eshta	eshtaphal
estaph	estaphal
ethp	passive of quadriliteral verb
ethpa	ethpaal
ethpe	ethpeel
ettaph	ettaphal
expr fut	expresses future
f	feminine
imperf	imperfect
impers	impersonal
incl	includes
incl idioms	includes idioms *(see lexicon for additional information)*
inf	infinitive
int	intransitive
intrj	interjection
Jac	Jacobite text
m	masculine
Nest	Nestorian text
non occ	nonoccurring in New Testament
num	ordinal number
p	active of quadriliteral verb
pa	pael
pa II	pael—second form
pe	peal
pl	plural
pn	proper noun
pp	passive participle
prep	preposition
pron	pronoun
saph	saphel
shaph	shaphel
subst	substantive
subst v	substantive verb
tr	transitive
v	verb
w/	with

ܐ

1 ܐܐܪ (c) air

1 CO 9:26
14:9
EPH 2:2
1 TH 4:17
REV 9:2
16:17

2 ܐܒ, ܐܒܐ (m) father

MAT 2:22
3:9
4:21,22
5:16,45,48
6:1,4,6,6,8,
9,14,15,
18,18,26,
32
7:11,21
8:21
10:20,21,
21,29,
32,33,
35,37
11:25,26,
27,27,
27
12:50
13:43
15:4,4,5,5,
13
16:17,27
18:10,14,
19,35
19:5,19,29
20:23
21:31
23:9,9,30,
32
24:36
25:34
26:39,42,
53
28:18,19
MRK 1:20
5:40
7:10,10,11,
12
8:38
9:21,24
10:7,19,29
11:10,25,
26
13:12,12,
32
MRK 14:36,36
15:21
LUK 1:17,32,55,
59,62,67,
72,73
2:27,48,49
3:8
6:23,26,36
8:50,51,56
9:26,42,59
10:21,21,
22,22,
22
11:2,11,13,
47,48
12:30,32,
53,53
14:26
15:12,17,
18,18,
20,20,
21,22,
27,28,
29,31
16:24,27,
27,30
18:20,29
21:16
22:29,42
23:34,46
24:49
JHN 1:14,18
2:16
3:35
4:12,20,21,
23,23,53
5:17,18,19,
19,20,21,
22,23,23,
26,36,36,
37,43,45
6:27,31,32,
37,40,42,
44,45,46,
46,49,57,
JHN 6:57,58,65
7:22
8:16,18,19,
19,19,27,
28,29,38,
38,39,41,
41,42,44,
44,44,49,
53,54,56
9:2,3,18,
20,22,23
10:15,15,
17,18,
25,29,
29,30,
32,36,
37,38,
38
11:41
12:26,27,
28,49,
50
13:1,3
14:2,6,7,8,
9,9,10,
10,10,
11,11,
12,13,
16,20,
21,23,
24,26,
28,28,
31,31
15:1,8,9,
10,15,
16,23,
24,26,
26
16:3,10,15,
16,17,
23,25,
26,27,
28,28,
32
17:1,5,11,
17,21,
24,25
18:11
20:17,17,
17,21
ACT 1:4,7
2:29,33
3:13,25
5:30
ACT 7:2,2,4,8,9,
11,12,14,
15,19,20,
32,38,39,
44,45,51,
52
13:17,32,
36
15:10
16:1,3
22:1,3,14
24:14
26:6
28:8,17,25
ROM 1:7,30
4:1,11,12,
12,16,17,
18
6:4
8:15,15
9:5,10
11:28
15:6,8
1 CO 1:3
4:15
5:1
8:6
10:1
15:24
2 CO 1:2,3,3
6:18
11:31
12:14,14
GAL 1:1,3,4,14
4:2,6,6
EPH 1:2,3,17
2:18
3:14
4:6
5:20,31
6:1,2,4,23
PHL 1:2
2:11,22
4:20
COL 1:2,3,12
2:2
3:17,20,21
1 TH 1:1,3
2:11
3:11,13
2 TH 1:1,2
2:16
1 TM 1:2,9
5:1,4

2 TM 1:2,3
TIT 1:4
PLM 3
HEB 1:1,5; 3:9; 7:3,4,10; 8:9; 11:23; 12:7,9,9
JAM 1:17,27; 2:21; 3:9
1 PT 1:2,3,17,18
2 PT 1:17
2 PT 3:4,18
1 JN 1:2,3; 2:1,13,13,14,15,16,22,23,23,24; 3:1; 4:14
2 JN 3,3,4,9
JUD 1
REV 1:6; 2:27; 3:5,21; 14:1

6 ܐܒܗܘܬܐ (f) family

EPH 3:15

3 ܐܒܐ (m) fruit

JUD 12
REV 18:14

7 (ܐܒܒ), ܐܒܘܒܐ (m) pipe

1 CO 14:7

4 ܐܒܕ (v) perish; (aph) destroy, lose

[a]PEAL

Perfect

MAT 10:6
LUK 15:4[2]
JHN 17:12
1 CO 10:10
1 CO 15:18
HEB 11:31
2 PT 3:6
JUD 11

Imperfect

MAT 5:29,30; 18:14
LUK 13:3,5,33; 15:4[1]; 21:18
JHN 3:15,16
JHN 6:12; 10:28; 11:50
ACT 3:23
ROM 2:12
2 PT 3:9

Active Participle

MAT 8:25; 9:17
MRK 2:22; 4:38
LUK 5:37; 8:24; 15:17
JHN 6:27
ACT 27:22,34
1 CO 8:11
2 CO 2:15; 4:3,9
JAM 1:11

10 ܐܒܝܕܐ (pp) lost

MAT 18:11
LUK 15:6,9,24,32
LUK 19:10
1 CO 1:18
2 TH 2:10

5 ܐܒܕܢܐ (m) loss, destruction

MAT 7:13; 26:8
MRK 14:4
JHN 17:12
ACT 8:20
ROM 9:22
1 CO 5:5
PHL 1:28; 3:19
1 TH 5:3
2 TH 1:9; 2:3
1 TM 6:9
HEB 10:39
2 PT 2:1,1,3; 3:7,16
REV 17:8,11

[e]APHEL

Perfect

MAT 22:7
LUK 17:27,29
JHN 18:9
1 CO 10:9
JUD 5

Imperfect

MAT 2:13; 10:28,39[1],39[2],42; 12:14; 16:25[1],25[2]; 21:41; 27:20
MRK 3:6; 8:35[1],35[2]; 9:22,41; 11:18; 12:9
LUK 9:24[2],25; 15:8; 17:33[1],33[2]; 20:16
JHN 6:39; 10:10; 12:25
ROM 14:15
1 CO 1:19
HEB 10:35
JAM 4:12
2 JN 8

Infinitive

MRK 1:24; 3:4
LUK 4:34
LUK 6:9; 9:56; 19:47

Active Participle

LUK 9:24[1]

15 ܐܒܠ (v) mourn

[a]PEAL (non occ)

12 ܐܒܝܠܐ (pp) sad, mourner

MAT 5:4
MRK 16:10
REV 18:15,19

16 ܐܒܠܐ (m) mourning

1 CO 5:2	REV 18:7,7,8
2 CO 7:7	21:4
JAM 4:9	

[b]ETHPEEL

Perfect

ACT 8:2

Imperfect

LUK 6:25	REV 18:11
2 CO 12:21	

Imperative

JAM 4:9

17 ܐܒܢܐ (c) stone

1 PT 2:8

20 (ܐܓܢܐ), ܐܓܘܢܐ (m)

contest

1 CO 9:25	2 TM 4:7
PHL 1:30	HEB 10:32
COL 2:1	12:1,4
1 TH 2:2	JUD 3
1 TM 6:12	

24 ܐܓܢܐ (f) waterpot

JHN 2:6,7

25 ܐܓܪ (v) hire

[a]PEAL

Perfect

MAT 20:7	ACT 28:30

Imperfect

MAT 20:1

23 ܐܓܝܪܐ (pp) hired servant, hireling

MRK 1:20	JHN 10:12,13,13
LUK 15:17,19	

26 ܐܓܪܐ (m) pay, reward

MAT 5:12,46	1 CO 3:8,14
6:1,2,5,16	9:17,18
10:41,41,42	1 TM 5:18
20:8	HEB 10:35
MRK 9:41	11:26
LUK 6:23,35	JAM 5:4
10:7	2 PT 2:13,15
JHN 4:36	2 JN 8
ACT 1:18	JUD 11
ROM 4:4	REV 11:18
	22:12

27 ܐܓܪܐ (m) roof

see also 439 ܒܪ ܐܓܪܐ

MAT 10:27	LUK 5:19
24:17	12:3
MRK 2:4	17:31
13:15	ACT 10:9

29 (ܐܓܪܐ), ܐܓܪܬܐ (f)

letter

ACT 9:2	1 CO 16:3
15:23,30	2 CO 3:1,2,3
17:15	7:8,8
22:5	10:9,10,11
23:25,33,34	COL 4:16
28:21	1 TH 5:27
ROM 16:22	2 TH 2:2,15
1 CO 5:9	3:14,17
	2 PT 3:1,16

22 (ܐܓܘܪܣܐ), ܐܓܪܘܣܐ (m) field

MAT 27:7,8,10	MRK 6:36

33 ܐܕܢܐ (f) ear

MAT 10:27	LUK 12:3
11:15	14:35
13:9,15,15,16,43	22:50,51
26:51	JHN 18:10,26
MRK 4:9,23	ACT 7:57
7:16,33,35	11:22
8:18	28:27
14:47	ROM 6:16
LUK 1:44	10:17,17
4:21	11:8
8:8	1 CO 2:9
9:44	12:16
	2 TM 4:4

JAM 5:4	REV 2:29
1 PT 3:12	3:6,13,22
REV 2:7,11,17,	13:9

34 ܐܕܪ, ܐܕܪܐ (m) threshing floor

MAT 3:12	LUK 3:17

36 ܐܕܫ, ܐܕܫܐ (m) profit, fruit

ROM 1:13	ROM 15:28
6:21	

38 ܐܘ (intrj) behold

MAT 15:28 LUK 24:25 ACT 1:1; 7:51; 13:10; 18:14; 26:13 ROM 2:1,3; 9:20; 11:33 1 CO 15:55 GAL 3:1 1 TM 6:11,20 JAM 2:20; 5:1

39 ܐܘ (conj) or; (ܐܘ...ܐܘ) either...or

MAT 5:17,18,36; 6:24,24,31,31,31; 7:4,9,16; 9:5; 10:11,14,15,19,37,37; 11:3,22,24; 12:5, 29,33,33; 13:21; 15:5,5; 16:14,26; 17:25; 18:8,8,8,16,16,20; 19:24,29,29,29,29,29,29, 29; 20:15,15,22; 21:25; 22:17; 23:17,19; 24:23,26; 25:37,38,39,44,44,44,44,44; 26:53; 27:17 MRK 2:9; 3:4,4; 4:17,21; 6:11; 7:12; 8:37; 9:43,45,47; 10:25,29,29,29,29,29,29, 29; 11:30; 12:14,14; 13:35,35,35
LUK 2:24; 5:23; 6:9,9,42; 7:19,20; 8:16; 9:25; 10:12,14; 11:33; 12:11,38,41; 13:4,15; 14:5,12,12,31; 15:7,8; 16:13,13,17; 17:2,7; 18:25,29,29,29,29; 20:4,22; 22:27,68
JHN 2:6; 4:27; 6:19; 7:17,48; 9:2,21; 13:29; 18:34 ACT 1:7; 3:12,12; 4:7; 7:42,49; 8:34; 9:2; 10:28; 17:29,29; 18:14,14; 19:12; 20:33,33; 23:9,29; 24:20; 25:6,11; 26:31
ROM 2:4,15; 3:1,8; 4:9,10; 6:3; 7:1; 8:35,35, 35,35,35,35; 9:11,21; 10:14,14,15; 11:2,34; 14:10 1 CO 1:13,13,20,20; 3:5,12,12,12, 12,12; 4:3,7,21; 5:10,10,10,11,11,11,11,11; 6:2,9,16,19; 7:11,15,16; 8:5,5; 9:1,1,1,6,7,7; 10:19,22; 11:4,5,6,22; 12:30; 13:1; 14:6,6,6, 6,7,23,24,29,36,36,37; 15:37,37; 16:6
2 CO 1:17; 3:1,1; 6:14,15,15; 9:7; 10:12; 11:4,4,7; 13:5 GAL 1:8,10,10; 2:2; 3:2,5, 15 EPH 5:4,4,5,5 PHL 2:3; 3:12
COL 2:16 1 TM 2:9,9; 5:4,16
2 TM 2:20 TIT 3:12 PLM 18
HEB 6:1; 12:15,16 JAM 2:2,3,15; 3:12,12, 14; 4:5,11,13,15 1 PT 3:3,3; 4:15,15
2 PT 2:21 REV 3:15,15; 9:20; 13:16,17, 17; 20:4

40 ܐܘܐ (v) agree; (pa) reconcile

[a]PEAL (non occ)

45 ܐܘܝܘܬܐ (f) unity

2 CO 6:16	PHL 3:16
13:11	1 PT 3:8
EPH 4:3	

53 ܐܘܢܐ (m) dwelling place

JHN 14:2,23

[d]ETHPAAL

Participle

MAT 5:25

47 ܐܘܟܪܝܣܛܝܐ (f) breaking of bread

ACT 2:42	ACT 20:7

52 ܐܘ (intrj) oh

MAT 17:17	MRK 15:29
MRK 9:19	LUK 9:41

54 ܐܘܢܓܠܝܘܢ (m) gospel

MRK 1:1	GAL 2:14
ROM 1:1,9,16	EPH 3:6
2:16	6:15
10:16	PHL 1:5,7,12,
11:28	16,27
15:16,29	4:3
16:24	COL 1:23
1 CO 9:18	1 TM 1:11
15:1	2 TM 1:8,10
2 CO 4:3,4	2:8
8:18	PLM 13

57 ܐܘܓܝܐ (m) anchor

ACT 27:28,29,	HEB 6:19
40	

86 (.ܐܝܙܓܕ), ܐܝܙܓܕܐ. (m)

ambassador

LUK 14:32; 19:14
2 CO 5:20
EPH 6:20

72 ܐܙܠ (v) go

[a]PEAL

Perfect

MAT 2:9[1],12,13; 4:20,22,25; 8:33; 9:7,9,19; 11:7; 12:15; 13:25,44,46; 14:13; 16:4; 18:30; 19:15,22; 20:5,34; 21:6,29,30; 22:5,15,22; 25:10,16,18,25; 26:14,42,44; 27:3,5,60,66; 28:8,11,16
MRK 1:18,20,35,42; 2:14; 3:7; 5:20,24; 6:27,32,46; 7:30; 8:13; 10:1,22; 11:4; 12:12; 14:10,39; 16:10,13
LUK 1:23,38,39; 2:15; 4:20,30,42[1]; 5:13,25,28; 7:14,24; 8:39; 9:11,13,52,56; 10:30; 15:13,15; 19:12,32; 22:4,13,39[1],39[2]; 24:12,24
JHN 1:37,40; 4:28,43,47,50[2]; 5:15; 6:1,2,66; 7:53; 8:1,59; 9:7[2],11[2]; 10:40; 11:28,31[1],46,54; 12:19,36; 18:6; 20:10
ACT 5:22,26,36[1]; 7:13; 8:27; 9:17,26,39; 10:7,23[1],23[2]; 12:17; 13:13,43; 15:38,39; 16:38; 18:22,27[2]; 19:21[2],29; 20:1,5,13; 21:26; 28:14
GAL 1:17[1],17[2],18
2 TM 4:10
2 PT 2:15
JUD 7,11
REV 9:12; 10:9; 11:14; 12:17; 16:2; 18:14[1],14[2]; 21:1,5

Imperfect

MAT 2:8[2],22[1],22[2]; 8:18,21,31; 10:5; 13:28; 14:15,22; 16:21; 25:46; 26:36,46; 28:10[2]
MRK 5:17,37; 6:31[1],36,37,45; 9:43; 14:12,42
LUK 1:17,76; 4:42[2]; 8:37; 9:12,51,59,61; 11:5; 13:33; 14:8; 15:18; 16:28,30; 17:23; 19:28; 21:8
JHN 6:68; 11:7,16; 14:3,31; 15:16; 16:7[1],7[3]; 20:15
ACT 1:25; 7:40; 8:20,28; 14:16; 16:7; 17:15; 18:18,27[1]; 19:21[1]; 20:11,30; 21:4,5,12; 22:5; 23:23[2]; 25:20; 27:3,7,30
1 CO 16:4[1],4[2]
1 TM 4:1
HEB 11:15
2 PT 2:2
REV 14:4

Imperative

MAT 2:8[1],20; 4:10; 5:24,41; 8:4,9[1],13,32; 9:6,13; 10:6; 11:4; 16:23; 17:27; 18:15; 19:21; 20:4,7,14; 21:2,28; 22:9; 25:9,41; 26:18; 27:65; 28:7,10[1],19
MRK 1:44; 2:11; 5:19,34; 6:38; 7:29; 8:33; 10:21; 11:2; 14:13[1],13[2]; 16:7,15
LUK 5:14,24; 7:8[1],22,50; 8:48; 9:60; 10:3,37; 13:31,32; 14:10; 17:14[1],19; 18:22; 19:30; 22:8,10
JHN 4:16,50[1]; 7:3; 8:11; 9:7[1],11[1]; 20:17
ACT 5:20; 8:26; 9:11,15; 10:20; 11:12; 16:36; 21:24; 22:10,21; 23:23[1]; 24:25; 28:26
JAM 2:16
REV 10:8; 16:1

Infinitive

MAT 14:16; 24:1
LUK 8:31; 9:53; 10:1
JHN 6:67; 7:35[1],35[2]
ACT 20:3
1 CO 10:27

Active Participle

MAT 2:9[2] 5:13 7:13 8:9[2],19 10:7 12:45 15:17 18:12 21:9 26:24,58
MRK 2:23 6:31[2],33 10:32,52 14:21 16:12
LUK 2:3,41 7:6,8[2],11 8:42 9:57[1],57[2] 11:24,26 12:58 13:15,22 14:19,25,31,35 15:4 17:11,14[2] 18:39 19:36 22:22 24:13,28[1],28[2]
JHN 3:8 6:21 7:33 8:14[1],14[2],21[1],21[2],22 10:4[1],4[2],5 11:8,11,31[2],44 12:11,35 13:3,33,36[1],36[2] 14:2,4,5,12,28[1],28[2] 16:5[1],5[2],7[2],10,16,17,28 18:8 21:3
ACT 1:10 5:36[2],37 8:36,39 9:3,7 12:9 16:4,16 18:6 20:22,29 21:2 22:6 25:12 26:12 27:2,6
ROM 15:24,25
1 CO 16:6
GAL 2:14
1 TM 1:3 5:24
HEB 11:8
JAM 4:13
2 PT 1:16 2:10 3:17
1 JN 2:11
JUD 18
REV 13:10 16:14 17:8,11 18:17

73 ܐܚܐ (m) brother

MAT 1:2,11 4:18,18,21,21 5:22,22,23,24,47 7:3,4,5 10:2,2,21,21 12:46,47,48,49,50 13:55 14:3 17:1 18:15,15,21,35 19:29 20:24 22:24,24,25,25 23:8 25:40 28:10
MRK 1:16,19 3:17,31,32,33,34,35 5:37 6:3,17,18 10:29,30 12:19,19,19,20 13:12,12
LUK 3:1,19 6:14,41,42,42,42 8:19,20,21 12:13 14:12,26 15:27,32 16:28 17:3 18:29 20:28,28,28,29 21:16 22:32
JHN 1:40,41 2:12 6:8 7:3,5,10 11:1,2,19,21,23,32 20:17 21:23
ACT 1:14,16 2:29,37 3:17,22 4:23 6:3 7:2,13,23,25,26,37 9:17,30 10:23,45 11:1,12,29 12:2,12,17 13:15,26,38 14:2 15:1,3,7,13,22,23,23,32,33,36,40 16:40 17:6,9,10,14 18:18,27 21:7,16,17,20 22:1,5,13 23:1,5,6 28:14,15,17,21
ROM 1:13 7:1,4 8:12,29 9:3 10:1 11:25 12:1,10,16 14:10,10,13,15,21 15:14,15,30 16:14,17,23
1 CO 1:1,10,11,26 2:1 3:1 4:6 5:11 6:1,5,5,6,6,8 7:12,15,24,29 8:12,13,13 9:5 10:1 11:2,33 12:1 14:6,20,26,39 15:1,6,31,50,58 16:11,12,12,15,20
2 CO 1:1,8 2:13 7:2 8:1,18,22,23 9:3,5 11:9,26 12:18 13:11
GAL 1:2,11,19 2:4 3:15 4:12,28,31 5:11,13 6:1,18
EPH 6:10,21,23
PHL 1:12,14 2:25 3:1,13,17 4:1,8,21
COL 1:1,2 4:7,9,15
1 TH 1:4 2:1,9,14,17 3:2,7 4:1,6,9,10,10,13 5:1,4,12,14,25,26,27
2 TH 1:3 2:1,13,15 3:1,6,6,13,15,18
1 TM 4:6 5:1 6:2
2 TM 4:21
PLM 1,16,20
HEB 2:11,12,17 3:1,12 6:9 7:5 8:11 10:19 13:1,22,23
JAM 1:2,9,16,

JAM 1:19; 2:1,5,14,15; 3:1,10,12; 4:11,11,11; 5:7,9,10,12,19
1 PT 2:17; 5:9,12
2 PT 1:10; 3:15
1 JN 2:9,10,11; 3:10,12,12,13,14,14,15,16,17; 4:20,20,21; 5:16
3 JN 3,5,10
JUD 1
REV 1:9; 6:11; 19:10; 22:9

75 ܐܚܘܬܐ (f) brotherhood

2 PT 1:7,7

78 ܐܚܝܢܐ (adj) kinsman

MRK 3:21; 6:4
LUK 1:36; 14:12; 21:16
JHN 18:26
ROM 9:3; 16:7,11,21

1124 ܚܬܐ (f) sister

MAT 12:50; 13:56; 19:29
MRK 3:35; 6:3; 10:29,30
LUK 10:39,40; 14:26
JHN 11:3,28,39; 19:25
ACT 23:16
ROM 16:1,15
1 CO 7:15; 9:5
1 TM 5:2
JAM 2:15
2 JN 13

74 ܐܚܕ (v) take, hold; (aph) cause to take, lease; (aph w/ ܢܘܪܐ) kindle

[a]PEAL

see below 77 ܐܚܕ ܒܠ

Perfect

MAT 9:25; 14:3,31; 18:28; 21:35,39; 22:6; 26:50,55[2],57; 28:9
MRK 1:31; 5:41; 6:17; 8:23; 9:10,27; 14:46,49,51
LUK 4:36,42; 5:5,9,26; 7:16; 8:37,54; 14:4; 22:54; 23:26
JHN 8:20; 18:12; 21:6
ACT 1:16; 3:7; 5:18; 7:58; 9:27; 12:4; 16:19; 17:19; 18:17; 21:30[1],33; 22:11; 23:19,27; 24:6; 26:21; 27:16,20
HEB 8:9
REV 20:3

Imperfect

MAT 21:38; 26:4,55[1]
MRK 14:1,48
LUK 13:25; 20:20; 22:52
JHN 7:32,44; 10:39; 11:57; 20:23[1]
ACT 13:11
1 CO 7:2[1],2[2]
2 TH 3:15
1 TM 3:9; 6:1
2 TM 2:17
PLM 13,15
HEB 3:6; 6:18; 12:28
1 JN 3:17
REV 11:6

Imperative

MAT 6:6; 26:48
ROM 14:22
EPH 6:17
PHL 2:29
1 TH 5:21
1 PT 3:7
REV 2:25; 3:11

Infinitive

MAT 21:46[1]
MRK 3:21; 12:12
LUK 11:54; 20:26
JHN 7:30; 16:12
ACT 12:3
2 CO 11:32
REV 3:8

Active Participle

MAT 12:11
MRK 2:2
LUK 8:15; 14:9
JHN 2:6
1 CO 3:19; 9:25
COL 2:19
JAM 1:26
REV 3:7[1],7[2]

Passive Participle

MAT 5:23; 8:14; 14:5; 21:26,46[2]; 23:14
MRK 7:3,8; 11:32; 16:8
LUK 3:17; 11:7; 22:63; 24:16
JHN 20:19,23[2],26
ACT 3:11; 5:23; 8:7; 9:8
ROM 1:18; 3:9; 7:6
1 CO 7:25; 11:2
2 CO 4:1; 6:10
EPH 6:12
2 TH 2:6,7
1 TM 3:4
HEB 2:14
JAM 2:1
1 PT 3:19
1 JN 5:12[1],12[2],12[3]
REV 2:1,13,14,15; 7:1; 11:17

43 ܐܘܚܕܢܐ (m) dominion

LUK	2:1	REV	1:6
1 PT	5:11		5:13
JUD	25		

77 ܐܚܝܕ ܟܠ (idiom) holder of all, almighty

from 1425 ܟܠ and 74 ܐܚܕ (above)

2 CO	6:18	REV	15:3
HEB	1:3		16:7,14
REV	1:8		19:6,15
	4:8		21:22

---

[b]ETHPEEL

Perfect

MAT	25:10	JHN	8:3,4
LUK	4:25	ACT	21:30[2]

Imperfect

ACT	2:24	REV	21:25

---

[e]APHEL

Perfect

MAT	21:33	LUK	22:55
MRK	12:1	ACT	28:2
LUK	20:9		

Imperfect

MAT 21:41

Imperative

MRK 14:44

1110 (ܐܚܪ), ܚܪܬܐ (f) end

MAT	10:22,23	LUK	14:10
	12:45		20:32
	21:29,32		21:9
	22:27	JHN	13:1,36
	24:13	ACT	27:29
	25:11	ROM	6:21,22
	26:58	1 CO	10:11
MRK	3:26		15:8,24
	4:38	2 CO	11:15
	12:6	PHL	3:19
	13:7,13	1 TH	2:16
	14:41	HEB	3:6
LUK	4:2		6:8,11
	11:26		9:26
HEB	12:11	2 PT	2:20
JAM	5:11		3:3
1 PT	1:20	JUD	18
	4:7,17		

80 ܐܚܪܝܐ (adj) last

MAT	4:2	JHN	12:48
	5:26	ACT	2:17
	19:30,30		27:41
	20:8,12,14, 16,16	1 CO	1:8
			4:9
	21:37		15:26,45, 52
	26:60		
	27:64	2 CO	1:13
MRK	4:28	1 TM	4:1
	9:35	2 TM	3:1
	10:31,31	HEB	1:2
	12:6,22		3:14
	16:14	JAM	5:3
LUK	12:59	1 PT	1:5
	13:30,30	1 JN	2:18,18
	14:9	REV	1:17
JHN	6:39,40,44, 54		2:8,19
			15:1
	7:37		21:9
	11:24		22:13

81 ܐܚܪܢܐ (adj) another, other

MAT	2:12	MRK	16:12
	4:21	LUK	3:18
	5:39		4:43
	6:24,24		5:7,29
	8:9,21		6:6,29
	11:3		7:8,19,20, 41
	12:45		
	13:5,7,8, 24,31, 33		8:3,6,7,8
			9:8,8,19, 19,56,59, 61
	15:30		
	16:14,14		10:1
	19:9		11:16,26
	20:3,6		13:33
	21:8,30,33, 36,41		14:19,20
			16:7,13,13, 18
	22:4		
	25:11,16, 17,20, 20,22		17:34,35, 36
			18:10
	26:67,71		19:20
	27:42,61		20:11,16
	28:1		22:58,59, 65
MRK	4:5,7,8,19, 36		
			23:32,35
	6:15,15		24:1
	7:4	JHN	1:35,43
	8:28,28		4:37,37,38
	10:11,12		5:7,32,43
	11:8,12		6:22,23
	12:4,5,5,9, 31,32		7:12,41,41
			9:16
	14:58		10:1,16,21
	15:31,41		12:12,29,

JHN 12:35, 13:33, 14:16,18, 15:24, 18:15,16,34, 19:18,32,37, 20:2,3,30, 21:2,8,18,25
ACT 1:20, 2:13,40, 4:3,5,12,12, 5:13,16, 7:18,26, 8:7,34, 10:9,24, 12:6,17, 13:35,42,44, 14:20, 15:2,35, 16:11, 17:7,18,18,21,32,34, 19:32,32,39, 20:7,15,15,15, 21:1,8,18,26, 22:30, 23:32, 24:27, 25:6,17,23, 26:11,17, 27:1,3,18,44, 28:24
ROM 2:21, 7:3,3,4,23, 8:39, 13:9, 15:14
1 CO 1:16, 3:4,10,11, 8:4, 9:2,12,27, 10:29, 12:8,9,9,10,10,10,10,10, 14:19,21,30, 15:39,39,39,39,40,40,41,41,41
2 CO 1:13, 3:1, 8:13,23, 10:15,16, 11:4,4,4,8, 12:13,17, 13:2
GAL 1:6,19, 5:10, 6:4
EPH 3:5
PHL 2:20
1 TH 2:6
1 TM 6:3
2 TM 2:2,17
HEB 4:7,8, 5:6, 6:1, 7:11,13,15, 11:35,36,36,37,37,37,37
JAM 2:25, 5:12
JUD 7
REV 2:24, 5:2, 7:2, 8:3, 10:1, 12:3, 13:11, 14:6,8,9,15,17,18, 15:1, 17:10, 18:1,4, 19:17, 20:1,12

82 ܐܚܪܢܐܝܬ (adv) otherwise

2 CO 2:7 | PHL 3:15,18
GAL 2:7 | 1 TM 5:25

79 (ܐܚܪ) (v) tarry, delay

[e]APHEL

Perfect

MAT 25:5

Imperfect

1 CO 16:7 | HEB 10:37

Active Participle

MAT 24:48 | 1 TM 3:15
LUK 12:45 | JAM 1:19[1],19[2]

3345 ܬܘܚܪܬܐ (f) delay

LUK 1:21

---

[g]SHAPHEL (non occ)

3125 ܫܘܚܪܐ (m) delay

2 PT 3:9

---

[h]ESHTAPHAL

Imperfect

ACT 20:16

Participle

ACT 22:16 | 2 PT 3:9

ܐܒܐ see ܐܒܐ

ܐܒܐ see ܒ

---

84 ܐܘ (adv) well (done)

MAT 25:21,23 | LUK 19:17

---

91 ܐܝܟ (adv) as, like, according to

MAT 2:13,16,23; 3:16; 5:28; 6:1,2,2,4,5,5,7,16,16,18,29; 7:29,29; 8:4,10,17,28; 9:8,36; 10:16,16,16,25,25; 12:10,13,14; 13:2,32,35,43; 14:5; 15:28,31; 16:27; 17:2,2,20; 18:3,4,5,17,17; 19:14,19; 20:14; 21:26,46; 22:30,39; 23:3,28,37; 24:24; 25:14,15,32; 26:12,39,39,55,59; 27:1,10; 28:3,3,4,15 MRK 1:2,10,22,22; 4:1,26,31,32,33,33; 5:13; 6:2,15; 7:5,6; 8:9,24; 9:3,26,26,37; 10:1,14,15; 11:6; 12:25,31,33; 13:34; 14:8,10,48; 15:8 LUK 1:2,38,55,56,70; 2:15,22,23,29,35,37,39; 3:23; 5:7; 6:10,22,40; 7:3,9; 8:42; 9:14,28,48,52,54; 10:3,18,27; 11:2,36,44; 12:27,

47; 13:34; 14:22; 15:19; 17:6; 18:11,11,16, 17; 20:36; 21:35; 22:4,13,26,26,27,29,31,39, 41,44,52; 23:14,41,41,44,56; 24:11,24,28,39 JHN 1:14,32,39; 4:23; 5:23; 6:19,58; 7:10, 46; 8:5; 11:18,57; 15:6; 18:31; 19:7,14,39; 21:8,25 ACT 1:11,12,15; 2:2,3,4,22,41,45; 3:12,17,18; 4:35; 5:31,36,36; 6:15; 7:5,28,42, 44,48,51; 8:15,32,32; 9:12,17,21; 10:47,48; 11:15,17,29; 12:1,17; 13:22,23,33,34,47; 14:1; 15:8,10,15,17; 16:9,30,36; 17:28; 19:27,34,40; 20:24,30; 21:24; 22:3,5,12,24; 23:3,11,15,20,24,27; 24:6,27; 25:10,18; 26:18; 27:13,25; 28:19 ROM 1:5,13,17,21, 28,32; 2:6,16,24; 3:5,7,8,10; 4:4,4,17,18,20; 5:15,16,21; 6:12,13,19; 7:2; 8:26,27,36,36; 9:13,27,29,29,33; 10:15; 11:11; 12:3,6,6,18; 13:7,9,13; 14:11; 15:2,3,9; 16:2 1 CO 1:6, 31; 2:2,9; 3:1,1,5,8,10,10,15; 4:1,7,9,13,14, 14,17,18; 5:1,3; 7:6,17,17,25,29,30,30,30,36, 40; 8:2,7; 9:5,5,5,8,20,20,21,22,24,26,26; 10:7,15,33; 11:16,17,20; 12:7,11; 13:11,11, 11,12,12; 14:9,33; 15:3,4,8,32,49,52; 16:7 2 CO 1:14,17; 2:17,17,17; 3:1,5,10,13,18,18; 4:1,13; 5:20; 6:1,8,9,9,9,10,10,10,13; 7:14; 8:3,5,6,12,12,15; 9:5,5,7,7,7,9; 10:2,2,7,9,14, 15; 11:3,15,16,16,17,21,21; 12:16,20,20; 13:2,7,7,10 GAL 1:4; 2:7; 3:1,8,15,16,16; 4:14,14,28,29; 5:14,21 EPH 1:5,7,11,11, 19; 2:2,2,3; 3:4,5,7,16,20; 4:4,7,16,17,21; 5:1,2,3,8,15,15,22,25,28,33; 6:5,6,6,7,7,20 PHL 1:20,30; 2:3,7,15,15,20,22; 3:8,17,21; 4:19 COL 1:6,7,10,11,25; 2:8,8,8,20; 3:12, 18,22,23,23,25; 4:6 1 TH 2:2,4,4,5,6,7,11, 12,13; 4:1,5,13; 5:2,3,4,6 2 TH 1:3,4,12; 2:2,4,4; 3:1,6,15,15 1 TM 1:18,20; 5:1,1,2, 2 2 TM 1:9,9; 2:3,8,9,17; 4:3,14 TIT 1:7 PLM 9,12,14,16,17 HEB 1:4,11,12,12; 2:4,6; 3:2,5,6,8,8,11; 4:2,3,4,10; 5:6; 6:19; 7:9,21,26,27; 8:4,5,6,9; 9:25; 10:25,29; 11:1, 9,12,12,27,29,38; 12:1,5,7,10,16; 13:3,3,17 JAM 1:10; 2:8,8,9,12; 3:3,6,6; 4:3,16; 5:5,7 1 PT 1:14,15,17,23,24,24; 2:2,2,5,11,11,16, 16,16,25; 3:7,16,16; 4:6,10,11,11,12,15,15, 15,16,19,19; 5:3,3,8,12 2 PT 1:3,17,19; 2:1,12; 3:3,8,8,9,10,11,13,15,16 1 JN 1:7; 2:6,18,27,27; 3:2,3,7,12,23; 4:17; 5:14,16 2 JN 5,6,6 3 JN 2,3,6,8 JUD 10,16,18 REV 1:10,13,14,14,14,15,16,17; 2:18,18,23, 24,27; 3:3; 4:1,3,6,7; 5:6,11; 6:1,11,12,12,13, 14; 8:1,8,10,11; 9:2,5,7,7,7,8,8,9,9,10,17; 10:1,1,3,9,10; 12:15; 13:2,2,3,11; 14:2,2,2,3; 15:2; 16:3,13,15,18,21; 17:12; 18:7,17,21; 19:6,6,6,12; 20:8,12,13; 21:2,11,11,11,16,21; 22:1,12

92 ܐܝܟܐ (adv) where

incl comp with 747 ܗܘ

MAT 2:2,4,9; 6:19,20,20,21; 8:20; 12:44; 13:5; 18:20; 24:28; 25:24,24,26,26; 26:13,17, 57; 28:16 MRK 4:5; 5:40; 6:55,56; 8:21; 9:18,44,46,48; 13:14; 14:9,12,14,14,14; 15:47; 16:6 LUK 2:7; 4:16,17; 8:25; 9:58; 10:33; 12:17,33,34; 17:17,37,37; 22:9,11,11, 11 JHN 1:28,38,39; 3:8; 4:46; 7:11,34,35, 36; 8:10,14,14,19,21,22; 9:12; 10:40; 11:32, 34,57; 12:1,26,35; 13:33,36,36; 14:3,4,5; 16:5; 18:1,20; 20:2,12,13,15,19; 21:18,18 ACT 17:1; 27:39; 28:16 ROM 3:27 1 CO 1:20,20,20; 3:3; 12:17,19; 15:55,55 GAL 4:15 HEB 9:16; 10:18; 11:8 JAM 3:16; 4:1 1 PT 4:18 2 PT 2:11; 3:4 1 JN 2:11 REV 2:5,13; 7:13; 11:8; 17:9; 20:10

93 ܐܝܟ, ܐܝܟܢܐ (adv) how

MAT 1:24; 5:45,48; 6:10,12,28; 7:4; 8:13,24; 9:29; 10:19; 12:4,22,26,29,34,40; 13:40,54; 16:11; 18:33; 20:28; 21:6,20; 22:12,15,17,43, 45; 23:33,35; 24:27,37,38; 26:19,24,54; 27:65; 28:6,18 MRK 1:44,45; 2:2,12,26; 3:6,20,23; 4:13; 5:9,16; 9:3,12,13; 11:18; 12:26,35,37,41; 14:1,16,21; 15:5; 16:7 LUK 1:18,34,62; 2:20,24,27,42; 3:4; 4:16; 5:14,19; 6:31,36,42; 8:18,36,47; 10:26,26; 11:1,18,30; 12:1,11,27,56; 17:24,26,28; 18:24; 19:32; 20:41,44; 22:2,22; 23:55; 24:35 JHN 1:23; 3:4,9,12,14,16; 4:9; 5:21,26,30, 44,47; 6:31,42,52,57; 7:15,38; 8:6,28,33; 9:10,15,16,19,21,26; 10:15,26; 12:14,34,50; 13:15,33,34; 14:5,9,27,31; 15:4,9,10,12; 17:2,11,14,16,18,21,22,23; 19:40; 20:21 ACT 2:8,15; 3:19; 5:15; 8:31; 9:27,27,27; 11:13; 12:17; 15:14; 17:2; 20:18 ROM 3:4, 6; 4:6,10,17; 5:12; 6:2,4,19; 8:32; 9:25; 10:14,14,14,15; 11:8,26,30; 12:4; 15:7,8,15, 19,21 1 CO 3:10,13; 4:21; 5:7; 7:32,33,34; 8:5; 10:6,7,8,9,10,13,17; 11:1,2,12; 12:17,18; 13:2; 14:7,9,16,34; 15:3,12,21,22,35,38,48, 48; 16:1 2 CO 1:5,14; 3:7,8; 6:16; 7:9; 8:7, 11; 9:3; 10:11 GAL 1:6,9; 2:4,14; 3:6 EPH 1:4; 3:3; 4:1,32; 5:15,23,24,29; 6:11 PHL 1:8,20,27; 2:12; 4:10 COL 1:6; 2:6; 3:13; 4:4,6 1 TH 1:5,8,9; 2:10,11,13,14; 3:4,6,12; 4:1,6,11; 5:11 2 TH 2:4; 3:7 1 TM 2:10; 3:5,15 2 TM 3:8,9 TIT 1:5 HEB 2:3; 3:3,15; 4:3,7; 5:3,4; 7:12; 9:27 JAM 1:24; 2:26 1 PT 1:7,16; 3:6,16 2 PT 1:14; 3:15,16 1 JN 3:17; 4:20 2 JN 4 JUD 7 REV 3:3,21; 13:13; 18:6

95 ܐܝܠܐ (m-non occ) stag

96 ܐܝܠܢܐ (m) tree

MAT	3:10,10	MRK	8:24
	7:17,17,18, 18,19		11:8
	12:33,33, 33	LUK	3:9,9
	13:32		6:43,43,44
	21:8		13:19
			21:29
		JUD	12

REV 7:1,3 8:7	REV 9:4

97 ܐܡܟܐ (adv) from where

MAT 13:27,54, 56 15:33 21:25 MRK 6:2 8:4 11:30 LUK 1:43 11:24 13:25,27	LUK 20:7 JHN 1:48 2:9 3:8 4:11 6:5 7:27,27,28 8:14,14 9:29,30 19:9

99 ܐܝܢ (intrj) yes

MAT 5:37,37; 9:28; 11:9,26; 13:51; 15:27; 17:25; 21:16 MRK 7:28 LUK 7:26; 10:21; 11:51; 12:5 JHN 5:7; 11:27; 21:15, 16 ACT 5:8; 22:27 ROM 3:29 2 CO 1:17,17,18,19,19,20 PLM 20 JAM 5:12,12 REV 1:7; 14:13; 16:7; 22:20

100 ܐܝܢܐ (pron) who, what, which;

(w/ ܕ) he who

incl ܐܝܕܐ, ܐܝܠܝܢ

incl comp with 747 ܗܘ

MAT 2:7; 4:16,24,24; 5:6,8,10,15,44,46; 7:8, 11,13,13,14; 8:16; 9:12; 10:11,22,28; 11:4,6, 8,20,21,23; 12:3,4,7; 14:35,36; 15:13; 19:14, 18; 20:23; 21:9,23,24,27,41; 22:28,36; 23:14, 37; 24:16,18,19,21,42,43; 25:9,10; 27:15,39, 54; 28:4 MRK 1:32; 2:9,17,26; 3:11,13,22, 34; 4:18,24,30; 5:26; 6:2,10,22,55,56; 7:4,8; 10:14,23,24,40,42,44; 11:5,15,28,29,33; 12:23,28; 13:1,1,14,17; 14:32,69,70; 15:6,29, 43; 16:16,16,17 LUK 1:1,17,45,45,50,79; 2:18,33,47; 3:7; 4:40; 5:23,31; 6:3,4,18,21, 27,28,28,32,32,32,33,33,34; 7:2,25,42; 8:3, 14,15,21,36,47; 9:4,11,48,55; 10:5,8,9,10; 11:11,13,28,33,52; 12:4,9,25,37,39,47; 13:17,23,34; 14:17; 15:8; 16:26; 17:10; 18:9, 16,24,26,27,39; 19:27,42,45; 20:2,8,33; 21:1, 15,21,21,23,23,35; 22:26,26,47,49; 23:19,27, 48,49; 24:25,33,35 JHN 1:12,12,13,22,33; 2:10; 3:34; 4:24,32,36,52; 5:4,4,19,21,28,29, 29; 6:13,27,51,64; 7:39; 8:7,26,40; 9:8,39,39, 40; 10:8,16,32,36; 12:12,33,50; 13:18; 14:10, 12; 15:2,24; 17:12,20; 18:9,32; 20:29,30; 21:19,25 ACT 1:1,2,7,16,24; 2:9,10,22,39, 39,44,45,47; 3:2,20,21,23,24,25; 4:6,7,7,27, 32,34; 5:6,14,16,21,22,30,32,36,37; 7:3,18, 49,49,52,52,58; 8:19; 9:14,21,21,29; 10:7,15, 21,35,41; 11:5,17,29; 13:2,16,26,31,41,48, 50; 14:2; 15:5,10,16,17,19,23,24; 16:4,21; 17:4,17,17,21,31; 18:7; 19:1,4,13,13,13,18, 25; 20:19,25,34,35,35,35; 21:8,20,25,34; 22:19,20,22,24; 23:4,31,34; 24:15,19; 25:5,7; 26:10,22,29,30; 27:39,43; 28:9,30 ROM 1:32,32,32; 2:2,3,7,8,12,12,19,28,29, 29,29; 3:19,27; 4:6,7,11,12,12,16,16,17,24; 5:14,17; 6:2,3,7,21; 7:4; 8:1,5,5,8,14,18,28, 28,30,30,30; 9:15,15,25,30; 10:14,20,20; 11:2,4,22; 12:2,16; 13:1,4; 14:1,1,14,23; 15:21,21,31; 16:5,6,11,12,17,18 1 CO 1:2, 18,21,28,28,28; 2:9,11,13; 3:14,15; 5:1,11; 6:3,4,6; 7:1,8,10,13,14,14,22,22,28,29,30,30, 30,31,32,33,34,34,37,38,38; 8:11; 9:3,10,13, 13,14,18,20,21,24; 10:18; 11:19,22,27; 12:2, 22,23,23,24,24; 14:3,5,7,22,22,22,23,26,26, 26,26,26; 15:18,23,35; 16:3,16,18 2 CO 1:4,13,17; 2:3,15,15,16,16; 3:11; 4:3,4; 5:15,15; 6:14,14,14,15,15,16; 8:18,22; 10:2, 6,16; 11:4,4,4,5,12; 12:4,11,21 GAL 1:7; 2:2,18; 3:7,10,12,21,22,27; 4:5,19,21; 5:4,10, 21,24; 6:1,11,12,16 EPH 1:1,12,14,19; 3:9; 4:28,29,29; 6:24 PHL 1:10; 2:29; 3:3, 15,17; 4:8,8,8,8,8,8,8 COL 1:2,27; 2:1,1, 17,23 1 TH 1:9; 2:13,19; 3:9; 4:2,13,14,15, 15,17; 5:7,7,12 2 TH 2:12; 3:6 1 TM 1:9,9,9,16,19; 3:2,2,12,13; 4:3,3,16; 5:1,2,3,5,6,8,8,8,9,9,11,14,16,17,17,20,25; 6:1,2,5,9,21 2 TM 2:2,2,14,19,22,23,25; 3:5,11,11,12,14; 4:8 TIT 1:5,6,9,10,15; 2:4,6,8; 3:8,14,15,15 PLM 8,10 HEB 1:5,14; 2:3,3,15,18; 3:5,17,18; 4:3,10; 5:1,2,2,4,9,12,14; 6:9; 7:5,25; 8:1,13; 9:9,13, 15,15,28; 10:1,2,11,14,28,29,34; 11:1,1,3,6, 7,14,33; 12:5,6,7,11,26; 13:3,3,7,9,14 JAM 1:8,12; 2:5,10; 3:18; 4:4,13,13,17; 5:11, 16 1 PT 1:2,11,12,12,14,21,23; 2:7,10,12, 18,19,20,20; 3:1,5,8,14,19; 4:17,17,19; 5:5, 14 2 PT 1:1,3; 2:1,9,10,12,13,18,18; 3:11, 16,16,17 1 JN 2:22,26; 3:3,17,24; 5:13,16 2 JN 1,1,2,7,9 3 JN 6,10 JUD 3,4,5,6, 10,10,12,15,15,17,18,19 REV 1:11,12,19, 20,20; 2:2,6,9,10,11,13,22,24,24; 3:2,3,4,6,7, 8,9,12,19; 4:5; 5:6,8; 6:11; 7:9,14; 8:2; 9:4, 15,20; 11:1,5,8,11,16,18; 12:12,13; 13:6,8, 10,14,17; 14:2,4,8,9,11,12,13; 16:2,14; 17:12,18,18; 18:19,19; 19:2,9,12,18,20,20, 21; 20:4,8,12,15; 21:8,9,12,17,27; 22:9,18, 19,19

106 ܐܝܩܐ (adv) in vain

MAT 5:22 GAL 3:4,4	PHL 2:16

112 ܐܝܬ (subst.verb) is, are;

(ܐܝܬ ܕ... ܘܐܝܬ)

some...others

see also 1572 ܠܝܬ

MAT 2:9,18; 3:4,9; 4:18; 5:46; 6:21,22,30; 7:15; 8:9,20,30; 9:6,32; 10:2; 11:15,18; 12:6, 8,10,11; 13:4,8,8,8,9,12,13,23,23,23,27,37, 38,38,39,39,43,44,46; 15:30,34; 16:13,14,15, 28; 17:15; 18:8,9,25; 19:10,12,12,12,14,22; 21:25,28,33,35,35,35,42; 22:5,5,25,30; 23:20; 24:38,45,47; 25:15,15,15,25,28,29,29; 26:7,11,11; 27:55,61,62,65; 28:3 MRK 1:6,13,16,23,23; 2:4,6,15; 3:1,11,17, 22,30; 4:4,8,8,8,9,23,25,25,36; 5:2,5,11,15, 21,25,26,42; 6:31,38,44,47,55; 7:4,16,25,26; 8:1,1,5,7,9,18,18,27,29; 9:1,6,17,43,45,47; 10:14,21,22,23; 11:13,25; 12:6,11,20,25,37, 42,44; 14:3,3,4,7,7,8,22; 15:7,16,25,34,40,42 LUK 1:18,66,80; 2:4,8,11,25,25,40; 3:8,11, 11,23; 4:25,27,33,33,40; 5:10,17,29; 6:6,43; 7:8,25,33,37,40,41; 8:5,8,11,12,18,18,26,27, 32,42; 9:12,18,20,27,30,58; 10:6,33,39; 11:5, 13,14,34,41,44; 12:1,15,19,28,34,42,50; 13:6,11,11,30; 14:2,22,28,35; 15:4,8,11,14, 17; 16:1,1,19,20,28,29; 17:6,7; 18:2,3,9,22, 24; 19:20,24,25,26,26,42,46; 20:24,28,29,36; 22:3,7,24,27,36,38; 23:17,38,44; 24:1,10,39, 41,53 JHN 1:1,1,1,2,4,9,18,21,25,39,40, 44; 2:6,23,25; 3:1,8,13,19,23,29,36; 4:6,6,9, 11,18,23,32,34,37,46; 5:2,2,4,5,5,6,13,18,24, 25,26,36,39,45; 6:9,9,33,46,47,54,55,55,62, 64,68; 7:12,12,18,20,34,36,37,44; 8:7,9,10, 26,29,41,44,47,48,49,50,52,54,58; 9:9,9,14, 16,24; 10:16,20,33,40; 11:1,2,6,9,17,18,31, 32,38; 12:1,8,8,20,26,35,36,48; 13:13,23; 14:3,21,25; 16:12,15; 17:5; 18:1,10,13,14,28, 29,37,39,40; 19:5,7,14,23,40,41; 20:19; 21:2, 5,25 ACT 1:12,15,17,19; 2:5,29,44,45; 3:6; 4:4,6,12,22,24,32,32,33,37; 5:17,38; 6:3; 7:2,12,44; 8:9,23,32,36; 9:10,11,14,19,31,36, 38; 10:1,6,12,24,30; 11:6,20,21,26,29; 12:3, 19; 13:1,6,7,15,25; 14:4,9,13,15; 15:21,23; 16:1,3,12,16; 17:1,6,7,11,11,24,28,34; 18:2, 10,12,24; 19:1,2,4,13,14,16,24,32,33,38; 20:8,34; 21:3,8,9,10,16,18,20,23; 22:3,5,9; 23:6,9,17,18,19,25,34; 24:5,10,15,19,24; 25:5,5,19,24; 27:2,12,26,29,37; 28:2,7,9,11, 19 ROM 1:31; 2:2,11,19,20; 3:4,24; 4:2, 16,17,17; 5:8,10,13,14; 6:14,21,21,22; 7:3, 23,25; 8:16,23,34; 9:4,5,6,8,9,10,14,24; 10:2; 11:6,6,13; 12:4,4,6,6,7,7,7,8; 13:1,9; 14:2,5, 5,22; 15:17,26; 16:1,5,5,11 1 CO 1:11,12, 12,12,12,28; 2:16; 3:3,7,11,13; 4:7,17; 5:7, 11,11; 6:1,4,7,11,20; 7:7,7,10,12,12,13,29, 33,34,34,40; 8:1,5,5,7,10; 9:2,12,17,21; 10:16,16,19; 11:8,18,25; 12:4,5,6,8,12,12,20, 24,30; 13:3; 14:10,25,26,26,26,26,26; 15:10, 10,12,31,34,40,40,44,44,48,48 2 CO 1:1, 1; 2:4; 3:4,12; 4:7,13; 5:1,4; 6:14,14,15,15, 16; 7:1,4,4; 8:9,11,12,12; 9:7; 10:2,10,11,11, 15; 11:10,13 GAL 1:2,7,7,14; 2:2,4,6,6,9; 3:16; 4:2,6,24,24,26; 5:6,10,19,22; 6:3,3,10, 15 EPH 1:1,7,13,14,22,23; 2:11,12; 3:12; 4:11,11,11,11,11,21; 5:5,5,8,18; 6:9,17 PHL 1:1,22; 2:1,6,6,16,25; 3:3,4,9,18; 4:11 COL 1:2,7,14,18,24; 2:1,10,14,17,22,23; 3:13; 4:1,9,11,13 1 TH 1:7; 2:13; 3:6 2 TH 3:11,17 1 TM 1:5,10; 3:7,10,15; 4:8, 10,14; 5:4,4,8,10,16,24,24; 6:1,2,3,6,10,10 2 TM 1:6,15; 2:8,17,19,20; 3:5 TIT 1:6,6, 10,13,16 PLM 5,6,7,8,9,17 HEB 1:12, 14; 2:14; 3:6; 4:6,14,15; 5:8; 6:19; 7:1,2,2,5, 11; 8:1,3,4,7; 9:1,2,4,4,4,8,9,10,16,24; 10:1, 18,19,20,21,25,34,35; 11:1,1,6,10,15,16; 12:1,2; 13:5,6,10,15,18,20 JAM 2:14,18, 18; 3:2,6,14,15,16; 4:1 1 PT 1:19; 2:4,10, 18,19; 3:16,22; 4:2; 5:1 2 PT 1:3,9,13,15, 18,19; 2:7,14,14,19; 3:4,5,8,16 1 JN 1:1,1, 2,3,6,7,7; 2:1,6,7,7,8,9,9,11,13,15,16,20,27, 29; 3:2,3,7,9,12,17,17,19; 4:1,3,4,6,10,16,17, 18; 5:1,7,8,10,11,13,14,16,17 2 JN 2,5,6, 6,7,9,12 3 JN 5,11,12,13 JUD 3,4,12, 12,14,19 REV 1:4,4,8,8,8,16,17,18,18,19, 20; 2:2,3,4,6,7,7,9,11,12,14,14,15,17,18,20, 25,29; 3:1,1,4,6,7,8,9,11,13,16,22; 4:5,7,8,8, 8; 5:6,6,8,8,11,13; 6:2,5,9; 7:2,15; 8:3,9; 9:3, 8,9,10,11,11,14,17; 10:2,10; 11:6,6,17,17; 12:3,6,12,12,17; 13:1,9,11,14,17,18,18; 14:1, 4,6,12,14,17,18,18; 15:1,2,6,7; 16:2,5,5,9,14; 17:1,3,4,4,7,8,8,9,10,11,13,15,18; 18:1,19, 23; 19:9,9,10,10,10,12,16; 20:1,2,6,12,14; 21:5,8,9,11,12,12,12,14,15,17,21,21,22,23; 22:9

113 ܐܝܬܘܬܐ (f) substance

HEB 1:3

132 (ܐܟ), ܐܟܬܐ (m) grudge

MAT 5:23

116 ܐܟܕܢܐ (f) viper

MAT 3:7, 12:34, 23:33
LUK 3:7
ACT 28:3,5

118 ܐܟܘܬ (adv) likewise

MRK 13:19, 14:31
LUK 13:5
JHN 5:19, 8:55
ACT 3:22, 7:37, 10:26, 14:15, 15:11
ACT 26:29
1 CO 7:7,8, 16:10
2 CO 11:12
GAL 4:12,12
1 TM 1:8
HEB 4:15
JAM 5:17
REV 16:18

119 ܐܟܢܐ (adv) as

ROM 5:18,19
1 CO 12:12

120 ܐܟܚܕܐ (adv) as one

MAT	13:30	ACT	12:20
	22:34		18:12
LUK	17:35		19:29
JHN	4:36	ROM	1:12
	20:4		3:12
	21:2		6:5
ACT	1:14	1 CO	15:6
	2:1,44	2 CO	7:3
	3:1	PHL	1:27
	4:24,26	1 TH	4:17
	5:12		5:10
	11:26		

123 ܐܟܠ (v) eat, devour; (w/ ܩܪܨܐ) accuse; (aph) feed

[a]PEAL

see below 124 ܐܟܠ ܩܪܨܐ

see below 125 ܐܟܠ ܩܪܨܐ

Perfect

MAT	12:4[1]	LUK	24:43
	13:4	JHN	2:17
	14:20,21		6:13,23,26, 31[1],49, 58[1]
	15:37,38		
MRK	2:26[1]		
	4:4	ACT	1:4
	6:42,44		9:9
	8:8,9		10:14,41
LUK	6:4[1]	1 CO	10:3
	8:5	2 TH	3:8
	9:17	REV	10:10[1],10[2]
	13:26		20:9

Imperfect

MAT	6:25,31	JHN	4:32
	12:10		6:5,50,51, 53,57
	15:32		
MRK	8:1,2	ACT	23:12,21
	11:14	ROM	14:2[1],21
	14:12,14	1 CO	8:8[2],13
LUK	6:7		10:28
	11:54		11:22
	12:22,29		15:32
	14:1,15	JAM	5:3
	15:23	REV	12:4
	22:11,15, 16,30		17:16
			19:18

Imperative

MAT	26:26	1 CO	10:27
LUK	12:19		11:24
ACT	10:13	REV	10:9
	11:7		

Infinitive

MAT	12:4[2]	JHN	4:33
	14:16		6:31[2],52
	25:35,42	ACT	27:35
MRK	2:26[2]	1 CO	5:11
	3:20		8:10
	6:31,36		9:4
LUK	6:4[2]		10:7
	8:55		11:33
	9:13	HEB	13:10
	24:41	REV	2:7,14,20

Active Participle

MAT	11:18,19	JHN	18:28
	12:1	ROM	14:2[2],3[1],3[2], 3[3],3[4],6[1], 6[2],6[3],6[4], 20,23
	15:2,27		
	23:13		
	24:38,49		
	27:12	1 CO	8:7,8[1]
MRK	2:16		9:7[1],7[2]
	7:2,5,28		10:18,25, 31
	12:40		
	14:18		11:20,21, 26,27, 28,29[1], 29[2]
	15:3		
LUK	5:30,33		
	6:1		
	7:33,34	2 CO	11:20
	15:2,16	GAL	2:12
	17:27,28		5:15
	20:47	2 TH	3:12
	23:2,10	HEB	10:27
JHN	6:54,56, 58[2]		12:29
		REV	11:5
	13:18		

117 ܐܟܘܠܐ (adj) gluttonous

MAT	11:19	LUK	7:34

124 ܐܟܠ ܩܪܨܐ (idiom) backbiter

from 123 ܐܟܠ (above) and 2894 ܩܪܨܐ

1 TM	3:11	TIT	2:3
2 TM	3:3		

125 ܐܟܠ ܩܪܨܐ (pn) the Devil

from 123 ܐܟܠ (above) and 2894 ܩܪܨܐ

MAT	4:1,5,8,11	EPH	4:27
	25:41		6:11
LUK	4:2,3,6,13	JUD	9
	13:16	REV	2:10
JHN	8:44		12:9,12
ACT	13:10		20:2,10

126 ܐܟܠܐ (m) (Nest reading) devouring insect, consuming (thing); (Jac reading) hammer

MAT 6:19,20

1599 ܡܐܟܘܠܬܐ (f) food

MAT 3:4	1 CO 6:13,13
MRK 1:6	8:4,8,13
7:19	10:3
JHN 4:32,34	2 CO 9:10
6:27,27,55	1 TM 4:3
ACT 27:34,38	6:8
ROM 14:15,15, 20	HEB 5:12,13,14
1 CO 3:2	12:16
	13:9

1600 ܡܐܟܠ ܩܪ̈ܨܐ (idiom) backbiting

JHN 18:29	2 CO 12:20
ROM 1:30	1 PT 2:1

1601 ܡܐܟܠܐ (m) food

ROM 14:17	HEB 9:10
COL 2:16	

ᵇETHPEEL

Perfect

LUK 16:1	JAM 5:2

ᵉAPHEL

Imperfect

1 CO 13:3

Imperative

ROM 12:20

---

127 ܐܘܟܠܘܣ (m) multitude

ACT 14:14	ACT 21:34
17:5,5	

---

128 ܐܟܡ (v-non occ) make black

ᶜPAEL

46 ܐܘܟܡܐ (adj) black

MAT 5:36	REV 6:5,12

---

130 ܐܟܦ (v-non occ) take care

ᵃPEAL

122 ܐܟܦܐܝܬ (adv) diligently

PHL 2:20

---

131 ܐܟܪܐ (m) husbandman

2 TM 2:6	JAM 5:7

---

133 ܐܠܐ (conj) but

from 177 ܐܢ and 1511 ܠܐ

MAT 4:4; 5:13,15,17,20,37,39; 6:1,13,18,20; 7:21; 8:4,8; 9:12,13,17,18,24; 10:20,34; 11:8, 9,27,27; 12:4,24,29,39; 13:21,57; 14:17; 15:11,24; 16:4,11,12,17,23; 17:8,21; 18:3,16, 22,30,35; 19:6,11,17; 20:23,26,28; 21:19,21; 22:30,32; 24:6,36; 25:9; 26:39,42; 27:24; 28:10 MRK 1:44,45; 2:7,17,17,22,26; 3:26,27,29; 4:17; 5:19,26,37,39; 6:4,5,8,9,27; 7:4,5,15,19; 8:14,33; 9:8,9,13,22,29,37; 10:8, 18,27,40,43,45; 11:13,23; 12:14,25,27; 13:7, 11,11,20,32; 14:28,29,36,36,38,49; 16:7 LUK 1:60; 4:4,26,27; 5:14,21,31,32,38; 6:4; 7:7; 8:13,16,27,51,52; 9:13,56; 10:20,22,22; 11:4,29,33,42; 12:51; 13:3,9; 14:10,13; 16:21,30; 17:8,18; 18:12,13,19,34; 20:21,38; 21:9; 22:26,42,53; 23:15; 24:22 JHN 1:8, 13,31,33; 3:2,8,13,15,16,17,27,28,36; 4:2,14, 23; 5:7,18,19,22,24,30,30,34,42; 6:9,22,26, 27,32,36,38,39,44,46,53,64,65; 7:10,12,16, 22,24,27,28,44,49,51; 8:12,16,26,28,37,42, 49,55; 9:3,9,31; 10:1,5,8,10,18,26,33; 11:4, 11,15,22,30,42,51,52,54; 12:6,9,16,24,27,30, 42,44,47,49; 13:9,10,10,18; 14:6,24,31; 15:4, 4,16,19,21; 16:7,12,13,20,25,33; 17:9,12,15, 20; 18:40; 19:15,21,24,34; 20:7,27; 21:8,23 ACT 1:4,8; 2:16; 3:6; 4:17,32; 5:4,13; 7:39, 43; 8:31,39; 9:6; 10:35,41; 11:19; 12:14; 13:25,27,46; 15:11,20; 16:37; 17:21; 18:9,25; 19:26,27; 20:24; 21:13; 24:19,21; 26:20,22, 25,29; 27:10,22,39 ROM 1:21,32; 2:5,8, 13,29,29; 3:6,27,31; 4:2,4,5,10,12,13,16,20, 24; 5:3,11,14,15; 6:13,14,15; 7:7,7,13,15,17, 19,20; 8:4,9,15,20,23,26,32,37; 9:8,10,11,16, 24,32; 10:2,3,8,15,16,18,19; 11:1,6,6,11,15,

18,20,22,23; 12:2,3,6,9,16,17,19,19,21; 13:3,
4,5,8,14; 14:13,14,17,20; 15:2,3,21; 16:4,18
1 CO 1:7,10,14,17,27; 2:2,4,5,7,9,11,11,12,
13; 3:1,2,5,6,7; 4:3,4,14,15,19,19,20; 5:8,10;
6:4,6,8,11,12,12,13; 7:2,4,4,5,7,9,10,17,19,
21,35; 8:4,6,7,8; 9:2,10,12,12,16,21,24,27;
10:5,13,13,20,23,23,24,29,33; 11:8,9,17,21;
12:3,4,5,6,14,22,25; 13:6; 14:2,2,6,16,17,19,
20,22,22,33,34; 15:10,10,29,36,37,40,46,46,
58; 16:11 2 CO 1:9,13,19,24; 2:2,4,5,13,
17; 3:3,3,5,6,14; 4:2,2,5,8,8,9,9,16,18; 5:1,3,
4,12,15,16; 6:4; 7:5,6,7,9,9,12,14; 8:5,7,8,10,
14,21; 9:12; 10:1,3,4,11,12,13,15,18; 11:1,6,
6,12,16,17; 12:1,5,13,14,14,16; 13:3,4,4,5,7,
8 GAL 1:1,7,12,17,19,23; 2:7,16,20; 3:12,
16,22; 4:2,7,14,17,23,30,31; 5:6,13; 6:4,13,
14,15 EPH 1:21; 2:8,19; 4:9,15,22,28,29;
5:4,11,15,17,18,24,27,29; 6:4,6,12
PHL 1:17,20,24,29; 2:3,4,7,12,17,27,27; 3:7,
9,12; 4:6,10,15,17 COL 2:5,23; 3:9,11,22
1 TH 1:5,8; 2:2,4,4,7,8,13,19; 3:10; 4:7,8;
5:6,9,15 2 TH 2:3,12; 3:8,9,11,15
1 TM 1:9,13,16; 2:10,12; 3:3,9; 4:12; 5:1,13,
19,23; 6:2,4,17 2 TM 1:7,8,9,17; 2:9,20,
24; 3:9; 4:3,8,16 TIT 1:8,15; 2:10; 3:2,5
PLM 14,16 HEB 2:6,16; 3:13,17,18; 4:2,
13,15; 5:4,5; 6:4,8,12; 7:3,12,16; 9:10,12,24,
26; 10:3,25,27,39; 11:13; 12:11,13,26; 13:5,
14 JAM 1:14,25,26; 2:11; 3:1,15; 4:11,14;
5:12 1 PT 1:12,15,19,23; 2:16,18,20,23;
3:4,9,15,21; 4:2,13,16; 5:2,2,3 2 PT 1:16,
21; 2:4,5; 3:9,9 1 JN 2:2,7,16,19,19,21,22,
27,28; 3:12,18; 4:1,3,10,18; 5:5,7 2 JN 1,5,
8,12 3 JN 9,11,13 JUD 6,9 REV 2:4,
5,6,9,9,14,17,20,22; 3:4,9; 9:4,5; 10:9; 13:17;
17:12; 19:12; 20:6; 21:27

134 ܐܒܠ (v) mourn

aPEAL

Perfect

MAT 11:17 | LUK 7:32

Imperfect

JHN 16:20

Active Participle

LUK 23:27

144 ܐܒܠܐ (m) mourning

MAT 2:18

135 ܐܠܗܐ (m) God, a god

MAT 1:23; 3:9,16; 4:3,4,6,7,10; 5:8,9,34;
6:24,30,33; 8:29; 9:8; 12:4,28,28; 14:33;
15:3,4,6,31; 16:16,23; 19:6,17,24,26; 21:12,
31,43; 22:16,21,21,29,30,31,32,32,32,32,37;
23:22; 26:29,61,63,63; 27:40,43,43,54
MRK 1:1,14,15,24; 2:7,12,26; 3:11,35; 4:11,
26; 5:7,7; 7:8,9,13; 8:29,33; 9:1,47; 10:6,9,
14,15,18,23,24,25,27,27; 11:15,22; 12:14,17,
17,24,26,26,26,26,27,29,30,34; 13:19; 14:25;
15:34,34,39,43; 16:19 LUK 1:6,8,16,19,
26,30,32,35,37,47,58,64,68,78; 2:9,13,14,20,
28,40,52; 3:2,4,6,8,38; 4:3,4,8,9,12,34,41,43;
5:1,21,25,26; 6:4,12,20; 7:16,16,28,29,30;
8:1,10,11,21,28,39; 9:2,11,20,27,43,60,62;
10:9,11,27; 11:20,20,28,42,49; 12:6,8,9,20,
21,24,28,31; 13:13,18,20,28,29; 14:15;
15:10; 16:13,15,15,16; 17:15,18,20,20,21;
18:2,4,7,11,13,17,19,24,25,27,29,43,43;
19:11,37; 20:21,25,25,36,37,37,37,38; 21:4,
31; 22:16,69,70; 23:35,40,47,51; 24:19,53
JHN 1:1,1,2,6,12,13,18,18,29,34,36,49,51;
3:2,2,3,5,16,17,18,21,33,34,34,34,36; 4:10,
24; 5:18,18,25,42,44; 6:27,28,29,33,45,46,
69; 7:17; 8:40,41,42,42,47,47,47,54; 9:3,16,
24,29,31,33,35; 10:33,34,35,35,36; 11:4,4,
22,27,40,52; 12:43; 13:3,3,31,32,32; 14:1;
16:2,27,30; 17:3; 19:7; 20:17,17,28,31; 21:19
ACT 1:3; 2:5,11,22,22,23,24,30,32,33,36,39,
47; 3:8,9,13,13,15,18,21,25,26; 4:10,19,19,
21,24,24,31; 5:4,29,30,31,32,39,39; 6:2,7,11;
7:2,4,6,7,9,17,20,25,32,32,35,37,40,42,43,
45,46,46,55,55,56; 8:3,4,10,12,14,20,21,22,
24,25; 9:20,31,35; 10:2,2,3,4,7,15,22,28,31,
33,34,38,38,40,41,42,46; 11:1,9,17,17,18,18,
19,23; 12:5,22,23,24; 13:2,7,16,17,21,23,26,
30,33,34,36,37,43,43,44,46,48,50; 14:11,12,
13,15,22,27; 15:4,7,8,10,12,14,18,19,35,36,
40; 16:6,14,17,25,34; 17:4,13,17,18,23,24,
27,29,30; 18:7,8,11,13,21; 19:8,9,11,20,23,
26; 20:19,21,24,27,28,32; 21:19,20; 22:3,14;
23:1,3,4; 24:14,15,16; 26:6,8,18,20,22,29;
27:23,24,25,35; 28:6,15,23,28,31
ROM 1:1,4,7,7,8,9,10,16,17,18,19,19,20,21,
21,23,24,25,26,28,28,30,32; 2:2,3,4,5,11,13,
16,17,23,24,29; 3:2,3,4,5,5,6,7,11,18,19,21,
22,23,25,26,29,30; 4:2,3,6,8,17,20,20,21;
5:1,2,5,8,10,11,15; 6:10,11,13,13,17,22,23;
7:4,22,25,25; 8:3,7,7,8,9,14,14,16,17,19,21,
27,28,31,33,33,34,39; 9:5,6,8,11,14,16,20,
22,23,26; 10:1,2,3,3,9,17; 11:1,2,2,8,21,22,
23,29,30,32,33; 12:1,1,2,3,19; 13:1,1,2,4,4,6;
14:3,6,6,12,17,18,20,22; 15:5,6,7,8,9,13,15,
16,17,19,30,32,33; 16:20,24,25 1 CO 1:1,
2,3,4,4,9,14,18,20,21,21,21,24,24,25,25,27,
30; 2:1,5,7,7,9,10,10,11,11,12,12; 3:6,7,9,9,
9,10,16,16,17,17,17,19,23; 4:1,5,9,20; 5:13;
6:9,10,11,13,14,19,20,20; 7:7,15,17,19,22,
24,25,25,40; 8:3,4,5,5,6,8; 9:9,21; 10:5,13,
20,31,32; 11:3,7,12,13,16,22; 12:3,6,18,24,
28; 14:2,18,25,25,28,33,36; 15:9,10,15,15,
24,28,34,38,57 2 CO 1:1,1,2,3,3,4,9,12,
18,19,20,20,21,23; 2:14,15,17,17,17; 3:3,4,5;
4:2,2,4,4,6,6,7,15; 5:1,5,11,13,18,19,20,20,
21; 6:1,4,7,16,16,16; 7:1,6,9,10,11,12; 8:1,5,
16,19,21; 9:7,8,11,12,13,14,15; 10:4,5,13;
11:2,7,11,31; 12:2,3,19,21; 13:4,4,7,11,14
GAL 1:1,3,4,10,13,20,24; 2:6,19,20,21; 3:6,
8,11,17,18,20,21,26; 4:4,6,7,8,8,9,9,14; 5:21;
6:7,16 EPH 1:1,2,3,17; 2:4,8,10,12,16,19,

22; 3:2,7,9,10,19; 4:6,13,18,24,30,32; 5:1,2, 5,6,17,20; 6:6,11,13,17,23 PHL 1:2,3,8, 11,14,29; 2:6,6,9,11,13,15,27; 3:3,9,14,15, 19; 4:6,7,9,18,19,20 COL 1:1,2,3,6,9,10, 10,12,15,25,25,27; 2:2,12,19,23; 3:1,3,6,12, 16,17; 4:3,11,12 1 TH 1:1,2,3,4,8,9,9; 2:2, 4,4,5,8,10,10,12,13,13,13,14,15; 3:2,9,10,11, 13; 4:1,3,5,7,8,9,14,16; 5:9,18,23 2 TH 1:1,2,3,4,5,6,8,11,12; 2:4,4,4,4,11,13, 13,16; 3:5 1 TM 1:1,2,4,11,17; 2:1,2,3,5,5, 10; 3:5,15,15; 4:3,4,5,10; 5:4,5,21; 6:1,3,5,6, 11,13,15,17 2 TM 1:1,2,3,6,7,8; 2:9,15,19, 25; 3:4,5,12,17; 4:1 TIT 1:1,1,1,2,3,4,7, 16; 2:3,5,10,11,12,13; 3:4,8 PLM 3,4 HEB 1:1,5,6,8,9,9; 2:4,9,13,17; 3:4,12; 4:3,4, 9,10,12,14; 5:1,4,10,12; 6:1,5,6,7,10,13,17, 18; 7:1,3,19,25; 8:2,10; 9:14,14,20,24; 10:7, 9,12,21,29,31,36; 11:3,4,4,5,5,6,6,10,16,16, 19,25,27,40; 12:2,7,10,15,22,23,28,29; 13:4, 7,15,16,20 JAM 1:1,5,12,13,13,20,26,27; 2:5,5,8,19,23,23; 3:9; 4:4,4,6,7,8 1 PT 1:2, 3,5,21,21,23,25; 2:4,5,10,12,13,15,15,16,17, 19,20; 3:4,5,17,18,20,21,22; 4:2,5,6,10,10, 11,11,11,14,16,17,17,19; 5:2,5,6,7,10,12 2 PT 1:3,6,7,17,21; 2:4; 3:5,11,12,18 1 JN 1:5; 2:5,14,17,27; 3:2,8,9,9,10,10,17, 20,21; 4:1,2,2,3,4,6,6,6,7,7,7,8,8,9,9,10,11, 12,12,15,15,15,16,16,16,19,20,20,21; 5:1,2, 2,3,4,5,9,10,10,10,11,12,13,18,18,19,20,20 2 JN 3,9 3 JN 6,11,11 JUD 1,4,4,5,21, 25 REV 1:1,2,6,8,9; 2:7,18; 3:1,2,12,12, 12,14; 4:5,8,11; 5:6,9,10; 6:9; 7:2,3,10,12,15; 8:2,4; 9:4,13; 10:7; 11:1,11,13,15,16,16,17; 12:5,6,10,10,17; 13:6; 14:4,7,12,19; 15:1,2,3, 3,7,8; 16:1,7,9,11,14,19,21; 17:17,17; 18:5, 20; 19:1,4,5,9,10,13,15,17; 20:4,6,9; 21:2,3, 3,3,7,10,11,22,23; 22:1,3,5,6,9,18,19

136 ܐܠܗܘܬܐ (f) godhead

ACT 17:29
ROM 1:20
COL 2:9

137 ܐܠܗܝܐ (adj) divine

2 PT 1:3,4

138 ܐܠܗܬܐ (f) goddess

ACT 19:27,27, 19:37

139 ܐܠܘ (conj) if

MAT 11:21,23; 12:7; 23:30; 24:22,43; 26:24 MRK 9:42; 13:20; 14:21 LUK 7:39; 10:13; 12:39,49; 17:2; 19:42 JHN 4:10; 5:46; 8:19,39,42; 9:33,41; 11:21,32; 14:7,28; 15:19,22,24; 18:30,36; 19:11; 21:25 ACT 18:14; 26:32; 27:21 ROM 4:2,14; 7:7; 9:29 1 CO 2:8; 11:31; 12:17,17,19 GAL 1:10; 3:21; 4:15; 5:11 HEB 4:8; 7:11; 8:4,7; 10:2; 11:15 1 JN 2:19

ܐܠܦ see (pa) of ܠܦ

158 ܐܠܦ (f) the letter aleph

REV 1:8
21:6
REV 22:13

159 ܐܠܦ, ܐܠܦܐ (num) thousand

MAT 14:21
15:38
16:9,10
MRK 5:13
6:44
8:9,19,20
LUK 9:14
14:31,31
JHN 6:10
ACT 2:41
4:4
21:38
ROM 11:4
1 CO 10:8.
2 PT 3:8,8
REV 5:11,11
6:15
7:4,5,5,5,6, 6,6,7,7,7, 8,8,8
11:3,13
12:6
14:1,3,20
19:18
20:2,4,6,7
21:16

160 ܐܠܦ, ܐܠܦܐ (f) ship, boat

MAT 4:21,22
8:24
9:1
13:2
14:13,24, 29,32, 33
15:39
JHN 6:23,24
ACT 20:13,14, 38
21:2,3,6
27:2,2,6, 10,11,
ACT 27:15,17, 19,22, 29,30, 30,31, 32,37, 38,39, 40,41, 44
28:11
JAM 3:4
REV 8:9
18:17,17, 19

161 ܐܠܦܪܐ (m) sailor

REV 18:17

162 ܐܠܨ (v) urge, constrain

aPEAL

Perfect

MAT 14:22
MRK 6:45
LUK 24:29
ACT 16:15
2 CO 12:11
PHL 2:25

Imperfect

LUK 19:43

Imperative

LUK 14:23

Active Participle

LUK	8:45	GAL	2:14
ACT	15:28		6:12
	26:11	PHL	1:23,24
ROM	13:5	TIT	3:14
1 CO	7:37	1 PT	2:20
2 CO	5:14		

149 ܐܠܝܨܐ (pp) narrow, straight, afflicted, anxious

MAT	4:24	ACT	18:5
	7:13,14	2 CO	6:12,12
LUK	4:38	1 TM	5:10
	12:50	HEB	11:37
	13:24		13:3
	14:18		

48 ܐܘܠܨܢܐ (m) affliction, tribulation

MAT	13:21	2 CO	8:2,13
	24:9,21,29		12:10
MRK	4:17	EPH	3:13
	13:19,24	PHL	1:17
LUK	21:23,25		4:14
JHN	16:21,33	COL	1:24
ACT	7:10,11,34	1 TH	1:6
	11:19		3:3,7
	14:22	2 TH	1:4,6
	20:23	HEB	4:16
	27:10,21		7:27
ROM	2:9		10:32
	5:3,3		11:25
	8:35	JAM	1:27
	12:12		5:10,13
1 CO	7:28	1 PT	2:20
2 CO	1:4,4,8		5:10
	2:4	2 PT	2:9
	4:17	REV	1:9
	6:4		2:9,10,22
	7:4		7:14

142 ܐܠܘܨܐ (m) oppressor

2 TH 1:6

[b]ETHPEEL

Perfect

MRK	5:26	2 CO	1:8
ACT	28:19		7:5

Imperfect

2 CO 10:2

Infinitive

1 TH 3:4

Participle

LUK	6:18	2 CO	4:8
2 CO	1:6[1],6[2]	2 TH	1:7

163 ܐܡ, ܐܡܐ (f) mother

MAT	1:18	LUK	8:51
	2:11,13,14, 20,21		12:53,53
	10:35,37		14:26
	12:46,47, 48,49, 50		18:20
	13:55		24:10
	14:8,11	JHN	2:1,3,5,12
	15:4,4,5,5		3:4
	19:5,12,19, 29		6:42
	20:20		9:1
	27:56,56		19:25,25, 26,26, 27
MRK	3:31,32,33, 34,35	ACT	1:14
	5:40		3:2
	6:24,28		7:21
	7:10,10,11, 12		12:12
	10:7,19,29, 30		14:8
	15:40	ROM	16:13
LUK	1:15,43,60	GAL	1:15
	2:33,34,43, 48,51		4:26
	7:12,12,15	EPH	5:31
	8:19,20,21,		6:2
		1 TM	1:9
			5:2
		2 TM	1:5,5,5
		HEB	7:3
		REV	17:5

51 ܐܘܡܬܐ (c) people

LUK	2:31	REV	10:11
ACT	4:25		11:9
ROM	15:11		13:7
REV	5:9		14:6
	7:9		17:15

175 (ܐܡ), ܐܡܬܐ (f) handmaid, servant

MAT	26:69	ACT	2:18
LUK	1:38,48	GAL	4:22,23,30, 30,31
	12:45		

174 ܐܡܐ, ܐܡܬܐ (f) cubit

MAT	6:27	JHN	21:8
LUK	12:25	REV	21:17

49 (ܐܡܢ), ܐܘܡܢܐ (m)

craftsman

ACT	19:38	HEB	11:10

50 ܐܘܡܢܘܬܐ (f) craft

ACT	17:29	ACT	19:38
	18:3,3	2 PT	1:16
	19:24,25,		

---

166 (ܐܡܢ), ܐܡܝܢ (adv) amen, verily

MAT 5:18,26; 6:2,5,16; 8:10; 10:15,23,42; 11:11; 13:17; 16:28; 17:20; 18:3,13,18; 19:23,28; 21:21,31; 23:36; 24:2,34,47; 25:12, 40,45; 26:13,21,34; 28:20 MRK 3:28; 6:11; 8:12; 9:1,41; 10:15,29; 11:23; 12:43; 13:30; 14:9,18,25,30 LUK 4:24; 12:37; 18:17,29; 21:32; 23:43; 24:53 JHN 1:51, 51; 3:3,3,5,5,11,11; 5:19,19,24,24,25,25; 6:26,26,32,32,47,47,53,53; 8:34,34,51,51,58, 58; 10:1,1,7,7; 12:24,24; 13:16,16,20,20,21, 21,38,38; 14:12,12; 16:20,20,23,23; 21:18,18 ROM 1:25; 9:5; 11:36; 15:33; 16:26,27 1 CO 14:16 2 CO 1:20; 13:14 GAL 1:5; 6:18 EPH 3:21; 6:24 PHL 4:20,23 COL 4:18 1 TH 5:28 2 TH 3:18 1 TM 1:17; 6:16,21 2 TM 4:18,22 TIT 3:15 PLM 25 HEB 13:21,25 1 PT 4:11; 5:11,14 2 PT 3:18 2 JN 13 JUD 25 REV 1:6,7,18; 3:14; 4:9,10; 5:14; 7:12,12; 15:7; 19:4; 22:21

---

167 (ܐܡܢ), ܐܡܝܢܐ (adj)

steadfast

ACT	1:14	ROM	12:12
	2:42,46	1 CO	7:35
	6:4	PHL	1:3
	12:5	1 TM	5:5,23

168 ܐܡܝܢܐܝܬ (adv) steadfastly

LUK	5:33	1 TH	1:2
ACT	18:21		2:13
	24:16,26	2 TM	1:3
EPH	6:18	2 PT	1:12,15

169 (ܐܡܢ) (v) (ethpe) be constant, firm; (p) believe, trust

[b]ETHPEEL

Imperative

COL 4:2

---

[k]P ܗܝܡܢ

Perfect

MAT	8:13	ACT	13:12,48
	9:29		14:23
	21:25,32[1], 32[2]		15:5
			16:15
MRK	11:31		17:4,12,34
	16:11,13, 14		18:8[1]
			19:2,18
LUK	1:20,45		21:20,25
	20:5	ROM	3:3[1],3[2]
	24:11		4:3,5,17, 18,24
JHN	2:11,22,23		10:14[1],16
	3:18[3]		11:20
	4:39,41,50, 53		13:11
	5:46[1]	1 CO	3:5
	6:69		15:2,11
	7:5,31,48	2 CO	4:13[1]
	8:30,31	GAL	2:16
	9:18		3:6
	10:42	EPH	1:13
	11:45	COL	2:12
	12:37,38, 42	2 TH	2:12
		2 TM	1:12
	16:27,31	TIT	3:8
	17:8	HEB	3:19
	20:8,29[1], 29[2],31[2]		4:3
		JAM	2:23
ACT	2:41,44	1 PT	1:21
	4:4,32	1 JN	4:16
	8:12,13		5:10[3],13
	9:42	JUD	5
	11:17,21		

Imperfect

MAT	21:22,32[3]	JHN	13:19
	24:23,26		14:29
	27:42		17:21
MRK	9:23[1]		19:35
	11:23		20:31[1]
	13:21	ACT	13:41
	15:32		14:1
LUK	8:12		15:7
	22:67		19:4
JHN	1:7		26:8
	3:12[2]	ROM	6:8
	4:48		9:33
	5:47[2]		10:9,14[2]
	6:29,30	PHL	1:29[2]
	8:24	2 TH	2:11
	9:36	1 TM	1:16
	10:37,38[3]	2 TM	2:13
	11:15,40, 42	HEB	11:6
		1 JN	3:23
	12:39		4:1

Imperative

MRK	1:15	JHN	10:38[2]
	5:36		12:36
	11:24		14:1[1],1[2], 11[1],11[2]
LUK	8:50		
JHN	4:21	ACT	16:31

Infinitive

LUK	24:25
JHN	5:44
PHL	1:29[1]

Active Participle

MAT	9:28; 18:6
MRK	9:23[2],24,42; 16:16[1],16[2],17
LUK	16:11,31; 24:41
JHN	1:12,50; 2:24; 3:12[1],15,16,18[1],18[2],36; 4:42; 5:24,38,46[2],47[1]; 6:35,36;40,47,64[1],64[2]; 7:38,39; 8:45,46; 9:35,38; 10:25,26,38[1]; 11:25,26[1],26[2],27,48; 12:11,44[1],44[2],46; 14:10,12; 16:9,30; 17:20; 20:25
ACT	5:14,32; 9:26; 10:43; 13:39; 15:11; 18:8[2]; 22:19; 24:14; 26:27[1],27[2]; 27:25
ROM	1:16; 3:22; 4:11; 10:4,10,11; 14:2
1 CO	1:21; 6:6; 7:12,13,14[1],14[2],14[3],14[4],15; 11:18; 13:7; 14:22[1],22[2],22[3],23,24
2 CO	4:4,13[2]; 6:14,15[1],15[2]
GAL	3:22
EPH	1:19
1 TH	2:13; 4:14
1 TM	4:3; 5:8
TIT	1:15
HEB	3:12
JAM	2:19[1],19[2]
1 PT	2:6,7
1 JN	2:23; 5:1,5,10[1],10[2]

Passive Participle

1 CO	9:17

1647 ܡܗܝܡܢܐ (ap) believer, believing

see also pp (below) - some forms are the same

MAT	17:17
MRK	9:19
LUK	9:41; 12:46
JHN	20:27,27
ACT	8:2; 16:1; 18:27
1 CO	14:22
GAL	3:9,9
EPH	1:1
COL	1:2
1 TH	1:7; 2:10
2 TH	1:10
1 TM	4:10,12; 5:16,16; 6:2,2
TIT	1:6
REV	17:14; 21:8

1646 ܡܗܝܡܢܐ (pp) faithful, eunuch; (w/ ܠܐ) faithless

see also ap (above) - some forms are the same

MAT	19:12,12,12,12,12; 24:45; 25:21,21,23,23
LUK	12:42; 16:10,10,11,12; 19:17
ACT	8:27,34,36,38,39; 13:34
1 CO	1:9; 4:2,17; 7:25; 10:13
2 CO	1:18
EPH	6:21
COL	1:7; 4:7,9
1 TH	5:24
2 TH	3:3
1 TM	1:12,15; 3:1,11; 4:9
2 TM	2:2,11
TIT	3:8
HEB	2:17; 3:2; 10:23; 11:11
1 PT	4:19; 5:12
1 JN	1:9
REV	1:5; 2:10,13,13; 3:14; 19:11; 21:5; 22:6

759 ܗܝܡܢܘܬܐ (f) faith, believing

MAT	6:30; 8:10,26; 9:2,22; 13:58; 14:31; 15:28; 16:8; 17:20,20; 21:21; 23:23
MRK	2:5; 4:40; 5:34; 6:6; 9:24; 10:52; 11:22; 16:14
LUK	5:20; 7:9,50; 8:13,25,48; 12:28; 17:5,6,19; 18:8,42; 22:32
ACT	3:16,16; 6:5,7; 7:55; 8:21; 11:24; 13:8; 14:9,22,27; 15:9; 16:5,34; 17:31; 19:20; 20:21; 24:24; 26:18
ROM	1:5,8,12,17,17,17; 3:3,22,25,26,27,28,30,30,31; 4:5,9,11,12,13,14,16,16,19,20,20,23; 5:1,2; 9:30,32; 10:6,8,17; 11:20,23; 12:3,6; 14:1,22,23,23; 15:13; 16:25
1 CO	2:5; 12:9; 13:2,13

1 CO 15:14,17
16:13
2 CO 1:24,24
4:13
5:7
8:7
10:15
13:5
GAL 1:23
2:16,16,20
3:2,5,7,8,
11,12,14,
22,23,23,
24,25,26
5:5,6,22
6:10
EPH 1:15
2:8
3:12,17
4:5,13
6:16,23
PHL 1:25,27
2:17
3:9
COL 1:4,23
2:5,7
1 TH 1:3,8
3:2,5,6,7,
10
5:8
2 TH 1:3,4,11
2:13
3:2
1 TM 1:2,4,5,13,
14,19,19
2:7,15
3:9,13
4:1,6,12
5:8,8,12
6:10,11,12,
21
2 TM 1:5,13

2 TM 2:13,18,22
3:8,10,15
4:7
TIT 1:1,4,9,13
2:2
3:15
PLM 5,6
HEB 4:2
6:1,12
10:22,38,
39
11:1,3,4,5,
6,7,7,8,
9,11,13,
17,20,
21,22,
23,24,
27,28,
29,30,
31,33,
39
12:2
13:7
JAM 1:3,6
2:1,5,14,
14,17,18,
18,18,20,
22,22,24,
26
5:15
1 PT 1:5,7,8,9,
21
3:15
5:9
2 PT 1:1,5
1 JN 5:4
3 JN 5
JUD 3,20
REV 2:13,19
13:10
14:12

[m]ETHP

Perfect

ROM 3:2
GAL 2:7[1],7[2]
1 TM 1:11

1 TM 3:16
TIT 1:3
HEB 3:5

Imperfect

1 TH 2:4

2 TH 1:10

172 ܐܡܪ (v) say

[a]PEAL

Perfect

MAT 1:20; 2:5,8,13[1],17[2],20; 3:7,15; 4:3[1],3[2],
4,6,9,10,14[2],19; 8:2,3,4[1],8[1],10[1],13,17[2],19,21,
22; 9:2,3,4,6,9,12,18,22,24,29,30,37; 10:5;
11:3,4,25; 12:3,11,13,17[2],25,39,47,48[1],48[2],
49; 13:11,14,24,28[1],29,31,33,35[2],37,51[1],57;
14:2,8,15,16,17,27,28,29,30,31,33; 15:3,4,7,
10,13,15,16,24,25,26,27,28,32; 16:2[1],6,8,11,
12,14[1],16,17,22,23,24; 17:4,7,9[1],11,13,15,
17,22,24,25[2]; 18:3[1],21,26,28,29,32; 19:4,5,
11,14,16,17,18[2],23[1],26,27; 20:4,6,8,13,17,
21[1],22[1],25,32; 21:2,4[2],13,19,21[1],24[1],28,29,
30[1],30[2],38,45; 22:1,4[1],8,12,13,18,20,21[2],24[2],
29,31[2],37,42[1],44; 23:2; 24:2[1],4,25; 25:12[1],20,
22,24,26,40[1]; 26:1,8,10,15,17,18[1],21[1],23,25[1],
25[3],26,27,31,33,35[2],36,38,40,42,44,45,48,
49,50,52,55,61[2],62,63[1],64[2],65,70[1],73,75;
27:4[1],4[2],6,9[2],11[1],11[3],13,17,21[1],21[2],23[2],24,
25,46,54,63[2]; 28:5,6,7[2],9,10[1],11,18
MRK 1:15,17,24,25,30,40,41,44[1]; 2:5,8,10,
14,16,17,27; 3:3,4,5,9,23,32,33,34; 4:9,11,
13,21,24,26,30,35,39,40; 5:7,14,19,30,33,34,
36[1],36[2],39,41,43; 6:4,10,14,16,18,22,30,31,
37[1],38[1],50; 7:6,10,14,27,34; 8:1,7,12[1],15,17,
24,26[1],28,29[3],33,34; 9:1[1],5,17,18,19,25,35,
36; 10:5,11,14,20,21,23,24,27,29[1],38,42,51[2],
52; 11:2,5,6,14,21,22,29[1],31[1]; 12:6,7,12,15,
16[2],26,32[2],34,35[1],36[1],36[2],43[1]; 13:1,2,23;
14:4,6,13,16,18[1],20,22,24,27,31[2],32,34,36,
37,39,41,44,45,48,57,58,60,61,62,63,68[1],70,
72; 15:2[1],2[2],4,9,12,14,28,34,36,39; 16:6,7[2],
13,15 LUK 1:13,18,19,28,30,35,42,46,61,
63,67; 2:10,28,34,48,50; 3:4,7,11,13,16; 4:3[1],
4,6,8,9,12[1],24[1],34,35,43; 5:3,4,5,8,10,12,13,
20,22,27,31,34,36; 6:3,5,8,9,10,20,39; 7:6,
9[1],13,19,22[1],39,40[1],40[3],40[4],43[1],44,48,50;
8:4,10[1],20,21,22,25[1],28,38,45[1],46,47,48,49,
50,52,54; 9:3,9,18[1],20[3],22,33[1],36,38,41,43,
48,49,55,57,59[1],59[2]; 10:2,18,21,22,23,25,26,
27,28[2],29,35,37[1],40[2],41; 11:1,5[1],15,17,27,39,
45[1],46,49,53; 12:3,13[1],14,15,16,17,18,22[1],
54[1]; 13:1,2,6,7,12,14,15,18,20,24[1]; 14:3,5,7,
12,15,21[1],21[2],22,23,25; 15:3,11,12,17,21,22,
29; 16:1,2,5,7[1],15,24,30; 17:1,5,14,17,19,20,
22; 18:1,4,6[1],6[2],9,16,18,22,24,27,31,38,41[1],
41[2],42; 19:5,8,12,13,15,16,18,19,20,24,28,
30,32,34,42,46; 20:3[1],7,16,17,19,23,24,41[1],
42[1],42[2],45; 21:3[1],5[2],8[1],29; 22:8,9,13,15,19,
20,25,31,33,35[1],40,46,51,52,57,58[1],58[2],61;
23:3[1],3[3],4,14,22,28,34,40,42,46[1],46[2],47;
24:7,9,17,18,24,25,36,40,41,44,46
JHN 1:15[1],15[2],21[1],21[2],22[1],23[1],23[2],25,26,29,
30,32,33,36,37,38[1],41,42,43,45,47,49,50[2];
2:10,16,18,19,21,22[1],22[2]; 3:2,3[1],5[1],7,9,10,
12[1],26,27,28; 4:7,10[1],10[2],13,17[3],18,27,29,32,
39,50[2],53; 5:6,7,11[1],11[2],12,14,15,17,19[1]; 6:5,
6,12,20,26[1],29,36,41,43,59,61,65[1],65[2],67,68,
71; 7:3,9,16,21,28,33,36,38,39,42,45; 8:6,7,
10,11[1],11[2],12,14,19[2],23,24,27,31; 9:6,7,11[1],
11[2],15,20,22,23,25,27[2],30,35,36,38,39,40;
10:6,25[1],25[2],26,34[2],35,36[2],41[2]; 11:4,7,11[1],
11[2],13[1],13[2],14,21,28[1],34[1],37,39[1],40[2],41,43,
46,49,51; 12:4,6,7,22[1],22[2],23,30,33,38,39,
41,44,50; 13:7,11,12,21[1],21[2],22,24,25,26,27,
28,31,33[1],36[2]; 14:23,28,29; 15:20; 16:4[1],4[2],6,
15,17[1],17[2],18[2],19[1],19[2],33; 17:1; 18:1,4,6,7,
8[2],9,11,16,17[1],20,21,22[1],22[2],23,25[2],29,32,
33,34[2],34[3],37[3],38[2],38[3]; 19:4,5,9,14,21[1],21[2],
24[1],24[2],26,27,28,30,35,36,37; 20:14,18,19,

20,21,22[1],22[2],25[2],26,27,28; 21:5[1],7,10,12,
15[1],17[2],17[3],19[1],19[2],19[3],20,21,23 ACT 1:9,
15,16,24; 2:14,25,34[1],34[2],37; 3:4,12,22,25;
4:8,13,19,23,24; 5:3,8[3],19,29,35,36; 6:2,11[2],
14; 7:2,3,27,31,33,37,48,56,60[1],60[2]; 8:24[1],
24[2],26,29,30,31,34[1],34[2],36; 9:5[1],5[2],10[1],10[2],
11,13,15,17,34,40; 10:3,4[1],4[2],14,19,21,26,
28[1],31,34,46; 11:8,9,12,13,16; 12:7,8[1],8[2],11,
17; 13:2,10,15,16,22,34,35,46[1]; 14:10[1]; 15:7,
13,36; 16:18,28,30,36,38[1]; 17:22,28; 18:6,9,
14; 19:15,21,25,41; 20:10,18,35,36,38;
21:11[1],13,14,20,37[1],37[2],40; 22:2,8[1],8[2],10[1],
10[2],13,14,19,21,25,26,27[1],27[3],28[1]; 23:1,3,7,
11,17[1],18[1],20,23,35; 24:10,25; 25:9,10,12,
16,20,22[1],22[2],24; 26:1[1],15[1],15[2],16,22[2],29,32;
27:21,24,31,35; 28:6,17,21[2],25
ROM 3:19[1],19[2]; 4:3,6[1]; 7:7[2]; 9:15,17,25,29;
10:8,11,16,19[2],20,21; 11:2[1],9; 13:9; 15:10,
11,12 1 CO 9:8[2],10; 11:24,25; 14:34;
15:27 2 CO 4:6; 6:2; 7:3[2]; 9:3; 12:9; 13:2[1],
2[3] GAL 1:9[1]; 2:14; 3:8,16; 4:30; 5:21[1]
PHL 3:18[1] 1 TH 3:4; 4:6 2 TH 2:5
1 TM 5:18 TIT 1:12 HEB 1:5,6,7,8,13;
3:7,10; 4:3,4,5,7; 5:5,6; 6:14; 7:11,14,15,21;
8:8[1],9,13; 9:20; 10:5,7,8,9,15,30; 12:5,21,26,
27; 13:5 JAM 2:11[1],11[2],23; 4:5,6 JUD 9
REV 3:17; 5:5; 7:3,13,14[1],14[2]; 10:9[2],11;
12:10; 17:7[1],15; 18:21; 19:3,9[1],9[2],10,17;
21:5[1],5[2],6; 22:6,9,10

Imperfect

MAT 3:9[1]; 5:22[2],22[3]; 6:31; 7:22; 12:32[1],32[2],
36[2]; 13:54; 15:5[2]; 16:20; 17:9[2],20[3]; 21:21[3],
24[2],25[2],26; 23:3[1],39[2]; 24:5,23,26,48; 25:34,
37,41,44,45[1]; 26:63[2]; 27:64; 28:8
MRK 7:11[2],36; 8:26[2],30; 9:9,26; 10:32;
11:3[1],23[2],29[2],31[2],32; 13:6,21; 14:40,69
LUK 4:23[2],41[2]; 5:14; 7:40[2]; 8:56; 9:21,54[2];
11:5[2],7; 12:10,11,12,19,45; 13:25[2],27,35[2];
14:9,10,17; 15:18; 17:4,23; 20:5[2],6,9; 21:8[2];
22:67[4]; 23:29 JHN 3:12[2]; 12:27,49
ACT 6:11[1]; 10:28[2]; 15:27; 16:35; 23:17[2],18[2],
19,30; 24:20 ROM 3:5; 6:1; 8:31; 9:14,19,
30; 10:6[2]; 11:19; 15:18 1 CO 1:15; 10:28[1];
11:22; 12:15,16,21[1],21[2]; 14:9[1],16[1],25,26[2];
15:35 2 CO 9:4 1 TH 1:8; 5:3 TIT 2:8
PLM 19 HEB 7:9; 8:11; 9:5; 11:32; 13:6
JAM 1:13; 2:3[1],3[2],16; 4:13[1],15 1 JN 1:8;
4:20 2 JN 10 REV 18:10; 22:17[2]

Imperative

MAT 8:8[2]; 10:7,27[2]; 18:17; 20:21[3]; 21:3[2],5;
22:4[2],17; 24:3[2]; 26:18[2]; 28:7[1],10[2],13[2]
MRK 11:3[2],30; 13:4; 14:14[1]; 16:7[1]
LUK 4:3[2]; 7:7,22[2]; 10:5,9,10; 12:13[2]; 13:32[2];
17:10; 19:31; 20:2[2],3[2]; 22:11[1],67[2]
JHN 10:24[2]; 20:15[3],17[2] ACT 5:8[2]; 22:27[2];
28:26[2] GAL 4:21 COL 4:17

Infinitive

MAT 4:17; 9:5[1],5[2]; 11:7; 26:22 MRK 2:9[1],
9[2]; 10:28,47; 13:5 LUK 3:8[1]; 4:21; 5:23[1],
23[2]; 6:42; 7:24; 11:29; 12:1; 13:25[1],26; 19:11;
23:30 JHN 8:26; 16:12 ACT 2:29; 4:14;
5:27; 11:4; 17:21; 19:36 1 CO 12:3[2]
HEB 5:11 REV 1:17; 4:1,8; 11:17; 13:4,
14; 14:7,9; 17:1; 21:9

Active Participle

MAT 2:2,13[2],15[2]; 3:2,9[2],14,17; 4:7; 5:2,11,
18,20,22[1],26,28,32,34,39,44; 6:2,5,16,25,29;
7:4,21; 8:4[2],6,7,9,10[2],11,20,25,26,27,29,31,
32; 9:11,14,15,21,27,28[1],28[2],33,34; 10:15,
23,27[1],42; 11:9,11,17,18,19,21,22,24; 12:2,
6,10,23,24,31,36[1],38,44; 13:3,10,17,27,28[2],
30,36,51[2],52; 14:4,18,26; 15:1,5[1],12,22,23,
33,34[1],34[2]; 16:2[2],3,7,13[1],13[2],14[2],15[1],15[2],18,
28; 17:5,10[1],10[2],12,19,20[1],20[2],25[1],26[1],26[2];
18:1,3[2],10,13,18,19,22[1],22[2]; 19:3,7,8,9,10,
18[1],20,21,23[2],24,25,28[1],28[2]; 20:7[1],7[2],12,21[2],
22[2],23,30,31,33; 21:3[1],9,10,11,15,16[1],16[2],
16[3],20,21[2],23,24[3],25[1],25[3],27[1],27[2],27[3],31[1],
31[2],31[3],37,41,42,43; 22:16,21[1],23,24[1],42[2],
42[3],43[1],43[2]; 23:3[2],16,30,36,39[1]; 24:2[2],3[1],34,
47; 25:8,9,11,12[2],21,23,40[2],45[2]; 26:5,13,18[3],
21[2],25[2],29,34[1],34[2],35[1],39,61[1],64[1],64[3],66,68,
69,70[2],71; 27:11[2],19,22[1],22[2],23[1],29,40,42,
43,47,49,63[1],65; 28:13[1] MRK 1:7,27,37,
38,44[2]; 2:11,12,18,19,24,25; 3:11,21,22,28,
30; 4:2,38,41; 5:8,9,12,23,28,31[1],31[2],35; 6:2,
11,15,24[1],24[2],25,35,37[2],38[2]; 7:9,11[1],18,28,
29,37; 8:4,5,12[2],16,19,20[1],20[2],21,27[1],27[2],
29[1],29[2]; 9:1[2],6,7,11[1],11[2],12,13,21,23,24,29,
31,38,39[1],39[2],41; 10:3,4,15,17,18,26,29[2],35,
36,37,39[1],39[2],48,49,51[1]; 11:9,17,23[1],23[3],23[4],
24,28,29[3],31[3],33[1],33[2],33[3]; 12:16[1],17,18[1],18[2],
24,29,32[1],35[2],38,43[2]; 13:30,37[1],37[2]; 14:2,9,
12,14[2],18[2],19,25,29,30[1],30[2],31[1],65,67,68[2],
71; 15:29,31,35; 16:3,8,11 LUK 1:24,34,
38,60,66; 2:13,15,49; 3:8[2],10,12,14[1],14[2],22;
4:22,23[1],24[2],25,36,41[1]; 5:21,24[1],24[2],26,30,
33,39; 6:2,26,27,46; 7:4,8,9[2],14[1],14[2],16,20[1],
20[2],26,28,32,33,34,40[5],43[2],47,49; 8:8,24,25[2],
30,45[2],45[3]; 9:7,8,12,13[1],13[2],14,18[2],19,20[1],
20[2],23,27,31,33[2],34,35,50,54[1],58,60,61,62;
10:12,17,24,28[1],30,37[2],40[1]; 11:2[1],2[2],8,9,18,
24,28,45[2],51; 12:4,5,8,20,22[2],27,37,41[1],41[2],
42,44,51,54[2],55,59; 13:3,5,8,17,24[2],25[3],31,
32[1],35[1]; 14:16,18,19,20,24,30; 15:2,6,7,9,10,
27,31; 16:3,6[1],6[2],7[2],7[3],9,25,27,29,31; 17:6[1],
6[2],7,8,13,21,34,37[1],37[2]; 18:3,8,13,14,17,19,
21,26,28,29[1],29[2],37; 19:7,9,14,17,22,25,26[1],
26[2],33,38,39,40[1],40[2]; 20:2[1],5[1],5[3],8[1],8[2],13,14,
21,25,27,28,34,37,39[1],39[2],41[2]; 21:3[2],5[1],7,32;
22:10,11[2],16,34[1],34[2],35[2],36,37,38[1],38[2],42,
48,49,56,59,60[1],60[2],64,65,67[1],67[3],70[1],70[2],
70[3],71; 23:2[1],2[2],3[2],5,18,21,35,37,39,43[1],43[2];
24:5,10,19[1],19[2],23[1],23[2],29,32,34,38
JHN 1:22[2],38[2],39,46[1],46[2],48[1],48[2],50[1],51[1],
51[2]; 2:3,4,5[1],5[2],7,8,20; 3:3[2],4,5[2],11; 4:9,11,
15,16,17[1],17[2],19,20,21,25,26,28,31,33,34,
35[1],35[2],42,48,49,50[1],51,52; 5:8,10,18,19[2],24,
25,34; 6:7,8,10,14,25,26[2],28,30,32[1],32[2],34,
35,42[1],42[2],47,52,53[1],53[2],60,70; 7:6,11,12[1],
12[2],15,20,25,26,31,35,37,40,41[1],41[2],46,47,
50,52; 8:4,5,13,19[1],21,22[1],22[2],25[1],25[2],28,
33[1],33[2],34[1],34[2],39[1],39[2],41,42,48[1],48[2],49,51,
52[1],52[2],54[1],54[2],55,57,58[1],58[2]; 9:2,3,8,9[1],9[2],

9[3],10,12[1],12[2],16[1],16[2],17[1],17[2],17[3],17[4],19,24, 26,27[1],28,34,37,41[1],41[2]; 10:1,7[1],7[2],20,21, 24[1],32,33,34[1],36[1],41[1]; 11:3,8,9,12,16[1],23,24, 25,27,28[2],32,34[2],36,39[2],40[1],42,44,47,56; 12:13,19,21,24,29[1],29[2],34[1],34[2],35; 13:6,8[1], 8[2],9,10,13,16,18,19,20,21[3],33[2],36[1],37,38[1], 38[2]; 14:2,5,6,8,9[1],9[2],12,22,26; 16:7,18[1],20, 23,26,29[1],29[2],31; 18:5[1],5[2],8[1],17[2],25[1],26,30, 31[1],31[2],34[1],35,36,37[1],37[2],38[1],40; 19:3,6[1],6[2], 7,10,11,15[1],15[2],22,31; 20:2,13[1],13[2],15[1],15[2], 16[1],16[2],17[1],25[1],29; 21:3[1],3[2],5[2],6,15[2],15[3],16[1], 16[2],16[3],17[1],17[4],18,22 ACT 1:3,6,7,11; 2:7, 12,13,17,38,40; 3:6; 4:15,32; 5:8[1],9,23,38; 6:13; 7:6,7,26,35,40,49,59; 8:6,9,10,19,20; 9:4,21; 10:13,22[1],30; 11:3,7,18; 12:14,15[1], 15[2],22; 13:25,45; 14:10[2],11,15,18,22; 15:5, 17,19,24; 16:9,14,15,17,20,31,37; 17:7,18[1], 18[2],19,32; 18:13,21; 19:2,3[1],3[2],4[1],4[2],13,26, 28,35; 20:23; 21:4,11[2],21[2],23,28,36,39; 22:7, 18,28[2]; 23:4,5,8,9,14; 24:2,9,14,22; 25:14,19; 26:1[2],14,22[1],25,28,31; 27:10,33; 28:4,21[1],26[1] ROM 2:22; 3:8[1],8[2]; 4:1,6[2],9; 6:19; 7:7[1]; 9:1, 20; 10:6[1],18,19[1]; 11:1,2[2],11,13; 12:3,19; 14:11; 15:8 1 CO 1:12[1],12[2],12[3],12[4],12[5]; 3:4[1],4[2]; 5:10; 6:5; 7:6,8,12,29,35; 9:8[1]; 10:15[1],15[2],19,28[2],29[1],29[2]; 12:3[1]; 14:9[2],16[2], 21,23,26[1]; 15:12,34,50,51 2 CO 6:13,17, 18; 7:3[1]; 10:10,11; 11:16,21[1],21[2],23; 12:6; 13:2[2] GAL 1:9[2]; 3:15,17; 4:1; 5:2,16,21[2] EPH 4:17; 5:32 PHL 3:18[2]; 4:4,11 COL 2:4 1 TH 4:15 1 TM 2:7; 4:1 2 TM 2:7,18 PLM 21 HEB 2:6,12; 4:8; 8:8[2],10; 10:16; 11:14 JAM 2:14,18; 4:13[2] 2 PT 3:4 1 JN 1:6,10; 2:4,6,9; 5:16 2 JN 11 JUD 14,18 REV 1:8,10; 2:1,2, 8,9,12,18,20,24[1],24[2]; 3:1,7,9,14; 4:10; 5:9, 12,13,14; 6:1,3,5,6,7,10,16; 7:10,12; 8:13; 9:14; 10:4,8,9[1]; 11:1,12,15; 14:8,13[1],13[2]; 15:3; 16:1,5,7,17; 17:7[2]; 18:4,7,16,18,19; 19:1,4,5,6; 21:3; 22:17[1],20

Passive Participle

MAT 3:3 MRK 13:14 LUK 2:24,26; 4:12[2] ACT 2:16 1 CO 6:16 2 CO 6:16 EPH 4:8; 5:14 HEB 3:15 1 PT 2:6

---

[b]ETHPEEL

Perfect

MAT 1:22; 2:15[1],17[1],23; 4:14[1]; 5:21,27,31, 33,38,43; 8:17[1]; 12:17[1]; 13:35[1]; 21:4[1]; 22:31[1]; 24:15; 27:9[1] ACT 10:22[2]; 16:38[2]; 21:21[1], 24 ROM 9:7,12; 11:4; 15:21 HEB 7:13; 8:5; 11:18 2 PT 3:2 JUD 17 REV 6:11; 9:4

Imperfect

ACT 13:46[2]

Participle

LUK 8:10[2] JHN 11:16[2]; 19:17; 20:16[3],24; 21:2 REV 8:11

---

173 ܐܡܪ, ܐܡܪܐ (m) lamb

MAT	7:15	REV	7:9,10,14,17
	10:16		12:11
MRK	14:27		13:8,11
LUK	10:3		14:1,4,4,10
JHN	1:29,36		15:3
	21:15		17:14,14
ACT	8:32		19:7,9
ROM	8:36		21:9,23,23,27
HEB	11:37		22:1,3
1 PT	1:19		
REV	5:6,8,12,13		
	6:1,16		

---

176 ܐܡܬܝ, (adv) when

MAT 5:11; 6:2,6,16; 10:19; 12:43; 17:17,17; 24:3; 25:37,38,39,44 MRK 5:4; 9:19,19; 13:4,33,35; 14:7 LUK 9:41; 11:2,21,34; 12:36; 14:8; 17:20; 21:7 JHN 4:23; 5:25, 28; 6:25; 7:27; 8:28,44; 10:24; 16:25 ACT 5:15; 24:25 ROM 15:29 1 CO 7:5; 11:25,26,33; 12:26; 13:10; 14:26; 16:12 2 CO 3:14,15,16; 12:10 GAL 4:18 COL 3:4 HEB 1:6; 12:5 REV 6:10

---

165 (ܐܡܬܘܣܛܘܣ), ܐܡܬܘܣܛܘܣ (c)

amethyst

REV 21:20

---

177 ܐܢ (conj) if

incl comp with 747 ܗܘ

see below 180 ܐܢܝ

see also 133 ܐܠܐ

see also 254 ܐܦ

MAT 4:3,6,9; 5:13,23,29,30,46,47; 6:14,15, 22,23,23,30; 7:10,11; 8:2,31; 10:13,13,25; 11:14,27,27; 12:4,10,11,26,27,28,29; 14:28; 15:14,20; 16:26; 17:4,8,20; 18:8,9,12,13,15, 15,17,17,19,21; 19:3,10,17,17,21; 21:3,21, 24,25; 22:24,45; 24:23,24,26,48; 26:35,39, 42,42,63; 27:40,42,43,49; 28:14 MRK 1:40; 2:7,26; 3:2,24,25,26,27; 4:23; 6:4,5,8; 7:3,11; 8:3,36; 9:9,23,43,45,47,50;

10:2,12; 11:3,13,13,26,31; 12:19; 13:21,22, 32; 14:29,31,35; 15:36,44,44; 16:18 LUK 4:3,7,9,27; 5:12,21,37; 6:7,32,33,34; 7:25,26; 9:13; 10:6,6,22,22,22,35; 11:8,11, 12,13,18,19,20,22,25,34,36; 12:26,28,38,45; 13:5,9,23; 14:3,28,31,32,34; 15:4; 16:11,12, 30,31,31; 17:3,3,4,6,7,23; 18:4,19; 19:31,40; 20:5,6,28,44; 22:42,67,67,68; 23:6,31,35,37, 39 JHN 1:25; 3:3,5,12,12,27; 4:48; 5:31, 43,47; 6:22,44,51,62; 7:4,17,23,37,49,51; 8:16,24,31,36,46,54,55; 9:19,22,25; 10:9,24, 35,37,38; 11:9,10,12,40,48,57; 12:24,26; 13:8,14,17,17,32,35; 14:2,3,6,11,14,15; 15:6, 7,10,14,18,20,20; 16:7,7; 18:8,23,23; 19:12, 15; 20:15,23,23,25; 21:22,23 ACT 1:6; 3:26; 4:9,19; 5:8,38,39; 7:1; 8:30,31; 9:2; 10:18; 11:17; 13:15,41; 15:1; 16:15; 17:11; 18:15,25; 19:2,2,38,39; 20:16; 21:37; 23:9; 24:19,21; 25:11,11,20; 26:4; 27:12,22,31,39 ROM 1:10,16,16; 2:14,17,25,25,26; 3:3,5,7; 5:6,8,10,15,17; 6:5,8,16,16; 7:2,3,3,3,16,20; 8:9,9,10,11,13,13,17,17,24,25,31,32; 9:22, 27; 10:9; 11:6,6,12,15,16,16,17,18,21,22,24, 24; 12:18,20,20,20; 13:4,9; 14:4,4,8,8,8,8,15; 15:27 1 CO 1:16; 2:2,11,11; 3:12,22,22,22, 22,22,22,22,22; 4:7,15,19; 5:11; 6:2,4; 7:8, 11,12,14,15,16,16,18,18,21,28,28,36,39,40; 8:2,3,4,8,10,12,13; 9:2,11,11,12,17,17; 10:27,28,30,31,31,31; 11:6,6,16; 12:3,13,13, 13,13,15,16,26,31; 13:1,2,2,3,3; 14:5,5,6,6,7, 7,7,8,9,11,14,16,23,24,27,28,30,35,37,38; 15:2,2,11,11,12,13,14,16,17,19,29,32,32; 16:4,7,10 2 CO 1:6,7; 2:2,5,9; 3:7,9,11; 4:3,11; 5:1,9,9,10,10,13,13,16; 8:12,23,23; 9:1; 10:7,8; 11:4,14,15,22,22,22,23,30; 12:2, 2,3,3,5,6,13; 13:2,5 GAL 1:9,19; 2:14,17, 18,21; 3:18,29; 4:7; 5:2,15,18; 6:1,3 EPH 3:2; 4:9,21; 6:8,8 PHL 1:18,18,20, 20,21,22,27,27; 2:1,1,1,1; 3:4,15 COL 1:16,16,16,16,20,20,23; 2:20; 3:1,13; 4:10 1 TH 2:19; 3:8; 4:14; 5:10,10 2 TH 1:6; 2:7,15,15; 3:11,14 1 TM 1:8; 2:15; 3:1,5,15; 4:4,6; 5:4,8,10,10,10,10,10, 16; 6:3 2 TM 2:5,5,11,12,12,13,21 PLM 17,18 HEB 2:2,3; 3:6,7,14,15; 4:7; 6:3,8; 9:13; 10:26,28,38; 12:8,9,25,25; 13:23 JAM 1:5,23,26; 2:2,8,9,11,14,15; 3:14; 4:11, 14,15; 5:13,13,14,15,19 1 PT 1:17; 2:3; 3:13,14,17; 4:1,14,16,17,18 2 PT 2:4,20 1 JN 1:6,7,8,9,10; 2:1,3,22,24,27,29; 3:13, 20,21; 4:1,11,12,20; 5:9,15,16 2 JN 10 3 JN 10 REV 3:20; 9:4; 19:12; 21:27

180 ܐܢܕܝܢ (conj) but if

from 177 ܐܢ (above) and 670 ܕܝܢ

REV 2:5,16; 3:3

---

178 ܐܢܐ (pron) I, we

incl ܚܢܢ

MAT 2:8,13; 3:9,11,11,11,14,14; 5:18,22,28, 32,34,34,39,39,44,44; 6:2,12,16; 8:7,8,9,9,9, 10,11,25; 9:14,14,21; 10:16,32,33,42; 11:3, 10,10,22,28,29,29; 12:27,27,28,31,38; 14:27, 27; 15:32,32; 16:18; 17:19,20; 18:3,18,20,29, 33; 19:20,23,24,27,28; 20:4,13,15,15,18,22, 22,22,22,23,23; 21:21,24,24,24,26,27,27,27, 30; 22:16,32,32; 23:34,36; 24:5,5,47; 25:12, 12,26,26,27,40,45; 26:15,15,18,22,25,32,32, 33,34,39,48,53,61,63; 27:24,43,63; 28:13,14, 14,18,18,20,20 MRK 1:2,7,8,24,41; 2:11; 3:28; 4:38; 5:7,9,28; 6:16,50,50; 8:2; 9:1,24, 25,28; 10:28,29,33,35,38,38,39,39,39; 11:29, 29,33,33; 12:14,26,26; 13:6,6; 14:7,9,19,25, 28,29,30,32,44,49,58,58,58,58,62,62,68 LUK 1:1,1,18,19,19,19,38; 2:48; 3:14,16,16; 4:6; 5:8; 7:6,7,8,8,8,8,9,27,43; 8:24,46; 9:9,9, 27; 10:3,3,11,12,19,21,24,35,35; 11:4,7,8,9, 18,19,20,49; 12:8,37,44,50,51,59; 13:3,5,7, 25,32,32,35; 14:18,18,19,19; 15:7,10,17,17, 19,21,29; 16:2,3,3,9,24; 17:4,10; 18:4,4,12, 12,12,14,17,28,29,31; 19:8,13,14,22,22,22, 23; 20:3,7,8,8,21; 21:8,8,15,32; 22:16,27,29, 29,32,33,34,37,47,57,70,70,71; 23:4,4,14,41, 46; 24:21,36,36,39,39,49 JHN 1:16,20,20, 23,26,26,27,27,30,31,31,33,34,48,51; 2:19, 19; 3:2,5,11,11,11,28,28; 4:14,14,19,22,22, 22,26,26,26,38,42,42; 5:7,17,17,19,25,30,30, 30,31,31,32,34,36,41,43,45,45; 6:20,20,26, 35,35,40,41,41,42,44,47,48,48,51,51,51,51, 54,56,57,57,63,69,70; 7:7,8,8,17,17,27,28, 29,29,33,33,34,35,35,36; 8:11,11,12,12,14, 14,14,14,15,15,16,16,18,18,18,21,21,21,21, 23,23,23,24,24,26,26,28,28,28,29,29,33,38, 38,41,42,45,45,46,48,49,50,51,54,54,55,55, 55,55,55,58,58; 9:5,5,9,9,17,20,21,24,25,25, 28,28,31,38,40,40,41; 10:1,7,7,9,9,10,11,11, 14,14,14,14,15,15,15,15,17,17,18,18,18,18,25, 27,28,28,30,30,33,34,36,36,37,38; 11:11,15, 16,25,25,27,42,48; 12:21,26,28,32,34,46,47, 47,49,50,50,50; 13:7,8,14,15,19,19,26,26,33, 33,33,34,34,36,37,37,38; 14:2,3,4,5,5,6,6,9, 10,10,10,10,11,12,12,12,12,14,16,19,20,20, 20,21,23,23,26,27,27,27,28,28,28,28,31,31; 15:1,1,4,5,5,5,5,9,10,10,12,14,15,16,19,20, 22,26,26; 16:4,5,7,7,7,7,10,16,17,18,23,26, 26,27,28,28,30,30,33; 17:4,9,9,9,10,11,11, 11,12,13,14,14,16,18,19,19,21,22,22,22,23, 24,25,26,26; 18:5,5,6,6,8,8,20,26,35,35,37, 37,37,38,38; 19:4,4,6,6,10,10,21; 20:17,21, 25,25,25; 21:3,3,15,16,17,22,22,23,23,25 ACT 2:8,8,11,32; 3:6,15,17; 4:9,9,16,20; 5:32,32,38; 6:4,11,14; 7:7,32,32,40,56; 8:9,9, 23,31,34; 9:5,5,10,16; 10:20,21,26,26,29,30, 30,33,33,39,47; 11:17; 13:2,25,25,32,32,33, 41,46; 14:10,15,15,15; 15:10,11,19,19,24,25; 16:16,18,21,28; 17:3,19,20,22,23,28,28,29, 32; 18:6,6,6,10,10,15,15; 19:13,15,15,40,40; 20:6,7,13,19,22,22,22,22,25,26,26,29,29,29, 31,32; 21:7,12,13,13,23,25,39,39,39,39; 22:3,3,3,6,8,8,19,19,20,21,21,28,28; 23:1,6, 6,6,9,15,15,27,35; 24:2,3,4,8,10,10,12,12,14, 14,14,16,18,21,21,22; 25:4,4,10,11,11,20,25, 26,27; 26:2,2,2,2,3,3,6,6,7,9,15,17,22,22,22, 25,26,26,27; 27:8,10,22,23,23,25,34; 28:17, 20,21,22,22 ROM 1:8,9,9,10,11,13,14,15,

16; 2:2; 3:5,7,7,8,9,19,31,31; 4:1,9; 5:2,2,3; 6:4,6,9,19; 7:1,7,9,9,14,14,14,14,15,15,15, 15,15,15,16,16,16,17,17,18,18,19,19,19,19, 20,20,20,20,21,22,23,24,25,25,25; 8:4,12,15, 18,22,23,23,23,24,25,25,26,28,37,38; 9:1,1, 3,15,15,24,33; 10:2,8,18,19; 11:1,1,1,3,11, 13,13,13,19,25; 12:1,3,5,5,5,5,19; 14:8,8,8,8, 8,8,8,10,11,14,14; 15:1,1,8,14,14,18,20,24, 24,25,28,29,29,29,30,31; 16:1,4,4,17,19,19, 22,22 1 CO 1:4,10,12,12,12,12,12,12,12, 12,12,14,16,18,23,23; 2:1,2,3,6,7,12,13,13; 3:1,4,4,4,4,6,9; 4:3,3,4,8,9,10,10,10,11,11, 11,11,12,12,12,12,13,14,14,15,16,17,18,19; 5:3,3,3,4,10; 6:3,5; 7:6,7,7,8,10,12,12,17,25, 25,26,28,28,29,32,35,40,40; 8:1,4,6,6,8,8,8; 9:6,8,11,11,12,15,16,17,17,18,19,23,25,26, 26,26,27,27,27,27; 10:1,15,15,16,16,17,17, 19,20,22,22,29,30,30,30,30,30,33,33,33; 11:1,2,3,17,17,18,18,22,23,32,32; 12:1,3,13, 23,23,23,31; 13:3,9,12,12; 14:5,6,11,11,18, 18,19,26,37; 15:1,9,9,9,10,11,11,15,19,19, 30,30,31,31,32,34,50,52; 16:4,5,5,6,7,7,8,11, 15,17 2 CO 1:4,4,4,6,6,6,6,6,7,8,10,13,13, 14,17,20,23,23,23,24,24; 2:2,2,2,3,8,10,10, 15,17; 3:1,1,5,5,12,18,18,18; 4:1,2,2,2,2,5,5, 8,8,8,8,9,9,9,9,11,11,13,13,14,18; 5:1,2,2,4, 4,6,6,6,7,8,8,9,9,10,11,11,11,11,11,12,12, 13,13,14,16,16,16,20,20,21; 6:1,4,9,9,9,9,9, 10,10,13,17; 7:3,4,8,16,16; 8:1,3,6,8,8,10,20, 21; 9:1,1,2,4; 10:1,1,1,1,1,2,2,2,3,3,4,5,5,6,7, 8,9,9,11,11,12,13,13,14,14,15; 11:2,3,4,5,6, 9,11,12,16,16,16,17,17,18,21,21,21,21,21, 21,22,22,22,23,23,29,29,29,29,31; 12:1,2,2, 3,3,6,6,6,10,10,10,13,14,14,15,15,16,19,19, 20,20,20; 13:1,2,2,2,2,4,4,4,6,6,7,7,9,9,9,10, 10 GAL 1:6,8,10,10,11,12,20,20; 2:2,2,9, 10,15,15,16,16,17,17,18,18,19,20,20,20,20, 20,21; 3:2,14,15,17,23; 4:1,3,11,12,12,15,18, 19,20,28,28,31; 5:2,3,5,5,10,10,11,16,21; 6:9,14,14,17,17 EPH 1:11,12,15,16,19; 2:3,10; 3:1,1,7,8,13,14,20,20; 4:1,1,17,17,25; 5:30,30,32,32; 6:20,21 PHL 1:3,4,4,6,8,9, 12,16,18,19,20,20,22,23,25,25,25,27,27; 2:12,12,17,17,17,19,23,24,24,24; 3:3,3,3,4,8, 12,13,13,13,13,13,14,18,18,20; 4:2,3,11,11, 12,12,12,13,17,17,18 COL 1:3,3,9,9,23, 24,24,25,28,28,28,28,29,29; 2:1,4,5,5,5,5; 4:3,13 1 TH 1:2,2,3,4; 2:4,4,8,8,8,12,13, 13,17,18; 3:3,4,5,6,8,9,9,12,12; 4:1,1,10,13, 14,15,15,15,17,17,17; 5:8,8,10,10,12,14,27 2 TH 1:3,4,4,11; 2:1,13,13; 3:4,4,6,11,12,12, 17,17 1 TM 1:3,8,11,12,15,15,18; 2:1,7,7, 7,8,12; 3:14,14,14,15; 4:10,10,10,13; 5:14, 21; 6:7,13 2 TM 1:3,3,3,4,4,5,6,11,12,12, 12,12; 2:7,9,10; 4:1,6,6 TIT 1:3; 2:13; 3:3, 8 PLM 4,4,9,9,10,19,19,19,20,21,21,21, 22,22 HEB 1:5,5; 2:1,3,5,8,9,13,13; 3:6, 19; 4:2,3,13; 5:5; 6:4,9,9,11; 7:19; 8:9,10; 10:7,7,9,30,30,39; 11:3; 12:1,9,21,21,25,26; 13:13,13,14,18,19,22 JAM 1:13; 2:18,18; 3:1,2,3,3,9,9; 4:13,13,13,13,15; 5:11 1 PT 1:16,16; 2:6,11; 5:1,1,12,12,12 2 PT 1:12,12,14,15,18; 3:1,1 1 JN 1:1,2,2, 3,4,5,6,6,6,6,7,8,9,10,10; 2:1,3,3,5,5,7,8,12, 13,13,18; 3:2,2,2,2,2,14,14,14,16,16,19,19, 22,22,22,22,24; 4:6,6,6,10,11,11,13,13,14, 14,16,17,19,20; 5:2,2,2,2,9,14,15,15,15,16, 18,19,19,20 2 JN 1,1,1,5,5,12 3 JN 1,1, 2,8,12,13,14 JUD 3,3,5 REV 1:8,9,17; 2:2,5,5,6,6,9,16,19,22,23,23,24,25,27; 3:1,3, 8,9,9,10,11,15,16,17,18,19,19,19,19,21; 10:9; 17:7,7; 18:7; 21:5,6,6,6; 22:7,8,12,13, 13,16,16,16,18,20

---

185 ܐܢܚ (v) (ethpa) groan

[d]ETHPAAL

Perfect

MRK 7:34 | MRK 8:12

Imperfect

JAM 5:9

Participle

ROM 8:22,23 | 2 CO 5:2,4

3409 ܬܢܚܬܐ (f) groan

ACT 7:34 | HEB 13:17
ROM 8:26

---

189 ܐܢܛܝܟܪܝܣܛܘܣ (adj) antichrist

2 JN 7

---

192 ܐܢܢܩܐ (f) necessity, distress

MAT 18:7 | HEB 9:23
1 CO 7:26 | JUD 3
2 CO 6:4

---

193 ܐܢܣ (v) compel

[a]PEAL (non occ)

183 ܐܘܢܣܐ (f) distress

2 CO 2:4

[b]ETHPEEL

Perfect

GAL 2:3

195 ܐܢܫܐ (c) man, mankind

see also 440 ܒܪ ܐܢܫܐ
see also 1427 ܟܠ ܐܢܫ

MAT 5:13; 6:24; 8:4,20,27,28; 9:3,16,30; 11:27,27; 12:19,29,38,47; 13:25; 14:15,21, 35; 15:20; 16:13,20,27,27,28; 17:8,9; 18:12, 35; 19:3; 20:7,28; 21:3; 22:16,16,24,46,46; 23:7; 24:4,23,36; 25:15,15; 27:47; 28:11 MRK 1:44; 2:21,22; 3:27; 4:23,26; 5:3,4,19, 37,43; 6:54; 7:2,24,36; 8:3,4,9,26,27,30; 9:1, 8,9,30,38,39; 10:29,45; 11:2,3,5,14,16,25; 12:13,14,19,33,34; 13:5,21,32,34,34; 14:4, 57,65; 15:35; 16:8 LUK 1:61; 2:41; 3:14, 14; 5:14,18,36,37,39; 6:2,35; 7:16,31; 8:16, 35,43,46,49,51,56; 9:7,14,21,27,32,36,49,57, 62; 10:4,22,33; 11:15,31,33,44; 12:13,36; 13:1,6,23,31; 14:8,8,24; 15:16; 16:30,31; 17:12; 18:9,11,29; 19:30,31,39; 20:27,28,39; 21:5; 23:53; 24:7,24 JHN 1:18; 2:25; 3:2, 3,5,13,32; 4:27,28,30,33; 5:7,22,28,41; 6:10, 14,44,46,50,51,64,65; 7:4,13,19,25,27,30,37, 44,44,48; 8:10,11,15,20,33,44; 9:4,16,22,32; 10:9,18,28,29,41; 11:9,10,37,46,57; 12:20, 26; 13:28,29; 14:6; 15:6,13,24; 16:5,22,30, 32; 17:12; 18:31; 19:41; 20:23,23; 21:12 ACT 1:15; 2:6,6,8,8,38,38,41,45,45; 3:2; 4:12,17,32,32,34,35,35; 5:13,13,23,25,28,35, 37,38; 6:9; 8:31,34; 9:7; 10:23,23,28,28,47; 11:3,19,20,29,29; 12:1; 13:41; 14:18; 15:1,5, 24,26; 16:17,20,35,37; 17:4,5,18,18,28,29, 34; 18:10; 19:9,13,22,36,38; 20:31,31; 21:16, 26,26,34; 22:9; 23:9,12,22; 24:12,19,23; 25:11,19; 27:9,21; 28:21,22,24 ROM 5:7, 7; 6:13; 8:9; 11:14,33; 12:17; 13:8; 14:7,7; 15:2 1 CO 1:14,15,16; 2:11,15; 3:4,4,5,5,8, 11,12,18,21; 4:2,5,5,6,6,18; 6:1,11,11,12; 7:2,17,17,17,18,24,36; 8:2,3,7,10; 9:15; 10:24,27,28; 11:16,21,21,28; 12:3,3,7,7; 14:2,27,37,38; 15:12,23,23,34,35; 16:2,2,11 2 CO 2:5; 3:16; 5:10,10,16; 6:3; 7:2,2,2; 8:20; 9:7; 10:2,7,10; 11:9,16,21; 12:6,17 GAL 1:7,9; 2:12; 3:11,15; 6:1,3,4,17 EPH 2:9; 4:25; 5:6,29; 6:8 PHL 1:15,15, 15,15; 2:4; 3:4 COL 2:4,8,16,18; 3:13; 4:6, 6 1 TH 3:3; 4:4,4,6,12,13; 5:15 2 TH 2:3; 3:8,8,11,14 1 TM 1:3,3,6,8; 3:1; 4:1,1,12; 5:8,15,15,16,20,22; 6:3,10,16,16 2 TM 2:2,4,5,18,18,21; 3:2,8; 4:16 TIT 1:12; 2:5,8,15; 3:2 HEB 3:4,12,13; 4:1,6,6; 5:4; 6:11,11; 7:9,13; 8:11; 10:25,25, 26,33; 11:6,38; 12:14,15,16; 13:2,3,16,17 JAM 1:5,13,13,14,14,23,26,27; 2:2,12,14, 16,18; 3:8; 5:13,19,19 1 PT 1:23; 2:16; 3:9,16,16; 4:15 2 PT 2:19; 3:9,9 1 JN 2:1,27; 3:7,15,15; 4:12,20; 5:16,16 2 JN 10 JUD 4,4 REV 1:7; 2:17; 3:8,11, 20; 9:5,7; 13:17; 14:3,4; 16:2; 21:17

196 ܐܢܫܘܬܐ (f) mankind

LUK 2:44	JAM 3:7
ACT 17:13	

197 ܐܢܬ (pron) you

incl ܐܢܬܝ, ܐܢܬܘܢ, ܐܢܬܝܢ

MAT 2:6; 3:14; 4:3,6; 5:13,14,23,25,36,46, 47,47,48; 6:2,3,3,5,6,6,7,9,16,17,17,18,24, 26,26,28; 7:2,2,3,3,4,11,11,11,12,12; 8:2,2,4, 19,26,31; 9:4,28; 10:7,11,11,12,14,20,27,27, 31; 11:3,4,14,23,29; 12:34,34; 13:10,17,17, 18,29; 14:16,28,33; 15:3,3,5,5,12,16,16,17, 28; 16:2,3,3,3,8,9,15,15,16,18,23,23; 18:8, 28,33; 19:17,28,28; 20:4,6,7,7,22,22,22,25, 32; 21:2,13,16,23,32; 22:9,16,16,16,16,18, 29,29,42; 23:8,8,8,13,13,14,14,14,14,15,15, 16,23,25,27,28,28,28,29,29,30,31,31,32,34, 34,34; 24:2,6,32,33,42,44,44; 25:13,24,24, 24,37,37,38,38; 26:2,10,15,17,25,31,39,53, 62,63,64,66,69,73,73; 27:4,4,11,11,13,17,21, 24,40,65; 28:5,5 MRK 1:11,24,40,40,44; 2:8; 3:11; 4:13,24,24,39,40; 5:31,35,39; 6:10, 10,11,22,37; 7:8,9,11,11,12,13,13,18,18,18; 8:17,17,17,17,18,18,18,21,29,29,29,33; 9:16, 22,23,41; 10:18,19,36,38,38,38,42; 11:2,2,3, 5,5,17,24,24,24,25,26,26,28; 12:14,14,14,14, 15,24,24,27,27; 13:9,11,23,28,29,33,35,36; 14:6,7,7,12,30,36,60,61,67,70,70,71; 15:2,2, 4,9,12,12; 16:6 LUK 1:42,76; 2:12,29,49; 3:22; 4:3,9,34,41; 5:12,22,30,34; 6:2,31,31, 32,33,34,34,37,37,38,41,42,46,46; 7:19,20, 33,34,44,45,46; 8:45; 9:4,5,13,20,20,44,54, 55,55,57,60; 10:5,7,8,10,15,23,24,24,26,37; 11:2,13,13,18,39,39,42,42,43,45,45,46,46, 46,47,48,48,48,48,52; 12:7,24,24,26,26,29, 40,40,41,51,54,55,56,56,57,58,58; 13:2,4,25, 27,28; 14:8,9,9,12,13; 15:31,31; 16:2,5,7,7, 13,15,25; 17:8,10; 18:19,20,41; 19:19,21,21, 21,30,30,31,33,46; 20:2,21,21,21,21,23,39; 21:6,9,30,31; 22:9,10,26,28,32,34,42,46,48, 58,58,60,67,68,68,70,70,70; 23:3,3,14,37,39, 40,40,40; 24:5,17,17,17,18,18,38,39,48,49 JHN 1:19,19,21,21,22,22,25,25,26,26,33,38, 38,42,42,48,49,49,50; 2:10,18,18,20,20; 3:2, 2,8,8,10,10,11,12,26,28,28; 4:9,9,9,10,12,12, 19,20,20,22,22,22,27,27,32,32,35,35,38,38; 5:6,14,20,33,34,35,38,38,39,40,43,44,44,44, 45,47; 6:26,30,36,67,67,69; 7:3,4,8,20,21,22, 23,28,28,28,28,34,36,36,47,52,52; 8:5,5,13, 13,14,14,15,15,19,21,21,22,22,23,23,23,23, 25,25,31,31,33,37,37,37,38,38,40,41,41,43, 43,44,44,45,46,46,47,47,48,49,52,52,53,53, 53,54; 9:17,17,19,19,27,27,27,28,30,30,34, 34,34,35,35,41; 10:20,24,24,25,26,26,32,33, 33,34,36,36,38; 11:3,8,27,42,42,49,49,50,56; 12:19,19,34; 13:6,6,7,7,8,10,10,11,12,13,13, 13,14,14,15,17,27,33,33,34,35,36,36,38; 14:3,4,4,5,7,9,10,15,17,17,19,19,20,20,22, 24; 15:3,3,4,5,5,14,14,16,16,27,27,27; 16:5, 10,12,19,20,22,27,29,29,30,30; 17:3,3,5,8, 21,21,23,23,25; 18:4,7,8,17,17,21,22,25,25, 31,33,37,37,39; 19:6,9,10,10,12,35; 20:13, 15,15; 21:6,15,15,15,16,16,16,17,17,17,17, 17,17,18,18,22 ACT 1:5,6,11,24; 2:15,22, 22,27,33,33,36; 3:12,12,13,14,16,16,25; 4:10,11,24,25,27,30; 5:4,28,28,30,39; 7:4,26, 26,28,33,51,51,51,52; 8:24,30,30; 9:4,5,5,5, 17; 10:15,21,28,28,33,37,37; 11:9,14,16;

13:10,25,33,46; 14:15; 15:1,1,7,7,10,10; 16:15,31; 17:19,20,22,23,23; 18:15,15; 19:15,15,25,26,26,26,39; 20:18,18,25,34,34; 21:13,13,13,20,21,21,24,24,37,37,38; 22:3,7, 8,8,8,16,16,26,27,27; 23:3,3,3,3,3,4,11,15, 15,21; 24:8,8,11; 25:9,10,10,12,22,24; 26:3, 8,14,15,15,15,15,16,27,27,28; 27:31,31; 28:22 ROM 1:6,6; 2:1,1,1,1,1,3,3,3,3,3,4, 4,5,17,17,17,17,18,18,18,19,21,21,21,21,21, 21,22,22,22,22,22,22,23,23,23,23,27; 6:3,11, 11,11,16,16,16,16,21; 7:1,4; 8:9,13,13,13,13; 9:20,20,20; 11:2,17,17,18,18,20,22,24,24,30; 12:16; 13:3,4,6; 14:4,4,4,10,10,10,10,15,15, 22; 15:14,14,14,14,24; 16:17 1 CO 1:7,30, 30; 3:2,3,3,3,4,9,16,16,17,23; 4:7,10,10,10, 21; 5:2,2,6,12; 6:2,2,3,7,7,8,8,8,9,15,16,19; 7:16,16,16,21,27,27,28,35; 8:10,12,12,12; 9:2,13,24; 10:13,15,21,21,27,31,31,31; 11:2, 2,18,20,20,22,22,25,26,26,26,33; 12:21,21, 27,27,31; 14:9,9,9,12,12,16,16,17,17,26,31; 15:2,2,17,36,37,37,58; 16:1,3,6,15,16 2 CO 1:6,7,7,13,13,14,16,24; 2:9,10,10; 3:1, 1,2,3,3; 6:12,12,16,16,18; 7:3,11; 8:7,9,9; 9:4,4; 10:7; 11:1,7,19,19,19,20; 12:11,11,15, 15,19,20; 13:3,5,5,5,7,9,9 GAL 1:6; 2:14, 14,14,14; 3:3,3,26,28,29,29; 4:9,10,13,17,21, 21; 5:4,10,13,15,15,17,18; 6:1,1,1,2 EPH 1:13; 2:11,13,22,22; 3:4,4; 4:20; 5:8,33; 6:6,8,9,9,13,18,21 PHL 1:7,7,27,27,28,30; 2:13,18,22; 3:15,17; 4:15,15,15 COL 1:23; 2:7,7,10,10,20,20; 3:4,13,17,23,24,24; 4:2,16 1 TH 1:5,5,6,10; 2:1,1,2,5,8,9,10,11,14,14, 19,20; 3:3,3,4,6,8; 4:2,9,9,9,10; 5:1,2,2,4,5, 11 2 TH 1:4,5,7,12; 2:5,6; 3:4,7,7,13 1 TM 4:6,6,15; 6:5,11 2 TM 1:15,18; 2:1, 23; 3:10,11,14,14,15; 4:5,13,15 TIT 2:1; 3:8,10 PLM 9,12,19,21,21 HEB 1:5,10, 11,11,12,12; 5:5,6,12; 6:1,10; 7:17,21; 10:25, 29,34; 12:5,8,17,22; 13:3,3 JAM 1:3,19; 2:3,3,6,8,8,9,9,9,11,11,12,13,19,19,20,24; 4:2,2,2,2,2,2,3,3,3,4,5,11,12,12,12; 5:7,8 1 PT 1:5,6,8,8,17,18; 2:4,5,9,9,20,20,21; 3:1, 2,6,7,17,17,21,21,21,21; 4:1,4,11,13,14; 5:5, 9,12 2 PT 1:4,5,10,10,12,12,19,19,20; 3:3, 12,12,14,17,17,17 1 JN 2:14,20,20,21,21, 24,24,24,27,27; 3:5,15; 4:4 3 JN 3,3,5,5,6, 6,12 JUD 5,17,20,23 REV 2:9,10,13; 3:1,1,15,17,17,17; 4:11; 7:14,14; 14:18; 15:4, 4; 16:5

199 (ܐܢܬ), ܐܢܬܬܐ (f) woman, wife

MAT 1:6,20,24; 5:28,31,32; 9:20,22; 11:11; 13:33; 14:3,4,21; 15:22,28, 38; 18:25; 19:3,5,8,9, 10,10, 29; 22:24,25, 25,27, 28,30, 30; 24:38; 26:7,10; 27:19,55; 28:5

MRK 5:25,33; 6:17,18; 7:25,26; 10:2,7,11, 12,29; 12:19,19, 20,22, 23,25, 25; 14:3; 15:40

LUK 1:5,13,18, 24,28,42; 3:19; 4:26; 7:28,37,39, 44,44,48, 50; 8:2,3,43, 47; 10:38; 11:27; 13:11,12, 21; 14:20,26; 15:8; 16:18; 17:27,32; 18:29; 20:28,28, 29,30, 32,33, 34,34, 35,35; 22:57; 23:27,49, 55; 24:1,22,24

JHN 2:4; 4:7,9,9,11, 15,19,21, 25,27,28, 39,42; 8:3,4,9,10; 16:21; 19:26; 20:13,15

ACT 1:14; 5:1,2,7,14; 8:3,12; 9:2; 13:50; 16:13,14; 17:4,12,34; 18:2; 21:5; 22:4; 24:24

ROM 7:2

1 CO 5:1; 7:1,2,2,3,3, 4,4,8,9, 10,10,11, 12,13,14, 14,16,16, 27,27,27, 28,29,32, 33,33,34, 39; 9:5; 11:3,5,6,6, 7,8,8,9, 9,10,11, 11,12, 12,13, 15; 14:34,35

GAL 4:4

EPH 5:22,23,24, 25,28,28, 31,33,33

COL 3:18,19

1 TM 2:9,10,11, 12,14; 3:2,11,12

2 TM 3:6

TIT 1:6

HEB 11:35

1 PT 3:1,5,7

REV 2:20; 9:8; 12:1,4,6, 13,14, 15,16, 17; 14:4; 17:3,4,6,7, 9,18; 19:7; 21:9

198 ܐܢܬܘܦܛܘܣ (m) proconsul

ACT 13:7,7,8, 12; 18:12; 19:38

223 (ܐܣܐ), ܐܣܝܐ (m) physician

MAT 9:12
MRK 2:17; 5:26
LUK 4:23

LUK 5:31	COL 4:14
8:43	

224 ܐܣܝܘܬܐ (f) healing, cure

LUK 9:11	1 CO 12:9,28,30
13:32	REV 22:2
ACT 4:22,30	

201 (ܐܣܐ) (v) heal

cPAEL

Perfect

MAT 4:24	MRK 6:5
8:16	LUK 7:21
12:15,22	9:42
14:14	13:14[1]
15:30	14:4
19:2	22:51
21:14	ACT 3:16
MRK 1:34	

Imperfect

MAT 8:7	JHN 4:47
13:15	12:40
MRK 3:15	

Imperative

MAT 10:8	LUK 10:9
LUK 4:23	

Infinitive

MAT 10:1	LUK 5:17
12:10	9:1,2
17:16,19	14:3
LUK 4:18	

Active Participle

MAT 4:23	LUK 6:7,19
9:35	9:6,11
MRK 3:2,10	ACT 9:34
6:13	10:38
LUK 4:40	

dETHPAAL

Perfect

MAT 8:13	JHN 5:10,13
9:22	9:36
14:36	ACT 4:9,14
15:28	8:7
17:18	1 PT 2:24
MRK 5:29	REV 13:3
LUK 8:2,36,47	

Imperfect

MAT 8:8	LUK 8:43
LUK 6:18[1]	HEB 12:13
7:7	JAM 5:16

Infinitive

LUK 5:15

Participle

MAT 9:21	LUK 13:14[2]
MRK 6:56	ACT 28:9
LUK 6:18[2]	

238 ܐܣܐ, ܐܣܬܐ (f) wall

see also 3302 ܫܬܐܣܬܐ

ACT 23:3

202 ܐܣܕ̈ܐ (m) pillows

JHN 20:12

203 ܐܣܘܛܐ (adj-non occ) greedy

204 ܐܣܘܛܘܬܐ (f) excess

LUK 21:34	TIT 1:6
EPH 5:18	1 PT 4:3,4

208 ܐܣܛܕܝܐ (m) furlong, stadium

MAT 14:24	ACT 1:12
LUK 24:13	1 CO 9:24
JHN 6:19	REV 14:20
11:18	21:16

209 ܐܣܛܘܐ (m) porch

JHN 5:2	ACT 3:11
10:23	5:12

211 ܐܣܛܘܟܣܐ (m) element

GAL 4:3,9	2 PT 3:10,12
COL 2:8,20	

214 ܐܣܛܠ, ܐܣܛܠܐ (f) robe

MRK 12:38	LUK 20:46
16:5	REV 6:11
LUK 15:22	7:9,13,14

212 (ܐܣܛܘܡܟܘܢ), ܐܣܛܘܡܟܐ (m) stomach

1 TM 5:23

215 ܐܣܛܣܝܣ (f) insurrection

MRK 15:7,7	LUK 23:19,25

218 ܐܣܛܪܛܝܐ (f) army

LUK 3:14

219 ܐܣܛܪܛܓܐ (m) magistrate

ACT 16:20,22, 35,36,	ACT 16:38

220 ܐܣܛܪܛܝܘܛܐ (m) soldier

MAT 8:9	JHN 19:34
27:27	ACT 12:4,6,18
MRK 15:16	21:32,32, 35
LUK 7:8	27:31,32, 42
23:36	28:16
JHN 19:2,23,23, 24,32,	

221 ܐܣܛܪܢܝܐ (noun) pleasure

1 TM 5:6

226 (ܐܣܟܠ), ܐܣܟܘܠܐ (f) school

ACT 19:9

227 ܐܣܟܡܐ (m) manner, way

ROM 13:13	PHL 2:7
1 CO 7:31,35	1 TH 4:12
12:23	2 TH 2:3
14:40	1 TM 2:9
1 TM 4:2	TIT 2:3
2 TM 3:5	

228 ܐܣܢ (v) store up

aPEAL

Passive Participle

2 PT 3:7

229 ܐܣܦܘܓܐ (f) sponge

MAT 27:48	JHN 19:29
MRK 15:36	

233 ܐܣܦܣ (f) asp, snake

ROM 3:13

230 (ܐܣܦܘܩܠܛܪܐ), ܐܣܦܘܩܘܠܛܪܐ (m) executioner

MRK 6:27

231 (ܐܣܦܪ), ܐܣܦܝܪܐ (f) company of soldiers

MAT 27:27	ACT 10:1
MRK 15:16	21:31
JHN 18:3,12	27:1

234 ܐܣܦܪܝܕܐ (m) basket

MAT 15:37	MRK 8:8,20
16:10	ACT 9:25

235 ܐܣܪ (v) bind, fasten

aPEAL

Perfect

MAT 14:3	ACT 5:18
27:2	16:24
MRK 15:1,36	21:11[1]
LUK 13:16	REV 20:2
JHN 18:12	

Imperfect

MAT 12:29; 16:19[1]; 18:18[1]
MRK 3:27
LUK 12:37
JHN 21:18[2]
ACT 9:2,14,21; 21:11[2],33; 27:30

Imperative

MAT 13:30; 22:13
LUK 17:8
ACT 12:8

Infinitive

MRK 5:3

Active Participle

MAT 23:4
JHN 21:18[1]
ACT 22:4

Passive Participle

MAT 16:19[2]; 18:18[2]; 21:2; 27:16
MRK 1:6; 11:2,4; 15:7
LUK 12:35; 19:30
JHN 11:44[1],44[2]; 18:24
ACT 10:11; 11:5; 12:6
ACT 20:22; 22:5; 24:27; 28:20
ROM 7:2; 13:4
1 CO 7:27,39
COL 4:3
2 TM 2:9
HEB 10:34; 13:3[1],3[2]
REV 1:13; 9:14; 15:6

225 ܐܣܝܪܐ (pp) prisoner; (w/ ܪܒ) sergeant

see also 369 ܒܝܬ ܐܣܝܪ̈ܐ

MAT 27:15,16
MRK 15:6
ACT 16:25,27,35; 23:18; 25:14,27
ACT 27:1,42
EPH 3:1; 4:1
2 TM 1:8
PLM 1,9

206 ܐܣܘܪܐ (m) bond

LUK 8:29
ACT 16:26; 20:23; 23:29; 26:29,31; 28:17
2 CO 6:5; 11:23
PHL 1:7,13,14,17
COL 4:18
2 TM 1:16; 2:9
PLM 10,13
HEB 11:36
JUD 6

207 ܐܣܘܪܝܐ (m) bondage

LUK 13:16

236 ܐܣܪܐ (m) belt

MAT 3:4
MRK 7:35
REV 1:13; 15:6

1605 ܡܐܣܪܬܐ (f) bundle

MAT 13:30

---

[b]ETHPEEL

Imperfect

ACT 21:13

Participle

MRK 5:4
LUK 8:29

---

237 ܐܣܪܐ (m) farthing, coin

MAT 10:29
LUK 12:6

---

239 ܐܣܬܝܪܐ (f) shekel

MAT 17:27

---

241 ܐܥܦ (v-non occ) double

cf ܥܦ

[c]PAEL

242 ܐܥܦܐ (m) double

MAT 23:15
LUK 18:30
REV 18:6,6

---

243 ܐܦ (conj) also

incl comp with 1511 ܠܐ

see below 254 ܐܦܢ

MAT 2:6,8; 5:35,36,39,40,46,47; 6:10,12,14, 15,21,22,29,32; 7:12; 8:9,10; 10:30,32,33; 11:27; 13:13,26,29; 15:3,16,27; 16:18; 17:12; 18:17,17,33; 19:28; 20:4,7,10; 21:24,24,27, 32; 22:26,26,27,30; 23:26,28,32; 24:24,33,

36,44; 25:11,17,24,29,41,44,45; 26:13,35,69, 71,73,73; 27:14,41,44,57; 28:18 MRK 1:19,27,38; 2:2,26,28; 3:4; 4:25; 5:14, 16,26,28; 6:5,31; 7:18,28; 8:7,26,38; 9:13; 10:45; 11:25,26,29,33; 12:4,5,10,21,22,25; 13:22,29,32; 14:9,31,59,67,69,70; 15:29,31, 32,40,43; 16:13 LUK 1:3,36; 2:4,36,38; 3:12,14,18,20,21; 4:23,41,43; 5:10,33; 6:29, 31,32,33,34,36,43,44; 7:5,8,9,29,49; 8:18,25; 9:5,54; 10:11,17,32,37; 11:1,2,4,9,30,34,34, 45,46,49; 12:7,8,26,27,30,34,40,41; 13:3,8; 14:12,12,12,26,34; 16:9,10,10,21,22,26,28, 31; 17:8,10; 18:1,13,15; 19:9,19,19,26; 20:3, 11,12,31,32,35,36,37; 21:2,31; 22:20,24,32, 36,37,39,55,56,58,59,59; 23:15,35,36,38,39, 40,40; 24:22,24,35 JHN 1:3; 2:2; 3:23,26; 4:21,23,45; 5:17,18,19,21,25,26,27,46; 6:11, 24,57,67; 7:5,10,47,52; 8:11,19,44; 9:3,21, 27,40; 10:16,16,41; 11:16,22,31,37,52; 12:9, 10,20,26,42; 13:9,9,10,15,32,33,34; 14:3,7, 12,19; 15:4,9,16,20,20,23,24,24,27; 16:22; 17:18,19,20,21,23,24; 18:2,5,9,17,18,25,30, 38; 19:4,11,19,35,39; 20:8,21,31; 21:3,24,25, 25 ACT 1:3,8; 2:26,29,31; 4:6,29; 5:7,23, 37; 7:5,22,45,51; 8:1,13,19,21; 9:14,21,32; 10:24,26,37,45; 11:1,6,12,17,18,19; 12:3; 13:27,32,43; 14:15; 15:3,10,10,28,32; 17:4,9, 12,13,18,27,28; 19:2,12,12,13,19,21,26,26, 27,27,31,40; 20:30; 21:13,28; 22:3,5,19,20, 28; 23:11,24; 24:9,12,15,16,18,26; 25:10; 26:4,10,11,20,26,29; 27:9,10; 28:9,28 ROM 1:6,13,15,27,32; 2:1,3,12,28; 3:10,12, 22,29,30; 4:6,11,12,15,16,24,24; 5:3,11,14, 19; 6:4,5,11,13,19; 7:4; 8:11,17,17,21,23,26, 39; 9:7,10,15,24,25; 11:1,5,16,16,21,22,23, 30,31,31; 12:5,16; 13:5,6,9,11; 14:9,10; 15:3, 7,14,14,14,27,27; 16:2,2,4 1 CO 1:16,26, 30; 2:1,2,6,10,11,13; 3:2; 4:3,8; 5:1,10,11; 6:5,8; 7:3,4,17,19,22,34,40; 8:6; 9:8,14,16, 21; 10:7,7,8,10,33; 11:1,6,9,11,12,14,19,25; 12:3,12,13,14,21; 14:7,9,11,12,15,15,19,21, 34; 15:8,13,14,15,16,18,21,22,30,42,45,48, 48; 16:1,4,6,16 2 CO 1:4,5,6,7,13,14,14; 2:9,10,10; 3:10; 4:10,11,13,13,13,14; 5:2,3, 11; 7:5,5,12,14,15; 8:5,6,7,10,14,19,21,22; 9:6,12; 10:7,8,11,13,16; 11:1,12,15,16,18,21, 22,22,22; 12:15,20; 13:2,2,4,9 GAL 1:12; 2:3,5,8,13,13,16,17; 4:3,7,12,29; 5:12,21; 6:1,13 EPH 1:13,15,21; 2:1,3,22; 4:9,10; 5:2,3,12,23,24,25,33; 6:9,9,19,21 PHL 1:13,20,22,24,29; 2:4,5,9,13,13,18,19, 24,27,27; 3:4,8,15; 4:3,10,12,12,12,15,15,16 COL 1:6,6,9,21,29; 2:10; 3:4,7,13; 4:1,3,16 1 TH 1:5,5; 2:3,3,5,8,8,13,14,14; 3:4,5,6; 4:6,10,14; 5:11 2 TH 1:4,12; 2:4; 3:4,8,10, 10 1 TM 2:9; 3:7,8,11; 5:13,13,14,20,25; 6:7,16 2 TM 1:5,8,17; 2:2,10,11,12,12,20, 20; 3:8,9; 4:8,15 TIT 1:9; 2:3; 3:3,3,5,8,14 PLM 9,11,11,15,19,22 HEB 2:14; 4:2,2, 10; 5:2,3,5,6,7; 7:5,9,9,12,26; 8:3,4,6,9,11; 9:18,21,25,28; 10:15,33; 11:4,11,19,26; 12:1, 1,17,18,26; 13:12,13 JAM 1:11,17; 2:17, 19,25,26; 3:2,4,5,5,6,12,16; 5:8,12,17 1 PT 1:12,16; 2:5,10,18,21,22; 3:1,5,7,9,18, 21; 4:1,6,13; 5:9 2 PT 1:8,12,14,15,15,18, 19; 2:1,1,7,19; 3:15,16,18 1 JN 1:3; 2:2,22, 23,23,24,27,29; 3:1,1,7,16; 4:11,17,21; 5:1, 12 3 JN 12 JUD 8,14,23,25 REV 1:7, 8; 2:15; 6:11,11; 7:3; 9:4,19; 12:2; 14:10; 18:6; 22:1

254 ܐܦܢ (adv) although, even if

from 243 ܐܦ (above) and 177 ܐܢ

MAT 9:21; 14:36; 21:21; 26:33 MRK 6:56 LUK 18:5; 19:42 JHN 8:14,25; 10:38; 11:25; 14:11 ACT 5:15 1 CO 7:21; 8:5 2 CO 1:6; 4:16; 7:8,8,8; 10:1,3; 11:6,16; 12:11,15; 13:4 GAL 1:8 PHL 2:17 COL 2:5 HEB 6:9; 12:20 1 PT 1:6

244 ܐ̈ܦܐ (f) face; (w/ ܢܣܒ) hypocrite; (w/ ܠܚܡ) shewbread

MAT	6:2,5,16, 17	ACT	10:3,34
	7:5		17:26
	15:7		24:10
	16:3		25:16
	17:6		26:1,21
	20:6		27:40
	22:16,18	ROM	2:11
	23:13,14, 15,23, 25,27, 28,29	1 CO	1:13
			11:24
			13:12,12
			14:25
			15:3
	24:51	2 CO	1:6,6,11, 11,11
	26:39,67		3:13,18
	27:46,51		5:12,15
MRK	7:6		7:7,14
	10:34		10:1
	14:65		11:20,28
	15:19,38		12:10,15
LUK	5:12	GAL	1:22
	6:42		2:6,11,13
	9:29	EPH	1:16
	11:44		3:1,13
	12:1,56		5:2,20,25
	13:15		6:9,18
	17:16	PHL	1:4,20,29
	18:32	COL	1:24
	20:21		3:25
	21:35	1 TH	2:17,17
	22:19,64		3:10
	23:45		5:10,12
	24:5	2 TH	1:5
JHN	6:51		2:13
	7:24	1 TM	3:13
	11:44		5:21
	15:22	HEB	3:6
	17:19,20, 20		6:19
ACT	1:18		9:2,3
	3:13		10:19,20,

HEB 10:35
JAM 1:23; 2:1,9; 3:17
1 PT 1:17,22; 2:1; 3:12,14; 4:14
1 JN 2:2,28; 3:16,21; 4:10,17
REV 4:7; 6:16; 7:11; 9:7,7; 11:16; 12:14; 20:11; 21:4; 22:4

245 ܐܦܘܕܐ (f) ephod

REV 1:13

249 ܐܦܛܪܘܦܐ (m) guardian

GAL 4:2

256 (ܐܦܣ), ܐܦܣܘܢܝܬܐ (f)
wage

LUK 3:14

259 ܐܦܣܢܬܝܢ (m) wormwood

REV 8:11,11

250 (ܐܦܣܩܦ),
ܐܦܝܣܩܘܦܐ (m)
bishop, overseer

ACT 20:28

263 ܐܦܪܫܢܐ (m) plan, plot

ACT 9:24 | ACT 23:16

56 (ܐܨܪ), ܐܘܨܪܐ (m)
storehouse

MAT 3:12; 6:26; 13:30
LUK 3:17

ܐܪܒܥ see under (ܪܒܥ)

270 ܐܪܓܘܢ, ܐܪܓܘܢܐ (m)
purple (cloth)

MRK 15:17,20
LUK 16:19
JHN 19:2,5
ACT 16:14
REV 17:4; 18:12,16

271 ܐܪܕܝܟܠܐ (m) masterbuilder

1 CO 3:10

59 (ܐܪܕܥ), ܐܘܪܕܥܐ (f) frog

REV 16:13

ܐܪܕܐ see ܪܕܐ

61 (ܐܪܚ), ܐܘܪܚܐ (f) way, road

MAT 2:12; 3:3; 4:15; 5:25; 7:13,14; 8:28; 10:5,10; 11:10; 13:4,19; 15:32; 20:17,30; 21:8,8,19,32; 22:9,10,16
MRK 1:2,3; 4:4,15; 6:8; 8:3,27; 9:33,34; 10:17,32,46,52; 11:8,8; 12:14
LUK 1:76,79; 3:4; 7:27; 8:5,12; 9:3,57; 10:4,31,38; 11:6; 12:58; 14:23; 18:35; 19:36; 20:21; 24:32,35
JHN 1:23; 4:6; 14:4,5,6
ACT 2:28; 8:26,36,39; 9:2,7,17,27; 10:9; 13:10; 14:16; 16:17; 18:25,26; 19:9,23; 21:5; 22:4; 24:22; 25:3; 26:13
ROM 1:10; 3:16,17; 11:33
1 CO 4:17; 12:31; 16:7
2 CO 11:26
1 TH 3:11
HEB 3:10; 9:8; 10:20
JAM 1:8; 2:25; 5:19,20
2 PT 2:2,15,15,21
JUD 11
REV 16:12

63 (ܐܪܝ), ܐܘܪܝܐ (m) stall, stable

LUK 2:7,12,16	LUK 13:15

64 (ܐܪܝ), ܐܘܪܝܬܐ (f) the Law

MAT 11:13 12:5	MAT 22:40

275 ܐܪܝܐ (c) lion

2 TM 4:17 HEB 11:33 1 PT 5:8 REV 4:7	REV 5:5 9:8,17 10:3 13:2

277 (ܐܪܟ), ܐܪܝܟ (adj-non occ) long

cf ܝܪܟ

65 ܐܘܪܟܐ (m) length

EPH 3:18	REV 21:16,16

278 (ܐܪܟ) (v) (aph) lengthen

[e]APHEL

Active Participle

MAT 23:5,13 MRK 12:40	LUK 20:47

279 ܐܪܟܐ (f) principality

EPH 1:21 3:10 6:12	COL 1:16 2:10,15

280 ܐܪܟܘܢܐ (m) ruler

MAT 9:18,23 LUK 12:58 23:13,35 JHN 3:1 12:31	JHN 14:30 16:11 ACT 4:1,5,8 5:24,26

284 ܐܪܡ (pn-non occ) Syria

cf (pn) Syria, ܣܘܪܝܐ

285 ܐܪܡܐܝܬ (adv) manner of Gentiles, manner of pagans

GAL 2:14	REV 9:11

286 ܐܪܡܝܐ (adj) Gentile, pagan, Syrian

LUK 4:27 ACT 16:1,3 19:10,17 20:21 21:28 ROM 1:16 2:9,10 3:9	ROM 10:12 1 CO 1:22,23,24 10:32 12:13 GAL 2:3 3:28 COL 3:11

ܐܪܡܠܬܐ see under ܪܡܠ

289 ܐܪܡܘܢ (m) sail

ACT 27:17,40

293 ܐܪܥ (v) meet

[a]PEAL

Perfect

MAT 8:28 LUK 17:12 JHN 4:51 11:30	ACT 8:27 10:25 HEB 7:1,10

Imperfect

EPH 6:13

Infinitive

LUK 14:31

Active Participle

ACT 20:22

66 ܐܘܪܥܐ (m) meeting, reception

MAT 8:34 25:1,6 JHN 11:20	JHN 12:13 ACT 28:15 1 TH 4:17

294 ܐܪܥ, ܐܪܥܐ (f) earth

MAT 2:20,21 4:15,15	MAT 5:5,13,18, 35

MAT 6:10,19; 9:6,26,31; 10:15,29,34; 11:24,25; 12:40,42; 13:5,8,23; 14:19,24,34; 15:35; 16:19,19; 17:25; 18:18,18,19; 23:9,35; 24:30,35; 25:18,25; 27:45,51; 28:18
MRK 2:10; 4:1,5,5,8,20,26,28,31,31; 6:47,53,55; 8:6; 9:3,20; 13:27,31; 14:35; 15:33
LUK 2:14; 4:5,25; 5:11,24; 8:8,15,27; 10:21; 11:2,31; 12:16,49,51,56; 13:7; 14:35; 16:17; 18:8; 21:23,25,26,33,35; 22:44; 23:44; 24:5
JHN 3:12,22,31,31; 4:35; 6:21; 8:6,8; 9:6; 12:24,32; 17:4; 18:6; 21:8,9,11
ACT 1:8,18; 2:19; 3:25; 4:24,26; 7:3,3,4,4,6,11,29,33,36,40,45,49; 8:33; 9:4,8; 10:11,12,39; 11:6,28; 13:17,19,19,47; 14:15; 17:6,24,26,31; 22:7,22; 24:5; 26:14; 27:27,30,39,43,44; 28:6
ROM 1:23; 9:17,28; 10:18
1 CO 8:5; 10:26; 15:47
2 CO 5:1
EPH 1:10; 3:15; 4:9; 6:3
PHL 2:10,10; 3:19
COL 1:16,20; 3:2,5
HEB 1:10; 6:7; 8:4,9; 11:9,13,29,38; 12:25,26,26
JAM 5:4,5,7,12,17,18
2 PT 3:5,7,10,13
REV 1:5,7; 3:10; 5:3,3,6,10,13,13; 6:4,8,8,10,13,15; 7:1,1,2,3; 8:5,7,7,7,13; 9:1,3,3,4; 10:2,6,8; 11:4,6,10,10,18; 12:4,9,9,12,13,16,16; 13:3,8,11,12,13,14,14; 14:3,6,7,16,16,18,19,19; 16:1,2,18; 17:2,2,5,8,18; 18:1,3,3,9,11,23,24; 19:2,19; 20:8,9,11; 21:1,1,24

296 ܐܪܥܢܝܐ (adj) earthly

1 CO 15:40,40 | JAM 3:15

---

301 (ܐܫܐ), ܐܫܬܐ (f) fever

MAT 8:14,15
MRK 1:30,31
LUK 4:38,39
JHN 4:52
ACT 28:8

---

298 ܐܫܕ (v) pour out

[a]PEAL

Perfect

JHN 2:15
ACT 2:33
TIT 3:6
REV 16:2,3,4,6,8,10,12,17

Imperfect

ACT 2:17,18

Imperative

REV 16:1

Infinitive

ROM 3:15

---

[b]ETHPEEL

Perfect

MAT 23:35
LUK 11:50
ACT 1:18

Participle

MAT 9:17; 26:28
MRK 2:22; 14:24
LUK 5:37; 22:20
ACT 22:20

---

70 (ܐܫܥ), ܐܘܫܥܢܐ (intrj) hosanna

MAT 21:9,9,15
MRK 11:9,10
JHN 12:13

304 ܐܫܬܩܕܝ (adv) last year

2 CO	8:10	2 CO	9:2

305 ܐܬܐ (f) sign

MAT	12:38,39, 39,39	JHN	12:18,37
	16:1,3,4,4, 4		20:30
	24:3,15,24	ACT	1:3
	26:48		2:19,22,43
MRK	8:11,12,12		4:16,22,30
	13:4,14,22		5:12
	14:44		6:8
	16:17,20		7:36
LUK	2:12,34		8:6,13
	11:16,29, 29,29, 30		14:3
	21:7,11,25		15:12
	22:47		28:11
	23:8	ROM	4:11
JHN	2:11,18,23		15:19
	3:2	1 CO	1:22
	4:45,48,54		14:22
	6:2,14,26, 30	2 CO	12:12
	7:31	2 TH	2:9
	9:16		3:17
	10:41	HEB	2:4
	11:47	REV	12:1,3
			13:13,14
			15:1
			16:14
			19:20

308 ܐܬܘܬܐ (f) tittle, letter

LUK 16:17

306 ܐܬܐ (v) come; (aph) bring

[a]PEAL

Perfect

MAT 2:1,2,9,21,23; 3:1,13,14,16; 4:13; 5:17[1],17[2]; 7:25,27; 8:2,14,28,29; 9:1,10,13, 18[1],20,23,28; 10:34[1],34[2],35; 11:18,19; 12:9, 42,46; 13:4,25,36,54; 14:12,25,33,34; 15:21, 25,29,39; 16:5,13; 17:12,14,24; 18:11,31; 19:1,2,16,27,28; 20:9,10,28; 21:1,19,23,32, 40; 24:39; 25:10,11,19,36,39; 26:36,40,43, 45,47,50,60; 27:33,55,57; 28:1,11,13 MRK 1:9,14,24,29,38,40; 2:3[1],15,17,18; 3:8, 13,19,31; 4:4,38; 5:1,15,22,27,33,35,38; 6:1, 29,48,53; 7:1,24,25,31; 8:10,22[1]; 9:1,13,14, 33; 10:1,45,46,50; 11:13[1],13[2],14,27[1],27[2]; 12:14,18,42; 14:3,16,17,32,37,40,41[1],41[2],43, 66; 15:43; 16:2 LUK 1:59; 2:9,16,27,44, 51; 3:3,12; 4:16,34,42; 5:7[2],11,12,17,32; 6:8[2],18; 7:4,20[1],33,34,36; 8:19,26,35,47,49, 51; 9:49,56; 10:32,33,39,40; 11:6,25,31; 12:36,49,51; 13:1,6; 14:21; 15:17,20,25,27, 30; 17:27; 18:28; 19:5,10,16,18,20; 22:14,45, 52; 23:33,42,49,55; 24:1[1],15,23 JHN 1:7, 11,31; 2:4; 3:2,19,22,26[1],31[1],31[2]; 4:3,5,7,25[2], 27,40,45[1],45[2],46,47,54; 5:43[1]; 6:23,24,25; 7:28,30,45[1],50; 8:2[1],14[1],14[2],20,42[1],42[2]; 9:7, 39; 10:8,10[2],41; 11:17,20,28,30,32,33,38,45; 12:1,9,21,22,23,27,46,47; 13:6; 15:22,26; 16:4,6,8,13,28,32[2]; 17:1; 18:3,37; 19:32,33, 38,39[1],39[2]; 20:1,2,4,6,8,18,19,24,26; 21:7,8 ACT 2:10; 4:23; 5:22,25; 6:12[1]; 7:4; 8:27[2], 40; 9:39; 10:13,17,21,27,29,33,45; 11:5,11, 12,23,27; 12:10,12,20; 13:13,14,51; 14:1,19, 20,21,24,26; 15:4,30; 16:7,11,39; 17:1,5,6[2], 10,13,15; 18:1,2,5,18,22,24; 19:1,6; 20:2,6, 14,15[1],15[2],18; 21:7,8,16,17,22; 22:13,17; 23:35; 24:7,17,19,22,27; 25:1,7[1],17[1],23[1],23[2]; 28:12,13,21,23 ROM 7:9 1 CO 2:1; 11:17,34; 16:2,3,22 2 CO 1:23; 2:12; 7:5; 10:2; 11:4,9[1],9[2]; 13:10 GAL 1:21; 2:11, 12[2]; 3:25 EPH 2:17 1 TH 3:6 1 TM 1:15; 2:6 2 TM 1:17; 3:10 HEB 6:7; 9:11 2 PT 1:17,18,21 1 JN 4:2,3[1]; 5:6,20 2 JN 7 REV 5:7; 6:17; 7:13,14; 8:3; 11:18; 14:7,15; 17:1[1],10[1], 10[2]; 18:10; 19:7; 21:9[1]

Imperfect

MAT 6:10; 8:7,11,19; 10:13,23; 13:32; 14:28,29[2]; 16:24[1],24[2],27; 17:10; 18:7[1],7[2]; 23:35,36; 24:5,14,44,46,50; 27:64 MRK 2:20; 8:34[1],34[2]; 9:11; 12:9; 13:6,36; 16:1 LUK 1:35,43; 5:7[1],35; 7:3,7; 8:17; 9:23[1],23[2],57,61[1],61[2]; 11:2,22; 12:37,38,43, 46; 13:29; 14:9,20; 16:28; 17:1[1],1[2],7,18,22; 18:8; 19:43; 20:16; 21:6,8,34 JHN 4:4; 5:40,43[2]; 6:15,37[1],37[2],44,65; 7:37; 12:26; 13:36[1],36[2],37; 14:3; 16:2 ACT 1:8,11; 2:20; 3:19; 7:2; 8:24; 9:38; 10:32[2]; 13:40; 16:37; 22:30[2]; 23:10,30; 24:8; 25:16; 28:20 ROM 1:10,13; 3:8; 9:9; 11:26; 15:22,23,24, 32 1 CO 4:5,21; 13:10; 14:6; 16:10,11,12[1], 12[2] 2 CO 1:15,16; 2:1,3; 9:4,5; 12:14,20, 21; 13:1,2 GAL 2:12[1]; 3:19,23 PHL 1:26,27 1 TH 2:18 2 TH 2:3 2 TM 3:1,9; 4:9,21 TIT 3:12 HEB 6:1; 10:37[1]; 13:23 2 PT 3:3,9 1 JN 3:19 2 JN 12 3 JN 10 REV 3:9,10; 15:4; 18:8; 22:17[3]

Imperative

MAT 2:8; 4:19; 5:24; 8:9[1],22; 9:9,18[2]; 11:28; 14:29[1]; 19:21; 21:38; 22:4; 25:34; 28:6 MRK 1:17; 2:14; 5:23; 6:31[1]; 10:21; 12:7 LUK 5:27; 6:8[1]; 7:8[1]; 9:59; 14:17; 18:22; 20:14 JHN 1:39[1],39[2],43,46; 4:16,29; 11:7, 34,43; 21:12,19,22[2] ACT 7:3,34; 12:8; 16:9,15 REV 6:1,3,5,7; 17:1[2]; 21:9[2]; 22:17[1],17[2],20[2]

Infinitive

MAT 11:14; 22:3; 24:48 LUK 12:45; 21:26 JHN 7:34,36; 8:21,22; 13:33 2 TM 3:7

Active Participle

MAT 3:7[1],7[2],11; 7:15; 8:9[2],10; 9:15; 10:38; 11:3; 12:44; 13:19; 16:28; 17:11; 19:14; 20:29; 21:5,9[1],9[2]; 23:39; 24:30,42,43; 25:6, 27,31; 26:64; 27:49 MRK 1:7,45; 2:13; 4:15,21,29; 6:31[2]; 8:38; 9:12; 10:14,30; 11:9, 10; 13:26,35; 14:51,54,62; 15:21,36 LUK 3:7,16; 6:47; 7:8[2],9,19,20[2]; 8:4,12; 9:26; 12:39,40,54; 13:7,14,35; 14:10,26,27, 31; 15:6; 16:21; 17:20[1],20[2]; 18:3,5,16,30,43; 19:13,23,38; 21:27; 22:47,54[2]; 23:26,27,29, 32 JHN 1:9,15,27,29,30,38,47; 3:8,20,21, 23,26[2]; 4:15,21,23,25[1],30,35; 5:7,24,25,28; 6:5,14,17[1],35,45; 7:27,31,41,42; 8:2[2],12; 9:4; 10:10[1],12[1],12[2],27; 11:27,29,35,48,56; 12:12[1], 12[2],13,15; 14:6,18,23,28,30; 16:7,25,32[1]; 17:11,13; 18:4,15; 20:3; 21:3,20,22[1],23 ACT 5:15,16[1]; 8:27[1]; 9:17; 13:25; 16:17; 17:21; 18:21; 19:4,18; 21:3,36; 28:30 ROM 15:29[1],29[2] 1 CO 4:18,19; 10:4; 15:35; 16:5,12[3] 2 CO 12:1 EPH 2:7; 5:6 PHL 1:12; 2:24 COL 3:6; 4:10 1 TH 1:10; 5:2 2 TH 1:10 1 TM 3:14; 4:13,15 2 TM 4:13[1] HEB 8:8; 10:7,9,37[2] JAM 4:2; 5:1 1 PT 1:13; 2:19 2 PT 3:10 1 JN 2:18; 4:3[2] 2 JN 10[1] 3 JN 3 JUD 14 REV 1:4,7,8; 2:5,16,25; 3:3[1],3[2], 11; 4:8; 9:12; 11:14; 16:15; 22:7,12,20[1]

Passive Participle

MRK 8:3 JHN 11:19

1607 ܡܐܬܝܐ (m) arrival, presence

2 CO 10:10

1609 ܡܐܬܝܬܐ (f) coming

MAT	24:3,27,37, 39	1 TH	3:13
			4:15
ACT	7:52		5:23
	13:24	2 TH	2:1,8,9
1 CO	11:26	JAM	5:7,8
	15:23	2 PT	1:16
	16:17		3:4,12
2 CO	7:6,7	1 JN	2:28
1 TH	2:19		

---

[c]PAEL

Perfect

JHN 6:17[2]

---

[e]APHEL

Perfect

MAT 14:11[1],11[2]; 21:7 MRK 1:32; 2:3[2]; 6:28; 7:32; 8:22[2]; 9:17,20; 11:7; 12:16; 15:22 LUK 4:9,29,40; 5:18; 10:34; 19:35; 22:54[1]; 23:1; 24:1[2] JHN 1:42; 2:8[2]; 4:33; 7:45[2]; 8:3; 9:13; 18:13,28; 19:39[3] ACT 4:37; 5:2, 27; 6:12[2]; 7:14; 9:27,30; 14:13; 16:19; 17:6[1], 19; 18:12,26; 19:19,37; 20:17; 23:31,33 ROM 9:22 2 CO 7:9 COL 1:13 2 PT 2:5

Imperfect

MRK 6:27 LUK 18:40 JHN 15:2,8,16 ACT 5:21,26,28; 9:2; 22:5; 23:15,18; 25:3,6, 17[2] JUD 9 REV 21:26

Imperative

MAT 14:18; 17:17; 21:2 MRK 9:19; 11:2; 12:15 LUK 15:23; 19:27,30 JHN 2:8[1]; 20:27[1],27[2]; 21:10 ACT 10:5,32[1]; 11:13 2 TM 4:11,13[2]

Infinitive

MRK 6:55 JHN 10:16 ACT 25:26

Active Participle

MRK 4:28 JHN 2:10; 12:24; 15:5 ACT 3:2; 4:34; 5:16[2]; 19:12; 22:30[1]; 24:26; 25:7[2] ROM 2:4; 3:5 1 TH 4:14 2 PT 2:1,11 2 JN 10[2] REV 21:24

---

307 (ܐܬܢ), ܐܬܘܢܐ (m) furnace

MAT	13:42,50	REV	9:2
REV	1:15		

---

310 ܐܬܢܐ (f) ass

MAT	21:5	2 PT	2:16
JHN	12:15		

---

313 ܐܬܪ, ܐܬܪܐ (m) place

MAT	2:12,22	MRK	8:10
	3:5	LUK	2:8
	4:16		3:1,3,5
	6:19		4:14,37,42
	8:19,28		7:17
	12:43		8:26
	14:13,15, 35		9:10,12,57
			10:1
	16:13		11:24
MRK	1:28,35,45		14:22
	2:4		15:13,14, 15
	5:1,10		19:12
	6:31,32,35, 54		21:24

JHN 3:8; 4:20; 6:62; 7:35; 11:48,54; 14:2,3; 16:32; 17:24; 18:1; 19:18
ACT 1:19,25; 2:9,10,10; 4:31,36; 6:13,14; 7:7,49; 11:19; 12:17,20; 13:49; 14:11,13,24; 16:3,6,7,8; 18:2,2,23; 19:1; 20:2,2; 21:12,28,28; 24:25; 25:16; 27:2; 28:7
ROM 2:4; 3:26; 11:25; 12:19; 15:23
1 CO 1:2; 16:6,12
2 CO 2:14; 3:17; 11:10
GAL 1:21
EPH 4:27
COL 3:1
1 TH 1:8
HEB 4:6; 8:7; 11:8; 12:17
JAM 3:4
2 PT 1:19
REV 2:13; 12:6,8; 16:16; 20:11

476 **ܒܬܪ** (prep) after, behind

see below 477 ܒܬܪܟܢ

MAT 1:12; 3:11; 4:19,20,22,25; 8:19,22; 9:9,9,19; 10:38; 12:15; 14:13; 15:23; 16:24,24; 17:1; 19:2,21,27,28; 20:29,34; 21:9; 24:29; 25:19; 26:2,32,58,73; 27:53,55,62,63 MRK 1:7,14,17,18,20; 2:14,14,15; 4:28; 8:34,34; 9:2; 10:21,32; 11:9; 13:24; 14:1,13,51,54,70; 16:12,19 LUK 1:24; 2:46; 5:11,27,27,28; 7:9,11; 8:1; 9:11,23,23,28,37,49,57,59,61; 10:1; 12:5; 14:27; 15:13; 18:22,28,43; 19:14; 21:8; 22:10,20,39,54,58,59; 23:26,27 JHN 1:15,27,29,30,37,38,40,43; 2:12; 3:22; 4:35,43; 5:1,4,14; 6:1,2,22; 7:1; 8:12; 10:4,5,27; 11:31; 12:19,26; 13:27,36,37; 18:15; 19:4,28,38; 20:6,26; 21:1,19,20,22 ACT 1:2,3,5,13; 3:24; 5:7,36,36,37,37,37; 7:7; 10:23,29,29,37,41; 11:4,4; 12:4,8,9,25; 13:3,15,25,43; 15:13,16,36; 16:17,17; 18:23,23; 19:4; 20:1,6,29,30; 21:5,15,19,19,36; 24:1,24,25; 25:1,7; 27:14,27; 28:11,13,17,18 ROM 9:30,31; 14:19,19 1 CO 11:25; 12:28,28,28,28; 14:1; 15:5,7,7 GAL 1:18,21; 2:1; 3:17 1 TH 5:15 1 TM 4:1,1; 5:15,24; 6:11,11,11,11,11,11 2 TM 2:22; 3:10,10,10,10,10,10,10,11,11 TIT 3:10 HEB 4:7; 7:28; 8:10; 9:27; 10:9,16,26; 12:14,14 1 PT 3:11 2 PT 1:15,16; 2:2,10,21; 3:17 JUD 7,11,18 REV 1:19; 4:1,1; 7:1; 9:13; 11:11; 12:15; 13:3; 15:5; 17:1; 18:1; 19:1; 20:3

477 **ܒܬܪܟܢ** (adv) afterwards

from 476 ܒܬܪ (above) and 1452 ܟܢ

LUK 12:4; 17:8; 18:4 JHN 11:7,11; 13:7 ACT 1:12; 2:14; 28:1 1 CO 15:6,23 HEB 4:8; 12:17 1 PT 1:11 REV 7:9

ܒ

315 ܒܐܪܐ (f) well

LUK 14:5
JHN 4:11,12
REV 9:1,2,2

316 ܒܐܫ (v) be evil; (ethpe w/ ܠ) be offended; (aph) treat evilly

[a]PEAL (non occ)

366 ܒܝܫܐ (adj) evil

MAT 4:24,24; 5:11,37,39,45; 6:13,23,34; 7:11,17,17,18,18; 8:28; 9:4; 12:33,33,34,35,35,35,39,45,45,45; 13:19,38,48,49; 14:35,35; 15:19; 16:4; 18:32; 20:15; 21:41,41; 22:10; 24:48; 25:26; 27:23,64
MRK 2:17,17; 3:4; 7:21,22,23; 9:39; 15:14
LUK 3:19; 5:31,31; 6:9,22,35,43,43,45,45,45; 7:21; 8:2; 11:4,13,26,26,29,34,39; 16:25; 19:22; 23:22,32,33,39
JHN 3:19; 5:14,29; 7:7; 17:15; 18:23,30
ACT 3:26; 9:13; 10:38; 13:10; 16:28; 17:5; 18:14; 19:15,16; 21:38; 23:9; 25:18; 28:21
ROM 1:29,30; 2:9; 3:8; 7:19,21; 9:11; 12:9,17,17,21,21; 13:3,4,4,10; 14:20; 16:19
1 CO 5:13; 10:6; 13:5; 14:20; 15:33
2 CO 5:10; 13:7
GAL 1:4
EPH 5:16; 6:12,13,16
PHL 3:2
COL 1:21; 3:5
1 TH 5:15,15,22
2 TH 3:2,3,6,6,7,7,11,11
1 TM 5:8; 6:4,10
2 TM 1:8; 2:3,9,9; 3:13; 4:5,14,18
TIT 1:12
HEB 3:12; 5:14; 10:22
JAM 1:13; 2:4; 3:8,16; 4:16
1 PT 2:12; 3:9,9,10,11,12,13,16,17,17; 4:15
2 PT 2:20
1 JN 2:13,14; 3:12,12; 5:18,19
2 JN 11
3 JN 10,11,11
REV 2:2; 16:2

367 ܒܝܫܐܝܬ (adv) wickedly

MAT 8:6,16; 9:12; 15:22; 17:15
MRK 1:32,34; 5:23; 6:55
LUK 7:2
JHN 18:23
JAM 4:3

368 ܒܝܫܘܬܐ (f) wickedness

MAT 22:18
MRK 7:22
ACT 8:22
ROM 1:29
1 CO 5:8
EPH 4:31
COL 3:8
2 TM 3:13
TIT 3:3
HEB 7:26
JAM 1:21
1 PT 2:1,16

[b]ETHPEEL

Perfect

MAT 21:15; 26:8
MRK 10:14; 14:4

Participle

LUK 11:53

ᵉAPHEL

Perfect

ACT 7:19

Imperfect

ACT 7:6, 12:1 | ACT 14:2

---

321 ܒܓܠ (prep) before; (w/ ܩܪܐ or ܩܥܐ) appeal to

ACT 25:11,12, 26:32 | ACT 28:19

320 (ܒܓܠ) (v) cry out

ᶜPAEL

Active Participle

ACT 21:28 | ACT 22:23

---

322 ܒܕܐ (v-non occ) imagine, contrive

ᵃPEAL

323 ܒܕܝܐ (m) nonsense

2 PT 2:3

---

324 ܒܕܩ (v) show

ᶜPAEL

Perfect

LUK 20:37, ACT 7:52 | ACT 23:16,22

Imperfect

JHN 11:57 | JHN 16:25

ᵈETHPAAL

Perfect

ACT 9:24 | ACT 23:30

---

325 ܒܕܪ (v) scatter, disperse

ᶜPAEL

Perfect

MAT 25:24,26, LUK 1:51 | LUK 15:13, 2 CO 9:9

Infinitive

MAT 12:30[1] | LUK 11:23[1]

Active Participle

MAT 12:30[2], LUK 11:23[2] | JHN 10:12

Passive Participle

JHN 11:52

ᵈETHPAAL

Perfect

ACT 5:36,37, 8:1,4 | ACT 11:19

Imperfect

MAT 26:31, MRK 14:27 | JHN 16:32

---

326 ܒܗܠ (v) cease

ᵃPEAL

Perfect

ACT 21:32,40 | ACT 22:2

---

328 ܒܗܪܐ (m-non occ) faint light

327 (ܒܗܪ) (v) boast

ᵍSHAPHEL

Active Participle

2 CO 10:12

3083 ܫܒܗܪܐ (adj) boastful

ROM 1:30 | 2 TM 3:2

3084 ܫܒܗܪܘܬܐ (f) boastfulness

MRK 7:22

3117 ܫܘܒܗܪܐ (m) boasting

ROM 3:27	2 CO 11:10,17
4:2	12:11
15:17	GAL 6:4
1 CO 5:6	PHL 1:26
9:15,16	2:16
15:31	1 TH 2:19
2 CO 1:12,14	HEB 3:6
7:4,14	JAM 4:16
8:24	1 JN 2:16
9:3,4	

[h]ESHTAPHAL

Perfect

2 CO 7:14	2 CO 9:2,3,4

Imperfect

JHN 5:35	2 CO 11:16,18[2], 30[2]
ROM 5:11	12:5[1],5[2],6, 9
11:18[1]	GAL 6:12,13,14
1 CO 1:29,31[2]	EPH 2:9
3:21	JAM 1:9
2 CO 10:8,16, 17[2]	

Infinitive

2 CO 11:30[1]	2 CO 12:1

Participle

ROM 2:17,23	2 CO 10:13,15, 17[1]
5:2,3	11:12,18[1]
11:18[2]	PHL 3:3
1 CO 1:31[1]	2 TH 1:4
4:7	JAM 4:16
2 CO 5:12[1],12[2]	

329 ܒܗܬ (v) be ashamed; (aph) shame

[a]PEAL

Perfect

2 CO 7:14	HEB 2:11
2 TM 1:16	

Imperfect

MAT 21:37	PHL 1:20
MRK 8:38[1],38[2]	2 TH 3:14
12:6	2 TM 1:8
LUK 9:26[1],26[2]	TIT 2:8
14:9	1 PT 2:6
ROM 9:33	3:16
10:11	4:16
2 CO 9:4[1],4[2]	1 JN 2:28

Active Participle

LUK 13:17	2 CO 10:8
16:3	2 TM 1:12
ROM 1:16	HEB 12:9
6:21	

330 ܒܗܬܬܐ (f) shame

ROM 1:27	2 TM 2:15
1 CO 13:5	HEB 12:2
14:35	JUD 13
15:34	REV 3:18
2 CO 4:2	16:15
PHL 3:19	

[e]APHEL

Perfect

COL 2:15

Imperfect

1 CO 1:27[1],27[2]	1 CO 4:14

Active Participle

ROM 5:5	1 CO 11:4,5,22

335 ܒܘܠܐ (f-non occ) senate

336 ܒܘܠܘܛܐ (m) senator, counselor

MRK 15:43	LUK 23:50

338 ܒܘܨܐ (m) linen

LUK 16:19	REV 19:8,8,14
REV 18:12,16	

340 (ܒܘܪ) (v-non occ) be uncultivated

[a]PEAL

341 ܒܘܪܐ (adj) rude

2 CO 11:6

ܒܘܬ see under ܒܝܬܐ

346 ܒܙ (v) plunder

[a]PEAL

Imperfect

MAT 12:29[1],29[2] | MRK 3:27

351 ܒܙܬܐ (f) spoil

LUK 11:22

---

348 ܒܘܙܚܐ (m) mocking

EPH 5:4 | HEB 11:36

347 (ܒܙܚ) (v) mock

[c]PAEL

Perfect

MAT 27:31 | MRK 15:20

Imperfect

MAT 20:19 | LUK 18:32
MRK 10:34

Active Participle

MAT 27:29,41 | LUK 23:11,36
LUK 14:29 | 2 PT 3:3
22:63 | JUD 18

1611 ܡܒܙܚܢܐ (m) mocker

2 PT 3:3

---

[d]ETHPAAL

Perfect

MAT 2:16

Participle

1 CO 7:36 | GAL 6:7

---

349 ܒܙܥ (v) cut, burst

[a]PEAL (non occ)

350 ܒܙܥܐ (m) tear, rent

MAT 9:16

---

[c]PAEL

Imperfect

MAT 7:6

Active Participle

LUK 5:37

---

352 ܒܚܪ (v) prove, examine

[a]PEAL

Imperfect

ACT 28:26 | ROM 11:8

Active Participle

MAT 7:3

Passive Participle

1 PT 2:6 | REV 3:18

331 ܒܘܚܪܢܐ (m) trial

1 PT 1:7 | 1 PT 4:12
2:12

---

[b]ETHPEEL

Perfect

JAM 1:12

Imperfect

MAT 7:5

Participle

2 PT 3:12

---

357 ܒܛܠ (v) be idle, cease; (w/ ܠ) care; (pa) annul

[a]PEAL

Perfect

HEB 11:12

Active Participle

ACT 19:27 | 2 PT 2:3

Passive Participle

MRK 4:38 | JHN 10:13
LUK 10:40 | 12:6

ACT 17:21	GAL 2:6
1 CO 9:9	TIT 1:9
2 CO 8:17	1 PT 5:7

355 ܒܛܝܠܐܝܬ (adv) carefully

MRK 7:3	LUK 7:4
LUK 1:39	15:8

356 ܒܛܝܠܘܬܐ (f) diligence

MRK 6:25

---

[b]ETHPEEL

Perfect

LUK 10:34	GAL 2:10
2 CO 9:5	

Imperfect

ROM 12:17	2 TM 4:9,21
1 CO 7:21	TIT 3:8,12,13
2 TM 2:15	

---

[c]PAEL

Perfect

MAT 15:6	EPH 2:15
ROM 3:3	2 TM 1:10
1 CO 13:11	HEB 10:9
15:24	

Imperfect

ACT 5:39	2 TH 2:8
1 CO 1:28	HEB 2:14
GAL 3:17	9:26

Active Participle

LUK 13:7	1 CO 6:13
ROM 3:31	

Passive Participle

ROM 4:14

354 ܒܛܝܠܐ (adj) idle, vain

MAT 20:3,6	TIT 1:12
25:30	2 PT 1:8
LUK 17:10	

358 ܒܛܠܐ (adj) idle, vain

MAT 12:36	ACT 14:15
20:6	1 CO 15:17

359 ܒܛܠܐܝܬ (adv) needlessly

ACT 19:40

---

[d]ETHPAAL

Perfect

ROM 3:27	2 CO 3:7,11
7:6	GAL 5:4,11

Imperfect

ROM 6:6	1 CO 13:10
1 CO 13:8[1],8[2],	2 CO 11:10

Participle

1 CO 2:6	2 CO 3:13,14
15:26	

---

360 ܒܛܢ (v) conceive

[a]PEAL

Perfect

LUK 1:24

Imperfect

MAT 1:23

Active Participle

JAM 1:15

361 ܒܛܢܐ (m) conception

LUK 1:31

362 ܒܛܢܬܐ (adj) pregnant

MAT 1:18	LUK 2:5
24:19	21:23
MRK 13:17	1 TH 5:3
LUK 1:36	REV 12:2

---

[b]ETHPEEL

Imperfect

LUK 2:21

363 (ܒܝܐ)(v) comfort

[c]PAEL

Perfect

ACT 16:40; 20:1,2
2 CO 7:6[2]

Imperfect

2 CO 1:4[2]; 2:7
EPH 6:22
COL 4:8
2 TH 2:17

Imperative

1 TH 5:11

Infinitive

TIT 1:9

Active Participle

JHN 11:31
2 CO 1:4[1]
2 CO 7:6[1]
1 TH 4:18

332 ܒܘܝܐܐ (m) comfort

LUK 2:25; 6:24
ACT 4:36; 9:31; 13:15
ROM 12:8; 15:4,5
1 CO 14:3
2 CO 1:3,4,5,6,7
2 CO 7:4,13
PHL 2:1
COL 4:11
1 TH 2:3
2 TH 2:16
PLM 7
HEB 6:18; 13:22

1612 ܡܒܝܐܢܐ (m) comforter

ROM 12:8

[d]ETHPAAL

Perfect

ACT 15:31; 27:36
2 CO 7:13
1 TH 3:7

Imperfect

MAT 5:4
ROM 1:12
1 CO 14:31
2 CO 1:6[2]
COL 2:2

Imperative

2 CO 13:11

Infinitive

MAT 2:18

Participle

2 CO 1:4[3],6[1]

364 ܒܝܡ (f) judgement seat

MAT 27:19
JHN 19:13
ACT 12:21; 18:12,16,
ACT 18:17; 25:6,10,17
ROM 14:10
2 CO 5:10

365 (ܒܝܢ), ܒܝܬ (prep) between, among

MAT 10:16; 12:1; 13:7,22,25,49; 18:2,15,20; 19:10; 20:17,26; 21:38; 23:35; 24:3; 28:15 MRK 2:3,23; 4:7,18,34; 9:33; 10:26,43 LUK 1:25; 4:30; 6:1; 8:7,14,43; 10:3; 11:51; 14:23; 16:15,26; 17:11; 18:11; 19:39; 22:23, 24,27,55; 23:12; 24:36 JHN 1:26; 4:4,31, 33; 8:59; 9:16; 10:19,39; 11:38,54; 19:24; 20:19; 21:23 ACT 1:8; 2:22; 8:1; 12:6,18; 15:3,9; 17:33; 18:15; 22:30; 23:10; 24:21,22; 27:21,41 ROM 2:24; 6:19 1 CO 1:11; 2:2; 5:1,1,2,13; 6:5; 7:34; 11:13,18,19; 14:7, 28; 15:32 2 CO 6:17; 12:12 GAL 2:2; 3:15; 6:4 EPH 5:3 PHL 2:15 1 TH 1:5; 2:7 2 TH 3:7 2 TM 3:6 HEB 6:16 2 PT 2:8 REV 2:1; 6:6; 7:3; 9:4; 13:16; 14:1,9; 17:5; 20:4; 22:4

377 ܒܝܬܐ (f) house

incl idioms
see (pn) (eg Bethlehem)
see below 369 ܒܝܬ ܐܣܝܪ̈ܐ
see also 370 ܒܝܬ ܗܪܘܕܣ
see also 2909 ܪܒ ܒܝܬܐ

MAT 2:11; 5:15; 7:24,25,26, 27; 8:6,14,28; 9:6,7,9,10, 23,28; 10:6,12,12, 13,14, 17,23, 25,25, 36; 11:8; 12:4,25,29, 29,44; 13:1,27,36, 52,57; 14:2,6
MAT 15:24; 17:25; 19:29; 20:1,11; 21:13,13, 33; 22:10; 23:13,29, 38; 24:17,43, 43,45; 25:10; 26:6; 27:6,7,52, 60,60, 64; 28:7
MRK 1:29

MRK 2:1,11,14,15,26
3:19,25,25,27,27
5:2,3,5,19,35,38
6:4,4,10,14,16,21,29
7:17,24,30
8:3,26
9:10,28,33
10:10,29,30
11:17,17
12:40,41,41,43
13:15,34,35
14:3,14,14
16:2,3,5
LUK 1:5,23,27,33,40,56,69
2:4,49
4:27,38
5:24,25,27,29
6:4,48,48,49,49
7:5,6,10,25,36,37,44
8:27,27,39,41,49,51
9:4,7,61
10:5,5,7,7,7,38
11:17,24
12:18,24,36,39,39,52
13:25,35
14:1,8,21,23
15:6,8,12,17,18,25
16:4,27
17:31
18:14,29
19:5,9,29,37,46,46
20:35,47
21:1,4,37
22:11,11,39,54,66
23:53
24:1,2,22,24,46
JHN 2:16,16,17,22
4:53
JHN 7:53
8:20,35
11:17,20,31,38,38
12:1,3,9,17
14:2
19:41
20:1,2,3,4,6,8
21:14
ACT 1:12
2:2,29,36,46
3:15
4:2,8,10,34
5:42
7:10,20,47,49
8:3
9:11,15,17,43
10:2,6,7,17,22,30,32,41
11:12,13,14
12:7,12
13:29,30,34
15:32
16:13,15,15,16,24,31,32,33,34,34
17:3,5,19,23,31,32
18:7,7,8,26
19:16
20:20
21:6,8,16
24:15
25:23
26:23
28:7,30
ROM 1:3,4
2:22
4:24
6:4,9
7:4
8:11,11
10:7,9
11:15
16:5,10,11
1 CO 1:11,16
4:11
8:10
9:13,13
11:22,34
1 CO 14:35
15:12,20
16:2,15,19
2 CO 5:1,1,2,4
GAL 1:1
6:10
EPH 1:20
2:19
5:14
PHL 3:11
4:22
COL 1:18
2:12
4:15
1 TH 1:10
1 TM 3:4,5,12,15,16
5:4,8,13,13,14,24
2 TM 1:16
2:8,20
2 TM 3:6
4:13,19
TIT 1:11
2:5
PLM 2,22
HEB 3:2,3,4,5,6,6
6:2
8:2,8,8,8,8,10,10
9:1,2,4,12,24,25
10:19,21
11:7
13:11,20
JAM 2:6
1 PT 1:21
4:17
2 JN 10
REV 2:10

369 ܒܝܬ ܐܣܝܪܐ (idiom)

prison

from 377 ܒܝܬܐ (above) and 225 ܐܣܝܪܐ

MAT 5:25
11:2
14:3,10
18:30
25:36,39,43,44
MRK 6:17,27
LUK 3:20
12:58
21:12
22:33
23:19,25
JHN 3:24
ACT 5:18,19,21,22,23,25
8:3
12:4,5,6,17
16:23,23,24,26,27,27,36,37,40
22:4,19
26:10

345 (ܒܘܬ) (v) lodge, remain

aPEAL

Perfect

MAT 21:17

Imperfect

JHN 19:31

Active Participle

LUK 21:37

378 ܒܟܐ (v) weep

aPEAL

Perfect

MAT 26:75
LUK 7:32
19:41
LUK 22:62
REV 18:18

Imperfect

MRK 14:72
LUK 6:25
7:13
8:52[2]
LUK 23:28[1]
JHN 16:20
REV 5:5
18:9,11

Imperative

LUK 23:28[2]
ROM 12:15[1]
JAM 5:1

Infinitive

JHN 11:31

Active Participle

MAT 2:18
MRK 5:38,39
9:24
16:10
LUK 6:21
7:38
8:52[1]
JHN 11:33[1],33[2]
20:11[1],11[2],
JHN 20:13,15
ACT 9:39
21:13
ROM 12:15[2]
1 CO 7:30[1],30[2]
PHL 3:18
REV 5:4
18:15,19

379 ܒܟܝܐ (m) weeping

MAT 2:18
8:12
13:42,50
22:13
MAT 24:51
25:30
LUK 13:28

383 ܒܟܬܐ (f) weeping

ACT 20:37

---

382 ܒܟܪ (v-non occ) be first

aPEAL

333 ܒܘܟܪܐ (m) first-born

MAT 1:25
LUK 2:7
ROM 8:29
COL 1:15,18
HEB 1:6
11:28
12:23
REV 1:5

334 ܒܘܟܪܘܬܐ (f) birthright

HEB 12:16

380 ܒܟܝܪܐ (adj) early (spring)

JAM 5:7

---

384 ܒܠܐ (v) grow old

aPEAL

Imperfect

HEB 1:11

Active Participle

LUK 12:33
1 PT 1:18,23[1],
1 PT 1:23[2]

387 ܒܠܝܐ (adj) old, worn out

MAT 9:16,17
MRK 2:21,21,22
LUK 5:36,36,37

ܒܠܚܘܕ see (ܚܘܕ)

---

388 ܒܠܡ (v) muzzle

aPEAL

Imperfect

1 CO 9:9
1 TM 5:18

---

390 ܒܠܥ (v) swallow, be struck

aPEAL

Perfect

LUK 22:51
2 CO 11:24
REV 8:12
12:16

Imperfect

LUK 12:47,48
1 PT 5:8

Active Participle

MAT 23:24

385 ܒܠܘܥܐ (m) fishhook

MAT 17:27

[b]ETHPEEL

Perfect

1 CO 15:54	HEB 11:29

Imperfect

2 CO 2:7	2 CO 5:4

391 ܒܠܥܕ (prep) without

MAT 10:29	1 CO 4:8
LUK 22:6	PLM 14
JHN 1:3	HEB 11:40
ROM 7:8	12:14

393 ܒܠܛ (v) sprout

[a]PEAL

Perfect

MRK 4:5

395 ܒܢܐ (v) build, edify

[a]PEAL

Perfect

MAT 7:24,26	LUK 6:48,49
21:33	7:5
MRK 12:1	ACT 7:47

Imperfect

MAT 16:18	ACT 7:49
26:61	15:16
LUK 12:18	ROM 15:20
14:28	

Infinitive

LUK 14:30

Active Participle

MAT 23:29	1 CO 3:10[1],10[2],
27:40	12,14
MRK 14:58	8:1
15:29	14:4[1],4[2],5
LUK 11:47,48	GAL 2:18
17:28	HEB 3:4[2]
ACT 20:32	

Passive Participle

MAT 5:14	LUK 4:29

399 ܒܢܝܢܐ (m) building

MAT 24:1	2 CO 10:8
MRK 13:1,2	12:19
ROM 14:19	13:10
15:2	EPH 2:20,21
1 CO 3:9	4:12,16,29
14:3,12,26	1 TM 1:4
2 CO 5:1	HEB 3:3

[b]ETHPEEL

Perfect

JHN 2:20	EPH 2:20

Participle

EPH 2:22	HEB 3:4[1]
COL 2:7	

[c]PAEL

Imperative

1 TH 5:11

Active Participle

1 CO 10:23

397 ܒܢܝܐ (m) builder

MAT 21:42	ACT 4:11
MRK 12:10	HEB 3:3
LUK 20:17	

[d]ETHPAAL

Imperative

1 PT 2:5	JUD 20

Participle

ACT 9:31	1 CO 14:17

400 ܒܣܐ (v) despise; (aph) despise, neglect

[a]PEAL

Perfect

MAT 22:5	HEB 8:9
ACT 20:20	

Imperfect

MAT 18:10	1 TM 6:2
1 TM 4:14	

Active Participle

LUK 18:9	1 CO 11:22

Passive Participle

1 CO 6:4

ᵇETHPEEL

Participle

ACT 6:1

ᵉAPHEL

Imperfect

1 TM 4:12	HEB 2:3
TIT 2:15	

---

401 ܒܣܕܝܐ (m) pillow

MRK 4:38

---

405 ܒܣܡ (v) be merry, sweet; (pa) perfume; (ethpa) rejoice

ᵃPEAL

Perfect

JAM 5:5

Infinitive

LUK 15:32

406 ܒܣܡܐ (m) ointment

MAT 26:7,12	JHN 12:3,3
MRK 14:3,4	19:40
LUK 1:9,10,11	HEB 9:4
7:37,38,46	REV 5:8
23:56	8:3,4
JHN 11:2	18:12,13

ᶜPAEL

Perfect

MRK 14:8

337 ܒܘܣܡܐ (m) pleasure

2 PT 2:13

402 ܒܣܝܡܐ (adj) pleasant

MAT 11:30	1 CO 15:33
LUK 5:39	2 CO 2:15
6:35	EPH 4:32
ROM 16:18	5:2
1 CO 13:4	PHL 4:18

403 ܒܣܝܡܐܝܬ (adv) gladly

MRK 6:20	MRK 12:37

404 ܒܣܝܡܘܬܐ (f) goodness

ACT 2:28	2 CO 6:6
14:17	GAL 5:22
ROM 2:4,4	EPH 2:7
11:22,22, 22	COL 3:12
	TIT 3:2,4

ᵈETHPAAL

Perfect

ACT 2:26	ROM 15:24

Imperfect

LUK 15:23,29	HEB 11:25

Imperative

LUK 12:19	GAL 4:27
ROM 15:10	

Infinitive

LUK 15:24

Participle

LUK 16:19	2 PT 2:13
ACT 7:41	

---

407 ܒܣܪ (v) despise

ᵃPEAL

Active Participle

TIT 2:8	1 JN 3:20,21

[c]PAEL

Perfect

PHL 2:30

Active Participle

2 PT 2:10

1613 ܡܒܣܪܢܐ (adj) despiser

ACT 13:41

408 ܒܣܪ, ܒܣܪܐ (m) flesh

MAT 16:17	GAL 1:16
19:5	2:16,20
24:22	3:3
MRK 10:8,8	4:13,14,23, 29
13:20	5:13,16,17, 17,19,24
LUK 3:6	6:8,8,12, 13
24:39	EPH 2:3,3,11, 11,15
JHN 1:13,14	5:30,31
3:6,6	6:5,12
17:2	PHL 1:22
ACT 2:17	3:2,3,4,4
ROM 1:3	COL 1:22,24
2:28	2:1,5,11, 13,18,23
3:20	1 TM 3:16
4:1	PLM 16
6:19	HEB 2:14
7:5,14,18, 25	5:7
8:1,3,3,3,4, 5,5,6,7,8, 9,12,12, 13	9:10,13
9:3,5,8	10:20
11:14	12:9
13:14	13:3,11
14:21	JAM 5:3
15:27	1 PT 1:24
1 CO 1:26,29	4:1,6
3:3,3	2 PT 2:10,18
8:13	1 JN 4:2,3
10:18	2 JN 7
15:50	JUD 7,8,23
2 CO 1:17	REV 17:16
3:3	19:18,18, 18,18, 18,21
7:1	
10:2,3,3,4	
11:18	
12:7	

409 ܒܬܪ (adv) after, behind, backwards

MAT 9:20	MRK 8:33
16:23	LUK 7:38
MRK 5:27	8:44
LUK 9:62	REV 1:10
PHL 3:13	4:6

410 ܒܣܬܪܐ (m) back; (as prep) behind

MAT 24:18	JHN 6:66
MRK 13:16	18:6
LUK 17:31	20:14

411 ܒܥܐ (v) seek

[a]PEAL

Perfect

MAT 8:34	ACT 12:19
15:23	13:42
18:29,32	16:27,39
21:46	19:31
LUK 2:44	21:12
4:38	24:6
7:36	25:15,21, 25
9:40	27:30
11:37	28:14,20
13:6	ROM 10:3,20
15:28	1 CO 16:12
20:19	2 CO 8:4
22:32	12:8,18
JHN 4:40	1 TH 2:6
7:30	1 TM 1:3,7
10:39	2 TM 1:17
19:31,38	HEB 12:17
ACT 4:31	2 JN 12
8:31	
10:48	

Imperfect

MAT 26:53	ACT 9:38
LUK 11:24	15:17
12:29	23:20
13:24	1 CO 7:27[1],27[2]
19:10	2 CO 8:6
JHN 7:34,36	9:5
8:21	1 TH 3:2
13:33	1 PT 3:11
14:16	1 JN 5:16
16:26	REV 9:6

Imperative

MAT 6:33	ACT 23:15[1]
7:7	1 CO 14:12
9:38	COL 3:1
LUK 10:2	1 TM 6:2
11:9	TIT 2:6,15
12:31	HEB 3:13
ACT 8:22,24	10:25
9:11	

Infinitive

MAT 2:13	ACT 11:25
MRK 8:11	PLM 9[1]

Active Participle

MAT 2:20
6:32[1]
7:8
8:5,31
9:13
12:39,43,
46,47
13:45
14:36
16:4
18:12
26:16,59
28:5
MRK 1:27,36,37,
40
3:32
5:10,12,17,
18,23
6:56
7:26,32
8:12,22
9:10
11:18
12:12
14:1,11,55
16:6
LUK 2:45,48,49
4:42
5:8,12,18,
39
6:19
7:3,4
8:28,31,32,
37,38,41
9:38
11:10,29,
54
12:30[1]
13:7
14:18,19,
32
15:4,8
16:27
19:47
22:2,6
24:5,15
JHN 1:38
4:23,27,31,
47
5:16,18,30,
44
6:24,26
7:1,11,18[1],
18[2],20[1],
20[2],25
8:37,40,
50[1],50[2]
11:8,56
16:19[1],19[2]
17:9[1],9[2],
15,20
18:4,7,8
20:15

ACT 2:40
3:3
7:28
8:34
9:24
10:2,19,21
11:23
13:7,11
14:22
16:9,15
17:5,27
18:14,20
19:39
21:31,39
22:29
23:15[2],18,
28
24:4
25:2,20
26:3,29
27:34
ROM 2:7
3:11
8:34
11:3,7
12:1
15:30
16:2,17
1 CO 1:10,22
4:13,16
10:24,33
13:5
16:15
2 CO 2:8
5:20[1],20[2]
6:1
10:1,2
11:12
12:14
13:3,7
GAL 1:10
2:17
4:12
EPH 4:1
PHL 2:21
4:2,3,17[1],
17[2]
1 TH 2:11
4:1,10
5:12,14
2 TH 2:1
3:12
1 TM 2:1
5:11
PLM 9[2],10
HEB 11:6,14,15
13:19,22
1 PT 1:12
2:11
5:1,8
3 JN 9,13
REV 11:5

414 ܒܥܘܬܐ (f) prayer, request

ROM 10:1
2 CO 1:11
8:4,17
EPH 6:18
PHL 1:4,19
PHL 4:6
1 TM 2:1
4:13
5:5
HEB 5:7

428 ܒܥܬܐ (f) question

JHN 3:25
ACT 15:2,2,7
25:20
1 TM 6:4
TIT 3:9

---

[b]ETHPEEL

Imperfect

REV 22:5

Participle

MAT 6:8,32[2]
14:16
21:3
26:65
MRK 11:3
14:63
LUK 5:31
10:42
11:8
12:30[2]
15:7
LUK 19:31,34
22:71
JHN 13:29
1 CO 4:2
12:21[1],21[2],
24
EPH 5:4
HEB 7:11
10:18,36
REV 21:23

---

412 (ܒܥܪ)(v) send away

[e]APHEL

Perfect

LUK 20:9

---

416 ܒܥܛ(v) kick

[c]PAEL

Infinitive

ACT 9:4
ACT 26:14

---

420 ܒܥܠ, ܒܥܠܐ(m) husband, master

see below ܒܥܠܕܒܒܐ
see below ܒܥܠܕܒܒܘܬܐ
see below 424 ܒܥܠܕܝܢܐ

MAT 1:19
MRK 10:12

LUK 2:36	1 CO 7:39,39
JHN 4:16,17,17, 18,18	14:35
ACT 5:9,10	EPH 5:22,24,33
ROM 7:2,2,2,3,3	COL 3:18
11:34	1 TM 3:2
1 CO 7:2,3,4,10, 11,13,13, 16,34,34,	TIT 1:6
	2:4,5
	1 PT 3:1,5
	REV 21:2

422 ܒܥܠܕܒܒܐ (adj) enemy

MAT 5:43,44	ROM 5:10
10:36	11:28
13:25,28, 39	12:20
22:44	1 CO 15:25,26
MRK 12:36	GAL 4:16
LUK 1:71,74	PHL 3:18
6:27,35	COL 1:21
8:12	2 TH 3:15
10:19	1 TM 5:14
19:27,43	HEB 1:13
20:43	10:13,27
21:15	11:34
ACT 2:35	JAM 4:4
13:10	1 PT 5:8
	REV 11:5,12

423 ܒܥܠܕܒܒܘܬܐ (f) enmity

LUK 23:12	EPH 2:15,16
ROM 8:7	JAM 4:4
GAL 5:20	

424 ܒܥܠܕܝܢܐ (adj) adversary (at law)

from 420 ܒܥܠܐ (above) and 671 ܕܝܢܐ

MAT 5:25,25	LUK 18:3
LUK 12:58	ACT 25:16

419 ܒܥܠ (v-non occ) marry

[a]PEAL

417 ܒܥܝܠܬܐ (adj) married woman

GAL 4:27

---

426 ܒܥܛ (v) shake violently

[d]ETHPAAL

Participle

MRK 9:20

---

418 (ܒܥܪ), ܒܥܝܪܐ (c) cattle, beasts (of burden)

ACT 23:24	1 CO 15:39

427 ܒܥܪܝܪܐ (adj) fierce, wild

2 TM 3:3

---

429 ܒܨܐ (v) search, examine

[a]PEAL

Perfect

1 CO 4:7	1 PT 1:11

Imperfect

ACT 23:15

Imperative

JHN 5:39	ACT 6:3
7:52	

Active Participle

1 CO 2:10	REV 2:23
1 PT 1:12	

[b]ETHPEEL

Participle

1 CO 14:24

---

433 ܒܨܪ (v) decrease

[a]PEAL

Infinitive

JHN 3:30

430 ܒܨܝܪܐ (pp) small, less

MAT 2:6	2 CO 2:5
5:19	1 TM 5:9
JHN 2:10	HEB 7:7
1 CO 1:28	

431 ܒܨܝܪܐܝܬ (adv) less

2 CO 12:15

432 ܒܨܝܪܘܬܐ (f) trifle

1 CO 4:3	1 CO 11:17

[b]ETHPEEL

Participle

1 CO 8:8

---

[c]PAEL

Perfect

1 CO 16:17	2 CO 12:11
2 CO 11:5	PHL 2:30

Imperfect

REV 22:19[2]

Active Participle

REV 22:19[1]

---

[d]ETHPAAL

Perfect

1 CO 1:7	2 CO 12:13
2 CO 8:15	

---

434 ܒܩܐ (m) gnat

MAT 23:24

---

435 ܒܩܐ (v) prove, examine; (ethpa) consider

[a]PEAL

Perfect

HEB 3:9

Imperfect

MAT 16:3	LUK 14:19

Imperative

2 CO 13:5	1 TH 5:21

Active Participle

1 CO 11:28	1 TH 2:4[2]
GAL 6:4	

Passive Participle

ROM 14:18	2 CO 10:18
1 CO 11:19	1 TH 2:4[1]
2 CO 8:22	

339 ܒܘܩܝܐ (m) proof, experience

ROM 5:4,4	2 CO 13:3,7
2 CO 8:2	PHL 2:22
9:13	JAM 1:3

---

[b]ETHPEEL

Perfect

1 PT 1:7

Imperfect

1 TM 3:10

---

[d]ETHPAAL

Imperative

MAT 6:28	HEB 13:7
LUK 12:24,27	

Participle

ROM 4:19	PHL 3:17

---

436 ܒܩܪ (v-non occ) seek, bore

[c]PAEL

437 ܒܩܪܐ (f) herd

MAT 8:30,31,32	LUK 8:32,33
MRK 5:11,13	

---

449 ܒܪ, ܒܪܐ (m) countryside (wild), outside

MAT 3:4	LUK 11:39
23:25,26	ROM 11:17,24
MRK 1:6	

457 ܒܪܝܐ (adj) outer, without

MAT 8:12	COL 4:5
22:13	1 TH 4:12
25:30	1 TM 3:7
MRK 4:11	HEB 9:6
1 CO 5:12,13	1 PT 3:3
2 CO 4:16	

1522 ܠܒܪ (adv) outside

MAT 5:13,32	MAT 13:48
12:46,47	15:17

MAT 21:17,39
23:27,28
26:69,75
MRK 1:45
3:31,32
5:10
7:15,18
8:23
11:4,19
12:8,32
14:68
LUK 1:10
4:29
8:20,54
11:40
13:25,28,
33
14:35
20:15
22:62
JHN 6:37
9:34,35
11:43
12:31,42
13:30
15:6
18:16,29
19:4,4,5,

JHN 19:13
ACT 5:34
7:58
8:1
9:40
14:13,19
15:28
16:13,30
18:13
21:5,30
26:22,29
ROM 12:3
16:17
1 CO 6:18
7:31
11:11,11
2 CO 7:5
10:15
GAL 1:8,9
HEB 13:11,12,
13
1 JN 4:18
REV 3:12
5:1
11:2
14:20
22:15

450 ܒܪ, ܒܪܐ (m) son

incl idioms
see (pn) (eg Barabbas)
see below 439 ܒܪ ܐܓܪܐ
see below 440 ܒܪ ܐܢܫܐ
see below 441 ܒܪ ܚܐܪܐ
see below 447 ܒܪ ܥܡܬܗ
see also 2163 ܣܝܡܬ ܒܢܝܐ

MAT 1:1,1,20,
21,23,25
2:15,16,18
3:9,17
4:3,6,21
5:9,45
7:9,11
8:12,20,29
9:2,15,27
10:2,3,21,
21,25,
36,37
11:27,27,
27
12:23,27
13:38,38,
55
14:33
15:22,26
16:16
17:5,15,25,
26

MAT 18:25
19:29
20:20,20,
21,28,
30,31
21:5,9,15,
28,28,
37,37,
38
22:2,24,25,
42,42,
45
23:15,31,
35,37
24:45
26:37,63
27:9,25,40,
43,54,
56
28:19
MRK 1:1,5,11,
19

MRK 2:5,14,19
3:11,17,17,
18
5:7
6:3
7:27,27,28
8:29
9:7,17
10:24,29,
30,35,
45,47,
48
12:6,6,19,
35,37
13:12,12,
32
14:61
15:39
LUK 1:7,13,16,
17,31,32,
35,36,57,
58
2:7,42,44,
48
3:2,8,22,
23,23,23,
24,24,24,
24,24,25,
25,25,25,
25,26,26,
26,26,26,
27,27,27,
27,27,28,
28,28,28,
28,29,29,
29,29,29,
30,30,30,
30,30,31,
31,31,31,
31,32,32,
32,32,32,
33,33,33,
33,33,34,
34,34,34,
34,35,35,
35,35,35,
36,36,36,
36,36,37,
37,37,37,
37,38,38,
38
4:3,9,22,
41
5:10,34
6:15,16,35
7:12,35
8:28
9:35,38,41,
61
10:6,22,22,
22
11:7,11,13,
19,44
12:53,53
13:34

LUK 14:5,26
15:11,12,
13,15,
19,21,
21,24,
25,30,
31
16:8,8,25
18:29,38,
39
19:9,12,14,
44
20:13,28,
29,30,
31,34,
36,36,
41,44
22:70
23:28
JHN 1:12,34,45,
47,49
3:16,17,18,
35,36,36
4:5,12,46,
47,50,51,
53
5:19,19,20,
21,22,23,
23,25,26,
28,41
6:40,42,69,
71
8:35,36,39,
57
9:19,20,35
10:36
11:4,27,52
12:15,36
13:2,26,33
14:13
16:21
17:1,1,12
18:35
19:7,26
20:31
21:2
ACT 1:13,13
2:17,22,39
3:12,13,25,
26
4:22,27,30,
36
5:35
7:3,5,16,
21,23,23,
24,25,29,
37,42
9:15,20
10:7,24,28,
36
11:22
13:1,10,16,
21,22,
26,33,
33

ACT 14:21
16:1,15,32,33,34
18:3,8,22
19:14,24,25,26,29,38
21:5,12,21,28
23:6,16
24:17
25:12
28:19

ROM 1:3,4,9
4:19
5:10
8:3,14,16,17,17,19,21,29,32
9:4,7,8,8,8,9,11,26,27,27
11:14
16:10,11

1 CO 1:9,26
4:14,17
5:1
7:14
15:28

2 CO 1:19
3:7,13
6:13,14,18
12:14,14

GAL 1:14,16
2:20
3:7,26
4:4,6,6,7,7,19,22,25,27,27,28,30,30,30,31,31
6:10

EPH 1:5
2:2,3,19,19
3:6
4:13
5:1,6,8
6:1,4

PHL 2:15,22
3:5,5
4:3

COL 1:13
3:6,20,21
4:10

1 TH 1:10
2:7,11,14
5:5,5,5,5,8

2 TH 2:3

1 TM 1:2,18
3:4,12
5:4,4,4,4,8,10,14

2 TM 1:2
2:1

TIT 1:4,6,12
2:4

PLM 10

HEB 1:2,5,5,8
2:10,13,14
3:6
4:8,14
5:5,8
6:6
7:3,5,28
8:11
10:29
11:7,9,21,22,24,35
12:5,5,6,7,7,8

JAM 2:21

1 PT 1:14
5:13

2 PT 1:17
2:14,15

1 JN 1:3,7
2:1,12,18,22,23,23,24,28
3:1,2,7,8,10,10,18,23
4:4,9,10,14,15
5:2,5,9,10,10,11,12,12,13,20,20,21

2 JN 1,3,4,9,13

3 JN 4

REV 1:9
2:14,18,23
12:4,5,5
21:7,14

439 ܒܪ ܐܓܪܐ (idiom) lunatic

from 450 ܒܪܐ (above) and 27 ܐܓܪܐ

MAT 4:24

MAT 17:15

440 ܒܪ ܐܢܫܐ (idiom) man, mankind, son of man

from 450 ܒܪܐ (above) and 195 ܐܢܫܐ

MAT 4:4,19
5:16,19
6:1,2,5,14,15,16,18
7:12
9:6,8
10:17,23,32,33
11:19
12:8,12,31,31,32,36,40,43
13:37,41
15:9,11,11,18,20
16:13,23,26,26,27,28
17:9,12,22,22
18:11
19:6,12,26,28
20:18
21:25,26
23:4,5,14,28
24:27,30,30,37,39,44
25:31
26:2,24,24,45,64

MRK 1:17
2:10,27,27,28
3:28
5:8
7:7,8,15,15,18,20,20,21,23
8:24,31,33,36,37,38
9:3,9,12,31,31
10:9,27,33
11:2,30,32
12:14
13:26
14:21,21,41,62

LUK 1:25
2:14,52
4:4
5:10,24
6:5,22,22,26,31
7:34
8:29
9:22,25,26,44,44,56,58
11:24,26,30,46
12:8,8,9,10,40
13:4
16:15,15
17:22,24,26,30
18:2,4,8,27,31
19:10
20:4,6
21:26,27,36
22:22,48,69
24:7

JHN 1:4,6,51
2:25,25
3:13,14,19,27
5:34
6:27,53,62
7:22,23,23,46,51
8:28
10:33
12:23,34,34,43
13:31
16:21
17:6

ACT 4:9,12,17
5:4,29,38
7:56
8:6
10:26
12:22
14:11,15
15:17
17:25,26,26,29,30
18:13
19:26,35
22:15
24:16
25:16

ROM 1:18,23
2:1,3,9,16,29
3:4,5,28
5:12,12,15,18,18,19
6:6,19
7:22,24
9:20

ROM 12:17,18
14:18,20
16:19
1 CO 1:25,25
2:5,9,11,11,11,13,14
3:21
4:3,9
6:18
7:7,23,26
9:8
10:13
13:1
14:2,3
15:19,21,21,22,32,39,45,47,47
2 CO 4:2,16
5:11
8:21
12:3,4
GAL 1:1,1,10,10,10,11,12
2:6,16
3:15,15
5:3
6:7
EPH 2:15
3:5,16
4:8,14,22,24
6:6,7
PHL 2:7,7
COL 1:28,28
2:8,22
3:9,22,23
1 TH 2:4,6,13,15
1 TH 4:8
2 TH 2:3
3:2
1 TM 2:1,4,5,5
4:10
5:24
6:5,9,11,16
2 TM 3:2,13,17
TIT 1:10,14
2:11
3:2,8
HEB 2:6
5:1,1
6:16
7:8,28
8:2
9:27
13:6
JAM 1:7
2:20,24
3:9
5:17
1 PT 2:4,12,13
3:4
4:2,6
2 PT 1:21,21
2:16
3:7
1 JN 5:9
REV 1:13
4:7
8:11
9:4,6,10,15,18,20
13:13,18
14:14
16:8,9,18,21,21
18:13
21:3

441 ܒܪ ܚܐܪܐ (idiom) freeman

from 450 ܒܪܐ (above) and 882 ܚܐܪܐ

MAT 17:26
JHN 8:33,36
1 CO 7:22
9:1
12:13
GAL 3:28
EPH 6:8
COL 3:11
1 TM 1:10
1 PT 2:16
REV 6:15

447 ܒܪ ܫܥܬܗ (idiom) immediately

from 450 ܒܪܐ (above) and 3263 ܫܥܬܐ

MAT 13:5,20
14:27,31
20:34
21:20
MRK 2:12
MRK 3:6
4:5
5:42
6:50,54
9:15,20,24

MRK 11:2
14:45
LUK 5:13
6:49
8:6
18:43
JHN 5:9
13:30
ACT 9:18,20,34
10:33
16:33
17:10
21:30,32
28:6
GAL 1:16

471 ܒܪܬܐ (f) daughter; (w/ ܩܠܐ) voice

MAT 9:18,22
10:35,37
14:6
15:22,28
21:5
MRK 5:23,34,35,42
6:22
7:25,26,29,30
LUK 1:5
2:36
8:42,42,48,49
11:12
LUK 12:53,53
13:16
23:28
JHN 12:15
ACT 2:17
7:21
12:22
21:9
ROM 10:16,18
2 CO 6:18
GAL 4:20
1 TM 6:20
HEB 3:15
11:24
1 PT 3:6

460 (ܒܪ), ܒܪܝܪܘܬܐ (f) simplicity

cf ܒܗܪ

ACT 2:46

461 (ܒܪ), ܒܪܝܬܐ (f) street

LUK 14:21

451 ܒܪܐ (v) create, make

[a]PEAL

Perfect

MRK 13:19
EPH 3:9
1 TM 4:3
REV 4:11[1]
10:6

Imperfect

EPH 2:15

Passive Participle

1 TM 4:4

458 ܒܪܝܐ (ap) creator

COL 3:10

455 ܒܪܘܝܐ (m) creator

ROM 1:25	1 PT 4:19

462 ܒܪܝܬܐ (f) creature, creation

MRK 13:19	COL 1:15,23
16:15	HEB 4:13
ACT 17:27	9:11
ROM 1:20,25	JAM 1:18
8:19,20,21,	2 PT 3:4
22,39	REV 3:14
2 CO 5:17	5:13
GAL 6:15	8:9
EPH 2:10	

[b]ETHPEEL

Perfect

MRK 2:27	EPH 4:24
LUK 11:50	COL 1:16[1],16[2]
1 CO 11:9	REV 4:11[2]
EPH 2:10	

452 ܒܪܒܪܝܐ (adj) barbarian

ACT 28:2,4,6	1 CO 14:11,11
ROM 1:14	COL 3:11

453 ܒܪܕܐ (m) hail

REV 8:7	REV 16:21,21
11:19	

342 (ܒܪܟ), ܒܘܪܟܐ (f) knee

MAT 17:14	ACT 20:36
27:29	21:5
MRK 10:17	ROM 11:4
15:19	14:11
LUK 22:41	EPH 3:14
ACT 7:60	PHL 2:10
9:40	HEB 12:12

343 ܒܘܪܟܬܐ (f) blessing

ROM 1:25	EPH 1:3
9:5	HEB 6:7
11:36	12:17
15:29	JAM 3:10
16:18	1 PT 3:9
2 CO 9:5,5,6,6	REV 5:12,13
GAL 3:14	7:12

463 ܒܪܟ (v) kneel; (pa) bless

[a]PEAL

Perfect

MAT 17:14	ROM 11:4
27:29	

Active Participle

MRK 15:19

459 ܒܪܝܟܐ (pp) blessed

MAT 21:9	LUK 13:35
23:39	19:38
25:34	JHN 12:13
MRK 11:9,10	TIT 2:13
LUK 1:28	

[c]PAEL

Perfect

MAT 14:19	LUK 9:16
26:26	24:30,50
MRK 6:41	JHN 6:11,23
8:6,7	1 CO 11:24
10:16	EPH 1:3[2]
14:22,23	HEB 7:1,6
LUK 1:64	11:20,21
2:28,34	

Imperfect

HEB 6:14[2]

Imperative

MAT 5:44	ROM 12:14[1],14[2]
LUK 6:28	

Infinitive

HEB 6:14[1]

Active Participle

LUK 24:51,53	1 CO 14:16,17
ACT 3:26	JAM 3:9
1 CO 4:12	1 PT 3:9
10:16	

Passive Participle

MRK 14:61	EPH 1:3[1]
LUK 1:42[1],42[2],	1 TM 1:11
68	6:15
2 CO 1:3	1 PT 1:3
11:31	

dETHPAAL

Imperfect

ACT 3:25 | GAL 3:8

Participle

GAL 3:9 | HEB 7:7

---

456 (ܒܪܠ), ܒܪܘܠܐ (m) beryl

REV 21:20

---

465 ܒܪܡ (conj) but, however

MAT 11:22,24; 26:39 LUK 6:24,35; 10:11,14,20; 11:41; 12:31; 13:33; 18:8; 19:27; 22:21,22,42; 23:28 ACT 3:17; 8:22; 9:31; 10:29,32; 11:29; 16:5; 20:23; 24:14; 27:26 1 CO 11:11 EPH 5:33 PHL 3:16; 4:14

---

344 (ܒܪܣܝܐ), ܒܘܪܣܝܐ (m) tanner

ACT 9:43 | ACT 10:6,32

---

469 ܒܪܩ (v) shine; (aph) make shine

aPEAL

Active Participle

LUK 17:24

470 ܒܪܩܐ (m) lightning

MAT 24:27
28:3
LUK 10:18
17:24 | REV 4:5
8:5
11:19
16:18

eAPHEL

Active Participle

LUK 9:29 | LUK 24:4

---

472 ܒܬܘܠܐ (m) virgin

REV 14:4

---

473 ܒܬܘܠܘܬܐ (f) virginity

LUK 2:36 | 1 CO 7:25

474 ܒܬܘܠܬܐ (f) virgin

MAT 1:23
25:1,7,11
LUK 1:27,27
ACT 21:9 | 1 CO 7:28,34,36,
37,38,38
2 CO 11:2

ܒܬܪ see under ܐܬܪ

ܓ

478 (ܓܐܝܐ), ܓܐܝܐ (adj-non occ) lofty, proud

479 ܓܐܝܐܝܬ (adv) luxuriously

LUK 16:19

482 ܓܐܪܐ (m) arrow, dart

EPH 6:16

ܓܒܐ see under ܓܒ

484 ܓܒܐ (v) choose; (pa) gather

[a]PEAL

Perfect

MRK	3:14	ACT	13:17
	13:20		15:7,22,25, 40
LUK	6:13	1 CO	1:27[1],27[2], 28
	10:42	EPH	1:4
JHN	6:70	2 TH	2:13
	13:18	2 TM	2:4
	15:16[1],16[2], 19	HEB	11:25
ACT	1:2	JAM	2:5
	6:5		

Imperfect

PHL 1:22

Imperative

ACT 6:3 | 1 CO 7:21

Infinitive

ACT 15:14 | 2 CO 8:19

Active Participle

ACT	1:24	1 TM	5:9
1 CO	16:3		

486 ܓܒܝܐ (pp) chosen, elect

MAT	20:16	2 CO	8:19
	22:14	COL	3:12
	24:22,24, 31	1 TM	5:21
MRK	13:20,22, 27	2 TM	2:10
LUK	18:7	TIT	1:1
	23:35	1 PT	1:1
ACT	9:15		2:4,9
ROM	8:33		5:13
	16:10,13	2 JN	1,13
		REV	17:14

487 ܓܒܝܘܬܐ (f) election

ROM	9:11	1 TH	1:4
	11:28		

490 ܓܒܝܬܐ (f) election; (pl) collections

ROM	11:5,7	2 PT	1:10
1 CO	16:2		

[b]ETHPEEL

Perfect

ACT	10:41	1 PT	1:2
EPH	1:11		

[c]PAEL

Perfect

MAT 13:48

Imperfect

MAT 13:28,41

Imperative

MAT 13:30

Active Participle

MAT 13:29 | LUK 14:7

485 ܓܒܝܐ (m) official, tax collector

MAT 5:25 | LUK 12:58,58

---

dETHPAAL

Participle

MAT 13:40

---

491 ܓܒܠ (v) form, thicken

aPEAL

Perfect

JHN 9:6 | ROM 9:20[1],20[2]

488 ܓܒܝܠܬܐ (f) lump

ROM 9:20,21
11:16
1 CO 5:6,7
GAL 5:9

---

bETHPEEL

Perfect

1 TM 2:13

---

489 (ܓܒܢ), ܓܒܝܢܐ (m) brow (of a hill)

LUK 4:29

---

493 ܓܒܪ, ܓܒܪܐ (m) man, husband

MAT 1:16
7:9,24,26
8:9
9:9
10:35,36
11:8,19
12:10,11,13,35,35,41,45
13:24,28,31,44,45,52
15:38
17:14
18:7,23
19:5,10
20:1
21:28,33
MAT 22:2,11,30
24:38
25:14,24
26:24,24,72,74
27:32,57
MRK 1:23
3:1,3,5
5:2
6:20,44
7:11
10:2,7
12:1,25
13:34
14:13,21,21,71
15:39
LUK 1:27,34
2:25,25
LUK 4:33
5:8,12,18,20
6:6,8,45,45,48,49
7:8,25,34
8:27,33,35,36,38,41
9:14,30,38
10:30
11:32
12:14,16
13:19
14:2,16,30
15:4,11
16:1,19
17:27
18:10
19:2,7,12,21,22
20:9,34,35
22:10,22,60,63
23:4,6,14,14,47,50,50
24:4,19
JHN 1:13,30
3:1,4
4:29,50
5:5,9,12,15
6:10
7:46
8:17,40
9:1,11,16,16,24,24,30
10:41
11:47,50
18:14,17,29
19:5
ACT 1:10,11,16,21
2:5,14,22,22,29
3:2,12,14
4:4,16,22
5:1,14,25,28,35,36
6:3,5,11,13
7:2,26
8:2,3,9,12
9:2,7,12,13,33,38
10:1,5,17,19,21,22,28,30
11:11,12,
ACT 11:24
13:6,7,15,16,21,22,26
14:8,15
15:7,13,22,22,25
16:9
17:12,22,31
18:2,7,24
19:9,14,16,25,29,33,35,37
20:30
21:11,23,26,28,28,38,39
22:3,4,12,25,26
23:1,6,9,13,21,27
24:5
25:5,14,17,22,24,24,27
26:31,32
27:1,10,21,25
28:4,7,17
ROM 4:6,8
7:1,3,3
11:4
1 CO 7:1,3,4,11,11,14,14,16,25,28,34,36
11:3,3,4,7,7,8,8,9,9,11,11,12,12,14
13:11
2 CO 11:2
12:2,16
EPH 4:13
5:23,25,28,31
COL 3:19
1 TM 2:8,12
5:9,11
TIT 3:10
HEB 2:6
11:24
JAM 1:12,20
3:2
1 PT 3:7
REV 11:13

494 ܓܒܪܘܬܐ (f) (pl) mighty deeds

ACT	2:19,22,43	ACT	7:36
	4:30		15:12
	5:12	2 CO	12:12

492 ܓܒܪ (v) (ethpa) be a man

[d]ETHPAAL

Imperative

1 CO 16:13

---

542 (ܓܝܓܠ), ܓܝܓܠܐ (f) wheel, cycle

JAM 3:6

---

497 ܓܓܪܬܐ (f) throat

ROM 3:13

---

499 ܓܕ (v-non occ) cut, cut off

[a]PEAL

500 ܓܕܘܕܐ (m) young man

ACT 2:17

---

502 ܓܕܝܐ (m) goat

MAT	25:32,33	LUK	15:29

---

503 ܓܕܠ (v) weave

[a]PEAL

Perfect

MAT	27:29	JHN	19:2
MRK	15:17		

501 ܓܕܘܠܐ (m) braiding

1 TM	2:9	1 PT	3:3

1616 ܡܓܕܠܐ (m) tower

MAT	21:33	LUK	13:4
MRK	12:1		14:28

---

506 ܓܕܦ (v) blaspheme

[c]PAEL

Perfect

MAT	26:65	REV	16:9,11,21

Imperfect

MRK	3:28,29	TIT	3:2
LUK	12:10	REV	13:6[2]
TIT	2:5		

Infinitive

REV 13:6[1]

Active Participle

MAT	9:3	ACT	26:11
	27:39	ROM	3:8
MRK	15:29	1 TM	1:20
LUK	22:65	JAM	2:7
	23:39	1 PT	4:4
JHN	10:33,36	2 PT	2:10,12
ACT	13:45	JUD	8,10
	18:5		

513 ܓܘܕܦܐ (m) blasphemy

MAT	12:31,31	EPH	4:31
	15:19	COL	3:8
	26:65	1 TM	6:4
MRK	2:7	2 PT	2:11
	3:28	JUD	9
	7:22	REV	2:9
	14:64		13:1,5
LUK	5:21		17:3
ACT	6:11		

1618 ܡܓܕܦܢܐ (m) blasphemer

1 TM	1:13	2 TM	3:2

---

[d]ETHPAAL

Imperfect

ROM	14:16	2 PT	2:2

Participle

ROM	2:24	1 TM	6:1
1 CO	10:30		

---

508 ܓܕܫ (v) happen

[a]PEAL

Perfect

LUK	10:31	1 CO	10:11
	24:14	2 PT	2:22

Active Participle

1 PT 4:12

---

509 ܓܗܢ (v) stoop, bow

[a]PEAL

Imperfect

MRK 1:7

[b]ETHPEEL

Perfect

JHN 8:6,8

---

511 ܓܘ, ܓܘܐ (m) inside; (as adj, adv) common

MAT 23:26	TIT 1:4
ACT 2:44	JUD 3
4:32	REV 18:4

318 ܒܓܘ (adv, prep) in, within

MRK 11:16	LUK 24:32
LUK 19:44	HEB 2:12
21:21	

518 ܓܘܝܐ (adj) inner

ACT 16:24	HEB 9:3

519 ܓܘܝܐ (m) bowels

ACT 1:18

1525 ܠܓܘ (adv, prep) within

MAT 7:15	ROM 7:22
23:25,27, 28	1 CO 5:12
26:58	2 CO 4:16
MRK 7:21,23	7:5
14:54	EPH 3:16
15:16	HEB 6:19
LUK 11:7,39,40	9:3,7
17:21	REV 4:8
JHN 20:26	5:1
	11:2

---

514 (ܓܘܙ) (v) fail

[a]PEAL

Active Participle

LUK 12:33

---

524 ܓܘܣܐ (m-non occ) refuge

523 (ܓܘܣ) (v) (ethpa) flee

[d]ETHPAAL

Perfect

ACT 14:6	HEB 6:18

---

526 (ܓܘܪ) (v) commit adultery

[a]PEAL

Perfect

MAT 5:28

Imperfect

MAT 5:27,32[1]	ROM 2:22[1]
19:18	13:9
MRK 10:19	JAM 2:11[1]
LUK 18:20	

Active Participle

MAT 5:32[2]	ROM 2:22[2]
19:9[1],9[2]	JAM 2:11[2]
MRK 10:11,12	REV 2:22
LUK 16:18[1],18[2]	

527 ܓܘܪܐ (m) adultery

MAT 15:19	JHN 8:3,4
19:9	2 PT 2:14
MRK 7:21	

[c]PAEL (non occ)

546 ܓܝܪܐ (adj) adulterer

MAT 12:39	ROM 7:3,3
16:4	1 CO 6:9
MRK 8:38	HEB 13:4
LUK 18:11	JAM 4:4

[e]APHEL (non occ)

543 ܓܝܘܪܐ (m) proselyte

MAT 23:15	ACT 6:5
ACT 2:10	13:43

531 ܓܙ (v-non occ) shear

[a]PEAL

534 ܓܙܘܙܐ (m) shearer

ACT 8:32

533 ܓܙܐ (m) treasure; (w/ ܒܝܬ) treasury

MRK 12:41,41, 43	JHN 8:20
LUK 21:1	ACT 8:27

515 (ܓܙܠ), ܓܘܙܠ (v) inflame

[k]P (non occ)

516 ܓܘܙܠܐ (m) flame

2 TH 1:8

[m]ETHP

Participle

ACT 5:33

536 ܓܙܡ (v) rush at, threaten

[a]PEAL

Perfect

ACT 7:57

537 ܓܘܙܡܐ (m) assault, threat

ACT 14:5

538 ܓܙܪ (v) cut, circumcise

[a]PEAL

Perfect

ACT 7:8	ACT 16:3

Imperfect

1 CO 7:18[2]	GAL 2:3

Infinitive

LUK 1:59	ACT 15:5

Active Participle

JHN 7:22	ACT 21:21
ACT 15:1,24	GAL 6:13[1]

Passive Participle

ACT 7:51	1 CO 7:18[1]
10:45	PHL 3:5

535 ܓܙܘܪܬܐ (f) circumcision

JHN 7:22	GAL 2:7,8,9,12
ACT 7:8	5:6,11
11:2	6:15
ROM 2:25,25,26, 27,28,29	EPH 2:11
3:1,30	PHL 3:3
4:9,10,10, 11,12,12	COL 2:11,11
15:8	3:11
1 CO 7:19	4:11
	TIT 1:10

539 ܓܙܪܐ (m) flock

LUK 12:32

540 ܓܙܪܬܐ (f) island

ACT 13:6	ACT 28:11
20:15	REV 1:9
21:1,3	6:14
27:7,16,26	16:20
28:1,7,9,	

[b]ETHPEEL

Perfect

COL 2:11

Imperfect

LUK 2:21	GAL 6:12,13[2]
GAL 5:2	

Participle

JHN 7:23	GAL 5:3

541 ܓܚܟ (v) laugh

ªPEAL

Imperfect

LUK 6:21

Active Participle

MAT 9:24	LUK 6:25
MRK 5:40	8:53
15:31	

517 ܓܘܚܟܐ (m) laughter

JAM 4:9

544 ܓܝܣܐ (m) robber

MAT 26:55	JHN 10:1,8
27:44	18:40
MRK 14:48	2 CO 11:26
LUK 10:36	

545 ܓܝܪ (conj) for

MAT 1:20,21; 2:2,5,6,13,20; 3:3,9,15; 4:6, 10,17,18; 5:12,18,20,29,30,46; 6:7,8,14,16, 21,24,32,34; 7:2,8,12,25,29; 8:9; 9:5,13,21, 24; 10:10,17,19,20,23,26,35; 11:10,13,18,30; 12:8,33,34,36,37,40,50; 13:12,15,17; 14:4, 24; 15:4,19; 16:2,3,25,26,27; 17:15,20; 18:7, 10,11,20; 19:12,14,22; 20:1,16; 21:26,32; 22:14,16,28,30,43; 23:3,5,8,9,12,14,17,19, 39; 24:5,6,6,7,21,24,27,38; 25:14,29,35,42; 26:9,11,31,43,52,73; 27:18,19,23,43; 28:2,5, 6 MRK 1:16,22,38; 2:15; 3:10,21,24,35; 4:22,25,28; 5:8,28,42; 6:14,17,18,20,31,36, 48,50,52; 7:3,8,10,21,25,27; 8:3,35,36,38; 9:6,31,34,39,49; 10:14,22,27,45; 11:13,18, 23,32; 12:6,12,14,23,25,36,44; 13:6,7,8,9,11, 19,22,33,34; 14:5,7,27,56,70; 15:10,14; 16:4, 8,8 LUK 1:15,18,30,31,44,48,76; 2:10,11, 44; 3:8; 4:10,25; 5:9,39; 6:19,23,26,32,32,33, 34,38,40,44,44,45,48; 7:5,6,8,33; 8:10,17,18, 29,29,40,42,46,52; 9:14,24,25,44,48,50,56; 10:7,24; 11:4,10,11,30; 12:3,12,23,30,34,48, 52,53,58; 13:24,35; 14:14,24,28; 16:2,8,13, 28; 17:21,24; 18:14,16,23,32; 19:5,10,21,48; 20:6,19,33,36,36,37,38; 21:4,8,9,10,15,23, 35; 22:2,16,27,37,37,47,59,71; 23:8,12,15, 17,22,34,41; 24:22,37 JHN 1:9; 2:25; 3:2, 16,17,19,20,24,31,34,34; 4:8,9,18,23,24,37, 38,42,45,47; 5:4,13,19,20,21,22,26,30,36,46, 46; 6:6,27,33,40,45,55,64,71; 7:1,4,5,12,39; 8:20,24,42; 9:4,22,24,28; 10:18,29; 11:31,39; 12:8,43,47; 13:10,11,13,15,18; 14:18,30; 15:19; 16:2,6,7,13,27; 17:16; 19:6,12,31,36; 20:9,17; 21:8 ACT 1:20; 2:15,25,30,34,39; 3:22; 4:12,16,20,21,21,22,27,34; 5:26,36; 6:14; 7:33,52; 8:7,16,23; 9:11,16; 10:36,46; 12:9; 13:27,36,47; 15:21,28; 16:3,37; 17:11, 20,23,24,28,30; 18:15,28; 19:32,35,37; 20:13,16,27; 21:3,13,29,36; 22:22,26; 23:5,8, 17,21; 24:5,5,26; 25:27; 26:4,9,16; 27:22,23, 25,34; 28:20,27,28 ROM 1:9,16,17,18,19, 20,26; 2:1,1,11,12,13,14,24,25,28; 3:3,4,20, 22,29; 4:2,3,9,11,13,14,15,15; 5:7,7,10,12, 13,15,16,17,19; 6:2,5,6,7,9,10,14,20,21; 7:1, 5,7,8,11,14,15,18,18,19; 8:2,3,5,6,7,13,14, 15,18,19,20,22,24,26,38; 9:3,6,9,12,17,19, 26,32; 10:2,3,4,5,10,11,12,13,16; 11:1,15,21, 23,24,29,30,32,34; 12:4,19; 13:1,3,4,4,4,6,8, 9,11; 14:2,3,4,7,10,14,17,18,20,23,23; 15:4, 18,26,27; 16:18 1 CO 1:11,17,18,19,21, 26; 2:8,10,11,14,14,16; 3:2,3,3,4,5,9,11,13, 17,19,19,21; 4:4,4,7,9,15,15,20; 5:3,7,12; 6:7,16,18,20; 7:7,9,14,16,19,22,31,32; 8:5,7, 8,10; 9:9,10,15,16,16,17,19; 10:4,5,17,26,29; 11:5,6,7,8,9,12,18,19,23,26,29,31; 12:12,13, 14,15,17,24,28; 13:8,9,13; 14:2,2,5,7,10,14, 17,31,32,34,35; 15:3,9,16,22,25,27,27,32,34, 39,44,53; 16:5,7,7,9,10,11,18 2 CO 1:5,7, 12,19,20,24; 2:2,9,10,11,15,17; 3:3,6,9,10, 11,14; 4:5,8,11,15,16,17,18; 5:1,2,4,7,10,13, 14,19,21; 6:2,14; 7:3,5,7,8,9,10,11; 8:3,9,12, 13,17,21; 9:2,7,13; 10:3,4,8,12,14,14,18; 11:2,2,4,5,6,9,13,14,19,31; 12:1,6,6,9,10,11, 13,14,20; 13:4,8,9 GAL 1:10,10,12,13; 2:6,7,8,15,18,19,21; 3:8,10,10,13,21,26,27, 28; 4:8,13,15,22,25,27; 5:5,6,14,17,19; 6:3,5, 7,8,9,13,15,17 EPH 2:8,10,14; 4:5,25; 5:6, 8,9,12,13,28,29; 6:1 PHL 1:7,8,19,21,23; 2:13,20,21,27,30; 3:3,4,18; 4:11
COL 1:29; 2:5,20; 3:3,6,20,24; 4:13
1 TH 1:4,8,9; 2:3,5,9,19,20; 3:3,4,9; 4:2,3,7, 9,14; 5:2,5,7,18 2 TH 2:7,9,14; 3:2,7,10, 11 1 TM 1:19; 2:3,5,12,13; 3:5,13; 4:5,8, 10,16; 5:4,8,11,15,18; 6:6,7,21 2 TM 1:7, 12; 2:11,13,16,23; 3:6,9,14; 4:3,6,10,11,15
TIT 1:7,10,11,15; 2:11; 3:3,9,12 PLM 7, 13,22 HEB 1:5; 2:2,5,9,10,11,14,16,18; 3:3,4,14,16; 4:2,8,10,12,15; 5:1,12; 6:7,10, 13,16; 7:5,10,13,14,17,19,21,25,26,27,28; 8:3,7,8; 9:2,13,16,19,23,24; 10:1,2,4,10,11, 14,23,26,28,36; 11:3,5,6,10,16,18,26,32; 12:4,6,7,10,17,17,18,20,25,29; 13:2,5,9,11, 14,16,17,18 JAM 1:3,6,11,13,20,23,24,27; 2:2,10,11,13,18; 3:2,3,7,16; 4:11,14; 5:2,5,8, 9,11,16 1 PT 2:6,19,21,24; 3:5,9,17; 4:1,3, 6,8 2 PT 1:8,9,10,11,16,17,21; 2:4,8,18, 19,20,21; 3:4,5 1 JN 2:2,4,5,15,16,19,24; 3:4,15; 4:16,20; 5:3,5,16,17,18 2 JN 11
3 JN 3,7 JUD 4 REV 1:3; 2:27; 3:2; 13:18; 14:4,5; 16:14; 17:17; 19:8,10; 21:1,22, 23,25; 22:10

547 ܓܠܠܐ (m) wave

MAT 8:24	ACT 27:41
14:24	JAM 1:6
MRK 4:37	JUD 13

548 ܓܠܐ (m-non occ) cloak

549 ܓܠܐ (m) straw, chip (of wood)

MAT 7:3,4,5	LUK 6:41,42,42

550 ܓܠܐ (m-non occ) curved (thing)

1623 ܓܠܝܘܢܐ (f) roll, parchment

2 TM 4:13

551 ܓܠܐ (v) reveal

aPEAL

Perfect

MAT 11:25	ROM 1:19
16:17	1 CO 2:10
LUK 10:21	GAL 1:16[2]
ACT 2:28	2:2
28:23	TIT 1:3

Imperfect

MAT 11:27	GAL 1:16[1]
12:16	PHL 3:15
MRK 3:12	COL 4:4
LUK 10:22	

Active Participle

1 CO 3:13[2]	2 CO 2:14
4:5	1 JN 3:21

558 ܓܠܝܐ (pp) manifest, uncovered

see below 2339 ܡܢ ܓܠܝܐ

ACT 4:16	GAL 3:11
ROM 1:19	EPH 5:13
1 CO 11:5,13	HEB 4:13
2 CO 3:18	7:14
5:11,11	

319 ܒܓܠܝܐ (adv) openly

MAT 6:4,6	ROM 2:28
JHN 7:4,10	

554 ܓܠܘܬܐ (f) captivity

MAT 1:11,12,17,	MAT 1:17

559 ܓܠܝܐܝܬ (adv) openly

MRK 1:45	JHN 11:54
JHN 7:13,26	16:29
8:4	ACT 10:3
10:24	COL 2:15

561 ܓܠܝܘܬܐ (f) manifestation; (w/ ܐܦܐ) boldness

2 CO 4:2	HEB 10:19,35
PHL 1:20	1 JN 2:28
HEB 3:6	4:17

564 ܓܠܝܢܐ (m) manifestation, revelation

LUK 2:32	EPH 3:3
ROM 2:5	2 TH 1:7
8:19	2:8
11:4	1 TM 6:14
16:24	2 TM 1:10
1 CO 1:7	4:1,8
12:7	TIT 2:13
14:6,26	HEB 11:1
2 CO 12:1,7	1 PT 1:7,13
GAL 1:12	4:13
2:2	REV 1:1
EPH 1:17	

1527 ܓܠܝܐ (adv) openly

LUK 8:17

1621 ܒܓܠܐ (m) (w/ ܐܦܐ) boldness

1 TM 3:13

2339 ܡܢ ܓܠܝܐ (idiom) openly, boldly

from 2341 ܡܢ and 558 ܓܠܝܐ (above)

MRK 8:32	ACT 14:3
JHN 16:25	18:26
18:20	19:8
ACT 2:29	26:26
4:13,29,31	28:31
9:27,29	2 CO 3:12
10:40	EPH 6:19
13:46	HEB 4:16

[b]ETHPEEL

Perfect

JHN 12:38	2 TM 1:10
ROM 3:21	TIT 2:11
16:25	3:4
2 CO 11:6	HEB 9:8
EPH 3:5	1 PT 1:12[1],12[2],
PHL 1:13	20
COL 1:26	1 JN 1:2[1],2[2]
1 TM 3:16	3:2[1],2[2],5

Imperfect

MAT 10:26	1 CO 14:30
MRK 4:22[1]	2 CO 4:10,11
LUK 2:35	COL 3:4[2]
8:17	2 TH 2:3,6,8
12:2	1 PT 1:5
19:11	5:1,4
ROM 8:18	REV 3:18

Infinitive

GAL 3:23

Participle

MRK 4:22[2]	2 CO 3:14
LUK 17:30	EPH 5:13
ROM 1:17,18	COL 3:4[1]
1 CO 3:13[1],13[3]	1 JN 2:28
14:25	

552 ܓܠܕܐ (m-non occ) hide (animal), skin

560 ܓܠܝܕܐ (m) crystal, ice

REV 4:6	REV 22:1

555 ܓܠܙ (v) defraud

[a]PEAL

Perfect

LUK 19:8

Imperfect

MRK 6:26	1 CO 7:5
1 CO 1:19	

Active Participle

1 CO 6:8

Passive Participle

1 TM 6:5

[b]ETHPEEL

Participle

1 CO 6:7

553 (ܓܠܘܣܩ), ܓܠܘܣܩܡܐ (m) bag, money box

JHN 12:6	JHN 13:29

565 ܓܠܦ (v) engrave

[a]PEAL

Passive Participle

ACT 17:29

571 ܓܡܠ, ܓܡܠܐ (c) camel

MAT 3:4	MRK 1:6
19:24	10:25
23:24	LUK 18:25

520 (ܓܘܡܨ), ܓܘܡܨܐ (m) ditch

MAT 15:14	LUK 6:39

573 ܓܡܪ (v) perfect, accomplish

[a]PEAL

Perfect

LUK 16:9	HEB 7:19
ROM 7:8,13	10:14

Imperfect

ROM 2:25	HEB 8:8
1 TH 3:10	10:1
HEB 1:12	13:21
2:10	

Infinitive

ROM 4:21	HEB 9:9

Active Participle

ROM 2:27	2 CO 9:11
5:3	HEB 10:2

568 ܓܡܝܪܐ (pp) perfect, mature

MAT 5:48,48	EPH 4:13
19:21	PHL 3:15
LUK 1:17	COL 1:28
6:40	4:12
JHN 17:23	2 TM 3:17
ROM 9:22	HEB 5:14
12:2	7:28
1 CO 1:10	JAM 1:4
2:6	3:2
14:20	1 PT 1:22

566 ܓܡܘܪܐ (adj) finisher

HEB 12:2

567 ܓܘܡܪܬܐ (f) live coal

JHN 21:9	ROM 12:20

569 ܓܡܝܪܐܝܬ (adv) perfectly

ACT 22:3	2 TM 2:15
1 TH 5:23	1 PT 1:13

570 ܓܡܝܪܘܬܐ (f) perfection

1 CO 13:10	HEB 6:1
COL 3:14	7:11

574 ܓܡܪܐ (m) perfection

EPH 4:12

1528 ܓܡܪ (adv) absolutely

LUK 13:11	ACT 4:18

---

bETHPEEL

Perfect

PHL 3:12	JAM 1:15
HEB 5:9	2:22
12:23	

Imperfect

2 CO 13:9	HEB 11:40

Imperative

2 CO 13:11

Participle

2 CO 12:9	GAL 5:6

---

cPAEL

Perfect

LUK 15:14	ROM 15:28

---

589 (ܓܢ), ܓܢܬܐ (f) garden

LUK 13:19	JHN 19:41,41
JHN 18:1,26	

582 ܓܢܘܢܐ (m) bridal chamber

MAT 9:15	LUK 5:34
MRK 2:19	

586 ܓܢܢܐ (m) gardener

JHN 20:15

575 ܓܢ (v) descend upon, make rest

eAPHEL

Perfect

JHN 1:14	ACT 11:15
ACT 10:44	

Imperfect

LUK 1:35	2 CO 12:9
ACT 2:26	REV 7:15
5:15	

---

576 ܓܢܐ (v) hide

bETHPEEL

Perfect

JHN 5:13

---

577 (ܓܢܐ) (v-non occ) reprimand

cPAEL

522 ܓܘܢܝܐ (m) blame, insult

2 CO 6:8

---

578 ܓܢܒ (v) steal

possibly denom from ܓܢܒ - side

[a]PEAL

Perfect

MAT 28:13	2 CO 12:16

Imperfect

MAT 19:18	JHN 10:10
27:64	ROM 2:21[1]
MRK 10:19	13:9
LUK 18:20	EPH 4:28[2]

Active Participle

MAT 6:19,20	EPH 4:28[1]
ROM 2:21[2]	TIT 2:10

[c]PAEL (non occ)

580 ܓܢܒܐ (adj) thief

MAT 6:19,20	1 TH 5:2,4
24:43	1 TM 1:10
LUK 12:33,39	1 PT 4:15
JHN 10:1,8,10	2 PT 3:10
12:6	REV 3:3
1 CO 6:10	16:15

581 ܓܢܒܘܬܐ (f) theft

MAT 15:19	MRK 7:21

579 ܓܢܒ (m) side

MAT 15:29	JHN 6:23
21:1	11:18
MRK 11:1	ACT 1:12
LUK 5:2	5:10
19:29	9:38
JHN 3:23	22:3
4:5	27:39

483 ܓܒܐ (m) side

JHN 20:27	ACT 23:2,9,19
21:6	27:41,41
ACT 12:7	

584 (ܓܢܐ), ܓܢܝܐ (adj) unknown, hidden

ACT 17:23

583 ܓܢܚ (v) be touched, stupified

[a]PEAL (non occ)

521 ܓܘܢܚܐ (m) terrible event

2 PT 2:18

585 ܓܢܝܚܘܬܐ (f) terror

JUD 16

[b]ETHPEEL

Perfect

ACT 2:37

587 ܓܢܣ, ܓܢܣܐ (m) family, kind

MAT 13:47	MRK 9:29
17:21	1 CO 14:10

590 ܓܥܪ (v) roar

[a]PEAL

Active Participle

REV 10:3

591 ܓܥܐ (v) call out

[a]PEAL

Imperative

GAL 4:27

594 ܓܥܬܐ (f) cry, crying out

HEB 5:7	JAM 5:4

525 (ܓܥܠ), ܓܘܥܠܢܐ (m) deposit

2 TM 1:12,14

592 (ܓܥܠ) (v) (ethpe) be committed; (aph) commit, commend

[b]ETHPEEL

Perfect

1 TM 6:20

[e]APHEL

Perfect

LUK 12:48

Imperfect

1 PT 4:19

Imperative

2 TM 2:2

Active Participle

ACT 14:23, 20:32 | ROM 16:1 | 1 TM 1:18

Passive Participle

ACT 14:26 | ACT 15:40

593 ܓܥܪ (v) rebuke

[a]PEAL

Imperfect

1 TM 5:1 | JUD 9

595 ܓܦ, ܓܦܐ (m) wing

MAT 23:37 | LUK 13:34 | REV 4:8 | REV 9:9, 12:14

597 (ܓܦܢ), ܓܦܬܐ (f) vine

MAT 26:29 | MRK 14:25 | JHN 15:1,4,5 | JAM 3:12

598 ܓܪ (v) drag away

[a]PEAL

Perfect

ACT 14:19, 17:6 | ACT 21:30

[k]P ܓܪܪ

Active Participle

ACT 8:3

599 ܓܪܐ (v) flow; (pa) incite

[c]PAEL

Perfect

ACT 21:27

600 ܓܪܒ (v-non occ) be leprous

[a]PEAL

602 ܓܪܒܐ (m) leper

MAT 8:2, 10:8, 11:5, 26:6 | MRK 1:40 | MRK 14:3 | LUK 4:27, 7:22, 17:12

603 ܓܪܒܐ (m) leprosy

MAT 8:3 | MRK 1:42 | LUK 5:12,13

601 ܓܪܒܐ (m) leather bottle, jar

LUK 22:10

604 ܓܪܒܝܐ (f) north

LUK 13:29 | REV 21:13

605 (ܓܪܓ) (v) stir up

[c]PAEL

Perfect

ACT 13:50, 14:2 | 2 CO 9:2

528 ܓܘܪܓܐ (m) provocation

HEB 10:24

ܓܪܓܪ see under ܓܪ

607 ܓܕܡ (v) cut off, decide

[a]PEAL

Perfect

ROM 9:28

608 ܓܪܡ, ܓܪܡܐ (m) bone

MAT 23:27
LUK 24:39
JHN 19:36
EPH 5:30
HEB 3:17
4:12
11:22

609 ܓܪܥ (v) shave

[a]PEAL

Imperfect

ACT 21:24

Infinitive

1 CO 11:6

Passive Participle

1 CO 11:5

606 (ܓܪܝܨ), ܓܪܝܨܬܐ (f) loaf

MAT 14:17
MRK 8:14
LUK 11:5
JHN 6:9

610 ܓܪܫ (v) drag, draw

[a]PEAL

Active Participle

REV 12:4

611 ܓܫ (v) touch, explore

[a]PEAL

Perfect

ACT 27:41
1 JN 1:1

Imperfect

GAL 2:4

Imperative

LUK 24:39

612 ܓܫܘܫܐ (m) a spy

LUK 20:20
HEB 11:31
JAM 2:25

[d]ETHPAAL

Participle

HEB 12:18

529 (ܓܫܡ), ܓܘܫܡܐ (m) body

MAT 26:12
MRK 14:8
LUK 3:22
ACT 19:12
2 CO 10:10
EPH 1:23
JAM 3:3

530 ܓܘܫܡܐܝܬ (adv) bodily

COL 2:9

ܕ

613 ܕܐܒܐ (c) wolf

MAT	7:15	JHN	10:12,12
	10:16	ACT	20:29
LUK	10:3		

615 ܕܒܐ (c) bear

REV 13:2

616 ܕܒܚ (v) sacrifice

[a]PEAL

Perfect

HEB 9:28

Active Participle

MRK	14:12	1 CO	10:20[1],20[2]

Passive Participle

ACT	15:20,29	1 CO	8:7,10
	21:25		10:28

617 ܕܒܚܐ (m) sacrifice

MRK	12:33	HEB	7:27
LUK	13:1		8:3
ACT	7:41		9:9,23
1 CO	8:1,4		10:1,3,5,8,
	10:18,19		11,12
EPH	5:2		13:15,16
PHL	4:18	1 PT	2:5
HEB	5:1	REV	2:14,20

618 ܕܒܚܬܐ (f) sacrifice

MAT	9:13	ROM	12:1
	12:7	PHL	2:17
MRK	9:49	HEB	10:26
LUK	2:24		11:4
ACT	7:42		

619 ܕܒܚܘܬܐ (f) sacrificing

HEB 9:26

1627 ܡܕܒܚܐ (m) altar

MAT	5:23,24	HEB	11:17
	23:18,19,		13:10
	20,35	JAM	2:21
LUK	1:11	REV	6:9
	11:51		8:3,3,5
ROM	11:3		9:13
1 CO	9:13,13		11:1
	10:18		14:18
HEB	7:13		16:7

[c]PAEL

Perfect

ACT 7:41

Imperfect

ACT 14:13,18

621 ܕܒܩ (v) remain with

[a]PEAL

Perfect

MAT	9:27	REV	18:5
LUK	10:11		

[c]PAEL (non occ)

620 ܕܒܘܩܐ (adj) follower, attendant

MRK	5:24	ACT	13:7
	6:1		

622 ܕܒܪ (v) lead, take; (pa) rule, guide

[a]PEAL

Perfect

MAT	1:24	MAT	17:1
	2:21		20:17
	4:5,8		26:37
	16:22		27:27

MRK 4:36	JHN 18:3[1],3[2]
5:40	19:16,27
8:32	ACT 12:25
9:2	15:39
10:32	16:33,34
14:33	20:12
LUK 4:1	21:26,32
9:10,28	22:30
18:31	23:18,31
JHN 6:19	GAL 2:1

Imperfect

MAT 15:14	ACT 15:37,38
LUK 5:3	16:3
JHN 14:3	

Imperative

MAT 2:13,20	JHN 19:6
18:16	ACT 21:24
LUK 5:4	2 TM 4:11
JHN 18:31	

Active Participle

MAT 5:44	LUK 11:26
12:45	17:7
LUK 6:28	

Passive Participle

ACT 21:16	JAM 3:4[1]

623 ܕܒܪܐ (m) open country

MAT 6:28	LUK 5:16
MRK 6:31	15:4

1628 ܡܕܒܪܐ (m) wilderness

MAT 4:1	ACT 7:30,36,38,
MRK 1:3,4,12,	42,44
13	13:18
JHN 1:23	21:38
3:14	1 CO 10:5
6:31,49	HEB 3:8,17

1629 ܡܕܒܪܝܐ (adj) desert

ACT 8:26

---

[b]ETHPEEL

Perfect

MAT 4:1	GAL 2:13
ACT 8:32,33	

Imperfect

MAT 24:40	LUK 17:36
LUK 17:34,35,	HEB 13:9

Participle

MAT 11:12	ACT 7:24
15:22	1 CO 12:2
24:41	2 TM 3:6
LUK 8:29	

---

[c]PAEL

Perfect

1 TM 3:12

Imperfect

JHN 16:13	1 TM 3:5[1],5[2]
COL 3:15	5:14

Infinitive

LUK 6:39

Active Participle

1 TM 3:4	REV 18:17
JAM 3:4[2]	

632 ܕܘܒܪܐ (m) custom, manner

ACT 26:4	HEB 13:7
EPH 2:12	1 PT 3:1,16
2 TM 3:10	

1630 ܡܕܒܪܢܐ (m) ruler, guide

MAT 23:10,10	1 CO 12:28
ACT 1:16	HEB 13:7,17,24
ROM 2:19	

1631 ܡܕܒܪܢܘܬܐ (f) administration

EPH 1:10	COL 1:25
3:2,9	

---

[d]ETHPAAL

Perfect

ACT 23:1

Imperfect

1 TM 1:8	HEB 13:18

Imperative

1 PT 1:17

Participle

ROM 8:14	1 TM 5:17
2 CO 3:12	TIT 1:7
GAL 5:18	1 PT 3:2
PHL 1:27	

624 ܕܒܫ, ܕܒܫܐ (m) honey

MAT 3:4	LUK 24:42
MRK 1:6	REV 10:9,10

625 (ܕܓܠ) (v) lie

cPAEL

Perfect

ACT 5:4

Imperfect

MAT 5:33	HEB 7:21
ACT 5:3	JAM 3:14
HEB 6:18	

Active Participle

ROM 9:1	1 TM 2:7
COL 3:9	REV 3:9

626 ܕܓܠܐ (adj) false

MAT 7:15	1 TM 4:2
14:26	6:20
24:11,24	TIT 1:12
MRK 6:49	2 PT 2:1,1
10:19	1 JN 1:6,10
JHN 8:44	2:4,18,18, 22,22
ACT 6:13	4:1,3,20
13:6	5:10
21:24	REV 2:2
ROM 3:4	16:13
1 CO 15:15	19:20
2 CO 11:13,26	20:10
GAL 2:4	21:8
2 TH 2:9	
1 TM 1:10	

627 ܕܓܠܘܬܐ (f) falsehood

MAT 5:11	1 JN 2:21,27
MRK 13:22	REV 14:5
LUK 6:26	21:27
ROM 3:7	22:15

630 ܕܗܒ, ܕܗܒܐ (m) gold

MAT 2:11	MAT 10:9
MAT 23:16,17, 17	REV 1:12,13,20
ACT 3:6	2:1
17:29	3:18
20:33	4:4
1 CO 3:12	5:8
1 TM 2:9	8:3
2 TM 2:20	9:7,13,20
HEB 9:4,4,4	14:14
JAM 2:2	15:6
5:3	17:4,4
1 PT 1:7,18	18:12,16
3:3	21:15,18, 20,21

629 (ܕܗܒ) (v) gild

eAPHEL

Passive Participle

REV 17:4	REV 18:16

631 ܕܘܐ (v-non occ) be miserable

aPEAL

636 ܕܘܝܐ (ap) miserable

ROM 7:24	REV 3:17
1 CO 15:19	

635 ܕܘܘܝܐ (m) misery

ROM 3:16	JAM 5:1
1 TM 6:10	

628 (ܕܘܕܐ), ܕܕܐ (m) uncle

COL 4:10

634 ܕܘܕܐ (adj-non occ) mad

633 (ܕܘܕ) (v) trouble

cPAEL

Perfect

GAL 5:7

Imperfect

COL 2:16

[d]ETHPAAL

Imperfect

MAT 24:6	JHN 14:1,27

642 ܕܘܠܐ (m) bucket

JHN 4:11

671 (ܕܘܢ), ܕܝܢܐ (m) judgement

see also 424 ܒܝܬ ܕܝܢܐ

MAT 5:21,22	ACT 25:21,23,
7:2	25,26
10:15	ROM 1:32
11:22,24	2:2,3,5
12:18,20,	3:8
36,41,	5:16
42	11:33
23:13,23,	12:19,19
33	13:2
MRK 3:29	1 CO 6:1,2,4,4,7
6:11	GAL 5:10
12:40	2 TH 1:5,9
LUK 10:14	1 TM 3:6
11:31,32,	5:12,24
42	HEB 6:2
20:47	9:27
23:40	10:27
24:20	JAM 2:6,13,13
JHN 3:19	3:1
5:22,24,27,	5:9,12
29,30	1 PT 2:23
7:24	4:17
8:16	2 PT 2:3,4,9,11
9:39	3:7
12:31	1 JN 4:17
16:8,11	JUD 6,7,9,15
ACT 7:24	REV 14:7
8:33	16:7
17:19	17:1
19:38	18:10,20
24:25	19:2
25:14,15,	20:4,12

647 (ܕܘܢ) (v) judge

[a]PEAL

Perfect

MRK 14:64	1 CO 5:3
LUK 7:43	7:37
ACT 12:19	2 CO 2:1
13:27	REV 16:5
ROM 1:28	18:8,20
14:22	19:2
1 CO 2:2	

Imperfect

MAT 5:40	ACT 17:31
7:1[1]	19:38
19:28	24:6
LUK 6:37[1]	ROM 2:27
19:22	3:6
22:30	14:3,13[1]
JHN 3:17	1 CO 6:1,2[1]
12:47[2]	HEB 10:30
ACT 7:7	

Imperative

JHN 7:24[2]	1 CO 5:12[2]
18:31	10:15
ACT 4:19	11:13
ROM 14:13[2]	

Infinitive

JHN 8:26	2 TM 4:1
1 CO 5:12[1]	1 PT 4:5
6:2[3]	

Active Participle

MAT 7:2[1]	ROM 14:10
LUK 12:57	1 CO 2:15[1]
JHN 5:22,30	4:3[2],5
7:24[1]	5:13
8:15[1],15[2],	6:3
16,50	9:3
12:47[1],48[1],	11:31[1]
48[2]	HEB 4:12
ACT 11:2	13:4
23:3	JAM 4:11[1],11[2],
26:8	11[3],12
ROM 2:1[1],1[2],1[3],	1 PT 1:17
3,16	JUD 9
3:4	REV 6:10
14:4,5[1],5[2],	19:11

Passive Participle

JHN 16:11

672 ܕܝܢܐ (m) judge

MAT 5:25,25	ACT 13:20
10:17	17:34
12:27	18:15
MRK 13:9	24:10
LUK 11:19	ROM 13:3
12:14,58,	1 CO 4:4
58	2 TM 4:8
18:2,6	HEB 12:23
20:20	JAM 4:11,12
ACT 7:27,35	1 PT 2:14,23
10:42	

1635 ܡܕܝܢܬܐ (f) city

MAT 2:23	MAT 5:14,35
4:5	8:33,34

MAT 9:1,35
10:5,11,15,
23,23
11:1,20
12:25
13:54,57
14:13
21:10,17,
18
22:7
23:34,34
26:18
27:53
28:11
MRK 1:33,38,45
5:14
6:1,4,11,
33,56
11:19
14:13,16
LUK 1:26,39
2:3,4,4,11,
39
4:23,24,29,
29,31,43
5:12
7:11,12,12,
37
8:1,4,27,
34,39
9:5,6
10:1,8,10,
11,12
13:22
14:21
15:15
18:2,3
19:14,41
22:10
23:19,50
24:49
JHN 1:44
2:1
4:5,8,28,
30,39,44
19:20
ACT 4:27
5:16
7:58
8:5,8,9,40
9:6,11,24,
32,32,36,
38,42
10:5,9,32
11:13
13:1,5,6,
13,13,
14,14,
44,50,
51

ACT 14:4,6,8,
13,19,
20,20,
21,21,
25
15:21,36
16:1,4,11,
12,13,
14,20,
20,39
17:1,5,5,6,
8,10,13,
14,15,
16
18:10
19:29,35,
35,38
20:4,4,6,
23
21:5,7,29,
30,31,
39
22:3
23:31
24:12
25:23
26:11
27:2,2,5,7,
8
28:12,13,
13
ROM 16:23
2 CO 11:26,32
EPH 2:19
2 TM 4:20
TIT 1:5,5
HEB 8:11
11:10,14,
15,16
12:22
13:12,14
JAM 4:13
2 PT 2:6
JUD 7
REV 3:12
11:2,8,13
14:20
16:19,19
17:18
18:10,10,
16,18,
19,21
20:9,9
21:2,10,14,
15,16,
16,18,
19,21,
23
22:14,19

^{b}ETHPEEL

Perfect

REV 20:12,13

Imperfect

MAT 7:1^2,2^2
ACT 25:9,20
ROM 2:12
1 CO 4:3^1
2 TH 2:12
JAM 5:9
1 PT 4:6
REV 11:18

Infinitive

ACT 25:10
JAM 2:12

Participle

LUK 6:37^2
JHN 3:18
ACT 4:9
23:6
24:21
26:6
ROM 3:7
1 CO 2:14,15^2
6:2^2,6
10:29
11:31^2,32
COL 2:20

650 (ܕܘܨ)(v) leap for joy, rejoice

^{a}PEAL

Perfect

LUK 1:41,44

Imperative

LUK 6:23

651 (ܕܘܩ)(v) look into, observe

^{c}PAEL

Imperfect

1 PT 1:12

^{e}APHEL

Perfect

LUK 24:12
JHN 20:5,11

1644 ܡܕܘܩ (pp) competent

ACT 18:24

718 (ܕܘܪ), ܕܪܐ(m) generation

LUK 1:50
ACT 8:33
ACT 14:16
15:21

EPH 3:5,21	COL 1:26
PHL 2:15	HEB 3:10

732 ܕܪܬܐ (f) house, enclosure

MAT 26:3,58,69	ACT 10:17
MRK 14:54,66	11:11
15:16	12:13,14
LUK 11:21	14:13
22:55	REV 11:2
JHN 18:15	

652 (ܕܘܪ) (v-non occ) dwell

[a]PEAL

675 ܕܝܪܐ (c) dwelling

ACT 1:20

1636 ܡܕܝܪܐ (m) loft

ACT 20:9

655 (ܕܘܫ)(v) trample

[a]PEAL

Perfect

HEB 10:29

Imperfect

MAT 7:6	REV 11:2

Active Participle

LUK 10:19	REV 19:15

[b]ETHPEEL

Perfect

LUK 8:5	REV 14:20

Imperfect

MAT 5:13

Participle

LUK 21:24

[c]PAEL

Imperfect

LUK 12:1

656 ܕܚܐ(v) push away

[a]PEAL

Imperfect

ACT 27:39

Active Participle

ACT 13:46

660 ܕܚܠ(v) fear; (pa) cause to fear

[a]PEAL

Perfect

MAT 2:22	LUK 8:35
9:8	9:34
14:30	19:21
17:6	20:19
21:46	JHN 6:19
25:25	19:8
27:54	ACT 10:4
MRK 4:41	16:38
5:15	22:29
6:50[1]	23:10
12:12	ROM 1:25
LUK 2:9	HEB 11:7,23,27

Imperfect

MAT 1:20	LUK 21:9
10:26,28[1], 31	24:36
14:27	JHN 6:20
17:7	12:15
28:5,10	14:27
MRK 5:36	ACT 18:9
6:50[2]	27:24
13:7	ROM 13:3
16:6	1 TM 5:20
LUK 1:13,30	HEB 4:1
2:10	13:6
5:10	1 PT 3:14[1]
8:50	REV 1:17
12:4,5[1],7, 32	2:10
	15:4

Imperative

MAT 10:28[2]	ROM 13:4
LUK 12:5[2]	1 PT 2:17
ROM 11:20	REV 14:7

Active Participle

MAT 14:5	LUK 1:50
15:9	9:45
21:26	18:2,4
MRK 6:20	22:2
7:7	23:40
9:32	JHN 9:22,31
11:18	ACT 2:5

ACT 5:26 9:26 10:2,7,22, 35 13:16,26, 43,50 16:14 17:4,17,23 18:7,13 27:17	2 CO 11:3 12:20 GAL 2:12 4:11 EPH 5:33 2 PT 2:9 1 JN 4:18 REV 11:18 19:5

658 ܕܚܝܠܐ (pp) terrible

ACT 2:20 HEB 10:27	HEB 12:21

661 ܕܚܠܐ (m) fear

LUK 1:74 1 CO 16:10 PHL 1:14	2 TH 2:4 1 PT 3:6

662 ܕܚܠܬܐ (f) fear

MAT 14:26 28:4,8 MRK 4:41 9:6 11:32 LUK 1:12,65 2:9 5:26 7:16 8:37 21:11,26 22:44 24:5,37 JHN 7:13 19:38 20:19 ACT 2:43 5:5,11 9:31 17:22,23 19:17 24:25 25:19 ROM 3:18 8:15 13:3,7,7 1 CO 2:3 2 CO 5:11	2 CO 7:1,5,11, 15 EPH 6:5 PHL 2:12 COL 2:23 3:5,22 1 TH 1:9 1 TM 2:2,10 6:3,5,6 2 TM 1:7 3:5,12 TIT 1:1 2:3,12 HEB 2:15 5:8 10:31 12:28 1 PT 1:17 2:18 3:2,15 2 PT 1:3,6,7 3:11 1 JN 4:18,18,18 5:21 JUD 12,23 REV 11:11,13 18:10,15

[c]PAEL

Infinitive

2 CO 10:9[1]

Active Participle

2 CO 10:9[2]	1 PT 3:14[2]

657 ܕܚܘܠܬܢܐ (adj) fearful

MAT 8:26	MRK 4:40

659 ܕܚܝܠܐ (adj) afraid

MRK 5:33 10:32 16:8	LUK 8:25 ACT 27:29 HEB 12:21

663 ܕܚܐ (v) reject

[a]PEAL

Perfect

ACT 7:27 ROM 11:1,2	1 TM 1:19

Imperative

2 TM 3:5

664 ܕܚܫܐ (m) guard, attendant

MAT 26:58 MRK 14:65 JHN 7:32,45,46 18:3,12,18,	JHN 18:22 19:6 ACT 5:26

665 ܕܝܘ, ܕܝܘܐ (m) devil

MAT 8:16 9:32,33,34, 34 10:8 11:18 12:24,27, 28 MRK 1:34,34 3:15,22,22	LUK 8:27,30 9:42 11:15,15, 18,19, 20 JHN 7:20 8:48,49,52 10:20,21 REV 9:20

667 ܕܝܘܢܐ (adj) possessed (w/ a devil)

MAT 4:24 8:16,28,33 12:22	MRK 1:32 LUK 8:36 JHN 10:21

669 ܕܝܠ (prt) own

MAT 5:3,10; 6:13,34; 10:2,18,30; 13:16; 15:6; 20:14,15,23; 24:31; 25:25,27; 27:19,60 MRK 2:18; 10:40; 12:7; 14:36,36 LUK 1:2; 2:35; 4:7; 5:33; 6:20,30,42; 10:7, 35; 12:7; 15:31,31; 16:12,12; 18:16; 20:14; 22:30,42; 23:23 JHN 1:11,11; 3:29; 4:34; 5:47; 7:6,6,8,16,42,51; 8:39,44; 9:30; 10:4,

12,14,14,27; 13:1; 14:24,27; 15:9,10,19,20, 21; 16:14,15,15; 17:6,9,10,10,10,17,24; 18:36,36; 19:11 ACT 1:7; 2:11; 3:12; 4:32; 5:4; 7:50; 15:7; 18:15,16; 20:30; 21:28; 24:17; 27:10,19,23; 28:30 ROM 1:12,12; 2:16; 3:7; 6:16; 8:9; 9:4,25; 11:11; 14:4; 15:4; 16:13,13,19,24 1 CO 1:2,2; 2:7; 3:21,22; 4:6; 5:7; 7:35,40; 8:6,11; 10:11,29; 13:5; 14:16; 16:18,18,21 2 CO 1:12,14; 3:2; 4:3; 5:11,19; 8:14,14,19,19,23; 9:2; 10:8; 11:8; 12:14,19; 13:7 GAL 6:13 EPH 2:10; 4:15,16; 5:29; 6:9 PHL 1:12,21,25,28; 2:16,20,25; 3:20; 4:10 COL 4:18 2 TH 2:1,14,15 1 TM 5:8; 6:6 2 TM 2:8,19 TIT 1:12; 3:5,14 PLM 12, 16,16 HEB 1:4,8; 4:10; 8:9; 9:25; 10:1,29, 30,38; 11:9,40 1 PT 1:12; 2:24; 4:11 2 PT 1:3,15,16,20; 2:2,12; 3:3,7,13,16,17 1 JN 1:3; 2:2,6 2 JN 12 3 JN 4,9,12 JUD 3,6,16,18,20,21 REV 1:1,1,1,4,5,5,6; 2:13,13; 3:12,21,21; 11:19; 17:13; 21:3

670 ܕܝܢ (conj) but

see also 180 ܐܕܝܢ

see also 757 ܗܝܕܝܢ

see also 1634 ܡܕܝܢ

MAT 1:12,18,19,20,21,22,24; 2:1,3,5,9,10, 13,14,19,22; 3:1,4,7,10,11,14,15,16; 4:2,4, 12,20,22; 5:1,13,19,22,28,29,32,33,34,39,44; 6:1,3,6,15,16,17,23,27,29,30,32,33; 7:3,15, 16,17; 8:1,5,10,11,12,16,18,20,21,22,24,27, 30,31,33; 9:3,4,6,8,12,15,18,22,31,34,36; 10:2,6,11,13,14,17,19,21,22,23,28,28,30,33; 11:2,7,11,12,16,21; 12:2,3,6,7,11,12,15,24, 25,31,32,39,43,46,47,48; 13:1,6,11,11,16,18, 20,21,22,23,26,28,29,30,32,37,38,38,39,39, 39,46,57; 14:1,3,6,8,9,13,15,16,17,21,25,27, 29; 15:5,8,13,14,16,18,20,23,24,25,27,32,38; 16:2,6,7,8,13,14,14,15,23; 17:2,4,12,21,22, 27; 18:7,8,15,17,17,28,30,31; 19:4,8,9,11,14, 17,17,18,22,23,24,25,26,30; 20:2,5,8,13,14, 17,21,23,24,31; 21:4,8,9,11,13,15,18,25,28, 29,29,30,32,32,34,37,38; 22:5,6,7,12,18,19, 25,27,31,34,37,41; 23:3,4,8,8,11,16,18,23, 25,27; 24:2,8,13,15,19,20,22,28,29,32,36,37, 43,48; 25:2,4,5,8,11,12,16,18,19,24,29,31; 26:8,10,11,12,15,17,18,23,24,26,29,32,41, 50,56,58,59,60,63,64,67,69,70,73; 27:1,4,6, 11,15,16,19,20,20,21,23,24,39,45,47,49,50, 54,55,57,61,62,66; 28:1,3,5,9,11,15,16,17 MRK 1:6,8,14,32,41,45; 2:5,6,8,10,17,18, 20; 3:4,29,32; 4:1,5,6,8,10,11,15,28,29,34, 38; 5:6,11,25,30,33,34,36,40; 6:16,19,24,26, 37,38,44,47,49; 7:6,6,11,17,20,26,28; 8:1,9, 17,28,29,33; 9:6,25,27,28,32,34,41,43,50; 10:4,6,13,14,20,21,22,23,24,26,27,31,32,38, 40,43,48,50,51; 11:6,8,11,17,26,29; 12:3,5,6, 7,14,15,16,26,34,44; 13:2,5,7,9,10,11,12,13, 14,17,18,23,24,28,32,37; 14:1,4,6,7,10,11, 19,20,21,31,46,47,48,52,54,55,57,59,61,62, 63,64,68,70,71; 15:2,4,5,6,9,11,12,13,14,15, 16,23,25,29,32,36,37,39,40,44,47; 16:2,3,6, 9,14,17,19,20 LUK 1:6,7,8,21,22,26,29, 39,56,57,80; 2:1,4,8,19,25,33,35,36,40,43, 50,51,52; 3:1,9,13,15,16,18,19,21,23; 4:1,12, 20,24,30,40,40,43; 5:1,5,8,10,10,16,20,22, 24,33,33,34,35,37; 6:1,2,6,8,11,12,27,41,41, 48; 7:2,4,6,6,9,13,21,24,28,30,36,39,40,40, 44,45,46,47,49,50; 8:10,10,11,12,13,14,15, 19,21,22,24,25,28,30,32,34,37,38,40,43,46, 47,48,50,51,52,52,54,56; 9:7,8,9,11,12,13, 19,20,21,24,25,26,28,31,41,45,47,58,59,61; 10:6,7,10,13,18,26,29,33,37,40,42,42; 11:15, 16,17,20,22,34,36,37,38,39,39,42,46; 12:2,4, 5,7,8,9,10,11,13,14,20,25,26,27,28,30,39, 45,47,48,56,57; 13:1,3,5,10,12,14,15,16,18, 23,24,28; 14:4,12,15,32,34; 15:1,22,25,29, 30,32; 16:14,15,15,17,19,22,22,30; 17:1,7, 15,17,25,29; 18:1,3,4,7,13,15,16,22,23,27, 34,39,41; 19:7,8,14,26,36,39,42,43,46,47; 20:5,6,10,11,12,14,16,17,19,23,24,27,29,35, 37,38; 21:1,4,8,8,12,13,14,16,19,20,23,28, 34,37; 22:1,3,9,24,25,26,27,33,49,51,55,57, 58,70; 23:3,5,6,8,9,10,11,13,18,20,21,22,23, 24,25,34,35,38,39,41,44,47,50,55; 24:1,10, 12,21,24,42,49,52 JHN 1:12,17,24,26,39, 40,44; 2:6,9,10,18,21,22,23,24; 3:1,18,19,21, 23,25,29,33; 4:1,4,6,14,22,27,32,39,44,45, 46,51; 5:2,5,7,11,13,17,19,28,34,36; 6:4,6, 10,14,15,18,20,23,39,41,50,52,54,61,71; 7:6, 7,10,11,13,14,18,27,29,31,37,39,40; 8:1,2,3, 5,6,7,9,10,11,11,12,14,16,17,35,40,41,45, 50,55; 9:8,9,14,15,16,18,20,21,25,28,29,31, 38,41; 10:2,5,6,7,12,13,16,21,22,38,41; 11:1, 2,4,5,10,13,16,18,20,20,30,31,32,33,37,38, 49,51,54,55,57; 12:1,3,6,7,8,14,16,19,20,23, 24,29,33,42,44; 13:1,3,6,7,12,22,23,28,29, 30,30,36; 14:10,17,19,21,24,26; 15:6,7,15, 22,24,26; 16:4,5,7,10,11,13,19,21,22,25; 17:3,10,13,25; 18:2,4,5,7,10,10,14,15,15,16, 17,18,19,23,24,28,29,33,36,39,40; 19:6,8,9, 12,13,13,15,17,19,23,23,25,26,29,30,31,41; 20:1,4,5,6,11,15,17,19,21,24,25,30,31; 21:1, 4,7,8,9,12,13,15,18,19,23,25 ACT 1:6,15; 2:5,7,12,13,24; 3:5,14; 4:32,36; 5:8,16,21,28, 39; 6:8; 7:2,27,47; 8:1,3,5,9,12,16,25,32,40; 9:1,7,10,22,24,27,29,31,36,37,40,40,43; 10:1,16,24,34,41; 11:16,19,20,29; 12:1,19, 21,22,25; 13:1,8,9,13,14,30,37,46,50; 14:2,5, 14,19; 15:1,5,6,30,35,37,38,40; 16:1,6,10,12, 24; 17:8,10,16,21; 18:3,11,15; 19:7,13,14,15, 19,21,22,23,24,32,33,38; 20:3,6,11,13,14,38; 21:7,21,25,37; 22:3,8,9,28; 23:8,9,13,24; 24:4,7,9,14,17,22,27; 25:11,19,21,25; 26:22; 27:11,30,33,37,41; 28:5,6,7,8,11,22 ROM 1:13; 2:3,8,10,17,25,26; 3:5,7,19,21, 22; 4:4,5; 5:5,6,16,20; 6:17,23; 7:2,3,3,6,9,9, 14,17,18,18,22,23,25; 8:9,9,10,10,24,25,27, 28,30; 9:6,8,22,27,30,31; 10:6,20,21; 11:6,6, 7,7,11,13,16,18,20,22,25,28; 12:3,5; 14:1,3, 4,5,10,15; 15:5,8,13,14,15,23,25,29,30,33; 16:1,17,19,20,24,25 1 CO 1:10,12,16,16, 18,23,24,30; 2:6,10,12,15,16; 3:8,10,10,12, 15,15; 4:3,6,8,10,18; 5:2,10,11,13; 6:5,13,13, 14,17,18; 7:1,6,8,9,10,12,14,15,25,25,28,28, 34,35,36,37,39,40,40; 8:1,1,2,3,8,9; 9:15,16, 17,23,25,25; 10:1,4,6,11,13,20,27,28,29;

11:2,3,6,7,11,12,16,17,32,34,34; 12:1,4,7,8, 10,10,10,10,10,11,12,18,19,20,20,24,27,31; 13:10,11,12,12,13; 14:1,3,5,5,5,14,22,29,37, 38,40; 15:1,8,10,12,15,20,38,39,50,51,54,56, 57; 16:1,4,5,8,10,12,12,15,17 2 CO 1:6,8, 13,21,23; 2:1,3,5,6,10,12,14; 3:2,4,6,7,17,18; 4:3,5,7,18; 5:11,11; 6:12,13,16,16; 7:10,12; 8:1,10,11,16,18,20,22,22; 9:1,3,6,8,10,15; 10:1,2,9,10,13,17; 11:1,3,16; 12:2,3,5,6,15; 13:6,7,9 GAL 1:8,11,15,19,20; 2:1,2,4,6,6, 6,11,12,17; 3:4,11,12,13,16,17,18,18,20,20, 23,25; 4:1,4,6,9,11,18,20,23,24,26,28; 5:3, 11,12,13,15,16,18,22,24; 6:6,14 EPH 2:4, 13; 3:20; 4:7,9,17,20; 5:3,5,8,32,33; 6:21 PHL 1:12,15,17,22; 2:8,19,22,25,25,27; 3:13,18,20; 4:10,11,14,15,20 COL 1:26; 2:1,4,17; 3:8,25; 4:7 1 TH 2:14,16,17; 3:6, 11; 4:9,10,13,15; 5:1,4,8,12,14,23 2 TH 2:1,13,16; 3:3,4,6,12,13,16 1 TM 1:5,8,14,17; 2:14,15; 3:2,7,15; 4:1,7,8; 5:5,6,11,13; 6:2,3,5,9,10,11 2 TM 1:5; 2:12,17,19,20,24; 3:1,8,10,12,13,14; 4:4,5,8, 12,13,15,17,20 TIT 1:15,16; 2:1,7; 3:4,9, 13 PLM 9,9,11,12,14,15,22 HEB 1:6,7, 8,13; 2:8,8,9; 3:4,6; 4:3,3; 5:11,12,13,14; 6:8, 9,11; 7:1,2,4,6,7,8,11,18,19,21,24,28; 8:1,6, 10; 9:1,3,5,7,8,11,17,23,26,28; 10:2,5,12,15, 16,18,38,39; 11:1,6,14,16,36; 12:10,11,11, 22,26,27; 13:4,10,20,22,23 JAM 1:4,5,6,9, 15,22,25; 2:5,6,9,11,20; 3:8,14,17,18; 4:6,12, 13; 5:7,12,16 1 PT 2:7,9,10,10,20; 3:8; 4:7,16,17; 5:1,10 2 PT 1:5,5,6,6,6,7,7,13, 15; 2:1,9,10,12,16,22; 3:7,8,10,10,13,18 1 JN 1:3,7,9; 2:5,7,10,11,17,26; 3:2,4; 4:4,6, 12,18,20 2 JN 1 3 JN 12,14 JUD 1,5, 8,9,10,10,14,17,20,21,23,24 REV 1:14; 4:4; 9:10; 10:2; 17:3; 19:12,21; 21:8,21

668 (ܕܝܬ), ܕܝܘܬܐ (f) ink

2 CO 3:3
2 JN 12
3 JN 13

676 ܕܝܬܩܐ (f) testament, covenant

MAT 26:28
MRK 14:24
LUK 1:72
22:20
ACT 3:25
7:8
ROM 11:27
1 CO 11:25
2 CO 3:6,14
GAL 3:15,17
4:24
EPH 2:12
HEB 7:22
8:6,8,9,9, 10
9:4,4,15, 15,16,20
10:16,29
12:24
13:20
REV 11:19

638 (ܕܘܟ), ܕܘܟ (m) place

LUK 9:6

641 ܕܘܟܬܐ (f) place

MAT 24:7,7,15
26:36,52
27:33
28:6
MRK 1:45
13:8,8
14:32
15:22
16:6,20
LUK 2:7
4:17
10:32
11:1
14:7,9,9
16:28
19:5,43
21:11,11
22:40
23:33
24:28
JHN 5:2,13
6:10,23
10:1,40
11:6,30
JHN 18:2
19:13,17, 20,41
20:7,10,25
ACT 8:36
13:35
17:30
19:39
21:28
24:3,27
27:8,29,41
ROM 9:26
11:17,19
15:23
1 CO 12:27
14:16
2 CO 11:17
PHL 2:16
2 TH 3:1
1 TM 2:8
HEB 5:6
REV 6:14
12:6,14
18:17

677 ܕܟܐ (v) be pure; (pa) cleanse

aPEAL (non occ)

678 ܕܟܐ (pp) clean, pure

MAT 5:8
23:26
LUK 11:41
JHN 13:10,10, 11
15:3
ACT 18:6
20:26
24:16
ROM 14:20
1 CO 7:14
2 CO 7:11
11:2
PHL 1:10
2:15
4:8
1 TM 1:5,9
3:8,9
2 TM 1:3
2 TM 2:21,22
TIT 1:15,15,15
2:2
HEB 7:26
10:22,22
13:4
JAM 1:27
3:17
1 PT 1:22
3:21
1 JN 3:3
REV 15:6
16:13
18:2
19:8,14
21:18,18, 21
22:1

679 ܕܟܝܐܝܬ (adv) purely

PHL 1:17
1 TH 2:10
1 TM 2:8

680 ܕܟܝܘܬܐ (f) purity

1 CO 5:8	1 TM 2:2
7:7	3:4
2 CO 1:12	4:12
6:6	5:2,22

[c]PAEL

Perfect

ACT 10:15	ACT 15:9
11:9	

Imperfect

JHN 11:55	TIT 2:14
2 CO 7:1	HEB 9:14
EPH 5:26	1 JN 1:9
2 TM 2:21	

Imperative

MAT 10:8	1 CO 5:7
23:26	JAM 4:8

Infinitive

MAT 8:2	LUK 5:12
MRK 1:40	HEB 10:4,11

Active Participle

MAT 3:12	LUK 11:39
23:25	JHN 15:2
MRK 7:19	1 JN 1:7
LUK 3:17	3:3

Passive Participle

ACT 24:18

639 ܕܘܟܝܐ (m) cleansing

HEB 1:3	2 PT 1:9
9:13	

3329 ܬܕܟܝܬܐ (f) purification, excrement

MAT 15:17	LUK 5:14
MRK 1:44	JHN 2:6
7:19	3:25
LUK 2:22	ACT 21:26

[d]ETHPAAL

Perfect

MAT 8:3[2]	LUK 4:27
MRK 1:42	17:14,15,
LUK 17:17	HEB 10:2
ACT 21:26	

Imperfect

ACT 21:23

Imperative

MAT 8:3[1]	ACT 21:24
MRK 1:41	22:16
LUK 5:13	

Participle

MAT 11:5	HEB 9:22,23
LUK 7:22	

681 (ܕܟܪ), ܕܟܝܪ (adj-non occ) mindful

640 ܕܘܟܪܢܐ (m) remembrance

MAT 26:13	ACT 10:4,31
MRK 14:9	1 CO 11:24,25
LUK 22:19	

682 (ܕܟܪ) (v) (ethpe, aph) remember

[b]ETHPEEL

Perfect

MAT 26:75	LUK 24:8
27:63	JHN 2:17,22
MRK 11:21	12:16
14:72	ACT 11:16
LUK 1:54	REV 16:19
22:61	18:5

Imperfect

MAT 5:23	HEB 10:17
HEB 8:12	

Imperative

LUK 16:25	HEB 13:3
17:32	JUD 17
23:42	REV 2:5
2 TM 2:8	3:3
HEB 10:32	

Participle

ROM 1:9	2 TM 1:3,4
2 CO 7:15	PLM 4
1 TH 1:2	

[e]APHEL

Perfect

LUK 20:37

Active Participle

HEB 10:3

683 ܕܟܪ, ܕܟܪܐ (adj) male

MAT 19:4	1 CO 6:9
MRK 10:6	GAL 3:28
LUK 2:23	1 TM 1:10
ROM 1:27,27,27	REV 12:5,13

684 (ܕܠ) (v-non occ) put away

[c]PAEL

643 ܕܘܠܠܐ (m) repudiation, divorce

MAT 5:31

688 (ܕܠ), ܕܠܝܠܐ (adj) easy

MAT 19:24	1 TM 6:18
LUK 18:25	

685 ܕܠܐ (v) draw out

[a]PEAL

Active Participle

LUK 14:5 | JHN 4:15

687 ܕܠܚ (v) trouble

[a]PEAL

Active Participle

GAL 1:7 | GAL 5:10,12

686 ܕܘܠܚܐ (m) confusion

JAM 3:16

[c]PAEL

Perfect

ACT 15:24 | ACT 17:5,6

Infinitive

ACT 17:13

Active Participle

ACT 16:20

[d]ETHPAAL

Perfect

ACT 17:8

692 ܕܠܩ (v) shine

[a]PEAL

Active Participle

JHN 5:35

693 ܕܠܩܐ (m) flame

LUK 11:36

695 ܕܡ (prt) lest

GAL 2:2

696 ܕܡ, ܕܡܐ (m) blood

MAT 9:20	ROM 5:9
16:17	1 CO 10:16
23:30,35, 35,35	11:25,27
26:28	15:50
27:4,6,8, 24,25	GAL 1:16
MRK 5:25,29	EPH 1:7
14:24	2:13
LUK 8:43,44	6:12
11:50,51, 51	COL 1:20
13:1	HEB 2:14
22:20,44	9:7,12,12, 13,14,18, 19,20,21, 22,22,25
JHN 1:13	10:4,19,29
6:53,54,55, 56	11:28
19:34	12:4,24
ACT 1:19	13:11,12, 20
2:19,20	1 PT 1:2,19
5:28	1 JN 1:7
15:20,29	5:6,7,8
17:26	REV 1:5
20:26,28	5:9
21:25	6:12
22:20	7:14
ROM 3:15,25	8:8

REV 11:6	REV 17:6,6
12:11	18:24
14:20	19:2,13
16:4,6,6	

697 ܕܡܐ (v) resemble; (pa) liken to

ᵃPEAL

Perfect

MRK 4:16,31

Imperfect

MAT 6:8	MRK 4:30

Infinitive

JHN 9:9

700 ܕܡܐ (ap) alike, like, it seems

MAT 11:16	LUK 12:36
13:24,31,	13:18,19,
33,44,	21
45,47,	JHN 9:9
52	ACT 9:18
20:1	10:11
22:39	11:5
23:27	17:29
MRK 6:34	GAL 5:21
7:8,13	EPH 5:27
12:31	JAM 1:6,23
14:70	REV 4:7
LUK 6:47,48,49	13:4,11
7:31,32	18:18

644 ܕܘܡܝܐ (m) likeness

ROM 2:20	REV 21:11
REV 4:6	

698 ܕܡܘܬܐ (f) form, image

MRK 16:12	HEB 1:1
LUK 3:22	2:14
ACT 7:43,44	4:11
ROM 1:23,23	5:6,10
5:14,14	6:20
6:5,17	7:3,11,11,
8:3,29	15,17,21
1 CO 11:7	8:5,5
15:49,49	9:23,24
2 CO 3:18	JAM 3:9
4:4	5:10
PHL 2:6,7,7	1 PT 5:3
3:17,21	1 JN 3:2
COL 1:15	JUD 7,8
3:10	REV 1:13,15
1 TH 1:7	4:3,3,7,7
1 TM 4:12	9:7,7,7,10
TIT 2:7	11:1

REV 13:2	REV 21:11,18
14:14	

701 ܕܡܝܐ (m) price

MAT 13:46	ACT 4:34,37
26:7	5:3,4,8,8
27:9	19:19
MRK 14:3	1 CO 6:20
JHN 12:3	7:23

ᶜPAEL

Imperfect

MAT 11:16	LUK 13:18,20
LUK 7:31	

Active Participle

2 CO 11:13

ᵈETHPAAL

Perfect

MAT 18:23	1 TH 1:6
22:2	2:14
ACT 14:11	

Imperfect

MAT 7:24,26	PHL 3:10
25:1	2 TH 3:9
ROM 12:2	HEB 2:17
1 CO 4:16	3 JN 11

Imperative

1 CO 11:1	PHL 3:17

Infinitive

2 TH 3:7

Participle

LUK 20:20	2 CO 11:14,15
ROM 9:29	EPH 5:1

702 ܕܡܟ (v) sleep

ᵃPEAL

Perfect

MAT 13:25	JHN 11:12
25:5	ACT 12:6
MRK 4:38	1 CO 15:6,18
14:37²	1 TH 4:14,15
LUK 8:23	

Imperfect

MRK 4:27	1 CO 15:51
1 CO 7:39	1 TH 5:6

Imperative

MAT 26:45	MRK 14:41

Active Participle

MAT 9:24	LUK 22:45,46
26:40,43	1 CO 11:30
28:13	15:20
MRK 5:39	EPH 5:14
13:36	1 TH 4:13
14:37[1],40	5:7[1],7[2],10
LUK 8:52	

Passive Participle

MAT 8:24

1640 ܡܕܡܟܐ (m) bed, sleep

JHN 11:13	ROM 13:13

---

645 (ܕܡܣ), ܕܘܡܣܐ (f) building

REV 21:18

---

703 ܕܡܥܬܐ (f) tear

LUK 7:38,44	HEB 5:7
JHN 11:35	12:17
ACT 20:19,31	REV 7:17
2 CO 2:4	21:4
2 TM 1:4	

---

704 (ܕܡܪ) (v) (pa) admire; (ethpa) marvel, be amazed

^c^PAEL (non occ)

646 ܕܘܡܪܐ (m) wonder, amazement

MRK 5:42	REV 17:6
ACT 3:10	

---

^d^ETHPAAL

Perfect

MAT 8:10,27	MAT 27:14
9:33	MRK 1:27
22:22	6:2
LUK 1:63	LUK 20:26
2:18	ACT 7:31
7:9	13:12
9:43[1]	REV 13:3
11:14,38	17:6,7

Imperfect

MAT 15:31	JHN 5:20,28
MRK 2:12	1 PT 4:12
15:5	1 JN 3:13
JHN 3:7	REV 17:8

Infinitive

JHN 9:30	2 CO 11:14

Participle

MAT 12:23	JHN 4:27
MRK 5:42	7:15,21
6:6,51	ACT 2:7,12
7:37	3:12
10:24,26	8:13
LUK 4:22	10:17
8:25	GAL 1:6
9:7,43[2]	1 PT 4:4
24:12	

3330 ܬܕܡܘܪܬܐ (f) wonder

MAT 21:15,42	ACT 7:36
MRK 12:11	14:3
13:22	ROM 15:19
LUK 5:26	2 CO 12:12
JHN 4:48	2 TH 1:10
ACT 2:11	2:9
6:8	HEB 2:4

---

706 ܕܢܐ (v) (ethpe) obey

^b^ETHPEEL

Infinitive

ACT 7:39

Participle

ACT 10:7	2 CO 11:20

---

648 (ܕܢܒ), ܕܘܢܒܐ (f) tail

REV 9:10,10,19	REV 12:4

707 ܕ.ܢܚ (v) rise, shine; (aph) make rise

[a]PEAL

Perfect

MAT 4:16, 13:6; MRK 4:6 | MRK 16:2; 2 CO 4:6[2]; HEB 7:14

Imperfect

2 CO 4:4,6[1] | 2 PT 1:19

Active Participle

LUK 12:54 | JAM 1:11

708 ܕ.ܢܚܐ (m) dawn

LUK 1:78

1641 ܡܕ.ܢܚܐ (f) east

MAT 2:1,2,9; 8:11; 24:27; LUK 13:29 | REV 7:2; 16:12; 21:13

[e]APHEL

Active Participle

MAT 5:45

[c]PAEL

Perfect

HEB 11:34

Imperfect

1 TH 5:19

Infinitive

EPH 6:16

[e]APHEL

Imperfect

MAT 12:20

---

674 (ܕ.ܝܢܪ), ܕ.ܝܢܪܐ (m) Roman penny

MAT 18:28; 20:2,9,9, 10,10, 13; 22:19,19; MRK 6:37; 12:15 | MRK 14:5; LUK 7:41,41; 10:35; 20:24; JHN 6:7; 12:5; REV 6:6,6

---

710 ܕ.ܥܟ (v) go out (fire); (pa, aph) quench

[a]PEAL

Perfect

MAT 25:8

Active Participle

MAT 3:12; MRK 9:44,46,48 | LUK 3:17

---

711 ܕ.ܥܪ (v-non occ) prick; (pa) blind

[c]PAEL

1643 ܡܕ.ܥܪܢܐ (adj) quarrelsome

ROM 11:8

---

649 (ܕ.ܥܬ), ܕ.ܘܥܬܐ (c) sweat

LUK 22:44

---

712 ܕ.ܦܐ (m) board

JHN 19:20 | ACT 27:44

---

713 ܕ.ܦܢܐ (f) side (of a body)

JHN 19:34 | JHN 20:25

---

714 ܕ.ܩ (v-non occ) break in pieces

[k]P ܕ.ܩܕܩ

715 ܕ.ܩܕܩܐ (adj) small

MAT 15:34; ACT 8:10 | 1 CO 6:2

716 ܕܩܠܐ (f) palm tree

JHN 12:13 | REV 7:9

717 ܕܩܪ (v) hit, pierce

aPEAL

Perfect

JHN 19:37
ACT 12:7 | REV 1:7

719 ܕܪܐ (v) scatter

aPEAL

Imperfect

MAT 21:44 | LUK 20:18

721 ܕܪܓ, ܕܪܓܐ (m) stair, rank

ACT 21:35,40 | 1 TM 3:13

722 ܕܪ̈ܕܪܐ (m) thistles

HEB 6:8

725 ܕܪܟ (v) walk; (aph) overtake, comprehend

aPEAL (non occ)

653 ܕܘܪܟܬܐ (f) treading

ACT 7:5

726 ܕܪܟܬܐ (f) treading out

1 TM 5:18

eAPHEL

Perfect

JHN 1:5
ACT 10:34
25:25 | ROM 9:30,31
PHL 3:12[2],13

Imperfect

JHN 12:35
1 CO 9:24
PHL 3:12[1] | 1 TH 4:15
5:4
1 TM 6:19

Imperative

1 TM 6:12

Infinitive

EPH 3:18

Active Participle

MRK 9:18 | 1 CO 9:9,10

729 ܕܪܥܐ (m) arm, shoulder

MRK 9:36
10:16
LUK 1:51
2:28 | LUK 4:11
JHN 12:38
ACT 13:17

730 ܕܪܫ (v) train, debate

aPEAL

Active Participle

MRK 9:14,16
12:28
ACT 6:9 | ACT 9:29
17:18
18:28

724 ܕܪܘܫܐ (m) disputer

1 CO 1:20

731 ܕܪܫܐ (m) disputation

1 TM 6:4

cPAEL

Imperative

1 TM 4:7

Passive Participle

PHL 4:12
HEB 5:14 | 2 PT 2:14

654 ܕܘܪܫܐ (m) exercise

1 TM 4:8

dETHPAAL

Perfect

HEB 12:11

ܗ

733 ܗܐ (intrj) lo, behold

MAT 1:23; 2:9; 3:10,17; 4:11; 5:46,47; 6:25, 26; 7:4; 8:2,24; 9:20; 10:16; 11:8,10,19; 12:2, 18,41,42,47,49,49; 13:3,27,56; 15:22,32; 17:5,12; 19:27; 20:18,30; 21:5; 22:4; 23:34, 38; 24:2,23,23,25,26,26; 25:6,8,20,22,25; 26:45,46,47,51,65,65; 28:2,7,7,9,20 MRK 1:2,7; 3:32,34,34; 4:3; 6:3; 8:2; 9:21, 21; 10:28,33; 11:21; 13:1,21,21,23; 14:13,15, 41,42,64; 16:6,7 LUK 1:31,36,38,44,48; 2:9,10,30,34,48; 3:9,16; 6:42; 7:25,27,34,45; 9:30; 10:3,19,25; 11:7,31,32,41,49; 13:7,16, 30,32,35; 14:2,17; 15:29; 16:24,25; 17:21,21, 21,23,23; 18:28,31; 19:8,20,30; 22:10,12,21, 31,38,47; 23:14,15,29; 24:4,13,21,21 JHN 1:29,36,47; 3:26,29; 4:35; 5:14; 7:26; 8:40; 9:25; 11:3; 12:15,19,27; 14:29; 16:29, 32; 18:21; 19:4,5,14,26,27,30 ACT 2:7,11, 15,33; 3:2; 4:10,16; 5:9,25,28; 7:44,50,56; 8:36; 9:10,11,14; 10:6,19,30,32,33,47; 12:14; 13:25,32,33,46; 17:6; 19:38; 23:21,21; 26:22; 27:24,33 ROM 2:26; 9:15,33; 10:18; 11:4 1 CO 1:20; 3:3,4; 8:10; 9:8; 14:10; 15:51 2 CO 6:2,2,9; 7:11; 12:11,14 GAL 1:20, 23; 3:1; 5:2 EPH 1:15; 6:21 COL 1:4 2 TH 2:2 PLM 5 HEB 1:14; 2:13; 4:3; 8:8; 10:7,9 JAM 2:4,6,7; 3:3; 5:4,9,11 1 PT 2:6; 4:4 JUD 14 REV 1:7,18; 2:10, 22; 3:8,9,9,20; 4:1,2; 5:5; 6:2,5; 9:12; 11:14, 14; 12:3,10; 14:1,14; 16:15; 19:11; 21:3,5; 22:7,12

737 ܗܒܬܐ (f-non occ) flower

734 ܗܒ (v-non occ) bloom; (pa) shine

[c]PAEL

735 ܗܒܒܐ (m) flower

JAM 1:10,11

738 ܗܓܐ (v) (ethpa) meditate

ETHPAAL

Imperative

1 TM 4:15

739 ܗܓܡ (v) destroy

[a]PEAL

Perfect

ACT 13:19

740 ܗܓܡܘܢܐ (m) governor

MAT 10:18
27:2,11,11,
15,19,
21,23,
27
28:14
MRK 13:9
MRK 15:1
LUK 20:20
21:12
ACT 23:24,26,
33
24:1,10,27
26:30

741 ܗܓܡܘܢܘܬܐ (f) governorship

LUK 2:2
LUK 3:1

743 ܗܕܝܘܛܐ (adj) ignorant

ACT 4:13
1 CO 14:16,23,
1 CO 14:24

744 ܗܕܡܐ (m) member

MAT 5:29,30
ROM 6:13,13,19,
19
7:5,23,23
12:4,4,5
1 CO 6:15,15,15
12:12,12,
14,18,
19,20,
22,24,
1 CO 12:24,25,
26,26,
26,27
EPH 4:16,25
5:30
COL 2:19
3:5
HEB 12:13
JAM 3:5,6
4:1

745 ܗܕܪܐ (m) ornament, splendor

EPH 1:12

747 ܗܘ (pron) he, she, it, they; (as enclitic) is

incl ܗܝ, ܗܢܘܢ, ܗܢܝܢ, etc

see also 92 ܐܝܕܐ

see also 100 ܐܝܢܐ

see also 177 ܐܢ

see also 770 ܗܢܐ

see also 1380 ܒܝܘ

see also 1533 ܠܘ

see also 1769 ܡܢ

see also 1771 ܡܢܐ

MAT 1:20,21; 2:5,6,8,9,13; 3:4,11,11,14,15; 4:4,20,21,22,24; 5:3,4,5,6,8,10,13,13,14,15, 21,22,22,22,23,34,35,35,37,46,47,48; 6:4,13, 18,21,22,23,25,32,34; 7:6,13,13,14,16,20; 8:16,17,24; 9:13,24,31; 10:5,10,21,22,23,30; 11:3,3,8,11,14,25,30,30; 12:2,3,5,7,11,12,23, 27,30,33,39,41,45,46,48,48,48,50; 13:11,11, 15,19,20,21,22,23,28,28,29,30,30,32,32,32, 37,38,38,39,42,50,56,57; 14:2,8,15,16,17,18, 19,22,26,27,28; 15:8,11,13,14,16,17,18,19, 20,23,24,25,27,28,30,30,32,32; 16:1,2,2,3,4, 6,7,14,16,18,20,21,23,27; 17:1,4,5,9,22,26, 27; 18:4,8,9,9,25,30; 19:2,4,4,11,12,14,14, 14,17,18,20,23,24; 20:2,5,10,12,13,16,20,21, 25,25,31,32; 21:9,13,14,17,25,25,29,30,41, 42,44; 22:5,12,14,19,41,45; 23:4,8,9,10,34, 39; 24:2,3,8,13,16,17,18,23,26,26; 25:12,32, 40,44; 26:15,18,23,23,25,38,40,43,44,46,47, 48,50,63,66,70; 27:4,6,10,11,11,12,15,21,23, 42,50,57,66; 28:9,15,15,16,19,20
MRK 1:6,8,11,20,27,27,41,45; 2:1,2,10,19, 25,28; 3:4,11,14,23,26,26,29,33,33,35; 4:10, 15,16,17,18,20,26,27,31,31,36,38; 5:34,35, 39,40,43; 6:2,7,8,15,15,16,17,19,20,24,28, 33,33,34,35,36,37,38,45,46,47,48,48,49; 7:3, 6,6,15,15,20,26,28,36,36,36; 8:3,5,5,7,10,13, 15,28,29,31,31,33; 9:2,5,10,21,27,32,34,37, 40,43,45,47,50; 10:4,6,14,14,16,16,20,20,22, 25,26,32,38,42,42,46,47,48,50,51; 11:6,6,6, 9,10,29,30,32,32; 12:3,10,14,15,16,21,22,28, 29,32,33,35,36,37,40; 13:5,7,8,12,13,14,15, 16,21,29,33,37; 14:3,6,11,18,19,20,22,31,34, 37,39,40,43,44,46,48,52,61,61,62,64,64,68, 69,70,71; 15:2,2,4,5,9,12,13,14,14,23,26,37, 39,41,43; 16:6,10,11,11,13,18,20
LUK 1:15,17,18,22,29,29,35,36,42,63,68; 2:6,27,34,36,38,44,50; 3:13,15,16,22,23; 4:2, 4,8,12,15,24,30,36,40,40,41,41,43,43,44; 5:1,7,7,11,16,24,33,34,37; 6:3,5,8,11,13,20, 32,33,35,35,36,44; 7:4,4,5,12,19,19,19,20, 20,25,28,39,39,40,44; 8:9,10,10,13,13,14,15, 21,21,22,23,24,25,25,37,37,42,46,48,49,52, 54,56,56; 9:2,10,11,13,14,18,21,21,22,29,33, 36,38,45,48,50,54,59; 10:1,7,16,18,21,26,29, 37,38,42; 11:1,7,12,19,21,23,28,31,35,36,40, 41,46,47,48,48; 12:7,18,21,30,37,37,37,38; 13:2,4,14,16,23,25,35; 14:1,4,4,12,19,32,34; 15:8,15,20,29,31; 16:8,10,10,15,15,17,28,28, 29,30; 17:14,16,17,18,21,21,21,23,23,25,31, 31,31; 18:15,16,16,16,16,16,21,23,25,34,36, 39,41; 19:9,27,27,38,47; 20:5,6,7,11,12,17, 17,17,18,23,24,36,38,41,42,44,47; 21:7,8,9, 21,21,22,31; 22:9,12,25,25,26,28,38,41,45, 47,47,49,53,55,57,59,60,67,70; 23:2,3,5,6,7, 11,21,22,23,34,35,37,39; 24:4,6,7,8,11,14, 15,15,15,17,18,21,23,28,31,35,37,40,42,44, 44,48,50,50,52 JHN 1:1,1,5,8,15,18,19, 30,30,33,38,39,44,45,49,49; 2:2,7,7,9,11,12, 21,24,24,25; 3:6,6,10,18,26,29,30,31,31,31, 33; 4:2,6,12,12,20,22,23,24,25,29,32,37,42, 44,45,50,52,53; 5:9,10,11,11,15,17,28,28,30, 32,32,36,36,37,38,39; 6:6,9,15,20,29,29,46, 51,56,57,60,63,63,63,64,69,70,71; 7:4,7,10, 12,22,22,27,27,28,29,32,36,49; 8:9,14,16,17, 26,26,28,32,34,39,42,44,44,44,50,54; 9:3,4, 9,9,15,16,17,19,21,21,22,24,25,25,28,28,29, 30,30,31,37,38,41; 10:1,2,6,8,8,12,13,16,16, 24,25,27,28,29,41; 11:5,13,13,13,27,30,32, 38,41,54,57; 12:1,6,9,13,22,31,34,35,40,48, 49,50; 13:1,3,10,17,26,30; 14:2,10,12,21,26, 26,26,28; 15:1,16,26; 16:4,8,11,13,14,15,17, 18,27,32; 17:3,6,7,8,9,10,10,11,11,14,15,15, 17,17,18,19,21,23,24,25,26; 18:1,3,7,7,21, 25,28,33,35; 19:7,11,12,15,21,21,29,31,35, 35; 20:10,15,15,20,25,31; 21:4,7,12,24,24,25
ACT 1:2,4,6,7,7,10,19,21,22,25; 2:7,12,15, 16,25,33,34,39,39; 3:5,10,13,13,16,25; 4:3,7, 11,13,13,15,18,18,21,24,24,25,32,33; 5:8,9, 18,19,21,22,24,25,26,26,27,27,33,34,36,36, 37,39,40,40,40,40; 6:3,11,14; 7:1,2,9,15,26, 33,34,36,38,38,42,55; 8:11,13,25,27,31,36, 36; 9:2,2,4,5,11,15,20,21,26,29,38,40; 10:2, 4,8,9,10,20,20,21,21,23,23,32,35,36,38,44; 11:14,22,25,28; 12:5,15,15,15,19,22; 13:2,2, 3,4,8,14,15,17,17,18,22,26,31,31,43,46,50; 14:3,3,5,5,12,16; 15:3,5,5,24,27,27,32,32,33, 38,38; 16:6,10,12,12,15,15,17,19,20,20,22, 23,23,23,24,24,30,31,33,33,34,34,36,37,38, 40; 17:3,5,5,6,6,6,9,16,20,24,25,28,28,29; 18:2,4,5,5,8,15,16,21,22,28; 19:16,19,21,22, 25,25,26,27,27,28,34,34,35,35,38; 20:1,1,2, 2,10,13,32,35; 21:5,6,20,22,24,24,26,34,37, 37; 22:5,8,8,19,22,25,26,29,30; 23:3,5,5,27; 24:5,9,9,15,20,22; 25:10,21,25; 26:4,4,10,11, 14,15,22; 27:15,24,33,39,40,42,43,44; 28:4, 5,6,7,15,18,21,25,28,28 ROM 1:9,16,18, 19,22,24,26,28; 2:1,1,4,8,15,23,24,28,29,29, 29; 3:1,5,5,8,9,19,21,22,26,26,28,29,30,31, 31; 4:9,11,12,15,16,16,24,25; 5:11; 6:3,10, 10,23; 7:1,2,7,12,12,13,13,14,15,16,18,21; 8:5,5,5,5,6,7,8,10,10,13,14,16,21,23,24,26, 26,27,27,27,29,29,29; 9:2,7,11,18,29,30; 10:4,8,8,12,17; 11:3,5,16,18,23,23,28,28; 12:7,8,19; 13:1,1,4,4,6,10,11,11,11; 14:2,4,8, 9,14,20,20,21,23; 15:4,14,27,27,29; 16:2,4,7, 18,26 1 CO 1:8,9,18,18,20,25,25,28; 2:14, 14,15; 3:8,9,15,17,17,18,19,19,20,21,22; 4:3, 4,6,9,15,17; 5:7,11; 6:3,5,15,16,18,18,19; 7:1,3,12,13,14,14,14,14,15,22,22,28,35,39, 39; 8:4,6,10,12; 9:2,10,10,11,17,20,20,21,24, 24,27; 10:4,6,6,9,13,17,17,19,20,26,28,28; 11:3,3,3,5,6,7,7,12,14,14,15,15,19,26,27,29; 12:3,3,4,5,6,11,11,12,12,18,20,22,23,23; 13:4,9,13; 14:4,5,14,14,14,22,23,35,36,36,

37,37,37; 15:6,11,14,17,19,19,23,25,28,34, 39,40,41,41,53,54,55,56,56; 16:4,15,15,16, 17,18 2 CO 1:3,4,6,6,6,7,12,17,18,20,21, 21,24; 2:3,3,7,10,13; 3:2,5,14,14,17,17; 4:3, 3,4,6,6,13,15,18,18; 5:5,7,12,12,15,17,17; 6:11,16; 7:8,9,10,11; 8:22,23,23; 9:2,7,8,10, 11; 10:7,7,8,18; 11:1,11,12,14,21,22,22,22, 23,31; 12:2,2,3,4,6,9,10,14,19; 13:1,3,4,5 GAL 1:7,10,10; 2:6,9,10,17,20,21; 3:7,7,7,8, 9,10,10,10,11,13,13,17,18,18,19,20,21; 4:1, 5,17,18,25,25,26; 5:3,10,13,17,19,24; 6:7,8, 12,13 EPH 1:3,19; 2:8,8,11,14,18,20; 3:11,13; 4:5,9,10,11,15,18; 5:6,9,12,13,16, 23,23,23,28,32; 6:4,7,8,8 PHL 1:6,8,21, 21,29; 2:11,13,20,21,29,29; 3:1,1,4,7,18,19, 19,20,21; 4:3,5,12 COL 1:7,8,15,17,18,19, 27,29; 2:10,15,17,22,23; 3:4,5,5,11,14; 4:1,9, 11,11 1 TH 1:9,10; 2:13,14,20; 3:3,8,11; 4:6,16; 5:3,7,7,23,24,24 2 TH 1:9; 2:2,4,4, 6,9,14,16; 3:2,3,3,16 1 TM 1:4,8,15,15,17; 2:5,5; 3:1,10,15,16; 4:3,4,8,9,10; 5:3,5,5,6,8, 8,9,12,16,16,18,24,25,25; 6:2,2,2,5,6,16 2 TM 2:10,11,12,13,19,19,23; 3:5,5,6,8,9, 16; 4:8,11 TIT 1:5,6,7,10,12,15,15; 2:14; 3:8,8,9,11,11,11,13,14,15 PLM 9 HEB 1:3,3,5,10,11,12,12; 2:3,3,9,9,11,11,14, 18; 3:3,4,4,10,10,16; 4:2,2,8,9,10; 5:1,2,3,6, 11,12,13,13,14; 6:8,8,11; 7:1,5,5,8,9,13,14, 17,21,25,28; 8:5,9,9,10,12,13; 9:5,7,15,15, 16,17,20,22,23,23,26; 10:1,1,11,11,16,23,27, 30,31,34,36,37; 11:4,6,10,11,13,26,32; 12:1, 2,3,6,10,11,27,29; 13:4,4,5,8,9,17,21,21,22 JAM 1:13,14,18,21,21,26,27; 2:6,7,11,17, 19,20,25,26,26; 3:5,6,6,6,6,8,17,17; 4:4,12, 12,13,14,16; 5:3,11,16 1 PT 1:3,17,25; 2:3,6,8,15,24; 3:1,7,7,12,14,17,17; 4:11,12, 17,17; 5:4,5,6,9,12,14 2 PT 1:5; 2:1,4,4,6, 9,17,19; 3:16,17 1 JN 1:5,5,7,9; 2:2,4,11, 16,16,17,18,18,20,22,27,27,29; 3:3,3,4,7,7,8, 8,8,15,16,19,20,21,24; 4:2,3,4,5,7,8,10,13, 15,15,16,17,19,20; 5:3,4,5,7,8,9,9,11,11,17, 17,19 2 JN 11 3 JN 10,10,12,12 JUD 16 REV 1:3,3,20; 2:2,19,20,27; 3:4, 9,17,20; 4:11; 5:1,9,10,12; 7:13,14,14,17,17; 9:5; 11:4,5,5,7,7; 12:4; 13:7,10,18; 14:4,5,10; 15:4; 16:6,14,21; 17:9,10,11,12,14,14; 18:6, 14,15,18; 19:8,12,15,15,15; 20:5,6,8,9; 21:3, 3,4,7,16,22

748 ܗܘ (pron) that, those; (w/ ܕ) he who

incl ܗܝ, ܗܢܘܢ, ܗܢܝܢ

see also 757 ܗܢܐ

MAT 1:20; 2:9,20; 3:1,3,11,11,12; 4:3; 5:45; 7:22,24,25,27; 8:8,13,28,31,32,33,33; 9:2,6, 8,16,22,22,26,28,31,33; 10:4,14,15,19; 11:3, 23,25; 12:1,4,13; 13:1,11,13,19,20,20,22,22, 23,23,33,36,37,44,44; 14:1,3,19,21,33,35; 15:11,22,28,31,38; 16:9,10; 17:18,24,27; 18:1,12,17,26,27,28,29,32; 19:4,20,22; 20:9, 24; 21:12,19,31,40; 22:7,8,10,23,26,26,46; 23:11,31,35; 24:15,17,19,22,22,29,36,36,46, 48,50; 25:3,4,7,8,9,11,13,16,17,18,19,20,22, 24,28,29,29,34,37,41,41; 26:24,24,48,50,51, 52,55,57,68,73; 27:8,19,33,44,47,55,63,66; 28:11 MRK 1:7,9; 2:5,20,21,26; 3:3,5,19, 24,25; 4:10,16,18,20,24,25,31,35; 5:12,12, 13,14,15,15,16,16,16,18,21,33,36,38,40; 6:11,16,17,41,41,49,52,55; 7:15,17,20; 8:1,6, 13; 9:25,26; 11:2,9,9,15,20,21,23; 12:4,5,7,9, 18,32,40; 13:11,11,14,14,19,20,20,24,24,32, 32; 14:8,21,21,25,42,44,44,47,69; 15:7,32, 35,39,41,43,47; 16:4,6,9,10,13,14 LUK 1:2,24,35,36,39,49; 2:1,20,31; 3:16,16, 17; 4:2,28,29; 5:9,20,35; 6:4,8,12,13,14,16, 23,38,48,49,49; 7:7,10,10,14,15,19,20,21,36, 37,37,39,39,43,44,47,48,49,50; 8:2,2,10,12, 12,14,15,18,22,33,35,36,38,43,47; 9:5,16,32, 32,36,38,42,42; 10:12,12,15,17,31,32,36,37, 42; 11:7,14,14,22,26,38,51; 12:5,12,13,37, 38,40,43,45,46,46,48,48; 13:1,1,4,19,21,31; 14:7,9,10,12,15,21,24,31; 15:4,13,14,15,16, 25; 16:3,20,21,22,22; 17:1,9,31,34; 18:3,11, 13,14; 19:5,10,11,15,20,24,24,26,26,27,30, 32,33; 20:2,11,12,16,17,18,19,27,35,35,47; 21:23,34; 22:22,23,27,27,27,27,47,51,52; 23:7,12,19,25,25,33,39,53; 24:19,28 JHN 1:15,18,24,26,27,27,29,39,40,45; 2:9,9, 9,14,16; 3:13,13,21,26,29,30,31,31,31,33; 4:9,11,12,14,15,19,25,38,39,39,40,42,49,50, 53; 5:7,9,9,10,11,13,13,15,15,23,25,32,35, 38,43,45,47; 6:10,11,13,14,21,21,22,22,23, 33,42,46,64; 7:11,16,18,18,25,28,45,50; 8:11,31,44,44,54; 9:6,8,13,17,18,19,24,28, 30,31,36,37; 10:1,2,35; 11:2,3,30,31,33,37, 39,41,44,49,51,53; 12:1,4,9,16,17,21; 13:10, 11,18,23,24,25,26,28; 14:17,17,20,21,21,24, 26; 15:26,26; 16:13,23,26; 17:4,5,6,9,11,24, 24,26; 18:2,13,13,14,15,16,21,26; 19:11,25, 26,27,27,27,30,31,31,32,38,39,41; 20:2,2,3, 4,7,8,14,19,24; 21:2,3,7,7,8,10,11,20,20,23 ACT 1:2,3,4,13,15,16,16,19; 2:2,6,18,41; 3:2,10,12,13,15,23,23,24; 4:10,10,10,14,22, 36; 5:10,11,25,28,32,37; 6:1,15; 7:20,24,27, 35,37,38,41,44,45,46,49,52; 8:1,4,8,34,36, 38,39; 9:5,17,19,21,22,37,38; 10:1,6,17,21, 38,45,47; 11:2,19,27; 12:1,1,6,9,12,25; 13:9, 25,32,49; 14:13,15,16,21,23,26; 15:30,37; 16:18; 17:11,11,13,14,15,23; 18:2; 19:15,16, 16,22,23,26; 20:8,28,28,38; 21:38; 22:5,9,11, 11,29; 23:2,13; 25:19,19; 26:20,20; 27:12,23; 28:1,7,16 ROM 1:3,18; 2:1,6,14,23,28,29; 3:8; 4:5,17; 5:12,14,14; 6:16; 7:6,10,15,21; 8:11,11; 10:14; 11:7,23,24,24,27,30; 13:9; 14:3,3,3,3,14,15; 16:24,24 1 CO 1:24,30; 2:7,8; 3:7,7,13,14; 4:5,7,18,19; 5:2,3; 6:19, 20; 7:15; 8:11; 9:21,26; 10:4,16,16,17,17,20, 29; 11:5,23,23; 13:10; 14:5,9,11,11,13,16,28; 15:27,28,29,37,37,48,48,49,49; 16:2 2 CO 1:4,4,6,9,10,19,21; 2:2,3,3,7; 3:6,7,10, 10,13,14; 4:14; 5:5,12,15,18,19,20,21; 7:6,7, 12; 8:11,14,15,15; 9:4,5,8,10; 10:9,12,12,17, 18; 11:4,12,15,21; 13:3 GAL 1:1,4,6,15, 23,23; 2:6,8,9,12,20; 3:1,5,16,19; 4:6,8,9,23, 23,26,27,27,29,29; 5:1,8,12,14; 6:6,6,7 EPH 1:3,6,8,9,11,14,23; 2:3,10,12,14; 3:5,7, 8,9,9,12,15,20; 4:10,10,14,19,22,24; 6:6,8,20

PHL 1:6,17,28,30; 2:5,6,13; 3:8,9,9,18,18, 19,21; 4:3,7,11 COL 1:5,5,6,14,15,23,23, 25,26,28; 2:1,3,7,14,20; 3:22; 4:9,10,11,12, 13,16,17 1 TH 1:10; 2:4,12,15; 4:5,8; 5:4, 10 2 TH 1:5,8,8,10; 2:4,7,8,9,16
1 TM 1:11,17; 2:4,6,7; 4:14; 6:13,13,15,16, 16,17 2 TM 1:3,5,6,9,9,11,12,14,18; 2:2,4, 8,16; 3:6,9; 4:1,8 TIT 1:3; 3:6 PLM 11
HEB 2:3,8,9,10,11,11,14,15,18; 3:4,10,16, 17,18; 4:2,2,6,11,11; 5:5; 6:4,7,10,12,19; 7:6, 7,7,8,9,13,15,16,21,23; 8:2,5,6,6,6,9,10,13; 9:4,4,7,9,16,17,20,24; 10:8,16,25,30,32,37; 11:1,8,9,11,15,16,17,27,28,31; 12:3,8,10,19, 19,24,25,27,27; 13:3,10,20 JAM 1:6,7,12, 17,23; 2:3,5,11,13; 3:4; 4:11,15; 5:4,10,15,20
1 PT 1:3,4,8,10,15,18,20,21,25; 2:4,7,9,15, 22,23; 3:6,16,21,22; 4:3,4,5,5,11,11; 5:1,10, 10 2 PT 1:3,9,10,17,17,19; 2:8,15,19; 3:10,12 1 JN 1:1,1,1,2; 2:4,5,6,7,7,8,10, 11,13,14,17,23; 3:5,7,8,12,14,15,24; 4:3,4,4, 6,6,18,20,20; 5:1,5,18 2 JN 5,9,11
3 JN 1,5,6,9,10,11,11 JUD 4,5,9,14,24
REV 1:1,1,2,3,3,3,4,4,4,4,5,5,5,5,7,8,8,8,8, 9; 2:1,1,7,7,8,12,14,17,17,18,20,25; 3:1,7,11; 4:1,8; 5:7; 6:8,9,11; 7:2; 8:7; 9:6; 10:4,5,6,6, 7; 11:13; 12:5,9,9,9,10,11,16; 13:2,8,8,12; 14:16; 15:6; 16:5,14,15; 17:8,10,11,11,17; 18:6,9; 19:19,20,21; 20:2,11; 21:15

756 (ܗܘ), ܐܬܘܗ (f) chasm

LUK 16:26

749 ܐܘܗ (v) be; (as enclitic) was

[a]PEAL

Perfect

MAT 1:18[1],18[2],19[1],19[2],22; 2:4,6,9,15,20,22; 3:1,4,5,6,14; 4:4,11,18,23[1],23[2]; 5:2,25; 6:7; 7:21,25,27,28[1],28[2],29; 8:5,15,16[1],16[2],24[1], 24[2],26,30,31,33[1],33[2]; 9:18,20,21,24,34,35[1], 35[2],36; 10:11,20; 11:1,20,21[1],21[2],21[3],23[1], 23[2],23[3],26; 12:1,4,7[1],7[2],10[1],10[2],23,30,40[1]; 13:2,3,5[1],5[2],6,21,34,45,53,54,55,57; 14:3,4[1], 5[1],5[2],5[3],6,8,15,21[2],23,24[1],24[2],26,36; 15:11, 30,38[2]; 16:2,7,11,13; 17:5; 18:6[1],11,28[1],28[2], 31[1],31[2],33; 19:1,3,6,8,12,22,25; 20:8,13,17, 20,23,29,30,31; 21:4,8[1],8[2],9[1],9[2],10,11,25,26, 28,33,42[1],42[2],46; 22:8[1],8[2],25[1],25[2],32,33; 23:15,16,18,23,26,30[1],30[3]; 24:1,21[2],22,38, 43[1],43[2]; 25:2,6,10,20,21,23,24,26,27[1],27[2], 27[3],34,35,36[1],36[2],36[3],43[1],43[2],43[3],43[4]; 26:1, 5[1],6,9,16,20[1],20[2],24,39,43,48,55,56,57,58, 59,63,67[1],67[2],69[1],69[2],71; 27:1,12,15[1],15[2],16, 18,29,30,36,39[1],39[2],41,44,45,47[1],47[2],48,49, 52,54[1],54[2],54[3],55[1],55[2],55[3],55[4],57[1],57[2],61[1], 61[2],63; 28:2[1],2[2],3[1],3[2],4[1],4[2],6[1],6[2],11,17
MRK 1:4,5[1],5[2],6[1],6[2],6[3],7,9,11,13[1],13[2],13[3], 14,16,21,22[1],22[2],23,27,30,31,33,34[1],34[2],34[3], 35,36,39,40,45[1],45[2],45[3],45[4]; 2:2,4[1],4[2],6[1],6[2], 13[1],13[2],15[1],15[2],15[3],18,23[1],23[2],26,27; 3:1,2,4, 7,8,10[1],11[1],11[2],12,20,21,22,30,32; 4:1[1],1[2],2[1], 2[2],5,6,9,10,17,21,22,26,33[1],33[2],34[1],34[2],36, 37[1],37[2],37[3],38,39,41; 5:3[1],3[2],4[1],4[2],4[3],4[4],5[1],5[2], 8,10,11,12,14[1],14[2],15,16,18[1],20,23,24[1],24[2], 25,28,32,33,34,40[1],40[2],42[1],42[2],42[3]; 6:1,2[1],2[2], 3[1],3[2],5,6,10,12,13[1],13[2],13[3],14[1],14[2],15,17,18, 19[1],19[2],19[3],20[1],20[2],20[3],20[4],20[5],21[1],21[2],31[1], 31[2],34[1],34[2],35,44,47[1],47[2],48[1],48[2],51,52[1],52[2], 55,56[1],56[2],56[3],56[4],56[5]; 7:19,24,25,26[1],26[2], 27,32,36[1],36[2],37; 8:1[1],1[2],7,9,14,16,22,25,27, 31,32; 9:1,3,6[1],6[2],7[1],7[2],7[3],9,10,11,16,20,26, 30[1],30[2],31,32[1],32[2],33[1],33[2],34[1],34[2],37,40,42[1], 42[2],50[2]; 10:1[1],1[2],8[2],13[1],13[2],17,22,24,26,32[1], 32[2],32[3],40,46,48[1],48[2],52; 11:8[1],8[2],9,11,13[1], 13[2],16,17,18[1],18[2],18[3],19,23[1],27,32,33; 12:6, 10,11,12,17,18,20,24,27,34,37,38,41[1],41[2], 44; 13:11,19[2],20,37; 14:1[2],1[3],2[1],4[1],4[2],5[1],5[2],8, 11,17,21,31[1],35,40[1],40[2],49[1],49[2],51[1],51[2],54[1], 54[2],55,56[1],56[2],59,61,65,67,71,72; 15:3,6,7[1], 7[2],8,10,14,19[1],19[2],19[3],21[1],21[2],25,26,29[1],29[2], 31,32[1],32[2],33[1],33[2],35,39,40[1],40[2],41[1],41[2],42, 43,46; 16:3,4,6[1],6[2],8[1],8[2],9,10[1],10[2],20[1],20[2]
LUK 1:2,3,5[1],5[2],5[3],6,7[1],7[2],7[3],8[1],8[2],8[3],10,21[1], 21[2],22[1],22[2],24[1],24[2],24[3],29,41,45,57[1],57[2],58, 59[1],59[2],65[1],65[2],66[1],66[3],80[1],80[2]; 2:1,2,3,4[1],4[2], 6,7[1],7[2],8[1],8[2],15[1],15[2],19,25[1],25[2],25[3],25[4],25[5], 26,27,33[1],33[2],36,37[1],37[2],37[3],38[1],38[2],40[1],40[2], 41,42[1],42[2],44,45,47[1],47[2],48,49[1],51[1],51[2],52; 3:2,7[1],7[2],10,14,15[1],15[2],18[1],18[2],19[1],19[2],21, 22,23[1],23[2]; 4:4,15[1],15[2],16,20,22[1],22[2],22[3], 22[4],22[5],25[1],25[2],27,29,31,32[1],32[2],33[1],33[2],36, 38,39,40[1],40[2],40[3],41[1],41[2],41[3],42,44; 5:1[1],1[2], 3[1],3[2],6,7,9,10[1],12[1],12[2],15,16,17[1],17[2],17[3],17[4], 17[5],18,26,29[1],29[2],30; 6:1[1],1[2],4,6[1],6[2],6[3],6[4],7, 11,12[1],12[2],16,18,19[1],19[2],19[3],23,26[2],39,48[1], 48[2],49; 7:2[1],2[2],2[3],3,4,6,10,11[1],11[2],12[1],12[2], 14,16,21,37,38[1],38[2],39[1],39[2],41[1],41[2],42; 8:1[1], 1[2],1[3],3,4[1],4[2],6,8,19,22,23[1],23[2],24,25,27[1],27[2], 29[1],29[2],29[3],29[4],29[5],29[6],29[7],30,31,32[1],32[2],34, 35,37,38[1],39,40,41,42[1],42[2],42[3],43,52,53[1], 53[2],56; 9:6[1],6[2],7[2],7[3],7[4],8,9,11[1],11[2],11[3],14[2], 23,28,29,30,31[1],31[2],32[1],32[2],33[2],34[1],34[2],35, 36,37,43,45[1],45[2],50,51,53; 10:1,13[1],13[2],18, 19,21,30,31,33[1],33[2],36,37,38,39[1],39[2],40; 11:1,2[1],14,16,17,23,27,29,30[1],40,42,53[1],53[2]; 12:15,17,39[1],39[2],39[3]; 13:2[1],2[2],4,6,11[1],11[2], 11[3],11[4],14,16,17[1],17[2],17[3],17[4],17[6],18,19,22; 14:1[1],1[2],2[1],2[2],7[1],7[2],22,24,25; 15:1,2,6,9,11[1], 11[2],14[1],14[2],16[1],16[2],16[3],24[1],24[2],25,28,32[1], 32[2],32[3]; 16:1[1],1[2],11,14[1],14[2],19[1],19[2],19[3],20[1], 20[2],21[1],21[2],22; 17:1,2,6[1],6[2],6[3],10,11[1],11[2],15, 16,17[1],26[1],27,28[1],28[2],28[3]; 18:2[1],2[2],2[3],3[1],3[2],4, 9,11[1],11[2],11[3],13[1],13[2],13[3],15,23,34[1],34[2],35, 36,39[1],39[2],39[3],43[1],43[2]; 19:2,3[1],3[2],3[3],4,7,9, 10,11[1],11[2],11[3],14,20,22,23,36,38,47[1],47[2], 48[1],48[2]; 20:1,4,5,14[1],17,19,29,36,38,41,45; 21:1,4[1],4[2],5,7[1],29,37[1],37[2],38; 22:1,2[1],2[2],3[1], 3[2],6,7,14,19,24,27,39,41,44[1],44[2],44[3],47,49, 53,54,55[1],55[2],56,58,59[1],59[2],61,63[1],63[2],63[3], 64,65; 23:5,7,8[1],8[2],8[3],9,10[1],10[2],12[1],12[2],17, 19[1],19[2],21,23[1],23[2],23[3],25,27[1],27[2],32,34,35[1], 35[2],36,38,39[1],39[2],41,44[1],44[2],47[1],47[2],48[1],48[2], 49[1],49[2],49[3],50,51[1],51[2],53,54[1],54[2],55; 24:1[1], 1[2],4[1],4[2],5,7,10[1],10[2],12,13,14,15,16,18,19[1], 19[2],21[1],21[2],21[3],22,26[1],26[2],27[1],27[2],28[1],28[2],

28[3],30,32[1],32[2],32[3],35,36,37[1],37[2],41[1],41[2],44,
46[1],46[2],51,53 JHN 1:1[1],1[2],1[3],2,3[1],3[2],3[3],4,
6,8,9,10[1],10[2],14,15,17,24,27,28[1],28[2],30,31,
33,35,39[1],39[2],39[3],40,44; 2:1[1],1[2],3,6,9[1],9[2],9[3],
9[4],12,13,21,22,23,24[1],24[2],25[1],25[2]; 3:1[1],1[2],13,
19,22,23[1],23[2],23[3],24,25[1],25[2],26,28,34; 4:2[1],
2[2],4,5,6[1],6[2],6[3],6[4],8,10[1],10[2],10[3],15,18[1],18[2],27,
30,31,38,39,40[2],42[1],42[2],45,46[1],46[2],47[1],47[2],
51; 5:1,2[1],2[2],3[1],3[2],4[1],4[2],4[3],4[4],4[5],5[1],5[2],9,13[1],
13[2],13[3],16[1],16[2],16[3],18[1],18[2],18[3],18[4],22,31,34,
35,46; 6:2,3,4,6,10,14,16,17[1],17[2],17[3],18[1],
18[2],21[1],21[2],21[3],22[1],22[2],22[3],23,24[1],24[2],24[3],
26,32,38,41,42[1],42[2],46,52,58,62,64,65,66,
70,71; 7:1[1],1[2],1[3],2,5,11[1],11[2],12[1],12[2],12[3],13,
14,15,16,19,22,25,30,37,39[1],39[2],39[3],40,41,
42,43[1],43[2],44[1],44[2],50; 8:2[1],2[2],6[2],8,9,13,16,
19[1],19[2],20,23,30,39[1],39[2],41,42[1],42[2],42[3],47,
54,56,57; 9:8[1],8[2],8[3],8[4],8[5],9[1],9[2],9[3],13,14,16[1],
16[2],16[3],16[4],18[1],18[2],22[1],22[2],24,25,33[1],33[2],40,
41[1],41[2]; 10:12,16[1],18,19,20,21[1],21[2],22[1],22[2],
23,26,33,34,35,39,40[1],40[2],40[3],41; 11:1,2[1],2[2],
4,5,6,8;15,18,19,20,21[1],21[2],29,30[1],30[2],31[1],
31[2],32[1],32[2],32[3],35;36[1],36[2],37,38[1],38[2],47,49,
51[1],51[2],53,54[1],54[2],55,56[1],56[2],57; 12:1,2[1],2[2],
4,6[1],6[2],6[3],6[4],6[5],6[6],10,11,12,13,16,17[1],17[2],19,
20,29[1],29[2],30[1],30[2],39,42[1],44; 13:1,2[1],2[2],3,5,
11[1],11[2],18,19[2],22,23[1],23[2],23[3],29,30,34; 14:2,
7[1],7[2],22[1],22[2],24,27,28[1],28[2],29[2]; 15:16,19[1],
19[2],19[3],22,24; 16:4,17,18,19,32; 17:5[1],6,9,
11[1],12[1],12[2],14[1],14[2],15,16[1],16[2],20; 18:1,2[1],2[2],
4,5,10,13[1],13[2],14,15[1],15[2],16[1],16[2],18[1],18[2],
18[3],18[4],22,25[1],25[2],26,28,30[1],30[2],36[1],36[2],36[3],
36[4],40; 19:3[1],3[2],11[1],11[2],12[1],12[2],12[3],14[1],14[2],
15,20[1],20[2],23,25,26,29,31[1],31[2],36,38[1],38[2],
39,41[1],41[2],42[1],42[2]; 20:2,3,4,7,9[1],9[2],11,12,14,
19[1],19[2],19[3],24[1],24[2],26; 21:2,4,7[1],7[2],8[1],8[2],12[1],
12[2],18[1],18[2],18[3],18[4],20[1],20[2],23,25[1],25[2],25[3]
ACT 1:2,3,7,10[1],10[2],13[2],14,15,16[1],16[2],17[1],
17[2],21; 2:1,2[1],2[2],2[3],2[4],3,4,5,6[1],6[2],6[3],7[1],7[2],12,
13,23,24,25,30[1],30[2],34,39,40[1],40[2],42[1],42[2],
43[2],43[4],44[1],44[2],44[3],44[4],45[1],45[2],45[3],45[4],46[1],
46[2],46[3],47[1],47[2]; 3:1,2[1],2[2],3,5,10[1],10[2],11,13,
20,24; 4:1,2,3,4[1],4[2],4[3],6,7,9,11,13,14[1],14[2],
14[3],15,16,21[1],21[2],22[1],22[2],31[1],31[2],32[1],32[2],
32[3],32[4],32[5],32[6],33[1],33[2],34[1],34[2],34[3],35[1],35[2],
37; 5:1[1],1[2],1[3],2,4[1],4[2],4[3],5,7[1],7[2],7[3],11,12[2],12[3],
13[1],13[2],14[1],14[2],15[1],15[2],16[1],16[2],16[4],16[5],17[1],
17[2],21,24[1],24[2],26,27,28[1],28[2],33[1],33[2],34[1],34[2],
36[1],36[2],36[3],37[1],37[2],41,42; 6:1[1],1[2],5,7[1],7[2],7[3],
8[1],8[2],9[1],9[2],10[1],10[2],15; 7:2,3,5[1],5[2],6[1],9,10,11[1],
11[2],12,14[1],14[3],16,17[1],17[2],17[3],18,20,22,23[1],
23[2],24,26,27,29[1],29[2],32[1],32[2],38[1],38[2],40,41,
44,54[1],54[2],55,58,59; 8:1[1],1[2],1[3],1[4],3[1],3[2],3[3],4,
5,6[1],6[2],6[3],6[4],6[5],6[6],7[1],7[2],7[3],8,9[1],9[2],9[3],9[4],10[1],
10[2],11[1],11[2],12[1],12[2],13[1],13[2],13[3],13[5],16[1],16[2],
17[1],17[2],21,27[1],27[2],27[3],28[1],28[2],32[1],32[2],32[3],
36,38,39,40; 9:1,3[1],3[2],7[1],7[2],7[3],7[4],8[1],8[2],9,10[1],
10[2],19[1],19[2],20,21[1],21[2],21[3],21[4],21[5],21[6],21[7],
22[1],22[2],22[3],22[4],24[1],24[2],26[1],26[2],26[3],28,29[1],
29[2],29[3],29[4],31[1],31[2],31[3],32[1],32[2],33[1],33[2],36[1],
36[2],36[3],36[4],38[1],38[2],39,43[1],43[2]; 10:1[1],1[2],2[1],2[2],
2[3],2[4],7,10,11[1],11[2],12,15,16,17,18,19,23,24[1],
24[2],27,28,31,34,37,38[1],38[2],44[1],44[2],46[1],46[2],
46[3]; 11:1,2,4,5[1],5[2],5[3],5[4],5[5],6,7[1],7[2],10,11,15,
16,17[1],17[2],18,19[1],19[2],19[3],19[4],19[5],20[1],20[2],
20[3],20[4],21,22,23[1],24[1],24[2],24[3],25,26,28[1],28[3],

29; 12:1[1],1[2],3[1],3[2],5[1],5[2],6[1],6[2],6[3],6[4],9[1],9[2],9[3],9[5],
9[6],9[7],11,12,15,16,17,18[1],18[2],18[3],18[4],19,20[1],
20[3],21[1],21[2],22[1],22[2],24; 13:1,2,5[1],5[2],6[1],6[2],7[1],
7[2],7[3],7[4],7[5],8[1],8[2],9,11[2],12,17,25[1],25[2],25[3],29,
32,42,43[1],43[2],45[1],45[2],45[3],46,48[1],48[2],48[3],49,
50,52; 14:2,3[1],3[2],3[3],3[4],4[1],4[2],4[3],5,7,8[1],8[2],8[3],
12[1],12[2],13[1],13[2],13[3],14,16,17[1],17[2],17[3],18,19,
21[1],21[2],22[1],22[2],22[3],23[1],23[2],26,27,28; 15:1[1],
1[2],2[1],2[2],3[1],3[2],3[3],5[1],5[2],7,12[1],12[2],21,22,28,32,
33,35[1],35[2],37,38[1],38[2],41; 16:1[1],1[2],1[3],2,3[1],3[2],
3[3],3[4],4[1],4[2],5[1],5[2],7,12,13[1],13[2],13[3],14[1],14[2],14[3],
15[1],15[2],16[1],16[2],16[3],16[4],17[1],17[2],18,20,25[1],
25[2],25[3],26,27,30,31,34,35; 17:1,2,3[1],3[2],4,5[1],
5[2],5[3],6[1],6[2],6[3],10,11[1],11[2],11[3],11[4],14,16[1],16[2],
16[3],16[4],17[1],17[2],18[1],18[2],18[3],18[4],23[1],23[2],23[3],
27[2],32[1],32[2],34[1],34[2]; 18:2[1],2[2],2[3],2[4],3[1],3[2],3[3],4[1],
4[2],5[1],5[2],5[3],5[4],5[5],7[1],7[2],8[1],8[2],11[1],11[2],12,14[1],
14[2],14[3],17[1],17[2],17[3],18[1],18[2],19,20,23[1],23[2],
24[1],24[2],24[3],24[4],25[1],25[2],25[3],25[4],28[1],28[2];
19:1[1],1[2],4,6[1],6[2],8[1],8[2],8[3],9[1],9[2],10,11,12[1],12[2],
12[3],13[1],13[2],13[3],13[4],14[1],14[2],14[3],16,17[1],17[2],
18[1],18[2],20,22[1],22[2],23[1],23[2],24[1],24[2],24[3],24[4],
26,28,30,31,32[1],32[2],32[3],32[4],33[1],33[2]; 20:3[1],
3[2],6,7[1],7[2],7[3],8[1],8[2],9[1],9[2],9[3],9[4],11,13[1],13[2],13[3],
16[1],16[2],18,19,20,21,31,37[1],37[2],38; 21:3,4,5,
8,9[1],9[2],10[1],10[2],13,16[1],16[2],16[3],18,19,29[1],29[2],
31,32,33,34[1],34[2],34[3],36,38,40; 22:2,3,4[1],4[2],
5,6,7,9[1],9[2],11[1],11[2],12,19[1],19[2],19[3],20[1],20[2],
20[3],20[4],20[5],23[1],23[2],23[3],24,25,29[1],29[2],30[1],
30[2]; 23:4,5,6,9[1],9[2],10[1],10[2],11,12[1],12[2],13[2],14,
16,19,28[1],28[2],29[1],29[2],34; 24:2[1],2[2],19,22,24,
26[1],26[2],26[3],27[1],27[2]; 25:2,3,6,7[1],7[2],8,9,13,14,
15,18,19[1],19[2],20[1],20[2],22; 26:1,4,6[1],6[2],10,11[1],
11[2],11[4],11[5],12,13,21,24,26,29[1],29[2],30,31,32;
27:1,2[1],2[2],2[3],2[4],4,6,7[1],7[2],8,9[1],9[2],9[3],11,12[1],
12[2],12[3],12[4],12[5],13,17[1],17[2],17[3],20[1],20[2],21[1],
21[2],21[3],25,27,29[1],29[2],33[1],33[2],37,39[1],39[2],40,
41,42,43[1],43[2]; 28:2[1],2[2],4,5,6[1],6[2],7[1],7[2],7[3],8,9[1],
9[2],9[3],9[4],10,11[1],11[2],14,19,23,24[1],24[2],30[1],30[2],
30[3],31[1],31[2] ROM 1:27,32; 2:13,14[1],14[2],
25,28,29; 4:2[1],2[2],10,12,13[1],13[2],14[1],14[2],14[3],
19,23; 5:8,13[1],13[2],13[3],15,16[1],16[2],16[3],18[1],
19[1],20; 6:15,17,20[1],20[2],21,22; 7:3[1],5[1],5[2],6,7,
8,9,13,15,17,19,20; 8:3,4,9[1],9[2],24; 9:3[1],4,6[1],
6[2],8,10,23,24,25,26[2],29[2],29[3],30,31,32; 10:16;
11:2[1],2[2],6[1],6[2],7,11,12,15,17,18,25[2],30,34;
12:2,4,9[2],10[1],10[2],11[1],11[2],11[3],12[1],12[2],12[3],13[1],
13[2],16,19; 13:1,3[1],4; 14:15,17,23; 15:3,9,23;
16:2,4,7[1],7[2],24 1 CO 1:30; 2:3,4,7[1],7[2],8,
12,13; 3:2; 4:1,9,13,14,20; 5:10; 6:11,19,20;
7:19,34[1],35[1]; 8:4,7; 9:1[1],1[2],1[3],2,20[1],20[2],21,
22[1],22[2],26; 10:1,4[1],4[2],4[3],5,6[1],6[2],11,16[1],16[2],
18[1],25,29,31,32; 11:17,23[1],23[2],24,25,31[1],
31[2],33; 12:2[1],2[2],14,15[1],15[2],16[1],16[2],17[1],17[2],
17[3],17[4],19[1],19[2]; 13:1[2],2[3],10,11[1],11[2],11[3],11[4],
11[5]; 14:2,9[2],14,20[1],22,33; 15:2,10,20,21[1],23,
37[1],39,45,46,58[4]; 16:12[1],18 2 CO 1:8[1],8[2],
13,15,17[1],18,19[1],19[2],20,24; 2:3,5,13,17; 3:7,
9,11[1],13; 4:1,5; 5:9,12[1],12[2],18,19,21[1]; 7:3,5,
7,8,12[2]; 8:2,5,8,11,12,13[1],14[1]; 9:5[2],12; 10:3,
4,14,18; 11:1,4,15[1],17,25[1],25[2],26[1],26[2],32;
12:11[1],11[2],11[3]; 13:2[1],2[2],3,6 GAL 1:10[1],
10[3],11,13[1],13[2],14[1],14[2],14[3],22,23[1],23[2],23[3],24;
2:2,3,9,10,11,12[1],12[2],12[3],13[1],13[2],15,20; 3:1,
12,13,17,18,19,20,21[1],21[2],21[4],23[1],23[2],24,25;
4:3[1],3[2],4[1],4[2],7,8[1],8[2],12[2],13,15[1],15[2],16,17[1],

20[1],22,23,29[1],29[2],31; 5:7,8,11[1],11[2],13[2],16,
18; 6:1,9[1] EPH 1:9,13; 2:1,2,3[1],3[2],5,7,8,
11[1],11[2],11[3],12[1],12[2],12[3],12[4],13[1],13[2],14,18,19,
20; 3:7,9,11; 4:2,3,15,20,28[1],32[1],32[2]; 5:1,5,8,
10,11[1],11[2],18,19,20,21,22; 6:9[1],9[2],12,18
PHL 1:17,23[2],27; 2:6,7,14,16,26[1],26[2],27[1],30;
3:4,6,7,12,17; 4:10[1],10[2],11[1] COL 1:21,23,
25,26; 2:13,14; 3:7[1],7[2],13,15,16[1],16[2],17[1],17[2];
4:1,2,6[2],11,18 1 TH 1:5[1],5[2],5[3],7,9; 2:1[1],1[2],
3,6[1],7,9,10,11[1],11[2],13,17; 3:4[1],4[2]; 4:8,11[2];
5:4,5,6,8,12,13 2 TH 2:5[1],5[2]; 3:6,8,9,10[1],
10[2],14,15 1 TM 1:3,13[1],13[2],18; 2:7,8,11;
3:2[2],12[2]; 5:7[1],9[1],9[2],23 2 TM 1:5; 2:14[1],18,
20; 3:1; 4:5,16 TIT 1:5,6,13[1]; 3:1[1],3[1],3[2],3[3],
3[4],3[5],3[6],8,11 PLM 11,13[1] HEB 2:5,10,
15,16[1],16[2],16[3],17[1]; 3:5; 4:2,3,6,8[1],8[2]; 5:4,5[1],
7[1],7[2],7[3],9,11,12[1],12[3]; 6:10,13,16[1],20; 7:2,5[1],
5[2],9,10,11[1],11[2],12[1],12[2],16[1],18[1],18[2],21,22,
23[1],23[2],23[3],26,28; 8:2,3[1],4[1],4[3],4[4],4[5],5,7[1],7[2];
9:1,2[1],2[2],3,4[1],4[2],5[1],5[2],6[1],6[2],7[1],7[2],8[1],8[2],9[1],9[2],
9[3],11[1],11[2],13[1],13[2],15[1],15[2],19,24,25,26;
10:1[1],1[2],1[3],2[1],2[2],8,11[1],11[2],11[3],33,39; 11:1,2,
3,4,5,7[1],7[2],8[1],8[2],9,10,11,15[1],15[2],16,17,18,19,
20,23,24,26,27,28,34,38,39; 12:2[1],2[2],3,8,9[1],
9[2],10[1],10[2],15,17,20,21; 13:5,7,11[1],11[2]
JAM 1:4[3],24,25[1]; 2:4,5[1],11,12[1],12[2],21,24,25;
3:1[2]; 4:1,11[2]; 5:12[1],16[1],16[2],17 1 PT 1:10[1],
10[2],12[1],12[2],12[3],14,16,20; 2:10[1],10[2],13,23[1],
23[2],23[3],25; 3:5[1],5[2],5[3],6[1],6[2],6[3],8[2],8[3],9,15,19,
20[1]; 4:9 2 PT 1:8,15[1],16[1],16[2],18,21; 2:1[1],
7[1],7[2],8[1],8[2],12,13[1],13[2],16,20,21; 3:5,18
1 JN 1:1,2; 2:7,13,16,18,19[1],19[2],19[3],19[4],21,
22; 3:12[1],12[2]; 4:1,10,17[2]; 5:6,16[1],16[2],17
2 JN 1,5[1],5[2],6,12[1] 3 JN 9[1],13 JUD 9,18[1]
REV 1:4,8,9,10,18; 2:8; 3:2[2],15[1]; 4:2,8,11;
5:4,11; 6:9,12[1],12[2],12[3]; 7:9,11; 8:1,2,5,7,8[1],
8[2],11; 9:9; 10:4,10; 11:1,11,13[1],13[2],15[1],15[2],
17,19; 12:4,6,7,10[1],10[2]; 13:2,11[1],11[2]; 14:8;
15:8; 16:2,3,4,5,10[1],10[2],17,18[1],18[2],18[3],18[4],
18[5],19; 17:4,8[1],8[2]; 18:2,23; 19:14; 21:6,15[1],
15[2],21

Imperfect

MAT 4:3,19; 5:7,18,37,45; 6:4,5,10,16,22,
23[1],23[2],23[3]; 8:12,13; 9:16,29; 10:15,22,25;
11:22,24; 12:27,40[2],45[2]; 13:40,42,49,50;
14:4[2]; 15:28; 16:19[1],19[2],22; 17:4,17,20; 18:3,
4,6[2],12,17,18[1],18[2],19; 19:5,16,21[2],27,30;
20:16,26[1],26[2],26[3],27[1],27[2]; 21:19,21[1],21[2];
22:13,28; 23:7,11; 24:3,6,7,9,20,21[1],21[3],27,
28,34,37,39,40,41,49,51; 25:30; 26:5[2],35,42,
54; 27:64 MRK 3:10[2],14,15; 5:18[2]; 6:23,
11; 9:5,19,23,35[1],35[2],50[1]; 10:8[1],12,21,31,
32[4],43[1],43[2],43[3],44[1],44[2]; 11:22,23[2],24; 12:7,
23; 13:4,7,8[1],8[2],13,18,19[1],19[3],30,34; 14:2[2],
31[2] LUK 1:14,15,20[1],20[2],32,33,34,38,66[2];
2:10,49[2]; 3:5; 4:3,7; 5:10[2]; 6:26[1],35[1],35[2],40;
8:38[2]; 9:3,33[1],41,48; 10:12,14; 11:2[2],19,30[2],
34[1],34[2],34[3],36; 12:20,34,35,52; 13:25,28[1],
28[2],30; 14:8,10,12[1],12[2],14,26,27,29,33; 15:7,
10; 16:2; 17:24,26[2],30,34,35,36; 18:5,22;
19:5,17,19; 20:14[2],16,33; 21:7[2],7[3],11[1],11[2],
11[3],14,17,23,24,25,28,32; 22:26,42,69;
23:24,31,43; 24:47 JHN 1:12; 3:15,16;
4:14,40[1]; 5:14,26,27,40; 6:40,45; 7:4,24;
8:6[1],33,36,58; 10:10[1],10[2],16[2]; 12:26,36,42[2];
13:19[1],35; 14:3,16,29[1]; 15:7,8,11; 16:20,24,
33[1]; 17:5[2],11[2],13,19,21[1],21[2],22,23,24[1],24[2],
26[1],26[2]; 19:24; 20:27,31 ACT 1:8,20[1],20[2],
22; 2:17,21; 3:2[3],23; 4:28,29,30; 5:15[3],40;
6:4; 7:6[2],19,42,43; 8:19; 10:41; 11:23[2];
12:20[2]; 13:11[1],43[3],47; 15:19,20,24,29[1];
16:4[3]; 17:26,27[1]; 18:13,15; 19:36; 21:14,21[1],
21[2],25; 22:15; 24:15,16,23,25; 26:11[3],22,23,
28,29[3]; 27:22,29[3] ROM 1:13,20,28; 3:4,
26; 4:11,13[3],16,18[1],18[2]; 5:1,18[2]; 6:5,13; 7:3[2],
4; 8:28,29; 9:3[2],9,12,26[1],27; 11:9,10,25[1],27,
31; 12:3[1],3[2],9[1]; 13:3[2]; 14:1,9; 15:4,12[1],12[2],
16[1],16[2],26,33; 16:19,20 1 CO 1:8,10[1],10[2],
10[3]; 2:5; 3:18[1],18[2]; 4:5[1],5[2],15; 5:7; 6:16; 7:7,
23,25,26,28[1],29,32,34[2],35[2],39; 8:9; 9:15,23;
10:7,20,24; 11:10,19,28,34; 12:25[1],25[2],26[1],
26[2],26[3]; 13:1[1],2[1],2[2],3; 14:9[1],24,26,34,40;
15:24,28,54,58[2]; 16:2[1],2[2],10,12[2],14,16,22
2 CO 1:6,9,11,17[2]; 3:6,8,11[2]; 4:7; 5:8,21[2];
6:3,14,16[1],16[2],18[1],18[2]; 7:12[1]; 8:13[2],14[2],14[3],
14[4]; 9:3,5[1],8; 11:15[2]; 12:7; 13:7[1],7[2],7[3],11[1],11[2]
GAL 1:8,9; 3:14; 4:17[2],20[2],21; 5:13[1],17,26;
6:4[1],4[2],9[2],14,16 EPH 1:4,12; 3:6,17; 4:4,
13,14,17,28[2],30; 5:7,17,27,31,33; 6:3
PHL 1:10[1],10[2],23[1]; 2:2,15,19,27[2],28; 3:21;
4:2,3,9,11[2] COL 1:18; 2:4; 3:9,19; 4:6[1],17
1 TH 3:5; 4:3,4,6,11[1],12,13,17 2 TH 1:4;
2:14; 3:1,12 1 TM 1:20; 2:1,9,12; 3:2[1],3,6,
8[1],8[2],11[1],11[2],11[3],11[4],12[1]; 4:6[1],6[2]; 5:7[2]; 6:1,18
2 TM 1:13; 2:14[2],24,25; 3:2,17; 4:3
TIT 1:7[1],7[2],7[3],7[4],7[5],7[6],8[1],8[2],8[3],8[4],8[5],13[2]; 2:2[1],
2[2],2[3],2[4],3[1],3[2],3[3],3[4],5[1],5[2],6,7; 3:1[2],2[1],2[2],7,14[1],
14[2] PLM 6,13[2],14 HEB 1:5[1],5[2]; 2:1,13,
17[2],17[3]; 3:12; 5:5[2]; 6:12[1],18; 7:11[3]; 8:3[2],10[1],
10[2]; 10:25; 11:25,35; 13:17 JAM 1:2,4[1],4[2],
18,19,23,25[2]; 2:1,5[2],15; 3:1[1]; 4:4[1],11[1]; 5:12[2],
13[1],13[2],13[3] 1 PT 1:2,21,22[1],22[2],22[3]; 2:12;
3:7,8[1],13,20[2]; 4:8,15; 5:3 2 PT 1:4,15[2];
2:1[2],6; 3:11 1 JN 1:3,4; 2:28; 3:2[1]; 4:17[1];
5:20 2 JN 3,12[2] 3 JN 2,8,9[2],15
JUD 18[2] REV 2:10[1]; 3:15[2]; 10:6,9; 20:6;
21:3[1],3[2],4[1],4[2],7[1],7[2],25,27; 22:3[1],3[2],5,14

Imperative

MAT 2:13; 5:48; 10:16; 24:44 LUK 6:36;
9:4; 10:7; 12:36,40; 21:36[1] ACT 15:29[2];
23:30 ROM 15:7 1 CO 14:20[2],20[3];
15:58[1],58[3] GAL 4:12[1] 1 TH 4:18; 5:16,
18 1 TM 4:12,15 TIT 2:9,10
HEB 6:12[2] JAM 1:22 1 PT 1:15; 2:2,5
REV 2:10[2]; 3:2[1]

Infinitive

MAT 19:21[1] LUK 18:27; 21:9,36[2]
JHN 1:46; 3:9; 9:27 1 CO 15:37[2]
1 TH 2:6[2] 1 TM 1:7; 5:11 HEB 5:12[2]
REV 1:1,19; 4:1; 22:6

Active Participle

MAT 12:45[1]; 13:22,32; 14:21[1]; 15:38[1];
22:30; 23:30[2]; 26:2; 27:24 MRK 2:21;
4:11,19,28,32; 12:25; 13:29; 14:1[1]

LUK 9:7[1],14[1]; 11:26; 12:54,55[1],55[2]; 13:17[5]; 17:17[2]; 20:34,35; 21:13,31 JHN 1:38; 8:55; 16:33[2] ACT 1:13[1]; 2:43[1],43[3]; 5:12[1], 16[3]; 7:14[2]; 8:13[4]; 11:28[2]; 12:9[4]; 19:7; 23:13[1]; 27:10 ROM 5:19[2]; 9:29[1] 1 CO 6:17; 7:28[2]; 10:18[2]; 11:21; 14:11[1],11[2]; 15:21[2] 2 CO 12:6 GAL 1:10[2]; 3:21[3] 2 TH 2:10 1 TM 6:4 2 TM 2:21 HEB 5:1; 6:8,16[2]; 7:16[2]; 8:4[2]; 11:6 JAM 2:13; 4:4[2],14,17; 5:3 1 PT 2:20; 4:12[1],12[2] 2 PT 1:14,20 1 JN 3:2[2]

---

752 ܗܘܢܐ (m) mind, reason

MRK 3:21
REV 13:18
REV 17:9

751 (ܗܘܢ) (v) be wise, prudent

[c]PAEL

Passive Participle

1 TH 5:6

---

757 ܗܝܕܝܢ (adv) then

from 748 ܗܘ and 670 ܕܝܢ

MAT 2:7,16,17; 3:5,13,15; 4:1,5,10,11,17; 5:12,24; 7:5,23; 8:26; 9:14,15,29; 11:20; 12:13,22,29,38,44,45; 13:26,36,43; 15:1,12, 28; 16:12,20,21,24,27; 17:13,19; 18:21,32; 19:13,27; 20:20; 22:8,13,15; 23:1; 24:9,10, 14,16,21,23,30,30,40; 25:1,7,31,34,37,41,44, 45; 26:3,14,16,31,36,45,50,52,56,65,67,74; 27:3,9,13,26,27; 28:10 MRK 2:20; 3:27; 13:14,21,26,27; 14:50 LUK 5:35; 6:42; 11:26; 14:21; 16:16; 21:20,21,27; 23:30; 24:25,45 JHN 2:10; 7:10; 8:28; 11:14; 13:27; 18:12; 19:1,16; 20:8,18 ACT 4:8, 15; 5:19,26; 6:11; 7:4,8; 8:17,35; 9:17,25; 10:21,48; 11:26; 12:11; 13:21; 15:22; 16:22; 17:9; 19:9; 20:11; 21:13,26; 23:31; 25:12; 26:1; 27:21,32; 28:14 ROM 6:21; 11:26,27 1 CO 4:5; 11:28; 13:10,12,12; 14:25; 15:24, 28,46,54; 16:2 2 CO 12:10 GAL 4:8,29; 6:4 COL 3:4 1 TH 2:2; 4:17; 5:3 2 TH 2:8 1 TM 2:13; 3:10 HEB 7:27; 10:7 1 PT 2:20 2 PT 3:6

---

758 ܗܝܟܠ, ܗܝܟܠܐ (m) temple

MAT 4:5
12:5,6
21:12,12,14,15,23
23:16,16,17,21,
MAT 23:35
24:1,1
26:55,61
27:5,40,51
MRK 11:11,15,15,16,27
MRK 12:35
13:1,3
14:49,58
15:29,38
LUK 1:9,21,22
2:27,37,46
4:9
11:51
18:10
19:45,47
20:1
21:5,37,38
22:4,52,53
23:45
24:53
JHN 2:14,15,19,20,21
5:14
7:14,28
8:2,20,59
10:23
11:56
18:20
ACT 2:46
3:1,2,2,3,8
4:1
ACT 5:20,21,24,25,42
17:24
19:27,37
21:26,27,28,29,30
22:17
24:6,12,18
25:8
26:21
1 CO 3:16,17,17
6:19
2 CO 6:16,16
EPH 2:21
2 TH 2:4
1 PT 2:5
REV 3:12
7:15
11:1,2,19,19
14:15,17
15:5,6,8,8
16:1,17
21:22,22

ܗܟܢܐ see under ܐܟܢܐ

---

760 ܗܟܘܬ (adv) likewise

MAT 20:5; 21:30,36; 22:26; 25:17; 26:35; 27:41,44 MRK 12:21 LUK 5:10; 6:31, 34; 9:15; 19:4; 20:31; 22:20 JHN 8:28; 14:31 ACT 27:17 2 CO 8:12 REV 2:15; 8:12

---

761 ܗܟܝܠ (conj) therefore

cf ܗܟܝܠ

MAT 1:17; 3:8,10; 5:19,23,48; 6:2,8,9,22,23, 31,34; 7:11,24; 9:38; 10:16,26,31,32; 12:26; 13:40,56; 17:10; 18:4; 19:6,7; 21:40; 22:9,17, 21,28,45; 23:3,20; 24:26,42; 25:13,28; 26:54; 27:64; 28:19 MRK 2:28; 9:11,40; 10:9; 12:9,23,27,37; 13:35; 15:12 LUK 3:8,9, 10; 4:7; 6:36; 7:31,42; 10:2,36; 11:34,35,48; 12:7,24,40; 16:11; 20:15,25,33,44; 21:36; 22:70; 23:16,22 JHN 1:21,25; 3:29; 6:45, 62; 7:53; 8:5,36; 9:30; 12:50; 13:14; 18:3,39 ACT 1:21; 2:36; 3:19; 6:3; 11:17; 13:38,40; 17:23,29; 19:36; 20:28; 21:22; 23:21; 25:5; 28:28 ROM 2:21; 3:1,7,9,27,28,31; 4:1,9, 10; 5:1,9,10,15,18; 6:1,8,12,15; 7:7,13,21,25; 8:31; 9:14,16,20,30; 10:14; 11:7,12,15,22,24; 12:1; 13:2,3,7,12; 14:8; 15:1,17,28; 16:19 1 CO 3:7; 4:16; 6:7,20; 7:5,38; 8:4; 9:18,26; 10:19,31; 11:20,27; 14:15,23,26,39; 15:11;

16:11,18 2 CO 1:17; 3:8,12; 4:13; 5:6,11, 17,20,20; 7:1; 8:23; 12:9 GAL 3:5,7,19,21, 24; 4:15,31; 5:1,25; 6:10 EPH 4:1; 5:1,7,8, 15; 6:14 PHL 2:1,28,29; 3:15 COL 2:6, 16; 3:1,5,12 1 TH 4:18; 5:6 1 TM 2:1,8; 5:9,14 2 TM 1:8; 2:1,21 PLM 17 HEB 3:12; 4:1,6,11,14,16; 7:11; 9:14; 10:19, 22,32,35; 12:3,7,9,25,28; 13:13 JAM 4:4,7 1 PT 2:1,7; 3:10; 4:1; 5:6,9 2 PT 3:11,17 1 JN 2:9; 4:19 3 JN 8 REV 1:19; 2:16, 25; 3:19

---

762 ܗܟܢ, ܗܟܢܐ (conj) thus

MAT 1:18; 2:5; 3:15; 5:12,16,19; 6:9,30; 7:12,17; 9:33; 11:26; 12:40,45; 13:40,49; 17:12; 18:14,35; 19:8,10,12; 20:16,26; 23:28; 24:27,33,37,39,46; 26:40,54 MRK 2:12; 4:26,40; 7:18; 9:21; 10:43; 13:29; 14:59; 15:31,39 LUK 1:60; 2:48; 3:11; 6:23,26, 33; 10:21,32,37; 11:2,30; 12:21,28,38,43,54; 13:2,3; 14:33; 15:7,10; 17:10,24,26,30; 19:31; 21:31; 22:26,36; 24:24,46,46 JHN 3:8,14,16; 5:21,26; 6:11; 7:46; 10:34; 11:48; 12:50; 15:4; 18:22; 19:19; 21:1 ACT 1:11,19; 3:18; 5:3; 7:1; 8:32; 12:8,15; 13:34,47; 14:1; 15:23; 16:18; 17:11,12,33; 19:12,20; 20:13,35; 21:11,11; 22:22; 23:11, 25; 24:9; 26:24; 27:25,44 ROM 1:15,27; 4:18; 5:3,11,12,15,16,18,19,21; 6:4,5,11,19; 8:26; 9:20; 10:5,6,19; 11:5,31; 12:5; 16:18 1 CO 2:11; 3:15; 4:1; 5:11; 6:5; 7:3,4,7,7,17, 17,22,26,28,37,40; 8:12; 9:14,15,24,26,26; 10:17; 11:12,24,25,25; 12:12; 14:9,12,21; 15:11,11,21,22,42,45,48,48,49; 16:1,16,18 2 CO 1:5; 2:7; 3:4; 4:11; 7:14; 8:6,7,11,19; 9:5; 10:7,11,11; 11:3 GAL 2:13; 3:3; 4:3, 29; 6:2 EPH 4:20; 5:8,24,28,33; 6:9 PHL 1:7,13; 2:18,22,29; 3:17; 4:1 COL 3:13,20 1 TH 2:4,8,14; 4:10,14,17; 5:2 2 TH 3:17 1 TM 2:9; 3:8,11; 5:25 2 TM 3:5,8 TIT 2:3,6; 3:11 PLM 12 HEB 1:7; 5:3,5,9; 6:9,15; 7:12; 9:5,28; 12:21 JAM 1:10,11; 2:12,12,17,25,26; 3:5,10,12; 5:8 1 PT 2:15; 3:1,5,7,17; 4:13 2 PT 1:11; 3:4 1 JN 4:11,17 REV 2:1,8, 12,15,18,27; 3:1,5,7,14; 9:17; 11:5; 16:18; 18:7,21

---

763 (ܗܠܠ)(v) praise

cPAEL

Active Participle

LUK 2:20

767 ܗܠܠܘܝܐ (intrj) hallelujah

REV 19:1,3,4,6

1532 (ܗܠ), ܠܗܠ (adv) far, far off

MAT	8:30	HEB	7:8
ACT	7:43	JAM	2:3
2 CO	10:16		

---

765 ܗܠܟ (v) walk

aPEAL (non occ)

766 ܗܠܟܬܐ (f) walk, way

1 JN 2:6

---

cPAEL

Perfect

MAT	14:29	EPH	2:2
JHN	5:9	COL	3:7
ACT	3:8[1]	2 TH	3:7
	14:8,10	1 TM	5:10
	16:6	HEB	13:9
2 CO	12:18		

Imperfect

MRK	12:38	EPH	4:1
JHN	8:12		5:15
	11:10	COL	1:10
ACT	3:12	1 TH	2:12
ROM	6:4		4:1
	8:12	1 PT	2:21
	13:13	1 JN	2:6
1 CO	7:17	2 JN	6[1]
2 CO	6:16	REV	16:15
EPH	2:10		

Imperative

MAT	9:5	JHN	12:35[1]
MRK	1:38	ACT	3:6
	2:9	EPH	5:2,8
LUK	5:23	COL	2:6
JHN	5:8,11,12		4:5
	11:15		

Infinitive

LUK	20:46	REV	9:20
JHN	7:1[2]		

Active Participle

MAT	4:18	MRK	5:42
	11:5		6:48,49
	12:1		7:5
	14:25,26		8:24
	15:31		11:27
MRK	1:16		16:12
	2:23	LUK	1:6

LUK	6:1	2 CO	5:7
	7:22		10:2,3
	11:44	GAL	5:16
	24:15,17	EPH	4:17[1],17[2]
JHN	1:36	PHL	3:17,18
	6:19,66	1 TH	4:12
	7:1[1]	2 TH	3:6,11
	10:23	1 PT	5:8
	11:9,54	2 PT	3:3
	12:35[2]	1 JN	1:6,7
	21:18		2:11
ACT	3:8[2],9	2 JN	4,6[2]
	21:21	3 JN	3,4
ROM	8:1,4	JUD	16
	14:15	REV	2:1
1 CO	3:3		3:4
2 CO	4:2		21:24

769 (ܗܡܐ)(v) neglect, cease

eAPHEL

Imperfect

HEB 12:5

Active Participle

ACT 18:17 | 2 CO 10:9

770 ܗܢ, ܗܢܐ (pron) this, these

incl ܗܕܐ, ܗܠܝܢ

incl comp with 747 ܗܘ

see also 1694 ܡܛܠ

MAT 1:20,22; 3:3,9,17; 4:3,9; 5:19,19,37,46,47; 6:25,32,32,33; 7:12,24,26,28; 8:9,9,10,27; 9:3,8,18,26,28; 10:2,5,23,42; 11:10,16,25; 12:23,24,27,31,32,41,42,45; 13:13,15,19,22,28,34,40,51,52,53,54,54,55,56,56; 14:2,2,7; 15:8,12,15,20,32,33,36; 16:3,18,22; 17:5,9,20,21; 18:4,5,6,10,14,23; 19:1,5,11,14,20,22,26; 20:12,14,21; 21:2,4,10,11,16,21,21,23,23,24,27,31,38,42,43,44; 22:20,28,38,40; 23:13,23,23,34,36,36; 24:2,3,8,14,33,34,34,43,44; 25:1,40,45,46; 26:1,8,9,12,12,13,13,26,28,29,31,34,39,42,56,61,62,71; 27:3,8,14,24,32,37,47,54,58; 28:14,15 MRK 1:27,27,38; 2:7,8,8; 4:13,15,15,16,18,19,20,33,41; 5:13,32,43; 6:2,2,2,3,14,25,35; 7:6,8,13,23,29; 8:2,4,12,12,19,38; 9:7,10,29,37,42; 10:5,7,10,13,14,20,22,27,30; 11:3,23,28,28,28,29,33; 12:7,10,11,12,16,24,30,31,43,44; 13:2,4,4,8,17,29,30,30; 14:4,8,9,9,22,24,27,30,36,49,58,60,69,71; 15:12,26,39; 16:12,17 LUK 1:18,19,20,20,25,29,32,34,35,36,43,61,65,66; 2:2,12,15,19,25,27,34; 3:8,20; 4:3,6,18,21,22,23,36,43; 5:6,21,27; 6:3; 7:4,8,8,9,9,17,18,27,31,39,44,44,45,46,47,49; 8:1,8,9,11,13,13,14,15,21,25; 9:9,9,13,21,24,28,34,35,44,45,45,48,48; 10:1,5,11,20,21,28,36; 11:15,19,27,29,30,31,32,42,42,45,49,50,51,53; 12:5,18,20,20,22,27,29,30,30,31,39,41,56; 13:2,6,7,8,16,16,17,32; 14:6,9,12,15,20,21,30; 15:2,3,24,26,30,32; 16:2,8,8,9,14,24,26,28; 17:2,6,16,17,18,25; 18:5,9,11,11,14,16,21,23,30,34,34,34,36; 19:9,9,11,14,19,28,40,42; 20:2,2,8,9,14,16,19,30,34; 21:3,4,4,6,7,7,9,12,22,23,28,31,32,32,36; 22:15,19,19,20,23,37,42,47,51,53,56,59; 23:2,4,14,14,18,22,31,38,41,46,47,48,49,51,52,55; 24:1,4,9,10,11,14,17,18,21,26,36,40,44,48 JHN 1:2,7,15,19,27,28,30,31,33,34,41,50; 2:11,12,16,18,19,20,22; 3:2,2,9,10,19,22,29; 4:10,12,13,15,18,18,20,21,23,31,37,42,47,54; 5:1,3,6,12,16,16,18,19,20,28,34; 6:1,5,6,9,9,14,24,27,29,34,39,40,42,42,50,51,52,58,58,59,60,61,61,65,66; 7:1,4,8,8,9,15,22,25,26,27,31,31,32,35,36,39,40,41,46,49; 8:4,5,6,20,23,23,26,30,40,47; 9:2,6,8,16,16,19,20,22,23,24,29,30,33,33,39,40; 10:3,6,16,17,18,19,21,41; 11:2,2,4,9,11,26,28,37,37,39,42,42,43,47,51; 12:5,6,16,16,16,18,18,21,25,27,27,27,30,31,31,33,34,36,37,39,41; 13:1,1,11,15,17,21,24,25,28,35; 14:9,10,12,24,25; 15:5,8,11,12,13,17,19,21; 16:1,3,4,4,6,11,15,17,18,19,25,30,33; 17:1,3,11,13,20; 18:1,8,17,22,29,34,36,36,37,37,38,39,40,40; 19:8,11,12,12,13,19,20,24,28,31,36,38; 20:14,18,20,22,30,31; 21:1,7,11,14,15,19,19,21,21,22,23,23,24,24 ACT 1:6,7,9,11,14,17,18,19,21,21,24; 2:7,12,13,14,15,16,22,23,23,26,32,33,36,37,40; 3:3,12,12,12,16,16,17; 4:1,7,9,10,10,11,16,17,17,22,27; 5:4,5,5,8,8,20,24,24,28,31,32,33,35,36,38,38,38; 6:3,5,6,13,13,14,14; 7:1,4,7,7,29,35,35,36,37,38,40,45,50,54,60,60; 8:10,19,21,22,24,32,34,35; 9:2,13,21,21,21,22,36,39,42; 10:3,16,36,39,42,44; 11:10,12,18,20,22,28; 12:3,15,17,22; 13:7,8,17,23,27,37,38,39,42; 14:9,15,18; 15:2,6,15,16,17,19,25,27,28,29,39; 16:3,10,12,14,17,20,24,35,36,38; 17:3,6,7,7,8,11,18,19,20,23,30,32; 18:10,13,15,17,25; 19:5,10,14,17,21,25,25,26,27,28,36,37,38,40,41; 20:2,5,26,31,34,36; 21:4,5,11,12,14,15,20,26,28,28,28,38; 22:3,4,22,26; 23:7,9,9,13,16,17,18,22,27; 24:2,5,8,9,10,10,14,14,15,16,18,20,21,22,26; 25:3,9,11,20,20,22,24,24,26; 26:3,7,7,10,12,16,19,21,22,26,26,26,29,31,32; 27:21,23,25,31,34,35,43; 28:4,9,20,20,20,22,25,26,27,28,28 ROM 1:24,26,32,32; 2:1,3; 3:25,26; 4:9,14,22,23; 5:2,6; 7:8,17,18,24; 8:9,14,18,31,37; 9:8,9,9,10,17; 10:3,5,8,12; 11:5,20,25,31; 12:2,20; 13:2,5,6,6,9,11; 14:9,13,18; 15:7,22,23,26,28,28; 16:4,25 1 CO 1:12,20,20; 2:6,6,8; 3:11,12,18,19; 4:3,4,6,11,14,17; 5:1,2,3,5,10,11; 6:3,10,11; 7:6,15,26,29,31,31,35; 8:3,9; 9:3,8,8,12,15,15,17,23,25; 10:6,11,28; 11:10,16,16,17,22,24,25,26,26,28,28,28,30; 12:11,15,16,23; 13:11,13; 14:21,23,37; 15:7,19,50,53,53,54,54 2 CO 1:12,15,17,20; 2:1,3,4,6,8,9,16; 3:10,12; 4:1,1,4,7,11,13,16,17,18,18; 5:1,2,4,5,14; 6:17; 7:1,11,12,13; 8:6,7,10,14,14,16,19,20,20; 9:2,3,5,5,6,12,13; 10:7,11; 11:10,12,13,14,17; 12:2,3,5,8,10,13,13,14; 13:1,2,9,10,10 GAL 1:4,20,21,22,23; 2:6,

10,13,20; 3:2,4,10,11,17; 4:24,25; 5:21,21, 23; 6:13,16 EPH 1:15,21; 2:2,2,2,8,11; 3:1,8,13,13; 4:8,17,25; 5:4,4,5,6,14,27,31,32; 6:1,2,12,13,16,22 PHL 1:6,9,18,19,22,23, 25,29; 2:5,6,9,22,23; 3:7,15,15,16,19; 4:8,9, 9,22 COL 1:9,27,29; 2:4,17,22; 3:6,7,8,14; 4:8,8,11,16,18 1 TH 2:13,14; 3:3,3,5,7; 4:3,6,6,15,18; 5:18,27 2 TH 1:11; 2:5,14; 3:10,12,14,14 1 TM 1:4,6,18,18,19,20; 2:3; 3:10,14,16; 4:2,6,8,10,11,15,16; 5:4,5,7, 8,21; 6:2,2,4,5,11,17 2 TM 1:12,12,15,15; 2:14,18,19,21; 3:1; 4:10,16 TIT 1:5,11,13; 2:12,15; 3:8,8 PLM 8,15,18 HEB 1:2,4, 9; 2:1,11,14,17; 3:1,3,10,14,16; 5:11; 6:1,3, 11,17; 7:1,4,6,13,21,22,22,24,26,27; 8:3,3,5, 7,10; 9:5,8,9,11,15,18,20,23,23,23,23; 10:1, 5,9,10,12,16,33; 11:2,3,12,13,14,16,19,39; 12:1,1,1,12,27; 13:2,11,12,16,17,19 JAM 1:15,21,23,25,26,27; 2:8; 3:2,8,10,15; 4:4,4,6,15,16 1 PT 1:6,12,13,17,20,25; 2:7,8,11,19,21,21; 3:9,9,20; 4:1,6,7,16,19; 5:9,10,12,12,12 2 PT 1:4,5,8,9,10,12,12, 12,13,15,17,17,18,20; 2:2,3,7,12,17,17,19, 20,22; 3:1,1,3,5,6,8,11,13,14,14,16,16,16 1 JN 1:4,5; 2:1,3,5,5,16,18,22,25,26; 3:1,3,8, 10,11,14,16,19,23,24; 4:2,3,5,5,6,9,10,13,17, 17,21; 5:2,3,4,6,9,10,11,13,14,16,20 2 JN 6,6,7,9,10 3 JN 4,8,10,10 JUD 4, 7,8,10,12,13,14,16,19 REV 1:2,3,4,19; 2:6,24; 4:1,1; 7:1,13,14,15; 9:13,18,20; 11:4, 6; 12:17; 13:4; 14:4,4,4; 15:5; 16:5,9,18; 17:13,14,16; 18:1,15,17; 19:1,9,10; 20:3,4,5, 6,14; 21:5,7; 22:6,7,8,8,9,9,10,16,18,18,19, 19,20

---

771 ܗܢܐ (v) profit

aPEAL (non occ)

772 ܗܢܝܘܬܐ (f) pleasure

2 PT 2:13

773 ܗܢܝܐ (m) profit

JAM 2:14,16

---

bETHPEEL

Perfect

1 CO 15:32

Imperfect

MAT 15:5

Participle

MAT 16:26

---

eAPHEL

Active Participle

JHN 6:63
ROM 2:25
GAL 5:2

---

775 ܗܦܟ (v) turn, return

aPEAL

Perfect

MAT 21:18
MRK 11:15
14:40
LUK 1:56
2:20,39,43,45
4:1,14
7:10
8:37,40,55
9:10
10:17
17:15
19:15
23:48,56
24:9,33,52
JHN 2:15
ACT 1:12
5:22
7:39,42
8:25,28
12:14
14:21
21:6
22:17
GAL 1:17
4:9
2 TM 1:15
HEB 7:1
2 PT 2:22
REV 1:12

Imperfect

MAT 2:12
7:6
12:44
LUK 10:6
11:24
19:12
ACT 13:34
ACT 15:16
20:3
23:32
26:18
1 CO 7:18
HEB 11:15
2 PT 2:21

Imperative

LUK 8:39

Active Participle

LUK 10:35
ROM 11:29
2 CO 7:10

774 ܗܘܦܟܐ (m) overthrow

2 PT 2:6

776 ܗܘܦܟܬܐ (f) return, answer

1 TM 6:20

---

bETHPEEL

Imperfect

MAT 18:3
24:18
MRK 13:16
LUK 17:31
JAM 4:9

Participle

GAL 1:6

---

[c]PAEL (non occ)

753 ܗܘܦܟܐ (m) conduct, behavior

ROM 8:13	JAM 3:13
GAL 1:13	1 PT 1:15
EPH 4:22	2:12
COL 3:9	2 PT 2:7
1 TM 4:12	3:11
JAM 1:11	

---

[d]ETHPAAL

Perfect

2 CO 1:12	EPH 2:3

Infinitive

1 TM 3:15

Participle

MAT 17:22	ROM 2:1,2,3[1],3[2]
JHN 3:22	COL 3:7
11:54	TIT 3:3
ACT 4:13	2 PT 2:18

---

[e]APHEL

Perfect

MAT 27:3	ACT 19:26
ACT 15:24	

Imperfect

ACT 20:30	2 TM 4:4
ROM 11:26	REV 11:6

Imperative

MAT 26:52

Active Participle

LUK 23:14	JAM 5:20
2 TM 2:18	JUD 4
JAM 3:3	

---

777 ܗܓܡܘܢܐ (m-non occ) prefect

754 ܗܓܡܘܢܝܐ (f) province

ACT 23:34

---

778 ܗܪ (v) fight, hurt

[a]PEAL

Imperfect

REV 2:11

---

[e]APHEL

Imperfect

MRK 16:18	REV 6:6
LUK 10:19	7:2,3
11:7	9:4
HEB 12:15	11:5[1],5[2]

Infinitive

ACT 18:10	REV 9:10

Active Participle

MRK 14:6	LUK 18:5

---

785 ܗܪܟܐ (adv) here

see also 792 ܗܪܬܡܢ

MAT 12:6,42; 14:8,18; 24:2,23,23; 26:36,38 MRK 6:38; 8:4; 9:5; 13:2,21; 14:32,34 LUK 4:23; 9:27,33; 11:31,32; 15:17; 16:25; 17:21,23; 22:38; 23:5 JHN 4:15,16; 6:25; 20:27 ACT 9:14,21; 10:18; 16:28; 17:6; 25:10,24 ROM 5:8 1 CO 4:2 PHL 2:20 HEB 4:5; 7:8; 13:14 JAM 2:3, 3 REV 4:1; 13:10,18; 14:12; 17:9

---

784 (ܗܪܡ),

ܗܪܘܡܐ (m)

spices

MRK 16:1	LUK 24:1
LUK 23:56	

---

791 ܗܪܣܝܣ (f) heresy

2 PT 2:1

790 ܗܪܣܝܘܛܐ (adj) heretic

TIT 3:10

792 ܗܪܬܡܢ (adv) there

from 785 ܗܪܟܐ and 3402 ܬܡܢ

MRK 13:21 | LUK 17:21,23

793 ܗܫ, ܗܫܐ (adv) now

MAT 3:15; 9:18; 11:12; 15:16; 16:9; 23:39; 24:21; 26:29,53,64,65; 27:42,43
MRK 8:17,21; 10:30; 13:19; 15:32
LUK 1:48; 5:10; 6:21,21,25; 11:39; 12:52; 15:17; 16:25; 19:42; 22:36,69; 24:29,41
JHN 1:51; 2:10; 4:18,23; 5:17,25; 7:6,8; 8:11,40,52; 9:19,21,25,41; 11:8,22; 12:27,31, 31; 13:7,19,31,33,36,37; 14:7,29; 15:22,24; 16:5,12,22,24,29,30,32; 17:5,7,13; 18:36; 20:29; 21:10 ACT 2:15; 3:17; 4:29; 5:38; 7:34; 10:5,30; 12:11; 13:11,31; 15:10; 16:36, 37; 18:6; 19:40; 20:22,25,32; 22:16; 23:15; 24:13,25; 26:6; 27:22 ROM 1:13; 3:21; 5:9,11; 6:19,22; 7:4,6,17,25; 8:12; 11:30,31; 13:11; 14:19; 15:23,25 1 CO 3:2; 4:13; 7:14; 8:7; 12:18,20; 13:12,12; 14:6; 15:6,20; 16:7 2 CO 4:12; 5:4,16; 6:2,2; 8:11,22; 13:2 GAL 1:9,10,10,23; 2:20; 3:3; 4:9,20, 29; 5:21; 6:10 EPH 2:13; 3:5; 4:17; 5:8
PHL 1:5,20,30; 2:12,25; 3:18 COL 1:21, 26; 3:8 1 TH 3:6,8 2 TH 2:6,7; 3:1
1 TM 5:15 2 TM 1:10; 4:8 PLM 9,11
HEB 2:8; 5:12; 8:6; 9:26; 10:20; 11:16; 12:26
1 PT 1:12; 2:10,10,25; 4:4 2 PT 3:7,18
1 JN 2:9,18,28; 3:2,2; 4:3 2 JN 5
JUD 25 REV 14:13

ܘ

794 ܘܝ (intrj) woe

MAT 11:21,21; 18:7,7; 23:13,14,15,16,23, 25,27,29; 24:19; 26:24 MRK 13:17; 14:21 LUK 6:24,25,25,26; 10:13,13; 11:42,43,44, 46,47,52; 17:1; 21:23; 22:22 1 CO 9:16 JUD 11 REV 8:13,13,13; 9:12,12; 11:14, 14; 12:12; 18:10,10,10,16,16,19,19

795 (ܘܠܐ)(v) it is right

[a]PEAL

Active Participle

MAT 17:10
18:33
20:4,7
23:23
24:6
25:27
26:54
MRK 9:11
13:14
LUK 2:49
4:43
11:42
12:12
13:14,16,33
15:32
19:5
22:37
24:44
JHN 3:7,30
4:20,24
9:4
10:16
ACT 1:21
3:21
4:12
5:29,35
9:6
13:46
14:22
15:5
16:30

ACT 18:14,21
19:21,36
20:35
22:22
24:19
25:24,27
26:8
ROM 1:28
2:18
8:26
12:3
1 CO 7:36
8:2
9:10,12
2 CO 1:17
2:3,7
11:30
12:1
EPH 5:28
6:20
COL 4:4,6
1 TH 4:1
2 TH 1:3
3:7
1 TM 3:2,7,15
5:13
2 TM 2:6
TIT 1:11[1],11[2]
JAM 3:10
1 JN 2:6
REV 3:15

797 ܘܥܕܐ (m) appointed (place)

ACT 20:13

796 (ܘܥܕ) (v) appoint

[c]PAEL

Perfect

MAT 28:16

ܘܥܕܬܐ see under ܥܕܬܐ

ܙ

803 ܙܒܠܐ (m) dung

LUK 14:35	PHL 3:8

802 (ܙܒܠ) (v) manure

[c]PAEL

Imperfect

LUK 13:8

804 ܙܒܢ (v) buy; (pa) sell

[a]PEAL

Perfect

MAT 13:44[2],46[2]	LUK 14:18,19
27:7	ACT 7:16
MRK 15:46	GAL 3:13
16:1	2 PT 2:1
LUK 9:13	REV 5:9

Imperfect

MAT 14:15	JHN 13:29
MRK 6:36,37	GAL 4:5
LUK 22:36[2]	REV 3:18
JHN 4:8	13:17[1]
6:5	

Imperative

MAT 25:9[2]	COL 4:5

Infinitive

MAT 25:10

Active Participle

MAT 21:12[1]	1 CO 7:30
MRK 11:15[1]	EPH 5:16
LUK 17:28[1]	REV 18:11
19:45[1]	

Passive Participle

REV 14:3

[b]ETHPEEL

Perfect

1 CO 6:20	REV 14:4
7:23	

[c]PAEL

Perfect

MAT 13:44[1],46[1]	ACT 7:9
ACT 4:37	HEB 12:16
5:1,8	

Imperfect

LUK 22:36[1]	REV 13:17[2]

Imperative

MAT 19:21	LUK 12:33
MRK 10:21	18:22

Active Participle

MAT 21:12[2],12[3]	JHN 2:14,16
25:9[1]	ACT 2:45
MRK 11:15[2],15[3]	4:34[1]
LUK 17:28[2]	16:14
19:45[2]	

Passive Participle

ROM 7:14

[d]ETHPAAL

Perfect

JHN 12:5	ACT 5:4[2]

Imperfect

MAT 18:25	ACT 5:4[1]
26:9	

Infinitive

MRK 14:5

Participle

MAT 10:29
LUK 12:6
ACT 4:34[2]
1 CO 10:25

805 ܙܒܢ, ܙܒܢܐ (m) (incl f) time

see also 1428 ܟܠ ܙܒܢ

MAT 2:7,16; 8:29; 11:25; 12:1; 13:21,30; 14:1; 16:3; 17:15,15; 18:21,21,22; 21:34,41; 23:37; 24:45; 25:19; 26:18,34,42,44,75
MRK 1:15; 4:17; 9:21,22; 10:30; 11:13; 12:2; 13:33; 14:30,41,72,72
LUK 1:20,57; 4:13; 8:13,13,27,29; 12:42,56; 13:1,34; 17:4,4; 18:4,30; 19:44; 20:9,10; 21:8,24; 22:32,34,61; 23:8,22
JHN 3:4; 5:4,4,6,14; 7:6,6,8,33; 9:24; 12:16,35; 13:38; 18:2; 21:14,16,17,17
ACT 1:6,7,7,21; 3:19,21; 5:36; 7:13,17,20; 8:9,11; 10:15,16; 11:10; 12:1; 13:11; 14:3,17,28; 15:33; 17:26,30,30,32; 18:2; 19:22,23; 27:9
ROM 1:13; 3:26; 5:6; 6:10; 8:18; 9:9; 11:5; 13:11; 15:22; 16:24,25
1 CO 4:5; 7:5,26,29,36; 16:7
2 CO 4:17,18; 6:2,2; 8:14; 11:23,24,25,25,25; 12:8,14; 13:1,2
GAL 1:23; 4:1,2,4,10; 6:9,10
EPH 1:10; 2:12
PHL 3:18; 4:16
1 TH 2:17,18; 4:6; 5:1
2 TH 2:6
1 TM 2:6; 4:1,8,8; 6:15
2 TM 1:9,16; 3:1; 4:2,2,3,6
TIT 1:2,3; 3:10
PLM 11
HEB 4:7,16; 5:12; 6:4,7; 7:27; 9:5,8,9,10,12,25,26,26,27,28,28; 10:2,10,37; 11:11,15,25,32; 12:10,11,26,27
1 PT 1:5,6,11,17,20; 3:18; 4:2,3,17; 5:6
1 JN 2:18,18
JUD 3,5,18
REV 1:3; 2:21; 6:11; 10:6,11; 11:18; 12:12; 20:3; 22:10

801 (ܙܒܪ), ܙܒܘܪܐ (m) bowl, platter

MAT 23:25,26
REV 5:8; 15:7; 16:1,2,3,4,8,10,12,17; 17:1; 21:9

806 ܙܓܘܓܝܐ (adj-non occ) glass

807 ܙܓܘܓܝܬܐ (f) glass

REV 4:6; 15:2,2; 21:18,21

808 ܙܓܪ (v) confine, hinder

[a]PEAL

Passive Participle

MRK 4:39

815 (ܙܕܩ), ܙܕܩܐ (adj) just; (impers) it is right

LUK 24:46
ACT 1:16; 25:10
ROM 1:27; 16:2
1 CO 11:20
PHL 1:7
COL 1:10; 3:18
PLM 8
HEB 2:17; 7:26; 8:3
1 PT 5:6
2 PT 3:11
1 JN 3:16
REV 1:1

816 ܙܕܩܐ (m) just

1 CO 7:31

817 ܙܕܩܬܐ (f) alms

MAT	6:1,2,3,4	ACT	9:36
LUK	11:41		10:2,4,31
	12:33		24:17
ACT	3:2,3,10		

814 (ܙܕܩ) (v) justify, approve

cPAEL

Perfect

LUK	7:29	ROM	8:30¹,30²
ACT	3:13		

Imperfect

ROM	3:26	ROM	4:25

Infinitive

LUK 10:29

Active Participle

LUK	16:15	ROM	4:5
ROM	3:30		8:33

Passive Participle

LUK 18:14

811 ܙܕܝܩܐ (adj) righteous, just

MAT	9:13	LUK	20:20
	10:41,41, 41		23:47,50
		ACT	3:14
	13:17,43, 49		7:52
			10:2
	23:28,29, 35,35		22:14
		GAL	3:11
	25:37,46	JAM	5:6,16
	27:19,24	1 PT	3:12,18
MRK	2:17		4:18
	6:20	2 PT	2:7,8
LUK	1:6	1 JN	1:9
	2:25		2:1,29
	5:32		3:7,7,12
	14:14	REV	16:5,7
	15:7		22:11
	18:9		

812 ܙܕܝܩܐܝܬ (adv) justly

1 CO 15:34

813 ܙܕܝܩܘܬܐ (f) righteousness

MAT	6:33	1 CO	1:30
LUK	1:75	2 CO	3:9
JHN	16:8,10		5:21
ACT	24:25		6:7,14
ROM	4:3,6		9:9,10
2 CO	11:15	HEB	12:11
GAL	2:21	JAM	1:20
	3:6,21		2:23
	5:5		3:18
EPH	4:24	1 PT	2:24
	5:9	2 PT	1:1
	6:14		2:21
PHL	1:11		3:13
	3:6,9,9	1 JN	2:29
1 TM	6:11		3:7,10
TIT	3:5	REV	22:11

dETHPAAL

Perfect

MAT	11:19	1 CO	4:4
LUK	7:35		6:11
ROM	4:2	1 TM	3:16
	5:1	JAM	2:21,25

Imperfect

MAT	12:37	GAL	2:16²,17
ACT	13:39¹		3:24
ROM	4:16	1 TM	5:4
	5:9	TIT	3:7

Participle

ACT	13:39²	GAL	2:16¹,16³
ROM	2:13		3:8,11
	3:20,24,28		5:4
	10:10	JAM	2:24

818 ܙܗܝ (v-non occ) be pure

aPEAL

819 ܙܗܝܐܝܬ (adv) perfectly, circumspectly

EPH 5:15

822 ܙܗܪ (v) shine

eAPHEL

Passive Participle

MRK 9:3

824 ܙܗܪܐ (m-non occ) caution

820 ܙܗܝܪܐ (adj) cautious

GAL	6:1	HEB	12:15
HEB	2:1		

821 ܙܗܝܪܐܝܬ (adv) surely, safely

MRK 14:44; ACT 5:23; ACT 16:23

823 (ܙܗܪ) (v) (ethpe) take heed; (w/ ܡܢ) beware of; (w/ ܒ) take care of; (pa) warn

[b]ETHPEEL

Perfect

MAT 27:66

Imperfect

MAT 16:11,12; ROM 16:17; 1 CO 10:12

Imperative

MAT 7:15, 10:17, 16:6, 24:4, 27:65; MRK 8:15, 12:38, 13:23; LUK 11:35, 12:1,15, 17:3, 20:46, 21:34; ACT 5:35; ACT 13:40, 20:28; PHL 3:2[1],2[2],2[3]; COL 2:8, 4:17; 1 TH 5:15; 1 TM 4:16, 6:20; 2 TM 4:15; HEB 3:12, 12:25; 2 JN 8; REV 3:3

Participle

MAT 27:64

---

[c]PAEL

Perfect

MRK 7:36[1]; LUK 8:56; LUK 9:21

Active Participle

MRK 7:36[2]; PHL 3:1

---

833 (ܙܘܐ), ܙܘܝܬܐ (f) corner

MAT 6:5, 21:42; MRK 12:10; LUK 20:17; 1 PT 2:6; REV 7:1, 20:8

---

826 ܙܘܓܐ (m) yoke, pair

LUK 2:24, 14:19; 2 CO 6:14; PHL 4:3

825 (ܙܘܓ) (v) join together, marry

[c]PAEL

Perfect

MAT 19:6; MRK 10:9

829 ܙܘܘܓܐ (m) marriage

HEB 13:4

---

[d]ETHPAAL

Imperfect

1 CO 7:9,36; 1 TM 5:14

Infinitive

1 TM 4:3

---

828 ܙܘܕܐ (m-non occ) provision

827 (ܙܘܕ) (v) supply provision

[c]PAEL

Perfect

ACT 28:10

Active Participle

3 JN 6

---

830 ܙܘܙܐ (m) coin

MAT 17:24,24; LUK 15:8,9

---

831 (ܙܘܚ) (v-non occ) be exalted

[a]PEAL

832 ܙܘܚܐ (m) pomp, magnificence

ACT 25:23

835 (ܙܘܥ)(v) be shaken, confused;
(aph, p) shake, trouble

[a]PEAL

Perfect

ACT 12:15[2]

Imperfect

ACT 2:25

Infinitive

ACT 12:15[1]

Passive Participle

2 PT 2:10

836 ܙܘܥܐ (m) earthquake, shaking

MAT 8:24	LUK 21:11,26
24:7	JHN 5:3,4
27:54	ACT 16:26
28:2	REV 11:13,13
MRK 13:8	16:18

[e]APHEL

Perfect

JHN 11:33	HEB 12:26[1]
ACT 21:38,40	

Imperfect

LUK 6:48	HEB 12:26[2]

Infinitive

ACT 17:13

Active Participle

JHN 5:4	REV 2:5
ACT 9:22	

[f]ETTAPHAL

Perfect

MAT 2:3	JHN 5:7
14:26	ACT 4:31
21:10	16:26
27:51	21:31
28:4	REV 6:14

Imperfect

MAT 24:29	ACT 20:10
MRK 13:25	2 TH 2:2
LUK 21:26	HEB 6:19

Participle

MAT 11:7	PHL 1:28
LUK 7:24	COL 1:23
24:38	HEB 12:27[1],27[2],28
ACT 17:28	
27:41	1 PT 3:6
1 CO 15:58	REV 6:13

[m]ETHP ܐܙܕܘܥ

Participle

EPH 4:14

837 ܙܘܦܐ (f) hissop

JHN 19:29	HEB 9:19

839 ܙܚܘܪܝܬܐ (f) scarlet

MAT 27:28	REV 17:4
LUK 23:11	18:12,16
HEB 9:19	

840 ܙܛܡܐ (m) question

ACT 18:15	ACT 25:19
23:29	26:3

841 ܙܝܙܢܐ (m) tare, weed

MAT 13:25,26,27,29,	MAT 13:30,36,38,40

842 ܙܝܢܐ (m) armor

LUK 11:22	2 CO 6:7
JHN 18:3	10:4
ROM 6:13,13	EPH 6:11,13
13:12	

834 (ܙܝܢ) (v) arm

[c]PAEL

Passive Participle

LUK 11:21

[d]ETHPAAL

Imperative

1 PT 4:1

843 ܙܝܬܐ (m) olive; (w/ ܛܘܪܐ) Mt of Olives

MAT 21:1	LUK 22:39
24:3	JHN 8:1
26:30	ACT 1:12
MRK 11:1	ROM 11:17,17,
13:3	24,24,
14:26	24
LUK 19:29,37	JAM 3:12
21:37	REV 11:4

844 ܙܟܐ (v) overcome

[a]PEAL

Perfect

JHN 16:33	REV 3:21[2]
HEB 11:33	5:5
1 JN 2:13,14	12:11
4:4	15:2
5:4[2]	21:7
REV 2:26	

Imperfect

LUK 11:22	REV 6:2[2]
ROM 3:4	11:7
12:21[1]	17:14

Imperative

ROM 12:21[2]

Infinitive

REV 13:7

Active Participle

1 JN 5:4[1],5	REV 3:5,12,21[1]
REV 2:7,11,17	6:2[1]

Passive Participle

2 PT 2:19

845 ܙܟܘܬܐ (f) victory

MAT 12:20	1 CO 15:54,55,
LUK 1:51	57
ROM 5:18	PHL 3:14
1 CO 9:24	1 JN 5:4

[b]ETHPEEL

Participle

2 PT 2:20

[c]PAEL (non occ)

847 ܙܟܝܐ (adj) victorious, innocent

MAT 27:4	REV 6:2
ROM 8:37	

851 ܙܠܓܐ (m-non occ) brilliance

850 (ܙܠܓ) (v) shine

[e]APHEL

Perfect

ACT 9:3	ACT 22:6
12:7	26:13

852 ܙܠܗܙ (v) be lacking

[m]ETHP

Perfect

1 CO 7:29

853 ܙܠܚ (v) draw out

[a]PEAL

Imperative

JHN 2:8

Passive Participle

REV 19:13

854 ܙܡ (v) sound, ring

[a]PEAL

Active Participle

1 CO 13:1

855 (ܙܡܢ), ܙܘܡܢܐ (m-non occ) invitation, guest

857 (ܙܡܢ) (v) invite

[c]PAEL

Passive Participle

MAT 22:3,4,8 | LUK 14:7,8[2]

[d]ETHPAAL

Perfect

LUK 14:10

Participle

LUK 14:8[1]

858 ܙܡܪ (v) sing, pipe

[a]PEAL

Perfect

MAT 11:17 | LUK 7:32

Active Participle

EPH 5:19 | COL 3:16

856 ܙܡܝܪܬܐ (f) song

EPH 5:19 | COL 3:16

859 ܙܡܪܐ (m) music

LUK 15:25
ROM 13:13
GAL 5:21
1 PT 4:3
REV 18:22

1671 ܡܙܡܘܪܐ (m) psalm

LUK 20:42
24:44
ACT 1:20
13:33
1 CO 14:26
EPH 5:19
COL 3:16

[c]PAEL

Imperfect

ROM 15:9 | 1 CO 14:15[1],15[2]

Active Participle

JAM 5:13

860 ܙܡܪܐ (adj) musician

MAT 9:23

[d]ETHPAAL

Participle

1 CO 14:7

861 ܙܡܪܓܕܐ (m) emerald

REV 4:3 | REV 21:19

862 ܙܢܐ, ܙܢ (m) kind

1 CO 12:10,28
HEB 9:10,10
REV 18:22

866 (ܙܢܐ), ܙܢܝܬܐ (f) harlot, prostitute

MAT 21:31,32
LUK 15:30
1 CO 6:15,16
HEB 11:31
JAM 2:25
REV 17:1,5,15,16
19:2

865 ܙܢܝܘܬܐ (f) fornication, adultery

MAT 5:32
15:19
MRK 7:21
JHN 8:41
ACT 15:20,29
21:25
ROM 1:29
1 CO 5:1,1
6:13,18
7:2
2 CO 12:21
GAL 5:19
EPH 5:3
COL 3:5
1 TH 4:3
REV 2:21
9:21
14:8
17:2,4
18:3
19:2

863 (ܙܢܐ) (v) commit fornication

[c]PAEL

Perfect

1 CO 10:8[2]
JUD 7
REV 17:2
18:3,9

Imperfect

1 CO 10:8[1]

Infinitive

REV 2:14,20

Active Participle

1 CO 6:18

864 ܙܢܝܐ (adj) fornicator, adulterer

1 CO 5:9,10,11
6:9
EPH 5:5
1 TM 1:10
HEB 12:16
13:4
REV 21:8
22:15

869 ܙܥܦ (v) (ethpe) be angry

[b]ETHPEEL

Participle

MRK 14:5

870 ܙܥܩ (v) cry out

[a]PEAL

Perfect

LUK 4:33
REV 8:8,10,12
REV 9:1,13
11:15

Infinitive

REV 10:7

1672 ܡܙܥܩܢܐ (m) trumpeters

REV 18:22

[e]APHEL

Perfect

REV 8:7

Infinitive

REV 8:6,13

Active Participle

LUK 4:41
LUK 23:5

871 ܙܥܪ (v-non occ) diminish

[a]PEAL

867 ܙܥܘܪܐ (adj) little, least

MAT 5:19
6:30
MAT 7:14
8:26
9:37
10:42
11:11
13:32
14:31
16:8
18:6,10,14
20:16
22:14
25:40,45
28:12
MRK 4:31
9:42
15:40
LUK 4:5
7:28
9:48
10:2
12:26,28,
32,48
13:23
15:12,13
17:2
19:3
22:26
ACT 5:34
9:43
17:4
26:22
27:40
ROM 9:12
1 CO 12:24
15:9
2 CO 4:17
EPH 3:3,8
1 TH 5:14
1 TM 4:8
HEB 8:11
10:37
11:25,32
12:10
13:22
JAM 3:4,5,5
1 PT 5:10,12
REV 2:14
6:11
11:18
13:16
19:5,18
20:12

868 ܙܥܘܪܘܬܐ (f) smallness

MRK 16:14

872 ܙܩܐ (f) wineskin

MAT 9:17,17,17,
17
MRK 2:22,22,22,
MRK 2:22
LUK 5:37,37,37,
38

874 ܙܩܦ (v) crucify, lift up

[a]PEAL

Perfect

MAT 27:35
MRK 15:24,25,
27
LUK 23:33
24:20
JHN 19:18,23
ACT 2:23,36
4:10
GAL 5:24

Imperfect

MAT 20:19
MRK 15:20
LUK 23:23
JHN 19:10,15,
16
HEB 6:6

Imperative

MRK 15:13,14
LUK 23:21[1],21[2]
JHN 19:6

Active Participle

MAT 23:34
1 CO 2:8

Passive Participle

MRK 15:32	GAL 2:20
JHN 19:31,32	6:14[1],14[2]
1 CO 1:23	2 TM 4:15
2:2	

873 ܙܩܝܦܐ (m) cross

MAT 10:38	JHN 19:25,31
16:24	1 CO 1:17,18
27:32,40,	GAL 5:11
42	6:12,14
MRK 8:34	EPH 2:16
15:21,30,	PHL 2:8
32	3:18
LUK 9:23	COL 1:20
23:26	2:14
JHN 19:17,19,	

[b]ETHPEEL

Perfect

MAT 27:38,44	JHN 19:20,41
28:5	ROM 6:6
MRK 16:6	1 CO 1:13
JHN 6:18	2 CO 13:4

Imperfect

MAT 26:2	MAT 27:26,31
27:22,23,	MRK 15:15

875 ܙܩܪ (v) weave

[a]PEAL

Passive Participle

JHN 19:23

878 ܙܪܥ (v) sow

[a]PEAL

Perfect

MAT 13:4,24,25,	MRK 4:14[2]
27,31,	LUK 8:5[2]
37,39	19:21,22
25:24,26	1 CO 9:11
MRK 4:4,14[1],	

Imperfect

MAT 13:3

Infinitive

MRK 4:3	LUK 8:5[1]

Active Participle

MAT 6:26	1 CO 15:36,37[1],
LUK 12:24	37[2]
JHN 4:37	2 CO 9:6[1],6[2]
ACT 17:20	GAL 6:7,8[1],8[2]

Passive Participle

MAT 13:19[1]	JAM 1:1
MRK 4:15[2]	1 PT 1:1

876 ܙܪܘܥܐ (m) sower

MAT 13:3	JHN 4:36
MRK 4:3,14	2 CO 9:10
LUK 8:5	

879 ܙܪܥܐ (m) seed

MAT 12:1	ACT 13:23
13:18,24,	ROM 1:3
27,37,	4:13,16,18
38	9:7,7,8
22:24	11:1
MRK 2:23	1 CO 15:36
4:26,27	2 CO 9:10,10
12:19,20,	11:22
21,22	GAL 3:16,16,16,
LUK 1:55	19,29
6:1	2 TM 2:8
8:5,11	HEB 2:16
20:28	11:11,18
JHN 7:42	1 PT 1:23
8:33,37	1 JN 3:9
ACT 3:25	REV 12:17
7:5,6	

880 ܙܪܥܘܢܐ (m) grain, seed

MAT 13:32	1 CO 15:37,38
MRK 4:31	

[b]ETHPEEL

Perfect

MAT 13:19[2],20,	MRK 4:16,20,31,
22,23	32

Participle

MRK 4:15[1],18	1 CO 15:43[2],44
1 CO 15:42,43[1],	JAM 3:18

ܚ

881 ܚܐܦܐ (m) violence

REV 18:21

884 ܚܒ (v) be kindled, dear; (pa, aph) love

[a]PEAL

Perfect

LUK 12:49

888 ܚܒܝܒܐ (pp) beloved

MAT 3:17; 12:18; 17:5
MRK 1:11; 9:7; 12:6
LUK 3:22; 9:35; 20:13
ACT 10:24; 15:25
ROM 1:7; 11:28; 12:19; 16:5,8,9,12
1 CO 4:14,17; 10:14; 15:58
2 CO 7:1; 12:19
EPH 1:6; 5:1; 6:21
PHL 2:12; 4:1,1
COL 1:7,13; 3:12; 4:7,9,14
1 TH 1:4; 2:8
2 TH 2:13
1 TM 6:2
2 TM 1:2
PLM 1,2,16
JAM 1:16,19; 2:5
1 PT 2:11; 4:12
2 PT 1:17; 3:1,8,14,15,17
1 JN 2:7; 3:2,21; 4:1,7,11
3 JN 1,2,5,11
JUD 3,17,20
REV 20:9

885 ܚܒܘܒܐ (m) twig, stick

ACT 28:3

905 ܚܒܬܐ (f) stubble

1 CO 3:12

929 ܚܘܒܐ (m) love

MAT 24:12
LUK 11:42
JHN 5:42; 13:35; 15:10,10,13; 17:26
ROM 1:31; 5:5,8; 8:35,39; 12:9; 13:10,10; 14:15; 15:30
1 CO 4:21; 7:3; 8:1; 13:1,2,3,4,4,4,8,13,13; 14:1; 16:14,24
2 CO 2:4,8; 5:14; 6:6,13; 7:7,11; 8:7,8,24; 9:14; 13:11,14
GAL 5:6,13,22
EPH 1:4,15; 2:4; 3:17,19; 4:2,15,16; 5:2,21; 6:7,23
PHL 1:9,15; 2:1,2
COL 1:4,8; 2:2; 3:14
1 TH 1:3; 2:17; 3:6,12; 4:9; 5:8,13
2 TH 1:3; 2:10; 3:5
1 TM 1:5,14; 2:15; 4:12; 6:11
2 TM 1:7,13; 2:22; 3:4,10
TIT 2:2
PLM 5,7,9
HEB 6:10; 10:24; 13:1
1 PT 1:22; 4:8,8
2 PT 1:7
1 JN 2:5,15; 3:1,16,17; 4:7,8,9,10,12,16,16,16,17,18,18,18; 5:3
2 JN 3,6
3 JN 6
JUD 2,21
REV 2:4,19

[c]PAEL

Active Participle

1 TH 2:7,8

[e]APHEL

Perfect

MRK 10:21
LUK 7:47[1]
JHN 3:16,19; 13:1[1],1[2],34[2]; 15:9[1],9[2],12[2]; 17:23[1],23[2],24,26
ROM 8:37
GAL 2:20
EPH 2:4

EPH 5:2,25[2]	1 JN 4:10[1],10[2], 11[1],19[2]
2 TH 2:16	REV 3:9
2 TM 4:8,10	12:11
2 PT 2:15	

Imperfect

MAT 19:19	1 TH 4:9
MRK 12:31	1 JN 3:11,18,23
LUK 7:42	4:7[1],12, 19[1],20[3], 21[2]
JHN 13:34[3] 15:12[1],17	
GAL 5:14	2 JN 5
EPH 5:28[1]	

Imperative

MAT 5:44	COL 3:19
LUK 6:27,35	1 PT 2:17
EPH 5:25[1]	

Infinitive

ROM 13:8[1]	1 JN 4:11[2]

Active Participle

MAT 5:46[1],46[2]	EPH 5:28[2],28[3] 6:24
LUK 6:32[1],32[2], 32[3] 7:47[2]	PHL 1:8
	1 TH 3:12
JHN 3:35 8:42 11:5 13:34[1] 14:21	1 PT 1:8,22
	1 JN 2:10 3:10,14[1], 14[2] 4:7[2],8,20[1], 20[2],21[1] 5:1[1],1[2],2[1], 2[2]
ROM 8:28 12:10 13:8[2]	
1 CO 8:3	2 JN 1
2 CO 11:11 12:15[1],15[2]	3 JN 1
	REV 1:5

887 ܚܒܛ (v) knock down

aPEAL

Perfect

MRK 9:20

Active Participle

MRK 9:18

890 ܚܒܠ (v) be destroyed; (pa) corrupt, destroy, alter

aPEAL (non occ)

892 ܚܒܠܐ (m) corruption

ACT 2:27,31 13:34,35, 36,37	GAL 6:8
	EPH 6:24
	1 TM 6:9
ROM 8:21	HEB 8:13
1 CO 15:42,42, 50,52	2 PT 1:4 2:12,12,19

cPAEL

Perfect

2 CO 7:2	REV 19:2
REV 11:18[2]	

Imperfect

REV 11:18[1]

Active Participle

MAT 6:16,19,20	1 CO 15:33
LUK 12:33	TIT 1:11
1 CO 3:17[1],17[2]	HEB 11:28

Passive Participle

1 CO 6:9	2 TM 3:8
1 TM 6:5	TIT 2:8

1674 ܡܚܒܠܢܐ (m) destroyer

1 CO 10:10

dETHPAAL

Perfect

JAM 5:2	REV 8:9

Imperfect

ACT 13:41	2 PT 2:12
2 CO 11:3	

Participle

ROM 1:23[1],23[2]	1 TM 1:17 6:16
1 CO 9:25[1],25[2] 15:53,54	1 PT 1:4 3:4
2 CO 4:16	
EPH 4:22	JUD 10
COL 2:22	

1935 ܡܬܚܒܠܢܘܬܐ (f) (w/ ܠܐ) incorruptibility

ROM 2:7	1 CO 15:54
1 CO 15:50,53,	2 TM 1:10

891 ܚܒܠ (v) travail, labor

[a]PEAL (non occ)

894 ܚܒܠܐ (m) sorrow, pain

MAT 24:8	ACT 2:24
MRK 13:8	1 TH 5:3

[c]PAEL

Active Participle

ROM 8:22	REV 12:2
GAL 4:19,27	

893 ܚܒܠ, ܚܒܠܐ (m) rope

JHN 2:15	ACT 27:32

930 (ܚܒܠ), ܚܘܒܠܐ (m) compensation

2 CO 6:13	1 TM 5:4

896 ܚܒܢܐ (adj-non occ) lazy

895 (ܚܒܢ) (v-non occ) (ethpa) cease

[d]ETHPAAL

897 ܚܒܢܢܐ (adj) lazy

MAT 25:26	ROM 12:11

898 ܚܒܢܢܘܬܐ (f) laziness

1 TM 5:13,13

899 ܚܒܨ (v) crowd together, throng

[a]PEAL

Imperfect

MRK 3:9

Active Participle

MRK 5:24,31	LUK 16:16
LUK 8:42,45	

900 ܚܒܨܐ (m) crowd

MRK 5:27

889 (ܚܒܪ), ܚܒܝܪܐ (adj-non occ) obscure

901 ܚܒܪܐ (m) pit

MAT 12:11

902 ܚܒܪ, ܚܒܪܐ (m) friend, companion

MAT 11:16	ROM 2:1,1
20:13	13:8
22:12	1 CO 4:6
26:50	10:24
LUK 5:7	14:17
7:32	2 CO 8:8
14:31	PHL 2:3,4
23:40	COL 3:13
JHN 11:16	2 TH 1:3
ACT 5:21	HEB 1:9
7:27	1 PT 4:10
23:32	5:1

903 ܚܒܪܬܐ (f) friend, companion

MAT 12:13	1 CO 14:7
LUK 6:10	

904 ܚܒܫ (v) confine

[a]PEAL

Perfect

LUK 3:20	ROM 11:32
5:6	GAL 3:22
ACT 5:25	HEB 6:17
16:24	

Infinitive

GAL 4:17

Passive Participle

GAL 3:23

886 ܚܒܘܫܝܐ (m) imprisonment, distress

ACT	8:33	HEB	11:36
ROM	8:35	REV	2:10
2 CO	6:4		20:7
	12:10		

906 (ܚܓܣ), ܚܓܝܣܐ (adj) lame

MAT	18:8	LUK	14:13
	21:14	JHN	5:3
MRK	9:45		

908 ܚܓܪ (v-non occ) lame

[a]PEAL

907 ܚܓܝܪܐ (pp) lame

MAT	11:5	ACT	4:14
	15:30,31		14:8
LUK	7:22	HEB	12:13
ACT	3:2		

[c]PAEL

1675 ܡܚܓܪܐ (pp) lame

LUK	14:21	ACT	8:7

909 ܚܕ (num) one; (as adj) certain one; (ܚܕ ܚܕ) each one

cf (ܚܘܕ)

see below 910 ܚܕ ܙܒܢܐ

see below 918 ܚܕܒܫܒܐ

see below 1676 ܡܚܕܐ

see also 1429 ܟܠ ܚܕ

MAT 5:18,18,19,29,30,36,41; 6:24,24,27,29; 8:2,5,19; 9:18; 10:25,29,42; 12:10,11,22; 13:46; 16:14; 17:4,4,4; 18:6,9,10,12,14,16, 24,28; 19:5,6,16,17,29; 20:12,13,21,21; 21:19,24,28,33; 22:35; 23:8,9,10,15; 24:10, 10,10,10,40,40,41,41; 25:15,18,24,32,32,40, 45; 26:7,14,21,22,22,40,47,51,69; 27:14,15, 38,38,48,56 MRK 1:27,27; 2:7; 3:1; 4:41, 41; 5:22,25; 6:5,15; 7:24,25,32; 8:14,16,16, 28; 9:5,5,5,17,34,34,36,42,47,50,50; 10:8,8, 17,18,21,30,37,37; 11:13,29; 12:1,6,28,29, 32,42; 13:1; 14:10,18,19,19,20,37,43,47,51, 66; 15:6,7,21,27,27,31,31,36 LUK 1:5; 2:15,15,25,44; 4:26,27,40,40; 5:3,12,12,17, 18; 6:11,11; 7:2,36,41,41; 8:8,22,25,25,27, 41,43; 9:19,33,33,33,38; 10:25,30,31,38,42; 11:1,1,27,37,45,46; 12:1,1,6,16,25,27,52; 13:10,15,15; 14:1,2,15,16,18,24; 15:4,7,8,10, 11,15,19,26; 16:1,5,5,13,13,17,19,20; 17:2, 12,15,22,34,34,35,36; 18:2,2,3,10,18,19,22, 34,35; 19:2,8,12; 20:1,9; 21:2; 22:12,47,50, 56,59; 23:17,33,33,33,39,50; 24:14,14,15,15, 17,17,18,32,32 JHN 1:3,40; 3:1,25,25; 4:46; 5:2,5,44,44,44; 6:7,7,8,9,43,43,52,52, 70,71; 7:21,50; 8:9,9,41; 9:25; 10:16,30,41; 11:1,49,50,52,56,56; 12:2,4,19,19; 13:14,14, 21,22,22,23,34,34,34,34,35,35; 15:12,12,17, 17; 16:17,17,29; 17:11,21,21,22,22,23; 18:9, 14,15,22,25,26,38,39; 19:4,11,18,18,23,24, 24,34; 20:7,12,12,24; 21:25,25 ACT 1:14, 21,24; 2:3,3,7,7,12,12,46; 3:2; 4:15,15,32,32; 5:1,34; 7:24,26,26,26,26,58; 8:9,16,27,36; 9:10,33,36; 10:1,7,11,22,30; 11:5,28; 12:10; 13:6; 14:8; 15:39,39; 16:1,1,9,14,16; 17:23, 26,34,34; 18:2,11,24; 19:14,24,34,38,38; 20:9; 21:7,10,16; 22:12; 23:7,7,17,19; 24:21; 25:14; 26:26,31,31; 27:1,12,16,22,26,34,39; 28:7,13 ROM 1:27,27; 3:10,12,30; 5:12, 15,15,16,16,17,17,18,18,19,19; 6:10; 9:10, 21,21; 10:12; 12:4,4,5,5,5,10,10,10,10; 13:8, 8; 14:13,13,19,19; 15:5,5,6,6; 16:16,16 1 CO 1:7,10,10,10; 2:8; 3:8; 6:3,5,7,7,16,16, 17; 7:5,5; 8:4,6,6; 9:15,24; 10:3,4,8,17,17,17; 11:21,21,33,33; 12:4,5,6,11,12,12,13,13,13, 14,18,19,20,25,25,26,26; 14:10,27,27,27,31, 31; 15:38,38; 16:20,20 2 CO 3:9; 4:13; 5:14; 7:5; 11:2,24,25; 12:18; 13:12,12 GAL 3:16,20,20,28; 4:22,22,24; 5:13,13,14, 15,15,15,15,17,17,26,26,26,26 EPH 2:14, 15,16,18; 4:2,2,4,4,4,5,5,5,6,7,7,13,13,25,25, 32,32,32,32; 5:21,21,31,33,33 PHL 1:27, 27; 2:2,2,2,2; 3:13,16,16; 4:2,15,16 COL 3:9,9,13,13,13,13,15 1 TH 2:9,11, 11,18; 3:12,12; 4:9,9,18,18; 5:11,11,11,11 2 TH 2:3 1 TM 1:17; 2:5,5; 3:2,12; 5:9,14 2 TM 2:17 TIT 1:6; 3:3,3,10 PLM 16, 22 HEB 2:11; 6:4; 7:27; 9:5,5,7,12,26,27, 28; 10:2,10,12,14,24,24,25,25; 11:12,21,21; 12:16,25,26,27 JAM 2:10,19; 3:11; 4:12, 13; 5:9,9,16,16,16,16 1 PT 1:22,22; 3:8,8, 18; 5:14,14 2 PT 3:8,8,8 1 JN 3:11,11, 18,18,23,23; 4:7,7,11,11,12,12; 5:8,9 2 JN 5,5 JUD 3,5 REV 5:5,8; 6:1,1,11; 7:13; 8:13; 9:12,13; 11:13; 13:3; 15:7; 17:1, 10,12,13,17; 18:8,10,17,19,21; 20:13,13; 21:9,21,21,21

910 ܚܕ ܒܫܒܐ (idiom) Sunday

from 909 ܚܕ (above) and 3100 ܫܒܬܐ

MAT	28:1	ACT	20:7
MRK	16:2,9	1 CO	16:2
LUK	24:1	REV	1:10
JHN	20:1,19		

911 ܚܕ̈ܕܐ (pron) one another

LUK	4:36	GAL	6:2
	23:12	1 TH	5:15
JHN	16:19	JAM	4:11
ACT	21:6	1 PT	4:8
	28:25		5:5
ROM	2:15	1 JN	1:7
	12:5	REV	6:4
	15:7		11:10

918 ܚܕܥܣܪ (num) eleven

from 909 ܚܕ (above) and 2400 ܥܣܪ

MAT	20:6,9	ACT	1:26
	28:16		2:14
MRK	16:14	REV	21:20
LUK	24:9,33		

1676 ܡܚܕܐ (adv) immediately

from 1770 ܡܢ and 909 ܚܕ (above)

MAT	3:16	LUK	1:64
	4:20,22		4:39
	5:28		5:25,39
	8:32		8:44,47,55
	9:30		12:36,54
	14:22		13:13
	21:2,3,19		14:5
	24:29,32		17:7
	25:15		21:30
	26:49		22:60
	27:51		24:31
MRK	1:10,12,18, 20,21,28, 31	JHN	13:32
			19:34
		ACT	16:10,26
	4:15,16,29		22:29
	5:29,30		23:30
	6:25,27,45	REV	2:16
	7:25		3:11
	8:10		4:2
	10:52		11:14
	11:3		22:12
	15:1		

914 ܚܕܝ (v) be glad, rejoice; (pa) gladden

aPEAL

Perfect

MAT	2:10	ACT	15:31
MRK	14:11		20:12
LUK	1:47	2 CO	7:13
	22:5	PHL	1:18[1]
	23:8		4:10
JHN	8:56	HEB	11:13
	20:20	2 JN	4
ACT	11:23	3 JN	3

Imperfect

LUK	1:14	PHL	2:28
	10:20[1]	1 PT	1:6
JHN	4:36		4:13[2]
	16:20,22	REV	11:10

Imperative

MAT	5:12	PHL	2:18
LUK	6:23		3:1
	10:20[2]		4:4[1],4[2]
	15:6,9	1 PT	4:13[1]
ROM	12:15[1]	2 JN	10,11
2 CO	13:11		

Infinitive

LUK 15:32

Active Participle

MAT	18:13	1 CO	13:6[1],6[2]
LUK	1:58		16:17
	13:17	2 CO	4:18
	15:5		6:10
	19:6,37		7:16
JHN	3:29		13:9
	11:15	PHL	1:4,18[2]
	14:28		2:17
ACT	5:41	COL	1:24
	8:39		2:5
	13:48	1 TH	3:9
ROM	7:22		5:16
	12:12,15[2]	JAM	5:13
	16:19	REV	19:7
1 CO	7:30[1],30[2]		

913 ܚܕܘܬܐ (f) joy, gladness

MAT	2:10	JHN	3:29,29
	13:20,44		15:11,11
	25:21,23		16:20,21, 22,24
	28:8		
MRK	4:16		17:13
LUK	1:14,44	ACT	8:8
	2:10		12:14
	8:13		13:52
	10:17		15:3
	15:7,10	ROM	14:17
	24:41,52		15:13,32

2 CO 1:24
2:3
7:4,7,9,13
8:2
GAL 5:22
PHL 1:25
2:2,29
4:1
COL 1:11
1 TH 1:6
2:19,20
3:9
2 TM 1:4
PLM 7
HEB 1:9
10:34
12:2,11
13:17
JAM 1:2
4:9
1 PT 1:8,13
1 JN 1:4
2 JN 12
3 JN 4
JUD 25

916 ܚܕܝܐ (adj) joyous

2 CO 9:7

917 ܚܕܝܐܝܬ (adv) gladly

ACT 17:11
21:17
24:10
ACT 28:7
2 CO 12:9,15

[c]PAEL

Imperfect

2 CO 2:2,3

915 ܚܕܝܐ (m) breast

LUK 18:13
23:48
JHN 13:25
JHN 21:20
REV 15:6

919 ܚܕܪ (v) surround, wander, beg

[a]PEAL

Perfect

JHN 10:24
ACT 25:7
REV 20:9

Imperfect

LUK 19:43

Infinitive

LUK 16:3

Active Participle

MRK 10:46
LUK 18:35
JHN $9:8^1,8^2$

Passive Participle

MAT 8:18
LUK 21:20
HEB 12:1

912 ܚܕܘܪܐ (adj) beggar

ACT 3:10

920 ܚܕܪܐ (m) surrounding area

MAT 3:5
14:35
MRK 1:16
3:32
6:36
LUK 3:3
4:14,37
7:17
9:12
LUK 22:55
ACT 5:16
9:39
14:6
27:8,13
JUD 7
REV 4:3,4,6
5:11
7:11

932 ܚܘܕܪܐܝܬ (adv) round about

REV 4:8

[e]APHEL

Perfect

MAT 21:33
MRK 12:1

921 ܚܕܬ (v) be new; (pa) renew

[a]PEAL (non occ)

922 ܚܕܬܐ (adj) new

MAT 9:16,17,17,
17
13:52
19:28
26:28,29
27:60
MRK 1:27
2:21,21,22,
22,22
14:24
16:17
LUK 5:36,36,36,
37,37,38,
38,39
22:20
JHN 13:34
19:41
ACT 17:19,21
ROM 6:4
1 CO 5:7
1 CO 11:25
2 CO 3:6
5:17,18
GAL 6:15
EPH 2:15
4:24
COL 3:10
TIT 2:14
HEB 8:8,13
9:15
12:24
2 PT 3:13,13
1 JN 2:7,8
2 JN 5
REV 2:17
3:12,12
5:9
14:3
21:1,1,2,5

923 ܚܕܬܐܝܬ (adv) anew

MRK 14:25

924 ܚܕܬܘܬܐ (f) newness

ROM 7:6

---

[c]PAEL

Perfect

HEB 10:20

933 ܚܘܕܬܐ (m) renewal

JHN 10:22
ROM 12:2
TIT 3:5

---

[d]ETHPAAL

Imperfect

EPH 1:10
4:23
HEB 6:6

Participle

2 CO 4:16
COL 3:10

---

926 (ܚܘܐ)(v) show

[c]PAEL

Perfect

MAT 3:7
4:8
8:33
14:12
LUK 3:7
4:5
24:40
JHN 10:32
20:20
21:1[1],1[2]
ACT 1:3
7:44
ACT 10:28
18:26
20:35
28:2
2 CO 7:11
GAL 2:2,18
2 TM 1:10
4:14
HEB 6:10
REV 8:12
21:10
22:1

Imperfect

MAT 16:1
24:29
LUK 6:47
12:5
JHN 12:33
14:21
16:14,15
21:19
ACT 7:3
9:16
ACT 24:13
25:7,18
ROM 9:17,22
1 CO 12:31
2 CO 3:1
6:4
EPH 2:7
2 TH 1:10
2:4
1 TM 1:16
6:15
TIT 2:10
3:2
HEB 6:11,17
JAM 3:13
REV 4:1
17:1
21:9

Imperative

MAT 2:8
8:4
22:19
MRK 1:44
LUK 5:14
17:14
20:24
JHN 7:4
14:8,9
ACT 1:24
2 CO 8:24
TIT 2:7
JAM 2:18[1]

Infinitive

MAT 16:21
JHN 14:22
REV 1:1
22:6

Active Participle

MAT 24:1
MRK 14:15
LUK 22:12
JHN 2:18
5:20[1],20[2]
ACT 9:22,39
17:3
18:28
ROM 2:15
5:8
2 CO 4:2
HEB 9:16
11:14
12:27
JAM 2:18[2]
1 PT 1:11
JUD 13
REV 1:16
22:8

3364 ܬܚܘܝܬܐ (f) example, appearance

LUK 1:80
ROM 3:26
1 CO 2:4
2 CO 8:24
PHL 1:28
2 TH 1:5
1 TM 1:16
2 PT 2:6
JUD 7

---

927 (ܚܘܒ)(v) be condemned, owe; (pa) condemn

[a]PEAL

Perfect

1 CO 6:7

Imperfect

ROM 13:8

Active Participle

MAT 23:16,18

928 ܚܘܒܐ (m) debt

MAT 6:12
LUK 7:41
COL 2:14

931 ܚܘܒܬܐ (f) debt

MAT 18:27,32

[b]ETHPEEL

Participle

ROM 4:4, 13:7	1 CO 7:3

[c]PAEL

Perfect

JHN 8:10	HEB 11:7
ACT 26:10	JAM 5:6
TIT 3:11	2 PT 2:6

Imperfect

MAT 12:41,42; 20:18	LUK 6:37[1]; 11:31,32
MRK 10:33	ROM 8:3

Infinitive

2 CO 7:3	COL 2:18

Active Participle

MAT 12:7	ROM 1:32; 2:1; 8:34
JHN 7:51; 8:11	

Passive Participle

MAT 5:21,22[1], 22[2],22[3]	1 CO 11:27
MRK 3:29	1 JN 5:16
ACT 22:25	JUD 7

938 ܚܘܒܐ (m) condemnation

ROM 5:16,18	2 CO 3:9
1 CO 11:29	JUD 4

981 ܚܝܒܐ (adj) debtor

MAT 6:12; 18:24,28, 28,30, 34; 26:66	ROM 1:14; 8:12; 15:1,27,27
MRK 14:64	1 CO 5:10; 11:7,10
LUK 7:41,41; 11:4; 16:5,5,7; 17:10	2 CO 4:8; 12:11,14
JHN 13:14; 19:7	GAL 5:3
ACT 17:29	2 TH 1:3; 2:13
	2 TM 2:24
	TIT 1:7
	PLM 18,19
HEB 2:1; 5:3,12; 9:26; 11:6	HEB 12:9
	JAM 3:1
	1 JN 4:11
	3 JN 8

982 ܚܝܒܘܬܐ (f) condemnation

ROM 8:1; 11:12	1 CO 11:34

[d]ETHPAAL

Perfect

MAT 27:3	JAM 2:10
ROM 14:23	

Imperfect

MAT 12:37	1 CO 11:32
ROM 3:19; 7:13	JAM 5:12

Participle

MRK 16:16	LUK 6:37[2]

1564 (ܚܘܕ), ܠܚܘܕ (adj) alone

cf ܚܕ

JHN 8:9

386 ܒܠܚܘܕ (adv) only, alone

MAT 4:4,10; 5:47; 8:8; 9:21; 10:42; 12:4; 14:13,23,23,36; 17:1,8,19; 18:15; 21:19,21; 24:36 MRK 4:10; 5:36; 6:8, 31,32,47; 7:33; 9:2,8,28,41; 13:3 LUK 4:4,8; 5:21; 6:4; 8:50; 9:10,18,36; 10:23,40; 24:12,18 JHN 5:18; 6:15; 8:16,29; 11:52; 12:9,24; 13:9,10; 16:32, 32; 17:3,20 ACT 8:1,16; 9:7; 11:19; 19:26,27; 21:13; 26:29; 27:10 ROM 1:32; 3:29; 4:5,12,16,23; 5:3,11; 8:23; 9:10,24; 11:3; 13:5; 14:14; 16:4,26 1 CO 7:39; 9:6; 14:36; 15:19 2 CO 7:7; 8:10,21; 9:12 GAL 1:23; 2:10; 3:2; 4:18; 5:13; 6:12 EPH 1:21 PHL 1:26,29; 2:12,27; 4:15 COL 4:11 1 TH 1:5,8; 2:8; 3:1 2 TH 2:7 1 TM 5:13; 6:15,16 2 TM 2:20; 4:8, 11 HEB 9:7,10,17; 12:26 JAM 1:22; 2:17,24 1 PT 2:18; 3:20; 4:15 1 JN 2:2; 5:6 2 JN 1 JUD 4, 25 REV 15:4

935 ܚܘܛܐ (m-non occ) thread

934 (ܚܘܛ) (v) sew

aPEAL

Active Participle

MRK 2:21

Passive Participle

JHN 19:23

ܚܘܝ see (ܚܘܐ)

937 ܚܘܝܐ (m) serpent

MAT 7:10	JHN 3:14
10:16	1 CO 10:9
23:33	2 CO 11:3
MRK 16:18	REV 12:9,14,15
LUK 10:19	20:2
11:11	

996 (ܚܘܠ), ܚܠܐ (m) sand

MAT 7:26	REV 13:1
ROM 9:27	20:8
HEB 11:12	

943 (ܚܘܣ) (v) spare, pity

aPEAL

Perfect

ROM 8:32	2 PT 2:4,5
11:21[1]	

Imperfect

ROM 11:21[2]	2 CO 13:2

Active Participle

ACT 20:29	2 CO 12:6
1 CO 7:28	COL 2:23
2 CO 1:23	

945 ܚܘܣܢܐ (m) moderation

2 CO 9:6,6

1053 (ܚܘܣ), ܚܣ (prt) God forbid, let it not be

MAT 16:22 ACT 10:14; 11:8 ROM 3:4, 6,31; 6:2,15; 7:7,13; 9:14; 11:1,11 1 CO 6:15 GAL 2:17; 3:21

947 (ܚܘܨ) (v) tighten, strengthen

aPEAL (non occ)

987 ܚܝܨܐ (m) bond, shroud

MAT 27:59	LUK 23:53

988 ܚܝܨܐܝܬ (adv) strongly

1 PT 5:5

cPAEL

Active Participle

ACT 27:17

948 (ܚܘܪ) (v) look

aPEAL

Perfect

MAT 14:19	LUK 21:1
19:26	22:56,61
MRK 3:5,34	JHN 1:36,42
6:41	13:22
7:34	ACT 3:4[1],5
8:24,33	6:15
9:8	7:55
10:21,23,	10:4
27	11:6
14:67	13:9
16:4	22:13
LUK 1:25,48	23:1
6:10	27:39
9:16	HEB 11:40
20:17	JAM 1:25

Imperfect

JHN 19:37	HEB 10:24
ACT 7:32	12:2
2 CO 3:13	JAM 2:3

Imperative

MAT 6:1,26	ACT 4:29
ACT 3:4[2]	

Infinitive

2 CO 3:7

Active Participle

MRK 5:32, 12:14,41
LUK 4:20, 8:40, 9:62
ACT 1:10,11
ACT 3:12, 27:12
2 CO 10:7
HEB 11:26
JAM 3:4
2 PT 1:19

951 ܚܘܪܐ (m) example

2 TM 1:13

949 ܚܘܪ (v) be white; (pa, aph) make white

ªPEAL

Perfect

MAT 17:2
LUK 9:29
JHN 4:35

950 ܚܘܪܐ (adj) white

MAT 5:36, 28:3
MRK 16:5
JHN 20:12
ACT 1:10, 10:30
REV 1:14, 3:4,5,18
REV 4:4, 6:2,11, 7:9,13, 14:14, 19:11,14,14, 20:11

ᶜPAEL

Perfect

REV 7:14

Passive Participle

ACT 23:3

ᵉAPHEL

Infinitive

MRK 9:3[2]

Passive Participle

MRK 9:3[1]

959 ܚܙܐ (v) see

ªPEAL

Perfect

MAT 2:2,9,10,11,16, 3:7,16, 4:16,18,21, 5:1, 8:14,18,34, 9:2,8,9,11,22,23,36, 12:2, 13:17[3], 14:14,26,30, 17:8, 18:31, 20:3, 21:15,19,20,32,38, 22:11[2], 24:15,33, 25:37,38,39,44, 26:8,71, 27:3,24,54, 28:17
MRK 1:10,16,19, 2:5,12,14,16, 3:11, 5:6,15,16,22,38, 6:33,34,38[2],48,49,50, 7:2, 9:8,9,14,15,20,25,38, 10:14, 11:11,13,20, 12:28,34, 13:14,29, 14:67,69, 15:39,47, 16:4,5,14[2]
LUK 1:12,22,29, 2:17,20,30,48, 5:2,8,12,20,26,27, 7:12,13,22[1],39, 8:28,34,36,47, 9:32,34,36,49,54, 10:18,24[3],31,32,33, 11:38, 12:54, 13:12, 15:20, 16:23, 17:14,15, 18:15,24,43[1],43[2], 19:5,7,37,41, 20:14, 21:2,20,31, 22:49,56,58, 23:8[1],47,48,55, 24:12,23,24
JHN 1:14,18,29,32,34,38,39[2],41,47,48,50[1], 2:23, 3:11,32, 4:45, 5:6,37, 6:5,14,19,22,24,26,36, 8:38[1],38[2],56[2],57, 9:1,8,18[1],18[2],37, 10:12, 11:31,32,33,45, 12:41,45[2], 14:7,9[2],17, 15:24, 18:26, 19:6,26,33,35, 20:1,5,6,8,12,14,18,20,25[1],29[1],29[2], 21:9,20,21
ACT 1:11, 2:31[1],31[2], 3:3,9,12, 4:20, 6:15, 7:24,31[1],34[2],55, 8:13,18,39, 9:12,27,35,40, 10:3,8,11,

ACT 10:17
11:5,13,23
12:3,9,16
13:12,36,37,45
14:9,11
16:10,19,27,40
21:27,29,32
22:9,15,18
26:13,16[2]
27:31
28:4,6,15
1 CO 2:9
9:1
GAL 1:19
2:7,14
PHL 1:30
2:23
4:9
COL 2:1,18
1 TM 6:16[1]
HEB 3:9
11:13,23
JAM 1:23,24
5:11
1 PT 1:8
2:3
1 JN 1:1[1],1[2],2,3
1 JN 3:6
4:12,14
3 JN 11
REV 1:2,12,17,19,20[1],20[2]
4:1
5:1,2,6,11
6:1[1],2,8,9,12
7:1,2,9
8:2
9:1,17
10:1,5
12:13
13:1,2,11
14:1,6
15:1,2,5
16:13
17:3,6[1],6[2],8[1],12,15,16,18
18:1
19:11,17,19
20:1,4,11,12
21:1,2,22
22:8[1],8[2]

Imperfect

MAT 5:8,16
12:22,38
13:14[2],15,17[1]
16:28
22:11[1]
23:39
24:30[2]
26:58,64
27:42,49
28:1,7,10
MRK 4:12[2],12[3]
5:32
9:1
10:51
12:15
13:26
14:62
15:32,36
16:7
LUK 2:15,26[1],26[2]
3:6
8:10[2],16,35
9:9,27
10:24[1]
11:33
13:28,35
14:18
17:22[2]
18:41
19:3,4
LUK 20:13
21:27
23:8[3]
JHN 1:39[1],46,50[2],51
3:3,36
4:48
6:30,62
7:3
8:51,56[1]
9:39[2]
11:40
12:9,21,40
14:19[2]
16:16[1],16[2],17[1],17[2],19[1],19[2],22
ACT 2:17,27
7:31[2]
13:11,34,35
15:6,36
19:21
20:38
22:14
26:16[3]
28:20,26,27
ROM 1:11
11:10
15:21,24
1 CO 3:10
1 CO 8:10
16:7
GAL 1:18
PHL 1:27
2:28
1 TH 3:10
HEB 13:23
1 PT 2:12
1 JN 3:17
5:16
3 JN 14
REV 1:7
3:18
16:15
18:7,14
22:4

Imperative

MAT 8:4
9:30
16:6
18:10[1]
24:6
28:6
MRK 1:44
2:24
4:24
6:38[1]
8:15
10:52[1]
13:1,5,9,33
15:4
LUK 8:18
18:42
21:8,29
24:39[1]
JHN 4:29,35
7:52
JHN 11:34,36
20:27
ACT 4:29
5:35
13:41
ROM 11:22
1 CO 1:26
8:9
10:18
16:10
GAL 5:15
6:11
EPH 5:15
HEB 3:1
7:4
8:5[1]
12:3
1 JN 3:1
REV 6:1[2]
22:9

Infinitive

MAT 11:7,8,9
13:14[1]
MRK 5:14
LUK 7:21,24,25,26
8:20
17:22[1]
23:8[2]
ACT 7:34[1]
PHL 2:26
1 TH 2:17
3:6
1 TM 6:16[2]
2 TM 1:4
1 PT 3:10
REV 5:3
9:20

Active Participle

MAT 5:28
6:4,6,18[2]
7:3
11:4,5
13:13[1],13[2],16,17[2]
15:31[1],31[2]
18:10[2]
24:2
27:55
MRK 4:12[1]
5:31
8:18,23,24,25
13:2
15:40
LUK 6:41[1]
7:22[2],44
8:10[1]
LUK 10:23[1],23[2],24[2]
14:7,29
21:6
23:35,49
24:37,39[2]
JHN 1:33
4:19
5:19
6:2,40,46[1],46[2]
9:7,19,21,25,39[1],39[3],41
11:9
12:19,45[1]
14:9[1],19[1]
16:10
17:24

JHN 20:25[2]
ACT 1:9
2:25,33
3:16
4:14
7:56
8:6,23
11:6
17:16,22,23
19:26
20:25
21:20
25:24
27:10
ROM 7:23
8:24[2]
1 CO 13:12
2 CO 3:18
7:8
12:6
PHL 3:17
COL 2:5
HEB 2:8,9
3:19
10:25
11:27[1]
12:14
JAM 2:22,24
1 PT 3:2
2 PT 1:9
1 JN 3:2
REV 1:11
11:9,11
17:8[2]
18:9,18

960 ܚܙܘܐ (m) vision, appearance

MAT 14:26
17:9
28:3
MRK 6:49
LUK 1:22
9:29
JHN 5:37
ACT 2:17
7:31,32
9:10,12
10:3,17,19,22
11:5
12:9
16:9,10
18:9
22:18
26:19
2 CO 12:1
HEB 10:33
12:21
JAM 1:11
REV 4:3,3
9:17
10:1

961 ܚܙܝܐ (m) observer

LUK 1:2
2 PT 1:16
REV 22:15

962 ܚܙܝܐ (m) sight

LUK 4:18
2 CO 5:7

968 ܚܙܝܬܐ (f) sight

LUK 23:48
ROM 15:24
2 CO 2:14
2 PT 2:8
REV 1:16

1678 ܡܚܙܝܐ (m) sight; (w/ ܥܝܢܐ) eyeservice

EPH 6:6
COL 3:22

1679 ܡܚܙܝܬܐ (f) mirror

1 CO 13:12
2 CO 3:18
JAM 1:23

[b]ETHPEEL

Perfect

MAT 1:20
2:7,12,13,19,22
9:33
13:26
17:3
27:53
MRK 9:4
10:52[2]
16:9,11,12,14[1]
LUK 1:3,11
2:13
9:8,31
22:43
24:11,34
JHN 9:11,15[1],15[2]
21:14
ACT 2:3,22
7:2,26,30,35
9:17
13:31
16:9
23:11
26:16[1]
27:23
ROM 9:5
10:20
1 CO 15:5,6,7,8
1 TM 3:16
HEB 8:5[2]
1 JN 3:8
REV 2:13
11:19
12:1,3

Imperfect

MAT 6:1,5,16,18[1]
23:5
24:30[1]
LUK 6:42[2]
21:11
JHN 9:3
ACT 10:40
ROM 7:13
2 CO 13:7
HEB 9:24
1 PT 1:7
REV 18:23

Imperative

PHL 2:15

Participle

MAT 17:25
18:12
21:28
22:17
23:27,28
24:27
MRK 14:64
LUK 6:41[2],42[1]
10:36
ACT 1:3
9:7,8,9
16:13
22:11
27:20
ROM 1:20
ROM 2:28
8:24[1],25
2 CO 4:18[1],18[2],18[3],18[4]
COL 1:15,16[1],16[2]
2:23
1 TM 1:17
HEB 9:28
11:1,3[1],3[2],7,27[2]
JAM 4:14
1 JN 2:8
4:20[1],20[2]

965 ܚܙܩ (v) gird, journey

[a]PEAL

Perfect

MAT 21:33
25:14,15
MRK 12:1
13:34

Imperfect

ACT 25:4

Imperative

EPH 6:14
1 PT 1:13

Passive Participle

JHN 20:7

966 ܚܙܩܐ (m) bond, belt

EPH 4:3
COL 3:14

---

963 (ܚܙܪ), ܚܙܝܪܐ (m) swine

MAT 7:6
8:30,31,32
MRK 5:11,12,13,
MRK 5:16
LUK 8:32,32,33
15:15,16

964 ܚܙܝܪܬܐ (f) sow

2 PT 2:22

---

969 ܚܛ (v-non occ) dig

[a]PEAL

1680 ܡܚܛܐ (f) needle

MAT 19:24
MRK 10:25
LUK 18:25

---

977 (ܚܛ), ܚܛܬܐ (f) wheat

MAT 3:12
13:25,29,
30
MRK 4:28
LUK 3:17
16:7
LUK 22:31
JHN 12:24
ACT 27:38
1 CO 15:37
REV 6:6

---

970 ܚܛܐ (v) sin

[a]PEAL

Perfect

MAT 27:4
LUK 15:18,21
JHN 9:2,3
ACT 25:10
ROM 2:12[1],12[2]
3:23,25
ROM 5:12,14
2 CO 12:21
13:2
HEB 3:17
2 PT 2:4
1 JN 1:10

Imperfect

LUK 17:3
JHN 5:14
8:11
ROM 6:15
1 CO 15:34
EPH 4:26
HEB 6:6
10:26
1 JN 2:1[1],1[2]

Infinitive

1 JN 3:9

Active Participle

1 CO 6:18
7:28[1],28[2],
36
1 TM 5:20
TIT 3:11
1 JN 3:6[1],6[2]
5:16[1],16[2],
18

971 ܚܛܗܐ (m) sin

MAT 1:21
3:6
9:2,5,6
12:31
26:28
MRK 1:4,5
2:5,7,9,10
3:28
4:12
LUK 1:77
3:3
5:20,21,23,
24
7:47,48,49
11:4
24:47
JHN 8:7,21,24,
24
9:34
15:22
20:23
ACT 2:38
3:19
5:31
10:43
13:38
22:16
26:18
ROM 3:25
4:7,25
5:16
7:5
11:27
1 CO 15:3,17
2 CO 5:19
GAL 1:4
EPH 1:7
2:1,5
COL 1:14
2:11,13,13
1 TH 2:16
1 TM 5:22,24
2 TM 3:6
HEB 1:3
2:17
5:1,3
7:26,27
8:12
9:28,28
10:2,3,4,6,
8,11,12,
17,18,
18,26
13:11
JAM 4:17
5:15,20
1 PT 2:24
3:18
4:1,8
2 PT 1:9
2:14
1 JN 1:7,9,9
2:2,12
3:5
4:10
5:16,16,17
REV 1:5
18:4,5

974 ܚܛܝܐ (adj) sinner

MAT 9:10,11,13
11:19
26:45
MRK 2:15,16,16,
17
8:38
14:41
LUK 5:8,30,32
6:32,33,34,
34
7:34,37,39
13:2,4
15:1,2,7,
10

LUK 18:13
19:7
24:7
JHN 9:16,24,25,31
ROM 3:7
4:5
5:8,19
GAL 2:15,17
1 TM 1:9,15
HEB 12:3
JAM 4:8
5:20
1 PT 3:18
4:18
1 JN 3:8
JUD 15

975 ܚܛܝܬܐ (f) sin

JHN 1:29
8:34,34,46
9:41,41
15:22,24
16:8,9
19:11
ACT 1:18
7:60
ROM 3:9,20
4:8
5:12,12,13,13,20,20,21
6:1,2,6,6,7,10,11,12,13,14,16,17,18,20,22,23
7:7,7,8,8,9,11,13,13,13,14,17,20,23,25
ROM 8:2,3,3,3,10
14:23
1 CO 6:18
15:56,56
2 CO 5:21,21
GAL 2:17
3:22
2 TH 2:3
HEB 3:13
4:15
9:26
11:25
12:1,4
JAM 1:15,15
2:9
3:6
1 PT 2:22,24
1 JN 1:8
3:4,4,5,8,9
5:17

976 ܚܛܦ (v) seize

ᵃPEAL

Perfect

ACT 6:12
8:39
ACT 19:29

Imperfect

MRK 3:27
JHN 6:15
JHN 10:28,29
ACT 23:10

Imperative

JUD 22

Active Participle

MAT 13:19
JHN 10:12

972 ܚܛܘܦܐ (adj) ravenous, extortioner

MAT 7:15
LUK 18:11
1 CO 5:10,11
6:10

973 ܚܛܘܦܝܐ (m) extortion, robbery

MAT 23:25
LUK 11:39
PHL 2:6
HEB 10:34

ᵇETHPEEL

Perfect

ACT 27:15
2 CO 12:2,4
REV 12:5

Imperfect

1 TH 4:17

ᶜPAEL

Active Participle

MAT 11:12

936 (ܚܛܪ), ܚܘܛܪܐ (m) rod, staff

MAT 26:47,55
MRK 14:43,48
LUK 22:52
1 CO 4:21
HEB 11:21

978 ܚܝܐ (v) live; (aph) make live

ᵃPEAL

Perfect

LUK 2:36
15:24,32
JHN 4:51,53
ACT 26:5
ROM 6:13
7:9
ROM 8:24
14:9
1 PT 3:18,20
REV 2:8
13:14
20:4

Imperfect

MAT 9:18
10:22
19:25
24:13
MRK 5:23
13:13
LUK 8:12
10:28
JHN 3:17
5:25,34
6:51,57,58
10:9
11:25
14:19
ACT 2:21
ACT 7:19
11:14
14:9
15:11
16:30,31
25:24
27:31
28:4
ROM 1:17
5:10
6:2,8
9:27
10:1,5,9,13
11:26

1 CO 5:5
9:14
10:33
2 CO 5:15
GAL 2:14[2],19
3:11,12
5:25
1 TH 2:16
5:10
2 TH 2:10
1 TM 2:4
2 TM 2:11
3:12
TIT 2:12
HEB 10:38
12:9
JAM 4:15
1 PT 2:24
4:2,6
1 JN 4:9

Imperative

ACT 2:40

Infinitive

MRK 10:26
LUK 18:26
ACT 4:12
ACT 15:1
22:22
2 CO 7:3

Active Participle

MAT 4:4
15:27
24:22
MRK 5:28
13:20
16:16
LUK 4:4
8:50
13:23
15:13
ACT 2:47
ROM 8:13[1],13[2]
10:10
14:8[1],8[2]
1 CO 15:2,22,36
2 CO 2:15
GAL 2:14[1]
EPH 1:14
1 TM 2:15
1 PT 3:21
4:18

979 ܚܝܐ (adj) alive, living

MAT 16:16
22:32
26:63
27:63
MRK 8:29
12:27
16:11
LUK 5:10
20:38,38
24:5,23
JHN 4:10,11,50
6:51,57,57,
69
7:38
11:26
14:19
ACT 1:3
7:38
9:39,41
10:42
14:15
17:28
20:12
25:19
ROM 6:10,10,11
7:1,2,3,9
8:10
9:26
ROM 12:1
14:7,8,9,
11
1 CO 1:18
7:39
15:45
2 CO 3:3
5:15
6:9,16
13:4,4
GAL 2:20,20,20,
20
COL 2:20
1 TH 1:9
3:8
4:15,17
1 TM 3:15
4:10
5:6
6:17
2 TM 4:1
HEB 3:12
4:12
7:8,25
9:14,17
10:31
12:22
1 PT 1:23
1 PT 2:4,5
4:5
REV 1:18,18
3:1
4:9,10
REV 7:2
10:6
11:11
15:7
16:3

980 ܚܝ̈ܐ (m) life, salvation

MAT 7:14
18:8,9
19:16,17,
29
25:46
MRK 9:43,45
10:17,30
LUK 1:77
3:6
10:25
12:15
16:25
18:18,30
19:9
JHN 1:4,4
3:15,16,36,
36
4:14,22,36
5:24,24,26,
26,29,39,
40
6:27,33,35,
40,47,48,
51,53,54,
63,68
8:12
10:10,28
11:25
12:25,50
14:6
17:2,3
20:31
ACT 2:28
3:15
5:20
8:33
11:18
13:26,46,
47,48
16:17
17:25
27:20,34
ROM 1:16
2:7
5:10,17,18,
21
6:4,22,23
7:10
8:2,6,38
11:11,15
13:11
1 CO 3:22
15:19
2 CO 1:6,8
2:16,16
2 CO 4:10,11,11,
12
5:4
6:2,2
7:10
GAL 6:8
EPH 1:13
4:18
6:3
PHL 1:19,20,21,
22,28
2:12,16
4:3
COL 3:3,4
1 TH 5:8,9
2 TH 2:13
1 TM 1:16
4:8
6:12,19
2 TM 1:1,10
2:10
3:15
TIT 1:2
3:7
HEB 1:14
2:3,10,15
5:9
6:9
7:3,16
9:28
10:20
11:7
JAM 1:12
4:14
1 PT 1:3,5,9,10
2:2
3:7,10
2 PT 1:3
1 JN 1:1,2,2
2:25
3:14,15
5:11,11,12,
12,13,16,
20
JUD 3,21
REV 2:7,10
3:5
7:17
11:11
13:8
17:8
20:15
21:6
22:1,2,14,
17,19

983 ܚܝܘܬܐ (f) living creature, animal

MRK 1:13
ACT 10:12
11:6
1 CO 15:32
TIT 1:12
HEB 12:20
13:11
JAM 3:7
2 PT 2:12
JUD 10
REV 4:6,7,7,7,7,
8,9
5:6,8,11,
14
6:1,3,5,6,7,
8
7:11

REV 11:7
13:1,2,3,4,
4,4,11,
12,12,
14,14,
15,15,
17,18
14:3,9,11
15:2,7
16:2,10,13
17:3,7,8,8,
11,12,
13,16,
17
19:4,19,20,
20
20:4,10

989 ܚܝܬܐ (f) (w/ ܡܝܬܐ) resurrection

MAT 22:23
1 CO 15:12,13,

1 CO 15:21,42

[e]APHEL

Perfect

MAT 9:22
27:42[1]
MRK 5:34
10:52
15:31[1]
LUK 7:50
8:48

LUK 17:19
18:42
23:35[1]
EPH 2:5
COL 2:13
2 TM 1:9
TIT 3:5

Imperfect

MAT 1:21
16:25
18:11
MRK 8:35[1],35[2]
LUK 7:3
9:24[1]
17:33[1],33[2]
19:10
23:35[2]
JHN 12:47
ACT 27:43
ROM 8:11

ROM 11:14
1 CO 1:21
7:16[1],16[2]
9:22
2 TH 1:7
1 TM 4:16
2 TM 4:18
HEB 5:7
JAM 1:21
2:14
4:12

Imperative

LUK 23:37

Infinitive

MAT 27:42[2]
MRK 3:4
15:31[2]
LUK 6:9

LUK 9:56
GAL 3:21
1 TM 1:15
HEB 7:25

Active Participle

LUK 9:24[2]
JHN 5:21[1],21[2]
6:63
ROM 4:17

2 CO 3:6
1 TM 6:13
TIT 2:11
JAM 5:20

1683 ܡܚܝܢܐ (adj) life-giving, savior

LUK 1:47
JHN 4:42
ACT 5:31
1 CO 15:45
EPH 5:23
PHL 3:20
1 TM 1:1

1 TM 2:3
4:10
2 TM 1:10
TIT 1:3,4
2:10,13
3:4,6

985 ܚܝܠ, ܚܝܠܐ (m) power, mighty work; (w/ ܡܨܐ) be able

see also 2910 ܒܪ ܚܝܠܐ

MAT 6:13
7:22
11:20,21,
23
13:54,58
14:2
22:7,29,37
24:29,30
25:15
26:64
MRK 5:30
6:2,5,14
9:1,39
12:24,30,
33
13:25,26
14:62
LUK 1:17,35
2:13
4:14,36
5:17
6:19
8:46
9:1
10:13,19,
27
19:37
21:20,26,
27
22:69
24:49
ACT 1:8
2:22
3:12
4:7,33
6:8
7:42
8:10,13
10:38
19:11,20
ROM 1:4,16,20

ROM 8:38
9:17,22
15:13,19,
19
1 CO 1:18,24
2:4,5
4:19,20
5:4
6:14
12:6,10,28,
29
14:11
15:24,43,
56
2 CO 1:8
3:5
4:7
6:7
8:3,3
10:4
12:9,9,12
13:4,4
GAL 3:5
EPH 1:19,19,21
3:7,16,20,
20
6:10,16
PHL 3:10,21
4:13
COL 1:11,29
2:12
1 TH 1:5
2 TH 1:7,9,11
2:9
2 TM 1:7,8
3:5
HEB 1:3
2:4
6:5
7:16
11:11,34

JAM 5:16	REV 6:15
1 PT 1:5	7:12
3:22	9:16
4:11	11:17
2 PT 1:3,16	12:10
2:11	13:2
REV 1:16	15:8
3:8	17:13
4:11	18:3
5:12	19:1,14,19

986 ܚܝܠܬܢܐ (adj) strong, mighty

MRK 1:7	2 CO 13:3,9
LUK 1:49	1 TM 6:15
3:16	HEB 5:7
24:19	11:34
ROM 15:1	1 JN 2:14
1 CO 1:25,26,27	REV 5:2
4:10	18:8,21
2 CO 12:10	19:6

984 (ܚܝܠ) (v) strengthen

[c]PAEL

Perfect

ACT 15:32	2 TM 4:17
1 TM 1:12	

Active Participle

LUK 22:43	PHL 4:13

---

[d]ETHPAAL

Perfect

ACT 9:19	ROM 4:20
19:16	HEB 11:34
28:15	

Imperfect

COL 1:11	1 PT 5:10

Imperative

ACT 23:11	2 TM 2:1
EPH 6:10	

Participle

LUK 1:80	ACT 9:22
2:40	

---

992 ܚܟܡ (v) know; (pa) make wise

[a]PEAL

Perfect

MAT 1:25

Active Participle

JHN 21:17

Passive Participle

LUK 1:34

990 ܚܟܝܡܐ (adj) wise

MAT 7:24	ROM 12:16
10:16	16:19,26
11:25	1 CO 1:19,20,25, 26,27
23:34	3:10,18,18, 19,20
24:45	4:10
25:2,4,8,9	6:5
LUK 10:21	10:15
12:42	2 CO 11:19
16:8	EPH 5:15
ACT 13:7	JAM 3:13
17:28	
ROM 1:14,22	
11:25	

991 ܚܟܝܡܐܝܬ (adv) wisely

MRK 12:34	LUK 16:8

993 ܚܟܡܬܐ (f) wisdom

MAT 11:19	1 CO 12:8
12:42	2 CO 1:12
13:54	EPH 1:8,17
MRK 6:2	3:10
LUK 2:40,47,52	COL 1:9,28
7:35	2:3,23
11:31,49	3:16
21:15	4:5
ACT 6:3,10	2 TM 2:7
7:10,22	JAM 1:5
ROM 11:33	3:13,15,17
1 CO 1:17,19,20, 21,21,22, 24,30	2 PT 3:15
2:1,4,5,6,6, 7,13	REV 5:12
3:19	7:12
	13:18
	17:9

---

[c]PAEL

Imperfect

2 TM 3:15

939 (ܚܠ), ܚܘܠܐ (adj-non occ) profane

994 (ܚܠ) (v) wash; (aph) profane

[c]PAEL

Perfect

REV 7:14

[e]APHEL

Active Participle

MAT 12:5

---

995 ܚܠ (v-non occ) cut asunder, sap

[a]PEAL

997 ܚܠܐ (m) vinegar

MAT 27:34,48 MRK 15:36 LUK 23:36	JHN 19:29,29, 30

998 ܚܠܐ (m) dust

MAT 10:14 MRK 6:11 LUK 9:5	LUK 10:11 ACT 13:51 22:23

1018 ܚܠܬܐ (f) sheath

JHN 18:11

1002 (ܚܠ), ܚܠܘܠܐ (m) banquet, wedding

MAT 25:10

ܚܠܐ see ܚܠ

---

999 ܚܠܒ, ܚܠܒܐ (m) milk

1 CO 3:2 9:7	HEB 5:12,13 1 PT 2:2

1000 ܚܠܠ (v) (pa) penetrate

[c]PAEL

Active Participle

2 TM 3:6

1001 ܚܠܠܡܬܐ (f) gangrene

2 TM 2:17

1003 ܚܠܛ (v) mingle, company with

[a]PEAL

Perfect

LUK 13:1

Passive Participle

MAT 27:34	MRK 15:23

940 ܚܘܠܛܐ (m) mingling

2 CO 6:14

1004 ܚܠܛܐ (m) mixture

REV 14:10

[d]ETHPAAL

Perfect

HEB 3:14

Imperfect

1 CO 5:9*,11*

Participle

2 TH 3:14*

1005 ܚܠܐ (v-non occ) be sweet

[a]PEAL

1006 ܚܠܝܐ (pp) sweet, agreeable

JAM 3:11,12	REV 10:10

1007 (ܚܠܡ), ܚܠܝܡܐ (adj) whole, healthy

MAT 9:12	ACT 23:30
MRK 2:17	1 TM 1:10
5:34	6:3
LUK 5:31	2 TM 1:13
7:10	4:3
15:27	TIT 1:9,13
JHN 5:11,14	2:1,2,7
ACT 4:10	3 JN 2

1008 ܚܠܝܡܘܬܐ (f) health

ACT 3:16

1010 (ܚܠܡ) (v) (ethpe) be cured; (aph) cure

[b]ETHPEEL

Perfect

JHN 4:52	REV 13:12
5:9	

Imperfect

MRK 5:23	JHN 5:6
16:18	

Participle

MAT 15:31	JHN 11:12
JHN 5:4	ACT 5:16

[e]APHEL

Perfect

JHN 5:15	ACT 28:8
7:23	

Active Participle

JAM 5:15

1011 ܚܠܡ (v) dream

[a]PEAL

Imperfect

ACT 2:17

1012 ܚܠܡܐ (m) dream

MAT 1:20	MAT 27:19
2:12,13,19,	ACT 2:17
22	JUD 8

1013 ܚܠܦ (v) change

[a]PEAL (non occ)

1014 ܚܠܦ (prep) for, instead

MAT 2:22; 5:38,38; 17:27,27; 20:28; 26:28 MRK 1:44; 9:40; 10:45; 14:24 LUK 2:27; 5:14; 6:22; 7:47; 9:50; 11:11; 19:44; 22:20 JHN 1:16; 9:21; 10:11, 15; 11:4,50,51,52; 13:37,38; 15:13; 18:14 ACT 8:24; 12:5,23; 15:26; 21:13 ROM 1:26; 5:6,7,7,8; 8:26,27, 31,32,34; 9:3; 10:1; 12:17; 14:12; 15:8,9, 30; 16:4 1 CO 1:4; 5:7; 11:15; 15:29, 29 2 CO 5:14,15,20,20; 8:16; 9:14; 13:8 GAL 1:4; 2:20; 3:13 EPH 5:4 COL 1:7,24; 2:1,1,1; 4:12,13,13 1 TH 3:9; 5:15 1 TM 2:1,2,6 TIT 2:14 PLM 13 HEB 2:9; 5:1,1, 3,3; 6:20; 7:19,25,27,27; 9:7,7,24; 10:6, 8,12,18,26; 12:2; 13:11,17 JAM 4:15 1 PT 2:21; 3:9,9,18,18; 4:1 1 JN 2:2, 2; 3:16 3 JN 7 JUD 3

3367 ܬܚܠܘܦܐ (m) exchange

MAT 16:26	MRK 8:37

[c]PAEL

Perfect

ROM 1:23,25

Imperfect

ACT 6:14	PHL 3:21

[d]ETHPAAL

Perfect

MRK 9:2	LUK 9:29

Imperfect

ACT 2:20	HEB 1:12
1 CO 15:51,52	

[g]SHAPHEL

Perfect

ACT 28:6

Imperfect

GAL 1:7	GAL 4:20

Active Participle

GAL 3:15

1908 ܡܫܚܠܦܐ (pp) different, diverse

MAT 4:24	TIT 3:3
MRK 1:34	HEB 2:4
LUK 4:40	13:9
ROM 12:6	JAM 1:2
1 TM 1:3	1 PT 1:6
2 TM 3:6	

3131 ܫܘܚܠܦܐ (m) change, variety

HEB 7:12,12,18	JAM 1:17
12:27	

---

[h]ESHTAPHAL

Perfect

MAT 17:2

Imperative

ROM 12:2

Participle

2 CO 3:18	HEB 6:17,18

1009 (ܚܠܨ), ܚܠܝܨܐ (adj-non occ) strong

1016 ܚܠܨ (v) (pa) steal, spoil

[c]PAEL

Perfect

ACT 19:37	2 CO 11:8

Imperfect

COL 2:8

Active Participle

ROM 2:22

1017 ܚܠܝܫܐ (adj) weak

JAM 2:20

1019 ܚܡ (v) be hot; (aph) burn

[a]PEAL

Perfect

MAT 13:6

941 ܚܘܡܐ (m) heat

MAT 20:12	JAM 1:11
LUK 12:55	REV 16:9

1024 ܚܡܝܡܐ (adj) hot

REV 3:15,15,16

---

[b]ETHPEEL

Perfect

REV 16:9

---

[e]APHEL

Imperfect

REV 16:8

Passive Participle

REV 1:15

1020 ܚܡ (v) sweep

[a]PEAL

Active Participle

LUK 15:8

Passive Participle

MAT 12:44	LUK 11:25

1021 (ܚܡ), ܚܡܐ (m) father-in-law

JHN 18:13

1037 ܚܡܬܐ (f) mother-in-law

MAT 8:14	LUK 4:38
10:35	12:53,53
MRK 1:30	

1022 ܚܡܐ (v) wither, fade

aPEAL

Perfect

MRK 4:6

Active Participle

JAM 1:11
1 PT 1:4,24
1 PT 5:4

1026 ܚܡܠ (v) gather in

aPEAL

Imperfect

LUK 12:17,18

Active Participle

MAT 6:26

1027 ܚܡܣܢ (v) forbear, hold

cf ܚܣܢ

kP

Perfect

1 TH 3:1,5

Imperfect

HEB 3:14
4:14
HEB 10:23

Imperative

2 TH 2:15
1 TM 4:16

1685 ܚܡܣܢܘܬܐ (f) temperance, self-control

2 PT 1:6,6

1028 ܚܡܥ (v) leaven; (aph) make leaven

aPEAL

Perfect

MAT 13:33
LUK 13:21

ePAHEL

Active Participle

1 CO 5:6
GAL 5:9

1029 (ܚܡܨ) (v-non occ) shame

cPAEL

3368 ܬܚܡܨܬܐ (f) shame, modesty

1 TM 2:9
HEB 12:28

1030 ܚܡܪܐ (c) ass

MAT 18:6
21:2,5,7
MRK 9:42
LUK 10:34
LUK 13:15
17:2
JHN 12:14

1031 ܚܡܪܐ (m) wine

MAT 9:17,17,17
11:19
MRK 2:22,22,22,
22
15:23
LUK 1:15
5:37,37,37,
38,39
7:33,34
10:34
JHN 2:3,3,9,10,
10
JHN 4:46
ROM 14:21
EPH 5:18
1 TM 3:3,8
5:23
TIT 1:7
2:3
REV 6:6
14:10
16:19
17:2
18:3,13

1025 ܚܡܝܪܐ (m) leaven

MAT 13:33
16:6,11,12
MRK 8:15,15
LUK 12:1
LUK 13:21
1 CO 5:6,7,8,8,8
GAL 5:9

1032 ܚܡܫ (num) five

see below 1034 ܚܡܫܡܐܐ

see below 1035 ܚܡܫܝܢ

MAT 14:17,19,
21
16:9,9
25:2,2,15,
16,16,
20,20,
20,20
MRK 6:38,41,44
MRK 8:19,19
LUK 1:24
9:13,14,16
12:6,52
14:19
16:28
19:18,19
JHN 4:18

JHN 5:2	1 CO 14:19
6:9,10,13, 19	2 CO 11:24
ACT 4:4	REV 6:9
7:14	9:1,5,10
19:19	16:10
20:6	17:10
24:1	21:20

1033 ܚܡܫܝܢ (num) fifty

MRK 6:40,40	JHN 8:57
LUK 7:41	21:11
9:14	ACT 13:20
16:6	

1034 ܚܡܫܡܐܐ (num) five hundred

from 1032 ܚܡܫ (above) and 1598 ܡܐܐ

LUK 7:41	1 CO 15:6

1035 ܚܡܫܬܥܣܪ (num) fifteen

from 1032 ܚܡܫ (above) and 2400 ܥܣܪ

LUK 3:1	ACT 27:28
JHN 11:18	GAL 1:18

1038 ܚܡܬܐ (f) anger, wrath

MRK 3:5	GAL 5:20
LUK 4:28	EPH 4:31
ACT 7:54	COL 3:8
9:1	HEB 11:27
19:28	REV 12:12
ROM 2:8	14:8,10,19
3:13	15:1,7
2 CO 12:20	16:1,19

1039 ܚܡܬܢܐ (adj) wrathful

TIT 1:7

1036 ܚܡܬ (v) (ethpa) grow angry

[d]ETHPAAL

Perfect

MAT 2:16

Participle

LUK 11:53	ACT 4:2
13:14	

1040 ܚܢ (v) have compassion; (ethpe) obtain mercy; (ethpa) implore

[a]PEAL

Perfect

MAT 18:33[2]

Imperfect

MAT 18:33[1]	ROM 9:15[1]

Imperative

LUK 18:13

Active Participle

ROM 9:15[2]

1047 ܚܢܢܐ (m) compassion

MAT 9:13	LUK 1:72,78
12:7	2:30
23:23	1 PT 1:3
LUK 1:50,54,58,	JUD 21

3369 ܬܚܢܢܬܐ (f) supplication

1 TM 2:1

[b]ETHPEEL

Perfect

ROM 11:30[1]	1 TM 1:13
1 CO 7:25	

[d]ETHPAAL

Participle

ROM 1:10

1042 ܚܢܐ (v-non occ) bend

[a]PEAL

1044 ܚܢܘܬܐ (f) tavern; (w/ ܬܠܬ) The Three Taverns

ACT 28:15

1045 ܚܢܛ (v-non occ) embalm

PEAL

942 ܚܘܢܛܬܐ (f) mixture of spices

JHN 19:39

1051 ܚܢܦܐ (adj) godless, Gentile, heathen

MAT 6:7
10:5
18:17
MRK 7:26
JHN 7:35
ACT 18:4,17
1 CO 5:1
10:20,27
12:2
1 PT 4:3

1052 ܚܢܩ (v) choke, strangle; (pa) drown

PEAL

Perfect

MAT 13:7
27:5
MRK 4:7
LUK 8:7

Active Participle

MAT 13:22
18:28
MRK 4:19

Passive Participle

ACT 15:20,29
ACT 21:25

1686 ܡܚܢܘܩܬܐ (f) noose

1 CO 7:35

ETHPAAL

Perfect

MRK 5:13
LUK 8:33

Participle

LUK 8:14*
2 CO 4:8*

1056 ܚܣܕܐ (m) reproach, disgrace

LUK 1:25
ROM 15:3
1 TM 3:7
HEB 10:32
11:26
13:13

1055 (ܚܣܕ) (v) revile, reproach

[c]PAEL

Perfect

MRK 16:14

Infinitive

MAT 11:20

Active Participle

MAT 5:11
27:44
MRK 15:32
LUK 6:22
JAM 1:5

1687 ܡܚܣܕܢܐ (adj) reviler

ROM 15:3

[d]ETHPAAL

Participle

1 TM 4:10
1 PT 4:14

1057 ܚܣܝܐ (adj) holy, pure

ACT 2:27
13:35
TIT 1:8
REV 15:4
16:5

1058 ܚܣܝܘܬܐ (f) holiness

EPH 4:24

1054 (ܚܣܐ) (v) absolve

[c]PAEL

Imperfect

HEB 8:12

Active Participle

HEB 2:17

Passive Participle

MAT 27:24

944 ܚܘܣܝܐ (m) propitiation

ROM 3:25
HEB 9:5
1 JN 2:2
4:10

1062 ܚܣܟ (v) withhold, spare

[b]ETHPEEL

Participle

ACT 27:21

1064 ܚܣܡ (v) envy, be jealous

[a]PEAL

Perfect

ACT 17:5	GAL 3:1

Active Participle

1 CO 13:4 GAL 4:17[1],17[2]	GAL 5:26 TIT 2:14

1065 ܚܣܡܐ (m) envy

MAT 27:18 MRK 15:10 LUK 6:11 ACT 5:17 13:45 ROM 1:29 13:13 1 CO 3:3	2 CO 12:20 GAL 5:21 PHL 1:15 1 TM 6:4 TIT 3:3 JAM 3:14,16 1 PT 2:1

[b]ETHPEEL

Imperfect

GAL 4:18

1066 ܚܣܢ (v) be strong, prevail; (pa) strengthen

cf ܡܚܣܢ

[a]PEAL

Imperfect

MAT 16:18	MAT 17:20

1067 ܚܣܢܐ (m) stronghold

2 CO 10:4

1582 ܠܡܚܣܢ (adv) scarcely, hardly

LUK 9:32,39 ACT 14:18 27:7,8,16	ROM 5:7 1 PT 4:18

[c]PAEL (non occ)

1059 ܚܣܝܢܐ (adj) strong

MAT 3:11 12:29,29 MRK 3:27,27 LUK 11:21,22	1 CO 10:22 2 CO 1:10 10:10

[d]ETHPAAL

Imperative

1 CO 16:13

1068 ܚܣܪ (v) lack, lose

[a]PEAL

Perfect

LUK 22:35 JHN 2:3 2 CO 11:9	PHL 3:8 4:11 PLM 18

Imperfect

MAT 16:26 MRK 8:36 LUK 9:25 22:32	1 CO 3:15 2 CO 7:9 TIT 3:13

Active Participle

LUK 15:14

946 ܚܘܣܪܢܐ (m) loss

ACT 27:10,21	PHL 3:7,8

1060 ܚܣܝܪܐ (adj) lacking

MAT 19:20 MRK 10:21 LUK 11:40 12:20 18:22 24:25 ROM 1:30 2:20 3:23 4:20	2 CO 11:19,24 12:11 GAL 3:1 EPH 5:17 1 TH 3:10 TIT 1:5 HEB 12:15 JAM 1:4,5 2:15

1061 ܚܣܝܪܘܬܐ (f) want, need

MRK 6:6 9:24 12:44 LUK 21:4 ROM 11:23	2 CO 8:14,14 9:12 11:21,23 PHL 4:12 COL 1:24

1069 ܚܦܐ (v) cover, hide

[c]PAEL

Active Participle

MRK 14:65	LUK 22:63
LUK 8:16	1 PT 4:8

3370 ܬܚܦܝܬܐ (f) veil

2 CO 3:13,14,15, 16	1 PT 2:16

1070 ܚܦܛ (v) be diligent; (pa) exhort

[a]PEAL (non occ)

1071 ܚܦܝܛܐ (pp) diligent, careful

ACT 26:7	2 CO 8:22,22
ROM 12:11	EPH 4:3

1072 ܚܦܝܛܐܝܬ (adv) diligently

MAT 2:8	PHL 2:28

1073 ܚܦܝܛܘܬܐ (f) diligence

ROM 12:8	2 TM 1:17
2 CO 1:6	4:2
7:11,12	HEB 6:11
8:7,8,16	

[c]PAEL

Perfect

MRK 15:11	GAL 2:8[1],8[2]
ACT 18:27	

Active Participle

PHL 2:13

[d]ETHPAAL

Perfect

1 TH 2:17

Imperfect

1 TH 4:11	HEB 4:11

Imperative

1 TM 4:13

Infinitive

2 TH 2:7

Participle

ROM 1:15	2 CO 4:12
7:5	5:9
15:20	EPH 2:2

1074 ܚܦܪ (v) dig

[a]PEAL

Perfect

MAT 21:33	MRK 12:1
25:18	LUK 6:48

Imperfect

LUK 16:3

1075 ܚܨܐ (m) back, loins

MAT 3:4,4	ACT 12:8
MRK 1:6	21:11
LUK 12:35,37	ROM 11:10
17:8	EPH 6:14
JHN 13:4,5	HEB 7:5,10
21:7,18,18	1 PT 1:13

1076 ܚܨܐ (v) pluck out

[a]PEAL

Imperative

MAT 5:29	MRK 9:47
18:9	

Active Participle

GAL 4:15

1077 ܚܨܕ (v) reap

[a]PEAL

Perfect

JAM 5:4

Imperfect

1 CO 9:11	GAL 6:8[2],9
2 CO 9:6[2]	

Imperative

REV 14:15[1]

Infinitive

JHN 4:38 | REV 14:15[2]

Active Participle

MAT 6:26
25:24,26
LUK 12:24
19:21,22
JHN 4:36,37
2 CO 9:6[1]
GAL 6:7,8[1]

1078 ܚܨܕܐ (m) harvest

MAT 9:37,38,38
13:30,30,
39
MRK 4:29
LUK 10:2,2,2
JHN 4:35,35

1079 ܚܨܘܕܐ (m) reaper

MAT 13:30,39
JHN 4:36
JAM 5:4

---

[b]ETHPEEL

Perfect

REV 14:16

1081 ܚܨܦ (v-non occ) be bold, obnoxious

[a]PEAL

1080 ܚܨܝܦܘܬܐ (f) importunity

LUK 11:8

1082 ܚܨܦܐ (m) earthen vessel

2 CO 4:7

1084 ܚܩܠ, ܚܩܠܐ (f) field

MAT 6:30
24:18
MRK 13:16
LUK 12:28
LUK 17:7,31,36
ACT 1:19
1 PT 1:24

---

882 (ܚܪ), ܚܐܪܐ (adj) free, noble

see also 441 ܒܪ ܚܐܪܐ

ACT 17:11
GAL 4:22,23,26,
GAL 4:30,31
REV 19:18

883 ܚܐܪܘܬܐ (f) freedom, liberty

1 CO 10:29
2 CO 3:17
GAL 2:4
5:1,13,13
JAM 1:25
2:12
1 PT 2:16
2 PT 2:19

1094 ܚܘܪܪܐ (m) freedom

ROM 8:21

1085 (ܚܪ) (v) set free

[c]PAEL

Perfect

ROM 8:2 | GAL 5:1

Imperfect

JHN 8:32,36

Passive Participle

ROM 6:20
1 CO 7:22,39
1 CO 9:19

---

[d]ETHPAAL

Perfect

ROM 6:7,18,22 | ROM 7:2,3

Imperfect

ROM 8:21

Infinitive

1 CO 7:21

---

952 (ܚܪ), ܚܘܪܐ (m-non occ) hole

1093 ܚܪܘܪܐ (m) hole, opening

MAT 19:24
MRK 10:25
LUK 18:25

1086 **(ܚܪܐ)**(v) (ethpe) hold on to, affirm, strive

[b]ETHPEEL

Perfect

MRK	9:34	ACT	27:41

Imperfect

MAT 12:19

Participle

LUK	22:59	1 CO	11:16
ACT	12:15	1 TM	1:7
	19:9	2 TM	2:14,25
ROM	10:21	TIT	1:9

1095 **ܚܪܝܢܐ** (m) contention, strife

LUK	2:34	GAL	5:20
	22:24	PHL	1:15,17
ACT	15:39		2:3
	26:19	1 TM	1:4
ROM	1:29		6:4
	13:13	2 TM	2:23
1 CO	1:11	TIT	3:9
	3:3	HEB	6:16
	11:19		7:7
2 CO	12:20	JAM	3:14,16

1087 **ܚܪܒ**(v) be desolate

int of ܚܪܒ below

[a]PEAL

Perfect

REV 18:19

Imperfect

MAT	12:25	LUK	11:17

1088 **ܚܪܒ** (v) lay waste

tr of ܚܪܒ (above)

Active Participle

GAL 1:13

953 **ܚܘܪܒܐ** (m) wilderness, plain

MAT	3:1,3	MAT	24:15,26
	11:7	MRK	1:35,45
	14:13,15		6:32,35
	15:33		8:4
MRK	13:14	LUK	21:20
LUK	1:80	JHN	11:54
	3:2,4	2 CO	11:26
	4:1,42	HEB	11:38
	7:24	REV	12:6,14
	8:29		17:3
	9:10,12		

1090 **ܚܪܒܐ** (adj) desolate

MAT	23:38	ACT	1:20
LUK	13:35	REV	17:16

1089 **ܚܪܒ, ܚܪܒܐ**(c) sword, slaughter

MAT	10:34	REV	2:12,16
LUK	9:62		6:4,8
	21:24		13:10,10,14
HEB	7:1		19:15,21
2 PT	2:12		
REV	1:16		

1092 **(ܚܪܒ), ܚܪܘܒܐ**(m) husk, carob

LUK 15:16

1091 **ܚܪܕܠܐ**(m) mustard seed

MAT	13:31	LUK	13:19
	17:20		17:6
MRK	4:31		

1098 **ܚܪܡ**(v) be forbidden; (aph) vow, curse

[a]PEAL (non occ)

1099 **ܚܪܡܐ** (m) curse

ACT	23:14	1 CO	16:22
ROM	9:3	GAL	1:8,9
1 CO	12:3	REV	22:3

[e]APHEL

Perfect

ACT	23:12,14,	ACT	23:21

Infinitive

MAT 26:74

Active Participle

MRK 14:71

1101 ܚܪܝܡܐ (adj) crafty

2 CO 12:16

1102 ܚܪܝܡܘܬܐ (f) craftiness

LUK 20:23	2 CO 4:2
1 CO 3:19	EPH 4:14

1103 ܚܪܦ (v-non occ) be sharp

[a]PEAL

1096 ܚܪܝܦܐ (adj) sharp

HEB 4:12	REV 14:14,17, 18,18
1 PT 4:8	19:15
REV 1:16	
2:12	

1097 ܚܪܝܦܐܝܬ (adv) suddenly

1 CO 15:52

1104 ܚܪܩ (v) gnash

[c]PAEL

Active Participle

MRK 9:18	ACT 7:54
LUK 9:39	

954 ܚܘܪܩܐ (m) gnashing

MAT 8:12	MAT 24:51
13:42,50	25:30
22:13	LUK 13:28

1105 ܚܪܫ (v-non occ) be dumb, silent

[a]PEAL

1106 ܚܪܫܐ (adj) dumb, mute

MAT 9:32,33	MAT 12:22,22
11:5	15:30,31
MRK 7:32,37	LUK 11:14,14
9:25	2 PT 2:12
LUK 1:22	JUD 10
7:22	

1108 ܚܪ̈ܫܐ (m) sorcery

ACT 8:9,11	REV 18:23
REV 9:21	

1107 ܚܪܫܐ (m) sorcerer

ACT 13:6,8	REV 21:8
19:19	22:15

1109 ܚܪܫܘܬܐ (f) witchcraft, magic

GAL 5:20

1111 ܚܫ (v) feel, suffer

[a]PEAL

Perfect

MAT 27:19	HEB 2:18
ACT 1:3	13:12
1 TH 2:2	1 PT 4:1

Imperfect

MAT 16:21	ACT 17:3
17:12	26:23
MRK 8:31	ROM 8:17
9:12	PHL 1:29
LUK 9:22	HEB 4:15
17:25	5:2
22:15	9:26
24:46	1 PT 3:14
ACT 3:18	

Infinitive

ACT 9:16	REV 2:10

Active Participle

1 CO 12:26	1 PT 2:23
2 CO 1:6	3:8[1],8[2]
2 TH 1:5	4:15,16,19

Passive Participle

1 CO 4:4

1112 ܚܫܐ (m) feeling, suffering

ROM 8:18	COL 1:24
2 CO 1:5,6,7	1 TH 4:5
PHL 3:10	2 TM 3:11

HEB 2:9,10	1 PT 1:11
5:8	4:13
10:32	5:1,9

1115 ܚܫܘܫܐ (adj) capable of feeling

ACT 14:15	JAM 5:17

1113 ܚܫܒ (v) think, reckon

ªPEAL

Perfect

ACT 19:19	PHL 3:7,8^{2}
2 CO 5:19	1 TM 1:12
PHL 2:6	HEB 10:29

Imperfect

ROM 4:8,24	2 PT 3:15
2 CO 10:12	REV 13:18
PHL 2:3	

Imperative

ROM 6:11	PLM 18

Active Participle

LUK 14:28	2 CO 10:2
ROM 4:6	PHL 3:8^{1}

Passive Participle

ACT 20:24	1 TH 5:13
ROM 5:13	1 PT 2:10
1 CO 4:1	2 PT 2:13

956 ܚܘܫܒܢܐ (m) reckoning

MAT 18:23	PHL 4:15
25:19	HEB 13:17
LUK 16:2	REV 2:17

1689 ܡܚܫܒܬܐ (f) thought, reasoning

MAT 9:4	ROM 1:21,29
12:25	2:15
15:19	14:1
MRK 7:21	1 CO 3:20
LUK 2:35	4:5
5:22	2 CO 2:11
6:8	10:5
9:46,47	1 TM 2:8
11:17	HEB 4:12
24:38	JAM 2:4
ACT 5:38	

ᵇETHPEEL

Perfect

MRK 15:28	ROM 8:36
ROM 4:3,9,10,	GAL 3:6
22,23	JAM 2:23

Imperfect

ROM 4:11	2 TM 4:16

Participle

ACT 19:27	ROM 4:4,5
ROM 2:26	9:8

ᶜPAEL (non occ)

955 ܚܘܫܒܐ (m) reckoning, thought

JAM 3:15

ᵈETHPAAL

Perfect

MRK 11:31	ACT 15:25
LUK 7:39	20:3
JHN 11:53	23:20

Imperfect

ROM 15:5

Participle

MAT 9:4	LUK 12:17
16:8	20:5,14
MRK 8:16	JHN 11:50
9:33	ACT 5:24,33
LUK 1:29,66	12:11
3:15	ROM 2:3
5:21,22	1 CO 13:11

1116 ܚܫܚ (v) be useful; (ethpa) use

ªPEAL

Active Participle

LUK 9:62	PLM 11
EPH 4:29	HEB 6:7

957 ܚܘܫܚܐ (m) use

1 TM 4:3	2 TM 2:21

1117 ܚܫܚܘܬܐ (f) advantage, usefulness

2 TM 2:16	HEB 9:17
PLM 11	

1118 ܚܫܚܬܐ (f) use

ROM 1:26,27	PHL 4:16
1 CO 7:31	COL 2:22,23
PHL 2:25	1 TM 6:6

[d]ETHPAAL

Perfect

ACT 27:3	1 CO 9:12,15
ROM 1:26	1 TH 2:5

Imperfect

1 CO 9:18

Participle

JHN 4:9	1 CO 10:30
1 CO 7:31	

1119 ܚܫܟ (v) grow dark; (pa, aph) darken

[a]PEAL

Perfect

MAT 14:23	REV 8:12
LUK 23:45	9:2
JHN 6:17	

Imperfect

MAT 24:29	ROM 11:10
MRK 13:24	

Infinitive

LUK 24:29

1114 ܚܫܘܟܐ (adj) dark, darkness (dark place)

MAT 4:16	LUK 11:36
6:23,23,23	12:3
8:12	22:53
10:27	23:44
22:13	24:1
25:30	JHN 1:5,5
27:45	3:19
MRK 15:33	8:12
LUK 1:79	12:35,35,
11:34,35,	46
JHN 20:1	COL 1:13
ACT 13:11	1 TH 5:4,5
26:18	HEB 12:18
ROM 2:19	1 PT 2:9
13:12	2 PT 2:17
1 CO 4:5	1 JN 1:5,6
2 CO 4:6	2:8,9,11,
6:14	11,11
EPH 4:18	JUD 13
5:8,11	REV 16:10
6:12	

[d]ETHPAAL

Perfect

ROM 1:21

[e]APHEL

Perfect

JHN 12:40

1120 ܚܫܠ (v-non occ) forge, excite

[a]PEAL

1121 ܚܫܠܬܐ (f) ornament

1 PT 3:3

[e]APHEL

1690 ܚܫܘܠܐ (m) storm

LUK 8:24,25

1123 (ܚܫܡ), ܚܫܡܝܬܐ (f) supper

MAT 23:6	JHN 12:2
MRK 6:21	13:2,4
12:39	21:20
LUK 14:12,16,	1 CO 11:21
17,24	REV 19:9,17
20:46	

1122 (ܚܫܡ) (v) eat supper

[e]APHEL

Perfect

LUK 22:20	1 CO 11:25

Imperfect

LUK 17:8 | REV 3:20

1125 ܚܬܚܬ (v-non occc) excite

[k]P

958 ܚܘܬܚܬܐ (m) itching, excitation

2 TM 4:3

1128 ܚܬܡ (v) seal

[a]PEAL

Perfect

MAT 27:66 | JHN 6:27
JHN 3:33 | 2 CO 1:22

Imperfect

REV 7:3 | REV 22:10

Imperative

REV 10:4

Passive Participle

REV 7:4,8

1129 ܚܬܡܐ (m) seal

ROM 4:11 | REV 7:2
1 CO 9:2 | 9:4
2 TM 2:19

[b]ETHPEEL

Perfect

EPH 1:13 | EPH 4:30

[c]PAEL

Perfect

ROM 15:28

1130 ܚܬܢܐ (m) bridegroom

MAT 9:15,15 | MAT 25:10
25:1,5,6, | MRK 2:19,20
LUK 5:34,35 | JHN 3:29,29,29
JHN 2:9 | REV 18:23

1131 ܚܬܪ (v) be puffed up, proud; (aph) make proud

[a]PEAL (non occ)

1126 ܚܬܝܪܐ (pp) proud

LUK 1:51 | 1 CO 5:2
ROM 1:30 | 2 TM 3:4

1127 ܚܬܝܪܘܬܐ (f) boasting

2 CO 12:20 | JAM 4:16

[b]ETHPEEL

Perfect

1 CO 4:18

Participle

1 CO 13:4 | COL 2:18

[d]ETHPAAL

Imperfect

JAM 3:14

[e]APHEL

Active Participle

1 CO 8:1

ܛ

1132 ܛܐܒ (v) do good

eAPHEL

Imperative

LUK 6:35

Active Participle

LUK 6:33

1133 ܛܒ (v) hear, know; (aph) inform

aPEAL (non occ)

1134 ܛܒܐ (m) fame, rumor

MAT 4:24	LUK 4:14,37
9:26	5:15
MRK 1:28	7:39
13:7	ACT 4:17

eAPHEL

Perfect

MAT 9:31	MRK 1:45

1138 ܛܒܥ (v) (tr) seal; (int) sink; (pa) drown

aPEAL

Perfect

ACT 20:9	REV 20:3

Infinitive

MAT 14:30	LUK 8:23
LUK 5:7	

Passive Participle

REV 5:1

1139 ܛܒܥܐ (m) seal

REV 5:1,2,3,4,5,	REV 5:9
REV 6:1,3,5,7,9, 12	REV 8:1

cPAEL

Active Participle

1 TM 6:9

Passive Participle

MAT 18:6

1142 (ܛܠܡ) (v) (ethpa) do violence, molest

dETHPAAL

Imperfect

LUK 3:14

1147 (ܛܘܗܡ), ܛܘܗܡܐ (m) kinsman

LUK 1:58	ACT 18:24
19:12	1 CO 1:26,28
ACT 7:3,13,14, 19	2 CO 11:26
10:24	GAL 1:14
17:28,29	PHL 3:5

1148 (ܛܘܐ), ܛܘܝܐ (adj) broiled

LUK 24:42

1135 (ܛܘܒ), ܛܒܐ (adj) good; (ܛܒ as adv) very

MAT 2:10,16	MAT 7:11,11,17, 18,18,19
3:10	8:28
4:8	12:34,35,
5:16,45	

MAT 12:35,35
13:8,23,24,27,37,38,45,48
17:6,23
18:8,9,31
19:16,16,17,17,25
20:15
22:10
25:21,23
26:22
27:14,54
MRK 1:35
3:4
4:8,20
6:51
9:3
10:17,18,18
16:4
LUK 1:53
2:14
3:9
5:6
6:9,33,38,43,43,45,45,45
8:8,15,15
10:42
11:13
12:18,19
16:25
18:18,19,19,23
19:17
22:25
23:8,50
JHN 1:46
2:10,10
5:29
7:12
10:11,11,14
ACT 6:7
9:36
11:24
14:17
19:32
23:1
ROM 1:11,25
2:7,10
3:8,12
5:7
7:12,13,13,18,18,19,21
8:28
9:11
10:15
ROM 11:24
12:2,9,17,21
13:3,3,4
14:16
15:2,14
16:19
1 CO 7:9
2 CO 4:17
5:10
8:17
9:8
11:5
12:11
13:7
GAL 1:14
6:6,9,10
EPH 2:10
4:28
PHL 1:6,15,23
COL 1:10
1 TH 3:6
5:15
2 TH 1:11
2:16,17
1 TM 1:5,19
2:10
3:1,13
4:6,6
5:10,25
6:12,12,18,19
2 TM 1:14
2:3,21
3:3,4,17
4:15
TIT 1:8,16
2:7,10,14
3:1,8,8,14
PLM 6,11,14
HEB 3:3,3
4:12
5:8,14
6:5
9:11
10:1,24,37
11:4,16,26
12:24
13:18,21
JAM 1:17
2:7
3:17
4:17
1 PT 2:3,14,18
3:6,10,11,13,16,17
4:10
2 PT 1:10,12
3 JN 11,11
REV 16:21
17:4

1136 ܛܒܘܬܐ (f) goodness

GAL 5:22
EPH 5:9

1144 ܛܘܒܐ (m) blessing; (w/ suff) blessed

MAT 5:3,4,5,6,7,8,9,10,11
11:6
13:16
16:17
24:46
LUK 1:45,48
6:20,21,21,22
7:23
10:23
11:27,28
12:37,38,43
14:14,15
LUK 23:29
JHN 20:29
ACT 20:35
ROM 4:6,7,8,9
14:22
1 CO 7:40
GAL 4:15
JAM 1:12
5:11
1 PT 3:14
4:14
REV 14:13
16:15
19:9
22:7,14

1145 ܛܘܒܢܐ (adj) blessed, happy

JHN 13:17
ACT 26:2
JAM 1:25
REV 20:6

1146 ܛܘܒܬܢܐ (adj) blessed

REV 1:3

1165 ܛܝܒܘܬܐ (f) grace, goodness

LUK 1:28,30
2:40,52
4:22
6:32,33,34
17:9
JHN 1:14,16,16,17
ACT 4:33
6:8
7:10
11:23
13:34,43
14:3,26
15:11,40
18:27
20:24,32
24:3,27
25:3,9
ROM 1:5,7
3:24
4:4,16
5:2,15,17,20,21
6:1,14,15,17
11:5,6,6,6,6
12:3,6
ROM 15:15
16:20,27
1 CO 1:3,4
3:10
10:30
15:10,10,10,57
16:3,23
2 CO 1:2,11,12,15
2:14
4:15
6:1
8:1,4,6,7,9,16,19
9:8,14,15
12:9
GAL 1:3,6,15
2:9,21
5:4
6:18
EPH 1:2,6,7
2:5,7,8
3:2,7,8
4:7,29
6:24
PHL 1:2,7
4:23

COL	1:2,6	HEB	2:9
	3:16		4:16,16
	4:6,18		10:29
1 TH	1:1		12:15,28
	5:28		13:9,25
2 TH	1:2,12	JAM	4:6,6
	2:16	1 PT	1:2,10
	3:18		2:19
1 TM	1:2,14		4:10
	6:21		5:5,10,12
2 TM	1:2,9	2 PT	1:2
	2:1		3:18
	3:2	2 JN	3,13
	4:22	JUD	4
TIT	1:4	REV	1:4
	2:11		4:9
	3:7,15		7:12
PLM	3,25		22:21

1143 (ܛܘܒ) (v) make ready

[c]PAEL

Perfect

MAT	26:19	ROM	6:19[1]
MRK	14:16	1 CO	2:9
LUK	2:31	EPH	2:10
	12:20,47	HEB	11:16
	22:13	REV	8:6
	23:56		19:7
	24:1		

Imperfect

MAT	26:17	LUK	22:9
MRK	14:12	JHN	14:2,3
LUK	1:17,76	ROM	6:13[1]

Imperative

MAT	3:3	LUK	22:8,12
MRK	1:3	ACT	23:24
LUK	3:4	ROM	6:13[2],19[2]
	17:8	PLM	22

Active Participle

ROM	6:16	REV	10:4
2 CO	4:17		

Passive Participle

MAT	22:4[1],4[2],8	ACT	23:15,21
	24:44	ROM	9:23
	25:10,41	2 CO	9:3,5
	26:41		10:6
MRK	10:40		12:14
	14:15,38	2 TM	2:21
LUK	12:40	HEB	12:1
	14:17	1 PT	1:4,5
	22:33		3:15
JHN	7:6	REV	9:7,15
ACT	3:20		12:6
	21:13		21:2

1149 ܛܘܝܒܐ (m) preparation

2 CO	9:2	EPH	6:15

[d]ETHPAAL

Perfect

MAT	20:23	ACT	21:15

Imperfect

1 CO	14:8	REV	16:12

1153 (ܛܘܦ)(v) overflow

[a]PEAL

Perfect

2 PT 3:6

1156 ܛܘܦܢܐ (m) flood

MAT	24:38,39	2 PT	2:5
LUK	17:27		

1171 (ܛܘܪ), ܛܝܪܐ (m) sheepfold

JHN 10:1,16

1158 ܛܘܪܐ (m) mountain

MAT	4:8	LUK	9:28,37
	5:1,14		19:29,37
	8:1		21:21,37
	14:23		22:39
	15:29		23:30
	17:1,9,20	JHN	4:20,21
	18:12		6:3,15
	21:1,21		8:1
	24:3,16	ACT	1:12
	26:30		7:30,38
	28:16	1 CO	13:2
MRK	3:13	GAL	4:24,25
	5:5,11	HEB	8:5
	6:46		11:38
	9:2,9		12:20,22
	11:1,23	2 PT	1:18
	13:3,14	REV	6:14,15,16
	14:26		8:8
LUK	1:39,65		14:1
	3:5		16:20
	4:5,29		17:9
	6:12		21:10
	8:32		

1161 (ܛܘܫ)(v) annoint; (pa) soil, defile

aPEAL

Perfect

JHN 9:6,11

cPAEL

Perfect

REV 3:4

dETHPAAL

Perfect

REV 14:4

Imperfect

JHN 18:28

Participle

1 CO 8:7

1162 ܛܚܢ(v) grind

PEAL

Active Participle

MAT 24:41 | LUK 17:35

1164 ܛܛܪܪܟܐ(m) tetrarch

MAT 14:1 | LUK 9:7
LUK 3:19 | ACT 13:1

166 ܛܝܡܐ(m) price

MAT 27:6 | ACT 5:2

170 ܛܝܢܐ(m) clay

JHN 9:6,11,14,15 | ROM 9:21

172 ܛܝܪܐ(f) bird

REV 19:21

1173 ܛܟ(adv) perhaps

ROM 5:7

1175 ܛܟܣܐ(m) order, arrangement

LUK 1:3,8 | 1 CO 15:23
1 CO 14:40

1174 (ܛܟܣ) (v) order, arrange

cPAEL

Passive Participle

1 TM 3:2

1693 ܛܟܣܘܬܐ(f) orderliness

COL 2:5

1180 (ܛܠ), ܛܠܠܐ(m) shadow

MAT 4:16 | LUK 1:79
MRK 4:32

1182 ܛܠܠܬܐ (f) shadow

ACT 5:15 | HEB 10:1
COL 2:17 | JAM 1:17
HEB 8:5

1695 ܡܛܠܠܐ (m) shelter

MAT 8:8,20 | LUK 9:58
LUK 7:6 | 16:9

1696 ܡܛܠܬܐ (f) booth, tabernacle

MAT 17:4 | LUK 9:33
MRK 9:5 | JHN 7:2

1176 (ܛܠܠ) (v) cover, overshadow

cPAEL (non occ)

3373 ܬܛܠܝܠܐ (m) roof

MRK 2:4 | LUK 5:19

eAPHEL

Perfect

MAT 17:5

Active Participle

MRK 9:7
LUK 9:34
HEB 9:5

1177 ܛܠܝܐ (m) young boy, youth

MAT 2:8,9,11, 13,13,14, 16,20,20, 21
8:6,8,13
11:16
14:21
15:38
17:18
18:2,3,4,5
19:13,14
21:15,16
MRK 9:24,36,37
10:13,14, 15
LUK 1:59,66,76, 80
LUK 2:17,21,27, 40,43
7:7,32
9:42,47,48
15:26
18:16,17
JHN 4:49
6:9
21:5,18
ROM 2:20
1 CO 14:20
GAL 4:1
1 TM 3:6
5:1
TIT 2:6
HEB 11:23
1 JN 2:13

1178 ܛܠܝܘܬܐ (f) youth, childhood

MAT 19:20
MRK 9:21
10:20
LUK 18:21
ACT 26:4
1 CO 13:11
1 TM 4:12
2 TM 2:22
3:15

1179 ܛܠܝܬܐ (f) young girl

MAT 9:24,25
14:11
MRK 5:39,40,40, 41,41,42
6:22,28,28
LUK 8:50,51,54
ACT 12:13
1 TM 5:2,11,14
TIT 2:4

1181 ܛܠܡ (v) wrong, reject

aPEAL

Perfect

LUK 7:30
1 TM 5:12
JAM 5:4

Imperfect

MRK 10:19

Active Participle

MRK 7:9
LUK 10:16[1],16[2], 16[3],16[4]
JHN 12:48
GAL 2:21
1 TH 4:8[1],8[2]
1 PT 3:16
JUD 8

1183 ܛܠܩ (v) vanish; (ethpa) be finished

aPEAL

Active Participle

JAM 4:14

dETHPAAL

Infinitive

2 CO 1:8

1184 ܛܠܪ̈ܐ (m) sandals

MRK 6:9
ACT 12:8

1185 ܛܠܫ (v-non occ) be soiled

aPEAL

1151 ܛܘܠܫܐ (m) spot, impurity

EPH 5:27
1 TM 6:14
HEB 7:26
JAM 1:27
1 PT 1:19

1187 ܛܡܐ, ܛܡܐܐ (adj) unclean, impure

MRK 1:23
ACT 10:14,28
11:8
ROM 1:24
14:14,14
1 CO 7:14
2 CO 6:17
REV 21:27
22:15

1188 ܛܡܐܘܬܐ (f) uncleaness, impurity

ACT 15:20
2 CO 7:1
2 PT 2:10
REV 17:4

1186 (ܛܡܐ) (v) consider unclean

dETHPAAL

Participle

HEB 9:13

1189 ܛܡܪ (v) hide, cover

aPEAL

Perfect

MAT 13:33	LUK 13:21

Passive Participle

2 TM 3:6

1190 ܛܢ (v) be eager, jealous; (aph) provoke jealousy

aPEAL

Perfect

ACT 7:9

Imperative

1 CO 14:1,39	REV 3:19

Active Participle

1 CO 12:31	GAL 1:14
2 CO 11:2	JAM 4:2

1191 ܛܢܢܐ (m) jealousy, zeal

JHN 2:17	GAL 5:20
ROM 10:2	PHL 3:6
11:11	COL 4:13
2 CO 7:7,11	HEB 10:27
9:2	JAM 4:5
11:2	

cPAEL (non occ)

1192 ܛܢܢܐ (adj) zealot, zealous

LUK 6:15	ACT 22:3
ACT 1:13	1 CO 14:12
21:20	1 PT 3:13

eAPHEL

Imperfect

ROM 10:19	ROM 11:14

Infinitive

1 CO 10:22[1]

Active Participle

1 CO 10:22[2]

1193 ܛܢܦ (v) be soiled; (pa) soil

aPEAL (non occ)

1194 ܛܢܦܐ (adj) defiled, unclean

MAT 10:1	LUK 9:42
12:43	11:24
24:15	ACT 5:16
MRK 1:26,27	8:7
3:11,30	19:13
5:2,8,13	ROM 13:13
6:7	EPH 5:5
7:25	COL 3:8
9:25	1 TM 3:8
13:14	TIT 1:7,11
LUK 4:33,36	1 PT 5:2
6:18	2 PT 2:18
8:29	

1195 ܛܢܦܘܬܐ (f) uncleanness

MAT 23:27	COL 3:5
ROM 6:19	1 TH 2:3
2 CO 12:21	4:7
GAL 5:19	JAM 1:21
EPH 4:19	2 PT 2:2,7,20
5:3	JUD 4

cPAEL

Active Participle

JUD 8

dETHPAAL

Participle

1 PT 1:4

1196 ܛܥܐ (v) wander, err, forget; (aph) deceive, seduce

aPEAL

Perfect

MAT 15:24	1 TM 1:6
16:5	2:14[1],14[2]
18:12[2],13	6:10,21
MRK 8:14	2 TM 2:18
LUK 8:47	HEB 12:5
JHN 7:47	JAM 1:24
ACT 27:27	2 PT 1:9

Imperfect

MAT 18:12[1]	LUK 21:8
24:5	1 CO 6:9

1 CO	15:33	JAM	1:16
GAL	6:7		5:19
HEB	6:10	2 PT	3:8
	13:2,16		

Active Participle

MAT	22:29	TIT	3:3
MRK	12:27	HEB	3:10
LUK	12:6		5:2
ACT	27:32		11:38
PHL	3:13	1 PT	2:25
1 TM	4:1	2 PT	3:5
2 TM	3:13[1]		

Passive Participle

MRK	12:24	ACT	26:26

1152 ܛܘܥܝܝ (f) error, deception

MAT	13:22	ACT	3:17
	27:64	EPH	4:22
MRK	4:19	2 TH	2:10,11

1197 ܛܘܥܝܘܬܐ (f) error, deception

ACT	17:30	JAM	5:19,20
ROM	1:27	2 PT	2:18
COL	2:8		3:17
1 TH	2:3	JUD	11
HEB	3:13		

---

[b]ETHPEEL

Participle

JAM 1:25

---

[e]APHEL

Perfect

ROM	7:11	REV	18:23
2 CO	11:3		19:20
REV	12:9		

Imperfect

MAT	24:4,11,24	2 TH	2:3
MRK	13:5,6,22	JAM	1:22
1 CO	3:18	1 JN	3:7
EPH	4:14	REV	13:14
	5:6		20:3

Infinitive

REV 20:8

Active Participle

LUK	23:2	JHN	7:12

ACT	8:9	TIT	1:10
ROM	16:18	JAM	1:26
GAL	6:3	1 JN	1:8
COL	2:4		2:26
1 TM	4:2	REV	2:20

Passive Participle

2 TM 3:13[2]

1697 ܛܥܝܢܐ (adj) deceiver

MAT	27:63	2 JN	7,7
2 CO	6:8	JUD	13
2 TM	3:13	REV	20:10

1698 ܛܥܝܢܘܬܐ (f) error, deception

1 JN 4:6

1198 ܛܥܡ (v) taste, perceive; (ethpe) be grafted; (aph) graft

[a]PEAL

Perfect

MAT	27:34	HEB	6:4,5
JHN	2:9		11:5
ACT	20:11	1 PT	2:3
HEB	2:9		

Imperfect

MAT	16:28	JHN	8:52
MRK	9:1	ACT	23:14
LUK	9:27	COL	2:21
	14:24		

Passive Participle

ACT 27:33

---

[b]ETHPEEL

Perfect

ROM	11:17,19,	ROM	11:24[1]

Imperfect

ROM 11:23[1],24[2]

---

[e]APHEL

Imperfect

ROM 11:23[2]

1199 ܛܥܢ (v) bear, carry; (aph) make carry

[a]PEAL

Perfect

LUK 11:27 | REV 2:3
ACT 21:35

Imperfect

MAT 8:17 | LUK 23:26

Imperative

GAL 6:2

Infinitive

ACT 15:10 | REV 2:2

Active Participle

ROM 15:7

Passive Participle

JHN 12:6 | REV 17:7

1200 ܛܥܢܐ (m) burden, load

see also 3278 ܫܩܠ ܛܥܢܐ

ACT 21:3 | 1 TH 5:14

[e]APHEL

Active Participle

LUK 11:46

1201 ܛܥܐ (v) stumble, deviate

[a]PEAL

Imperfect

HEB 12:13

1154 (ܛܦܙ), ܛܦܐܙܝܘܢ (m) topaz

REV 21:20

1202 ܛܦܛܦ (v) flicker

[k]P

Active Participle

MAT 12:20

1155 (ܛܦܘܢܣ), ܛܦܘܢܝܩܘܣ (adj) tempestuous

ACT 27:14

1157 (ܛܦܣ), ܛܦܣܐ (m) type, example

JHN 13:15 | 1 PT 2:21
1 CO 10:6,11 | 3:21
2 TH 3:9

1203 ܛܦܪܐ (f) claw, onyx

REV 4:8 | REV 21:20

1204 ܛܪܐ (v) trouble; (ethpa) beat upon

[a]PEAL

Active Participle

HEB 10:2

[d]ETHPAAL

Perfect

MAT 7:25,27 | LUK 6:48,49

1205 ܛܪܕ (v) expel, drive away

[a]PEAL

Perfect

ACT 18:16

1215 ܛܪܦ (v) smite, beat

[a]PEAL

Active Participle

LUK 18:13 | LUK 23:48

1217 ܛܪܦܐ (m) leaf

MAT 21:19, 24:32; MRK 11:13,13 | MRK 13:28; REV 22:2

1216 (ܛܪܦ) (v) tire

[c]PAEL

Passive Participle

HEB 11:37

1160 ܛܘܪܦܐ (m) anxiety, weariness

LUK 2:48 | ROM 2:9

[d]ETHPAAL

Perfect

ACT 27:27

Participle

2 CO 4:8

1218 ܛܫܐ (v) hide oneself, be hidden

[a]PEAL

Imperfect

MAT 5:14 | MRK 7:24

Imperative

REV 6:16

Infinitive

1 TM 5:25

Passive Participle

MRK 4:22 | HEB 4:13

353 ܒܛܘܫܝܐ (adv) secretly

MRK 4:22; JHN 7:4,10, 18:20 | ACT 26:26; EPH 5:12

[c]PAEL

Perfect

MAT 13:44[2], 25:18,25; ACT 5:2 | HEB 11:23; REV 6:15

Imperfect

ACT 5:3

Active Participle

LUK 1:24 | JHN 19:38

Passive Participle

MAT 10:26, 13:44[1] | LUK 8:17, 12:2

[d]ETHPAAL

Perfect

JHN 8:59 | JHN 12:36

[e]APHEL

Passive Participle

REV 2:17

1702 ܒܛܘܫܝܐܝܬ (adv) secretly, privately

MAT 1:19, 2:7 | ACT 16:37

1220 (ܝܐܐ), ܝܐܝܐ (adj)

beautiful, due, becoming

MAT 3:15	PHL 1:27
ROM 10:15	1 TH 2:12
1 CO 11:13	1 TM 2:10
EPH 4:1	TIT 2:1,3
5:3	HEB 2:10

1221 ܝܐܘܬܐ (f) glory, magnificence

1 PT 1:24

1219 ܝܐܒ (v) (ethpa) desire

[d]ETHPAAL

Participle

LUK 16:21

1224 (ܝܒܠ) (v) conduct, take away

[c]PAEL (non occ)

1251 ܝܘܒܠܐ (m) course, succession

JAM 3:6

[d]ETHPAAL

Perfect

ACT 7:45

[e]APHEL

Perfect

MAT 26:57	LUK 16:22
27:2,31	ACT 5:10
MRK 14:53	19:29
15:1,16	REV 21:10

Imperfect

LUK 12:58	ACT 21:34
JHN 21:18	1 CO 16:3
ACT 9:21	

Imperative

MRK 14:44	ACT 23:17

Active Participle

MAT 7:13,14	HEB 10:39
LUK 23:26	REV 13:10
ROM 15:31	

1649 ܡܘܒܠܐ (f) burden, load

MAT 11:28,30	ACT 27:10
23:4	GAL 6:5
LUK 11:46,46	REV 18:11,12

1225 ܝܒܫ (v) dry up, wither; (aph) cause to wither

[a]PEAL

Perfect

MAT 13:6	MRK 11:21
21:19,20	LUK 8:6
MRK 4:6	REV 16:12
5:29	

Active Participle

MRK 9:18	1 PT 1:24
JHN 15:6	

1226 ܝܒܫܐ (m) dry land, earth

MAT 14:13	ACT 20:11,13
23:15	27:39,40
MRK 6:33	JAM 3:7
LUK 5:3	REV 10:5

cPAEL (non occ)

1223 ܝܒܝܫܐ (adj) dry

MAT 12:10
MRK 3:1,3
11:20
LUK 6:6,8
LUK 23:31
JHN 5:3
HEB 11:29

eAPHEL

Active Participle

JAM 1:11

83 (ܐܝܕ), ܐܝܕܐ (f) hand; (w/ ܒ) through; (w/ ܥܠ) near

MAT 1:22
2:17
3:3,12
4:6,13,14,
18
5:30
8:3,9,15,
17
9:18,25
11:2
12:10,13,
13,17,
49
13:1,4,19,
35
14:31
15:2,20
17:22
18:7,8,8
19:13,15
20:30
21:4
22:13
26:23,24,
45,50,
51
27:9,24
MRK 1:31,41
3:1,3,5,5
4:1,1,4,15
5:21,23,41
6:2,5
7:2,3,5,32
8:23,23,25
9:27,31,43,
43
10:16,46
14:21,41,
46,58,
58
16:18
LUK 1:66,71,74
LUK 3:17
5:1,13
6:1,6,8,10,
10
7:8
8:5,12,54
9:7,44,62
10:36
12:48
13:13,17
15:22
17:1
18:35
20:19
21:12,25
22:21,22,
53
23:46
24:7,39,40,
50
JHN 1:3,7,10,
17,17
3:17,35
7:30,44
10:28,29,
39
11:44
13:3,9
20:20,25,
25,27,
27
21:4,18
ACT 2:22,23,43
3:7
4:3,16,25,
28,30
5:12,18,39
6:6
7:25,35,41,
48,50,53
8:13,17,18,
19
ACT 9:8,12,17,
41
10:6,32,36
11:21,30
12:1,7,9,
11,17
13:3,11,11,
16
14:3
15:12,23
16:13
17:24,25,
31
18:27
19:6,11,26,
33
20:34
21:5,11,11,
27,40
22:11
23:19
24:7,13
25:5,14
26:1,7
27:15,19
28:3,4,5,8,
17
ROM 1:2
2:16
3:22
5:11,12,12,
17,21
7:7,11,25
8:3,37
9:11,16,16,
16
10:21
11:36
14:4
15:18
16:25,26
1 CO 1:9
3:5
4:12
8:6,6
10:2,10
11:12
12:15,21
15:2,21,21,
57
16:2,21
2 CO 1:5,19,20
4:14,15
5:1,20
9:8,11
11:33
12:17
GAL 1:1,1
2:21
3:19,19
4:7
6:11
EPH 1:6
2:11
3:6,10
4:6,28
PHL 4:18
COL 1:16,20,20
2:11
3:17
4:18
1 TH 2:9
4:11
2 TH 3:17
1 TM 2:8,15
3:3
4:14
5:22
2 TM 1:6,12
2:2,2
TIT 1:3,7
3:6
PLM 7,19
HEB 1:10
2:2,7,10
3:5,16
6:2
7:9,11,21,
25
8:9
9:11,24
10:31
11:19
12:12
13:5,15,21
JAM 4:2,8
1 PT 1:12,21
2:5
4:11
5:6,10,12
2 PT 1:3,4,4,10
3:2,5,6
1 JN 1:1
4:9
5:6
2 JN 12
3 JN 13
JUD 13,25
REV 1:1,16,17
2:1
4:11
5:7
6:5
7:9
8:4
9:20
10:2,5,8,
10
12:11
13:14,16
14:14
17:4
19:2
20:1,4

1227 (ܐܕܝ)(v) (aph) confess, give thanks; (eshta) profess, promise

eAPHEL

Perfect

MAT 26:27	ACT 28:15
MRK 14:23	ROM 1:21
LUK 2:38	1 TM 6:12
22:19	HEB 11:13
JHN 1:20[1],20[2]	

Imperfect

MAT 7:23	ROM 15:9
10:32[1],32[2]	2 CO 1:11
LUK 12:8[1],8[2]	PHL 2:11
JHN 9:22	COL 1:12
ROM 10:9	REV 3:5
14:11	

Infinitive

EPH 1:16	2 TH 2:13
2 TH 1:3	

Active Participle

MAT 3:6	PHL 1:3
11:25	COL 1:3
MRK 1:5	3:15,17
LUK 10:21	4:2
17:16	1 TH 1:2
18:11	2:13
JHN 11:41	5:18
12:42	1 TM 1:12
ACT 19:18	2 TM 1:3
23:8	TIT 1:16
24:14	PLM 4
ROM 1:8	HEB 13:15
7:25	JAM 5:16
10:10	1 PT 3:21
14:6[1],6[2]	1 JN 1:9
16:4	2:23[1],23[2]
1 CO 1:4,14	4:2,3,15
10:30	2 JN 7
14:18	REV 11:17
EPH 5:20	

3341 ܬܘܕܝܬܐ (f) confession, thanksgiving

1 CO 10:16	1 TH 3:9
14:16	1 TM 2:1
2 CO 4:15	4:3,4
9:11,12,13	6:12
EPH 5:4	HEB 3:1
PHL 4:6	4:14
COL 2:7	10:23

gSHAPHEL (non occ)

3122 ܫܘܘܕܝܐ (m) promise

ACT 1:4	1 TM 4:8
2:33,39	HEB 6:17
13:32	8:6
23:21	2 PT 1:4
26:6	1 JN 2:25
GAL 3:14,19	

hESHTAPHAL

Perfect

MRK 14:11	ACT 13:23
LUK 22:6,29[2]	1 JN 2:25
ACT 7:5,17	

Participle

LUK 22:29[1]	1 TM 6:21
1 TM 2:10	2 PT 2:19

1231 ܝܕܥ(v) know; (aph, shaph) make known; (eshta) know, recognize

aPEAL

Perfect

MAT 7:23	JHN 8:55[1]
9:4	10:6
12:15,25	12:16
16:8	13:28
17:12	14:9,17[1]
21:45	16:3,19
22:18	17:7,8,25[1], 25[2],25[3]
24:39	19:28
26:10	21:4
MRK 2:8	ACT 9:30
5:30,33	12:11[2]
8:17[1]	14:6
12:12,15	17:13
LUK 2:43	19:34
5:22	23:6
6:8	ROM 1:21
7:37	3:17
8:46	8:29
9:11,47	10:3,19
16:4	11:34
19:44	1 CO 1:21
20:19	2:8[1],8[2],16
23:7	8:2[2]
JHN 1:10	2 CO 5:16[2]
4:1,42,53	GAL 2:9
5:6,42	3:8
6:15,61,69	4:9[1]
7:26	PHL 2:26
8:27,52,	

2 TH 1:8[1]
HEB 3:10
1 JN 2:3,13[1], 13[2],14, 29[1]
1 JN 3:1[2],6 4:16
2 JN 1
REV 2:24

Imperfect

MAT 6:3 7:16,20 9:6,30 13:14 27:24
MRK 2:10 4:13[2] 5:43 7:24 9:30
LUK 1:4,18 5:24 9:45[2] 19:15
JHN 7:51 8:28,32 10:38 11:57 13:7[2],17, 35 14:20,31 17:3,23 19:4
ACT 2:36 22:24 23:22
ROM 1:13,28 11:25
1 CO 2:12,14 4:19 10:1 11:3 12:1 13:2,12[2] 14:37,38[2]
2 CO 1:8 2:4,9 10:7 13:6
GAL 3:2
EPH 1:18 3:19 6:21[1],22
PHL 1:12
COL 2:1 4:8
1 TH 3:5 4:13
1 TM 3:15
2 TM 2:25
HEB 8:11[2]
JAM 2:20 5:20
1 JN 5:13,20[2]
REV 3:3,9

Imperative

MAT 24:33,43[1]
MRK 13:29
LUK 10:11 12:39[1] 21:20,31 24:39
JHN 15:18
ACT 13:38
ROM 13:11
GAL 3:7
COL 3:24
HEB 8:11[1] 13:23
1 PT 5:9
1 JN 2:29[2]

Infinitive

MAT 13:11
MRK 4:11
LUK 8:10
JHN 14:5[2]
ACT 1:7 17:19,20
ACT 21:34 22:14,30 23:28 24:11
1 CO 8:2[3]
REV 1:12

Active Participle

MAT 6:8,32 7:11 11:27[1],27[2] 12:7 15:12,17 16:3[1],3[2] 20:22,25
MAT 21:27 22:16,29, 35 24:32,36, 42,43[2], 50 25:12,13,
MAT 25:24,26 26:2,70,72, 74 27:4,18,65 28:5
MRK 1:24,34 4:13[1],27 6:20 7:18 8:17[2] 9:6,32 10:19,38, 42 11:33 12:14,24 13:28,32, 33,35 14:40,68, 71 15:10
LUK 2:44,49 4:34,41 7:39 8:53 9:33,55 10:22 11:13,17, 44 12:30,39[2], 46,47, 48,56 13:25,27 16:15 18:20,34 19:22,42 20:7,21 22:34,57, 60 23:34 24:18
JHN 1:26,31[1], 33,48 2:9[1],9[2],24, 25 3:2,8,10, 11 4:10,22[1], 22[2],25, 32 5:13,32 6:6,42,64 7:15,27[1], 27[2],28[1], 28[2],28[3], 29,49 8:14[1],14[2], 19[1],19[2], 19[3],37, 55[2],55[3], 55[4] 9:12,20,21, 24,25[1], 25[2],29[1], 29[2],30, 31
JHN 10:4,5,14[1], 15[1],15[2], 27 11:22,24, 42,49 12:35,50 13:1,3,7[1], 11,12, 18,22 14:4[1],4[2],5[1], 7[1],7[2],7[3], 17[2] 15:15[1],21 16:18,30[1], 30[2] 18:2,4,15, 16,21 19:10,35 20:2,9,13, 14 21:12,15, 16,17, 24
ACT 1:24 2:22,30 3:16,17 4:13[1] 5:7 7:18,40 9:29 10:28,37 12:9 15:7,8 16:3 17:23 18:15,25 19:15[2],25, 32,35 20:18,22, 25,29, 34 21:37 22:19 23:5 24:10,22 25:10,26 26:3,4,5, 26,27 28:22
ROM 1:32 2:2,4,18 3:19 5:3 6:3,6,9,16 7:1[1],1[2],7, 14,15,18 8:22,26,27, 28 11:2 14:14 15:29
1 CO 1:16 2:2,11[1], 11[2] 3:16,20

1 CO 5:6
6:2,3,9,15,16,19
7:16[1],16[2]
8:1,2[1],4
9:13,24
13:9,12[1]
14:11,16,38[1]
15:58
16:15
2 CO 1:7,13[1]
2:11
3:3
4:14
5:1,6,11,16[1],16[3],21
8:9
9:2
11:11,31
12:2[1],2[2],2[3],3[1],3[2],3[3]
GAL 1:22
2:16
4:8,13
EPH 5:5
6:8,9
PHL 1:16,19,22,25
2:22
3:13
4:12[1],12[2],15
COL 4:1,6
1 TH 1:4,5
2:1,2,5,11
3:3,4
4:2,4,5
5:2,12
2 TH 2:6

2 TH 3:7
1 TM 1:8,9,13
3:5
4:3
6:4
2 TM 1:12,15,18
2:19,23
3:1,11,14
TIT 1:16
3:11
PLM 9,21
HEB 5:2
10:30,34
11:8
12:17
JAM 1:3
3:1
4:4,14,17
1 PT 1:18
2:15
2 PT 1:12,14[1],20
2:9,12
3:3,17
1 JN 2:5,11,18,21[1],21[2]
3:1[1],2,5,14,15,16,20
4:6,7,8,13
5:2,18,19,20[1]
3 JN 12
JUD 5,10
REV 2:2,9,13,17,19,23
3:1,8,15,17
7:14
12:12
19:12

1229 ܝܕܝܥܐ (pp) apparent, known, certain (one)

MAT 27:16
MRK 6:21
LUK 11:44
ACT 12:21
15:18
16:12
17:4,12
18:23
21:39
ROM 11:2
16:7

1 CO 9:10,26
15:27
2 CO 3:2
6:9,9
GAL 5:19
1 TM 5:24,25
6:7
HEB 7:15
11:16
JUD 6

1228 ܝܕܘܥܐ (m) acquaintance

LUK 23:49

ACT 24:23

1230 ܝܕܘܥܬܐ (f) knowledge

ROM 1:19

1232 ܝܕܥܬܐ (f) knowledge

LUK 1:17
11:52
ACT 2:23
17:29
ROM 2:20
10:2
15:14
1 CO 1:5
8:1,1,7,10,11
12:8
13:2,8
14:6
15:34
2 CO 2:14
4:6
6:6
8:7
10:5
11:6

EPH 1:17
3:4,19
4:13,18
PHL 1:9
3:8
COL 1:9,10
2:2,3
3:10
1 TM 2:4
6:20
2 TM 3:7
TIT 1:1
PLM 6
HEB 10:26
1 PT 1:2,14
3:7
2 PT 1:5,6
3:18
1 JN 2:4

1642 ܡܕܥܐ (m) knowledge, understanding, mind

LUK 1:77
ROM 1:28
11:33
14:5
1 CO 14:14,15,15,19
2 CO 3:14

2 CO 4:4
5:11
EPH 4:18,23
PHL 4:7,7
HEB 8:10
10:16
1 JN 5:20

---

[b]ETHPEEL

Perfect

MRK 6:14
LUK 24:35
ACT 1:19
4:16
7:13[2]
9:42
19:17
ROM 1:4
3:20

ROM 9:11
16:19,25
1 CO 8:3
13:12[3]
GAL 4:9[2]
EPH 3:3,5
2 TM 3:9[2]
1 JN 4:9

Imperfect

MAT 10:26
LUK 8:17
12:2
JHN 1:31[2]
3:21
ACT 2:14
4:10

ACT 28:28
1 CO 11:19
2 CO 7:12
EPH 3:10
PHL 4:5,6
1 TM 4:15
1 JN 2:19

Participle

MAT 12:33
LUK 6:44
JHN 10:14[2]
ACT 21:24
1 CO 14:7,9
2 TM 3:9[1]
1 JN 4:2

[e]APHEL

Perfect

MAT 18:31
LUK 2:15,17
JHN 2:11
15:15[2]
17:6,26[1]
ACT 5:25
7:13[1]
ACT 11:28
24:1
25:2,15
EPH 1:9
COL 1:8
2 PT 1:14[2],16

Imperfect

JHN 16:13
ACT 20:27
ROM 9:22
COL 1:27
4:7,9

Active Participle

MAT 26:73
JHN 17:26[2]
18:32
ACT 21:26
1 CO 12:3
15:1
2 CO 8:1
GAL 1:11
EPH 6:21[2]
HEB 9:8
1 JN 1:3

[g]SHAPHEL

Perfect

REV 1:1

3123 ܬܘܕܝܬܐ (m)

acknowledgement

2 PT 1:2,3,8
2 PT 2:20

[h]ESHTAPHAL

Perfect

MAT 14:35
MRK 6:33
LUK 2:50
9:45[1]
24:31
ACT 3:10
4:13[2]
ACT 12:11[1],14
14:9
27:39
2 CO 1:14
COL 1:6
2 TH 1:8[2]
2 PT 2:21[2]

Imperfect

2 CO 1:13[3]
PHL 3:10
2 PT 2:21[1]

Participle

JHN 8:43
ACT 19:15[1]
1 CO 16:18
2 CO 1:13[2]
13:5
1 JN 3:19

1233 ܝܗܒ (v) give

imperf and inf use verb ܢܬܠ

[a]PEAL

Perfect

MAT 9:8
10:1
13:8
14:19
15:36[1],36[2]
20:30
21:23
25:15,20,
22,35,
42
26:26,27,
48
27:10,14,
34
28:12
MRK 2:26
4:7,8
6:7,28[1],
28[2],41
8:6
11:28
13:34
14:22,23,
44
15:5,23,45
LUK 4:20
6:4
7:15,21,44
9:1,16,42
10:35[1]
15:29
18:43
19:13,15,
23
20:2
22:19[1],47
24:30,42
JHN 1:12
3:34,35
4:5,12
5:22,26,36
6:31,32[1],
37,39
7:19,22
10:29
12:49
13:3,15,
26[2]
17:2[1],2[2],4,
JHN 17:6[1],6[2],7,
8[1],8[2],9,
11,12,
14,22[1],
22[2],24[1],
24[2]
18:9,11
19:9
21:13
ACT 3:16
5:32
7:5[1],8,10,
45
9:41
10:40
11:17,18
12:23
13:19,20,
21,35
15:8,30
17:25
18:18
21:7,19
23:25,33
27:15,24
ROM 2:4
3:26
4:20
11:8,35
16:4
1 CO 3:2,5
7:36[1]
9:18
11:25
12:24
15:57
2 CO 1:22
5:5,18
8:16
9:9
10:8[1],8[2]
13:10
GAL 1:4
2:9[2],20
3:5,18
EPH 1:22
4:8,11
PHL 2:9
1 TH 4:2,8

2 TH	2:16
1 TM	2:6
	6:17
2 TM	1:7
TIT	2:14
HEB	2:13
	7:4
	8:9
	11:35
JAM	4:6[1]
	5:18[1],18[2]
1 PT	1:21
	5:10
2 PT	1:3,4
1 JN	3:16[1],24
	4:13
	5:11,20
REV	1:1
	2:21
	3:8
	4:9
	11:13
	13:2,4
	15:7
	16:6
	20:13[1],13[2]

Imperfect

MAT	4:9
	5:26,31
	7:6,11[2]
	12:36
	14:7
	16:19,26
	18:30
	19:7
	20:14,23,28
	22:46
	24:24,45
MRK	5:43
	6:22,23,25,37[2]
	8:37
	10:45
	12:9,14[2],14[3]
	13:22,24
	14:11
LUK	1:32,48,73,77
	2:24
	3:11
	4:6[1]
	8:55
	11:7,8[1],8[2],13[2]
	12:32,42,59
	16:12
	17:18
	20:10,16,22
	21:15
	22:5
	23:2
JHN	1:22
	3:16
	4:14[1]
	6:27,51[1],52
	13:29
JHN	14:16
	15:4,16
	16:23
	17:2[3]
ACT	2:19
	3:3
	5:31
	7:5[2],38
	9:2
	13:34
	19:31
	24:17
	25:16[1]
ROM	1:11
	7:4,5
	8:32
	15:5
1 CO	7:36[2]
2 CO	6:3
	9:10[2]
	12:15
EPH	1:17
	3:16
	4:27,29
COL	1:10
2 TH	3:9,16
1 TM	5:14
2 TM	1:16,18
	2:7,25
HEB	8:10[1],10[2]
	10:16[1],16[2]
JAM	2:16
1 JN	3:16[2]
REV	2:7,10,17[1],17[2],23,26,28
	3:21
	8:3[2]
	11:3,18
	13:15[2]
	17:17[2]
	19:7
	21:6
	22:12

Imperative

MAT	5:42
	6:11
	10:8
MAT	14:8,16
	17:27
	18:28
MAT	19:21
	20:8
	22:21
	25:8,28
MRK	6:37[1]
	10:21,37
	12:17
LUK	6:30,38[1]
	9:13
	11:3,41
	12:33,58
	14:9
	15:12
LUK	16:2
	18:22
	19:24
	20:25
JHN	4:7,10[1],15
	6:34
ACT	4:29
	8:19
ROM	12:19
	14:1
	16:5
2 TM	4:19
REV	14:7

Infinitive

MAT	7:11[1]
	22:17
	26:15
MRK	10:40
	12:14[1]
LUK	11:13[1]
LUK	14:6
EPH	4:28
1 TH	2:8
1 TM	6:18
REV	10:9
	16:9,19

Active Participle

MAT	13:23
	17:24
	20:4
	21:41
	24:38
MRK	4:20
LUK	4:6[2]
	8:14,15
	10:19,35[2]
	15:16
	17:27
	19:8
JHN	4:10[2],14[2]
	6:32[2],33,51[2]
	10:28
	11:22
	13:26[1],34
	14:27[1],27[2],27[3]
	15:2[1],2[2]
	18:22
ACT	2:4,27
	3:6
	7:25
	9:39
	20:32,35
	25:11
ROM	2:7
	9:20
	12:8
	13:6
	14:12
1 CO	7:25,38[1],38[2]
	13:1
	14:7
	15:38
2 CO	1:20
	5:12
	9:10[1]
GAL	4:15
COL	1:6
PLM	6
HEB	4:13
	12:11
	13:17
JAM	1:5[1]
	4:6[2]
	5:11
1 PT	4:5,11
	5:5
REV	3:9
	17:13,17[1]
	22:2

Passive Participle

MAT	13:11[1],11[2]
	19:11
MRK	4:11
LUK	8:10
JHN	6:65
	19:11
ACT	2:47
	19:39
1 CO	7:7
	12:8
REV	4:1
	10:11
	11:5
	17:10
	20:3
	22:6

1234 ܝܗܘܒܐ (m) giver

2 CO 9:7

1650 ܡܘܗܒܬܐ (f) gift

MAT 7:11
LUK 11:13
JHN 4:10
ACT 2:33,38
8:20
10:45
11:17
25:11,16
27:24
ROM 1:11
5:15,15,16,16,17
6:23
11:29
12:6
1 CO 1:7
2:12
7:7
12:4,9,28,30,31
14:1,12
2 CO 1:11
9:15
EPH 2:8
3:7
4:7,8,16
PHL 1:19
4:17
1 TM 4:14
2 TM 1:6
HEB 6:4
JAM 1:17
1 PT 3:7
4:10
REV 11:10

1942 ܡܬܠܐ (m) (from ܝܬܠ) act of giving

PHL 4:15

---

[b]ETHPEEL

Perfect

MAT 14:11
28:18
MRK 6:2
LUK 4:17
12:48
JHN 1:17
3:27
7:39
12:5
ACT 4:12
ROM 5:5
12:3,6
15:15
1 CO 1:4
2:12
3:10
11:15
2 CO 8:1
GAL 2:9[1]
3:19,21
EPH 3:2,6,7,8
4:7
PHL 1:29
COL 1:25
1 TM 4:14
2 TM 1:9
HEB 2:4
8:6
11:19
1 PT 2:7
2 PT 3:15
REV 6:2,4[1],4[2],8,11
7:2
8:2,3[1]
9:1,3,5
11:1,2
12:14
13:5[1],5[2],7[1],7[2],14,15[1]
16:8
19:8
20:4

Imperfect

MAT 7:7
12:39
13:12
14:9
21:43
25:29
26:9
27:58
MRK 4:25
8:12
LUK 8:18
11:9,29
19:26
ACT 3:14
25:16[2]
GAL 3:22
EPH 6:19
1 PT 1:10
REV 13:16

Infinitive

MRK 14:5

Participle

MAT 10:19
16:4
MRK 13:11
LUK 6:38[2]
22:19[2]
ACT 4:35
8:18
24:26
1 CO 12:7
EPH 4:16
COL 1:29
PLM 22
JAM 1:5[2]
2 PT 1:11
1 JN 5:16

1235 ܝܗܘܕ (pn) Judea, Judah

MAT 2:1,5,6,6,22
3:1,5
4:25
19:1
24:16
MRK 1:5
3:7
10:1
13:14
LUK 1:5,39,65
2:4,15
3:1
5:17
6:17
7:17
21:21
23:5,50
JHN 3:22
4:3,47,54
7:1,3
11:7
ACT 1:8
8:1
9:31
10:37,39
11:1,29
12:19
15:1
21:10,20
26:20
28:21
ROM 15:31
2 CO 1:16
GAL 1:22
1 TH 2:14

1245 ܝܗܘܕܐܝܬ (adv) judaically

GAL 2:14,14

1246 ܝܗܘܕܝܐ (adj) Judean

MAT 2:2
27:11,29,37
28:15
MRK 7:3
14:12
15:2,9,12,18,26
LUK 7:3
23:3,37,38
JHN 1:19
2:6,13,18,20
3:1,25
4:9,9,22
5:1,10,15,16,18
6:4,41,52
7:1,2,11,13,15,35
8:22,25,31,48,52,57
9:18,22,22
10:19,24,31,33
11:8,19,31,

JHN 11:33,36,45,54,55
12:9,11
13:33
18:12,14,20,31,33,35,36,38,39
19:3,7,12,14,19,20,21,21,31,38,40
20:19
ACT 2:5,9,10,14
6:7
9:20,22,23,29
10:22,28,39
11:19
12:3,4,11
13:5,6,43,45,50
14:1,1,2,4,5,19
16:1,3,20
17:1,5,10,11,11,13,17
18:2,2,4,5,12,14,14,19,24,28

ACT 19:10,13,14,17,33,33,34
20:3,19,21
21:11,21,27,39
22:3,12,30
23:12,20,27,30
24:5,9,19,24,27
25:2,7,8,9,10,15,24
26:2,3,4,7,17,21
27:9
28:17,19
ROM 1:16
2:9,10,17,28,29
3:1,9,29
9:24
10:12
1 CO 1:22,23,24
9:20,20,20
10:32
12:13
2 CO 11:24
GAL 2:13,14,15
3:28
COL 3:11
1 TH 2:14
TIT 1:14
REV 2:9,9
3:9

1247 ܝܗܘܕܝܘܬܐ (f) Judaism

GAL 1:13,14

1252 ܝܘܕ (f) jot, the letter yud

MAT 5:18

1263 ܝܘܡ, ܝܘܡܐ (m) day

see also 1430 ܟܠ ܝܘܡ

MAT 2:1
3:1
4:2
6:34
7:22
9:15
10:15
11:12,22,24
12:11,36
13:1

MAT 15:32
16:21
17:1,23
20:2,6,12,19
22:23,46
23:30
24:19,22,22,29,36,37,38,50

MAT 25:13
26:2,17,29,61
27:40,62,63,64
MRK 1:9,13
2:1,20,20
6:11,21
8:1,2,31
9:2,31
10:34
11:12
13:17,19,20,20,24,32
14:1,12,25,58
15:29
LUK 1:5,7,18,20,23,24,25,39,59,75,80
2:1,6,21,22,36,43,44,46
4:2,2,16,25,27,42
5:17,35,35
6:12,23
7:11
8:22
9:12,22,28,36,37,51
10:12,14,35
12:46
13:14,14,16,31,32,33
14:1,5
15:13
17:4,4,22,22,24,26,26,27,28,29,30,31
18:33
19:42,43
20:1
21:6,22,23,34
22:7
23:7,12,29,54
24:7,13,18,21,29,46
JHN 1:29,35,39,43
2:1,12,19,20
4:40,43
5:9
6:22,39,40,

JHN 6:44,54
7:14,23,23,37
8:56
11:6,9,17,24,39,53
12:1,7,12,48
14:20
16:21,23,26
19:31,31
20:19,26
ACT 1:2,3,5,5,15,22
2:1,17,18,20,41
3:24
4:3,5
5:37
6:1
7:8,26,41,45
8:1
9:9,19,23,37,43
10:9,23,24,30,40,48
11:27,28
12:3,21
13:14,31,41
14:20
15:7,36
16:11,12,13,18
17:31
18:18,23
19:40
20:6,6,6,7,7,15,15,15,16,18,26
21:1,4,5,7,8,10,15,18,26,26,27,38
22:6,30
23:32
24:1,11,24
25:1,6,6,13,14,17,23
26:13,22
27:3,7,9,18,19,20,27,29,33,39
28:7,12,13,13,14,17,23

ROM 2:5,16
10:21
11:8
14:5,5,6,6
1 CO 1:8
3:13
5:5
10:8
11:20
15:4
2 CO 1:14
4:16,16
6:2,2
GAL 1:18
4:10
EPH 4:30
5:16
PHL 1:5,6,10
2:16
3:5
COL 1:6,9
1 TH 5:2,4
2 TH 1:10
2:2
2 TM 1:12,18
3:1
4:8
HEB 1:2

HEB 3:8,13
4:4,7,8
7:3
8:8,9,10
10:16,25,32
11:30
JAM 2:15
5:3,5
1 PT 2:12
3:10,20
2 PT 2:8,8,9
3:3,7,8,8,10,12,18
1 JN 4:17
JUD 6
REV 1:10
2:10,13
6:17
8:12
9:6,15
10:7
11:3,6,9,11
12:6
16:14
18:8

1264 ܝܘܡܢܐ (m) this day

MAT 6:11,30
11:23
16:3
21:28
27:8,19
28:15
MRK 14:30
LUK 2:11
4:21
5:26
12:28
13:32,33
19:5,9
22:34
23:43
ACT 2:29
4:9

ACT 7:4
13:33
20:26
23:1
24:21
26:2,29
27:33
ROM 6:21
8:22
11:8
2 CO 3:14,15
HEB 1:5
3:7,13,15
4:7
5:5
13:8
JAM 4:13

1265 ܝܘܢ (pn-non occ) Greece

1267 ܝܘܢܐܝܬ (adv) in Greek

LUK 23:38
JHN 19:20

ACT 9:29
21:37

1269 ܝܘܢܝܐ (adj) Greek, Grecian

ACT 6:1
11:20
14:1

ACT 17:4,12
ROM 1:14
COL 3:11

1266 ܝܘܢܐ (c) dove

MAT 3:16
10:16
21:12
MRK 1:10
11:15

LUK 2:24
3:22
JHN 1:32
2:14,16

1295 ܝܙܦ (v) borrow; (aph) lend

[a]PEAL

Imperfect

MAT 5:42

[e]APHEL

Imperative

LUK 6:35

Active Participle

LUK 6:34[1],34[2]

1298 (ܝܚܕ), ܝܚܝܕܝܐ (adj) only, only begotten

LUK 7:12
8:42
9:38
JHN 1:14,18

JHN 3:16,18
HEB 11:17
1 JN 4:9

1296 (ܝܚܕ) (v-non occ) (shaph) separate

[g]SHAPHEL

1902 ܡܫܘܚܕܬܐ (adj) desolate, solitary

1 TM 5:5

1297 ܝܚܛܐ (m) untimely birth

1 CO 15:8

1305 (ܐܠ), ܐܠܠܬܐ (f-non occ) lamentation

1299 (ܐܠ) (v) wail

eAPHEL

Imperative

JAM 5:1

Active Participle

MRK 5:38

1300 ܝܠܕ (v) beget, bear (a child)

aPEAL

Perfect

MAT 1:25
LUK 1:57[2]
2:7
23:29
JHN 16:21[2]
ACT 13:33
PLM 10
HEB 1:5
5:5
11:11
JAM 1:18
REV 12:4[2],5,13

Imperfect

MAT 1:21,23
LUK 1:13,31,
57[1]
LUK 2:6
1 TM 5:14
REV 12:2,4[1]

Active Participle

JHN 16:21[1]
GAL 4:24,27
JAM 1:15[1],15[2]

Passive Participle

MAT 11:11
LUK 7:28
JHN 3:6[1],6[2],8
18:37
ACT 2:8
21:39
ACT 22:3
GAL 4:29
1 JN 4:7
5:1[1],4,18[1],
18[2]

1301 ܝܠܕܐ (m) birth, offspring, fruit

MAT 1:18
3:7
12:34
14:6
23:33
26:29
MRK 6:21
14:25
LUK 3:7
1 TM 2:15
PLM 12

1303 ܝܠܘܕܐ (m) parent, begetter

1 JN 5:1

1304 ܬܘܠܕܬܐ (f) origin

MAT 1:1

1653 ܡܘܠܕܐ (m) birth

LUK 1:14
JHN 16:21
TIT 3:5

bETHPEEL

Perfect

MAT 1:16[2],20
2:1,2
19:12
26:24
MRK 14:21
LUK 2:11
JHN 1:13
9:19,20,32,
34
16:21[3]
ACT 7:20
22:28
ROM 1:3
GAL 4:23
HEB 7:13
11:12,23
1 PT 1:23
1 JN 3:9[1],9[2]
5:1[2]

Imperfect

JHN 3:4[1],4[2]
9:2
ROM 9:11

Infinitive

JHN 3:7

Participle

MAT 2:4
LUK 1:35
JHN 3:3,5

cPAEL (non occ)

1302 ܝܠܘܕܐ (m) infant

MAT 11:25
21:16
LUK 10:21
18:15
ACT 7:19
1 CO 3:1
1 CO 13:11,11,
11,11
14:20
GAL 4:3
EPH 4:14
1 PT 2:2

eAPHEL

Perfect

MAT 1:2[1],2[2],2[3],
3[1],3[2],3[3],
4[1],4[2],4[3],
5[1],5[2],5[3],
6[1],6[2],7[1],
7[2],7[3],8[1],
MAT 1:8[2],8[3],9[1],
9[2],9[3],10[1],
10[2],10[3],
11,12[1],
12[2],13[1],
13[2],13[3],

MAT 1:14[1],14[2],
14[3],15[1],
15[2],15[3],
16[1]
ACT 7:8[1],8[2],8[3]
1 CO 4:15
1 PT 1:3

Active Participle

2 TM 2:23

1306 ܝܠܦ (v) learn; (pa) teach

[a]PEAL

Perfect

MAT 2:7
MRK 15:45
JHN 7:15
ACT 22:29
23:27,34
28:1
ROM 7:7
16:17
GAL 1:12
EPH 4:20,21
PHL 4:9,11
COL 1:7
2:7
2 TH 2:15
2 TM 3:14[1],14[2]
HEB 5:8

Imperfect

ACT 23:20
24:8
1 CO 4:6
14:31,35
PHL 2:19
1 TM 5:4
TIT 3:14
HEB 5:12

Imperative

MAT 9:13
11:29
MAT 24:32
MRK 13:28

Infinitive

REV 14:3

Active Participle

JHN 6:45[2]
1 TM 2:11
1 TM 5:13
2 TM 3:7

Passive Participle

ROM 2:18
1 TM 4:6[2]
2 TM 3:15

1262 ܝܘܠܦܢܐ (m) teaching, instruction, doctrine

MAT 7:28
15:9
16:12
22:33
MRK 1:22,27
4:2
7:7
11:18
12:38
LUK 4:32
JHN 7:16,17
JHN 18:19
ACT 2:42
5:17,28
13:12
15:5
17:18,19
24:5,14
26:5
28:22
ROM 6:17
12:7

ROM 15:4
16:17
1 CO 2:13,13
14:6,26
GAL 1:14
EPH 4:14
6:4
COL 2:8,22
1 TM 1:3,10
4:1,6,13,
16
5:17
1 TM 6:1,3,3
2 TM 3:10,16
4:2,3
TIT 1:9,9
2:1,10
HEB 5:12
6:2
12:5
13:9
2 PT 3:16
2 JN 9,9,10
REV 2:15,24

[c]PAEL

Perfect

MAT 28:15
MRK 6:30
LUK 11:1[2]
13:26
JHN 8:28
18:20
ACT 6:11
8:25
11:26
1 JN 2:27[3]
REV 2:14

Imperfect

MAT 5:19[1],19[2]
LUK 12:12
JHN 7:35
14:26
ACT 4:18
5:28
ACT 20:20
1 CO 2:16
14:19
1 TM 1:3
HEB 8:11
1 JN 2:27[1]

Imperative

MAT 28:20
LUK 11:1[1]
1 TM 4:11
1 TM 6:2
TIT 2:2

Infinitive

MAT 11:1
MRK 6:2,34
8:31
ACT 1:1
ACT 5:42
1 TM 2:12
2 TM 2:2

Active Participle

MAT 4:23
5:2
7:29
9:35
13:54
15:9
21:23
22:16
26:55
MRK 1:21,22
2:13
4:1,2
6:6
7:7
9:31
10:1
MRK 11:17
12:14,35
14:49
LUK 3:18
4:15,31
5:3,17[1]
6:6
13:10,22
19:47
20:1,21[1],
21[2]
21:37
23:5
JHN 4:25
6:59
7:14,28

JHN 8:2,20
9:34
ACT 4:2
5:21,25,34
15:1,35
16:4
18:11,25
21:21,28
28:31
ROM 2:21[1],21[2]
1 CO 4:17
11:14
COL 1:28
3:16
1 TH 5:12
1 TM 4:6[1]
6:3
TIT 1:11
2:3
REV 2:20

Passive Participle

MAT 14:8
LUK 5:17[2]
JHN 6:45[1]
1 TH 4:9
1 JN 2:27[2]

1759 ܡܠܦܢܐ (m) teacher

MAT 12:38
19:16
22:16,24,
36
MRK 5:35
9:17
10:17,20,
35
12:14,19
13:1
LUK 2:46
3:12
8:49
9:38
10:25
11:45
12:13
18:18
20:21,28,
LUK 20:39
21:7
JHN 3:2,10
8:4
20:16
ACT 13:1
ROM 2:20
12:7
1 CO 12:28,29
EPH 4:11
1 TM 1:7
2:7
3:2
2 TM 1:11
2:24
4:3
HEB 5:12
JAM 3:1
2 PT 2:1

1760 ܡܠܦܢܘܬܐ (f) teaching, doctrine

TIT 2:7
REV 2:14

ETHPAAL

Participle

LUK 21:14

---

8 (ܝܡܐ), ܐܝܡܡܐ (m) daytime

MAT 12:40,40
MRK 4:27
5:5
LUK 2:37
18:7
21:37
JHN 9:4
JHN 11:9
ACT 9:24
10:3
20:31
26:7
ROM 13:12,13
2 CO 11:25
1 TH 2:9
3:10
5:5,8
2 TH 3:8
1 TM 5:5
2 TM 1:3
2 PT 1:19
2 PT 2:13
REV 4:8
7:15
12:10
14:11
20:10
21:25

1307 ܝܡܐ (v) swear; (aph) make swear

[a]PEAL

Perfect

MAT 14:7
MRK 6:23
LUK 1:73
ACT 2:30
HEB 3:11,18
HEB 4:3
6:13[2]
7:21
REV 10:6

Imperfect

MAT 5:34,36
HEB 6:13[1]

Infinitive

MAT 26:74

Active Participle

MAT 23:16[1],16[2],
18[1],18[2],
20[1],20[2],
21[1],21[2],
22[1],22[2]
MRK 14:71
1 CO 15:31
HEB 6:16
JAM 5:12

1657 ܡܘܡܬܐ (f) oath, curse

MAT 5:33,33
14:7,9
26:72
MRK 6:26
LUK 1:73
ACT 2:30
7:17
ACT 23:13
1 TM 1:10
HEB 6:16,17
7:20,21,21,
28
JAM 5:12

---

[e]APHEL

Imperfect

ACT 19:13[2]

Active Participle

MAT 26:63
MRK 5:7
ACT 19:13[1],13[3]
1 TH 5:27

1308 ܝܡܐ (m) sea

see (pn) ܝܡܐ ܕܣܘܦ

MAT	4:13,15,18, 18	ACT	17:14
	8:24,26,27, 32		18:18,22
	13:1,2,47, 48		20:6
	15:29		21:5
	17:27		27:5,9,17, 18,27, 30,38, 39,40, 41
	18:6		28:4
	21:21	ROM	9:27
	23:15	1 CO	10:1,2
MRK	1:16,16	2 CO	11:25,26
	2:13	HEB	11:12
	3:7	JAM	1:6
	4:1,1,1,39, 41		3:7
	5:1,13,21	JUD	13
	6:47	REV	4:6
	7:31		5:13
	9:42		7:1,2,3
	11:23		8:8,8,9
LUK	6:17		10:2,5,8
	8:25		11:7
	17:2,6		12:12
	21:25		13:1,1
JHN	6:1,16,18, 22,25		14:7
	21:1,4,7		15:2,2
ACT	4:24		16:3,3,3
	10:6,32		17:8
	13:4,13		18:17,19, 21
	14:15,26		20:8,13
	15:39		21:1

1313 ܝܡܬܐ (f) lake

LUK	5:1,2	REV	20:10,14, 15
	8:22,23,33		21:8
JHN	6:19		
REV	19:20		

1311 (ܝܡܢ), ܝܡܝܢܐ (f) right, right hand

MAT	5:29,30,39	JHN	18:10
	6:3		21:6
	20:21,23	ACT	2:25,33,34
	22:44		3:7
	25:33,34		5:31
	26:64		7:55,56
	27:29,38		23:23
MRK	10:37,40	ROM	8:34
	12:36	2 CO	6:7
	14:62	GAL	2:9
	15:27	EPH	1:20
	16:5,19	COL	3:1
LUK	1:11	HEB	1:3,13
	6:6		8:1
	20:42		10:12
	22:50,69		12:2
	23:33	1 PT	3:22

REV	1:16,17,20	REV	10:2
	5:1		13:16

1312 (ܝܡܢ) (v-non occ) greet w/ right hand

cPAEL

3376 ܬܝܡܢܐ (f) south

MAT	12:42	ACT	8:26
LUK	11:31		27:12,13
	12:55		28:13
	13:29	REV	21:13

1315 ܝܢܩ (v) give suck, suck

eAPHEL

Perfect

LUK	11:27	LUK	23:29

Active Participle

MAT	24:19	LUK	21:23
MRK	13:17		

1316 (ܝܣܦ) (v) add, increase

eAPHEL

Perfect

LUK	3:20	ACT	12:3
	19:11	GAL	2:6
	20:11,12		

Imperfect

1 TH	4:1	2 TM	3:13
2 TM	2:16		

Imperative

LUK	17:5	2 PT	1:5

Infinitive

MAT	6:27	LUK	12:25

Active Participle

ACT	2:47	PHL	1:17

fETTAPHAL

Perfect

ACT	2:41	ACT	13:36
	11:24	GAL	3:19

Imperfect

MAT 25:29
HEB 12:19

Participle

MAT 6:33
MRK 4:24
LUK 12:31
ACT 5:14

1317 ܝܥܐ (v) spring up

[a]PEAL

Perfect

MAT 13:26
LUK 8:6,7,8

---

[e]APHEL

Perfect

HEB 6:7

1319 ܝܥܢ, ܝܥܢܐ (adj-non occ) greedy

1320 ܝܥܢܘܬܐ (f) greediness

LUK 12:15
2 CO 9:5
EPH 4:19
1 TH 2:5

1318 (ܝܥܢ) (v) (ethpa) take advantage

[d]ETHPAAL

Perfect

2 CO 12:17,18

1328 (ܝܦܐ) (v) cease, expire

[e]APHEL

Perfect

JUD 12

Active Participle

JAM 4:14
2 PT 2:14

1332 ܝܨܦ (v) be careful, anxious

[a]PEAL

Imperfect

MAT 6:25,31, 34[1]
10:19
MRK 13:11
LUK 12:11,22
ROM 13:14
PHL 2:4
4:6

Imperative

LUK 10:35
2 PT 1:10
2 PT 3:14

Infinitive

ACT 20:35
PHL 4:10[1]

Active Participle

MAT 6:27,28, 34[2]
LUK 10:41
12:25,26
1 CO 7:33
12:25
EPH 5:29
PHL 2:20
4:10[2]
1 TM 5:8
TIT 2:5
2 PT 1:15

2724 ܝܨܦܘܬܐ (f) care, anxiety

MAT 22:16
28:14
MRK 12:14
LUK 8:14
LUK 21:34
1 CO 7:32
2 CO 11:28
1 PT 5:7

---

[c]PAEL (non occ)

1329 ܝܨܝܦܐ (adj) careful, diligent

2 CO 8:21

1330 ܝܨܝܦܐܝܬ (adv) carefully

LUK 1:3

1331 ܝܨܝܦܘܬܐ (f) diligence

JUD 3

1333 ܝܩܕ (v) burn

[a]PEAL

Perfect

REV 8:7[1],7[2],7[3]

Imperfect

MAT 13:30
JHN 15:6
1 CO 3:15
1 CO 13:3
REV 18:8

Infinitive

1 CO 7:9

Active Participle

MAT 13:40
ACT 7:30

2 CO	11:29	2 PT	3:10,12
EPH	6:16	REV	4:5
HEB	1:7		8:8,10
	12:18		19:20
	13:11		21:8
JAM	3:6[2]		

1334 ܝܩܕܐ (m) burnt offering

MRK	12:33	HEB	10:6,8

1335 ܝܘܩܕܢܐ (m) burning

HEB	6:8	REV	18:9,18

eAPHEL

Perfect

MAT	22:7	2 PT	2:6
ACT	19:19		

Imperfect

LUK	3:17	REV	17:16

Active Participle

MAT	3:12	JAM	3:5,6[1]

1336 (ܝܩܢ), ܝܘܩܢܬܐ (m) jacinth

REV	21:20

1339 ܝܩܪ (v) be heavy, precious; (pa) honor; (aph) make heavy

aPEAL

Perfect

LUK	9:32	2 CO	12:13,16
2 CO	11:9[1]		

Imperfect

LUK	21:34	1 TH	2:9
2 CO	2:5	2 TH	3:8
	11:9[2]	1 TM	5:16
	12:14		

108 ܐܝܩܪܐ (m) honor

ACT	28:10	EPH	1:14
ROM	2:7,10	PHL	1:11
	9:21		2:29
	13:7,7		4:20
1 CO	12:23,24, 24	1 TH	4:4
		1 TM	1:17
1 TM	5:17	1 PT	4:11
	6:1,16		5:11
2 TM	2:20,21	2 PT	1:1,17
HEB	2:7,9	JUD	25
	3:3	REV	4:9,11
	5:4		5:12,13
1 PT	1:7		7:12
	2:7		18:19
	3:7		21:26

1285 ܝܘܩܪܐ (m) burden, load

MAT	20:12	GAL	6:2
JHN	21:11	HEB	12:1
ACT	15:28	REV	2:24
2 CO	5:4		

cPAEL

Perfect

ACT	28:10

Imperfect

MAT	6:24	JHN	5:23[1]
	15:5		12:26
LUK	16:13		

Imperative

MAT	15:4	LUK	18:20
	19:19	EPH	6:2
MRK	7:10	1 TM	5:3
	10:19	1 PT	2:17[1],17[2]

Active Participle

MAT	15:8	JHN	5:23[4]
MRK	7:6		8:49
JHN	5:23[2],23[3],	ROM	12:10

1714 ܡܝܩܪܐ (pp) honorable, precious

MRK	15:43	COL	2:23
LUK	14:8	HEB	13:4
ACT	5:34	1 PT	2:4
1 CO	12:24		

1337 ܝܩܝܪܐ (adj) heavy, precious

MAT	13:46	2 CO	10:10
	23:4,23	1 TH	2:6
	26:43	JAM	5:7
	27:9	1 PT	1:19
MRK	14:40		2:6
LUK	7:2	2 PT	1:4
	11:46	1 JN	5:3
	24:25,32	REV	18:12,12, 16
ACT	20:9		21:11,19
1 CO	3:12		

1338 ܒܥܣܩܐܝܬ (adv) with difficulty

MAT 13:15	ACT 27:7

[d]ETHPAAL

Participle

JHN 4:44

[e]APHEL

Perfect

ACT 28:27

1340 ܪܒ (v) be great; (aph) make great, magnify

[a]PEAL

Perfect

HEB 1:4

Active Participle

1 PT 2:20

[e]APHEL

Perfect

ACT 13:17

Imperfect

LUK 12:18

Active Participle

LUK 1:46	ACT 8:9
ACT 5:13	10:46

1342 ܝܪܚ, ܝܪܚܐ (m) month

LUK 1:24,26,36,	GAL 4:10
56	COL 2:16
4:25	HEB 11:23
JHN 4:35	JAM 5:17
ACT 7:20	REV 9:5,10,15
18:11	11:2
19:8	13:5
20:3	22:2
28:11	

1343 ܝܪܟ (v) be long

cf ܐܪܟ

[a]PEAL

Imperfect

MRK 4:27	EPH 6:3

1344 ܝܪܘܩܐ (m) herb, vegetable

MAT 13:32	ROM 14:2
MRK 4:32	

1289 ܝܘܪܩܐ (adj) pale; (as subst) herb

LUK 11:42	REV 9:4
REV 6:8	

1345 ܝܪܬ (v) inherit

[a]PEAL

Perfect

HEB 1:4

Imperfect

MAT 5:5	GAL 4:30
19:29	HEB 12:17
MRK 10:17	1 PT 3:9
LUK 10:25	REV 21:7
18:18	

Imperative

MAT 25:34

Infinitive

ACT 7:5	HEB 1:14
1 CO 15:50[1]	

Active Participle

MAT 21:38	GAL 4:1,7
MRK 12:7	5:21
LUK 20:14	TIT 3:7
ROM 4:13,14	HEB 1:2
8:17[1],17[2]	6:12,17
1 CO 6:9,10	11:7
15:50[2]	JAM 2:5
GAL 3:29	1 PT 3:7

1290 ܝܘܪܬܢܐ (m) inheritance, possession

ACT 7:45	ACT 20:32
13:19	

1346 ܝܪܬܘܬܐ (f) inheritance

MAT 21:38
MRK 12:7
LUK 12:13, 20:14
ACT 7:5
ROM 8:17
GAL 3:18
EPH 1:14,18
EPH 3:6, 5:5
COL 1:12, 3:24
HEB 9:15, 11:8,9
1 PT 1:4

1350 (ܝܫܛ)(v) stretch out

[e]APHEL

Perfect

MAT 26:51
LUK 22:53
ACT 9:41

Imperative

JHN 20:27

Active Participle

MAT 7:9,10
LUK 11:11[1],11[2], 12
JHN 20:25
ACT 4:30

[h]ESHTAPHAL

Participle

PHL 3:13

ܝܫܢ see (ܝܫܢܐ), ܝܫܢܬܐ

1351 ܝܫܦܗ (m) jasper

REV 4:3, 21:11,18,
REV 21:19

1352 ܝܬܒ (v) sit; (aph) seat, establish

[a]PEAL

Perfect

MAT 5:1, 13:1,48, 15:29, 23:2, 24:3, 26:58, 27:19
MRK 9:35
MRK 12:41, 13:3, 16:19
LUK 4:20, 5:3[1], 7:15, 8:22, 10:39
JHN 4:6, 6:17, 12:14, 19:13
ACT 2:3, 9:40, 12:21, 13:14, 16:13, 18:11
ACT 25:6,17
1 CO 5:2, 10:7
HEB 1:3, 8:1, 10:12, 12:2
REV 3:21[2], 20:4

Imperfect

MAT 13:2, 19:28[2], 20:21,23, 25:31
MRK 4:1
MRK 10:37,40
LUK 22:30
ACT 8:31
2 TH 2:4

Imperative

MAT 22:44, 26:36
MRK 12:36, 14:32
LUK 16:6,7
LUK 20:42
ACT 2:34
HEB 1:13
JAM 2:3[1],3[2]

Infinitive

REV 3:21[1]

Active Participle

MAT 4:16[1],16[2], 9:9, 11:16, 19:28[1], 20:30, 23:22, 26:55,64, 69, 27:36,61, 28:2
MRK 2:6,14, 3:32,34, 5:15, 10:46, 14:54,62, 16:5
LUK 1:79, 2:46, 5:3[2],17,27, 7:32, 8:35, 14:28, 18:35, 21:35, 22:55[1],55[2], 56,69
JHN 2:14, 6:3, 8:2
JHN 9:8, 11:20, 20:12
ACT 2:2, 3:10, 6:15, 8:28, 14:8, 20:9, 23:3, 26:30
1 CO 14:30
COL 3:1
REV 4:2,3,4,9, 10, 5:1,7,13, 6:2,4,5,8, 7:10,15, 9:17, 11:16, 14:6,14,15, 16, 17:1,3,9, 15, 18:7, 19:4,11,18, 19,21, 20:11, 21:5

1667 ܡܘܬܒܐ (m) seat

MAT 23:6	LUK 20:46
MRK 12:39	COL 1:16
LUK 11:43	REV 20:4

3361 ܬܘܬܒܐ (adj) stranger, sojourner

ACT 7:6,29	HEB 11:9,13
13:17	1 PT 1:1
EPH 2:19	2:11

3362 ܬܘܬܒܘܬܐ (f) sojourning

1 PT 1:17

---

[e]APHEL

Perfect

ACT 27:6	EPH 2:6
EPH 1:20	

Imperfect

ACT 2:30

Imperative

1 CO 6:4

1356 ܝܬܡ, ܝܬܡܐ (adj) desolate, orphan

JHN 14:18	JAM 1:27
1 TH 2:17	

1357 ܝܬܪ (v) gain, be left over, abound; (pa) make abound; (w/ ܡܢ) prefer

[a]PEAL

Perfect

MAT 18:15	JHN 6:12,13
25:16	

Imperfect

MAT 5:20	1 CO 9:19,20[1],
MRK 7:11	20[2],21,
8:36	22
LUK 9:25	PHL 3:8

Active Participle

1 CO 13:3	JAM 4:13

1293 ܝܘܬܪܢܐ (m) profit, gain

ACT 19:24	TIT 1:7,11
ROM 3:1	3:9
PHL 1:21	HEB 7:18
3:7	1 PT 5:2
1 TM 3:8	JUD 16
2 TM 2:14	

3363 ܬܘܬܪܐ (m) remainder

MAT 12:34	MRK 8:8
14:20	LUK 6:45
15:37	

---

[c]PAEL

Imperfect

2 CO 9:8[1]	1 TH 3:12

1717 ܡܝܬܪܐ (pp) excellent

MAT 6:26	PHL 2:3,9
10:31	HEB 1:4
LUK 12:7	7:7,19,22
ACT 26:13	8:6,6,6
1 CO 12:31	9:23
15:41	10:34
2 CO 3:10	11:4,26,35
9:12	1 PT 1:7
11:5	2:9
12:11	3:3,4

1353 ܝܬܝܪܐ (adj) more, excessive

MAT 5:20,37,47	LUK 12:4,23,24,
6:25,30	28
9:16	13:2,4
10:24,37,	15:17
37	18:14
11:9	20:47
12:12,42	21:3,4
18:13	JHN 3:19
20:10	4:1
23:13	5:20
26:53	7:31
MRK 2:21	10:10
7:36	12:43
12:33,40,	14:12
43,44	21:15
14:5	ACT 4:19,22
LUK 3:13	5:14,29
6:40	9:22
7:26,42	15:28
9:13	17:22
10:35	20:35
11:31,32	23:13,20,

ACT	23:21	2 CO	10:8,13
	24:11		11:23,23,
	25:10		23,23,
	27:11,20		28
ROM	3:9		12:6
	13:11	GAL	4:27
1 CO	4:6	EPH	3:20,20
	10:13	PHL	3:4
	12:23,23,		4:18
	24	1 TH	5:13
	14:18,19	PLM	16,21
	15:6,10	HEB	1:9
2 CO	1:8	JAM	3:1
	2:4,7		4:6
	8:3	2 PT	1:8
	9:1		

1354 ܝܬܝܪܐܝܬ (adv) abundantly, especially

MAT	7:11	2 CO	7:13,15
	10:6,28		8:22
	20:31		12:15
	27:23,24	GAL	1:13,14
MRK	5:26		4:9
	7:37		6:10
	10:26,48	PHL	1:12,14
	14:31		2:12
	15:11,14		4:22
LUK	5:15	1 TH	2:17
	11:13		3:10
	12:48		4:1
	18:7,39	2 TH	1:3
JHN	5:18	1 TM	1:4
	19:8		4:10
ACT	4:17		5:8,17
	20:38		6:2
	22:2	2 TM	1:18
	25:26		2:16
	26:3,26		4:13
ROM	5:9,10,15,	TIT	1:10
	17	HEB	2:1
	7:13		6:17
	14:13		7:15
1 CO	5:2		9:14
	7:38		10:25,29
	9:12		13:19
	12:22	2 PT	1:10
	14:1,5		2:10
2 CO	1:12	3 JN	5
	3:8,11,12	REV	19:10

1355 ܝܬܝܪܘܬܐ (f) abundance, excellence

LUK	12:15	2 CO	12:7
ROM	3:1	EPH	1:19
2 CO	8:2,14,14		

1718 ܡܝܬܪܘܬܐ (f) excellence, virtue

2 PT 1:3,5,5

[d]ETHPAAL

Perfect

ROM	3:7	2 CO	8:2,15
	5:20	EPH	1:8

Imperfect

MAT	13:12	2 CO	9:8[2]
ROM	5:15		10:15
	6:1	PHL	1:9,26
	15:13		4:12
1 CO	14:12	COL	2:7
2 CO	3:9	1 TH	4:10
	8:7[2]		

Participle

1 CO	8:8	2 CO	7:4
	15:58		8:7[1]
2 CO	1:5[1],5[2]	GAL	1:14
	4:15		

[e]APHEL

Perfect

LUK	9:17	ROM	9:29
	19:16	HEB	4:2

Active Participle

JHN	12:19	1 CO	14:6
ACT	19:24	1 TM	4:8[1],8[2]

Passive Participle

MAT	27:24	TIT	3:8

1669 ܡܘܬܪܢܐ (adj) profitable

2 TM 3:16

ܟ

1358 ܟܐ (adv) (only as comp) here

see also 1573 ܠܟܐ
see also 1720 ܡܟܐ

1359 ܟܐܐ (v) rebuke, reprove

[a]PEAL

Perfect

MAT	8:26	MRK	8:30,33
	9:30		9:25
	12:16	LUK	4:35,39
	17:18		8:24
	19:13		9:21,42,55
MRK	1:25,43		18:15
	4:39		23:40

Imperative

LUK	17:3	LUK	19:39

Infinitive

MAT	16:22	MRK	8:32

Active Participle

MAT	20:31	LUK	4:41
MRK	3:12		18:39
	10:13,48		

1369 ܟܐܬܐ (f) reproof

2 CO 2:6

1360 ܟܐܒ (v) suffer, grieve

[a]PEAL

Perfect

HEB 10:34

Active Participle

1 CO 12:26

1361 ܟܐܒܐ (m) pain

MAT	4:23	ROM	7:5
	8:17		9:2
	9:35	GAL	5:24
	10:1	COL	3:5
JHN	5:4	REV	16:10,11
ACT	28:8		21:4
ROM	1:26		

1362 ܟܐܒܢܐ (adj) painful

REV 16:2

---

[e]APHEL (non occ)

1721 ܡܟܐܒܐ (pp) afflicted

LUK 14:21

1366 ܟܐܦܐ (f) stone

see also (pn) Peter, ܟܐܦܐ

MAT	3:9	JHN	2:6
	4:3,6		8:7,59
	7:9		10:31
	16:18		11:38,39,41
	21:42,44		19:13
	24:2,2		20:1
	27:51,60,60,66	ACT	4:11
	28:2		14:5
MRK	5:5		17:29
	12:10	ROM	9:32,33,33
	13:1,2,2	1 CO	3:12
	15:46		10:4,4
	16:3,4	2 CO	3:3,7
LUK	3:8	1 PT	2:4,5,6,8
	4:3,11	REV	4:3
	11:11		9:20
	19:40,44,44		17:4
	20:17,18		18:12,16,21
	21:5,6,6		21:11,19,20
	22:41		
	24:2		

1368 (ܒܗܬ)(v-non occ) shame

ᶜPAEL

1387 ܒܗܬܬܐ (m) shame

1 CO 6:5

1388 (ܟܒ), ܟܘܒܐ(m) thorn

MAT 7:16; 13:7,7,22
MRK 4:7,7,18; 15:17
LUK 6:44; 8:7,7,14
JHN 19:2,5

1370 ܟܒܕܐ(f) liver, gall

ACT 8:23

1371 ܟܒܠܐ(m) bond

LUK 8:29

1373 ܟܒܪ(v-non occ) multiply

ᵃPEAL

1372 ܟܒܪ (prt) perhaps, long ago

MAT 11:21; 21:37 MRK 12:6
LUK 4:23; 10:13; 20:13 ACT 11:18;
12:15; 28:4 ROM 9:19; 11:19
1 CO 15:18; 16:6,12 2 CO 12:16
PLM 15 HEB 10:2

1374 ܟܒܪܝܬܐ(f) sulphur, brimstone

LUK 17:29
REV 9:17,17,18; 14:10
REV 19:20; 20:10; 21:8

1375 ܟܒܫ(v) overcome, subdue

ᵃPEAL

Imperfect

JAM 3:8

Infinitive

MRK 5:4

Active Participle

1 CO 9:27
2 CO 10:4

1389 ܟܘܒܫܐ (m) footstool

MAT 5:35
MRK 12:36
ACT 2:35; 7:49
HEB 1:13; 10:13
JAM 2:3

1376 ܟܕ(adv) when, after

incl comp with 1511 ܠܐ

see also 1380 ܟܕܘ

MAT 1:18,20,24; 2:1,9,10,13,16,19,22; 3:6,7,16; 4:12,18,21; 5:1,1; 6:27; 7:28; 8:1,5,10,16,18,23,28,34; 9:2,8,9,10,11,12,15,18,25,27,28,32,36; 10:7,14; 11:1,2,7; 12:2,3,24,46; 13:4,6,25,26,29,46,48,53; 14:6,13,13,15,20,23,23,24,25,30,32; 15:9,20,32,39; 16:5,13; 17:3,6,9,14,22,24,25; 18:8,8,8,9,24,25,31; 19:1,22,25; 20:8,10,11,24,29,30; 21:1,10,15,18,23,23,32,34,37,38,45; 22:7,12,22,24,33,34,35,41; 24:3; 25:5,10; 26:1,6,7,20,21,26,40,43,71; 27:1,3,12,17,19,24,31,32,35,47,54,57,63; 28:11,13,15,17 MRK 1:5,13,16,19,21,37,45; 2:1,3,5,12,14,15,16,17,23,25,26; 3:5; 4:4,6,10,12,12,27,36; 5:2,6,15,18,21,21,22,27,33; 6:2,6,16,21,33,35,38,43,46,47,48,48,53,54,55; 7:2,5,7,17,30; 8:1,3,11,19,19,20,20; 9:4,8,9,14,14,20,24,25,28,30,33,43,45,47; 10:14,17,22,32,32,41,46; 11:1,4,11,12,13,19,20,20,27; 12:3,21,35,41; 13:1,3,26,36; 14:3,3,11,17,18,22,37,40,49,56,66; 15:15,20,24,25,33,39,41,42,45; 16:1,2,8,11,12,14 LUK 1:8,12,22,22,23,29,41,44; 2:5,6,13,15,17,20,21,22,27,39,42,43,44,46,48; 3:1,3,15,21,21; 4:1,2,13,25,28,35,38,41; 5:1,4,6,7,8,12,17,19,20,25,35; 6:1,3,8,13,26,48,49; 7:1,4,6,9,10,12,12,24,37,39; 8:4,5,8,10,10,23,25,27,28,34,35,40,42,45,47,47; 9:10,11,12,18,29,33,34,34,36,37,42,43,51,54,57; 10:7,29,30,33,38; 11:1,1,14,14,16,21,27,29,37,38,45,53,54; 12:1,25,37; 13:10,14,17,22,28; 14:1,9,15,25,29; 15:13,14,17,25,27,30; 16:14,20,23; 17:11,12,14,14,15,16,20; 18:22,23,24,35,40; 19:1,5,6,7,11,15,20,28,29,30,33,36,37,41,45; 20:1,10,11,14,16,37,45; 21:5; 22:14,35,40,44,45,47,49,60,66; 23:5,6,7,8,11,20,26,33,36,47,48,48; 24:4,6,12,15,17,23,30,32,34,35,36,40,41,44,51,53
JHN 1:19,36,37,47,48,51; 2:9,22,23; 4:2,27,40,45,51,54; 6:6,7,12,16,19,19,23,24,25,59; 7:10,14,15,28; 8:2,3,6,6,7,7,8,9,9,9,10,20,30; 9:1,2,6,7,14,19,20; 10:33,40; 11:6,18,20,28,29,32,33,38,43,44,45; 12:12,16,37,41; 13:2,6,12,30; 14:25; 17:12; 18:6,22,24,32,38; 19:5,6,8,13,17,23,30,33; 20:5,6,7,11,19,22,24,26; 21:4,7,9,9,9,11,14,15,18,19,21
ACT 1:3,3,4,6,8,9,9,10,10,24; 2:1,1,6,7,12,13,37,40,46,47; 3:1,3,5,8,9,11,11,12,13,25,

26; 4:1,2,7,10,13,23,24,30,31; 5:2,5,7,10,15, 16,22,24,27,30,33,41; 6:1,6; 7:2,4,5,6,12,13, 17,21,23,26,26,30,31,31,32,35,36,40,54,55, 55,56,56,59,60,60; 8:3,6,9,12,13,14,18,19, 25,28,30,36,39,39; 9:3,7,8,8,11,17,22,23,30, 31,32,39,39,39,40,41,43; 10:7,9,10,11,11,17, 19,20,24,25,27,29,30,30,44,46; 11:2,3,5,15, 18,19,23,26; 12:3,5,6,9,10,10,12,18,19; 13:2, 4,5,6,12,17,25,28,29,42,45,48,51; 14:6,9,11, 14,17,18,21,22,23,24,25,27; 15:3,4,7,24,25, 29,31,33,38,40; 16:4,7,8,9,10,13,16,19,23, 24,27,29,35,36,38,40; 17:3,6,6,7,8,10,11,13, 15,16,16,19,22,23,23,32; 18:1,5,5,12,13,14, 18,18,21,21,23,23,25,26,27,27,28; 19:1,4,5, 13,16,21,26,28,33,34,35,37,41; 20:2,3,7,9,9, 11,12,13,14,18,19,21,31,36; 21:4,10,12,14, 16,17,18,20,21,26,27,28,31,32,35,37,40,40; 22:2,4,5,6,11,16,18,20,22,23,25,26,29; 23:1, 3,6,7,10,11,12,22,27,28,30,34,34; 24:2,6,8,9, 11,14,15,18,20,21,22,25,27,27; 25:1,3,3,6,7, 8,13,14,14,15,17,24,27; 26:10,11,12,14,22, 24,31; 27:2,8,13,16,17,18,20,21,29,31,35,38, 39; 28:4,4,6,6,9,10,15,15,17,17,18,19,23,25, 26 ROM 1:22,29,32; 2:3,14,15,15; 3:4; 4:6,19; 5:8,10,13; 6:18,20; 7:3,5,9; 9:10; 11:2; 13:11; 15:20 1 CO 1:23; 2:1,2; 4:2, 12; 5:3; 6:1; 7:18,35; 9:18,19,21; 11:4,5,13, 29,32; 12:12; 13:11,11; 14:27,30; 15:15,52, 58 2 CO 2:3,12; 4:15,17; 5:4; 7:7,15; 8:9; 9:4; 10:1,11,15; 11:9,19; 12:15,21; 13:2,10 GAL 1:15; 2:9,11,12,14,17; 3:1,23,25; 4:1,3, 4,8; 6:3,9 EPH 2:5,22; 3:4,17; 5:27; 6:8, 13,18 PHL 1:4,26; 2:6,12,19,28; 3:1,4,9, 18; 4:15 COL 1:23,28; 2:7; 3:7; 4:12 1 TH 1:10; 2:6; 3:4; 5:3 2 TH 2:5; 3:10 1 TM 1:3,7,9,13; 2:8; 3:10,14; 4:6,16; 5:6,13; 6:4 2 TM 1:17; 2:18; 3:13; 4:20 TIT 2:8, 13; 3:4 HEB 2:4,12; 4:1; 5:7,8; 6:13; 7:1,5, 10; 8:5; 9:19; 10:1,1,5,22; 11:4,7,8,8,21,22, 23,24,29,37; 12:17; 13:2,13 JAM 1:2,6,13; 3:4,6 1 PT 1:5,10,18,22; 2:24; 3:2,6,16,17, 17,20,21,21; 5:4,9,10 2 PT 1:4,5,8,10,12, 14,16,16,17,17,18,19,20,21; 2:1,5,6,6,8,9,10, 12,13,13,14,14,15,18,19,20,20,21; 3:3,3,4,5, 7,10,11,12,12,12,14,17,17 2 JN 12 3 JN 7,10 JUD 3,3,5,5,7,9,12,12,14,16, 20,21,23,23 REV 1:1,12,17; 2:9; 4:10; 5:8, 8; 6:1,3,5,7,9,12; 7:12; 8:1; 10:3,4,9,10; 11:3; 12:12,13; 15:6; 17:6; 18:10,15,18,19; 22:8,20

1377 (ܟܕܒ)(v) lie

[c]PAEL

Active Participle

2 CO 11:31 | GAL 1:20

1378 ܟܕܒܐ (adj) liar

JHN 8:55

1379 ܟܕܒܘܬܐ (f) lie

MAT 24:24 | ROM 1:25
MRK 13:22 | EPH 4:25
JHN 8:44 | 1 TM 4:2

1380 ܟܕܘ (adv) it suffices; (w/ ܡܢ) already

from 1376 ܟܕ and 747 ܗܘ

MRK 15:44 LUK 12:49; 22:51
JHN 3:18; 4:35; 11:39; 14:8; 15:3; 19:33
ROM 1:10 1 CO 4:8; 5:3; 6:7 2 CO 2:6
PHL 3:12,12 2 TH 2:7 2 PT 3:1
1 JN 4:3; 5:15

1381 ܟܕܢ (v) yoke, subdue

[b]ETHPEEL

Imperfect

GAL 5:1

1383 ܟܗܢ, ܟܗܢܐ (m) priest

see also 2911 ܪܒ ܟܗܢܐ

MAT 8:4
12:4,5
MRK 1:44
2:26
LUK 1:5
5:14
6:4
10:31
17:14
JHN 1:19
7:45
ACT 4:1,23
23:2,4,5,
14
1 PT 2:5
REV 5:10
20:6

1384 ܟܗܢܘܬܐ (f) priesthood

LUK 1:9 | LUK 3:2

1385 ܟܗܢܝܐ (adj) priestly

REV 1:6

1382 (ܟܗܢ) (v) be a priest

[c]PAEL

Active Participle

LUK 1:8 | 1 PT 2:9

1386 ܟܘܐ (v) sear, burn

aPEAL

Passive Participle

1 TM 4:2

1409 ܟܘܐ, ܟܘܬܐ (f) window

ACT 20:9	2 CO 11:33

1393 ܟܘܟܒ, ܟܘܟܒܐ (m) star, planet

MAT 2:2,7,9,10	JUD 13
24:29	REV 1:16,20,20
MRK 13:25	2:1,28
LUK 21:25	3:1
ACT 7:43	6:13
27:20	8:10,11,12
1 CO 15:41,41, 41	9:1
	12:1,4
HEB 11:12	22:16

1392 (ܟܘܠ), ܟܘܠܬܐ (f) ark

MAT 24:38	LUK 17:27

1399 (ܟܘܢ) (v) be, exist; (pa II) reprove, rebuke; (aph) create

aPEAL (non occ)

1363 ܟܐܢܐ (adj) right, just

MAT 1:19	ROM 7:12
5:45	EPH 6:1
LUK 1:17	PHL 4:8
2:25	2 TH 1:5,6
JHN 5:30	1 TM 1:9
7:24	2 TM 4:8
17:25	TIT 1:8
ACT 4:19	HEB 10:38
10:22	11:4
22:12	12:23
24:15	2 PT 1:13
ROM 1:17	2:8
2:5,13	REV 15:3
3:4,10,26	19:2
5:19	

1364 ܟܐܢܐܝܬ (adv) rightly, justly

LUK 23:41	1 TH 2:10

1365 ܟܐܢܘܬܐ (f) righteousness, uprightness, godliness

MAT 3:15	ROM 10:3,3,3,4, 5,6
5:6,10,20	14:17
21:32	
LUK 1:6,75	COL 4:1
ACT 10:35	1 TM 3:16
13:10	4:7,8
17:31	6:11
28:4	2 TM 2:22
ROM 1:17	3:16
3:5,8,21, 22,26,26	4:8
	TIT 2:12
4:5,9,11, 11,13,22, 23	HEB 1:9
	2:2
	5:13
5:16,17,18, 21	7:2
	11:7,33
6:13,16,18, 19,20	1 PT 2:23
	3:14
8:4,10	2 PT 2:5
9:30,30,30, 31,31	REV 19:11

1420 ܟܝܢܐ (m) nature

ROM 1:26,27	GAL 2:15
2:14,27	4:8
11:21,24, 24,24	JAM 1:21
	3:7,7
1 CO 11:14	2 PT 1:4
15:38	2:12

1421 ܟܝܢܐܝܬ (adv) naturally

JUD 10

cPAEL ܟܘܢ

Imperative

1 TM 5:20	TIT 2:15
2 TM 4:2	

Active Participle

ROM 2:15	EPH 5:11

1390 ܟܘܢܝܐ (m) reproof

2 TM 3:16

dETHPAAL

Participle

1 CO 14:24	HEB 12:5
EPH 5:13	JAM 2:9

eAPHEL (non occ)

1726 ܟܝܢܝܐ (adj) natural, created

ROM 1:26

1463 (ܟܣܣ), ܟܣܐ (m) cup

MAT	10:42	LUK	22:42
	20:22,23	JHN	18:11
	23:25,26	1 CO	10:16,21,21
	26:27,39,42		11:25,25,26,27,28
MRK	7:4,8	REV	14:10
	9:41		16:19
	10:38,39		17:4
	14:23,36		18:6
LUK	11:39		
	22:20,20,		

1402 ܟܘܪܐ (c) region, district

MRK 1:5

1412 ܟܚܕ (v) (ethpa) fear, reverence

dETHPAAL

Imperfect

LUK 20:13

Participle

LUK 18:2,4

1414 ܟܚܠܐ (m-non occ) paint

1413 ܟܚܠ (v) paint

aPEAL

Imperative

REV 3:18

1415 ܟܝ (prt) now, indeed, perhaps

MAT 18:1; 19:25,27; 24:45 MRK 4:41 LUK 1:66; 4:36; 8:25; 9:46; 12:42; 18:8; 19:42; 22:23; 24:18 JHN 7:35; 8:22

1417 ܟܝܠܐ (m) measure

JHN 3:34

1418 ܟܝܠܬܐ (f) measure

MAT 7:2
MRK 4:24
LUK 6:38,38

1394 (ܟܘܠ) (v) measure

eAPHEL

Active Participle

MAT 7:2[1]
MRK 4:24[1]
LUK 6:38[1]

---

fETTAPHAL

Participle

MAT 7:2[2]
MRK 4:24[2]
LUK 6:38[2]

1422 ܟܝܣܐ (m) small bag

MAT 10:9
MRK 6:8
LUK 10:4
LUK 12:33
22:35,36

1423 ܟܟܪܐ (f) talent

MAT 18:24
25:15,16,20,20,22,22,
MAT 25:24,25,28,28
REV 16:21

1424 ܟܟܪܘܬܐ (f) honeycomb

LUK 24:42

1425 ܟܠ (noun) all, every

incl comp with 1597 ܡܐ
incl comp with 1769 ܡܢ
see below 1427 ܟܠ ܐܢܫ
see below 1428 ܟܠ ܕܡܢ
see below 1429 ܟܠ ܚܕ
see below 1430 ܟܠ ܝܘܡ
see below 1431 ܟܠ ܡܕܡ
see below 1432 ܟܠ ܒܪ

see also 77 ܐܢܫ ܟܠ

MAT 1:17,22; 2:3,4,16,16; 3:5,5,10,15; 4:4,
8,9,23,23,24,24; 5:11,15,18,19,19,21,22,22,
28,29,30,32; 6:22,23,29,32,32,33; 7:8,12,17,
19,21,24,26; 8:16,32,34; 9:26,31,35,35,35;
10:1,23,30,38,42; 11:13,28; 12:15,23,25,25,
31,32,32,36; 13:2,19,32,32,33,34,41,41,44,
46,47,51,52,56,56; 14:20,35,35; 15:5,13,33,
37; 16:26; 17:12; 18:6,16,18,19,31,32; 19:3,
20; 20:6; 21:10,12,26,44; 22:9,10,27,28,37,
37,37,37; 23:5,8,20,27,35,36; 24:2,6,8,9,14,
14,22,30,33,34,39,47; 25:5,7,31,32; 26:1,13,
27,31,35,52,56,59,70; 27:1,15,22,25,27,45;
28:18,19,20 MRK 1:5,5,27,28,32,33,39,
39,45; 2:12,12,13; 3:8,28; 4:1,13,31,32,34;
5:4,20,33,40; 6:11,30,30,33,41,42,50,55,56;
7:3,14,14,19,23; 8:4,35,35,36,38; 9:13,15,37,
41,42,49,49; 10:11,15,20,35; 11:17,18,32;
12:22,28,29,30,30,30,30,33,33,33,33,33,37,
44,44; 13:4,10,20,30,37; 14:9,9,23,27,29,31,
53,55,64; 15:1,6,16,33; 16:15,15,20
LUK 1:3,6,10,48,65,65,66,71,75; 2:1,10,18,
19,20,23,31,41,47,51; 3:3,5,5,6,9,15,19,20,
21; 4:4,5,6,7,13,14,20,22,23,25,28,37,40;
5:5,9,12,17; 6:10,17,19,19,30,44; 7:1,16,17,
17,18,29,35; 8:4,16,33,37,39,40,43,45,47,52;
9:1,6,7,13,15,17,25,43,43,48,48; 10:1,19,27,
27,27,27; 11:4,10,17,22,34,36,36,42,50;
12:3,7,8,10,15,18,27,30,31,44,48; 13:2,3,4,5,
17,17,17,21,28; 14:10,11,11,18,29,33; 16:14,
16,18,18,26; 17:10,24,29; 18:14,21,31,43;
19:7,26,37,37,43,48; 20:6,18,18,38,45; 21:4,
4,12,15,22,24,29,32,35,35,38; 22:37,70;
23:1,5,14,18,44,48,49; 24:9,14,19,21,25,27,
27,47 JHN 1:3,16; 2:15,25; 3:16,20,31,31;
4:13,14,45,53; 5:4,22,28; 6:9,10,37,39,40,45,
45; 7:21,23,38; 8:2,34; 9:34; 10:8,29; 11:26,
50; 12:19,37,46; 13:10,10,10,11,18; 14:26;
15:2,7,14,15,16,21; 16:2,13,13; 17:2,2,7,21;
18:20,37,40; 19:12,23; 21:11,24 ACT 1:1,
8,14,18,19,21,24; 2:1,2,4,5,6,7,7,12,14,17,
21,32,36,39,43,44,45,47; 3:9,11,15,16,18,21,
22,23,24,25; 4:10,16,23,24,28,31,33; 5:5,11,
11,12,16,17,20,27,34,37; 6:2,5,15; 7:10,10,
11,14,22,50,57; 8:1,6,10,11,27,40; 9:14,21,
21,26,31,35,39,42; 10:2,12,14,22,24,33,33,
35,36,37,39,39,41,43,43,44; 11:14,23,26,28;
12:7,22; 13:6,10,10,10,22,24,27,27,39,39,44,
49; 14:4,15,16,23,27; 15:3,3,4,12,12,17,17,
21,21,22,25,30,36; 16:2,3,26,26,28,31,32,33,
37; 17:6,7,8,16,21,22,24,26,26,27,30,30,31;
18:2,4,8,17,23,27; 19:10,17,17,21,25,25,26,
27,27,27,29,34; 20:23,25,26,27,28,32,37; 21:5,
18,19,20,21,27,28,30,31; 22:3,5,12,15,15,19,
30; 23:1,8; 24:3,3,5,5,8,14; 25:5,24,24; 26:2,
3,11,13,14,20,29; 27:20,20,24,33,35,36,44;
28:2,30 ROM 1:5,7,8,8,16,18,29; 2:9,10;
3:4,9,12,19,19,20,23; 4:11,16,16; 5:12,12,18,
18; 7:8; 8:19,22,32,37; 9:5,6,7,17; 10:4,11,
12,12,13,16,18,21; 11:26,36,36,36; 12:3,4,
17,18; 13:1; 14:6,10,11,11; 15:11,11,13,14,
33; 16:2,4,15,16,19,23,25,27 1 CO 1:2,2,
5,5,10,29; 4:3,17; 5:4,6; 6:12,12,12,18; 7:7,
17,24; 8:1,6,6; 9:19,22,24; 10:1,1,2,3,4,11,
17,17; 11:3,4,5,25,26; 12:6,11,12,13,13,17,
17,19,25,26,26,29,29,29,29,30,30,30; 13:1,2,
2,2,3,7,7; 14:5,18,23,23,24,24,24,26,31,33;
15:7,8,10,19,22,22,24,24,24,25,27,27,28,28,
28,28,30,39,51,51; 16:2,14,19,20,24
2 CO 1:1,1,3,4,4,20; 2:3,3,5,14; 3:18; 4:2;
5:10,17; 7:1,4,13,15; 8:7,18,24; 9:7,8,8,11;
10:5,5; 11:28; 12:12,19; 13:1,13,14
GAL 1:2; 2:14,16; 3:4,8,10,10,13,26,28; 4:1;
5:3,3,9,14,21,24; 6:6 EPH 1:3,8,8,11,21,
21,22,23,23; 2:21; 3:8,9,15,18,19,20,21; 4:2,
6,6,6,6,10,10,13,14,16,16,16,19,29,31,31;
5:3,9,33; 6:7,11,13,16,18,18,18,24
PHL 1:1,4,7,9,13,18; 2:9,10,11,17,21,26,29;
3:8,21; 4:7,12,18,19,21,22,23 COL 1:4,6,
9,9,10,11,11,15,16,16,17,18,19,23,28,28,28;
2:2,3,9,10,13,19; 3:8,9,11,14,16,23,23; 4:12
1 TH 1:2,7,8; 2:10,15; 3:7,9,13; 4:3,6,10,10;
5:5,22,23,23,26,27 2 TH 1:3,4,11; 2:4,9,
10,12,17,17; 3:1,6,10,16,17,18 1 TM 1:16;
2:1,2,4,8,11; 3:4; 4:4,10; 5:2,10; 6:1,10,13,17
2 TM 1:15; 2:19,21,22; 3:11,12,16,17; 4:2,
16,17,18,21 TIT 1:16; 2:7,11,11,14,15;
3:1,2,15,15,15 PLM 5,6 HEB 1:1,1,4,6,
11,14; 2:2,10,10,11,15; 3:2,4,4,5,16; 4:4,12;
5:1,9; 6:16; 7:22; 8:1,3,11; 9:4,19,19,19,21,
25; 10:1,3,11; 11:13,21,39; 12:1,1,11,23;
13:4,21,24,24,24,25 JAM 1:2,5,8,17,21,
25; 2:10,10; 3:2,2,2,3,6,7; 4:16 1 PT 1:12,
15,24,24; 2:1,1,11,12,13,24; 3:6,8,15; 4:1,1,
7,11,11,11; 5:2,7,14 2 PT 1:3,5,20; 3:11,
16 1 JN 1:5,5,7,9; 2:2,21,29; 3:3,4,6,6,9,
10,15,15; 4:1,2,3,7,8,15,16,21; 5:1,1,4,10,10,
12,12,14,17,18,19 2 JN 1,9 3 JN 6
JUD 3,5,15,15,15,15,16,25 REV 1:2,7,7;
2:13,23,24; 3:10; 4:11; 5:6,9,13,13; 6:12,14,
14,15; 7:1,4,9,11,16,17; 8:3,7,9; 9:4; 11:4,6,
17; 12:5,9; 13:3,7,8,12,15,16; 14:4,6,8; 15:4;
16:3,20; 17:2; 18:2,3,12,12,12,14,17,17,17,
23; 19:5,5,21; 20:3,8; 21:4,5,8,27; 22:2,3,15,
18,21

1427 ܟܠ ܐܢܫ (idiom) everyone

from 1425 ܟܠ (above) and 195 ܐܢܫܐ

MAT 10:22,32; 12:50; 19:11,29; 26:33
MRK 1:37; 6:39; 9:35,35; 10:44; 12:43;
13:13 LUK 1:63; 2:3,38; 4:15,36;
5:26; 6:40,47; 8:54; 9:23,43; 12:41;
14:33; 17:27; 18:9,14; 19:8; 21:3,17
JHN 1:7,9; 2:10,24; 3:8,15; 5:23; 11:48;
12:32; 13:35 ACT 4:21; 9:40; 17:25,
30,31; 19:7,19; 20:36; 21:24
ROM 1:14; 2:6; 3:22,22; 11:32,32; 12:3;
13:7; 14:5,12 1 CO 3:10,13,13; 4:13;
7:7,20; 8:7; 9:19,22,22,25; 10:24,33;
12:6,11; 14:31,31; 16:16 2 CO 3:2;
5:14,14,15; 9:13 GAL 6:5,10
EPH 3:9; 5:5,20 PHL 1:13; 2:3,4; 4:5
COL 3:11 1 TH 3:12; 5:14,15
2 TH 1:3; 3:2 1 TM 2:6; 4:15; 5:20
2 TM 2:24; 3:9 HEB 2:9; 5:13; 10:29;
12:8,14 JAM 1:19 1 PT 1:17; 2:17;
4:10 2 PT 3:9 1 JN 2:20 3 JN 12,
15 REV 2:23; 22:12

1428 ܟܠ ܙܒܢ (idiom) always

from 1425 ܟܠ (above) and 805 ܙܒܢܐ

MAT 18:10; 26:11,11 MRK 5:5; 14:7,7 LUK 15:31; 21:36; 24:53 JHN 6:34; 8:29; 11:42; 12:8,8; 14:9; 18:20 ACT 2:25; 7:51; 10:2; 20:18 ROM 1:9; 11:10 1 CO 1:4; 15:58 2 CO 2:14; 4:10; 6:10; 8:22; 9:8 GAL 4:18 EPH 5:20; 6:18 PHL 1:20; 2:12; 4:4,6 COL 1:3; 4:6, 12 1 TH 1:2; 2:16; 4:17; 5:15,16 2 TH 1:3,11; 2:13; 3:16 2 TM 3:7 TIT 1:12 PLM 4 HEB 7:25; 9:6; 12:1; 13:15 2 PT 3:18

1429 ܟܠ ܚܕ (idiom) each one; (ܟܠ ܚܕ...ܚܕ) each and every one

from 1425 ܟܠ (above) and 909 ܚܕ

LUK 19:15 JHN 7:53; 10:16 1 CO 12:18 REV 4:8; 5:8; 6:11; 21:21

1430 ܟܠ ܝܘܡ (idiom) everyday

from 1425 ܟܠ (above) and 1263 ܝܘܡܐ

MAT 26:55; 28:20 MRK 14:49 LUK 9:23; 11:3; 16:19; 19:47; 22:53 ACT 2:46,47; 3:10; 5:42; 6:1; 16:5; 17:17; 19:9; 21:4 ROM 8:36; 14:5 1 CO 15:31 2 CO 11:28 HEB 3:13; 7:27; 10:11

1431 ܟܠ ܡܕܡ (idiom) everything

from 1425 ܟܠ (above) and 1639 ܡܕܡ

MAT 8:33; 11:27; 14:7; 16:19; 17:11; 18:25,26,34; 19:26,27; 21:22; 22:4; 23:3; 28:11 MRK 4:11; 5:26; 7:18,37; 8:25; 9:12,23; 10:21,27,28; 11:11,24; 12:44; 13:23; 14:36 LUK 1:3; 2:39; 5:11,28; 7:22; 9:10; 10:22; 11:41; 14:17; 15:13,14,31; 18:12,22,28; 24:44 JHN 3:35; 4:25,29,39; 5:20; 10:41; 13:3; 14:26; 16:15,23,30; 17:10; 18:4,21; 19:28; 21:17 ACT 2:44; 4:32; 10:8; 11:10; 13:29; 14:27; 20:35; 22:10 ROM 3:2; 8:28,32; 14:2,20,23; 15:4 1 CO 1:5; 2:10,15; 3:21,22; 9:12,25; 10:23,23,23,23,25,27,31,33; 11:2,12; 13:7,7; 14:40; 15:27 2 CO 2:9; 4:8,15; 5:18; 6:4,10; 7:5,11,14,16; 8:7; 9:8,11; 11:6,9,21 GAL 3:22 EPH 1:10,22; 4:15; 5:13,13,24; 6:13 PHL 2:14; 3:8; 4:12,13,18 COL 1:16,16,17,20; 3:17, 20,22 1 TH 5:18,21 2 TH 3:16 1 TM 1:10; 2:1; 3:11; 4:8 2 TM 2:7, 10; 4:5 TIT 1:15; 2:7,9,10,10; 3:2 HEB 1:2; 2:8,8,8,17; 4:13,15; 7:2; 8:5; 9:22; 13:18 JAM 3:16; 5:12 1 PT 4:8 2 PT 3:4 1 JN 2:16,27; 3:20,22 3 JN 2

1432 ܟܠ ܥܕܢ (idiom) always

from 1425 ܟܠ (above) and 2281 ܥܕܢܐ

LUK 18:1,5 JHN 7:6 EPH 6:18 1 TH 3:6

1437 ܟܠܝܠܐ (m) crown

MAT	27:29	1 PT	5:4
MRK	15:17	REV	2:10
JHN	19:2,5		3:11
ACT	14:13		4:4,10
1 CO	9:25		6:2
PHL	4:1		9:7
1 TH	2:19		12:1
2 TM	4:8		14:14
JAM	1:12		

1444 ܟܠܬܐ (f) bride, daughter-in-law

MAT	10:35	REV	18:23
	25:1		21:2,9
LUK	12:53,53		22:17
JHN	3:29		

1426 (ܟܠܠ) (v) crown

[d]ETHPAAL

Participle

2 TM 2:5

1433 ܟܠܐ (v) hinder, forbid

[a]PEAL

Perfect

MRK	9:38	ACT	16:6
LUK	9:49		19:30
	11:52		27:43
ACT	14:18	2 PT	2:16

Imperfect

MAT	5:42	LUK	9:50
	19:14		18:16
MRK	9:39	ACT	11:17
	10:14	1 CO	14:39
LUK	6:29		

Active Participle

MAT 3:14	1 TH 2:16
LUK 23:2	1 TM 4:3
ACT 10:47	3 JN 10

1438 ܟܠܝܢܐ (m) hindrance

ACT 28:31

1440 ܟܠܝܬܐ (f) obstacle

ACT 8:36

[b]ETHPEEL

Perfect

ROM 1:13

Imperfect

ACT 24:23

1435 ܟܠܒ, ܟܠܒܐ (m) dog

MAT 7:6 15:26,27	LUK 16:21
	PHL 3:2
MRK 7:27,28	2 PT 2:22

1395 (ܟܠܝ), ܟܘܠܝܬܐ (f) rein, kidney

REV 2:23

1439 ܟܠܝܪܟܐ (m) captain of a thousand

MRK 6:21	ACT 22:29
JHN 18:12	23:10,15, 17,18, 19,22
ACT 21:31,32, 33,37 22:24,26, 27,28,	24:7,22 25:23

1441 ܟܠܡܘܣ (f) robe

MAT 27:28,31

1443 ܟܠܫܐ (m-non occ) lime

1442 (ܟܠܫ) (v) whitewash

[e]APHEL

Passive Participle

MAT 23:27

1445 ܟܡܐ (adv) how much, how many

MAT 6:23; 7:11; 9:15; 10:25; 12:12; 15:34; 16:9,10; 17:15,15; 18:21; 23:37; 25:40,45; 27:13 MRK 2:19; 6:38; 7:36; 8:5,19,20; 9:21; 10:23,24; 15:4 LUK 5:34; 11:8,13; 12:24,28; 13:34; 15:17,29; 16:5 JHN 6:11; 9:5; 11:22,36; 13:14 ACT 9:13,16; 21:20 ROM 5:9,10,15; 7:1,2; 11:12,15,24 1 CO 6:3; 7:39 2 CO 3:9; 5:6; 7:11 GAL 4:1 2 TM 1:18 PLM 16 HEB 7:4; 9:8,14,17; 10:25,29; 12:3,9,25 1 PT 4:2 2 PT 1:13 1 JN 3:1,20; 5:9 REV 11:6

1419 (ܟܡܢ), ܟܡܘܢܐ (m) storm

ACT 27:18

1447 (ܟܡܢ), ܟܡܘܢܐ (m) cummin

MAT 23:23

1450 ܟܡܢ (v-non occ) ambush

[a]PEAL

1446 ܟܡܐܢܐ (m) ambush

ACT 23:21,30	ACT 25:3

1396 (ܟܗܢ), ܟܘܗܢܐ (m) priest

see also 2912 ܪܒ ܟܘܗܢܐ

ACT 14:13	HEB 7:23,26,28 8:4,4 9:6 10:21
HEB 5:6 6:20 7:1,11,15, 17,21,21,	

1397 ܟܘܡܪܘܬܐ (f) priesthood

HEB 7:3,5,11, | HEB 7:12,14,24

1398 ܟܘܡܪܬܐ (f) priestess

ACT 19:35

1451 ܟܡܪ (v) be sad

[a]PEAL (non occ)

1448 ܟܡܝܪܐ (pp) sad

MAT 6:16 | LUK 24:17

1449 ܟܡܝܪܐܝܬ (adv) sadly

MAT 16:3

[b]ETHPEEL

Perfect

MRK 10:22

Infinitive

MAT 26:37 | MRK 14:33

1452 ܟܡ (adv) afterwards

see also 477 ܒܬܪܟܡ

ROM 11:35

1461 (ܟܢܐ), ܟܢܬܐ (m)

companion, fellow servant

MAT 18:28,29,
31,33
24:49
COL 1:7
COL 4:7
REV 6:11
19:10
22:9

1453 (ܟܢܐ) (v) name

[d]ETHPAAL

Perfect

MAT 10:3
ACT 4:36
ACT 12:12,25
15:37

Participle

ACT 12:1

1458 ܟܢܦ, ܟܢܦܐ (f) side, outer edge

MAT 4:5
14:36
MRK 6:56
LUK 4:9
8:44
ACT 27:39

1459 ܟܢܫ (v) assemble, gather

[a]PEAL

Perfect

MAT 13:47
27:27
MRK 7:1
LUK 5:1
8:4
ACT 2:6
ACT 5:6
9:39
13:44
14:20,27
15:30
28:23

Active Participle

MAT 3:12
12:30
23:37[2]
LUK 3:17
11:23
LUK 13:34[2]
JHN 4:36
18:2
ACT 24:12

Passive Participle

MAT 18:20
22:41
26:57
27:17
MRK 1:33
LUK 14:2
23:48
24:33
ACT 1:6
ACT 2:1
4:31
5:12
11:26
12:12
15:25
16:13
20:7,8

1454 ܟܢܫܐ (m) congregation

ACT 19:39
2 CO 11:28
2 TH 2:1
HEB 10:25

1455 ܟܢܘܫܬܐ (f) synagogue

see also 2913 ܪܫ ܟܢܘܫܬܐ

MAT 4:23
5:22
6:2,5
9:35
10:17
12:9
13:54
23:6,34
26:59
MRK 1:21,23,29,
39
3:1
6:2
12:39
13:9
15:1
LUK 4:15,16,20,
28,33,38,
44
6:6,8
7:5
8:41
11:43
12:11
13:10
20:46
21:12
22:66
JHN 6:59
9:22
12:42
16:2

JHN 18:20
ACT 6:9,15; 7:38; 9:2,20; 13:5,14,15,43; 14:1; 15:21; 17:1,10,17; 18:4,7,17, 18:19,26; 19:8; 22:19; 23:15; 24:12; 26:11
JAM 2:2
REV 2:9; 3:9

1460 ܟܢܫܐ (m) gathering, multitude

MAT 4:25; 5:1; 7:28; 8:1,18; 9:8,23,25,33,36; 11:7; 12:15,23,46; 13:2,2,34,36; 14:13,14,15,19,19,22,23; 15:10,30,31,32,33,35,36,39; 17:14; 19:2; 20:29,31; 21:8,9,11,26,46; 22:33; 23:1; 26:47,55; 27:20,24
MRK 2:4,13; 3:8,9,20,32; 4:1,1,36; 5:21,24,27,30,31; 6:34,45; 7:14,17,33; 8:1,2,6,6,34; 9:14,15,17; 10:1,46; 12:37,41; 14:55; 15:11,15
LUK 1:10; 3:7,10; 4:42; 5:1,3,29; 6:17,17,19; 7:9,11,12,24; 8:4,19,37,40,42,45; 9:11,12,16,18,37,38; 11:14,27,29; 12:1,13,54; 13:14; 14:25; 18:36; 19:3,37,39; 22:6,47; 23:1,4,18,48
JHN 5:13; 6:2,5,22,24; 7:12,20,31,32,40,43; 11:42; 12:9,12,17,18,29,34
ACT 1:15; 4:15,27,32; 5:14,27; 6:2,12; 12:21; 13:45; 14:4,11; 15:12; 16:22; 18:28; 19:9,32,40,41; 21:31; 22:30; 23:1,6,20,28; 24:12,18,20
HEB 12:22
1 PT 2:9
REV 7:9; 17:15; 19:1,6

cPAEL

Perfect

MAT 2:4; 22:10; 25:35,38,43
LUK 15:13
JHN 6:13
ACT 19:19,25
JAM 5:3

Imperfect

MAT 23:37[1]; 24:31
MRK 13:27
JHN 11:52
REV 16:16

Imperative

MAT 13:30
JHN 6:12

Infinitive

LUK 13:34[1]
REV 16:14
REV 20:8

Active Participle

MAT 25:24,26
REV 19:19

Passive Participle

ACT 10:24

dETHPAAL

Perfect

MAT 13:2; 22:34; 26:3; 27:62; 28:12
MRK 2:2; 3:20; 4:1; 5:21; 6:30; 14:53
LUK 12:1
LUK 22:66
JHN 11:47
ACT 4:5,27; 12:20; 15:6; 16:22; 18:12; 19:32,40; 21:30; 23:12; 28:17

Imperfect

MAT 24:28*; 25:32*
LUK 17:37*
1 CO 5:4*; 14:23

Imperative

REV 19:17

Participle

MRK 9:25
LUK 5:15; 11:29*
JHN 18:20*
1 CO 11:18*, 11:20*, 33*, 34*; 14:26*; 16:1

1466 (ܟܣܣ), ܟܘܣܣܐ (m-non occ)
admonition

1462 (ܟܣܣ) (v) (ethpe) be reproved; (aph) rebuke, admonish

[b]ETHPEEL

Imperfect

JHN 3:20

Participle

LUK 3:19

---

[e]APHEL

Perfect

GAL 2:11

Imperfect

JHN 16:8 | ACT 25:16

Imperative

MAT 18:15 | 2 TM 4:2

Infinitive

TIT 1:9 | JUD 15

Active Participle

JHN 8:46 | REV 3:19
TIT 1:13

1729 ܡܟܣܢܘܬܐ (f) reproof

2 PT 2:16

1464 ܟܣܐ (v) cover, conceal

[a]PEAL

Passive Participle

MAT 10:26 | 1 CO 14:25
13:35 | 2 CO 4:2
LUK 8:17 | EPH 3:9
12:2 | COL 2:3
ROM 1:20 | 3:3
2:16 | 1 PT 3:4
1 CO 4:5

381 ܟܣܝܐ (adv) secretly

MAT 6:4,4,6,6, 18,18 | LUK 11:33
ROM 2:29

1465 ܟܣܝܐܝܬ (adv) secretly

JHN 11:28

---

[c]PAEL

Perfect

MAT 11:25 | LUK 10:21
25:36,38, 43 | JHN 19:2

Imperfect

1 CO 11:7

Imperative

LUK 23:30

Passive Participle

LUK 9:45 | 1 CO 11:4
18:34 | 2 CO 4:3[1],3[2]
ROM 16:24 | COL 1:26
1 CO 2:7

3384 ܬܟܣܝܬܐ (f) covering

ACT 12:8 | 1 TM 6:8
1 CO 11:15 | HEB 1:12

---

[d]ETHPAAL

Perfect

MAT 6:29 | ACT 1:9
LUK 12:27 | ROM 4:7
19:42

Imperfect

MAT 6:31 | 1 CO 11:6[2]
8:24

Participle

1 CO 11:6[1]

---

129 (ܟܣܢ), ܐܟܣܢܝܐ (adj)
stranger

MAT 25:35,38, 43,44 | 1 TM 5:10
27:7 | TIT 1:8
ROM 12:13 | HEB 11:13
EPH 2:12,19 | 13:2
1 TM 3:2 | 1 PT 4:9
 | 3 JN 5

1467 ܟܣܦ, ܟܣܦܐ (m) silver, money

MAT	17:24,25	LUK	23:2
	22:17,19	ACT	5:2,3,37
	25:18,27		7:16
	26:15		8:18,20
	27:3,5,6,9		19:19
	28:12,15		20:33
MRK	12:14		22:28
	14:11	ROM	13:6,7,7
LUK	9:3	1 TM	3:3
	16:14		6:10
	19:15,23	2 TM	3:2
	20:22	HEB	13:5
	22:5	1 PT	1:18

1468 ܟܦ (v) bend, bow

[a]PEAL

Perfect

LUK 24:5

Imperfect

ROM	14:11	PHL	2:10

Active Participle

EPH 3:14

1470 ܟܦܝܦܐ (pp) bent, hump-backed

LUK	13:11	ROM	11:10

1471 ܟܦܢ (v) hunger

[a]PEAL

Perfect

MAT	4:2	MRK	11:12
	12:1,3	LUK	4:2
	21:18		6:3
	25:35,42	ACT	10:10
MRK	2:25		

Imperfect

LUK	6:25	REV	7:16
JHN	6:35		

1472 ܟܦܢܐ (m) hunger, famine

MAT	24:7	ACT	11:28,28
MRK	13:8	ROM	8:35
LUK	4:25	2 CO	11:27
	15:14,17	PHL	4:12
	21:11	REV	6:8
ACT	7:11		18:8

1473 ܟܦܢܐ (adj) hungry

MAT	5:6	ROM	12:20
	25:37,44	1 CO	4:11
LUK	1:53		11:21,34
	6:21		

1474 ܟܦܪ (v) deny, refuse

[a]PEAL

Perfect

MAT	26:70,72	ACT	7:35
MRK	14:68,70	1 TM	5:8
LUK	22:57	HEB	11:24
JHN	1:20	REV	2:13
	18:25,27		3:8
ACT	3:13,14		

Imperfect

MAT	10:33[1],33[2]	LUK	9:23
	16:24		22:34,61
	26:34,35, 75	JHN	13:38
		ACT	4:16
MRK	8:34	2 TM	2:12[1],12[2], 13
	14:30,31, 72	TIT	2:12

Active Participle

LUK	8:45	2 PT	2:1
	12:9[1]	1 JN	2:22[1],22[2], 22[3],23
2 TM	3:2		
TIT	1:16	JUD	4

1469 ܟܦܘܪܐ (adj) unthankful

LUK 6:35

[b]ETHPEEL

Imperfect

LUK 12:9[2]

[c]PAEL (non occ)

1400 ܟܘܣܦܪܐ (m) rubbish

1 CO 4:13

1475 ܟܦܪ, ܟܦܪܐ (m-non occ) village

1476 ܟܦܪܘܢܐ (m) small villages

LUK 9:12

1401 (ܟܪ), ܟܘܪܐ (m) measure

LUK 16:7,7

1478 ܟܪ (adv) where

ACT 10:23	ROM 15:20
28:23	COL 3:11
ROM 4:15	HEB 6:20
5:20	REV 14:4
9:26	

1479 ܟܪܐ (v) sorrow; (pa) shorten; (aph) make sorry

[a]PEAL

Perfect

MAT 14:9	MRK 6:26
17:23	LUK 18:23,24
18:31	JHN 21:17
26:22	2 CO 7:9[1],9[2]

Imperfect

JHN 16:20	2 CO 2:4

Active Participle

JHN 16:21	1 TH 4:13

Passive Participle

MAT 19:22	MRK 14:34
26:38	JHN 16:22
MRK 3:5	2 CO 6:10

1491 ܟܪܝܘܬܐ (f) sorrowfulness, sadness

JHN 16:6,20	2 CO 7:9,10,10
ROM 9:2	9:7
2 CO 2:1,7	HEB 12:11

[c]PAEL

Perfect

MRK 13:20[1],20[2]

[d]ETHPAAL

Perfect

MAT 24:22[1]

Imperfect

MAT 24:22[2]

[e]APHEL

Perfect

2 CO 2:2[2],5[1],5[2]	2 CO 7:8[1],8[2]

Imperfect

2 CO 2:3

Active Participle

2 CO 2:2[1]

1480 ܟܪܒ (v) plough

[a]PEAL

Imperfect

1 CO 9:10

1483 ܟܪܘܒܐ (m) ploughman

1 CO 9:10

1482 (ܟܪܒ), ܟܪܘܒܐ (m) cherub

HEB 9:5

1481 ܟܪܗ (v) (pe, ethpe) be sick, weak

[a]PEAL (non occ)

1489 ܟܪܝܗܐ (pp) sick, weak

MAT 10:8	MRK 3:15
14:14	6:5,13,56
25:36,39,	14:38
43,44	16:18
26:41	LUK 4:40,40

LUK 7:10
9:2
10:9
JHN 4:46
5:3,7
6:2
11:1,2,3,6
ACT 4:9
5:15,16
19:12
20:35
28:8,9
ROM 14:1,2
1 CO 1:27
4:10
8:7,9,10
9:22,22,22
11:30
2 CO 10:10
12:10
13:9
1 TM 6:4
2 TM 4:20
HEB 5:11
7:28
JAM 5:14,15

1403 ܟܘܪܗܢܐ (m) sickness, infirmity

MAT 4:23,24
8:17
9:35
10:1
MRK 1:34
LUK 4:40
5:15
6:18
7:21
8:2
LUK 9:1
13:11,12
JHN 5:5
11:4
ACT 19:12
ROM 15:1
2 CO 11:30
12:5,9,10
1 TM 5:23
HEB 11:34

1490 ܟܪܝܗܘܬܐ (f) sickness, infirmity

ROM 5:6
6:19
8:3,26
1 CO 1:25
15:43
2 CO 12:9
GAL 4:13
HEB 4:15
5:2

---

b ETHPEEL

Perfect

ACT 9:37
ROM 4:19
PHL 2:26,27

Participle

2 CO 11:29[1],29[2]

1484 (ܟܪܙ), ܟܪܘܙܐ (adj) preacher

ACT 15:21
1 TM 2:7
2 TM 1:11
2 PT 2:5

1485 ܟܪܘܙܘܬܐ (f) preaching, proclamation

MAT 12:41
LUK 11:32
1 CO 1:21
2:4
1 CO 15:14
2 TM 4:17
TIT 1:3

1487 (ܟܪܙ) (v) (ethpe) be preached, declared; (aph) preach

b ETHPEEL

Perfect

ACT 17:13
ROM 16:24
2 CO 1:19
COL 1:6,23
1 TM 3:16

Imperfect

MAT 24:14
26:13
MRK 13:10
14:9
LUK 12:3
24:47
ROM 9:17
PHL 1:18

Participle

ACT 12:24
13:38
1 CO 15:12

---

e APHEL

Perfect

MRK 6:12
16:20
ACT 3:18,24
10:37
15:36
20:25
26:20[1],20[2]
ROM 9:27
1 CO 9:27
2 CO 11:4[1],4[2],7
GAL 4:16
1 TH 2:10
1 PT 3:19

Imperfect

MAT 12:18
MRK 1:38
3:14
ACT 10:42
13:24
ACT 20:20
26:23
ROM 1:14
10:15
EPH 6:19

Imperative

MAT 10:7,27
MRK 16:15
2 TM 4:2

Infinitive

MAT 4:17
11:1
LUK 4:18,19
LUK 9:2
ACT 22:21

Active Participle

MAT 3:1
4:23
9:35
MRK 1:4,7,14,
39,45
5:20
7:36
LUK 3:3
4:44
LUK 8:1,39
ACT 4:2,29
8:4,5
9:20
16:4,21
17:18[1],18[2],
19
19:13
28:31

ROM 2:21	GAL 5:11
10:8	PHL 1:15,17
1 CO 1:23	COL 1:28
9:14	2 TM 2:15
15:11	1 JN 1:2
2 CO 4:5	REV 5:2
GAL 2:2	

1731 ܡܟܪܙܢܐ (m) preacher

ROM 10:14

1488 ܟܪܛܝܣܐ (c) paper

2 JN 12

1492 ܟܪܟ (v) wrap; (ethpe) go around; (aph) lead about

[a]PEAL

Perfect

MAT 27:59	LUK 4:20
MRK 15:46	23:53
LUK 2:7	JHN 19:40

Passive Participle

LUK 2:12	JHN 20:7

1493 ܟܪܟܐ (m) scroll

2 TM 4:13

1494 ܟܪܟܐ (m) walled city

LUK 19:17,19	JHN 11:54

[b]ETHPEEL

Perfect

ACT 13:6	ACT 27:4,7
14:24	28:13
18:23	HEB 11:30,37
19:1	REV 6:14
20:2,25	

Imperfect

ACT 19:21	ROM 15:19

Participle

MAT 4:23	MRK 6:6
9:35	LUK 8:1
12:43	9:6
23:15	11:24

ACT 8:4,40	ACT 17:23
9:32	19:13
10:38	1 TM 5:13
13:11	

[e]APHEL

Infinitive

1 CO 9:5

1495 ܟܪܡ, ܟܪܡܐ (m) vineyard

MAT 20:1,2,4,7, 8	LUK 13:6
21:28,33, 34,39, 40,41	20:9,10,13, 15,15, 16
MRK 12:1,2,8,9, 9	1 CO 9:7
	REV 14:18,19

1496 ܟܪܣ, ܟܪܣܐ (f) belly, womb

MAT 12:40	JHN 7:38
15:17	9:1
19:12	ACT 2:30
MRK 7:19	3:2
LUK 1:15,41,42, 44	14:8
2:21	ROM 16:18
11:27	1 CO 6:13,13
15:16	GAL 1:15
16:21	PHL 3:19
23:29	TIT 1:12
JHN 3:4	REV 10:9,10

1405 (ܟܪܣ), ܟܘܪܣܝܐ (m) throne, seat

MAT 5:34	REV 4:6,9,10, 10
19:28	5:1,6,7,11, 13
21:12	7:9,10,11, 11,15,15, 17
23:2,22	8:3
MRK 11:15	11:16
LUK 1:32,52	12:5
22:30	13:2
ACT 2:30	14:3
7:49	16:10,17
HEB 1:8	19:4,5
4:16	20:11,12
8:1	21:5
12:2	22:1,3
REV 1:4	
2:13	
3:21,21	
4:2,2,3,4,4, 4,5,5,6,6,	

1486 (ܟܪܘܣܦܪܣܘܣ), ܟܪܘܣܘܦܪܣܘܣܐ(m)

chrysoprase

REV 21:20

1499 ܟܫܠ, ܟܫܠܐ(m) offense

GAL 5:11
1 PT 2:8
1 JN 2:10
REV 2:14

1732 ܡܟܫܘܠܐ (m) offense

MAT 13:41
18:7,7,7
LUK 17:1
ROM 9:33
16:17

1498 (ܟܫܠ) (v) (ethpe) be offended; (aph) make stumble

[b]ETHPEEL

Perfect

MAT 15:12

Imperfect

MAT 11:6
24:10
26:31,33[1], 33[2]
MRK 14:27,29
LUK 7:23
JHN 16:1

Participle

MAT 13:21,57
MRK 4:17
6:3
LUK 8:13
2 CO 11:29

[e]APHEL

Imperfect

MAT 17:27
18:6
MRK 9:42
LUK 17:2
1 CO 8:13[2]

Active Participle

MAT 5:29,30
18:8,9
MRK 9:43,45,47
JHN 6:61
1 CO 8:13[1]

1408 (ܟܫܦ), ܟܘܫܦܐ(m-non occ) covering

1500 (ܟܫܦ) (v) (ethpa) pray

[d]ETHPAAL

Perfect

ACT 4:31

Imperfect

1 TH 3:10

Participle

ACT 13:2
EPH 6:18
PHL 1:4
1 TH 4:1

3385 ܬܟܫܦܬܐ (f) supplication

HEB 5:7

1501 ܟܬܒ(v) write

[a]PEAL

Perfect

MRK 10:5
12:19
LUK 1:63
20:28
JHN 1:45
5:46
19:19[1],22[1], 22[2]
21:24
ACT 1:1
15:23
16:4
18:27
21:25
23:25
ROM 10:5
15:15
ROM 16:22
1 CO 5:9,11
7:1
9:15
2 CO 2:3,4,9
7:12
GAL 6:11[2]
EPH 3:3
2 TH 3:17[1]
PLM 19,21
HEB 13:22
1 PT 5:12
2 PT 3:15
1 JN 2:13[3],14[1], 14[2],21, 26
5:13

Imperfect

MRK 10:4
LUK 1:3
JHN 19:21
ACT 25:26[1],26[2], 27
2 CO 3:1[2]
PHL 3:1
HEB 8:10
10:16
3 JN 9,13[2]
REV 3:12
10:4[2]

Imperative

LUK 16:6,7
REV 1:11,19
2:1,8,12, 18
REV 3:1,7,14
14:13
19:9
21:5

Infinitive

1 TH	4:9	3 JN	13[1]
	5:1	JUD	3[1],3[2]
2 JN	12	REV	10:4[1]

Active Participle

JHN	8:8	2 TH	3:17[2]
1 CO	4:14	1 TM	3:14
	14:37	2 PT	3:1
2 CO	1:13	1 JN	1:4
	9:1		2:1,7,8,12, 13[1],13[2]
	13:2,10		
GAL	1:20	2 JN	5

Passive Participle

MAT	2:5	ROM	2:15,24
	4:4,6,7,10		3:4,10
	11:10		4:17,18
	21:13		8:36
	26:24,31		9:13,33
MRK	1:2		10:15
	7:6		11:8,26
	9:12,13		12:19
	11:17		14:11
	14:21,27		15:3,9,21
	15:26	1 CO	1:19,31
LUK	2:23		2:9
	3:4		3:19
	4:4,8,10, 17		4:6
			9:9
	7:27		10:7
	10:26		14:21
	18:31		15:3,4,45, 54
	19:46		
	20:17,24	2 CO	3:2,3
	21:22		4:13
	22:37		8:15
	23:38		9:9
	24:44,46	GAL	3:10[1],10[2], 11,12,13
JHN	2:17		
	6:31,45		4:22,27
	8:17		6:11[1]
	10:34	PHL	4:3
	12:14,16	HEB	4:7
	15:25		5:12
	19:19[2],20		7:6
	20:30,31		10:7
ACT	1:20	JAM	2:8
	7:42	1 PT	1:16
	13:27,29, 33,40, 47	REV	1:3
			13:8
			14:1
	15:15		17:5,8
	17:23		19:12,16
	23:5		20:12
	24:14		21:12,27
ROM	1:17		22:18,19

1502 ܟܬܒܐ (m) book, writing

MAT	1:1	MAT	19:7
	5:31		21:42
MAT	22:20,29	ROM	4:3
	26:54,56		7:6
	27:37		9:17
MRK	10:4		10:11
	12:10,16, 24,26		11:2
			15:4
	14:49		16:25
	15:26,28	2 CO	3:6,6,7
LUK	3:4	GAL	3:8,22
	4:21		4:30
	16:6,7	PHL	4:3
	20:42	1 TM	5:18
	23:38	2 TM	3:16
	24:27,32,		4:13,13
	45	HEB	2:6
JHN	2:22		7:8
	5:39,47		10:7
	7:38,42	JAM	2:23
	10:35		4:5
	13:18	1 PT	2:6
	17:12	2 PT	1:20
	19:24,28,		3:16
	36,37	REV	1:11
	20:9,30		2:17
	21:25		5:1,2,3,4,5, 7,8,9
ACT	1:1,16		
	7:42		6:14
	8:32,35		13:8
	13:27		20:15
	17:2,11		21:27
	18:24,28		22:7,9,10, 18,18, 19,19
	19:19		
ROM	1:2		
	2:27,29		

1503 ܟܬܒܘܢܐ (m) little book

REV	10:2,8,9,	REV	10:10

1504 ܟܬܒܬܐ (f) (w/ ܐܝܕܐ) handwriting

1 CO	16:21	2 TH	3:17

---

[b]ETHPEEL

Perfect

LUK	10:20	COL	4:16
ROM	4:23	2 TM	3:16
	15:4[1],4[2]	HEB	7:3
1 CO	9:10	JUD	4
	10:11		

Imperfect

LUK	2:1,3,5	2 CO	3:1[1]

Participle

JHN	21:25[1],25[2]	HEB	12:23
ACT	5:37		

---

eAPHEL

Imperfect

LUK 1:1

Active Participle

JHN 8:6

1733 ܡܟܬܒܢܘܬܐ (f) enrollment

LUK 2:2

1505 ܟܬܡ (v) defile

aPEAL (non occ)

1411 ܟܘܬܡܬܐ (f) spot, mark

GAL 6:17	JUD 24
2 PT 3:14	

cPAEL

Active Participle

JAM 3:6	JUD 12

Passive Participle

2 PT 2:13	JUD 23

1506 ܟܬܢܐ (m) linen cloth

MAT 27:59	JHN 20:5,6,7
MRK 15:46	ACT 10:11
LUK 23:53	11:5
24:12	REV 15:6
JHN 19:40	

1410 ܟܘܬܝܢܐ (f) coat, linen garment

MAT 5:40	LUK 9:3
10:10	JHN 19:23
MRK 6:9	21:7
14:63	ACT 9:39
LUK 3:11	JUD 23
6:29	

1507 ܟܬܦ, ܟܬܦܐ (f) shoulder

MAT 23:4	LUK 15:5

1508 (ܟܬܪ) (v) abide, continue

cPAEL

Perfect

LUK 22:28	JHN 11:6
JHN 8:7	

Imperfect

JHN 8:31	HEB 13:1

Infinitive

REV 17:10

Active Participle

ACT 27:31	2 PT 3:4
1 CO 13:13	1 JN 2:10,19

1509 ܟܬܫ (v) strike; (ethpa) strive, endeavor

aPEAL

Active Participle

1 CO 9:26[2]

3386 ܬܟܬܘܫܐ (m) contest, strife

EPH 6:12	TIT 3:9
2 TM 2:23	

dETHPAAL

Perfect

2 TM 4:7

Imperative

LUK 13:24	1 TM 6:12

Infinitive

LUK 14:31	2 TM 2:24

Participle

JHN 18:36	2 TM 2:5[1],5[2]
1 CO 9:26[1]	TIT 3:2
COL 1:29	

ܠ

1511 ܠܐ (prt) no, not; (w/ ܕ) lest, without

see also 133 ܐܠܐ

see also 243 ܐܦ

see also 1376 ܟܕ

see also 1533 ܠܘ

see also 1572 ܠܝܬ

see also 2278 ܕܠܐ

MAT 1:18,19,20,25; 2:6,12,18,18; 3:9,10,11, 12; 4:4,6,7; 5:13,14,15,17,17,18,20,21,26,27, 29,30,33,34,34,35,36,36,37,37,39,42,46,47; 6:1,2,3,5,7,8,8,13,15,16,18,19,20,20,20,20, 24,24,25,25,25,26,26,26,26,28,28,30,31,34; 7:1,1,3,6,6,18,18,19,21,22,23,25,26,29; 8:8, 10,28; 9:12,13,13,14,16,16,17,17,24,30,33; 10:5,5,9,9,9,10,10,10,10,13,14,14,19,20,23, 24,26,26,26,28,28,29,29,31,34,34,37,37,38, 38,42; 11:6,11,17,17,18,18,20,27,27; 12:2,3, 4,4,5,5,7,7,7,11,16,19,19,19,20,20,24,25,30, 30,31,32,32,32,39,43; 13:11,13,13,13,14,14, 15,17,17,19,22,27,34,34,55,55,56,58,58; 14:4,16,27; 15:2,5,11,13,16,17,20,23,24,26, 32; 16:3,4,7,8,9,9,10,11,11,12,17,18,20,23, 28; 17:7,8,9,12,16,17,19,20,20,21,24,27; 18:3,8,9,10,12,13,17,17,22,30,33; 19:4,6,6,8, 9,10,11,14,18,18,18,18,26; 20:7,13,13,15,22, 23,26,28; 21:16,19,19,21,21,25,27,29,30,32, 32,42; 22:3,8,11,16,16,17,29,29,30,31,32,46, 46; 23:3,3,4,8,9,10,14,14,16,18,23,30,37,39; 24:2,2,2,4,6,6,17,18,20,20,21,21,22,22,23, 26,26,29,34,35,36,39,42,43,44,50,50; 25:3,9, 12,13,13,24,24,26,26,42,42,43,43,43,44,45; 26:5,5,11,24,29,33,35,39,40,41,42,53,55,60, 62,70,72,74; 27:6,12,13,14,19,24,34,42; 28:5,6,10,12,14 MRK 1:7,22,34,45; 2:2,4, 12,17,17,18,19,21,21,22,22,24,25,26,27; 3:9, 12,20,24,25,26,27; 4:7,12,12,13,19,21,22,22, 22,27,34,34,38; 5:3,4,7,10,19,26,36,37,39, 43; 6:3,3,5,8,8,8,8,9,11,11,18,19,26,50,52; 7:3,3,4,5,12,18,18,19,24,24,27,36,37; 8:1,12, 17,17,18,18,18,21,26,26,30,33; 9:1,3,6,8,9, 17,18,19,25,25,28,29,30,32,37,38,39,40,41, 44,44,46,46,48,48; 10:8,9,14,15,15,19,19,19, 19,19,27,30,38,40,43,45; 11:2,13,13,14,16, 17,23,26,31,33; 12:14,14,14,14,19,20,22,24, 24,24,25,26,27,34,34; 13:2,2,7,7,11,11,11, 14,15,15,16,18,19,19,20,20,21,24,30,31,32, 32,33,35; 14:2,7,21,25,29,31,36,37,38,40,49, 55,56,58,59,60,61,68,71; 15:4,5,23,29,31; 16:6,6,8,11,13,14,16,18 LUK 1:6,13,15, 17,20,20,22,30,33,34,37,60,74; 2:10,26,37, 43,45,49,50; 3:8,9,13,14,14,16,17; 4:2,4,11, 12,22,26,27,41,42; 5:5,10,14,19,31,32,34,36, 36,36,37,37,39; 6:2,3,4,29,30,35,37,37,37, 37,39,41,42,43,44,46,48,49,49; 7:6,6,6,7,9, 13,23,25,26,30,32,32,33,33,44,45,45,46; 8:10,10,12,14,16,17,17,17,19,27,27,28,31, 43,47,49,50,51,52,52,56; 9:3,3,3,3,3,3,5,21, 27,33,36,40,41,45,45,49,50,50,53,55,56,62; 10:4,4,4,4,6,7,10,19,20,22,24,24,40,42; 11:4, 7,7,8,23,23,24,29,33,38,40,42,44,44,46,52; 12:2,2,2,4,6,6,7,10,11,15,21,22,22,24,24,27, 27,29,29,32,33,33,33,33,39,40,46,46,46,47, 48,51,56,57,59; 13:3,5,5,6,7,11,14,15,16,24, 25,27,33,34,35; 14:5,6,8,12,12,12,20,24,26, 26,27,27,28,29,29,30,31,32,33,33,35,35; 15:4,7,8,16,19,21,28,29,29; 16:2,3,11,12,12, 13,26,28,30,31; 17:1,1,9,17,20,21,22,23,31, 31; 18:1,2,2,4,4,4,5,7,11,11,13,13,16,17,17, 20,20,20,20,27,30,34,34; 19:3,14,21,21,22, 22,23,27,30,44,44,48; 20:5,7,8,16,21,22,26, 28,29,30,31,35,38,40; 21:6,6,8,9,9,14,15,18, 21,32,33,34; 22:16,26,27,32,34,34,35,35,35, 40,42,46,53,57,58,60,67,68; 23:2,4,9,14,15, 22,28,29,29,34,40,41,51,53; 24:3,11,16,18, 23,24,26,32,36,41 JHN 1:3,5,8,10,11,13, 18,20,21,21,25,25,25,26,27,31,33; 2:4,9,16, 24,25; 3:2,3,3,5,5,7,8,10,11,12,13,15,16,17, 18,18,18,20,20,24,27,28,32,34,36,36; 4:2,9, 11,14,15,15,18,21,22,27,32,35,38,42,44,48, 48; 5:10,13,14,18,19,22,23,23,24,28,30,30, 31,34,37,37,38,38,40,41,43,44,47; 6:7,12,17, 20,22,24,26,27,32,35,35,36,37,38,39,42,43, 44,46,50,58,63,64,64,65,66,70; 7:1,6,7,8,8, 10,12,13,15,16,18,19,19,22,23,24,26,27,28, 28,30,30,34,34,35,36,36,39,39,42,44,45,46, 49,52; 8:7,10,11,11,12,13,14,14,15,16,19,19, 20,20,21,22,23,24,27,28,29,33,35,37,40,41, 42,43,43,44,45,46,47,47,48,49,50,51,52,54, 55,55,57; 9:3,3,4,8,9,12,16,16,18,21,25,27, 29,30,31,32,33,33,39; 10:1,5,5,6,8,10,12,13, 16,18,21,25,26,26,28,28,29,33,34,35,37,37, 38; 11:4,9,9,15,21,26,30,32,37,37,40,49,50, 50,51,52,54,56; 12:5,6,8,9,15,16,19,30,35, 35,37,39,40,42,42,44,46,47,47,47,48,49; 13:7,8,8,9,10,10,11,18,22,28,33,36,37,38; 14:1,2,5,6,9,10,10,11,17,17,17,18,19,22,22, 24,24,24,27,27,27,29,30; 15:2,4,5,5,6,15,15, 16,19,21,22,24,24; 16:1,3,3,3,4,5,7,7,9,10, 12,13,16,17,18,19,21,22,23,24,25,26,29,30, 32; 17:9,11,12,14,14,15,16,16,20,25; 18:9, 11,17,20,25,26,28,28,30,30,31,36,36,36,40; 19:4,6,9,10,10,11,12,21,23,24,31,33,36,41; 20:2,5,7,9,13,14,17,17,24,25,25,27,27,29, 30; 21:3,4,5,6,8,11,12,18,23,23,23

ACT 1:4,5,7,20; 2:7,15,24,25,27,27,31,31,
34; 3:23; 4:12,13,14,16,17,17,18,18,20,20,
21,32; 5:4,4,7,13,22,23,26,28,28,36,39,40,
42; 6:2,10,13; 7:5,5,18,19,25,32,39,40,48,50,
51,52,53,60; 8:21,21,24,32,39; 9:7,8,9,9,9,
21,26,38,43; 10:14,15,20,28,28,28,34,41,47;
11:8,9,12,19; 12:9,14,19,22,23; 13:10,11,25,
25,27,27,28,34,35,37,39,41,46; 14:2,8,17,17,
18; 15:1,1,9,10,10,19,24,28,38,38; 16:6,7,21,
28,37,37; 17:4,6,13,21,23,24,25,25,29; 18:9,
9,10,15,20,25; 19:26,27,31,32,35,36,36,37,
37,40,40; 20:10,20,22,24,25,27,29,31,33,38;
21:4,12,13,14,21,21,34,38; 22:9,11,18,22,25;
23:5,5,8,8,9,12,12,14,21,21,21,22; 24:4,12,
12,12,12,13,18,18,23; 25:7,8,8,8,8,10,11,11,
17,18,20,24,25,26,27,27; 26:8,19,22,25,26,
26,29,31,32; 27:7,12,15,20,20,20,21,21,22,
22,24,31,31,33,34,39,41,42; 28:4,5,6,17,18,
19,21,21,22,24,25,26,26,27,31 ROM 1:9,
16,20,21,21,23,26,28,28,30,31,31,31,32; 2:4,
5,7,8,11,12,12,13,21,21,22,26,28,29,29; 3:3,
3,11,11,12,17,20,21,27,28,29; 4:2,4,5,6,8,10,
12,13,15,16,17,18,19,20,23; 5:3,5,11,13,14,
15,16,19; 6:3,6,9,9,12,14,14,15,16; 7:1,3,6,7,
7,7,7,9,15,15,16,17,18,18,19,19,20,20; 8:1,4,
7,7,8,9,9,15,18,20,23,24,25,26,26,32,32,38,
38,38,38,38,38,38,39,39,39; 9:1,2,6,6,8,11,
11,11,16,16,21,24,25,25,26,29,30,31,32,33;
10:3,3,6,11,12,12,12,14,14,14,16,18,19,19,
19,20,20,21; 11:2,2,4,4,6,6,6,6,7,8,8,10,18,
18,20,20,21,21,24,25,29,30,30,31,32,33,33;
12:2,3,4,9,11,14,16,16,17,19,21; 13:1,3,3,4,
5,8,9,9,9,9,10,13,13,13,13,14; 14:1,3,3,3,3,4,
6,6,6,6,13,13,15,15,16,17,20,21,21,21,21,22,
23; 15:1,3,18,18,20,20,21,21,31; 16:4,18
1 CO 1:7,8,10,14,15,16,17,17,17,20,21,26,
26,26,29; 2:1,2,4,5,6,8,9,9,9,11,12,13,14,14,
15; 3:1,2,2,2,3,4,7,7,11,16,18,21; 4:3,4,5,6,6,
7,7,14,15,18,19,20; 5:1,2,6,6,8,8,9,10,11;
6:1,2,2,3,5,6,7,7,9,9,9,9,9,9,9,10,10,10,10,
10,10,12,12,13,15,16,19,19; 7:1,4,4,5,5,10,
10,11,11,12,12,12,13,13,14,14,14,15,15,18,
18,19,21,23,25,27,27,28,28,30,30,30,31,32,
34,35,35,36,36,37,38; 8:2,4,7,8,8,8,10,13,13;
9:1,1,1,1,2,4,5,6,7,7,9,12,12,12,13,15,15,17,
18,18,21,21,21,21,24,25,26,26,26; 10:5,6,7,
8,9,10,12,13,13,16,16,18,19,20,20,21,21,23,
23,24,25,27,28,29,32,33; 11:6,7,8,11,11,16,
17,17,22,27,29,29,31,32,34; 12:2,14,15,15,
16,16,21,21,21,24,25; 13:1,2,3,3,4,4,4,5,5,5,
5,6,8; 14:2,2,5,7,8,9,10,11,14,16,17,20,21,
22,22,22,22,23,23,24,33,34,38,38,39; 15:2,9,
10,10,13,14,16,16,17,29,32,33,34,36,37,39,
42,46,50,50,50,52,53,53,54,54,58,58; 16:2,7,
10,12,22 2 CO 1:9,12,13,17,17,18,18,19,
19,23,24; 2:1,3,4,5,5,11,13,13,17; 3:3,3,6,7,
8,10,13,13,14; 4:1,2,2,4,4,5,7,8,8,9,9,16,17,
18,18,18; 5:1,4,7,12,12,15,16,16,19,21; 6:1,
3,6,9,9,12,14,14,15,17; 7:2,2,2,3,5,7,8,9,9,
10,12,12,14; 8:5,8,12,13,15,15,20,21; 9:3,4,
4,5,7,12,15; 10:2,3,4,6,8,8,9,12,12,13,14,14,
15,16,18; 11:4,4,4,5,6,9,9,10,11,15,17,25,29,
29,31; 12:1,2,2,3,3,4,4,5,6,7,7,11,11,13,14,
14,14,16,20,20,21; 13:2,3,5,6,7,8,10,10
GAL 1:1,1,7,10,11,16,17,19,20,22; 2:3,6,6,
6,12,14,14,15,16,16,16,20,21; 3:10,11,12,15,
16,17,18,20,23,25,28,28,28; 4:1,7,8,8,12,14,
14,17,18,21,27,27,30,31; 5:1,2,6,6,7,8,10,13,
16,17,18,21,23,26; 6:3,4,7,7,9,9,12,13,14,15,
15,17 EPH 1:4,16,21; 2:2,8,9,9,12,12,12,
19,19; 3:5,8,13; 4:14,17,20,26,26,27,28,29,
30; 5:3,4,4,4,6,7,11,15,17,18,27,27,27,29;
6:4,6,7,12,24 PHL 1:10,14,17,20,22,28,
29; 2:3,4,6,12,14,14,15,16,16,21,27,27; 3:1,
3,6,12,13; 4:6,10,11,15 COL 1:9,15,16,22,
22,23; 2:1,4,8,11,16,18,19,21,21,21,23; 3:2,
6,9,11,11,11,19,21,21,22,23 1 TH 1:5,8,8;
2:1,3,3,4,5,6,6,6,8,9,10,13,15,17; 3:1,3,5,13;
4:5,5,6,7,8,9,12,13,15; 5:1,3,4,5,5,6,9,17,19,
20,23 2 TH 1:8,8; 2:2,2,2,2,2,5,10,12; 3:6,
7,8,9,9,10,11,13,14,14,15 1 TM 1:3,4,4,7,
9,9,13,13,17,17,20; 2:7,8,8,9,12,12,14; 3:2,3,
3,3,3,5,6,6,7,8,8,8,10,11; 4:12,14; 5:1,7,8,8,
9,13,13,14,16,18,19,21,21,22,22,23,25; 6:1,
2,3,4,7,14,14,16,16,16,17,17 2 TM 1:7,8,
10,12,16; 2:4,5,5,9,13,13,14,14,15,20,23,24;
3:2,7,9; 4:2,3,8,16,16 TIT 1:6,6,6,6,7,7,7,
7,7,7,10,11,14,15,16; 2:3,3,5,8,8,8,9,10,15;
3:2,2,3,3,5,13,14,14 PLM 14,14,16,19
HEB 1:12,14; 2:1,5,8,8,8,11,16; 3:8,10,11,
12,13,15,16,18,18,19,19; 4:2,2,3,5,6,6,7,8,
11,11,15,15; 5:2,4,5,12,13; 6:4,8,10,12,17,
18,18,19; 7:3,3,3,3,6,7,13,14,16,16,19,21,21,
23,24,26,26; 8:2,4,7,9,9,11,11,12; 9:5,8,9,11,
11,12,14,18,18,22,24,25,25,28; 10:1,1,2,4,5,
6,8,11,17,18,23,25,28,34,35,37,38,39; 11:1,
3,5,5,6,6,7,8,11,13,16,23,24,25,27,27,28,31,
31,35,38,39,40; 12:3,3,4,5,5,7,8,8,11,13,14,
17,18,18,19,19,20,25,26,27,28; 13:2,2,5,5,5,
6,9,9,9,10,16,17,17 JAM 1:4,5,6,7,13,13,
13,16,20,22,22,23,25,26,27; 2:1,4,5,6,7,11,
11,11,13,13,16,17,18,20,21,24,25,26,26; 3:1,
2,8,8,10,14,15,17,17; 4:1,2,2,3,4,11,11,14,
17; 5:6,9,9,12,12,12,12,12,12,17,17
1 PT 1:4,4,4,8,8,14,14,18,18,22,23,23; 2:6,7,
8,10,10,15,16,18,22,22,23,23; 3:1,1,3,4,6,7,
9,9,10,14,14,17,20; 4:2,4,9,12,15,16,17; 5:2,
2,3,4 2 PT 1:8,8,9,9,10,12,16,20,21; 2:3,3,
4,5,7,8,10,11,12,14,14,16,17,21; 3:8,9,9,14,
14,16,16,17 1 JN 1:10; 2:1,4,11,15,15,16,
21,21,21,22,27,28; 3:1,1,2,6,6,6,7,9,9,10,10,
13,14,15,18,21; 4:1,3,6,6,8,8,10,12,18,20,20;
5:3,6,10,10,12,16,16,16,17,18,18 2 JN 1,
5,7,8,9,10,10,10,12 3 JN 7,9,10,10,11,11,
13 JUD 5,6,6,9,10,12,12,12,24,24,24
REV 1:17; 2:2,3,5,9,10,11,13,16,17,21,24,
24; 3:2,3,3,4,5,8,8,9,11,12,15,15,16,16,17,
17,18; 5:3,3,5; 6:6,10; 7:1,1,1,3,3,16,16,16,
16; 8:12; 9:4,5,6,20,20,20,20,20,21; 10:4,6,7;
11:2,6,9; 12:8,8,11; 13:8,15,17; 14:3,4,5,5,
10; 15:4; 16:9,11,13,15,18,20; 17:8,10,12;
18:2,4,7,14,15,21,22,23,23; 19:10,12; 20:3,4,
4,4,11,15; 21:4,4,4,4,8,22,23,23,25,25,27;
22:3,5,5,9,10

1512 ܠܐܐ (v) toil, labor; (aph) tire

[a]PEAL

Perfect

LUK 5:5
JHN 4:38[1],38[2]
ROM 16:6,12[1], 12[2]
1 CO 15:10
GAL 4:11
PHL 4:3
REV 2:3

Imperfect

EPH 4:28

Infinitive

ACT 20:35

Active Participle

MAT 6:28
LUK 12:27
1 CO 4:12
16:16
1 TH 2:9
1 TH 5:12
1 TM 4:10
5:17
2 TM 2:6

Passive Participle

MAT 9:36
11:28
JHN 4:6

1513 ܠܐܘܬܐ (f) weariness, labor

2 CO 6:5
11:23,27
2 TH 3:8

[e]APHEL

Imperfect

ACT 24:4

Active Participle

MAT 26:10
LUK 18:5

1737 (ܠܐܟ), ܡܠܐܟܐ (m) messenger, angel

MAT 1:20,24
2:13,19
4:6,11
11:10
13:39,41, 49
16:27
18:10
22:30
24:31,36
25:31,41
26:53
MAT 28:2,5
MRK 1:2,13
8:38
12:25
13:27,32
LUK 1:11,13,18, 19,26,28, 30,34,35, 38
2:9,10,13, 15,21
4:10
LUK 7:27
9:26,52
12:8,9
15:10
16:22
20:36
22:43
24:23
JHN 1:51
5:4
12:29
20:12
ACT 5:19
6:15
7:30,35,38, 53
8:26
10:3,4,7, 22
11:13
12:7,8,9, 10,11, 15,23
23:8,9
27:23
ROM 8:38
1 CO 4:9
6:3
11:10
13:1
2 CO 11:14
12:7
GAL 1:8
3:19
4:14
COL 2:18
1 TH 4:16
2 TH 1:7
1 TM 3:16
1 TM 5:21
HEB 1:4,5,6,7,7, 13
2:2,5,7,9, 16
12:22
13:2
1 PT 1:12
3:22
2 PT 2:4,11
JUD 6,9
REV 1:1,20
2:1,8,12, 18
3:1,5,7,14
5:2,11
7:1,2,2,11
8:2,4,5,6, 13
9:11,11,13, 14,14,15
10:1,5,7,8, 9,10
11:1,15
12:7,7,9
14:6,9,10, 15,17, 18,19
15:1,6,7,8
16:1,3,4,5, 8,10,12, 17
17:1,7
18:1,21
19:17
20:1
21:9,12,17
22:6,8,16

1516 ܠܒܐ (m) heart

MAT 5:8,28
6:21
9:4
11:29
12:34,40
13:15,15, 19
15:8,18,19
18:35
19:8
22:37
24:48
MRK 2:6,8
3:5
4:15
6:52
7:6,19,21
8:17
10:5
11:23
12:30,33
MRK 16:14
LUK 1:17,51,66
2:19,35,51
3:15
4:18
5:22
6:45,45,45
8:12,15
9:47
10:27
12:34,45
16:15
21:14,34
24:25,32, 38
JHN 7:18
11:19
12:40,40
13:2
14:1,27
16:6,22

ACT	1:24	EPH	3:17
	2:26,37,46		4:18
	5:3,4		5:19
	7:23,39,51		6:5,22
	8:21,22	PHL	1:7
	11:23		2:1
	13:22		4:7
	14:17	COL	2:2
	15:8,9		3:15,16,22
	16:14		4:8
	21:13	1 TH	2:4,11,17
	28:27,27		3:13
ROM	1:21,24	2 TH	2:17
	2:5,15,29		3:5
	5:5	1 TM	1:5
	6:17	2 TM	2:22
	8:27	HEB	3:8,10,12, 15
	9:2		4:7,12
	10:1,6,8,9, 10		8:10
	11:7,25		10:16,22, 22
	16:18		13:9
1 CO	2:9	JAM	1:26
	4:5		3:14
	7:37		4:8
	14:25		5:8
	15:34	1 PT	1:22
2 CO	1:22		3:4,15
	2:4		5:2
	3:2,3,15	2 PT	1:19
	4:6		2:14
	5:12	1 JN	3:19,20,20, 21
	6:11		
	7:3	REV	2:23
	8:16		17:17
GAL	4:6		18:7
EPH	1:18		

1515 (ܠܒܒ) (v) encourage

[c]PAEL

Imperative

1 TH 5:14

1537 ܠܘܒܒܐ (m) encouragement

1 CO	14:3	2 CO	8:19

[d]ETHPAAL

Imperative

MAT	9:2,22	LUK	8:48
	14:27		21:28
MRK	6:50	JHN	16:33
	10:49	ACT	27:25

1520 ܠܒܟ (v) seize, lay hold of

[a]PEAL

Perfect

REV 20:2

Passive Participle

TIT	1:8	HEB	6:19

1517 (ܠܒܢ), ܠܒܘܢܬܐ (f) frankincense

MAT	2:11	REV	18:13

1523 ܠܒܫ (v) put on, be clothed; (aph) clothe

[a]PEAL

Perfect

ACT	12:21	2 CO	5:3
1 CO	15:49[1]	GAL	3:27

Imperfect

MAT	6:25	1 CO	15:49[2],53[1], 53[2]
MRK	6:9		
LUK	12:22	2 CO	5:2,4
	24:49	EPH	4:24
ROM	13:12		

Imperative

ROM	13:14	COL	3:10,12
EPH	6:11,13,14		

Active Participle

LUK	8:27	1 CO	15:54
	16:19		

Passive Participle

MAT	11:8[1],8[2]	HEB	5:2,7
	22:11		11:37
MRK	1:6		13:3
	5:15	JAM	2:3
LUK	7:25	REV	1:13
	8:35		15:6
ACT	10:30		19:14
1 TH	5:8		

1518 ܠܒܘܫܐ (m) clothing

MAT	3:4	MAT	14:36
	6:25,28		22:11
	7:15		28:3
	9:20	MRK	1:6

MRK 5:27,28; 6:56; 9:3; 10:50; 13:16
LUK 7:25; 12:23
LUK 24:4
JHN 19:24
ACT 1:10; 12:21
1 TM 2:9
1 PT 3:3

1524 ܠܒܘܫܐ (m) clothes

MAT 24:18

---

[e]APHEL

Perfect

MAT 27:28,31
MRK 15:17,20
LUK 23:11
HEB 10:5

Imperative

LUK 15:22

Active Participle

MAT 6:30
LUK 12:28

1529 (ܠܓܢ), ܠܓܢܬܐ (f) dish

MAT 26:23
MRK 14:20

1526 ܠܓܝܘܢܐ (f) legion

MAT 26:53
MRK 5:9,15
LUK 8:30

3200 (ܠܗܒ), ܫܠܗܒ (v-non occ) inflame

[g]SHAPHEL

3201 ܫܠܗܒܝܬܐ (f) flame

LUK 16:24
REV 1:14; 2:18
REV 8:10; 19:12

1531 ܠܗܓܐ (m) vapor

JAM 4:14

ܠܗܠ see (ܗܠ)

1533 ܠܘ (adv) no, not

from 1511 ܠܐ and 747 ܗܘ

JHN 1:13,13,20; 7:25; 10:12 ACT 19:26, 27; 27:10 ROM 8:12; 9:10; 10:2; 14:23 1 CO 2:8; 4:4; 7:6; 9:15; 11:20; 12:15,16; 15:51 2 CO 3:5; 8:10; 12:18 PHL 4:17 COL 2:23 2 TH 3:2 2 TM 1:9 1 PT 1:12; 3:21 1 JN 1:6; 2:2,7,19,19; 3:12

1534 ܠܘܐ (v) accompany; (pa, ethpa) escort, aid (on a trip)

[a]PEAL (non occ)

1550 ܠܘܝܬܐ (f) company

LUK 2:44
ACT 19:29

---

[c]PAEL

Perfect

ACT 15:3
ACT 20:38

Imperfect

ROM 15:24
1 CO 16:6
2 CO 1:16
TIT 3:13

Imperative

1 CO 16:11

Active Participle

LUK 7:12
ACT 21:5

---

[d]ETHPAAL

Perfect

ACT 17:15

1540 ܠܘܚܐ (f) table, tablet

JHN 19:19
2 CO 3:3,3
HEB 9:4

1543 (ܠܛ) (v) curse

[a]PEAL

Perfect

MRK 11:21

Imperfect

ACT 23:5 | ROM 12:14

Active Participle

MAT 5:44 | JAM 3:9
LUK 6:28

Passive Participle

MAT 25:41 | GAL 3:10,13
JHN 7:49

1544 ܠܘܛܬܐ (f) curse

ROM 3:14 | JAM 3:10
GAL 3:10,13,13 | 2 PT 2:14
HEB 6:8

1551 ܠܘܟܝܬܐ (f) spear

JHN 19:34

1552 ܠܘܠܪܐ (m) worker of rough cloth

ACT 18:3

1562 ܠܘܬ (prep) to, toward

MAT 2:12; 3:5,13,14; 5:1; 6:1; 7:15; 10:6; 11:28; 12:49; 13:2,36,56; 14:15,25,28,29; 15:1,24,30,30,32; 17:7,14,19,24; 18:1,19,21; 19:3,14,26,26; 21:19,28,30,32,34,37,42; 22:16,25; 23:34,37; 25:9,36,39; 26:10,14,17, 18,18,40,45,47,49,55,57,69; 27:58,62
MRK 1:5,32,40,45; 2:3,4,13,13; 3:7,8,13,34; 4:1; 5:11,15,19,22,30; 6:3,25,30,35,48,51; 7:1; 8:2; 9:14,14,17,19,19,20,25; 10:1,14,27, 27,27,35,50; 11:1,7,13,27; 12:2,4,6,11,13,18; 14:6,7,10,43,49,53,53; 15:39,43
LUK 1:16,26,27,28,30,38,43,45,49,56,58, 80; 2:9,15,44,44,52; 3:7; 4:13,21,26,26,40, 42,42; 6:47; 7:3,4,6,7,19,20,20,38,44; 8:4,19, 35,35,37,37,38; 9:32,41,47; 10:22,23,39; 11:5,6,37; 12:16,41,41,58,58; 13:34; 14:7,26; 15:1,17,20,25; 16:1,20,26,26,30; 17:4; 18:3, 16,27,27,40,40; 19:7,20,24,25,35; 20:10,20; 21:38; 22:28,45,47,56; 23:1,7,11,15,28,36, 52; 24:29,29,44 JHN 1:1,2,19,29,39,42, 47,51; 3:2,21,26,26; 4:30,40,40,40,47; 5:33, 40; 6:5,17,19,21,35,37,37,44,45,65,68; 7:29, 33,37,45,50; 8:2,38,38; 9:13; 10:32,35,41; 11:3,19,29,45,46; 12:6,21,32; 13:1,3,6,35; 14:3,6,12,17,18,21,23,23,25,28,28; 15:26,26; 16:5,7,7,10,16,17,27,28,28; 17:5,5,7,8,11,13; 18:3,13,16,24,28,29,38; 19:25,27,29,33,39; 20:2,2,11,17,17,17; 21:7 ACT 1:10,22; 2:22,29,29; 3:11; 4:23,24,35; 5:13,16; 7:3,27, 58; 8:10,14; 9:17,19,27,32,35,38,40; 10:3,15, 21,33,33,35,48; 11:3,5,11,21; 12:10,20; 13:31,32,46; 14:11,14,15,28; 15:2,19,25,33; 16:39,40; 17:2,6,15,15,28; 18:2,3,6,20,21; 20:18,21; 21:3,4,11,18,18,33; 22:1,5,13,15, 26; 23:14,14,15,15,17,18,18,24,29,30; 24:8, 17; 25:12,14,19,21; 26:17,18,20; 27:1,3,3; 28:2,8,9,14,23,25,26,27,30 ROM 1:10,13; 2:11; 4:2; 5:1,8; 8:7; 9:14; 10:1,21; 11:27; 12:18; 14:14; 15:17,22,23,29,30,32
1 CO 2:1,3; 3:19; 4:17,18,19,21; 7:24,35; 14:6,24,36; 16:5,6,6,7,10,11,12,12,12,17
2 CO 1:11,12,15,16,18; 2:1,4; 3:4,16; 4:14; 5:8,12; 6:11,13,13; 7:4,7,14; 8:7; 9:5; 10:1, 13,14,14; 11:3,4,6; 12:14,17,20,21; 13:1,2
GAL 1:17,18; 2:5,12; 3:11,24; 4:18,20; 6:10, 10 EPH 1:15; 2:18; 3:14; 4:32; 5:11; 6:9, 21,22,22 PHL 1:26; 2:19,23,23,24,25,28, 30; 4:5 COL 1:4; 4:1,5,7,8,8,9,10,16
1 TH 1:5,9,9; 2:1,10,18; 3:2,4,6,6,11,12,12; 4:12; 5:14,15,15 2 TH 1:3; 2:1,2,5; 3:1,10
1 TM 3:14 2 TM 1:18; 2:24; 4:9,13
TIT 3:2,12,12 PLM 5,5,13 HEB 11:6; 12:7,20; 13:13 JAM 1:17; 4:4,8
1 PT 1:2; 2:4,20,25; 4:8; 5:5 2 PT 1:3; 3:16
1 JN 1:2,10; 2:1,19,24,24,27; 3:1,16; 4:9; 5:14 2 JN 10,12,12 3 JN 5,14
REV 10:9; 12:5,5,12

1563 ܠܚܐ (v) blot out, wipe away

[a]PEAL

Imperfect

REV 3:5 | REV 21:4
7:17

ܠܚܘܕ. see (ܚܘܕ.)

1565 ܠܚܟ (v) lick

[c]PAEL

Active Participle

LUK 16:21

1566 ܠܚܡ (v) threaten; (ethpa) threaten

[a]PEAL

Passive Participle

MRK 6:19

1567 ܠܚܡܐ (m) bread; (w/ ܐܦ̈ܐ) shewbread

MAT	4:3,4	LUK	15:17
	6:11		22:19
	7:9		24:30,35
	12:4	JHN	6:5,7,11, 13,23,26, 31,32,32, 33,34,35, 41,48,50, 51,51,51, 58,58
	14:19		13:18,26, 26,27, 30
	15:2,26,33, 34,36		21:9,13
	16:5,7,8,9, 10,11, 12	ACT	1:4
	26:26		20:11
MRK	2:26		27:35
	3:20	1 CO	5:11
	6:8,36,37, 38,38,41, 41,44,52		10:16,17, 17
	7:2,5,27		11:23,26, 27,28
	8:4,5,6,14, 16,17,19	2 CO	9:10
	14:22	2 TH	3:8,12
LUK	4:3,4	HEB	9:2
	6:4		
	7:33		
	9:3,13,16		
	11:3,11		
	14:1,15		

cPAEL (non occ)

1541 ܠܘܚܡܐ (m) threat

ACT 4:29 | ACT 9:1

dETHPAAL

Perfect

ACT 4:21

Imperfect

ACT 4:17

Participle

1 PT 2:23

1568 ܠܚܫ (v) murmur, mutter

cPAEL

Perfect

LUK 12:3

1570 (ܠܛܪ), ܠܝܛܪܐ (m) pound (Roman)

JHN 19:39

1577 (ܠܠܘ), ܠܠܝܐ (m) night

MAT	2:14	ACT	5:19
	4:2		9:24,25,30
	12:40,40		12:6
	14:25		16:9,25,33
	25:6		17:10
	26:31,34		20:7,31
	27:64		23:11,23, 31
	28:13		26:7
MRK	4:27		27:23,27
	5:5	ROM	13:12
	6:48	1 CO	11:23
	13:35	2 CO	11:25
	14:27,30	1 TH	2:9
LUK	2:8,37		3:10
	5:5		5:2,5,7,7
	11:5	2 TH	3:8
	12:20	1 TM	5:5
	17:34	2 TM	1:3
	18:7	REV	4:8
	21:37		7:15
JHN	3:2		8:12
	7:50		12:10
	9:4		14:11
	11:10		20:10
	13:30		21:25
	19:39		22:5
	21:3		

1572 ܠܝܬ (subst.verb) there is not

from 1511 ܠܐ and 112 ܐܝܬ

MAT 6:1; 8:20; 9:36; 10:24,26; 12:43; 13:5, 5,6,13,21,57; 14:17; 15:32; 18:14,25; 19:17; 22:12,23,24,25; 25:29 MRK 3:29; 4:5,5,6, 17,22,25,40; 6:4,31,34,36; 7:15; 8:2,14,16, 17; 9:39; 10:18,29; 12:18,31,32 LUK 1:7, 61; 2:7; 3:11; 4:24; 6:40; 7:28,42; 8:6,13,17, 18; 9:13,58; 11:6,24,36; 12:2,4,17,24; 14:14; 16:13; 18:19,29; 19:26; 20:27; 22:36; 24:6,39 JHN 1:47; 2:3; 4:17,17; 5:7,42; 6:22,53; 7:4; 8:44; 9:41; 11:10; 13:8,16,16; 14:30; 15:13, 20,22,22,24; 19:11,15 ACT 3:6; 4:12,34; 7:5,11; 8:16,21; 23:8,29; 24:11; 25:11,16 ROM 1:31; 2:1,14,14; 3:10,12,18,22; 4:15; 5:13; 8:1,9; 13:1; 14:7,7,14; 15:23 1 CO 1:28; 4:11; 6:5; 7:8,29,32; 8:4; 9:6,16, 21; 11:16,22,22; 12:2,3,15,16; 13:2; 14:7,10, 28; 15:12,13,34 2 CO 6:10; 8:12; 11:14 GAL 3:28,28,28 EPH 4:18; 5:5,11,27; 6:9 PHL 2:20; 3:9 COL 3:11,25 1 TH 4:13 1 TM 1:4; 4:4; 6:17 2 TM 2:16 TIT 1:15; 3:9 PLM 11 HEB 4:13; 6:13; 7:18,27; 8:7; 9:17,22; 10:26; 11:12; 13:14

JAM 1:17; 2:14; 4:2,2 1 PT 1:17,19
1 JN 1:5,8,8,10; 2:4,10,15,27; 3:5,10; 4:3,18; 5:12 2 JN 9 3 JN 4 JUD 19
REV 2:2,24; 3:7,7; 4:8; 5:3,4; 7:9; 9:4; 14:11; 15:8; 17:8,8,11; 18:7,11; 20:6; 21:1

1573 ܠܟܐ (adv) hence, hither

from 1510 ܠ and 1358 ܟܐ

MAT 8:29
17:17
21:3
22:12
MRK 11:3
LUK 9:41
LUK 14:21
ACT 21:22
22:17
25:17
REV 11:12

1574 ܠܠ (v-non occ) speak foolishly

ªPEAL

1575 ܠܠܐ (adj) fool

MAT 5:22

1576 ܠܠܘܬܐ (f) foolishness

1 CO 3:19

1578 ܠܡ (prt) surely, clearly

COL 2:21
2 TH 2:2

1581 ܠܡܕ (v-non occ) join

ᵈETHPAAL

3392 ܬܠܡܝܕܐ (adj) disciple

MAT 5:1
8:21,23,25
9:10,11,14,
14,19,37
10:1,24,25,
42
11:1,2
12:1,2,49
13:10,36
14:12,15,
19,19,
22,26
15:2,12,23,
32,33,
36,36
16:5,13,20,
MAT 16:21,24
17:6,10,13,
16,19
18:1
19:10,13,
23,25
20:17
21:1,6,20
22:16
23:1
24:1,3
26:1,8,17,
18,19,
20,26,
35,36,
40,45,
MAT 26:56
27:64
28:7,8,13,
16
MRK 2:15,16,18,
18,18,23
3:7,9
4:34
5:31
6:1,29,35,
41,45
7:2,5,17
8:1,4,6,10,
27,27,33,
34
9:8,14,18,
28,31
10:10,13,
23,24,
46
11:1,14
12:43
13:1
14:4,12,13,
14,16,
31,32,
50
16:7
LUK 5:30,33
6:1,13,17,
20,40
7:11,18,19,
24
8:9,22
9:12,15,16,
18,40,43,
54
10:1,22,23
11:1,1
12:1,15,22
14:26,27,
33
16:1
17:1,22
18:15
19:29,37,
39
20:45
22:11,39,
45
JHN 1:35,37
JHN 2:2,11,12,
17,22
3:22,25
4:1,2,8,27,
31,33
6:3,8,12,
16,22,22,
24,60,61,
66
7:3
8:31
9:2,27,28,
28
11:7,8,12,
16,54
12:4,16,16
13:5,22,23,
25,35
15:8
16:17,29
18:1,1,2,
15,15,
16,17,
19,25
19:26,27,
27,38
20:2,3,4,8,
10,18,
19,20,
25,26,
30
21:1,2,4,7,
8,12,14,
20,23,
24
ACT 1:15
6:1,1,2,7
9:1,10,19,
25,26,26,
36,38
11:26,29
13:52
14:20,22,
28
15:10
16:1,2
18:23,27
19:1,9,30
20:1,30
21:4,16,16

3391 ܬܠܡܕ (v) teach, instruct

ᵏP

Perfect

ACT 14:21

Imperative

MAT 28:19

Participle

ACT 18:25

3348 ܬܘܠܡܕܐ (m)
doctrine

1 TM 3:6

---

[m]ETHP

Perfect

MAT 27:57 | LUK 1:4

Participle

MAT 13:52

1580 (ܠܡܐ), ܠܡܐܢܐ (m) port, haven

ACT 27:8,12,12

1585 ܠܡܦܐܕܐ (m) lamp

MAT 25:1,3,4,7,8 | JHN 18:3; ACT 20:8

1586 ܠܣܛܐ (m) robber

MAT 21:13; 27:38; MRK 11:17; 15:27 | LUK 10:30; 19:46; 22:52

1588 ܠܥܒܐ (adj-non occ) greedy

1587 (ܠܥܒ) (v) (ethpa) be greedy

[d]ETHPAAL

Perfect

JAM 5:5

1591 ܠܥܣ (v) eat, chew

[a]PEAL

Perfect

LUK 4:2 | ACT 11:3

Imperfect

MAT 15:20; 26:17; LUK 7:36; 17:8[1],8[2] | LUK 22:8; ACT 10:10; 1 CO 11:34; 2 TH 3:10

Imperative

LUK 10:8 | JHN 4:31

Infinitive

MRK 5:43; 6:37[1] | LUK 12:45; JHN 21:5

Active Participle

MAT 9:11; 26:21,26; MRK 2:16; 6:37[2] | MRK 7:3,4; 14:18,22; LUK 10:7

---

[c]PAEL

Active Participle

REV 16:10

1593 ܠܩܛ (v) gather

[a]PEAL

Active Participle

MAT 7:16; LUK 6:44 | JHN 15:6

---

[c]PAEL

Active Participle

ACT 17:18

1595 ܠܩܫܐ (m-non occ) aftermath

1594 ܠܩܫܝܐ (adj) latter

JAM 5:7

1596 ܠܫܢܐ (m) tongue

MRK 7:33,35; 16:17; LUK 1:64; 16:24; ACT 1:19 | ACT 2:3,4,4,6,8,11; 10:46,46; 14:11; 19:6,6

ROM	3:13	PHL	2:11
	14:11	JAM	1:26
1 CO	12:10,10,		3:5,6,6,8
	28,30	1 PT	3:10
	13:1,8	1 JN	3:18
	14:2,4,5,5,	REV	7:9
	6,9,10,		10:11
	13,14,		11:9
	18,19,		13:7
	21,22,		14:6
	23,26,		16:10
	27,28,		17:15
	39		

ܡ

1597 ܡܢܐ (pron) what

see also 1425 ܟܠ

see also 1634 ܡܕܡ

MAT 2:8; 6:3,5,7,17; 7:12,14; 8:29; 10:12, 19,23; 13:21,32,46; 15:2,28,32; 16:2; 17:12; 18:18,30; 19:28; 21:40; 23:15,20; 24:15,33; 25:31; 27:4; 28:20 MRK 1:24; 2:20; 3:11; 4:15,17,29,32; 5:7,33; 6:11,30,30; 8:2,38; 9:9,10,13,31; 11:25; 12:25; 13:4,7,11,14,28, 29; 14:28 LUK 3:13; 4:34; 6:22; 7:39; 8:13,28; 9:5,26,39; 10:35; 11:24,24; 12:11, 36,54,55,58; 14:10,10,12,13; 15:5,9; 16:4,9; 17:10; 21:4,7,9,20,22,28,30,31; 22:10; 23:42; 24:24 JHN 2:4,10; 4:25; 5:7; 7:31; 10:4, 12; 12:32; 13:19; 14:29; 15:7,26; 16:4,8,13, 21,21; 17:2,7; 20:31; 21:18,22,23
ACT 1:11,19; 2:4; 3:22; 4:20,23,28; 7:44; 9:6; 10:33,39,47; 11:15,29; 13:23; 15:4,12, 15; 17:24; 19:21; 21:19; 22:3,5,15; 23:35; 24:22; 25:16,18,26; 26:2; 27:25
ROM 8:26; 10:15; 11:27; 12:3; 15:24,24,28
1 CO 3:4; 4:6; 5:12; 8:2; 11:14,15,18,20,34; 13:12; 15:24,24,27,28,54; 16:2,3,5
2 CO 5:3; 8:5,11,12,12; 9:8; 10:2,6,11; 12:6, 20; 13:9,10 GAL 1:8,9 EPH 3:4,20; 4:4, 21; 6:22 PHL 2:23,23 COL 1:7; 4:8,16
1 TH 2:4; 3:10 2 TH 1:3,8,10; 2:6,7
2 TM 4:13 TIT 3:12 PLM 21
HEB 1:4; 8:6 JAM 1:12,15 1 PT 2:20
1 JN 2:28; 3:2; 5:2 2 JN 6 3 JN 2,3,5,6
REV 1:19; 3:11; 4:1,9; 6:13; 9:5; 10:4,7; 11:7; 12:4; 17:10; 18:9; 20:7; 22:6

689 ܕܠܡܐ (prt) lest

MAT 5:25; 7:6; 9:15; 12:23; 13:29; 15:32; 26:25; 27:64 MRK 4:12,21; 13:5,36; 14:2 LUK 3:15; 11:35; 12:58; 14:8,12 JHN 3:4; 5:14; 7:26, 41,51 ACT 5:26,39; 7:28; 8:22; 10:47; 13:40; 20:16; 23:10; 27:17,29
ROM 3:3,8; 9:14,20; 10:18,19; 11:1,11, 14,21 1 CO 1:13; 8:9; 9:8,27; 10:22, 22; 11:22; 12:29,29,30; 14:36
2 CO 1:17; 2:7; 3:1; 9:4; 11:3,7; 12:6,20, 20,21 GAL 4:11,16; 5:11,15; 6:1
EPH 5:6 PHL 3:11,12 COL 2:8
1 TH 3:5; 5:15 2 TM 2:25
HEB 3:12; 4:1; 12:15,15,25
JAM 2:14; 3:11,12; 4:5 2 PT 3:17
REV 18:4

1579 ܠܡܢܐ (pron) why

MAT 7:9,10,16; 8:4; 25:9; 26:22
MRK 1:44; 2:19; 14:19 LUK 6:39; 11:11,11,12; 17:9,18; 21:8; 22:35
JHN 4:12,22,29,33; 5:45; 6:67; 7:31,35, 47,48,52; 8:22,53; 9:27,40; 10:21; 18:17,25,35; 21:5 ACT 7:42
ROM 3:5,29,31 1 CO 1:13; 9:1,4,5,9; 12:29,29,30,30; 16:11 2 CO 1:17; 6:3; 11:16; 12:17,18,19 COL 2:18
2 TH 2:3 HEB 6:1; 12:16

1598 ܡܐܐ (num) one hundred

see also 268 ܐܪܒܥܡܐܐ

see also 1034 ܚܡܫܡܐܐ

see also 3305 ܫܬܡܐܐ

see also 3396 ܬܠܬܡܐܐ

MAT	13:8,23	LUK	16:6,7
	18:12,28	JHN	19:39
	19:29		21:11
MRK	4:8,20	ACT	1:15
	6:40,40	ROM	4:19
	10:30	REV	7:4
LUK	8:8		14:1,3
	15:4		21:17

1608 ܡܐܬܝܢ (num) two hundred

MRK	6:37	ACT	27:37
JHN	6:7	REV	11:3
	21:8		12:6
ACT	23:23,23		14:20

1602 ܡܐܢ (v) be tired, weary; (aph) neglect

[a]PEAL

Perfect

HEB 3:10,17

Imperfect

LUK	18:1	EPH	3:13
ACT	9:38	2 TH	3:13
GAL	$6:9^2$	HEB	12:3

Active Participle

2 CO	4:1,16	PHL	3:1
GAL	6:9[1]		

[e]APHEL

Active Participle

2 PT 1:12

1603 ܡܐܢܐ (m) vessel, garment

MAT	9:21	ACT	10:11,16
	12:29		11:5
	13:48		18:6
	21:8		22:20,23
	25:4		27:18,19
	26:65	ROM	9:21,22,23
MRK	2:21	2 CO	4:7
	3:27	1 TH	4:4
	5:30	2 TM	2:20,21
	7:4	HEB	9:21
	11:7,16	JAM	2:2,2,3
	14:13		5:2
	15:20,24	1 PT	3:7
LUK	5:36,36	REV	2:27
	8:16,27,44		3:4,5,18
	17:31		4:4
	19:35,36		16:15
JHN	19:29		18:12,12
ACT	9:15		19:13,16

ܡܐܠܐ see under (ܐܠ)

1624 ܡܓܢ (adv) freely, in vain

MAT	10:8,8	GAL	2:21
JHN	15:25	2 TH	3:8
ROM	3:24	REV	21:6
2 CO	11:7		22:17

1620 (ܡܓܘܫ), ܡܓܘܫܐ (m)

magi

MAT	2:1,7,16,	MAT	2:16

1626 ܡܠܛ (v) escape

[e]APHEL

Imperfect

1 TH 5:3

1638 ܡܘܙܓܐ (m-non occ) mixture

1637 (ܡܙܓ) (v) season

[c]PAEL

Passive Participle

COL 4:6

1639 ܡܕܡ (c) thing

see also 1431 ܟܠ ܡܕܡ

MAT 1:22; 2:15,17,23; 4:14; 5:13,23,37; 8:17; 10:26,27,27; 12:2,17; 13:17,17,35; 15:5,11,11,17,18; 16:19; 17:20; 18:11,18,28, 31; 19:6; 20:4,7,15,20; 21:3,4,19; 22:31; 23:16,18; 26:13,62; 27:9,12,24 MRK 2:24; 4:22,34; 5:14,19,20,26; 6:8,22,23,36; 7:11, 12,15,15,20; 8:1; 9:9,22,29; 10:9,32; 11:13, 23,23,25; 12:44; 13:11,15,37; 14:9,61; 15:5; 16:8 LUK 1:2,37; 3:13; 4:2,35; 5:5; 6:2,3, 46; 7:40; 8:17,34,35,39,39,56; 9:3,17,36; 10:8,19,23,24,24,35; 11:6,36,41,54; 12:2,3,4, 12,48; 16:15; 17:8,9,10; 19:8,10,21,21,22,22; 20:40; 21:26; 22:35,35,49; 23:4,8,9,14,15,22, 41,47,48; 24:12,18,41 JHN 1:3,46; 2:5; 3:6,6,11,11,27,32; 4:22,33,38; 5:14,19,19,30; 6:12,63; 7:4,26; 8:28,29,38,38,54; 10:10; 11:45,46,49; 12:6,19; 13:7,27,29,29; 14:13, 30; 15:5; 16:23,24; 18:20; 19:22; 21:3,5 ACT 2:45; 3:5,6,10,18; 4:14,21,34,35; 5:36, 36; 7:17; 8:24; 9:8,18; 11:9; 12:11; 13:12,28, 40; 14:11; 15:9,16; 16:14,28; 17:21,21,25; 18:14,25; 19:18,27,36,39; 20:20,24; 21:23, 24,34,34; 23:9,14,17,18,20; 24:13,19; 25:8, 10,11,11,18,19,19,25; 26:16,22,28,31; 27:21, 33; 28:5,6,17,19,21,22 ROM 1:26,28; 3:19; 4:21; 7:15,15,15,16,20; 8:25; 9:29; 12:16; 13:8; 14:14,14,21,22; 15:18 1 CO 2:2,9; 3:7; 4:4,17; 7:19,24; 8:2,2,4; 9:12,26; 10:13,15,19,19,20,30,31,33,33; 11:18,18,23; 13:2,3,10; 14:2,7,7,9,35; 15:3, 10,37; 16:1,2,17 2 CO 2:10; 3:5,11; 5:10; 6:3,10; 7:9,14; 8:11; 10:8; 11:5,12,17; 12:11, 11,18; 13:7,8 GAL 2:2,6,6; 3:15; 4:12; 5:2, 6,10,17,17,17; 6:3,7,15 EPH 4:13; 5:12, 27; 6:8,21,21 PHL 1:20,28; 2:3,13,30; 3:12,15; 4:6,11 COL 2:18,23; 3:25; 4:7,9 1 TH 1:8 2 TH 3:4,11 1 TM 1:7,7; 4:4; 5:13,21,21; 6:4,7,19,20 2 TM 2:7 TIT 1:11,15; 2:1,8; 3:13 PLM 14,18 HEB 2:1,8; 7:14,19; 8:3; 11:20; 12:20; 13:5, 21 JAM 1:4,7,17 1 PT 4:12

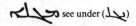

2 PT 2:19; 3:16 1 JN 1:3; 2:15,18,24,24; 3:2; 5:15 2 JN 8 3 JN 7 REV 2:10; 3:17; 18:7

1634 (ܡܟܝܠ), ܡܟܝܠ (adv) then, therefore

from 1597 ܡܐ and 670 ܟܝ

MAT 7:20; 12:12; 17:26; 19:6; 23:31 LUK 16:27 JHN 13:9; 18:37 ROM 7:12; 9:18; 14:12 1 CO 14:22 2 CO 5:14 GAL 2:17; 3:9 HEB 4:9

1645 ܡܟܝܪܐ (c) soil, dirt

MAT 13:5

1656 ܡܘܡܐ (m) spot, blemish

2 CO 6:3	1 TM 6:14
8:20	HEB 9:14
EPH 1:4	1 PT 1:19
5:27	2 PT 2:13
PHL 2:15	3:14
COL 1:22	JUD 24
1 TM 3:2	REV 14:5

1659 (ܡܘܩ) (v) deride, mock

cPAEL

Active Participle

LUK 16:14	ACT 2:13
23:35	17:32

1662 ܡܘܪܘܢ (m) ointment

REV 18:13

1663 (ܡܘܫ) (v) touch, search

aPEAL

Perfect

ROM 11:33

Active Participle

ROM 8:27

1665 (ܡܘܬ) (v) be dead, die; (aph) put to death

aPEAL

Perfect

MAT 2:19,20	ACT 25:19
8:32	ROM 5:6,8,15
9:18,24	6:2,7,8,10[1], 10[2]
22:25,27	7:2,4,6,9
MRK 5:35,39	8:34
9:26	14:9,15
12:20,21, 22	1 CO 8:11
15:44[1],44[2]	15:3
LUK 8:49,52,53	2 CO 5:14[1],14[2], 15[1],15[2]
16:22[1],22[2]	GAL 2:19,21
20:29,30, 31,32	COL 2:20
JHN 6:49,58	3:3
8:52,53[1], 53[2]	1 TH 4:14
11:14	5:10
19:33	2 TM 2:11
ACT 2:29	HEB 11:13,35, 37
5:5,10,37	1 PT 2:21
7:4,15	3:18[1],18[2]
9:37	JUD 12
12:23	REV 8:9,11
14:19	16:3

Imperfect

MAT 15:4[2]	JHN 11:26,37, 50,51
22:24	18:14,32
26:52	ACT 12:19
MRK 7:10	21:13
LUK 20:28	ROM 7:3
JHN 6:50	1 CO 9:15[2]
8:21,24[1], 24[2]	PHL 1:21
11:16,25,	HEB 9:27

Infinitive

MAT 15:4[1]	ROM 5:7[2]
26:35	8:13[1]
MRK 14:31	1 CO 9:15[1]
LUK 7:2	2 CO 7:3
8:42	REV 3:2
20:36	9:6
JHN 4:47	

Active Participle

MRK 9:44,46,48	ROM 14:8[3]
12:19	1 CO 15:22,31, 32,36, 53,54
JHN 4:49	2 CO 4:11
11:21,32	6:9
12:24[1],24[2], 33	HEB 7:8,23
21:23[1],23[2]	10:28
ROM 5:7[1]	11:21,22
6:9	1 PT 4:1
8:36	
14:7,8[1],8[2],	

1715 ܡܝܬܐ (pp) dead

MAT 8:22,22; 11:5; 14:2; 17:9; 22:23,30,31,32; 23:27; 27:64; 28:4,7
MRK 6:14,16; 9:9,10,26; 12:25,26,27
LUK 7:12,15,22; 9:7,60,60; 15:24,32; 16:30,31; 20:35,37,38; 24:5,46
JHN 2:22; 5:21,25; 11:39,44; 12:1,9,17; 20:9; 21:14
ACT 3:15; 4:2,10; 5:10; 10:41,42; 13:30,34; 17:3,31,32; 20:9; 23:6; 24:15,21; 26:8,23; 28:6
ROM 1:4; 4:17,19,19,24; 6:4,9,11,12,13; 7:4,8; 8:10,11,11,11; 10:7,9; 11:15; 14:9
1 CO 15:12,12,13,16,20,21,29,29,29,32,35,42,52
2 CO 1:9; 6:9
GAL 1:1
EPH 1:20; 2:1,5; 5:14
PHL 3:11
COL 1:18; 2:12,13
1 TH 1:10; 4:16
1 TM 5:6
2 TM 2:8,18; 4:1
HEB 6:1,2; 9:14,17; 11:19,35; 13:20
JAM 2:17,20,26,26
1 PT 1:21; 2:24; 4:5,6
REV 1:5,17,18; 2:8; 3:1; 11:18; 14:13; 16:3; 20:12,12,13,13

1666 ܡܘܬܐ (m) death

MAT 2:15; 4:16; 10:21; 16:28; 20:18; 26:38,66; 27:37
MRK 7:10; 9:1; 10:33; 13:12; 14:34,64; 15:26; 16:18
LUK 1:79; 2:26; 9:27; 22:33; 23:15,22; 24:20
JHN 5:24; 8:51,52; 11:4,13; 12:33; 18:32; 19:7; 21:19
ACT 13:28; 22:4; 23:29; 25:11,11,25; 26:31; 28:18
ROM 1:32; 5:10,12,12,14,17,21; 6:3,4,5,9,21,23; 7:5,10,13,13,24; 8:2,6,38
1 CO 3:22; 4:9; 11:26; 15:21,26,54,55,56
2 CO 1:9,10; 2:16,16; 3:7; 4:11,12; 7:10; 11:23
PHL 1:20; 2:8,8,27,30; 3:10
COL 1:22
2 TM 1:10
HEB 2:9,9,14,14,15,16; 5:7; 9:15,16,27; 11:5
JAM 1:15; 3:8; 5:20
1 JN 3:14,14; 5:16,16,16,17
REV 1:18; 2:10,11,23; 6:8,8; 9:6,6; 12:11; 13:3,3,12; 18:8; 20:6,13,14,14; 21:4,8

1668 ܡܘܬܢܐ (m) plague

MAT 24:7
LUK 21:11

1707 ܡܘܬܘܬܐ (f) (w/ ܠܐ) immortality

1 CO 15:53,54

1709 ܡܝܬܐ (adj) dead

HEB 11:4

1716 ܡܝܬܘܬܐ (f) mortality, death

2 CO 4:10
2 CO 5:4

---

[e]APHEL

Imperfect

MAT 10:21; 26:59; 27:1
MRK 13:12; 14:55
LUK 21:16

Imperative

COL 3:5

Active Participle

ROM 8:13[2]

1670 ܡܙܓ (v) mix, dilute

aPEAL

Perfect

1 CO 12:24 | REV 18:3,6[1]

Imperative

REV 18:6[2]

Passive Participle

REV 14:10

---

cPAEL

Active Participle

2 CO 2:17

Passive Participle

HEB 4:2

1651 (ܡܚ), ܡܘܚܐ (m) marrow

HEB 4:12

1673 ܡܚܐ (v) strike, gird

aPEAL

Perfect

MAT 21:35
26:51,68
MRK 12:3,5
14:47
LUK 10:30
20:10,11
22:50,64[2]
JHN 13:4
18:10,22,23
19:34
21:7
ACT 12:23

Imperfect

MAT 26:31
MRK 14:27
LUK 22:49
ACT 23:2,3[1],3[2]
REV 11:6

Infinitive

MAT 24:49
LUK 12:45
1 TM 3:3
TIT 1:7

Active Participle

MAT 5:39
26:67
27:30
MRK 14:65
15:19
LUK 6:29
22:64[1]
JHN 19:3
ACT 18:17
21:32
ACT 22:19
2 CO 11:20
1 TM 1:9[1],9[2]

Passive Participle

JHN 13:5

1677 ܡܚܘܬܐ (f) wound, plague

MRK 3:11
5:29,34
LUK 7:21
10:34
12:48,48
2 CO 11:23
REV 9:18,20
REV 11:6
13:3,12,14
15:1,6,8
16:9,21,21
18:4,8
21:9
22:18

---

cPAEL

Passive Participle

LUK 16:20

1684 ܡܚܠ (v-non occ) grow weak

aPEAL

1681 ܡܚܝܠܐ (pp) weak

ROM 8:3
15:1
1 CO 7:6
12:22
2 CO 11:21
2 CO 13:3,4
1 TH 5:14
1 PT 3:7
REV 3:17

1682 ܡܚܝܠܘܬܐ (f) weakness

2 CO 13:4 | HEB 7:18

1688 ܡܚܪ (adv) tomorrow

MAT 6:30,34,34
27:62
LUK 12:28
13:32,33
ACT 23:20
25:22
1 CO 15:32
JAM 4:13,14

1692 ܡܛܐ (v) arrive, reach; (ethpa) attain

aPEAL

Perfect

MAT 21:34
24:32,33
26:18,45,
MAT 26:46
MRK 1:15
13:28

MRK	14:41	JHN	13:1
LUK	1:9		16:21
	10:32	1 CO	14:36
	15:13	GAL	4:4
	21:9	2 TM	4:6
JHN	7:6		

Imperfect

ACT	23:15	2 CO	10:13

Active Participle

LUK	15:12	1 CO	16:2
ACT	5:39	2 CO	9:8
	24:13	2 TM	1:12
	25:5		2:2
ROM	14:4	HEB	11:19

^cPAEL

Perfect

MRK	4:29	ACT	21:27,35, 37
LUK	19:29		27:3,5,7,8
	22:7,40	1 CO	10:11,13
	24:15	2 CO	10:14²
JHN	4:35	PHL	2:30
ACT	7:17		3:16
	8:36	1 TH	2:16
	10:17	2 TH	2:2
	11:19	HEB	12:4
	16:1	1 PT	4:7
	18:19		
	21:3¹,3²,		

Imperfect

PHL 3:11

Active Participle

ACT	9:3	ACT	27:13
	22:6		

^dETHPAAL

Participle

2 CO 10:14¹

1694 ܡܛܠ (conj) because

incl comp with 770 ܗܘܐ

MAT 2:18; 5:10,11; 6:13,25; 10:18,22,39; 12:27,31; 13:5,6,13,13,21,52,58; 14:2,3,7,8, 9; 15:3,6; 16:25; 17:20; 18:23; 19:5,12,29; 21:43,46; 23:10,13,34; 24:9,12,22,44; 27:6,8, 19 MRK 1:34; 2:4,27,27; 3:9,10,30; 4:5,6, 17; 5:4,9; 6:14,17,26,26,52; 7:3,13,25,29; 8:35,35; 10:7,29,29; 11:18,24; 12:24; 13:9, 13,20; 14:40 LUK 1:1,3,7,13,35,37; 2:4,7; 3:19; 4:18,38; 5:8,19; 7:7,47; 8:19,30,37,47, 53; 9:7,12,24,45,53; 11:6,8,8,19,49; 12:15, 22; 13:31,33; 14:11,20; 16:14; 18:5,29; 19:3, 4,9,11; 20:5,36; 21:12,17,28; 23:7,8,19,25; 24:29 JHN 1:15,17,30,31; 2:24; 3:23,29; 4:39,41,42; 5:16,18,38; 6:2,18,26,57,57,65, 66; 7:1,7,8,12,13,22,22,23,30,39,43; 8:14,16, 29,37,43,44,44,47,47; 9:22,23,41; 10:4,13, 17,19,26,32,33,33,35; 11:4,9,10,15,19,42,51; 12:6,6,9,11,11,18,27,30,30,39,39,42; 13:3, 11,22,29; 14:11,17; 15:3,5,15,15,19,21; 16:3, 14,15,21; 18:2,13,18; 19:11,12,20,31,31,38, 42,42; 20:19; 21:7 ACT 1:17; 2:6,24,26, 34; 4:3,21; 5:9,41; 7:26,40; 8:11,20,21; 9:7, 15,16; 10:20,21,29,29,38; 11:24; 12:12,20, 20; 13:8,46; 14:12,19,26; 15:2,9,19,25,32,38, 39; 16:3,10,13,20,21,27,28; 17:18,25,27,31; 18:2,3,5,10,18; 19:31,32,36,40; 20:7,10,13, 16,26,31,35; 21:22,34,35; 22:11,18,24; 23:11,28; 24:2,10,16,22,26; 25:9,20,25,26; 26:3,5,12,16,19,26,26; 27:4,7,7,12,17,25,34, 43; 28:2,18,20,20,22 ROM 1:11,16,19,21, 24,26; 2:1,5,24; 3:20,23,25,30; 4:16,22,23, 24,25,25; 5:1,5,6,13,15,15,17,18,18,19,19; 6:19; 7:21; 8:3,3,7,7,10,10,11,20,24,36; 9:7, 7,32,32; 10:3; 11:20,28,28,30,36; 13:5,5,5,6, 10; 14:8,9,15,15,20,23; 15:3,7,22,23,27; 16:2 1 CO 1:21,22,25; 3:13,21; 4:5,6,6,10,17; 5:8; 6:7,7; 7:2,5,26,32; 8:7,10,11,13; 9:10,10,10, 15,23; 10:11,14,25,27,28,28; 11:7,9,9,10,10, 15,17,28,30; 12:3,15,15,16; 14:12,16,33; 15:9; 16:15 2 CO 1:6,17,20,23,24; 2:4,4,8, 9,10; 3:7,12; 4:1,5,6,11,13,13,15,16; 5:6,8, 11,21; 6:17; 7:1,9,10,11,12,12,12,12,13; 8:9, 10,17; 9:2,5,12,13,14; 10:8,10,12; 11:11,18; 12:10,11,14,19; 13:3,10 GAL 2:4,11,12, 16,16; 3:8,11,19; 4:12,20,27,30 EPH 1:15; 2:4,11,18; 3:1,13; 4:8,18,18,25; 5:6,14,16,17, 23,30,31; 6:9,12,13 PHL 1:6,7,16,24; 2:9, 19,26,30; 3:1,7,8,8,12; 4:11 COL 1:5,9,21; 3:6; 4:3 1 TH 1:5,5; 2:8,13; 3:1,5,7,7,9; 4:6,16; 5:9,11,13 2 TH 1:11; 2:3,11; 3:9 1 TM 1:13,16; 4:4,10; 5:23,23; 6:8 2 TM 1:6,12; 2:10,10 TIT 1:5,11,13 PLM 8,9,15,21 HEB 1:9,14; 2:1,9,10,11, 14,17; 3:7,10,19; 4:2,6,14; 5:2,3,11,12,13,14; 6:1,7,13,17; 7:18,23,24; 8:3,4,9,11; 9:15,17, 18,22; 10:1,2,5,34,37; 11:4,4,5,12,16,19,40; 12:1,7,12,27,28; 13:9,12,17,22 JAM 1:10, 21; 3:15; 4:2,3,6; 5:11 1 PT 1:12,13,16,20, 24; 2:13,13,14,19,20; 3:7,12,18; 4:6,7,12,17, 19; 5:5,8 2 PT 2:2; 3:9,14 1 JN 2:11,12, 26; 3:1,1,8,8,9,12,12,22; 4:1,4,5,7,8,17,18, 19; 5:4 2 JN 2,7 3 JN 10 JUD 9,15, 15,16 REV 1:9,9; 2:3,13; 3:8,17; 4:11; 5:4; 6:9,9,17; 7:15,17; 8:11; 9:19; 11:2,10; 12:12; 14:7,13,15,18; 15:4,4,4; 16:6,21; 17:14; 18:3, 5,7,8,8,10,17,20,23,23; 19:2,2,6,7; 20:4,4; 22:5

1700 ܡܛܪܐ (m) rain

MAT	5:45	HEB	6:7
	7:25,27	JAM	5:7,17,18
LUK	12:54	JUD	12
ACT	14:17	REV	11:6
	28:2		

1699 ܡܛܪ (v) rain; (aph) cause to rain

[e]APHEL

Perfect

LUK 17:29

1706 ܡܝܐ (m) water

MAT	3:11,16	JHN	9:11
	8:32		13:5
	12:43		19:34
	14:25,26, 28,29	ACT	1:5
	17:15		8:36,36,38, 39
	27:24		10:47
MRK	1:8,10		11:16
	5:13	EPH	5:26
	6:48,49	1 TM	5:23
	9:22,41	HEB	9:19
	14:13		10:22
LUK	3:16	JAM	3:11,12
	5:3	1 PT	3:20
	7:44	2 PT	2:17
	8:24		3:5,5,6
	11:24	1 JN	5:6,6,7,8
	14:2	REV	1:15
	16:24		7:17
	22:10		8:7,10,11, 11
JHN	1:26,31,33		11:6
	2:7,9,9		12:15,15
	3:5,23		14:2,7
	4:6,7,7,10, 11,13,14, 14,14,15, 46		16:4,5,12
			17:1,15
			19:6
	5:3,4,4,7		21:6
	7:38		22:1,17

1711 ܡܝܠܐ (m) mile (Roman)

MAT 5:41

1719 ܡܟ (v) be humble; (pa, aph) humble

[a]PEAL

Perfect

HEB 2:9

[c]PAEL

Perfect

2 CO	11:7	PHL	2:8

Imperfect

2 CO 12:21

Active Participle

MAT	18:4	JAM	4:6

1652 ܡܘܟܟܐ (m) humiliation

LUK	1:48	PHL	3:21
ACT	8:33	JAM	1:10

1722 ܡܟܝܟܐ (adj) humble

MAT	5:5	1 TM	3:3
	11:29	2 TM	2:24
	21:5	TIT	3:2
LUK	1:52	JAM	1:9
ROM	12:16		3:13,17
1 CO	4:21		4:6
2 CO	7:6	1 PT	2:18
	10:1		3:4,8
GAL	6:1		5:5
1 TH	2:7		

1723 ܡܟܝܟܘܬܐ (f) humility, meekness

ACT	20:19	COL	2:18,23
	24:4		3:12
2 CO	10:1	1 TM	6:11
GAL	5:23	2 TM	2:25
EPH	4:2	JAM	1:21
PHL	2:3	1 PT	3:15
	4:5		5:5

[d]ETHPAAL

Imperfect

MAT	23:12[1]	LUK	18:14[1]
LUK	3:5	PHL	4:12
	14:11[1]		

Imperative

JAM	4:9,10	1 PT	5:6

[e]APHEL

Perfect

HEB 2:7

Imperfect

MAT 23:12²
LUK 14:11²
LUK 18:14²
HEB 5:2

1720 ܡܟܐ (adv) hence;

(ܡܟܐ ܘܡܟܐ) here and there

from 1770 ܡܢ and 1358 ܟܐ

MAT 17:20
LUK 4:9
13:31
16:26
JHN 2:16
JHN 7:3
14:31
18:36
19:18,18
REV 22:2,2

1724 ܡܟܝܠ (adv) therefore, now

cf ܗܟܝܠ

MAT 26:45,65 MRK 5:35; 10:8; 11:14; 14:41,63 LUK 1:20; 2:29; 15:19; 16:2; 22:16 JHN 2:8; 4:42; 14:30; 15:15; 17:11 ROM 7:6; 8:1; 10:17; 13:11,12; 14:13 1 CO 4:2; 7:29; 10:12; 11:33; 15:58 2 CO 2:7; 5:16; 8:24; 13:11 GAL 2:20; 3:18,29; 4:7; 6:17 EPH 2:19; 4:28; 6:10 PHL 2:12; 3:1; 4:1,8 1 TH 4:1,8 2 TH 2:15 1 TM 5:23 2 TM 4:6 PLM 16 HEB 3:1; 10:2,13,26 1 PT 4:2 REV 21:4

1728 ܡܟܣܐ (m) tax, tribute

MAT 17:25
ROM 13:7,7

1727 ܡܟܣܐ (m) tax collector, publican

MAT 5:46,47
9:9,10,11
10:3
11:19
18:17
21:31,32
MRK 2:14,15,16,16
LUK 3:12
5:27,27,29,30
7:29,34
15:1
18:10,11,13
19:2

1730 ܡܟܪ (v) be engaged

ᵃPEAL

Perfect

2 CO 11:2

1725 ܡܟܝܪܐ (pp) engaged, married

MAT 1:18
LUK 1:27
LUK 2:5

1761 (ܡܠܠ), ܡܠܬܐ (f) word

MAT 4:4
5:11,32,37
7:24,26,28
8:8,16
10:14
12:32,36,37,37
13:19,19,20,21,22,22,23
15:6,12
18:16
19:1,11,22
21:24
22:15
24:35
26:1,44,75
27:14
28:15
MRK 1:45
2:2
4:14,15,15,16,17,18,19,20
5:36
7:13,29
8:32,38
9:10,10,32
10:22,24
11:29
12:13
13:31
14:39,72
16:20
LUK 1:2,4,20,29,38
2:15,17,19,29,50,51
3:2,4
4:22,32,36
5:1,5
6:18,47
7:1,7,17
8:11,12,12,13,14,15,21
9:26,28,44,45,45
10:39
11:28,53
12:10
18:34
20:3,20,26
21:33,38
22:61
LUK 23:9
24:8,11,17,19,44
JHN 1:1,1,1,14
2:22
3:34
4:37,39,41,42,50
5:24,38,47
6:60,63,66,68
7:36,40
8:20,31,37,43,43,47,51,52,55
10:19,21,35
12:38,47,48,48
14:10,23,24,24
15:3,7,20,20,25
17:6,8,14,17,20
18:9,32,37
19:8,13
21:23
ACT 2:14,22,40,41
4:1,4,13,29,31
5:5,20,24,32,33
6:2,4,5,7,11,13
7:22,29,38
8:4,6,14,25
10:22,36,37,44,44
11:1,14,16,18,19
13:5,7,15,26,42,44,45,46,49
14:3,12,25
15:6,7,15,24,27,32,35,36
16:6,32,36,38
17:11,13,

ACT 17:18,20
18:5,11,15,24
19:10
20:2,9,32,35,38
21:12
22:22
24:21
26:25,26
27:11
28:6,24,25
ROM 3:2,4
9:6,9,28
10:8,17,18
13:9
15:18
16:18
1 CO 1:5,10,17,18
2:4,4,13
4:19,20
12:8,8
14:9,19,19,36
15:2,54
2 CO 1:18
2:5,17
4:2
5:19
6:7
8:7
10:10,11
11:6
12:4
13:1
GAL 5:14
6:6
EPH 1:13
4:29
5:4,6,26
6:17,19
PHL 1:14
COL 1:5,25
2:4,23
3:16,17
4:3,6
1 TH 1:5,6,8
2:13,13,13
4:15,18
2 TH 2:2,15,17
3:1,14
1 TM 1:6,15
3:1
4:5,6,9,12
5:17
6:3,4
2 TM 1:13
2:9,11,14,15,16,17
4:2,15
TIT 1:3,9,10
2:5,7
3:8
HEB 1:3
2:2
4:2,12
5:11,12,13
6:1,5
7:28
11:3
12:19
13:7,22
JAM 1:18,21,22,23
3:2
5:12
1 PT 1:23,25,25
2:2,8,12
3:1,15
4:11
2 PT 1:19
2:3
3:2,5,7
1 JN 1:1,10
2:5,7,14
3:18
3 JN 10
JUD 15,17
REV 1:2,3,9
3:8,10
6:9
12:11
17:17
19:9,13
20:4
21:5
22:6,7,9,10,18,19

1747 ܡܠܝܠܐ (adj) reasonable

ROM 12:1

1764 ܡܡܠܠܐ (m) speech

MAT 6:7
26:73
MRK 14:70
LUK 5:4
1 CO 2:1
1 CO 14:21
COL 3:8
1 TH 2:5
1 TM 5:13

1734 (ܡܠܠ) (v) speak

ᶜPAEL

Perfect

MAT 9:33
13:34[1]
14:27
23:1
28:18
MRK 6:50
7:35
16:19
LUK 1:55,64,70
2:15
11:14
22:4
23:20
24:6,25,44
JHN 6:63
7:46[1],46[2]
8:12,20,40
9:29
10:6
12:29,36,41,48,49[1]
14:25
15:3,11,22
16:1,4,25[1]
17:1
18:20[1],20[2],21,23
ACT 2:31
3:21,24
ACT 4:25
7:6,38,44
8:26
9:27[1],27[2]
10:7
14:1,25
16:32
17:2
21:40
23:9
25:12
28:25
2 CO 4:13[1]
7:14
1 TH 2:2
HEB 1:1,2
12:25[1],25[2],25[3]
13:7
JAM 5:10
2 PT 1:21
2:16
3:16
JUD 15
REV 1:12
4:1
10:3,4[1],4[2]
17:1
21:9

Imperfect

MAT 10:19[1],19[2]
12:22,46[2],47
MRK 1:34
7:37[2]
12:1
13:11[1]
16:17
LUK 1:19,22
8:19
JHN 8:25
9:21
12:49[2]
14:30
16:13[1],13[2],25[2]
ACT 3:22
4:17,18,20
10:32
11:14
13:42
16:6
ACT 18:14
21:37
24:10
1 CO 3:1
13:1
14:5[1],6[1],6[2],19,21,23,27[1],27[2],27[3],28[2],29,34,35
2 CO 11:1
EPH 6:20[1]
COL 4:4
1 TH 2:16
1 TM 3:8
5:13
1 PT 3:10
4:11[2]
2 JN 12
3 JN 14

Imperative

MRK 13:11[2]
ACT 5:20
ACT 13:15
18:9

EPH 4:25, 5:19
TIT 2:1,15

Infinitive

MAT 12:34[1]
LUK 1:20, 7:15
ACT 2:4[1],4[2], 6:13, 11:15, 20:7[2], 21:39
ACT 26:1
1 CO 14:39
2 CO 12:4[2]
EPH 5:12, 6:20[2]
PHL 1:14
COL 4:3
JAM 1:19

Active Participle

MAT 9:18, 10:20[1],20[2], 12:34[2],46[1], 13:3,10,13, 34[2], 15:31, 17:3,5, 26:47
MRK 2:2,7, 4:33,34, 5:35, 7:37[1], 8:32, 9:4,17,25, 13:11[3], 14:43
LUK 2:38, 4:36, 5:21, 6:11,45, 8:49, 9:11,30, 11:27,37, 20:21, 22:47,60, 24:14,15, 17,32, 36
JHN 3:11,31,34, 4:26,27[1], 27[2],27[3], 7:13,17,18, 26,32, 8:26,28,30, 38,44[1], 44[2],45, 46, 9:37, 12:50[1],50[2], 14:10[1],10[2], 16:18,29, 17:13, 19:10
ACT 2:6,7,11, 4:1,31, 5:40, 6:10, 9:29, 10:27,44, 46
ACT 11:19,20, 12:21, 13:43, 14:3,9, 16:13, 17:17, 18:4,19,25, 26, 19:6,8,9, 20:7[1],11, 30, 22:2,9, 24:12,25, 26, 26:25,26, 31
ROM 3:5, 7:1
1 CO 2:6,7,13, 12:3,30, 13:11, 14:2[1],2[2],2[3], 2[4],3,4, 5[2],9, 11[1],11[2], 13,18, 28[1]
2 CO 2:17, 4:13[2], 11:17[1],17[2], 12:19, 13:3
1 TH 2:4
1 TM 1:7, 4:2
HEB 2:5, 6:9, 11:4, 12:24
JAM 2:12, 4:11[1],11[2], 11[3]
1 PT 2:12, 3:16, 4:11[1]
2 PT 2:18
1 JN 4:5
JUD 9,16
REV 2:7,11,17, 29

REV 3:6,13,22, 10:8
REV 13:5,11, 21:15

---

[d]ETHPAAL

Perfect

LUK 1:45, 2:17,18,20
ACT 27:25
HEB 2:2, 11:7

Imperfect

MAT 26:13
MRK 14:9
ACT 9:6
ACT 22:10
HEB 12:19

Infinitive

HEB 2:3
HEB 3:5

Participle

LUK 1:65, 2:33, 18:34
ACT 13:49
ROM 8:26
2 CO 9:15, 12:4[1]
1 PT 1:8

1735 ܡܠܐ (v) fill, complete

[a]PEAL

Perfect

MAT 13:48, 27:48
MRK 15:36
LUK 2:21, 5:7
JHN 2:7[2],9
JHN 6:13, 16:6, 19:29[2]
ACT 5:3,28, 7:30
REV 8:5

Imperfect

LUK 16:21
JHN 4:7, 11:19
ACT 2:28
ROM 15:13
2 TH 1:11

Imperative

JHN 2:7[1]

Infinitive

LUK 15:16

Active Participle

ACT 14:17
1 TH 2:11

Passive Participle

MAT 14:20, 15:37
MAT 23:25,27, 28

MRK 6:43
8:19,20
LUK 1:28
4:1
5:12
11:39
JHN 1:14
19:29[1]
21:11
ACT 6:3,5,8
7:55
9:1
13:10
17:16
26:11
ROM 1:29
3:14
ROM 15:14
1 CO 16:9
2 CO 7:4
GAL 2:5
EPH 3:10
PHL 1:11
4:18
JAM 3:8,17[1], 17[2]
1 PT 1:22
2 PT 2:13,14,18
REV 4:6,8
5:8
15:7
17:3,4
21:9

1736 ܡܠܐܐ (m) fullness

1 CO 10:26

1742 ܡܠܝܐ (m) flood

LUK 6:48,48

1744 ܡܠܝܐܝܬ (adv) fully, completely

ACT 18:25,26
24:22
EPH 2:3

1745 ܡܠܘܬܐ (f) fullness

MAT 9:16
JHN 1:16

1748 ܡܠܝܬܐ (f) patch

MRK 2:21

1763 ܡܡܠܝܐ (m) (w/ ܠܒܐ) consolation

PHL 2:1

ETHPEEL

Perfect

MAT 22:10
LUK 1:41,67
4:28
5:26
6:11
JHN 12:3
ACT 2:2,4
3:10
ACT 4:8,31
5:17
7:54
13:9,45
19:28
24:25
2 CO 10:6*
REV 15:8[1]

Imperfect

MRK 4:37
LUK 1:15

LUK 3:5
14:23
ACT 9:17
COL 1:9
2 TM 1:4

Imperative

EPH 5:18

Participle

ACT 13:52

---

[c]PAEL

Perfect

ACT 3:18
24:27
ROM 13:8
1 CO 16:17
2 CO 11:9

Imperfect

MAT 3:15
5:17
ROM 15:19
PHL 2:30
4:19

Imperative

MAT 23:32

Active Participle

1 CO 14:16
2 CO 9:12
GAL 6:2
COL 1:24

Passive Participle

JHN 3:29

1654 ܡܘܠܝܐ (m) fullness

ACT 3:21
21:26
ROM 11:25
13:10
15:29
EPH 1:10
3:19
COL 1:19
2:9

---

[d]ETHPAAL

Perfect

MAT 2:17
27:9
LUK 1:23
LUK 2:6,22
ACT 2:1

Imperfect

MAT 1:22
2:15,23
4:14
8:17
12:17
MAT 13:35
21:4
26:54,56
LUK 22:37
JHN 12:38

JHN 15:25
17:12
19:28,36
ACT 1:16
ROM 8:4
EPH 3:19

Participle

LUK 1:20
2:40
LUK 9:51
GAL 5:14

---

[g]SHAPHEL

Perfect

ACT 13:33
REV 11:7

Imperfect

COL 1:25

Active Participle

EPH 1:23
COL 4:17

1918 ܡܫܡܠܝܐ (pp) full, complete

MRK 4:28
JHN 16:24
17:13
ACT 11:24
ROM 15:14
COL 4:12
JAM 1:4,17
1 JN 1:4
4:18,18
2 JN 12
REV 3:2

3140 ܫܘܡܠܝܐ (m) fullness, completion

ROM 11:12
EPH 1:23
EPH 4:13
HEB 6:11

---

[h]ESHTAPHAL

Perfect

REV 15:1

Imperfect

LUK 12:50
JHN 15:11
REV 15:8[2]
17:17

Participle

LUK 13:32
COL 2:10
1 JN 4:12
REV 6:11

1738 ܡܠܓ (v) pluck

[a]PEAL

Active Participle

MAT 12:1
MRK 2:23
LUK 6:1

1741 ܡܠܚ, ܡܠܚܐ (f) salt

MAT 5:13,13
MRK 9:49,50,50,
50
LUK 14:34,34
COL 4:6

1739 ܡܠܚ (v) salt

[a]PEAL (non occ)

1746 ܡܠܝܚܐ (pp) salty

JAM 3:12

---

[b]ETHPEEL

Imperfect

MAT 5:13
MRK 9:49[1],49[2],
MRK 9:50
LUK 14:34

1740 ܡܠܚܐ (m) sailor

ACT 27:27,30

1750 ܡܠܟ (v) counsel, promise; (ethpa) deliberate; (aph) reign

[a]PEAL

Perfect

JHN 18:14
ROM 1:2
4:21
TIT 1:2
HEB 6:13
HEB 10:23
11:11
12:26
JAM 1:12
2:5

Infinitive

2 CO 8:10[1]

Active Participle

ACT 27:9,22
2 CO 8:10[2]
REV 3:18

Passive Participle

EPH 1:13
6:2
HEB 6:18

1655 ܡܘܠܟܢܐ (m) promise

LUK 24:49
ROM 4:13,14,16,
20
9:4,8,9
15:8
2 CO 1:20
7:1
GAL 3:16,17,18,
18,21,22,
29
4:23,28
EPH 2:12
3:6
2 TM 1:1
HEB 4:1
6:12,15,17
7:6
9:15
10:36
11:9,13,17,
33,39
2 PT 3:4,9,13

1751 ܡܠܟܐ (m) king

MAT 1:6
2:1,2,3,6,6,
9,19,22
5:35
10:18
11:8
14:9
17:25
18:23
21:5
22:2,7,11,
13
25:34,40
27:11,29,
37,42
MRK 6:14,22,25,
26,27
13:9
15:2,9,12,
18,26,
32
LUK 1:5
7:25
10:24
14:31,31
19:38
21:12
22:25
23:2,3,37,
38
JHN 1:49
4:46,49
6:15
12:13,15
18:33,37,
37,39
JHN 19:3,12,14,
15,15,
19,21,
21
ACT 4:26
7:10,18
9:15
12:1,11,20
13:21,22
17:7
25:13,14,
24,26
26:2,7,13,
19,26,
27,30
2 CO 11:32
1 TM 1:17
2:2
6:15,15
HEB 7:1,1,2,2,2
11:23,27
1 PT 2:13,17
REV 1:5
5:10
6:15
10:11
15:3
16:12,14
17:2,10,12,
12,14,
14,18
18:3,9
19:16,16,
18,19
21:24
22:5

1752 ܡܠܟܐ (m) counsel

MAT 12:14
22:15
27:1,7
28:12
MRK 3:6
MRK 15:1
ACT 25:12
ROM 11:34
1 CO 7:25
PLM 14

1754 ܡܠܟܘܬܐ (f) kingdom

MAT 3:2
4:8,17,23
5:3,10,19,
19,20
6:10,13,33
7:21
8:11,12
9:35
10:7
11:11,12
12:25,26,
28
13:11,19,
24,31,
33,38,
41,43,
44,45,
47,52
16:19,28
18:1,3,4,
23
19:12,14,
23,24
20:1,21
21:31,43
22:2
23:14
24:7,7,14
25:1,34
26:29
MRK 1:14,15
3:24,24
4:11,26,30
6:23
9:1,47
10:14,15,
23,24,
25
11:10
12:34
13:8,8
14:25
15:43
LUK 1:33
3:1
4:5,43
6:20
7:28
8:1,10
9:2,11,27,
60,62
10:9,11
11:2,17,18,
LUK 11:20
12:31,32
13:18,20,
28,29
14:15
16:16
17:20,20,
21
18:16,17,
24,25,
29
19:11,12,
15
21:10,10,
31
22:16,29,
30
23:42,51
JHN 3:3,5
18:36,36,
36
ACT 1:3,6
8:12
12:20,21
14:22
19:8
20:25
28:23,31
ROM 14:17
1 CO 4:20
6:9,10
15:24,50
GAL 5:21
EPH 5:5
COL 1:13
4:11
1 TH 2:12
2 TH 1:5
2 TM 4:1,18
HEB 1:8
11:33
12:28
JAM 2:5
1 PT 2:9
2 PT 1:11
REV 1:6
5:10
11:15
12:10
16:10
17:12,17,
18

1758 ܡܠܟܬܐ (f) queen

MAT 12:42
LUK 11:31
ACT 8:27
REV 18:7

[b]ETHPEEL

Perfect

GAL 3:16 | HEB 11:9

[d]ETHPAAL

Perfect

MAT 26:4 | ACT 4:26

[e]APHEL

Perfect

ROM 5:14,17[1], 21[1]
1 CO 4:8[1],8[2]
REV 11:15,17 19:6 20:4

Imperfect

LUK 1:33 19:14,27
ROM 5:17[2],21[2] 6:12
1 CO 4:8[3]
1 CO 15:25
2 TM 2:12
REV 5:10 20:6

1762 ܡܡܘܢܐ(m) mammon

MAT 6:24 | LUK 16:9,11,13

1768 ܡܢ(prt) indeed

JUD 8,22

1769 ܡܢ(pron) who; (w/ ܕ) he who

incl comp with 747 ܗܘ
see also 1425 ܟܠ

MAT 3:7; 5:19,22,22,28,31,32,32,39,40,41, 42,42,44,44; 6:27; 7:9,21,26; 8:27; 10:11,14, 28,33,37,39,39,40,40,40,41,41; 11:15,16,27; 12:11,30,30,32,48,48,48; 13:9,12,13,43; 15:4,5; 16:13,15,24,25,25; 17:25; 18:1,4,5; 19:9,9,11,12,25; 20:26,27; 21:10,23,31,44, 44; 22:9,20,42; 23:12,12,16,16,18,18,20,21, 21,22,22; 24:13,45; 25:29; 26:23,68; 27:17, 21 MRK 1:24; 2:7; 3:29,33,33,35; 4:9,25, 25,41; 5:30,31,32; 6:11; 7:10,16; 8:27,29,34, 35; 9:23,34,35,37,37,37,40,42; 10:11,26,43; 11:23,28; 12:16; 13:13,15,16; 15:24; 16:3 LUK 2:44; 3:7,11,11,11; 4:6,34; 5:21,21; 6:29,30,34; 7:23,31,31,39,49; 8:8,18,18,25, 30,45,45; 9:5,9,18,20,23,24,24,26,46,48,48, 48,50; 10:16,16,16,16,22,22,22,29,36; 11:5, 22,23,23,40; 12:5,10,14,20,21,42; 14:5,9,15, 26,27,28,31,35; 15:4; 16:10,10,11,12,18,18; 17:7,31,31,33,33; 18:17,26,36; 19:3,26; 20:2, 18,24; 22:23,24,27,36,36,64 JHN 1:19,22, 33; 3:2,16,18,18,29,36,36; 4:10,34; 5:12,13, 24,24,30,44,45; 6:29,35,35,37,38,39,39,45, 46,47,54,56,57,58,60,64,64,68; 7:17,18,18, 20,28,33,38; 8:12,25,26,29,34,46,47,51,52, 53; 9:2,4,21,31,36; 10:1; 11:25; 12:25,25,26, 34,35,38,38,44,44,45,45,46,47,48,48; 13:16, 20,20,20,20,22,24,25; 14:9,12,21,23; 15:5, 21,23; 16:5; 17:3; 18:4,7,37; 19:11,12,24,35, 37; 20:15; 21:12,20 ACT 7:27,35; 8:33,34; 9:5,25; 10:43; 11:17; 13:11,25; 19:15,35; 21:33; 22:8; 26:15 ROM 2:28; 3:26; 4:4,4, 5,24; 6:16; 7:24; 8:11,11,20,31,33,34,35,37; 9:11,16,16,18,18,19,20,20,33; 10:5,6,7,16; 11:34,34,35; 13:2,7,7,7,7,8; 14:3,3,3,4,6,18, 22; 15:12 1 CO 1:31; 2:16; 3:5,5,8,8,17,18; 4:7; 5:2,3; 6:16,17,18; 7:39; 9:7,7,7; 10:12, 13; 11:29,34; 14:2,8,24; 16:22 2 CO 2:2,7, 10,10,16; 4:14; 5:17; 7:12; 9:6,6; 10:11,18, 18; 11:20,20,20,20,20,29,29 GAL 1:15; 2:6; 3:1,10,12; 5:7,10; 6:6,8,8 EPH 1:18; 4:28; 5:28 PHL 1:6 1 TH 4:8; 5:24 2 TH 2:4 2 TM 1:12; 2:4; 3:14 TIT 3:11 HEB 1:13; 2:14; 3:2,16; 5:7; 9:9; 10:23; 11:6; 12:6,25,25,25 JAM 3:13; 4:12 1 PT 1:15; 2:6; 3:10,13; 4:1,11,11; 5:8 2 PT 1:3 1 JN 2:9,15,22,23; 3:4; 4:7; 5:5, 10 REV 3:22; 4:10,10; 5:2; 6:10,17; 7:13; 11:5; 13:4,4,9,10; 14:11; 15:4; 18:18; 20:6; 22:7

1770 ܡܢ(prep) from

see also 1676 ܡܢܝܐ
see also 1720 ܡܢܐ
see also 1767 ܡܢܡܘܡ

MAT 1:3,5,5,6,12,16,17,17,17,18,20,21,22, 24; 2:1,6,7,9,9,15,15,16,16,16; 3:6,7,7,7,9, 11,13,13,14,16,17; 4:1,1,4,17,21,25,25,25, 25,25; 5:12,13,18,19,20,26,29,30,30,32,37, 37,42; 6:2,13,25,25,26,27,29; 7:4,5,5,9,15, 15,16,16,16,20,23; 8:1,5,11,11,21,24,28,30, 31,34,34; 9:3,9,15,16,20,22,27,33,38; 10:6, 14,14,14,17,22,24,24,26,28,28,29,29,31,37, 37,37,42; 11:1,7,9,11,11,12,19,25,27,29; 12:6,9,11,12,15,33,34,35,35,37,37,38,38,38, 41,42,42,43,44,45,45; 13:1,13,27,32,32,35, 41,44,47,49,52,53; 14:2,5,13,13,21,24,24,26, 29,36; 15:1,5,8,11,17,18,18,19,21,22,22,23, 24,27,27,28,29,38; 16:1,6,11,12,12,14,21,21, 21; 17:5,9,9,12,18,18,25,25,25,26; 18:6,7,8, 9,10,12,13,14,19,19,23,28,29,32,35; 19:1,4, 8,12,12,15,20; 20:2,8,13,21,21,23,23,23,29; 21:1,8,11,16,17,25,25,25,25,26,26,31,36,37, 39,42,43,46; 22:28,31,35,37,37,37,37,44,46; 23:7,18,20,22,27,27,28,28,33,34,34,34,35, 39; 24:1,9,21,27,29,31,31,32; 25:2,8,19,24, 26,28,29,32,32,33,33,34,34,40,41,41,45; 26:14,16,21,22,27,29,29,32,47,47,51,53,53,

58,64,64,73,73; 27:9,18,21,24,37,38,38,40,
42,45,47,48,51,55,55,56,57,63,64,64; 28:2,2,
4,7,8,11,17 MRK 1:7,9,9,10,11,13,25,26,
29,40,42,45; 2:20,21; 3:7,7,8,8,8,8,8,21,22;
4:25,31,32; 5:2,2,6,8,10,10,12,17,17,18,22,
23,26,27,29,30,34,35; 6:1,10,11,14,15,16,20,
22,33,43,52,54,56; 7:1,2,4,6,11,15,15,17,18,
20,21,21,23,24,26,26,26,28,29,30,31,32,33;
8:3,3,11,15,15,22,23,28,31,31,31; 9:7,8,9,9,
10,17,21,21,25,30,42; 10:1,6,20,37,37,40,40,
44,46; 11:1,2,5,8,12,13,14,18,19,20,30,30,
30,31,32,32; 12:2,5,5,6,8,11,12,13,13,23,25,
26,28,29,30,30,30,30,31,32,33,33,33,33,33,
34,36,38,43,44,44; 13:1,1,13,15,19,25,27,27,
28,36; 14:4,5,10,13,18,20,23,25,35,36,43,43,
47,54,62,64,69,70; 15:10,21,27,27,30,32,35,
38,40,43,44,44; 16:3,5,8,9,19,19
LUK 1:2,5,5,11,16,24,26,27,35,38,45,48,52,
70,71,71,74,78; 2:1,4,4,4,13,15,18,21,26,36,
36,37,46,46; 3:7,8,16,19,22,38; 4:1,2,13,15,
22,26,27,29,29,35,35,38,38,39,40,41,42; 5:2,
3,3,3,4,8,8,10,12,12,13,15,15,17,17,19,35,
36,36; 6:2,13,17,17,17,18,18,19,29,30,34,40,
42,42,42,44,44,44,45,45,45; 7:3,4,6,19,21,
21,21,24,26,28,28,30,35,36,36,42,45; 8:1,2,
2,2,3,4,12,16,18,22,27,27,28,29,29,29,31,
32,33,37,37,37,38,38,41,43,44,46,49; 9:4,5,
5,7,8,13,19,22,33,35,37,38,38,39,39,40,45,
54; 10:1,2,7,7,11,18,21,22,27,27,27,27,30,
36,42; 11:1,4,5,6,7,11,13,15,16,22,24,26,26,
27,31,31,32,33,37,38,39,45,46,49,50,50,51,
51,54; 12:1,4,4,5,5,5,5,6,7,13,15,20,23,23,
24,25,27,36,48,49,52,54,57,58,59; 13:2,4,10,
12,15,15,16,25,27,29,29,29,29,31,33; 14:1,5,
8,8,11,15,18,18,19,24,24,28,32,33; 15:4,4,8,
12,13,15,16,19,26,28,29; 16:3,4,5,8,9,16,17,
21,21,23,26,27,30,31; 17:2,7,7,12,15,18,20,
21,22,24,25,29,29; 18:2,2,3,4,4,13,14,18,21,
34,34; 19:3,15,21,22,24,26,26,29,39,39,42,
43; 20:1,4,4,5,6,7,10,15,19,26,27,33,35,39,
42,46; 21:3,4,4,11,16,17,18,24,25,26,30,34,
36; 22:2,3,6,20,23,36,41,43,45,45,47,50,54,
58,69,69,71; 23:5,7,8,8,12,14,26,33,33,38,
39,40,45,49,49,50,55; 24:2,4,9,13,13,18,18,
19,21,22,24,27,27,27,31,41,42,42,46,47,49,
51 JHN 1:6,13,13,13,13,14,15,16,18,19,
24,30,32,35,40,40,44,44,45,46,48,50,51; 2:9,
15,15,22; 3:1,2,3,5,6,6,7,8,13,18,19,25,27,
27,31,31,31,31,31,31; 4:1,6,7,9,12,12,13,14,
15,15,22,30,31,35,39,40,43,47,47,54; 5:4,7,
14,19,20,24,30,34,36,37,41,44; 6:7,8,11,13,
23,31,32,32,33,38,39,41,42,45,45,46,50,50,
51,51,54,54,58,60,62,64,64,65,66,70,71;
7:17,17,18,19,22,22,22,25,27,27,28,28,29,
31,31,38,40,41,42,42,44,46,48,48,50,51,52,
52; 8:7,9,11,14,14,23,23,23,23,26,28,33,40,
41,42,42,44,44,44,46,47,47,53,53,59; 9:1,6,
8,13,16,16,22,22,29,30,31,32,33,40; 10:1,1,
2,5,14,16,18,18,18,20,26,28,29,29,32,32,39,
40; 11:1,18,19,37,39,45,46,49,51,53,54,55;
12:1,2,3,4,9,9,11,17,17,20,21,27,28,32,34,
36,42,42,43,49; 13:1,3,4,16,16,19,19,21,23,
28,29; 14:7,10,12,16,21,28; 15:3,4,13,15,19,
19,19,20,26,26,27; 16:2,4,5,13,14,15,17,22,
26,27,28,30; 17:5,6,7,8,12,14,14,15,15,16,
16,24; 18:3,9,15,17,22,25,26,28,34,36,36,37;
19:2,11,11,20,23,23,27,29,31,33,34,38,38,
38,39; 20:1,2,9,9,12,12,24; 21:2,2,6,6,8,10,
12,14,15 ACT 1:2,3,4,4,9,11,12,12,12,13,
18,18,21,22,22,24,25; 2:2,2,3,5,5,6,9,10,10,
11,11,22,30,33,34,38,40,40,41; 3:2,2,3,5,15,
19,21,22,23,24,24,26,26; 4:2,6,9,10,15,17,
19,22,32,36,36; 5:2,2,2,3,4,7,13,16,17,22,28,
29,34,34,36,37,38,38,39,41; 6:3,7,9,9,9; 7:3,
3,4,4,7,10,16,21,24,27,33,37,40,42,43,45,
45,52,55,56,58; 8:1,7,16,22,22,24,24,26,27,
31,31,33,33,33,34,35,35,39,40; 9:2,3,3,8,11,
13,14,18,26,30,38; 10:1,2,2,7,11,17,22,22,
22,23,30,33,33,35,37,38,38,41,41,41,42,48;
11:2,5,8,9,11,11,15,19,20,20,20,23,26,27,
28,29; 12:4,5,7,7,10,10,11,11,17,19,20,20,
25,25; 13:1,4,4,7,8,13,13,14,16,17,21,23,28,
29,30,31,34,39,42,42,43,43,46,50; 14:1,1,4,
4,5,5,8,13,15,17,18,19,19,19,20,22,26,26;
15:1,4,4,4,5,7,7,14,16,16,18,19,20,20,20,20,
21,22,23,24,28,29,29,29,29,29,39,40; 16:2,2,
7,8,9,11,11,12,13,14,14,15,18,19,26,33,39,
39,40; 17:2,3,4,4,4,5,5,9,9,11,11,11,12,12,
13,13,15,15,17,18,18,25,26,27,27,27,28,28,
29,31,32,32,32,33,34,34,34; 18:1,2,2,2,5,6,7,
7,13,16,20,24,28; 19:2,9,9,12,12,16,18,22,
25,31,32,33,35,35,39; 20:4,4,4,4,4,6,9,10,13,
14,15,17,17,18,24,26,29,30,31,35; 21:1,1,3,
5,5,7,8,10,12,16,16,16,21,25,25,25,25,25,
26,27,30,32,34,39,39; 22:5,6,6,14,16,18,22,
29; 23:6,6,9,10,12,13,15,17,18,20,20,21,21,
23,34,34; 24:1,4,7,8,10,11,15,19,23,24,24,
26; 25:2,7,11,11,14,15; 26:2,3,4,4,5,6,7,9,10,
10,13,13,17,17,18,18,20,22,23,26,29,29,31;
27:1,2,2,4,6,11,12,12,14,21,21,21,22,27,29,
30,30,30,32,33,34,34,34,38,40,41,42,43;
28:1,3,3,4,10,13,14,17,17,20,21,21,21,22,
23,23,23,24,25,30 ROM 1:2,3,4,6,7,7,10,
16,16,17,17,18,20,25; 2:3,12,14,18,25,27,29,
29; 3:3,20,20,23,25; 4:2,11,12,14,16,16,24;
5:9,14,16,16; 6:4,7,9,13,17,18,22; 7:2,3,4,6,
9,24; 8:2,11,11,21,29,35,39; 9:2,3,5,6,7,21,
21,24,24,27,30,32,32; 10:7,9,17,17; 11:1,1,1,
2,6,6,14,15,17,21,24,25,26,26,27,30,35,36;
12:1,3,5,18; 13:1,1,3,3,11,11,12; 14:5,7,12,
14,23; 15:2,4,15,19,23,24,30,31; 16:2,17,17,
17,17,24 1 CO 1:3,3,7,10,11,12,14,25,25,
30,30; 2:7,8,12,12,15; 3:4,11,15; 4:3,3,5,5,6,
8,13,16,18; 5:2,3,3,7,10,13; 6:1,7,11,18,18,
19; 7:6,7,9,10,25,25,27,31; 8:3,6; 9:7,7,11,
13,14,15,19,25; 10:4,7,8,9,10,14,17,22,27,
29; 11:8,8,11,11,12,12,23,25,27,27,28,28,29,
32; 12:15,15,15,15,16,16,16,16,18; 13:9,9,
12,13; 14:5,10,18,19,24,24,26,36,37; 15:3,6,
6,6,7,10,12,19,20,27,35,38,41,47,47,48,49,
49; 16:2,5,12,12,15 2 CO 1:2,2,4,8,10,14,
15,16; 2:4,4,6,8,17; 3:1,2,3,5,5,16,16,18,18;
4:6,7,7,16,16; 5:1,2,4,4,6,8,16,18,20; 6:1,17,
17; 7:1,5,5,5,9; 8:3,4,6,10,11,17,19,19,20;
9:2,5,5,7,7; 10:1,2,6,7,13,15,16; 11:3,5,9,9,
20,23,23,23,23,24,26,26,26,28,33,33,33;
12:2,6,6,8,8,11,13,18,21,21,21; 13:2,7
GAL 1:1,1,3,3,4,6,8,8,9,9,11,11,12,13,14,
15,17,18,19,21,23,23; 2:1,12,12,12,15,15,16,
16,16,16; 3:2,2,2,5,5,7,10,12,13,17,17,17,18,
18,21,24; 4:1,4,8,9,9,12,13,19,22,22,23,23,
24,27; 5:4,4,5,8,15,16,21; 6:1,8,8

EPH 1:2,2,4,10,15,20,20,21,21,22; 2:2,3,8,9,
10,11,11,12,13; 3:7,9,11,15,20,20; 4:1,7,10,
16,17,18,22,25,29,31; 5:8,13,14,29,30,30,33,
33; 6:7,8,23,23 PHL 1:2,2,5,15,28,29; 2:3,
9,10,12; 3:2,2,2,4,5,5,9,9,9,11,12,12,20; 4:2,
2,3,7,15,15,22 COL 1:2,4,5,6,7,9,13,17,
18,21,23,26,26; 2:5,12,14,19,20; 3:7,8,23,24;
4:9,11,12,16 1 TH 1:8,9,10,10,10; 2:3,3,5,
6,6,6,9,11,11,11,13,14,14,15,17; 3:2,3,6,6;
4:1,1,3,4,6,10,16; 5:3,12,14,15,22
2 TH 1:2,2,7,8,8,9,9; 2:1,2,2,2,2,3,7,7,13;
3:1,2,3,6,6,8,8,8,12 1 TM 1:2,3,5,5,5,6,6,
13,19,19; 2:1,1; 3:7; 4:1,3,7; 5:8,9,11; 6:2,4,
5,5,7,10,11,16,20,20,21 2 TM 1:2,2,3,9,
13,15,15; 2:2,6,8,8,16,17,18,19,20,20,21,22,
23,26; 3:4,5,5,6,7,8,11,14,15; 4:4,8,15,17,18
TIT 1:4,4,8,10,12; 2:6,14; 3:3,5,9,9,9,9,10,
10 PLM 3,3,5,9,10,16,21 HEB 1:1,4,4,
5,5,9,10,13,13; 2:3,3,3,7,9,11; 3:1,3,3,4,12,
12,13,13,14,16; 4:1,1,3,4,7,7,8,10,10,12,13,
15; 5:1,4,7,8,10; 6:1,2,4,6,6,7,8,11,13,16,19;
7:1,2,5,5,5,5,6,7,7,13,13,14,14,19,26,26; 8:1,
6,6,9,11,12; 9:3,5,5,7,11,14,19,20,21,21,23,
26,27; 10:2,8,22,25,26,38; 11:3,4,5,12,13,15,
16,19,21,23,26,27,30,34,34,35; 12:1,3,5,5,9,
15,17,24,25,25,25,25; 13:10,11,12,13,19,20,
22,24 JAM 1:5,5,5,7,13,14,17,17,19,21,
27; 2:9,16,18,21,22,24,24,25; 3:4,10,10,11,
13,15,15,15,17; 4:1,1,7; 5:2,13,19,19,19,20,
20 1 PT 1:3,7,11,12,18,18,20,21,22,23,23,
23; 2:1,9,10,11,11,14,17; 3:5,6,10,11,14,20,
21; 4:1,10,10,11,15,17,17; 5:1,2,4
2 PT 1:4,12,15,17,17,18,21,21; 2:3,7,8,9,10,
11,11,17,18,20,20,21; 3:1,2,4,4,5,5,10,17
1 JN 1:1,5,7,9; 2:7,13,14,16,16,16,18,19,19,
19,19,19,20,21,21,24,24,27,27,28,29; 3:8,8,
9,9,10,10,11,12,14,17,19,20,22,24; 4:1,2,3,3,
3,4,4,5,5,6,6,7,7,13,21; 5:1,1,4,15,15,15,18,
18,19,21 2 JN 3,3,4,4,5,6 3 JN 4,7,10,
11,12,12,12 JUD 4,5,12,12,14,17,20,22,
22,23 REV 1:4,4,5,5,10,16; 2:5,7,9,10,10,
11,13,17,19,21,22,27; 3:5,9,9,10,12,16,18,
18; 4:1,5,6,6,8,8,8; 5:1,1,3,5,5,7,8,9,13; 6:1,
1,4,6,9,10,11,13,14,16; 7:1,2,4,5,5,5,6,6,6,7,
7,7,8,8,8,9,13,13,14,17; 8:4,5,10,13; 9:1,2,2,
3,6,13,17,18,18,18,18,18,20,21,21,21; 10:1,
4,8,10; 11:2,2,5,7,9,11,11,12,13; 12:6,10,14,
15,16; 13:1,3,11,13; 14:2,3,4,7,8,10,13,13,
13,15,17,18,20,20; 15:2,2,2,2,5,6,7,8,8; 16:1,
10,11,11,11,12,13,13,13,17,17,18,21; 17:1,2,
6,6,8,8,11; 18:1,1,1,3,3,4,4,4,10,10,14,14,15,
15,15,17,19,20,21; 19:1,2,5,15,21,21; 20:1,3,
7,9,9,11,11,12,13; 21:2,2,3,4,6,9,10,10,13,
13,13,13,21,21; 22:1,19,19,19

1771 ܡܢ, ܡܢܐ (pron) why, what

incl comp with 747 ܗܘ

MAT 5:13,46,47; 6:3,8,25,25,25,28,31,31,
31; 7:3; 9:4,5,13; 10:19; 11:7,8,9; 12:3,7,27;
16:8,26,26; 17:25; 18:12; 19:16,17,20,27;
20:6,21,22,32; 21:16,25,28,40; 22:18,42;
23:17,19; 24:3; 26:10,15,62,65,66,70; 27:22,
23 MRK 1:27,27; 2:7,8,16,24,25; 4:24;
5:39; 6:24; 8:12,17,23,36,37; 9:6,10,11,16,
33,50; 10:3,17,18,36,38,51; 11:3,5; 12:9,15;
13:4,11; 14:6,40,60,63,64,68; 15:12,14,24
LUK 1:29,66; 2:49; 3:10,12,14; 4:36; 5:22;
6:2,9,11,41,46; 7:24,25,26; 8:9; 9:25,33;
10:25; 11:19; 12:11,17,22,22,26,29,29;
14:34; 15:26; 16:2,3,4,7; 18:6,18,19,41;
19:15,33,48; 20:5,13,15,17,23; 21:7; 22:46,
60,71; 23:22,31,34; 24:5,17,19,38,38
JHN 1:21,22,25,38; 2:18,25; 4:27,27; 6:6,9,
28,30,30; 7:20,36,51; 8:5,43; 9:17,26,27;
10:6,20; 11:47,56; 12:27,49,49; 13:12,28;
14:22; 15:15; 16:17,18,18; 18:21,21,29,35,
38; 20:13,15; 21:21 ACT 1:11; 2:12,37;
3:12,12; 4:9,16; 5:3,7,24,35; 7:26,40; 8:30,
36; 9:4; 10:4,17,29; 12:18; 14:15; 15:10,36;
16:30; 17:18,19,20; 19:3,32; 20:22; 21:13,33;
22:7,10,16,26,30; 23:9,19; 24:20; 25:26,26;
26:8,14 ROM 2:3; 3:1,5,9; 4:1,3; 6:1,15,
21; 7:7; 8:24,26,27,31; 9:14,30,32; 10:8;
11:2,7; 14:10 1 CO 4:7; 6:7,7; 7:16; 10:19,
30; 11:22; 14:6,15,16; 15:29,29,32
2 CO 3:1; 12:13 GAL 3:19; 4:30
EPH 1:18,19; 3:18; 4:9; 5:10,17 PHL 1:22
COL 1:27 HEB 2:6; 11:32; 13:6
JAM 2:14,16; 4:13,14,14 1 JN 3:2,12
REV 2:7,11,17,29; 3:6,13,22

1584 ܠܡܢܐ (pron) why

MAT 8:26; 9:11,14; 13:10; 14:31; 15:2,
3; 17:10,19; 19:7; 26:8; 27:46
MRK 2:18; 4:30,40,40; 5:35; 7:5; 9:28;
11:31; 14:4; 15:34,34 LUK 2:48;
5:30,33; 6:47; 12:57; 13:7,18,18,20;
19:23,31 JHN 7:45; 8:46; 12:5; 13:37;
18:23 ACT 4:25; 5:4 ROM 3:7;
9:19,20; 14:10 1 CO 4:7; 10:29; 15:30
2 CO 11:11 GAL 5:11 COL 2:20
HEB 7:11 REV 17:7

1786 (ܡܢ), ܡܢܬܐ (f) hair

MAT 5:36	LUK 21:18
10:30	ACT 27:34
LUK 12:7	

1772 ܡܢܐ (v) number, reckon

aPEAL

Passive Participle

MAT 10:30	ACT 1:17
LUK 12:7	

1776 ܡܢܝܐ (m) money, mite

MRK 12:42	LUK 19:18,20,
LUK 19:13,16,	24,24,
16,18,	25

1777 ܡܢܝܢܐ (m) number

LUK 22:3
JHN 6:10
ACT 4:4
6:7
7:14
16:5
ROM 9:27
HEB 11:12
REV 5:11
7:4,9
9:16,16
13:17,18,
18
15:2
20:8

1787 ܡܢܬܐ (f) part, portion

MAT 24:51
LUK 10:42
11:36
12:46
24:42
JHN 13:8
19:23,23
ACT 8:21
2 CO 6:15
COL 1:12
HEB 1:1
REV 16:19
20:6
21:8
22:19

[b]ETHPEEL

Perfect

ACT 1:26

Imperfect

LUK 22:37

1779 (ܡܢܐ), ܡܢܢܐ (m) manna

JHN 6:31,49,58
HEB 9:4
REV 2:17

1775 ܡܢܟܝܠ (adv) next year

LUK 13:9

1782 ܡܢܥ (v) arrive

[c]PAEL

Perfect

ACT 28:13

Imperfect

ACT 26:7
ACT 27:12

1788 ܡܣܐ (v) thicken, swell

[b]ETHPEEL

Participle

ACT 28:6

1789 (ܡܣܐ), ܡܣܐܬܐ (f)

balance

REV 6:5

1805 (ܡܣܐ), ܡܣܬܐ (f)

sufficiency

1 TM 6:6

1803 ܡܣܪ (v) accuse, despise

[a]PEAL

Active Participle

REV 12:10

1793 ܡܣܘܪܐ (m) accuser

REV 12:10

[e]APHEL

Perfect

HEB 12:2

1812 (ܡܥܐ), ܡܥܝ̈ܐ (m)

bowels

ACT 28:8

1820 ܡܥܣ (v) convulse

[a]PEAL

Perfect

LUK 9:42

1837 ܡܨܐ (v) (pe, ethpe) be able

aPEAL

Passive Participle

1 CO 10:13	REV 2:2
EPH 3:20	3:8
PHL 4:13	7:9
1 TM 6:16	9:20
HEB 4:15	15:8

bETHPEEL

Perfect

REV 5:3	REV 14:3
12:8	

Imperfect

EPH 6:16

1842 ܡܨܥܬܐ (f) middle, midst

MRK 3:3	ACT 4:7
6:47	6:12
9:36	23:10
14:60	EPH 2:14
LUK 2:46	COL 2:14
4:35	2 TH 2:7
5:19	REV 1:13
6:8	4:6
22:55	5:6
23:45	7:17
JHN 8:3,9	14:6
19:18	19:17
20:26	22:2
ACT 1:15,18	

1840 ܡܨܥܝܐ (m) mediator

GAL 3:19,20	HEB 9:15
1 TM 2:5	12:24
HEB 8:6	

1851 ܡܩܠܘܢ (m) marketplace

1 CO 10:25

1853 ܡܪ (v) be bitter; (aph, ethp) make bitter; (p) grieve

aPEAL

Perfect

REV 10:10

1660 ܡܘܪܐ (m) myrrh

MAT 2:11	JHN 19:39
MRK 15:23	

1885 ܡܪܝܪܐ (adj) bitter

ACT 8:23	JAM 3:11,14
COL 3:19	

1886 ܡܪܝܪܐܝܬ (adv) bitterly

MAT 26:75	LUK 22:62

1887 ܡܪܝܪܘܬܐ (f) bitterness

ROM 1:29	EPH 4:31
1 CO 5:8	

1894 ܡܪܪܐ (f) bitterness

HEB 12:15

1895 ܡܪܪܬܐ (f) gall

MAT 27:34

1897 ܡܪܬܐ (f) bitterness

ROM 3:14

eAPHEL

Imperfect

REV 10:9

kP (non occ) ܡܪܡܪ

1766 ܡܡܪܡܪܢܐ (adj) provoking, contentious

HEB 3:8

mETHP

Perfect

REV 8:11

Participle

ACT 17:16

1854 ܡܪܐ (m) lord, master

MAT 1:20,22,24; 2:13,15,19; 3:3; 4:7,10; 5:33; 6:24; 7:21,21,22,22; 8:2,6,8,21,25; 9:28,38; 10:24,25,25; 11:25; 12:4,8; 13:27, 27,51,52; 14:28,30,31; 15:15,22,25,27,27; 16:22; 17:4,15; 18:21,25,26,27,31,32,34; 20:1,8,11,25,30,31,33; 21:3,9,30,33,40,42; 22:37,43,44,44,45; 23:39; 24:42,43,45,46,48, 50; 25:11,11,18,19,20,21,21,22,23,23,24,26, 37,44; 26:22; 27:10,63; 28:2,6 MRK 1:3; 2:26,28; 5:19; 7:28; 10:42; 11:3,9; 12:9,11, 29,29,30,36,36,37; 13:20,35; 14:14,31; 16:19,20 LUK 1:6,9,11,15,16,17,25,28, 32,38,43,45,46,66,68,76; 2:9,11,15,22,23,23, 24,26,29,38,39; 3:4; 4:8,12,18,19; 5:8,12,17; 6:4,5,46,46; 7:6,41; 9:54,57,59,61; 10:2,17, 21,27,39,40; 11:1; 12:36,37,39,41,42,43,45, 45,46,47; 13:8,25,25,25,35; 14:21,21,22,23; 16:2,3,5,5,7,8,13; 17:5,29,37; 18:6,41; 19:8, 16,18,20,25,31,33,34,38; 20:13,15,37,42,42, 44; 22:11,25,33,38,49,61; 23:42; 24:34 JHN 1:23; 4:11,15,19,49; 5:7; 6:34,68; 8:11; 9:36,38; 11:3,12,21,27,32,34,39; 12:13,21, 38,38; 13:6,9,13,14,16,25,36,37; 14:5,8,22; 15:15,20; 20:2,13,15,18,20,25,28; 21:7,7,12, 15,16,17,20,21 ACT 1:1,6,21,24; 2:17,20, 21,25,34,34,36,38,47; 3:19,22; 4:24,26,29; 5:9,14,19,42; 6:3; 7:30,31,33,37,49,59,60; 8:12,16,26,35,39; 9:1,5,5,10,10,11,13,15,17, 27,42; 10:4,14,36,48; 11:8,16,17,20,21,21, 23,24; 12:7,11,17,23; 13:5,10,11,12,47,49; 14:3,10,12,13,23,25,26; 15:11,17,17,26,29; 16:10,14,15,16,19,30,31,32; 17:24; 18:8,9, 25,26; 19:5,10,13,17; 20:21,24,35; 21:11,13, 14; 22:8,10,10,19; 23:11; 26:15,15; 27:11; 28:31 ROM 1:4,7; 3:26; 4:24; 5:1,11,21; 6:11,23; 7:25; 8:11,39; 9:28,29; 10:9,12,13, 16; 11:3,34; 12:11; 13:14; 14:4,4,4,6,6,6,6,8, 8,8,9,11,14; 15:6,11,30; 16:2,8,10,11,12,12, 13,18,20,22,27 1 CO 1:2,3,7,8,9,10,31; 2:8,16; 3:5,20; 4:4,5,17,19; 5:4,4,5; 6:11,13, 13,14,17; 7:10,12,17,22,32,32,34,35,39; 8:5, 6; 9:1,1,5,14; 10:21,21,22,26; 11:11,20,23, 23,26,27,27,29,32; 12:3,5; 14:21,37; 15:31, 47,57,58,58; 16:7,10,19,22,22,23 2 CO 1:2,3,14,24; 2:12; 3:16,17,17,18,18; 4:5,14; 5:6,8,11; 6:17,18; 8:5,9; 10:8,17,18; 11:17,31; 12:1,8; 13:10,14 GAL 1:3,19; 4:1; 5:10; 6:14,17,18 EPH 1:2,3,15,17; 2:21; 3:11,14; 4:1,5,17; 5:8,10,19,20,22; 6:1, 4,5,7,8,9,9,10,21,23,24 PHL 1:2,6,14; 2:11,19,24,29; 3:1,8,20; 4:1,2,4,5,10,23 COL 1:3; 2:6; 3:17,20,22,22,23,24,24; 4:1,1, 7,17 1 TH 1:1,3,6,8; 2:15,19; 3:8,11,13; 4:1,2,6,15,15,16,17,17; 5:2,9,12,23,27,28 2 TH 1:1,2,7,8,9,12,12; 2:1,2,8,13,14,16; 3:1,3,4,5,6,12,16,16,18 1 TM 1:2,12,14; 5:21; 6:1,2,3,14,15,15 2 TM 1:2,8,16,18, 18; 2:7,14,19,19,21,22,24; 3:11; 4:1,8,14,17, 18,22 TIT 1:4; 2:9 PLM 3,5,16,20,25 HEB 2:3; 6:3; 7:14,21; 8:8,9,10,11; 10:16,30; 12:5,6,14; 13:5,6,20 JAM 1:1,7; 2:1; 3:9; 4:6,10,15; 5:4,7,8,10,11,11,14,15 1 PT 1:3,13; 2:3,18; 3:6,12,12,15; 5:3 2 PT 1:1,2,8,11,14,16; 2:1,9,11,20; 3:2,8,9, 10,15,18 2 JN 3 JUD 4,4,9,14,17,21,25 REV 1:8; 4:8,11; 6:10; 7:14; 11:4,8,17; 13:16; 14:10,13; 15:3,4; 16:7; 17:14,14; 18:8; 19:6,16,16; 21:22; 22:5,6,20,21

1867 ܡܪܘܬܐ (f) dominion

EPH	1:21	2 PT	2:10
COL	1:16	JUD	8

1855 (ܡܪܐ)(v) (w/ ܒ) imitate

cPAEL

Imperative

HEB 13:7

1765 ܡܡܪܝܢܐ (m) imitator

HEB 6:12

1859 ܡܪܓܢܝܬܐ (f) pearl

MAT	7:6	REV	17:4
	13:45,46		18:12,16
1 TM	2:9		21:21,21

1860 ܡܪܕ (v-non occ) rebel

aPEAL

1876 ܡܪܝܕܐ (pp) fortified

2 CO 10:4

1864 ܡܪܘܕܐ (adj) rebellious

1 TM 1:9

1865 ܡܪܘܕܘܬܐ (f) rebellion

2 TH 2:3

1869 ܡܪܝܚܐ (adj) bold, presumptuous

2 PT 2:10

1870 ܡܪܝܚܐܝܬ (adv) boldly

ROM 15:15

1868 (ܡܪܚ) (v) dare

eAPHEL

Perfect

MAT 22:46	ROM 10:20
MRK 12:34	HEB 11:29
15:43	JUD 9
LUK 20:40	

Infinitive

1 TM 2:12

Active Participle

JHN 21:12	ROM 15:18
ACT 5:13	1 CO 6:1
7:32	2 CO 10:12
ROM 2:4	11:21[1],21[2]
5:7	

1874 ܡܪܛ (v-non occ) pluck

dETHPAAL

1875 ܡܪܛܘܛܐ (m) cloak

MAT 5:40	LUK 6:29
23:5	ACT 9:39

1890 ܡܪܥ (v) be weak, sick

aPEAL

Perfect

1 CO 8:11

1891 ܡܪܥܐ (adj) weak, sick

1 CO 8:12	GAL 4:9
11:30	

1888 (ܡܪܬ), ܡܪܬܐ (f) new wine

ACT 2:13

1904 ܡܫܚ (v) annoint

aPEAL

Perfect

LUK 4:18	JHN 11:2
7:46[1],46[2]	12:3
ACT 4:27	2 CO 1:21
10:38	HEB 1:9

Imperfect

MRK 16:1	JAM 5:14

Imperative

MAT 6:17

Active Participle

MRK 6:13	LUK 7:38

1909 ܡܫܝܚܐ (pp) Messiah, annointed (one), Christ

MAT 1:1,16,17,18; 2:4; 11:2; 16:16,20; 22:42; 23:10; 24:5,23,24; 26:63,68; 27:17,22 MRK 1:1; 8:29; 9:41; 12:35; 13:21,22; 14:61; 15:32 LUK 2:11,26; 3:15; 4:41,41; 9:20; 20:41; 21:8; 22:67; 23:2,35,39; 24:26,46 JHN 1:17,20,25, 41; 3:28; 4:25,29,42; 6:69; 7:26,27,31, 41,41,42; 9:22; 10:24; 11:27; 12:34; 17:3; 20:31 ACT 1:1; 2:31,36; 3:6,18, 20; 4:2,10,26,33; 5:42; 8:5,12; 9:22,34; 10:36,48; 11:17; 14:10; 15:11,26; 16:18, 31; 17:3,3; 18:5,28; 19:4,17; 20:21; 24:24; 26:23; 28:31 ROM 1:1,4,6,7,8; 2:16; 3:22,24,26; 4:24; 5:1,6,8,11,15,17, 21; 6:3,4,8,8,9,11,23; 7:4,25; 8:1,2,9,10, 11,11,17,34,35,39; 9:1,3,5; 10:4,6,7; 12:5; 13:14; 14:9,10,15,18; 15:3,5,6,7,8, 16,17,18,19,20,29,30; 16:3,5,7,9,16,18, 20,24,26,27 1 CO 1:1,2,2,3,4,6,7,8,9, 10,12,13,17,17,23,24,30; 2:2,16; 3:1,11, 23,23; 4:1,10,10,15,15,17; 5:4,4,5,7; 6:11,15,15; 7:22; 8:6,11,12; 9:1,12,18, 21; 10:4,9,16,16; 11:1,3,3; 12:12,27; 15:3,12,13,14,15,16,17,18,19,20,22,23, 23,31,57; 16:22,23,24 2 CO 1:1,2,3,5, 5,14,19,20,21; 2:10,12,14,15,17; 3:3,4, 14; 4:4,5,6; 5:10,14,16,17,18,19,20,20; 6:15; 8:9,23; 9:13; 10:1,5,7,7,14; 11:2,3, 10,13,23,31; 12:2,9,10,19; 13:3,5,14 GAL 1:1,3,6,7,10,12,22; 2:4,16,16,16, 17,17,20,20,21; 3:1,13,14,16,17,22,24, 26,27,27,28,29; 4:7,14,19; 5:1,2,4,6,24; 6:2,12,14,18 EPH 1:1,1,2,3,3,5,10,12, 15,17,20; 2:5,6,7,10,12,13,13,20; 3:1,4, 8,11,14,17,19,21; 4:7,12,13,15,20,32; 5:2,5,14,20,21,23,24,25,29,32; 6:5,6,23, 24 PHL 1:1,1,2,6,8,10,11,13,15,17, 18,19,20,21,23,26,27,29; 2:1,5,11,16, 21,30; 3:3,7,8,8,9,12,14,18,20; 4:7,13, 19,21,23 COL 1:1,2,3,4,7,24,27,28; 2:2,5,6,8,11,17,20; 3:1,1,3,4,11,13,15, 15,17,18,24; 4:3,12 1 TH 1:1,3; 2:2,6, 14,15; 3:2,11,13; 4:16; 5:9,18,23,28 2 TH 1:1,2,7,8,12,12; 2:1,14,16; 3:5,6, 12,18 1 TM 1:1,1,2,12,14,15,16; 2:5; 3:13; 4:6; 5:11,21; 6:3,13,14 2 TM 1:1,1,2,9,10,13; 2:1,3,8,10; 3:12,

15; 4:1,22 TIT 1:1,4; 2:13; 3:6 PLM 1,3,6,8,9,20,23,25 HEB 3:1,6, 14; 4:14; 5:5; 6:1; 8:6; 9:11,14,24,28; 10:10; 11:26; 13:8,20,21 JAM 1:1; 2:1 1 PT 1:1,2,3,3,7,11,11,13,19; 2:5,21; 3:15,16,18,21; 4:1,11,13,14; 5:1,10,14 2 PT 1:1,1,2,8,11,14,16; 2:20; 3:18 1 JN 1:3; 2:1,18,18,22,22; 3:7,23; 4:2,3; 5:1,6,20 2 JN 3,7,9 JUD 1,1,4,17, 21,25 REV 1:1,2,5,9; 11:15; 20:4,6; 22:21

1906 ܡܫܚܐ (m) ointment, oil

MAT 25:3,4,8	JHN 12:5
26:7	HEB 1:9
MRK 6:13	JAM 5:14
LUK 7:46,46	REV 6:6
10:34	18:13
16:6	

1910 ܡܫܝܚܘܬܐ (f) annointing

1 JN 2:20,27,27

1905 ܡܫܚ (v) measure

aPEAL

Perfect

REV 21:16,17

Imperfect

REV 11:2

Imperative

REV 11:1

Infinitive

REV 21:15

1903 ܡܫܘܚܬܐ (f) measure

MAT 23:32	2 CO 10:16
ROM 12:3,6	EPH 4:7,13,16
2 CO 10:13,13,	REV 21:15,17
15,15,	

1911 ܡܫܟܐ (m) skin, leather

MAT 3:4	HEB 11:37
MRK 1:6	

1934 ܡܬܚ (v) stretch out

aPEAL

Perfect

ACT 22:25

Active Participle

2 CO 10:14

1941 ܡܬܠܐ (m) parable, proverb

MAT 13:18,24,	LUK 6:39
31,33,	8:4,9,11
35,36,	12:16,41
53	13:6
15:15	14:7
21:33,45	15:3
22:1	16:1
MRK 3:23	18:1,9
4:2,10,11,	19:11
13,13,30,	20:9,19
33,33,34	21:29
7:17	HEB 9:9
12:1,12	11:19
LUK 4:23	2 PT 1:16
5:36	2:22

1940 ܡܬܠ (v) use parables

eAPHEL

Perfect

MAT 13:24,31

Imperfect

MRK 4:30

1932 (ܡܬܡ), ܡܬܘܡ (adv)

always; (w/ ܠܐ) never

see below 1767 ܡܡܬܘܡ

MAT 9:33	ACT 11:8
21:16,42	1 CO 13:8
26:33	GAL 5:16
MRK 2:12,25	EPH 5:29
LUK 15:29,29	1 TH 2:5
19:30	2 TM 3:7
21:34	HEB 1:5,13
JHN 1:18	7:13
5:37	10:1
7:46	2 PT 1:10,21
8:33	1 JN 4:12

1767 ܡܢܡܬܘܡ (adv) always; (w/ ܠܐ) never

from 1770 ܡܢ and 1932 ܡܬܘܡ (above)

MAT 7:23	ACT 14:8
ACT 10:14	HEB 10:11

1945 ܡܬܪ̈ܝܢ (f) measures (liquid)

LUK 16:6,6

1952 (ܢܒܐ), ܢܒܝܐ (m) prophet

MAT 1:22; 2:5,15,17,23; 3:3; 4:14; 5:12,17; 7:12,15; 8:17; 10:41,41,41; 11:9,9,13; 12:17,39; 13:17,35,57; 14:5; 16:4,14; 21:4,11,26,46; 22:40; 23:29,30,31,34,37; 24:11,15,24; 26:56; 27:9
MRK 1:2; 6:4,15,15; 7:6; 8:28; 11:32; 13:14,22
LUK 1:17,70,76; 3:4; 4:17,24,25,27; 6:23,26; 7:16,26,26,28,39; 9:8,8,19,19; 10:24; 11:29,47,49,50; 13:28,33,34; 16:16,29,31; 18:31; 20:6; 24:19,25,27,44
JHN 1:21,23,25,45; 4:19,44; 6:14,45; 7:40,52; 8:52,53; 9:17; 12:38
ACT 2:16,30; 3:18,21,22,23,24,25; 7:37,42,48,52; 8:28,30,34; 10:43; 11:27; 13:1,6,15,20,27,40; 15:15,32; 21:10; 24:14; 26:22,27; 28:23,25
ROM 1:2; 3:21; 11:3; 16:25
1 CO 12:28,29; 14:29,32,32,37
EPH 2:20; 3:5; 4:11
1 TH 2:15
TIT 1:12
HEB 1:1; 11:32
JAM 5:10
1 PT 1:10
2 PT 2:1,16; 3:2
1 JN 4:1
REV 10:7; 11:10,18; 16:6,13; 18:20,24; 19:20; 20:10; 22:6,9

1953 ܢܒܝܘܬܐ (f) prophecy

MAT 13:14
ROM 12:6
1 CO 12:10; 13:2,8; 14:6,22
1 TH 5:20
1 TM 1:18; 4:14
2 PT 1:19,20,21
REV 1:3; 11:6; 19:10; 22:7,10,18,19

1954 ܢܒܝܬܐ (f) prophetess

LUK 2:36
REV 2:20

1951 (ܢܒܐ) (v) (ethpa) prophesy

[d]ETHPAAL

Perfect

MAT 7:22; 11:13; 15:7
MRK 7:6
LUK 1:67
JHN 11:51
1 PT 1:10
JUD 14

Imperfect

ACT 2:17,18
1 CO 14:1,5[1],31

Imperative

MAT 26:68
MRK 14:65
LUK 22:64

Infinitive

1 CO 14:39
REV 10:11; 11:3

Participle

ACT 19:6; 21:9
1 CO 11:4,5; 13:9; 14:3,4,5[2],24
1 PT 1:12

1955 ܢܒܥ (v) spring up; (aph) speak forth

[a]PEAL

Active Participle

JHN 4:14

1610 ܡܒܘܥܐ (m) fountain

JAM 3:11

[e]APHEL

Imperfect

MAT 13:35

1956 ܢܓܕ (v) lead, drag; (pa) beat, scourge; (ethpa) be beaten, constrained

[a]PEAL

Perfect

MRK 7:33
JHN 6:44
21:11
ACT 16:19
23:19
GAL 2:12

Imperfect

JHN 12:32

Infinitive

JHN 21:6

Active Participle

JHN 21:8
JAM 2:6

1957 ܢܓܕܐ (m) stripe

ACT 16:33
22:24
2 CO 6:5
HEB 11:36

1959 ܢܓܘܕܐ (m) guide

MAT 15:14
MAT 23:16,24

[b]ETHPEEL

Participle

JAM 1:14
2 PT 1:21

[c]PAEL

Perfect

MAT 27:26
JHN 19:1
ACT 5:40
16:23,37

Imperfect

MAT 10:17
20:19
MRK 10:34
LUK 18:33
ACT 16:22
22:25

Infinitive

ACT 22:29

Active Participle

MAT 23:34
HEB 12:6

Passive Participle

MRK 15:15

1774 ܡܢܓܕܢܐ (m) scourger

MAT 18:34

[d]ETHPAAL

Perfect

2 CO 11:25

Imperfect

MRK 13:9

1958 ܢܓܗ (v) dawn; (aph) spend the night

[a]PEAL

Perfect

LUK 6:13
LUK 22:66

Active Participle

MAT 28:1
LUK 23:54
JHN 19:31

[e]APHEL

Perfect

LUK 6:12

1622 (ܢܓܠ), ܡܓܠܐ (f) sickle

MRK 4:29
REV 14:14,15, 16,17,
REV 14:18,18, 19

1963 ܢܓܪ (v) be prolonged; (aph) make long; (w/ ܪܘܚܐ) be patient

[a]PEAL (non occ)

1961 ܢܓܝܪܐ (adj) (w/ ܪܘܚܐ) longsuffering

1 CO 13:4	2 TM 2:24

1962 ܢܓܝܪܘܬܐ (f) (w/ ܪܘܚܐ) longsuffering

2 CO 6:6	2 TM 3:10
EPH 4:2	HEB 6:12
COL 3:12	

1975 ܡܢܓܪܐ (m) long ago

ACT 26:5

[a]APHEL

see below 1625 ܡܓܪܬ ܪܘܚܐ

Perfect

ACT 20:7,9	HEB 6:15

Imperfect

ACT 18:20	HEB 13:22

Imperative

MAT 18:26,29	JAM 5:7[1],8
1 TH 5:14	

Active Participle

LUK 18:7	2 PT 3:9
JAM 5:7[2]	

1625 ܡܓܪܬ ܪܘܚܐ (idiom) longsuffering

from 1963 ܢܓܪ (above) and 2968 ܪܘܚܐ

ACT 26:3	1 TM 1:16
ROM 2:4	2 TM 4:2
3:26	JAM 5:10
9:22	1 PT 3:20
GAL 5:22	2 PT 3:15
COL 1:11	

1964 ܢܓܪܐ (m) carpenter

MAT 13:55	MRK 6:3

1965 ܢܕ (v) loathe

[a]PEAL

Perfect

GAL 4:14

1966 ܢܕܝܕܐ (pp) abominable, foul

LUK 16:15	EPH 5:12

1967 ܢܕܪ (v) vow

[a]PEAL

Passive Participle

ACT 18:18	ACT 21:23

1968 ܢܕܪܐ (m) vow

ACT 18:18

1971 ܢܗܡ (v) roar

[a]PEAL

Active Participle

1 PT 5:8

1972 ܢܗܪ (v) shine; (pa) bring to light, explain; (aph) light

[a]PEAL

Perfect

MAT 17:2	REV 18:1

Imperfect

MAT 5:16	EPH 1:18
13:43	

1978 ܢܘܗܪܐ (m) light

MAT 4:16,16	LUK 8:16
5:14,16	11:33,35
6:23	16:8
17:2	JHN 1:4,5,7,8,8,9
24:29	3:19,19,20,20,21
MRK 13:24	
LUK 2:32	

JHN 5:35, 8:12,12, 9:5, 11:9, 12:35,35,36,36,36,46
ACT 9:3, 12:7, 13:47, 22:6,9,11, 26:13,23
ROM 2:19, 13:12
2 CO 4:4,6, 11:14
EPH 5:8,8,9,13,13
COL 1:12
1 TH 5:5
1 TM 6:16
1 PT 2:9
1 JN 1:5,7,7, 2:8,9,10
REV 18:23, 21:11,24, 22:5,5

[c]PAEL

Imperfect

EPH 3:9

1969 ܢܗܝܪܐ (adj) light, bright

MAT 6:22, 10:27, 17:5
LUK 11:34,36, 12:3
JHN 11:10
ACT 26:18
2 CO 6:14
PHL 2:15
JAM 1:17
REV 4:5, 15:6, 19:8, 22:1,16

1970 ܢܗܝܪܐܝܬ (adv) clearly

MRK 8:25

[d]ETHPAAL

Imperfect

2 CO 4:6

[e]APHEL

Perfect

LUK 2:9
ACT 16:29
REV 21:23[2]

Imperfect

EPH 5:14
2 PT 1:19[2]
REV 21:23[1]

Infinitive

LUK 1:79

Active Participle

MAT 5:15[1],15[2]
LUK 8:16
LUK 11:33,36[1],36[2]

LUK 15:8, 17:24
JHN 1:5,9, 5:35
1 CO 4:5
2 PT 1:19[1]
REV 22:5

Passive Participle

LUK 12:35

1973 ܢܗܪ, ܢܗܪܐ (m) river

MAT 3:6, 7:25,27
LUK 6:49
JHN 7:38
ACT 16:13
2 CO 11:26
REV 8:10, 9:14, 12:15,16, 16:4,12, 22:1,2

1974 (ܢܦܓ) (v-non occ) be shipwrecke

[c]PAEL

1979 ܢܘܦܓܐ (m) shipwreck

2 CO 11:25

1976 (ܢܘܕ) (v) shake

[a]PEAL (non occ)

1977 ܢܘܕܐ (m) earthquake

REV 6:12, 8:5
REV 16:18

[e]APHEL

Active Participle

MAT 27:39
MRK 15:29

1981 (ܢܘܚ) (v) cease, rest; (aph) make rest, put off

[a]PEAL

Perfect

LUK 8:24

2009 ܢܝܚܐ (pp) quiet, tolerable

MAT 10:15, 11:22,24,29
MRK 6:11
LUK 10:12,14
1 TM 2:2

1982 ܢܘܚܐ (m) calm, rest

MRK 4:39

2008 ܢܝܚܐ (m) rest

MAT 11:29	2 CO 2:13
12:43	7:5,7
LUK 11:24	PHL 2:19
ACT 24:23	1 TM 6:17

2010 ܢܝܚܘܬܐ (f) quietness, meekness

2 CO 10:1	COL 3:12
EPH 4:2	

2011 ܢܝܚܬܐ (f) rest

ACT 3:19	HEB 4:10,11
7:49	2 PT 2:13
HEB 3:11,18	JUD 12
4:1,3,3,5,	

[e]APHEL

Perfect

1 CO 16:18	HEB 4:8
2 TM 1:16	

Imperfect

MAT 11:28	EPH 4:22
ROM 13:12	

Imperative

EPH 4:25	PLM 20[2]
COL 3:8	1 PT 2:1

Infinitive

ACT 21:3

Passive Participle

2 CO 11:19

[f]ETTAPHAL

Perfect

2 CO 7:7,13	HEB 4:4,10
PLM 7	10:2

Imperfect

LUK 10:6	PLM 20[1]
ACT 27:3	REV 6:11
ROM 15:32	14:13

Imperative

MAT 26:45	MRK 14:41
MRK 6:31	LUK 12:19

Participle

LUK 16:25	1 TM 6:2
ROM 2:17	1 PT 4:14

1986 (ܢܘܡ) (v) sleep

[a]PEAL

Perfect

MAT 25:5

Active Participle

2 PT 2:3

1987 ܢܘܡܐ (f) pasture, spreading (of a sore)

2 TM 2:17

1990 ܢܘܢܐ (m) fish

MAT 7:10	LUK 9:13,16
12:40	11:11,11
14:17,19	24:42
15:34,36	JHN 6:9,11
17:27	21:3,6,8,9,
MRK 6:38,41,41,	10,11,
43	13
8:7	1 CO 15:39
LUK 5:6,9	

1991 ܢܘܣܐ (m) shrine, temple

ACT 19:24

1992 (ܢܘܦ) (v) (aph) beckon, wave the hand

[e]APHEL

Perfect

ACT 13:16	ACT 28:5
19:33	

Active Participle

ACT 12:17

1993 ܢܘܪܐ (f) fire

MAT 3:10,11,12; 5:22; 7:19; 13:40,42, 50; 17:15; 18:8,9; 25:41
MRK 9:22,44,46, 47,48,49; 14:54
LUK 3:9,16,17; 9:54; 12:49; 17:29; 22:55,56
JHN 15:6; 18:18
ACT 2:3,19; 7:30; 20:8; 28:2,3,3,5
ROM 12:20
1 CO 3:13,13,15
2 TH 1:8
HEB 1:7
HEB 10:27; 11:34; 12:18,29
JAM 3:5,6,6; 5:3
1 PT 1:7
2 PT 3:7,12
JUD 7,22
REV 1:14; 2:18; 3:18; 8:5,7; 9:17,17,18; 10:1; 11:5,19; 12:3; 13:13; 14:10,18; 15:2; 16:8; 17:16; 18:8; 19:12,20; 20:9,10,14, 15; 21:8

1783 ܡܢܪܬܐ (f) candlestick

MAT 5:15
MRK 4:21
LUK 8:16; 11:33
HEB 9:2
REV 1:12,13,20, 20; 2:1,5; 11:4

1997 ܢܚܠ, ܢܚܠܐ (m) valley

LUK 3:5

1999 (ܢܚܡ), ܢܘܚܡܬܐ (f-non occ) resurrection

1998 (ܢܚܡ) (v-non occ) raise up

cPAEL

1983 ܢܘܚܡܐ (m) resurrection

JHN 11:24,25

2000 ܢܚܫܐ (m) brass

MAT 10:9
MRK 6:8
MRK 7:4
1 CO 13:1
REV 1:15; 2:18
REV 9:20; 18:12

2002 ܢܚܬ (v) descend; (aph) cause to descend

aPEAL

Perfect

MAT 7:25,27; 8:1; 14:29; 28:2
MRK 1:10; 3:22
LUK 2:51; 3:22; 4:31; 6:17; 18:14; 19:6
JHN 2:12; 3:13; 4:51; 6:16,33,38, 41,42,50, 51,58
ACT 7:15,34; 8:5,15,38; 9:32; 10:21
ACT 11:5; 13:4; 14:11,25; 15:1; 16:8; 19:35; 20:10,13; 21:10; 24:1; 25:6,7,13; 27:2
ROM 10:7
1 CO 11:17
EPH 4:9,10
HEB 6:4
JAM 3:15; 5:17[2]
REV 10:1; 16:21; 18:1; 19:20; 20:1,9

Imperfect

MAT 24:17; 27:42
MRK 13:15; 15:32
LUK 9:54; 17:31
JHN 4:47
ACT 17:14; 25:5
JAM 5:17[1]
REV 11:6

Imperative

MAT 27:40
MRK 15:30
LUK 19:5
JHN 4:49
ACT 10:20

Infinitive

REV 13:13

Active Participle

MAT 3:16; 17:9
MRK 9:9
LUK 9:37; 10:30,31
JHN 1:32,33,51; 5:4[1],4[2],7
ACT 8:26
1 TH 4:16
JAM 1:17
REV 3:12; 12:12; 21:2,10

1691 ܡܚܬܢܘܬܐ (f) descent

LUK	19:37	ACT	27:17

[e]APHEL

Perfect

MRK	15:46	ACT	23:28
LUK	23:53		27:17,30
ACT	13:29	ROM	10:6
	22:30		

Imperfect

JHN	19:31	ACT	23:20

Active Participle

MAT	5:45	ACT	14:17
MRK	15:36		

2003 ܢܚܬܐ (m) garment

MAT	9:16,16	JHN	13:4,12
	11:8		19:2,5,23, 24
	17:2		
	21:7	ACT	7:58
	22:12		14:14
	27:31,35		16:22
MRK	11:8		19:12
LUK	7:25		20:33
	9:29	1 TM	2:9
	22:36	HEB	1:11
	23:11,34		

2006 ܢܛܪ (v) guard, keep

[a]PEAL

Perfect

MAT	19:20	ACT	7:53
MRK	10:20	2 CO	11:9[1]
LUK	18:21	2 TM	4:7
JHN	2:10	2 PT	2:5
	12:7	JUD	6[1]
	15:10[2],20[1]	REV	2:26
	17:6,12[2]		3:8,10[1]
ACT	4:3		14:12

Imperfect

MAT	23:3[1]	ACT	15:5,29
	28:20		16:23[2]
MRK	7:4		23:35
LUK	11:21		24:23
JHN	12:25	ROM	2:26
	15:10[1],20[2]	1 CO	7:37
	17:15	1 TM	5:21
ACT	12:4		6:14
1 PT	3:10	JUD	21
2 PT	2:9	REV	3:10[2]
1 JN	5:3		

Imperative

MAT	19:17	1 TM	5:22
	23:3[2]	2 TM	1:14
JHN	14:15	2 PT	3:17
	17:11	1 JN	5:21

Infinitive

EPH	4:3	JAM	1:27
2 TM	1:12		

Active Participle

MAT	27:36,54	ACT	16:27
	28:4		21:24,25
MRK	3:2		22:20
LUK	2:8,19,51		23:21
	6:7		28:16
	11:28	1 CO	16:2
	14:1	2 CO	11:9[2],32
JHN	7:19	GAL	3:23
	8:51,52,55		4:10
	9:16		6:13
	10:3	JAM	2:10
	12:47	1 JN	2:3,4,5
	14:21,23, 24		3:22,24[1]
			5:18
	17:12[1]	JUD	6[2]
	18:16,17	REV	1:3
ACT	9:24		12:17
	12:6		16:15
	15:24		22:7,9
	16:4,23[1],		

Passive Participle

ROM	3:8	1 PT	1:5
COL	1:5	2 PT	2:17
2 TM	4:8	JUD	1,13

1701 ܡܛܪܬܐ (f) watch

MAT	14:25	LUK	2:8
	24:43		12:38,39
MRK	6:48	ACT	12:10

2004 ܢܛܘܪܐ (m) keeper, guard

ACT	5:23	ACT	12:19

2005 ܢܛܘܪܬܐ (f) watching

LUK	17:20	REV	18:2
1 CO	7:19		

[b]ETHPEEL

Imperfect

ACT 25:21[1],21[2], 25	2 PT 2:4

Participle

MAT 9:17	ACT 25:4
LUK 5:38	2 PT 3:7
8:29	1 JN 3:24[2]
ACT 12:5	

[c]PAEL

Imperfect

LUK 4:10	2 TH 3:3
PHL 4:7	JUD 24
1 TH 5:23	

Active Participle

MRK 6:20

2017 ܢܝܪܐ (m) yoke

MAT 11:29,30	GAL 5:1
ACT 15:10	1 TM 6:1

2018 ܢܝܫܐ (m) sign, mark, banner

MAT 24:30	PHL 3:14

2019 ܢܟܐ (v) harm, be opposed to

[a]PEAL

Active Participle

GAL 5:17[1],17[2]

[b]ETHPEEL

Perfect

ACT 10:38

2023 ܢܟܠ (v) deceive

[a]PEAL

Active Participle

LUK 11:54	2 CO 4:2

2021 ܢܟܝܠܐ (pp) deceitful

ACT 18:14	2 CO 11:13
ROM 12:9	EPH 4:14

2022 ܢܟܝܠܘܬܐ (f) deception, subtilt

2 CO 11:3

2024 ܢܟܠܐ (m) deceit, guilt, trickery

MAT 26:4	ACT 20:3,19
MRK 7:22	23:30
12:15	ROM 1:29
14:1	2 CO 6:6
JHN 1:47	12:16
ACT 8:22	1 TH 2:3
9:23	1 PT 2:1,22
13:10	3:10

[c]PAEL (non occ)

2020 ܢܟܘܠܬܢܐ (adj) deceitful

ROM 3:13

2025 ܢܟܣ (v) kill, sacrifice

[a]PEAL

Perfect

LUK 15:30

Imperative

ACT 10:13	ACT 11:7

Passive Participle

REV 5:6,12

2026 ܢܟܣܐ (m) a possession

MRK 10:22,23, 24	LUK 18:24
	19:8
LUK 12:15	ACT 4:32
15:30	HEB 10:34

2027 ܢܟܣܬܐ (f) slaughter, sacrifice

ACT 7:42	ROM 8:36
8:32	JAM 5:5

[b]ETHPEEL

Perfect

1 CO 5:7 | REV 5:9

Imperfect

LUK 22:7

---

[c]PAEL

Imperfect

REV 6:4

2028 ܢܟܦ (v) be modest, ashamed; (pa) make modest

[a]PEAL

Perfect

HEB 11:16

2029 ܢܟܦܐ (adj) modest, sober

PHL 4:8
1 TM 2:9
3:2,11
TIT 1:8
2:2,5,6,8

2030 ܢܟܦܘܬܐ (f) modesty, sobriety

ROM 12:3
1 TM 2:9,15
TIT 2:12
1 PT 3:2

---

[c]PAEL

Active Participle

TIT 2:4

1778 ܡܢܟܦܐ (pp) modest, prudent

MRK 5:15 | LUK 8:35

1984 ܢܘܟܦܐ (m) modesty

1 CO 12:23

---

[d]ETHPAAL

Imperative

1 PT 4:7

2031 (ܢܟܪ)(v-non occ) repudiate

[f]ETTAPHAL

1985 ܢܘܟܪܝܐ (adj) strange, foreign

MAT 17:25,26
LUK 17:18
24:18
JHN 10:5,5
ACT 7:6
10:28
17:18,20,21
ROM 15:20
1 CO 14:21
EPH 2:12
4:18
COL 1:21
1 TM 5:22
HEB 11:9
12:8
13:9
1 PT 4:12

2032 ܢܟܬ (v) bite

[a]PEAL

Perfect

ACT 28:3

---

[c]PAEL

Active Participle

GAL 5:15

2033 (ܢܡܣ), ܢܡܘܣܐ (m) law

MAT 5:17,18
7:12
22:35,36
23:23
LUK 2:22,23,24,27,39
5:17
10:26
16:16,17
24:44
JHN 1:17,45
7:19,19,23,49,51
8:5,17
10:34
12:34
15:25
18:31
19:7,7
ACT 5:34
6:13
7:53
13:15,39
15:1,5,24
18:13,15
19:39
21:20,21,24,28
ACT 22:3,12
23:3,3,29
24:6,14
25:8
26:3
28:17,23
ROM 2:12,12,12,12,13,13,14,14,14,14,15,17,18,20,23,23,25,25,26,27,27
3:19,19,20,20,21,21,27,27,28,31,31
4:13,14,15,15,15,16
5:13,13,14,20
6:14,15
7:1,1,2,2,3,4,5,6,7,7,7,8,9,12,14,16,21,22,23,23,23,25,25

ROM 8:2,2,3,4,7; 9:4,31,31,32; 10:4,5; 13:8,10
1 CO 7:39; 9:8,9,20,20,20,21,21,21,21,21; 14:21,34; 15:56
GAL 2:16,16,16,19,19,21; 3:2,5,10,10,11,12,13,17,18,19,19,21,21,21,23,24; 4:4,5,21,21; 5:3,4,14,18,23; 6:2,13
EPH 2:15
PHL 3:5,6,9
1 TM 1:7,8,8,9
2 TM 2:5
HEB 7:5,11,12,16,19,28,28; 8:4,10; 9:19,22; 10:1,8,16,28
JAM 1:25; 2:8,9,9,10,10,11,12; 4:11,11,11,11,12
2 PT 2:7,8; 3:17

2034 ܢܡܪܐ (m) leopard

REV 13:2

2035 ܢܢܥܐ (m) mint (herb)

MAT 23:23 | LUK 11:42

ܢܣܐ see (ܢܣܝܘܢܐ), ܢܣܝܘܢܬܐ

2037 ܢܣܒ (v) take, receive; (w/ ܐܦܐ) hypocrite

[a]PEAL

Perfect

MAT 10:8; 12:14; 13:31; 16:7; 20:9; 22:15,28; 25:1,3[1],3[2],4,16,18,19,20,24; 26:52; 27:1,7,9; 28:12,15
MRK 3:6; 6:17,41; 8:6; 9:36; 12:8,20,21,22,23; 14:22[1],23; 15:23
LUK 6:4; 7:37; 9:16,47; 13:19,21; 14:20; 19:15; 20:29,30,31,33; 22:19,50; 24:30,43
JHN 1:16; 13:30; 21:7
ACT 2:33; 13:22; 16:3,27; 17:9; 27:35
ROM 1:5; 5:17; 8:15[1],15[2]; 11:35
1 CO 2:12; 4:7[1],7[2],7[3]; 11:23
2 CO 11:4[1],4[2],8
GAL 3:2
PHL 2:7; 3:12; 4:18
HEB 6:4; 9:19; 11:11,13
2 PT 1:17
2 JN 4
3 JN 7
REV 2:17,27; 3:3; 5:7; 8:5; 10:10; 11:17; 17:12; 19:20; 20:4

Imperfect

MAT 8:17; 16:5; 18:23; 21:22; 22:24
MRK 6:18; 7:27; 8:14; 10:11; 12:2,19; 15:24
LUK 19:12; 20:28; 22:36
JHN 6:7; 10:17,18; 16:14,15,24
ACT 1:20
ROM 13:2
1 CO 5:1; 6:15; 7:28; 9:25
GAL 3:14
PHL 3:14
HEB 4:16; 7:5; 9:15; 10:36; 11:8
1 JN 3:5
REV 3:11; 18:4; 22:17

Imperative

MAT 17:27; 20:14; 25:28; 26:26,27
MRK 10:21; 14:22[2]
LUK 16:6; 19:24
1 CO 11:24
EPH 6:16
1 TH 5:14
JAM 5:10
REV 10:8,9

Infinitive

MAT 1:20; 15:26; 18:24; 19:10; 24:17,18
LUK 1:25
JHN 3:27
ACT 3:5
1 CO 7:9
GAL 2:13
REV 4:11; 5:9,12; 6:4

Active Participle

MAT 6:2,5,16; 7:5,8; 10:41[1],41[2]; 15:7; 16:3; 17:24,25; 19:9[1],9[2]; 20:7; 22:16,18,30

MAT 23:13,14, 15,23, 25,27, 29	JHN 5:34,41
24:38,51	10:24
MRK 2:21	16:22
7:6	ACT 10:34
11:24	20:35
12:25	1 CO 9:24
LUK 6:42	10:17
11:10,44	2 CO 11:20
12:56	GAL 2:6
13:15	HEB 5:4
16:18[1],18[2]	7:8,9
17:27	JAM 1:7,12
20:21,34, 35	2:9
JHN 4:36	3:17
	4:3
	5:7
	1 JN 3:22

1790 ܡܣܒܐ (m) taking; (w/ ܐܦܐ) hypocrisy, respect of persons

MAT 23:28	COL 3:25
LUK 12:1	1 TM 5:21
JHN 7:24	JAM 2:1
ROM 2:11	1 PT 1:17,22
EPH 6:9	2:1
PHL 4:15	

[b]ETHPEEL

Imperfect

LUK 10:42	1 TM 4:4
19:26	

2038 ܢܣܝܐ (m-non occ) temptation

2039 ܢܣܝܘܢܐ (m) trial, temptation

MAT 6:13	1 CO 10:13,13
26:41	GAL 4:14
MRK 14:38	1 TM 6:9
LUK 4:13	HEB 3:8
8:13	11:17
11:4	JAM 1:2,12
22:28,40, 46	1 PT 1:6
ACT 20:19	4:12
	REV 3:10

2040 ܢܣܝܢܐ (m) proof

2 CO 2:9

2036 (ܢܣܐ) (v) tempt, prove

[c]PAEL

Perfect

1 CO 10:9[2]	REV 2:2
HEB 3:9	

Imperfect

MAT 4:7	1 CO 10:9[1]
LUK 4:12	1 TH 3:5
10:25	REV 3:10
1 CO 7:5	

Infinitive

ACT 5:9

Active Participle

MAT 4:3	LUK 11:16
16:1	20:23
19:3	JHN 6:6
22:18,35	8:6
MRK 8:11	ACT 15:10
10:2	2 CO 8:8
12:15	JAM 1:13[4]

Passive Participle

HEB 4:15	JAM 1:13[3]

1781 ܡܢܣܝܢܐ (m) tempter

1 TH 3:5

[d]ETHPAAL

Perfect

HEB 2:18[1]

Imperfect

MAT 4:1	GAL 6:1
LUK 4:2	REV 2:10
1 CO 10:13	

Participle

MRK 1:13	JAM 1:13[1],13[2], 14
HEB 2:18[2]	

[e]APHEL

Imperative

2 CO 13:5

2041 ܢܣܪ (v) saw

[b]ETHPEEL

Perfect

HEB 11:37

2042 ܢܥܒܐ (m) raven

LUK 12:24

2054 (ܢܦܐ), ܢܦܘܬܐ (f) filth

1 CO 4:13

2045 ܢܦܚ (v) breathe

[a]PEAL

Perfect

JHN 20:22

2046 ܢܦܛܝܪܐ (m) lantern

JHN 18:3

2047 ܢܦܠ (v) fall

[a]PEAL

Perfect

MAT	2:11	LUK	15:20
	7:25,27		17:16
	8:32		22:44
	13:4,5,7,8, 47	JHN	3:24
	17:6		9:38
	18:26,29		11:32
	26:39		13:25
MRK	1:40		18:6
	4:4,5,7,8		21:20
	5:13,22,33	ACT	1:18
	7:25		5:5,10
	9:20		9:4
	10:17		10:10,25
	14:35		12:7
LUK	1:12,44		13:11
	5:8,12		15:16[1],16[2]
	6:49		16:29
	8:5,6,7,8, 14,28,33, 41,47		19:17
	10:18,30, 36		20:9,10
	13:4		22:7
			23:7
			26:14
		ROM	9:6[2]
			11:22
ROM	15:3	REV	8:10[2]
1 CO	10:5,8		9:1
GAL	5:4		11:11,13, 16
HEB	3:17		14:8[1],8[2]
	11:30		16:19
REV	1:17		17:10
	5:8,14		18:2[1],2[2]
	6:13		19:4,10
	7:11		22:8
	8:8,10[1],		

Imperfect

MAT	4:9	ACT	27:17
	5:25,29,30	ROM	11:11
	18:8,9	1 CO	10:12
	21:44[1],44[2]		14:25
	24:29	1 TM	3:6,7
MRK	9:45,47	HEB	2:1
	13:25		4:11
LUK	11:17	2 PT	3:17
	14:5	REV	4:10
	20:18[1],18[2]		7:16
	21:24		

Imperative

MAT	21:21	LUK	23:30
MRK	11:23	REV	6:16

Infinitive

ROM	9:6[1]	HEB	10:31

Active Participle

MAT	3:10	LUK	12:28
	6:30		16:21
	7:19	JHN	12:6,24
	10:29	ACT	9:18
	12:11		28:6
	15:14,27	ROM	14:4[1],4[2]
	17:15	1 CO	13:8
MRK	3:10,11	1 TM	6:9
	4:37	JAM	1:11
LUK	3:9	REV	9:5
	6:39		

1828 ܡܦܘܠܬܐ (f) fall

MAT	7:27	LUK	6:49
LUK	2:34		

2048 ܢܦܣ (v) cast lots

cf ܦܣܐ

[a]PEAL

Imperfect

JHN 19:24[1]

Infinitive

JHN 19:24[2]

2049 ܢܦܨ (v) shake off

[a]PEAL

Perfect

ACT 13:51

ACT 18:6

Imperative

MAT 10:14

MRK 6:11

LUK 9:5

Active Participle

LUK 10:11

2050 ܢܦܩ (v) go out; (w/ ܪܘܚܐ) defend; (ethpa) be exercised; (aph) make go out

[a]PEAL

Perfect

MAT 8:32,34; 9:26,31,32,33; 11:7,8,9; 12:14,44; 13:1,3; 14:14; 15:21,22; 17:18; 18:28; 20:1,3,5,6,29; 21:17; 22:10; 24:1; 25:1; 26:30,55,71,75; 27:53; 28:15

MRK 1:26,28,29,45; 2:12,13; 3:6,21[1],21[2]; 4:3; 5:2,13,14,30; 6:1,12,24,34,54; 7:29,31; 8:11,27; 9:26,30; 10:46; 11:11,12,19; 13:1; 14:16,26,48,68; 16:8,20

LUK 1:22; 2:1; 4:14,35[2],37,38,42; 5:15,27; 6:12; 7:17,24,25,26; 8:2,5,27,33,35[1],35[2],38,46; 9:6; 11:14[2],24[1],24[2]; 15:28; 16:4; 17:29; 19:28; 22:39,52,62

JHN 4:30,43; 8:42,59; 10:39; 11:20,31,44; 12:13,18; 13:3,30[1],30[2]; 16:27,28,30; 17:8; 18:1,4,16,29,38; 19:4[1],5,34; 20:3; 21:3,23

ACT 1:21; 5:21,41; 7:4; 10:23; 11:25; 12:9,10,13,16,17[2],19; 13:14,51; 14:14,20; 15:24,40; 16:8,13,18[2],19,40[1],40[2]; 17:33; 18:1,7,23; 20:1,4,6,11; 21:5,8; 27:14; 28:3,11,15

ROM 10:18

1 CO 14:36

2 CO 2:13; 8:17

PHL 4:15

HEB 3:16; 7:5; 11:8[2],15

1 JN 2:19[1],19[2]; 4:1

2 JN 7

3 JN 7

REV 2:5; 6:2,4; 9:3; 14:15,17,18,20; 15:6; 16:17

Imperfect

MAT 2:6; 5:26; 8:12; 12:43; 13:49; 24:26

LUK 12:11,59; 14:18

JHN 5:29; 10:9

ACT 4:17; 7:7; 16:18[1],39; 18:2; 19:33,40; 20:7; 23:23

2 CO 8:19

EPH 4:29

HEB 11:8[1]; 13:13

JAM 3:11

REV 3:12; 20:8

Imperative

MAT 25:6

MRK 1:25; 5:8; 9:25

LUK 4:35[1]; 9:4; 10:10; 13:31; 14:21,23

ACT 7:3; 16:36; 22:18

2 CO 6:17

REV 18:4

Infinitive

MRK 9:29

LUK 8:29

JHN 1:43

ACT 16:10

1 CO 5:10

Active Participle

MAT 3:5; 4:4; 8:28; 10:11,14; 15:11,18[1],18[2],19; 17:21; 24:27; 27:32

MRK 1:5; 6:10,11; 7:15,20,21,

MRK	7:23	ACT	25:8
LUK	4:22,36,41		26:1,2,11, 24
	6:19		28:10
	9:5	ROM	2:15
	21:37	2 CO	12:19
JHN	8:9	JAM	3:10
	15:26	REV	1:16
ACT	8:7		4:5
	9:28		9:17,18
	13:42		11:5
	17:15		19:15,21
	19:12		22:1
	24:10		

Passive Participle

MRK 7:30

1832 ܡܦܩܢܐ (m) (w/ ܪܘܚܐ)

defense; answer

LUK	21:14	1 CO	9:3
ACT	22:1	2 CO	7:11
	25:16	PHL	1:7,16
ROM	1:20	2 TM	4:16
	2:1	1 PT	3:15

1833 ܡܦܩܢܐ (m) exodus, a way out

MAT	22:9	1 CO	10:13
LUK	9:31	2 PT	1:15

1834 ܡܦܩܬܐ (f) exodus

HEB 11:22

2051 ܢܦܩܬܐ (f) expense, cost

LUK	14:28	2 CO	11:8
ACT	21:24		12:15
1 CO	9:7,18		

---

[d]ETHPAAL

Perfect

HEB 5:14

---

[e]APHEL

Perfect

MAT	7:22	MRK	12:8
	8:16		15:20
	9:25		16:9
	21:12,39	LUK	4:29
	22:13		8:43,54
MRK	1:12,34,43		10:35[1]
	5:26,40		20:12,15
	8:23		24:50

JHN	2:15	ACT	12:17[1]
	9:34,35		13:17,50
	10:4		16:30
	19:13,16		21:38
ACT	5:6,19	HEB	8:9
	7:36,40,58	JAM	2:25
	9:40	REV	17:3

Imperfect

MAT	7:4	LUK	10:2,35[2]
	9:38	JHN	6:37
	10:1		9:22
	12:20		16:2
MRK	3:15	ACT	4:15
	6:7		5:9,34
	7:26		16:37[2]
	9:18		17:5
	11:15	2 CO	12:15
	16:17	1 TM	6:7
LUK	6:42[1]	HEB	6:8
	9:40		12:15

Imperative

MAT	7:5[1]	LUK	15:22
	10:8	ACT	21:24
	25:30	GAL	4:30
LUK	6:42[2]	REV	11:2

Infinitive

MAT	7:5[2]	LUK	6:42[3]
MRK	3:23		19:45
	9:28		

Active Participle

MAT	8:31	LUK	6:45[2]
	9:34		9:49
	12:24,26, 27[1],27[2], 28,35[1], 35[2]		11:14[1],15 18,19 19[2],20
	13:52		13:28,32
MRK	1:39		21:26
	3:22	JHN	10:3
	6:13		19:4[2]
	9:38	ACT	5:15
LUK	6:22,45[1],		16:37[1]
		3 JN	10

2052 ܢܦܫ, ܢܦܫܐ (f) soul, breath of

life, self

MAT	2:20	MAT	12:18,25, 25,26
	3:9		16:7,8,24 25,25, 26,26
	4:6		18:4
	6:25,25		19:12,19
	8:4		20:28
	9:3,21		21:25
	10:28,28, 39,39		
	11:29		

MAT 22:37,39; 23:12,12,31; 26:38; 27:5,40,42
MRK 1:44; 2:8; 3:4,24,25,26; 4:17; 5:5,30; 6:51; 8:34,35,35,36,37; 9:10; 10:45; 11:31; 12:7,30,31,33,33; 13:9; 14:4,34; 15:30,31; 16:3
LUK 1:24,46; 2:35; 3:8; 4:9,23; 5:14; 6:9; 7:30,39,49; 9:23,24,24,25,56; 10:27,27,29,30; 11:17,18; 12:1,17,19,19,20,22,23,57; 14:11,11,26; 15:17; 16:3,15; 17:3,14,33,33; 18:4,9,11,14,14; 20:5,14; 21:19,26,34; 23:2,28,35,37,39; 24:12,27
JHN 1:22; 2:24; 3:27; 5:18,19,30,31,43; 6:61; 7:4,17,18,28,35; 8:13,14,18,22,28,42,53,54; 9:21; 10:11,15,17,24,33; 11:33,51,55; 12:25,25,27,49; 13:37,38; 14:10,21,22; 15:4,13; 16:13; 17:19; 18:34; 19:7,12; 21:1,7,18
ACT 1:3,7,14; 2:27,41,43,46; 3:23,23; 4:32; 5:35,36; 7:13,14,54; 8:9,34; 10:17; 12:10; 13:46; 14:16,17,22; 15:24,26,29; 16:27,28; 17:25; 19:31; 20:10,20,24,28; 21:11,25; 23:21; 24:10; 26:1,2; 27:10,22,37
ROM 1:22,28; 2:1,14,19,21; 6:11,13,16; 8:23; 10:3; 11:3,4,25; 12:16,16,19,19; 13:1,9; 14:5,7,7,12,22,22; 15:1,3; 16:4
1 CO 2:2,14; 3:18; 4:3,4,19; 6:19; 9:7,19; 10:24; 11:13,28,29,31; 14:4,7,28; 15:44,45; 16:15
2 CO 1:9,9,23; 2:1; 3:5; 4:2,5,5; 5:12,15; 6:4; 7:1,8,10,11; 8:3,5; 10:7,7,12,12,14,18; 11:7,9,13; 12:5,15; 13:5,5
GAL 1:4; 2:12,18,20; 5:14; 6:3,4,5
EPH 4:19; 5:2,19,25,27,28,33; 6:7
PHL 1:27; 2:2,4,5,7,8,20,21,30; 3:9,13
COL 3:16,23
1 TH 2:8; 5:14,23
2 TH 2:4; 3:9
1 TM 2:6; 3:5,13; 4:7,16,16; 5:22; 6:10,19
2 TM 2:13,15,21,26; 3:2; 4:3
TIT 1:7,8; 2:7,14,14; 3:11
PLM 19
HEB 3:13; 4:12; 5:2,3,4,5; 6:13,19; 7:27; 9:7,12,14,25,26; 10:38,39; 11:19; 12:3,3,5; 13:17
JAM 1:21,22,24,27; 2:4,8; 3:15; 4:8; 5:20
1 PT 1:9,12,22; 2:11,25; 3:5,19,20; 4:19
2 PT 2:1,8,14; 3:17
1 JN 1:8; 3:3,16,16; 5:10,18,21
2 JN 8
3 JN 2
JUD 12,15,21
REV 2:2,9,20; 3:9; 6:9,15; 8:6,9; 12:11; 16:3; 18:7,13,14; 19:7; 20:4

2044 ܢܘܦܫܐ (m) rest, time to breathe

PHL 2:28 | REV 14:11

2053 ܢܦܫܢܝܐ (adj) natural

1 CO 15:44,46 | JUD 19

2057 ܐܠܨ (v) strive

[a]PEAL

Active Participle

JHN 6:52; ACT 7:26 | ACT 23:9; JAM 4:2

1838 ܢܨܝܘܬܐ (f) strife

JAM 4:1

2061 ܢܨܝܐ (adj) contentious

1 TM 3:3

2058 ܢܨܒ (v) plant

[a]PEAL

Perfect

MAT 15:13	LUK 20:9
21:33	1 CO 3:6
MRK 12:1	

Active Participle

LUK 17:28	1 CO 9:7
1 CO 3:7,8	

Passive Participle

LUK 13:6	JAM 1:21

2059 ܢܨܒܬܐ (f) plant

MAT 15:13

[b]ETHPEEL

Perfect

ROM 6:5

Imperative

LUK 17:6

2060 ܢܨܚ (v) be famous; (ethpa) strive to excel

[c]PAEL (non occ)

2062 ܢܨܝܚܐ (adj) noble, excellent

LUK 1:3	ACT 24:3
ACT 23:26	26:25

[d]ETHPAAL

Participle

PHL 1:27

2063 ܢܨܠ (v) pour

[a]PEAL

Perfect

LUK 10:34

2066 ܢܩܐ (v) sacrifice; (pa) make a libation

[a]PEAL (non occ)

2070 ܢܩܝܐ (f) sheep

JHN 21:17	ACT 8:32

[d]ETHPAAL

Participle

PHL 2:17	2 TM 4:6

2067 ܢܩܒ (v-non occ) bore, pierce

[a]PEAL

2068 ܢܩܒܬܐ (f) female, woman

MAT 19:4	ROM 1:26,27
MRK 10:6	GAL 3:28

2069 ܢܩܕ ,ܢܩܕܐ (adj) clean

MAT 27:59	1 PT 2:2

2072 ܢܩܥܐ (m) hole, cavern

MAT 8:20	LUK 9:58

2073 ܢܩܦ (v) cleave to, follow

[a]PEAL

Perfect

MAT 8:1	LUK 15:15
MRK 3:7	ACT 17:4,34
9:38	REV 14:4,9
10:28	

Imperfect

MAT 19:5	MRK 10:7

MRK 16:17
ACT 10:28
ROM 7:3
EPH 5:31
COL 2:21

Imperative

ACT 8:29 | ROM 12:16

Active Participle

1 CO 6:16,17

Passive Participle

REV 6:8 | REV 14:8

[d]ETHPAAL

Infinitive

ACT 9:26

Participle

ROM 12:9

2071 ܢܩܝܦܐ (adj) following

MRK 15:41
ACT 8:13
11:23
13:43
ACT 14:4
18:7
REV 19:14

[e]APHEL

Perfect

ACT 1:22
2:4
5:27
10:37
11:4,15
ACT 17:5
24:2
27:35
PHL 4:10

2074 ܢܩܪ (v) hew out

[a]PEAL

Passive Participle

MAT 27:60
MRK 15:46
LUK 23:53

2075 ܢܩܫ (v) knock

[a]PEAL

Perfect

LUK 12:36 | ACT 12:13

Imperfect

REV 3:20

Imperative

MAT 7:7 | LUK 11:9

Active Participle

MAT 7:8
LUK 11:10
13:25
ACT 12:16
REV 14:2

[b]ETHPEEL

Participle

1 CO 14:7

2076 ܢܪܓܐ (m) axe

MAT 3:10 | LUK 3:9

2077 ܢܪܕܝܢ (m) spikenard

MRK 14:3 | JHN 12:3

ܢܫܐ man, see under ܐܢܫܐ

ܢܫ̈ܐ women, see under ܐܢܬܬܐ

2080 ܢܫܒ (v) blow

[a]PEAL

Perfect

MAT 7:25,27
JHN 6:18
ACT 27:13
28:13

Imperfect

REV 7:1

Active Participle

LUK 12:55
JHN 3:8
ACT 27:40

1899 ܢܫܒܐ (m) breeze

ACT 27:14

2081 ܢܫܩ (v) kiss

[a]PEAL

Perfect

MAT 26:49	LUK 15:20
MRK 14:45	22:47[1]
LUK 7:45[1]	

Active Participle

MAT 26:48	LUK 22:47[2]
MRK 14:44	

1994 ܢܘܫܩܬܐ (f) kiss

LUK 22:48	2 CO 13:12
ROM 16:16	1 TH 5:26
1 CO 16:20	1 PT 5:14

[c]PAEL

Perfect

ACT 20:1	ACT 21:6

Infinitive

LUK 7:45[2]

Active Participle

LUK 7:38	ACT 20:37

2082 ܢܫܪܐ (m) eagle

MAT 24:28	REV 8:13
LUK 17:37	12:14
REV 4:7	

ܢܬܠ see under imperf and inf of ܝܗܒ

2085 ܢܬܦ (v) drag, pull

[a]PEAL

Imperfect

MAT 9:16

---

[d]ETHPAAL

Participle

JAM 3:4

ܣ

2090 ܣܐܐ, ܣܐܬܐ (f)

measure, bushel

MAT 5:15	LUK 11:33
13:33	13:21
MRK 4:21	

2086 ܣܐܒ (v) grow old

cf (ܣܝܒ), ܣܒܐ

[a]PEAL

Perfect

JHN 21:18	HEB 8:13

2087 ܣܐܡܐ (m) silver, money

MAT 10:9	2 TM 2:20
ACT 3:6	JAM 5:3
17:29	REV 9:20
19:24,24	18:12
1 CO 3:12	

2088 ܣܐܢ (v) put on sandals

[a]PEAL

Imperfect

MRK 6:9

Imperative

ACT 12:8	EPH 6:15

1802 ܡܣܐܢܐ (m) sandal, shoe

MAT 3:11	LUK 15:22
10:10	22:35
MRK 1:7	JHN 1:27
LUK 3:16	ACT 7:33
10:4	13:25

[e]APHEL

Imperative

LUK 15:22

2092 ܣܒܠ (v) bear, suffer; (aph) cause to bear, impose

[a]PEAL

Perfect

MRK 5:26	HEB 5:8

Imperfect

1 PT 3:17

Active Participle

1 CO 13:7	2 TM 2:9

[e]APHEL

Perfect

ACT 9:13

2094 ܣܒܥ (v) be full, satisfied; (pa) satisfy

[a]PEAL

Perfect

MAT 14:20	JHN 6:12,26
15:37	ACT 27:38
MRK 6:42	1 CO 4:8
8:8	REV 19:21
LUK 9:17	

Imperfect

MAT 5:6	LUK 6:21
MRK 7:27	

Imperative

JAM 2:16

Infinitive

ACT 7:11

2095 ܣܒܝܥܐ (adj) full

LUK 6:25

2096 ܣܘܒܥܐ (m) fullness, plenty

PHL 4:12

ᶜPAEL

Perfect

LUK 1:53

Imperfect

MAT 15:33
MRK 8:4

2097 ܣܒܪ (v) think, suppose, hope

ᵃPEAL

Perfect

MAT 20:10
MRK 6:49
JHN 11:13,31
13:29
JHN 20:15
ACT 7:25
8:20
27:13,27

Imperfect

MAT 10:34

Infinitive

ACT 17:29

Active Participle

MAT 6:7
24:44,50
26:53
LUK 2:44
6:34
7:43
8:18
12:40,46,51
13:2,4
17:9
19:11
24:21,37
JHN 5:45[1]
11:56
21:25
ACT 2:15
3:5
12:9
ACT 13:25
14:19
16:27
21:29
24:26
25:18
26:2,26
28:6
ROM 1:22
1 CO 3:18
4:9
7:26,36,40
8:2
10:12
12:23
14:37
2 CO 5:11
8:5
12:19

GAL 6:3
PHL 1:17
3:4
1 TM 6:5
HEB 10:29
JAM 1:26
4:5
1 PT 5:12

2099 ܣܒܪܐ (m) hope

LUK 2:14
6:35
ACT 2:26
16:19
23:6
24:15
26:6,7,7
27:20
28:20
ROM 4:18,18
5:2,4,5
8:20,24,24,24
12:12
15:4,13,13
1 CO 9:10,10
13:13
2 CO 1:7
3:12
10:15
GAL 5:5
EPH 1:18
EPH 2:12
4:4,19
COL 1:5,23,27
1 TH 1:3
2:19
4:13
5:8
2 TH 2:16
1 TM 1:1
5:5
TIT 1:2
2:13
3:7
HEB 3:6
6:11,18
7:19
10:23
11:1
1 PT 1:3,21
3:15,20
1 JN 3:3

ᵇETHPEEL

Perfect

2 PT 1:13

Imperfect

2 CO 10:9

Participle

MRK 10:42
LUK 3:23
1 CO 12:22
GAL 2:2,6,9
HEB 12:11

ᶜPAEL

Perfect

JHN 5:45[2]
EPH 1:12

Imperfect

MAT 12:21
ROM 15:12

Imperative

1 PT 1:13

Active Participle

ACT 24:15	PHL 1:20
26:7	2:19,23
ROM 8:19,25	1 TM 3:14
15:24	4:10
1 CO 13:7	PLM 22
15:19	1 PT 3:5
16:7	2 JN 12
2 CO 1:10	3 JN 14
13:6	

[e]APHEL

Imperfect

MAT 3:9	2 CO 11:16
5:17	JAM 1:7
JHN 16:2	

Active Participle

LUK 3:15	JHN 5:39
23:8	2 PT 3:9
24:28	

1792 ܡܣܒܪܢܘܬܐ (f) beliefs, gospel

1 TH 1:5	2 TH 3:5
2 TH 2:14	

2100 (ܣܒܪ), ܣܒܪܬܐ (f) good tidings, gospel

MAT 4:23	2 CO 2:12
9:35	9:13
24:14	10:14
26:13	11:4,7
MRK 1:14,15	GAL 1:6,7,11
8:35	2:2,5,7
10:29	EPH 1:13
13:10	6:19
14:9	PHL 1:27
16:15	2:22
ACT 12:24	4:15
15:7	COL 1:5
20:24	1 TH 2:2,4,8,10
ROM 10:16	3:2
15:19	2 TH 1:8
1 CO 4:15	1 PT 4:17
9:12,14,14,	1 JN 1:5
18,23	REV 14:6

2098 (ܣܒܪ) (v) preach, declare; (p) bear, endure; (ethp) be nourished

[c]PAEL

Perfect

MRK 16:10	GAL 1:8[2]
JHN 4:51	3:8
20:18	4:13
ACT 8:25	EPH 2:17
10:36	1 TH 3:6
1 CO 2:1	1 PT 1:12
15:1,2	REV 10:7
2 CO 7:7	

Imperfect

LUK 1:19	GAL 1:8[1],16
ACT 16:10	EPH 3:8
ROM 1:15	HEB 2:12
15:20	1 PT 2:9
1 CO 9:16[2]	

Imperative

LUK 9:60

Infinitive

LUK 4:18,43	2 CO 10:16
ACT 5:42	REV 14:6
1 CO 1:17	

Active Participle

LUK 2:10	ACT 14:7,15,21
3:18	15:35
8:1	16:17
9:6	17:3,23
20:1	ROM 10:15[1],15[2]
ACT 8:12,35,40	1 CO 9:16[1],18
11:20	GAL 1:9,23
13:5,32	1 JN 1:1,5

1791 ܡܣܒܪܢܐ (adj) evangelist

ACT 21:8	2 TM 4:5
EPH 4:11	

[d]ETHPAAL

Perfect

GAL 1:11	1 PT 1:25
HEB 4:2,6	4:6

Participle

MAT 11:5	LUK 16:16
LUK 7:22	

[k]P ܣܝܒܪ

Perfect

GAL	3:4	HEB	10:34
1 TH	2:14		11:27
2 TM	3:11[1],11[2]		12:2,3
HEB	10:32,33,	JAM	5:11

Imperfect

MAT	10:22	LUK	24:26
	17:17	2 CO	1:6
	24:13	GAL	5:10
MRK	9:19	PHL	1:30
	13:13	2 TM	2:12
LUK	9:41	1 PT	5:10

Imperative

2 CO	7:2	2 TM	4:5
2 TM	2:3	HEB	12:7

Infinitive

1 CO	10:13	HEB	12:20

Active Participle

ROM	12:12	COL	3:13
1 CO	4:12	2 TH	1:4
	7:9	2 TM	1:12
	9:12		2:10
	13:7	JAM	1:12
2 CO	11:1[1],1[2]	1 PT	2:19,20[1],
EPH	4:2		20[2]

1796 ܡܣܝܒܪܢܘܬܐ (f) patience, endurance

LUK	8:15	2 TM	3:10
	21:19	TIT	2:2
ROM	2:7	HEB	10:36
	5:3,4		12:1
	8:25	JAM	1:3,4
	15:4,5		5:11
2 CO	6:4	2 PT	1:6,6
	12:12	REV	1:9
GAL	5:23		2:2,3,19
COL	1:11		3:10
1 TH	1:3		13:10
2 TH	1:4		14:12
1 TM	6:11		

2157 ܣܝܒܪܬܐ (f) food

MAT	6:25	LUK	12:23
	10:10	JHN	4:8
	14:15	ACT	2:46
	24:45		9:19
LUK	3:11		27:33
	9:12,13	JAM	2:15

[m]ETHP

Imperfect

2 TM	2:6

Participle

ACT	27:21	1 CO	9:13

2101 ܣܓܐ (v) increase, multiply

[a]PEAL

Perfect

MAT	5:12	ROM	5:20[2]
ACT	6:1	2 CO	7:15
	7:17	GAL	4:27
	9:23	1 TM	1:14

Imperfect

ROM	5:20[1]	1 PT	1:2
2 CO	4:15	2 PT	1:2
PHL	1:9	JUD	2
	4:17		

Active Participle

ACT	6:7	ACT	19:20
	9:31	2 TH	1:3
	16:5		

2121 ܣܘܓܐܐ (c) multitude, abundance

MAT	21:8	ROM	9:22
LUK	5:19	1 CO	10:5
	6:17	2 CO	7:4
	23:27		9:14
JHN	21:6	PHL	1:14
ACT	19:26	JAM	1:21
	24:2		5:20
	28:3	1 PT	4:8
ROM	4:17,18	REV	8:11
	5:17		

[c]PAEL (non occ)

2105 ܣܓܝܐܐ (adj) much, many

MAT	2:18	MAT	11:20
	3:7		12:15
	4:25		13:2,3,5,
	6:7,30		17,58
	7:13,22,22		14:14,24,
	8:1,11,16,		24
	18,30		15:8,30,3
	9:10,14,37		16:21
	10:31		19:2,22,3

MAT 20:16,28,
29
21:36
22:14
24:5,5,10,
11,11,
12,30
25:19,21,
23
26:7,9,28,
47,60
27:19,52,
53,55
MRK 1:34,34,45
2:2,15,15
3:7,8,10,
12
4:1,2,5
5:9,10,21,
23,24,26,
26,43
6:2,13,13,
20,26,31,
33,34,34,
35,35
7:4,6,8,13
8:1,31
9:12,14,22,
26,26
10:1,22,31,
45,46,
48
11:8
12:5,27,41,
41
13:6,6
14:3,24,43,
56
15:3,41
LUK 1:1,7,14,
16,18
2:13,34,35,
48
3:18
4:25,27,41
5:6,15,29
6:17,23,35
7:6,11,12,
21,21,43,
47,47
8:3,4,27,
29,30,32,
40,42
9:22,37
10:2,24,40,
41
11:54
12:1,7,16,
19,19,
47,48,
48,48,
50
13:24
14:16,25
15:25

LUK 16:10,10
17:25
18:4,30
20:9
21:8,27
22:65
23:8,8,9
JHN 2:23
3:23,26
4:1,39,41
5:3,6,13
6:2,5,10,
60,66
7:12,31,40
8:26,30
10:20,32,
41,42
11:19,45,
47,55
12:3,9,11,
12,18,
24,42
14:2,30
15:2,5,8
16:12
18:2
19:20
20:30
21:8,25
ACT 1:3,5
2:40,43
4:4
5:12,16,37
6:7
8:7,9,11,
25
9:13,42
10:2,27
11:21,24,
26
12:12,18
13:31,43,
45
14:1,3,21,
22,28
15:2,7,35
16:15,16,
18,22,
23
17:4,12,12
18:8,10,18,
27
19:18,19,
23,32
20:2,8,19
21:10,32,
36
22:6,28
24:2,4,7,
10,17
25:7,23
26:9,10,11,
24,29
27:7,9,10,
12

ACT 28:2,2,6,
23
ROM 1:13
3:2
5:15,15,16,
19,19
8:29
12:4,5
15:22,23,
24
16:2,6,12
1 CO 1:26,26,26
2:3
4:15
8:5,5
9:19
10:33
11:30,30
12:12,12,
14,20
13:9,9,12
14:10,27
15:6
16:9,12,19
2 CO 1:11,11,14
2:4,6
4:15
6:4,10
7:4,4,7,9
8:2,4,22,
22
9:2,12,14
11:18,23,
26,27,
27
12:21
GAL 1:14
3:16
EPH 2:4
PHL 3:18,18

COL 4:13
1 TH 2:17
1 TM 3:8,13
6:9,10,12
2 TM 1:16
2:2,17
4:14
TIT 1:10,11
2:3
PLM 7,8
HEB 2:10
3:3,3
4:7
5:11
6:7
7:23
9:25,26,28
10:35
11:12
12:15
JAM 1:2
3:1,2,5
1 PT 1:3
2 PT 2:2
1 JN 2:18
3:1
4:1
2 JN 4,7,12
3 JN 3,13
REV 1:15
2:19,20
5:4,11
7:9
8:3
9:9
10:11
14:2
17:1
19:1,6,6,
12

2106 ܣܓܝܐܘܬܐ (f) abundance

MAT 24:12

ᵉAPHEL

Perfect

LUK 1:58
2 CO 8:15
PHL 2:9

Imperfect

2 CO 9:10
1 TH 3:12
1 TM 5:13
2 TM 4:3
HEB 6:14[2]

Infinitive

HEB 6:14[1]

Active Participle

1 CO 12:23

2102 ܣܓܕ (v) worship

[a]PEAL

Perfect

MAT 2:11, 8:2, 9:18, 14:33, 15:25, 18:26, 20:20, 28:9,17
MRK 5:6
LUK 8:47, 24:52
JHN 4:20[1]
JHN 9:38
ACT 10:25
ROM 11:4
HEB 11:21
REV 5:14, 11:16, 13:4[1],4[2], 14:9, 19:4,10[1],20, 20:4

Imperfect

MAT 2:8, 4:9,10
LUK 4:7,8
JHN 4:21,23,24[2]
ACT 8:27
1 CO 14:25
HEB 1:6
REV 3:9, 4:10, 9:20, 13:8,12,15, 15:4

Imperative

REV 14:7, 19:10[2]
REV 22:9

Infinitive

MAT 2:2
JHN 4:20[2], 12:20
ACT 24:11
REV 22:8

Active Participle

MRK 15:19
JHN 4:22[1],22[2],24[1]
ACT 7:43
ACT 19:27
REV 11:1, 14:11, 16:2

2103 ܣܓܘܕܐ (adj) worshipper

JHN 4:23,23

2104 ܣܓܘܠܐ (m) cluster

REV 14:18

2107 (ܣܓܦ), ܣܓܝܦܐ (adj) afflicted

LUK 14:13 | ACT 14:8

2108 (ܣܓܦ) (v) hurt, maim

[c]PAEL

Active Participle

1 TM 6:9

2109 ܣܕܐ (m) stocks

ACT 16:24

2111 (ܣܕܢ), ܣܕܘܢܐ (m) linen cloth

MRK 14:51,52
LUK 19:20
JHN 13:4,5

2112 ܣܕܩ (v) tear, divide

[a]PEAL

Imperfect

JHN 19:24

2113 ܣܕܩܐ (m) tear, division

MRK 2:21 | GAL 5:20

---

[b]ETHPEEL

Perfect

MRK 1:10

---

[c]PAEL

Perfect

ACT 14:14 | ACT 16:22

2122 (ܣܕܪ), ܣܘܕܪܐ (m) cloth

JHN 11:44, 20:7
ACT 19:12

2114 ܣܗܕ (v) witness, testify

[a]PEAL

Perfect

JHN	1:15	JHN	4:44
	3:26	HEB	11:4

Imperfect

MAT	19:18	JHN	1:7,8
MRK	10:19		2:25
LUK	18:20	ACT	26:4

2115 ܣܗܕܐ (ap) witness

MAT	18:16	ROM	1:9
	26:59,60,		7:16
	65		8:27
MRK	14:57,63	1 CO	15:15
LUK	4:22	2 CO	8:3
	11:48		13:1
	22:71	GAL	4:15
	24:48	PHL	1:8
JHN	3:28	COL	4:13
	5:32,36,37,	1 TH	2:5,10
	39	1 TM	5:19
	8:18,18		6:12
	10:25	2 TM	2:2
	12:17	HEB	2:4
	15:27		10:15,28
ACT	1:8,22		12:1
	2:32	1 PT	5:1,12
	3:15	1 JN	1:2
	5:32		5:8
	6:13	3 JN	3,12
	10:39,41	REV	1:5
	13:31		2:13,13
	22:5,12,15,		3:14
	20		11:3
	26:16		17:6

2116 ܣܗܕܘܬܐ (f) testimony

MAT	8:4	JHN	19:35
	10:18		21:24
	15:19	ACT	6:3
	19:18		7:44
	24:14		14:17
MRK	1:44		22:18
	6:11	1 CO	1:6
	10:19	2 CO	1:12
	13:9	2 TH	1:10
	14:55,56,	1 TM	2:6
	59		3:7
LUK	5:14		5:10
	9:5		6:13
	18:20	2 TM	1:8
	21:13	TIT	1:13
JHN	1:7,19	HEB	3:5
	3:11,32,33		11:2,4,5,
	5:31,32,34,		39
	36	JAM	5:3
	8:13,14,17	1 JN	5:9,9,9,10,

1 JN	5:10,11	REV	12:11,17
3 JN	12,12		15:5
REV	1:2,9		19:10,10
	6:9		20:4
	11:7		

[c]PAEL

Perfect

ACT	8:25	1 TH	4:6

Imperfect

LUK	16:28	REV	22:16
ACT	10:42		

Active Participle

ACT	2:40	EPH	4:17
	18:5	1 TH	2:12
	20:21,23,	1 TM	5:21
	26		6:13[1]
	26:22	2 TM	2:14
	28:23		4:1
GAL	5:3	REV	22:18,20

[e]APHEL

Perfect

JHN	1:32,34	ACT	15:8
	5:33		23:11[1]
	13:21	1 CO	15:15
	19:35	1 TM	6:13[2]
	21:24	HEB	7:8
ACT	7:58	1 JN	5:9,10
	10:43	3 JN	6
	13:22	REV	1:2

Imperfect

JHN	15:26	ACT	23:11[2]
	18:37	2 CO	12:11
ACT	20:24		

Imperative

JHN 18:23

Active Participle

MAT	23:31	ACT	10:22
	26:62		14:3
	27:13		16:2
MRK	14:56,60	ROM	2:15
	15:4		3:21
JHN	3:11,32		8:16
	4:39		9:1
	5:31,32		10:2
	7:7	2 CO	1:23
	8:13,14	HEB	2:6
ACT	4:33		7:17

1 PT 1:11
1 JN 4:14
1 JN 5:7

2117 ܣܗܪܐ (c) moon

MAT 24:29
MRK 13:24
LUK 21:25
ACT 2:20
27:20
1 CO 15:41
REV 6:12
8:12
12:1
21:23

2118 (ܣܘܐ) (v) (as pp) desirous

[a]PEAL

Passive Participle

ROM 1:11
15:23
2 CO 5:2
PHL 2:26
1 TH 3:6
2 TM 1:4

2119 (ܣܘܒ) (v) defile

[c]PAEL

Perfect

ACT 21:28

Imperfect

ACT 10:15 | ACT 11:9

Infinitive

ACT 24:6

Active Participle

MAT 15:11[1],11[2], 18,20[1]
MRK 7:15[1],15[2], 18,20,23

Passive Participle

ACT 10:14,28
11:8
ROM 14:14
TIT 1:15[1],15[2]
REV 21:8

1795 ܣܢܝܘܬܐ (f) abomination

REV 21:27

2127 ܣܘܝܒܐ (m) abomination

REV 17:4,5

[d]ETHPAAL

Imperfect

HEB 12:15

Participle

MAT 15:20[2]

2120 (ܣܘܓ) (v-non occ) enclose

[a]PEAL

2158 ܣܝܓܐ (m) hedge, wall

MAT 21:33
MRK 12:1
LUK 14:23
EPH 2:14

2124 ܣܘܚ (v) long for, desire

[a]PEAL

Perfect

MAT 12:18

Active Participle

2 PT 3:12

[c]PAEL

Active Participle

JHN 8:56
2 CO 5:8
1 TH 2:8

2123 ܣܘܘܚܐ (m) eagerness

2 CO 8:11

2128 (ܣܘܦ) (v-non occ) be ended

[a]PEAL

2169 ܣܘܦܐ (m) end, summation; (w/ ܠܐ) by no means

MAT 5:34
ROM 10:4
1 CO 5:1
2 CO 4:17
1 TM 1:4,5

2129 ܣܘܟܐ (f) branch

MAT 13:32 21:8 24:32 MRK 4:32 11:8 13:28	LUK 13:19 JHN 12:13 ROM 11:16,17, 18,19, 21

2131 ܣܘܟܢܐ (m) rudder

ACT 27:40

ܣܘܩ see (ܣܝܩ)

2136 ܣܘܣܝܐ (m) horse

REV 6:2,4,5,8 19:11,19,	REV 19:21

ܣܘܟ see under (ܣܝܟ), ܣܟܬܐ

ܣܘܦ see (pn) ܝܡܐ ܕܣܘܦ

2141 (ܣܘܦ) (v) consume

[a]PEAL

Imperfect

GAL 5:15

2142 ܣܘܦܐ (m) end

LUK 1:33 ACT 1:8	ACT 13:47 ROM 10:18

[e]APHEL

Imperfect

LUK 9:54	2 TH 2:8

2147 ܣܚܐ (v) wash, swim

[a]PEAL

Perfect

1 CO 6:11	2 PT 2:22

Imperfect

ACT 27:43

Passive Participle

JHN 13:10

2148 ܣܚܘܐ (m) swimming

ACT 27:42,43

2149 ܣܚܝܐ (m) washing

EPH 5:26

2151 ܣܚܝܬܐ (f) washing

TIT 3:5

[e]APHEL

Perfect

ACT 9:37	ACT 16:33

Passive Participle

HEB 10:22

2150 ܣܚܦ (v) overturn, cast down

[a]PEAL

Imperfect

LUK 19:44

[b]ETHPEEL

Participle

2 CO 4:9*

[c]PAEL

Perfect

MAT 21:12 LUK 1:52	ROM 11:3 HEB 11:34

Active Participle

GAL 1:23

2125 ܣܘܚܦܐ (m) destruction

2 CO 10:8, 13:10 | 2 TM 2:14

2152 ܣܛܐ (v) turn aside; (aph) cause to turn

ᵃPEAL

Perfect

ROM 3:12 | 1 TM 1:6

Imperfect

2 TM 4:4

Infinitive

1 TM 5:15

ᵉAPHEL

Perfect

ACT 5:37

1794 ܣܛܝܘܬܐ (f) transgression

GAL 3:19

2153 ܣܛܒ (v-non occ) bind

ᵃPEAL

2126 ܣܛܒܐ (m) fetter, shackle

MRK 5:4,4

2154 ܣܛܢܐ (m) adversary; (as pn) Satan

MAT 4:10, 12:26,26, 13:39, 16:23
MRK 1:13, 3:23,23,26, 4:15, 8:33
LUK 4:5, 10:18, 11:18, 22:3,31
JHN 6:70, 13:2,27
ACT 5:3, 26:18
ROM 16:20
1 CO 5:5, 7:5
2 CO 2:11, 6:15, 11:14, 12:7
1 TH 2:18
2 TH 2:9
1 TM 1:20, 3:6,7, 5:15
2 TM 2:26
HEB 2:14
JAM 4:7
1 PT 5:8
1 JN 3:8,8,8,10
REV 2:9,13,24, 3:9, 12:9, 20:2,7

2155 ܣܛܪ, ܣܛܪܐ (m) side; (w/ ܡܢ) besides

MAT 14:21, 15:38
JHN 20:7,20
1 CO 3:11, 15:27
2 CO 11:28
HEB 4:15

2091 (ܣܝܒ), ܣܒܐ (adj) old, aged

cf ܣܝܒ

LUK 1:18
JHN 3:4
1 TM 4:7
PLM 9

2156 ܣܝܒܘܬܐ (f) old age

LUK 1:36 | HEB 11:12

2159 (ܣܝܡ) (v) put, place

incl idioms

ᵃPEAL

Perfect

MAT 14:19, 19:15, 21:7, 27:29,37, 48,60
MRK 3:17, 6:5,29, 8:6²,23,25, 10:16, 15:17,46
LUK 6:48¹, 10:34, 13:13, 19:21,22, 22:41, 23:26,53¹
JHN 9:15, 11:34, 13:4, 15:16, 19:2,19, 29²,42, 20:2,13,15
ACT 1:7, 3:25, 4:37, 5:2,4, 6:6, 7:58,60, 9:12,17,25, 37, 13:3,29,47, 16:34, 17:26, 19:6,21, 26:9, 28:3,8
ROM 3:25

ROM	4:17	1 TH	5:9
	8:28	1 TM	1:12
1 CO	3:10	TIT	3:12
	4:6,9	HEB	1:2,10
	12:18,28		2:7
	16:15	2 PT	2:6
2 CO	5:19	REV	1:17
GAL	4:2		10:2
EPH	1:5,9		

Imperfect

MAT	6:19	LUK	20:43
	12:18	JHN	10:18[2]
	19:13		15:13
	22:44	ACT	2:35
	24:51		4:21
MRK	6:41		8:19
	7:32		15:10
	8:6[1],7	ROM	14:13
	12:36	1 CO	15:25
	16:18	2 CO	8:20
LUK	1:9	1 TH	5:8
	5:18	1 TM	5:22
	9:16		6:19
	11:6	HEB	1:13
	12:46	REV	22:18[1],18[2]
	14:29		

Imperative

MAT	6:20	LUK	15:22
	9:18		21:14
MRK	5:23	JHN	18:11
LUK	9:44	EPH	6:17

Infinitive

ACT	22:5	1 TM	6:4
1 CO	3:11[2]	HEB	10:29
2 CO	12:14		

Active Participle

MAT	5:15	JHN	18:18
	23:4	ACT	3:2
MRK	6:56		4:35
LUK	4:40		8:17
	8:16[1],16[2]		19:12
	11:33	ROM	2:5
	12:21		9:33
	23:46	1 CO	16:2
JHN	10:11,15,	HEB	4:7
	17,18[1]	JAM	4:12
	13:37,38	1 PT	2:6

Passive Participle

MAT	3:10	LUK	12:19
	7:25		16:26
	28:6		19:20
MRK	16:6		24:12
LUK	2:12,16,34	JHN	2:6
	3:9		11:38
	6:48[2]		19:29[1]
	9:53		20:5,6,7,

JHN	20:12	HEB	2:9
	21:9[1],9[2]		7:11
ACT	13:48		9:10,27
1 CO	3:11[1]		12:1
	9:16	1 PT	2:8
	14:22	1 JN	5:19
GAL	5:23	JUD	7
PHL	1:7,16	REV	4:2
1 TH	3:3		21:16
1 TM	1:9		

2160 ܣܝܡܐ (m) (w/ ܐܝܕܐ)

laying on of hands

ACT	8:18	2 TM	1:6
1 TM	4:14	HEB	6:2

2162 ܣܝܡܬܐ (f) treasure

see below 2163 ܣܝܡܬ ܒܢܝܐ

MAT	2:11	LUK	12:34
	6:19,20,21		18:22
	12:35,35	ROM	2:5
	13:44,52	2 CO	4:7
	19:21		12:14
MRK	10:21	COL	2:3
LUK	6:45,45	HEB	11:26
	12:21,33,		

2163 ܣܝܡܬ ܒܢܝܐ (idiom)

adoption

from 2162 ܣܝܡܬܐ (above) and 450 ܒܪܐ

ROM	8:15,23	GAL	4:5
	9:4		

---

[b]ETHPEEL

Perfect

MRK	15:47	ACT	7:16
LUK	23:53[2],55	1 TM	2:7
JHN	19:41	2 TM	1:11

Imperfect

MRK	4:21[1],21[2]	HEB	10:13
ACT	15:28		

Infinitive

REV 11:9

Participle

LUK	10:8	1 CO	10:27

2164 ܣܝܢܐ (m) mud

2 PT 2:22

2166 (ܣܝܥ), ܣܝܥܬܐ (f-non occ) army

2139 (ܣܘܥ) (v) help, aid

[c]PAEL

Perfect

JAM 2:22

2167 ܣܝܦ, ܣܝܦܐ (m) sword

MAT 26:52,52	ACT 12:2
MRK 14:47,48	ROM 8:35
LUK 22:36,36, 38,49, 52	EPH 6:17
	HEB 11:34,37

2168 (ܣܟܐ) (v) expect, look for

[c]PAEL

Perfect

ACT 28:6	HEB 11:35

Active Participle

MAT 11:3	PHL 1:20
MRK 15:43	3:20
LUK 1:21	1 TH 1:10
2:25,38	TIT 2:13
7:19,20	HEB 9:28
12:36	11:10
23:51	13:14
JHN 5:3	JAM 5:7
ROM 8:19,23,24	2 PT 3:12,13,14
1 CO 1:7	JUD 21

2171 (ܣܟܠ) (v) (pa) make understand; (ethpa) understand

[c]PAEL

Active Participle

COL 1:28

2130 ܣܘܟܠܐ (m) understanding

ROM 1:20	COL 1:9
EPH 1:8	2:2
PHL 1:9	2 PT 3:16

2170 ܣܘܟܠܬܢܐ (adj) intelligent, prudent

MAT 11:25	1 CO 1:19
LUK 10:21	

[d]ETHPAAL

Perfect

MAT 13:51	LUK 20:23
16:9,11,12	ACT 4:13
17:13	7:25[2]
MRK 6:52,54	12:12
LUK 1:22	16:10
18:34	

Imperfect

MAT 13:14,15	LUK 24:16
24:15	JHN 12:40
MRK 4:12	ACT 8:31
13:14	28:26,27
LUK 8:10	

Imperative

MAT 15:10	EPH 5:17
MRK 7:14	2 TM 2:7

Infinitive

LUK 24:45	EPH 3:4

Participle

MAT 13:13,19, 23	ROM 1:21
	3:11
15:16	2 CO 10:12
MRK 8:17,21	1 TM 1:7
LUK 21:30	HEB 11:3
JHN 7:17	1 JN 3:24
ACT 7:25[1]	4:6
8:30	

2173 ܣܟܠܐ (adj) foolish

MAT 7:26	2 CO 11:16,16
23:17,19	GAL 3:3
25:2,3,8	EPH 5:15
ROM 1:14	1 TM 6:9
1 CO 1:27	2 TM 2:23
3:18	TIT 3:9
15:36	1 PT 2:15

2174 ܣܟܠܘܬܐ (f) foolishness, transgression

MAT 6:14,15	ACT 16:37
18:35	19:18
MRK 11:25,26	24:20

ACT 25:5,11,27	EPH 6:9
ROM 5:16,17,18	HEB 9:7
2 CO 12:13	JAM 5:16
GAL 6:1	1 PT 2:20
EPH 2:1	

2172 (ܣܟܠ) (v) (aph) offend, wrong

eAPHEL

Perfect

MAT 18:15	GAL 4:12
ACT 25:8	COL 3:25
2 CO 11:7²	

Imperfect

MAT 18:21 | LUK 17:4

Infinitive

2 CO 11:7¹

Active Participle

ACT 7:24,26,27 | 1 CO 8:12¹,12²

Passive Participle

2 CO 7:12

1797 ܡܣܟܠܢܐ (m) evil doer, offender

2 CO 7:12	1 TH 5:14
COL 3:25	1 PT 2:14

799 (ܡܣܟ), ܡܣܟܢܐ (adj) poor

MAT 5:3	LUK 21:2,3
11:5	JHN 12:5,6,8
19:21	13:29
26:9,11	ROM 15:26
MRK 10:21	1 CO 13:3
12:42,43	2 CO 6:10
14:5,7	9:9
LUK 4:18	GAL 2:10
6:20	4:9
7:22	HEB 13:16
14:13,21	JAM 2:2,3,5,6
16:20,22	REV. 3:17
18:22	13:16
19:8	

1800 ܡܣܟܢܘܬܐ (f) poverty

2 CO 8:2,9 | REV 2:9

1798 ܡܣܟܢ (v) (ethp) become poor

mETHP

Perfect

2 CO 8:9

2175 ܣܟܪ (v) stop, shut

aPEAL

Imperfect

1 PT 2:15

Imperative

MRK 1:25 | LUK 4:35

bETHPEEL

Imperfect

ROM 3:19

cPAEL

Perfect

ACT 7:57 | HEB 11:33

Infinitive

TIT 1:11

dETHPAAL (non occ)

2176 ܣܟܪܐ (f) shield

EPH 6:16

2178 ܣܠܐ (v) despise, reject

aPEAL

Passive Participle

2 TM 3:8

bETHPEEL

Perfect

ROM 3:12 | HEB 12:17

Imperfect

MRK 8:31
9:12
LUK 9:22
LUK 17:25
1 CO 9:27

1806 ܡܣܠܝܢܘܬܐ (f) rejection

ROM 11:15

ᵉAPHEL

Perfect

MAT 21:42
MRK 12:10
LUK 20:17
ACT 4:11
2 CO 4:2
1 PT 2:4

Imperfect

GAL 3:17
1 TH 5:20

Active Participle

MRK 7:13
GAL 3:15

1801 ܡܣܠܝܐ (pp) despised, rejected, reprobate

1 CO 1:28
2 CO 13:5,6,7
1 TM 4:4
TIT 1:16
HEB 6:8

2185 ܣܠܩ (v) go up, ascend; (pa, aph) make ascend

ᵃPEAL

Perfect

MAT 3:16
5:1
8:23[1],23[2]
9:1
13:7
14:23,32
15:29,39
MRK 1:10
2:4
3:13
4:7,8
5:18
6:51
8:10,13
15:41
16:19
LUK 2:4,42
5:2,3,19
8:22,37
9:28
18:10
LUK 19:4
24:51
JHN 2:13
3:13
5:1
6:3,22,24
7:10[1],10[2],
14
11:55
12:20
20:17[1]
21:3,9,11
ACT 1:11[2],13,
26
2:34
7:23
8:39
10:4,9
11:2
13:31
18:22
ACT 19:19
20:11[1],11[2]
21:2,6,15
24:11
25:1
ROM 10:6
1 CO 2:9
GAL 2:1,2
EPH 4:8,9,10
HEB 4:14
JUD 12
REV 7:2
8:4
9:2
11:12[2]
19:3
20:9

Imperfect

MAT 13:2
14:22
20:17
MRK 4:1
6:45
ACT 8:31
15:2
25:9
REV 14:11
17:8

Imperative

JHN 7:8[1]
REV 4:1
REV 11:12[1]

Active Participle

MAT 17:27
20:18
MRK 4:32
10:32,33
LUK 18:31
24:38
JHN 1:51
JHN 6:62
7:8[2]
10:1
20:17[2]
ACT 3:1
REV 11:7
13:1,11

ᶜPAEL (non occ)

2132 ܣܘܠܩܐ (m) ascension

LUK 9:51

ᵈETHPAAL

Perfect

ACT 1:2,9,11[1],
22
ACT 11:10
1 TM 3:16

ᵉAPHEL

Perfect

MAT 13:48
17:1
MRK 9:2
LUK 2:22
4:5
22:66
ACT 9:39
ACT 16:34
ROM 10:7
HEB 11:17
13:20
JAM 2:21
1 PT 2:24

Imperfect

HEB 13:15

Infinitive

1 PT 2:5

Active Participle

LUK 14:5	HEB 7:25
ACT 22:23	

2186 ܣܡܐ (m) drug, poison

MRK 16:18	JAM 3:8

2192 (ܣܡܝܕ), ܣܡܝܕܐ (m) flour

REV 18:13

2190 ܣܡܝ (v) be blind; (pa) blind

[a]PEAL

Imperfect

JHN 9:39

2191 ܣܡܝܐ (adj) blind

MAT 9:27,28	LUK 6:39,39
11:5	7:21,22
12:22	14:13
15:14,14,	18:35
14,14,	JHN 5:3
30,31	9:1,2,6,13,
20:30	17,18,19,
21:14	20,24,25,
23:16,17,	32,40,41
24	10:21
MRK 8:22,23	11:37
10:46,49,	ACT 13:11
50,51	2 PT 1:9

[c]PAEL

Perfect

1 JN 2:11

2194 ܣܡܟ (v) support, recline to eat; (aph) cause to recline

[a]PEAL

Imperfect

MAT 8:20	LUK 9:58

2193 ܣܡܝܟܐ (pp) steadfast, seated (at meals); (subst) guest

MAT 9:10	LUK 14:10,15
14:6,9	22:27,27
22:10,11	JHN 6:11
26:7,20	12:2
MRK 2:15,15	13:23,28
6:22,26	1 CO 8:10
14:3,18	2 PT 1:12
16:14	2:14
LUK 5:29	3:16
7:37,49	

2195 ܣܡܟܐ (m) pillar, steadfastness

2 PT 3:17

2196 ܣܡܟܐ (m) seat, feast, company

MAT 23:6	LUK 9:14,14
MRK 6:39,39,40,	14:7,8
40	20:46
12:39	JHN 2:8,9,9

[b]ETHPEEL

Perfect

MAT 9:10	LUK 22:14
MRK 6:40	24:30
LUK 7:36	JHN 6:10[2]
11:37	13:12

Imperfect

MAT 8:11	LUK 13:29
15:35	14:8
MRK 8:6	JHN 6:10[1]

Imperative

LUK 14:10[1],10[2]	LUK 17:7

Infinitive

MAT 14:19

[e]APHEL

Perfect

LUK 9:15

Imperfect

MRK 6:39	LUK 12:37

Imperative

LUK 9:14

Imperfect

MAT 6:24 24:10	LUK 16:13 REV 17:16

Imperative

MAT 5:43

Infinitive

JHN 7:7[1]

Active Participle

MAT 5:44 LUK 6:22,27 14:26 19:14 JHN 3:20 7:7[2] 12:25 15:18[1],19, 23[1],23[2] ROM 7:15	ROM 12:9 EPH 5:29 2 TM 3:3 TIT 1:14 3:3 1 JN 2:9,11 3:13,15 4:20 JUD 23 REV 2:6[1],6[2]

2197 ܣܡܠܐ (f) left, left hand

MAT 6:3 20:21,23 25:33,41 27:38 MRK 10:37,40	MRK 15:27 LUK 23:33 ACT 21:3 2 CO 6:7 REV 10:2

2198 ܣܡܩ (v) be red

[a]PEAL

Perfect

MAT 16:2,3

[c]PAEL (non occ)

2133 ܣܘܡܩܐ (adj) red

REV 6:4	REV 17:3

2199 ܣܢ (v-non occ) strain, purge

[a]PEAL

2206 ܣܢܝܢܐ (pp) refined

1 PT 1:7

2200 ܣܢܐ (v) hate

[a]PEAL

Perfect

JHN 15:18[2],24, 25 17:14	ROM 9:13 HEB 1:9

2201 ܣܢܝܐ (pp) hateful, shameful

LUK 23:41 ACT 18:14 28:5,6 ROM 1:30	EPH 4:29 TIT 2:8 3:3 REV 18:2

2202 ܣܢܐܐ (adj) enemy

LUK 1:71

2205 ܣܢܝܐܐ (adj) hated, hateful

MAT 10:22 24:9 MRK 13:13	LUK 21:17 JHN 3:20 TIT 1:16

2204 ܣܢܝܐ (m) bush

MRK 12:26 LUK 6:44	LUK 20:37 ACT 7:30,35

2208 ܣܢܩ (v) need

[a]PEAL

Passive Participle

MAT 3:14 9:12 MRK 2:17 LUK 9:11 JHN 2:25 13:10 16:30	ACT 2:45 4:35 17:25 2 CO 3:1 EPH 4:28 1 TH 4:9 5:1

HEB 5:12[1],12[2]
11:37
1 JN 2:27
1 JN 3:17
REV 3:17

2135 ܣܘܢܩܢܐ (m) need, necessity

MAT 6:11
LUK 11:3
1 CO 12:22

2207 ܣܢܝܩܘܬܐ (f) need, necessity, lack

ACT 20:34
ROM 12:13
2 CO 11:9
PHL 4:19
JAM 2:16

---

[b]ETHPEEL

Perfect

MRK 2:25

Imperfect

1 TH 1:8
1 TH 4:12

2203 (ܣܢܪ), ܣܢܘܪܬܐ (f) helmet

EPH 6:17
1 TH 5:8

2209 ܣܣܐ (c) moth

MAT 6:19,20
LUK 12:33
JAM 5:2

2210 ܣܥܐ (v) intrude into

[a]PEAL

Active Participle

COL 2:18

2212 ܣܥܪ (v) visit, do

[a]PEAL

Perfect

MAT 25:36,43
LUK 1:68
7:16
ROM 15:18
1 CO 5:2
HEB 2:6
9:11

Imperfect

LUK 1:78
13:33
ACT 7:23
15:36
26:9
ROM 7:18
ROM 9:11
2 CO 13:10
EPH 1:9
1 TM 5:21
HEB 13:21

Imperative

PHL 4:9
1 PT 5:2

Infinitive

LUK 22:23
PHL 2:13
JAM 1:27

Active Participle

JHN 6:30
ROM 1:32
7:15,17
13:10
1 CO 5:3
9:17
12:11,29
13:5
2 CO 13:7
GAL 3:5
GAL 5:21
EPH 1:11
6:21
COL 3:17
HEB 4:12
12:7
JAM 2:12
1 JN 3:4,8,22
3 JN 5

Passive Participle

LUK 23:15
ACT 25:25
ACT 26:26

2140 ܣܘܥܪܢܐ (m) deed, visitation

LUK 1:1
19:44
23:51
JHN 8:4
ACT 23:15
ROM 12:4
1 CO 5:2
16:4,9
PHL 1:12
1 TH 4:11
1 TM 6:18
HEB 11:1

2211 ܣܥܘܪܐ (m) overseer

1 PT 2:25

---

[b]ETHPEEL

Imperfect

JAM 3:10

Participle

MAT 14:2
MRK 6:14
EPH 3:20
1 TH 2:13

2213 ܣܥܪ, ܣܥܪܐ (m) hair

MAT 3:4	1 CO 11:14,15, 15
5:36	1 PT 3:3
MRK 1:6	REV 1:14
LUK 7:38,44	6:12
12:7	9:8,8
JHN 11:2	
12:3	

2214 ܣܥܪܬܐ (f) barley

JHN 6:9,13	REV 6:6
1 CO 15:37	

2215 ܣܦܐ (m) porch

MAT 26:71	MRK 14:68

2227 ܣܦܐ, ܣܦܬܐ (f) lip, edge

MAT 15:8	HEB 11:12
MRK 7:6	13:15
LUK 6:45	1 PT 3:10
ROM 3:13	

2216 ܣܦܝܠܐ (f) sapphire

REV 21:19

2217 (ܣܦܢ), ܣܦܝܢܬܐ (f) boat, ship

MAT 8:23	MRK 8:10,13,14
14:22	LUK 5:2,3,7,7, 11
MRK 1:19	8:22,23,37
3:9	JHN 6:17,19,21, 21,22,22
4:1,36,36, 37,38	21:3,6,8
5:2,18,21	2 CO 11:25
6:32,45,47, 51,54	

2220 ܣܦܢܐ (m) sailor

ACT 27:39

2221 ܣܦܣܪܐ (f) sword

MAT 26:47,51, 52,55	ACT 16:27
MRK 14:43	ROM 13:4
JHN 18:10,11	HEB 4:12

2222 ܣܦܩ (v) be sufficient, able

[a]PEAL

Perfect

3 JN 10

Imperfect

MAT 19:12[1],12[2]	ACT 11:17
25:9	1 TM 5:16
LUK 3:14	HEB 13:5

Active Participle

MAT 6:34	2 CO 3:5
10:25	9:8
19:11	12:9
LUK 22:38	PHL 4:11
JHN 6:7	1 TM 6:8
8:37	1 PT 4:3
21:25	

2218 ܣܦܝܩܐ (pp) empty, wanting

MRK 12:3	PHL 4:10

2219 ܣܦܝܩܐܝܬ (adv) empty handed

LUK 1:53

2223 (ܣܦܪ) (v) shave

[c]PAEL

Perfect

ACT 18:18

[d]ETHPAAL

Imperfect

1 CO 11:6[1]

Infinitive

1 CO 11:6[2]

2224 ܣܦܪܐ (m) book, scroll

LUK 4:17,17,20	HEB 9:19
JHN 7:15	REV 3:5
ACT 1:20	17:8
4:13	20:12,12, 12
26:24	
2 TM 3:15	

[a]PEAL (non occ)

2225 ܣܦܪܐ (m) scribe, lawyer

MAT 2:4; 5:20; 7:29; 8:19; 9:3; 12:38; 13:52; 15:1; 16:11,21; 17:10; 20:18; 23:2,13,14, 15,23, 25,27, 29,34; 26:3,57; 27:41
MRK 1:22; 2:6,16; 3:22; 7:1,5; 8:31; 9:11,14,16; 10:33; 11:18,27; 12:13,28,
MRK 12:32,35, 38; 14:1,43,53; 15:1,31
LUK 5:21,30; 6:7; 7:30; 9:22; 10:25; 11:44,45, 46,52, 53; 14:3; 15:2; 19:47; 20:1,19,39, 41,46; 22:2,4,66; 23:10
JHN 8:3
ACT 4:5; 6:12; 23:9
1 CO 1:20
TIT 3:9,13

2226 ܣܦܪܐ (m) shore

MAT 13:2,48 | LUK 6:17

2228 ܣܩܐ (m) sackcloth

MAT 11:21; LUK 10:13 | REV 6:12; 11:3

2233 ܣܪܐ (v) be rotten, stink

[a]PEAL

Perfect

JHN 11:39 | JAM 5:2

2234 ܣܪܓ (v-non occ) weave

[a]PEAL

2243 ܣܪܝܓܬܐ (f) net, basket

2 CO **11:33**

2236 ܣܪܕ (v-non occ) leave alone, be terrified

[a]PEAL

2244 ܣܪܝܕܐ (pp) survivor

ROM 9:29

[c]PAEL

2144 ܣܘܪܕܐ (m) terror

LUK 21:11

2237 ܣܪܕܘܢ (m) sardius

REV 4:3 | REV 21:20,20

2240 ܣܪܚ (v) hurt

[a]PEAL

Perfect

LUK 4:35

2241 ܣܪܛ (v-non occ) trace, draw

[a]PEAL

2242 ܣܪܛܐ (m) scratch, tittle

MAT 5:18

ܣܪܝ see ܣܪܐ

2248 ܣܪܩ (v) make vain

[a]PEAL (non occ)

2245 ܣܪܝܩܐ (pp) vain, empty

MAT 12:44; LUK 20:10,11; ROM 4:14; 1 CO 3:20; 15:10,14, 14,58; GAL 5:26
EPH 5:6; PHL 2:3; COL 2:8; 1 TH 3:5; 2 TH 3:11; 1 TM 1:6; 5:13

1 TM 6:20 | TIT 3:9
2 TM 2:16 | JAM 1:26
TIT 1:10 | 1 PT 1:18

2246 ܣܪܝܩܐܝܬ (adv) vainly

MAT 15:9 | GAL 4:11
MRK 7:7 | PHL 2:16
ROM 13:4 | COL 2:18
1 CO 15:2 | 1 TH 2:1
GAL 2:2 | JAM 4:5

2247 ܣܪܝܩܘܬܐ (f) vanity

ACT 4:25 | EPH 4:17
ROM 1:28 | 2 PT 2:18
8:20

---

[c]PAEL

Perfect

PHL 2:7

Imperfect

1 CO 9:15

---

[d]ETHPAAL

Perfect

ROM 1:21 | REV 18:17
1 TM 1:19

Imperfect

1 CO 1:17 | 2 CO 9:3
2 CO 6:1

2251 ܣܬܘܐ (m) winter, foul weather

MAT 16:3 | JHN 10:22
24:20 | ACT 27:12,20
MRK 13:18 | 2 TM 4:21
LUK 21:11

2250 (ܣܬܐ) (v) winter

[e]APHEL

Perfect

ACT 28:11

Imperfect

ACT 27:12[2] | TIT 3:12
1 CO 16:6

Infinitive

ACT 27:12[1]

2252 ܣܬܪ (v) pull down, destroy

[a]PEAL

Perfect

GAL 2:18

Imperfect

LUK 12:18

Imperative

JHN 2:19

Active Participle

MAT 27:40 | 3 JN 10
2 CO 10:5

---

[b]ETHPEEL

Imperfect

MAT 24:2 | LUK 21:6

Participle

MRK 13:2

ܥ

2288 (ܥܒ), ܥܘܒܐ (m) bosom

LUK 6:38; 16:22,23
JHN 1:18; 13:23

ܥܒܐ see ܥܒ

2255 ܥܒܕ (v) do, make, work; (shaph) subdue, subject

[a]PEAL

Perfect

MAT 1:24; 7:22; 12:3; 13:26,28,58; 17:12; 19:4[1],4[2],12; 20:5,12; 21:6,13,31,36; 22:2; 25:40[1],40[2],45[1],45[2]; 26:10,12,13,19; 27:23; 28:15
MRK 2:25; 5:19,20,32; 6:21,30; 9:13; 10:6; 11:17; 14:6,8,9; 15:1,7[2],14
LUK 1:25,49,51,68,72; 2:48; 4:23[1]; 5:6,29; 6:3; 8:8,39[1],39[2]; 9:10,15,54; 11:40[1],40[2]; 13:9; 14:16; 16:8; 17:9,10[1],10[3]; 19:18,46; 23:22,41[1]
JHN 2:11,15; 4:1,29,39,45,46,54; 5:11,29[1],29[2]; 6:14; 7:21,51; 8:40; 9:11,14,26; 10:41; 11:45,46; 12:2,16,18,37; 13:12,15[1]; 15:24[1],24[2]; 18:35; 19:7,23,24; 20:30; 21:25
ACT 2:22,36; 3:12,17[1],17[2]; 4:7,24; 7:24,36,41,43,50; 9:23; 10:33,39; 12:8; 14:11,15[2],27; 15:4,12,17; 17:5,24[2],26; 20:3; 21:19,33; 23:30; 26:10,24,31
ROM 1:27
2 CO 5:21; 7:9; 12:12,21
EPH 1:20; 2:14,15; 3:11
PHL 4:14
2 TH 3:4[1]
1 TM 1:13
TIT 3:5
HEB 1:2,3,7; 3:2; 7:27; 9:16,17; 11:7,28
JAM 5:11
1 PT 2:22
1 JN 3:1; 5:10
3 JN 10
REV 1:6; 5:10; 14:7; 19:20

Imperfect

MAT 4:19; 5:19; 6:1; 7:12[1]; 17:4; 18:35; 19:16; 20:15,32; 21:21,40; 23:3[2],15[1],23; 27:22
MRK 1:17; 3:35; 6:5; 7:12; 9:5; 10:17,35,36,51; 11:28[2]; 12:9; 14:7; 15:12,15
LUK 2:27; 3:10,11,12,14; 5:34; 6:11,31[1]; 7:4; 9:33; 10:25; 11:42; 12:17,18; 16:3,4; 18:7,8,18,41; 19:48; 20:13,15
JHN 2:16; 4:34; 6:15,28,38[1],38[2]; 7:17; 11:37,47[1]; 13:15[2],17; 14:12[2],12[3],13; 15:14,21; 16:3; 17:4
ACT 2:37; 4:16; 5:4; 13:22; 16:28; 18:21; 19:36; 20:16; 22:10[1],10[2]; 24:27; 25:15; 26:20
ROM 2:14; 3:8; 7:19[1],19[3],21; 9:21,28; 10:5; 12:17,19[1],19[2],20
1 CO 5:8; 6:15,18

1 CO 7:36; 9:18; 10:13; 14:15; 15:29
2 CO 11:12[2]; 13:8
GAL 2:10; 3:10,12; 5:3,16
PHL 2:3
1 TH 5:24
1 TM 4:16; 6:18
HEB 6:3; 10:7,9,36; 13:19,21
JAM 3:12[1]
1 PT 3:11,13
2 PT 1:10[1]
JUD 3[2],15
REV 3:9,12; 11:7; 12:15; 13:12[1],12[2],13[1],13[2],15,16; 17:16,17[1],17[2]; 22:11

Imperative

MAT 3:8; 5:44; 7:12[2]; 8:9[1]; 12:33[1],33[2]; 23:3[1]
LUK 3:8; 4:23[2]; 6:27,31[2]; 7:8[2]; 10:28; 12:33; 15:19; 16:9
JHN 2:5; 6:10; 13:27[2]
ACT 7:40; 21:23
ROM 12:18; 13:3
1 CO 16:1
COL 3:23[2]; 4:1,16
2 TM 4:5
HEB 8:5[2]; 12:13
REV 2:5

Infinitive

MAT 5:36; 7:18[1],18[2]; 9:28; 12:2[2],12
MRK 3:4
LUK 6:2[2],9; 12:4; 17:10[2]
JHN 3:2[1]; 5:30; 6:6; 8:44; 9:4,16,33; 15:5
ACT 1:1; 4:28; 5:35; 7:44; 9:6,24; 16:21,30
2 CO 8:10; 10:6
EPH 3:20
2 TH 3:13
PLM 14
REV 12:17; 13:5,7,14[1],14[2]; 19:19

Active Participle

MAT 3:10; 5:32,46,47[1],47[2]; 6:2[1],2[2],3[1],3[2]; 7:17[1],17[2],19,21,24,26; 8:9[2]; 12:2[1],50; 13:23,41; 21:15,23,24,27,43; 23:3[3],5,15[2]; 24:46; 26:18; 28:14
MRK 2:24; 3:8; 4:32; 6:20; 7:13,37[1],37[2]; 9:39; 11:3,5,28[1],29,33; 15:7[1],8; 16:20
LUK 3:9,19; 6:2[1],23,26,33[1],33[2],43[1],43[2],46,47,49; 7:8[3]; 8:21; 9:43; 10:37; 12:43,48; 13:32; 14:12,13; 20:2,8; 22:19,25; 23:31,32,33,34,39
JHN 2:18,23; 3:2[2],20,21[1]; 5:16,17[1],17[2],19[1],19[2],19[3],19[4],20,27,36; 6:2,30; 7:3,4[1],4[2],31[1],31[2]; 8:28,29,34,38,39,41,53; 9:31; 10:25,33,37,38; 11:47[2]; 13:7,27[1]; 14:10,12[1],14,23,31; 15:15; 18:30; 19:12
ACT 6:8; 8:6; 9:36; 10:2; 13:41; 14:3,15[1],17; 15:3; 16:16,18; 17:24[1]; 19:11,14,18,24[1],24[2]; 21:13,38; 22:26; 25:3
ROM 1:28,32[1],32[2]; 3:12; 7:15[1],15[2],16,19[2],19[4],20[1],20[2]; 13:4[1],4[2]; 16:17
1 CO 7:37,38[1],38[2]; 9:23,25; 10:31[1],31[2]; 11:24,25; 12:23,28; 14:7
2 CO 2:14; 7:10[1],10[2]; 9:1; 11:12[1]
GAL 5:17; 6:9
EPH 2:3; 5:12; 6:6,8,9
PHL 2:14
COL 3:17,23[1]
1 TH 4:10; 5:11
2 TH 1:8; 3:4[2]
1 TM 1:4
2 TM 2:9
PLM 21
HEB 8:5[1]; 9:25; 13:6,17
JAM 1:20; 2:8,9,13,19; 3:18; 4:2,13,15,17
1 PT 2:11,14,20; 3:17[1],17[2]; 4:11,15
2 PT 1:10[2],15,19
1 JN 1:10; 2:17,29; 3:4,7,9,10; 5:2
3 JN 5,6,11[1],11[2]
JUD 3[1]
REV 16:14; 21:5,27; 22:2,14,15

Passive Participle

MAT 4:24; 8:16; 9:12; 14:35; 17:15
MRK 1:32,34

MRK 2:17
5:23
6:55
14:58[1],58[2]
LUK 5:31
7:2
23:41[2]
JHN 3:21[2]
ACT 15:36
25:11
2 CO 1:11
5:10
1 TH 2:15
HEB 8:6
9:11,24
12:27
JAM 3:9
5:15
1 PT 2:16
2 PT 1:16

2256 ܥܒܕܐ (m) servant

MAT 8:9
10:24,25
12:18
13:27,28
14:2
18:23,26,27,28,32
20:27
21:34,35,36
22:3,4,6,8,10
24:45,46,48,50
25:14,19,21,23,26,30
26:51
MRK 10:44
12:2,4,5
13:34
14:47
LUK 1:54,69
2:29
7:2,3,8,10
12:37,38,43,45,45,46,47
14:17,21,21,22,23
15:22
16:13
17:7,9,10
19:13,15,17,22
20:10,11
22:50
JHN 4:46,49,51
8:34,35
13:16
15:15,15,
JHN 15:20
18:10,10,18,26
ACT 2:18
4:25,29
16:17
ROM 1:1
6:16,17,20,22
7:25,25
9:12
14:4
1 CO 7:21,22,22,23
12:13
2 CO 4:5
GAL 1:10
3:28
4:1,7
EPH 6:5,6,8,9
PHL 1:1
2:7
COL 3:11,22
4:1,12
2 TM 2:24
TIT 1:1
2:9
PLM 16,16
HEB 3:5
JAM 1:1
1 PT 2:16,18
2 PT 1:1
2:19
JUD 1
REV 1:1,1
2:20
6:15
7:3
10:7
11:18
13:16
15:3
19:2,5,18
22:3,6

2257 ܥܒܕܐ (m) deed, work

MAT 5:9,16
11:2,19
16:27
23:3,5
MAT 26:10
MRK 13:34
14:6
LUK 11:48
LUK 24:19
JHN 3:19,20,21
4:34
5:20,36,36
6:28,29
7:3,7,21
8:39,41
9:3,4
10:25,32,32,33,37,38
14:10,11,12
15:24
17:4
ACT 5:38
7:22,41,48
9:36
13:2,41
14:26
15:18
26:20
ROM 2:6,7,15
3:20,27,28
4:2,6
9:11,32
11:6,6,6,6
13:3,12
14:20
15:18
1 CO 3:13,13,14,15
9:1
15:58
16:10
2 CO 5:1
8:11,11
9:8
10:11
11:15
GAL 2:16,16,16
3:2,5,10
5:19
6:4
EPH 2:3,9,10,11
4:12
5:11
PHL 1:6,22
2:30
4:8
COL 1:10,21
3:17
1 TH 1:3
2:9,13
5:13
2 TH 1:11
2:17
1 TM 2:10
3:1
5:10,10,25
6:18
2 TM 1:9
2:21
3:17
4:5,14,18
TIT 1:16,16
2:7,14
3:1,5,8,14
PLM 6
HEB 1:10
2:7
3:9
4:3,4,10
6:1,10
9:14
10:24
13:21
JAM 1:4,25,25
2:14,17,18,18,18,20,21,22,22,24,25,26
3:13
1 PT 1:17,18
2:12,15
3:6,17
4:19
2 PT 1:10
2:8
3:10
1 JN 3:8,12,18
2 JN 11
3 JN 10
JUD 15
REV 2:2,5,6,19,19,22,23,26
3:1,2,8,15
9:20
15:3,3
16:11
18:6
20:12,13
22:12

2259 ܥܒܕܘܬܐ (f) service, bondage

LUK 15:29
JHN 8:33
ACT 7:7
ROM 6:16,19,19
8:15,21
GAL 4:24,25
5:1
1 TM 6:1
HEB 2:15

2260 ܥܒܘܕܐ (adj) doer, maker

ROM 2:13	JAM 1:22,23,25
HEB 11:10	4:11

[b]ETHPEEL

Perfect

HEB 9:2

Imperfect

JAM 3:12[2]

Participle

ACT 19:26

[e]APHEL

Perfect

2 CO 7:11

Active Participle

1 CO 12:6

Passive Participle

JHN 4:4

1807 ܡܥܒܕܢܐ (adj) worker, activator

ROM 4:15

1808 ܡܥܒܕܢܘܬܐ (f) operation, working

EPH 1:19	2 TH 2:9,11
3:7	

[g]SHAPHEL

Perfect

ROM 8:20[2]	1 CO 15:28[3]
1 CO 9:19	EPH 1:22
15:27[1],27[3],	HEB 2:5,8[1],8[2]

Imperfect

ACT 7:6	JAM 3:2
GAL 2:4	

Active Participle

1 CO 9:27	2 CO 11:20

Passive Participle

LUK 7:8[1]	TIT 2:3
1 CO 7:15	3:3
GAL 4:3	HEB 2:8[3],8[4],15
2 TM 3:3	2 PT 2:19

3145 ܫܘܥܒܕܐ (m) subjection

GAL 2:5	1 TM 3:4
1 TM 2:11	TIT 1:6

[h]ESHTAPHAL

Perfect

ROM 6:18	2 CO 9:13
8:20[1]	PHL 3:21
10:3	1 PT 3:22
1 CO 15:28[1]	

Imperfect

ROM 13:1,5	TIT 2:9
1 CO 14:34	3:1
15:28[2]	HEB 12:9
COL 2:18	JAM 3:3

Imperative

COL 3:18	1 PT 3:1
JAM 4:7	5:5
1 PT 2:18	

Infinitive

GAL 4:9

Participle

LUK 2:51	EPH 5:21,22,24
10:17,20	TIT 1:10
ROM 8:7	2:5
1 CO 14:32	JAM 3:7
15:27[2]	1 PT 2:13
GAL 5:13	3:5,6

2262 ܥܒܐ (v) thicken, harden

[c]PAEL

Passive Participle

MRK 6:52

[d]ETHPAAL

Perfect

MAT 13:15	ACT 28:27

2261 (ܥܒܪ), ܥܒܘܪܐ (m) crop

LUK 12:18 | ACT 7:12

2264 ܥܒܪ (v) cross over; (w/ ܥܠ) transgress; (w/ ܡܢ) turn away from; (aph) pass over

[a]PEAL

Perfect

MAT 4:21; 9:1,9,27; 14:15
MRK 1:19; 5:21; 6:53; 16:1
LUK 4:30; 10:31,32; 15:29; 19:1
JHN 8:59
ACT 12:10[1],10[2]; 17:1; 27:5,9,16
ROM 5:12; 13:12
1 CO 7:36; 10:1; 16:5[1]
2 CO 5:17
1 TM 2:14
HEB 2:2; 9:15; 10:28; 11:29
JAM 1:24
1 PT 4:3
1 JN 2:8

Imperfect

MAT 5:18[1],18[2]; 8:28; 24:34,35[1],35[2]; 26:39,42
MRK 4:35; 6:48; 13:30,31[1],31[2]; 14:35
LUK 2:35; 8:22; 12:37; 16:17[1],17[2],26[1],26[2]; 19:4; 21:32,33[1],33[2]; 22:42
JHN 4:4
ACT 20:16; 27:43
ROM 2:25
2 CO 1:16
HEB 1:11
1 PT 3:11

Imperative

LUK 17:7

Infinitive

1 TH 4:6

Active Participle

MAT 15:2,3; 20:30; 27:39
MRK 2:14; 9:30; 11:20; 15:21,29
LUK 11:42; 17:11; 18:36,37
JHN 9:1
ACT 5:38; 23:3
ROM 2:23,27; 15:28
1 CO 7:31; 16:5[2],7
GAL 2:18
1 TM 1:10; 3:3
TIT 1:7
HEB 7:24; 10:34
JAM 1:10; 2:9,11
2 PT 3:10
1 JN 2:17
2 JN 9

2265 ܥܒܪܐ (m) transgression

ROM 4:15 | ROM 5:14

2266 ܥܒܪܐ (m) crossing

MAT 4:15,25; 8:18,28; 12:42; 14:22; 16:5; 19:1
MRK 3:8; 4:35; 5:1,21; 6:45,53; 8:13; 10:1
LUK 8:22,26; 11:31
JHN 1:28; 3:26; 6:1,17,22,25; 10:40; 18:1

[b]ETHPEEL (non occ)

1944 ܡܬܥܒܪܢܘܬܐ (f) transgression

2 PT 2:16

[e]APHEL

Perfect

ACT 17:30 | ACT 27:44

Imperfect

MRK 11:16

Imperative

MRK 14:36

2268 ܥܒܪܝܐ (adj) Hebrew

ACT 6:1
2 CO 11:22
PHL 3:5,5

2267 ܥܒܪܐܝܬ (adv) Hebraically

LUK 23:38
JHN 5:2; 19:13,17,20; 20:16
ACT 21:40; 22:2; 26:14
REV 9:11; 16:16

2271 ܥܓܠܐ (m) calf

ACT 7:41; HEB 9:12,13 | REV 4:7

2270 ܥܓܠ (adv) quickly

MAT 5:25; 13:21; 28:7,8; MRK 4:17; 9:39; LUK 14:21; 16:6; 18:8; JHN 11:29,31; 13:27; ACT 12:7; 17:15; ROM 16:20 | 1 CO 4:19; GAL 1:6; PHL 2:19,23,24; 2 TH 2:2; 1 TM 3:14; 5:22; 2 TM 4:9; HEB 13:19,23; 2 PT 1:14; 3 JN 14; REV 1:1; 22:6,7,20

2272 ܥܓܠܬܐ (f) heifer

HEB 9:13,19

2269 (ܥܓܠ) (v) roll

cPAEL

Perfect

MAT 27:60; 28:2 | MRK 15:46; 16:3

Passive Participle

MRK 16:4 | LUK 24:2

kP (non occ) ܥܪܓܠ

2315 ܥܘܪܓܠܐ (m) rolling, wallowing

2 PT 2:22

2273 ܥܓ (v) cast down

cPAEL

Perfect

2 PT 2:4

2274 ܥܕ (adv) while, as

see below 2278 ܥܕܠܐ

MAT 1:18; 5:25; 6:8; 14:22; 17:5; 26:36,47 MRK 5:35; 6:45; 14:32,43 LUK 1:15; 4:13; 8:49; 12:58; 13:8; 14:32; 15:20; 19:13; 24:1 JHN 5:7; 9:4; 12:35,36; 14:29; 18:28; 20:1 ROM 9:11 1 CO 15:17 GAL 2:12; 3:23; 6:10 1 TM 4:13 REV 6:11

2278 ܥܕܠܐ (adv) before

from 2274 ܥܕ (above) and 1511 ܠܐ

JHN 1:48; 4:49; 8:58 ACT 2:20; 5:4; 7:2; 23:15

2275 ܥܕܐ (v) take, happen; (aph) sieze

aPEAL

Active Participle

LUK 9:39; ACT 20:19 | 1 PT 1:6

eAPHEL

Perfect

ACT 24:7

2276 ܥܕܟܠ (adv) yet, still

MAT 24:6 MRK 8:17; 13:7 LUK 21:9; 23:53 JHN 2:4; 3:24; 7:8,30,39,39; 8:20, 57; 11:30; 19:41; 20:9,17 ACT 8:16; 9:1 1 CO 3:2,3; 8:2 GAL 5:11 HEB 2:8; 7:10; 9:8; 12:4 REV 17:10,12

2277 ܥܕܠ (v) (pe, ethpa) find fault, complain

aPEAL

Active Participle

JUD 16

2279 ܥܕܠܬܐ (m) blame; (w/ ܕܠܐ) blameless

MAT 12:5,7; 19:10 | LUK 1:6

[d]ETHPAAL

Perfect

MRK 7:2

2280 ܥܕܡܐ (adv, prep) until

MAT 1:17,17,17,25; 2:9,13,15; 5:18,18,26; 10:11,22,23; 11:12,13,23,23,23; 12:20; 13:30,33; 15:16; 16:9,28; 17:9,17,17; 18:21, 22,22,30,34; 20:8; 22:26,44; 23:35,39; 24:13, 21,27,31,34,38,39; 26:29,38,58; 27:8,45,51, 64; 28:15,20 MRK 3:10; 6:10,23; 8:17,21; 9:1,19,19; 12:36; 13:13,19,27,30; 14:25,34, 54; 15:33,38 LUK 1:20,80; 2:15,26; 4:29, 42; 9:27,41; 10:15,15; 11:51; 12:50,59; 13:21,35; 15:4,8; 16:16; 17:8,27; 20:43; 21:24,32; 22:16,34,51; 23:5,44; 24:41,49,50 JHN 2:7,10; 5:17; 7:6; 9:18; 10:24; 13:1,38; 16:24; 21:22,23 ACT 1:2,8,22; 2:15,29,35; 3:21; 7:18,45; 8:40; 10:30; 11:5,19; 12:10; 13:4,6,11,20,47; 17:15; 19:10; 20:4,7,11,38; 21:3,5,26; 22:4,22; 23:1,12,14,21; 25:16,21; 26:22; 27:9,33; 28:15,15,23 ROM 1:13; 5:13,14; 8:22; 11:8,25; 15:19 1 CO 1:8; 4:5,11,13; 5:1; 8:7; 11:26; 15:6,25; 16:8 2 CO 1:8,13; 3:14,15; 10:13,14; 12:2 GAL 1:10; 3:19; 4:2,19 EPH 4:13 PHL 1:5,6; 2:8,27,30 1 TH 2:16; 3:5 1 TM 6:14 2 TM 2:9 HEB 1:13; 3:6,13, 14; 4:12; 6:11; 8:11; 9:10; 10:13; 12:4 JAM 5:7,7 2 PT 1:19 1 JN 2:9; 3:2 REV 2:10,25; 6:10,11; 7:3; 12:11; 14:20; 15:8; 17:17; 18:5

2281 ܥܕܢ, ܥܕܢܐ (m) moment, season, time

see also 1432 ܟܠ ܥܕܢ

MAT 14:15	JHN 16:4
MRK 6:35,35	ACT 3:1
11:11	5:21,34
15:44	28:6
LUK 1:10	1 TH 5:1
4:5	REV 6:11
14:17	12:14,14, 14
22:14	
JHN 4:52	

2283 ܥܕܪ (v) help, be of profit

[a]PEAL

Active Participle

1 CO 12:7	1 PT 3:17

2292 ܥܘܕܪܢܐ (m) help, profit

1 CO 7:35	HEB 11:40
HEB 4:16	12:10

[c]PAEL

Perfect

LUK 1:54	2 CO 6:2
ACT 18:27	COL 4:11
26:22	REV 12:16

Imperfect

LUK 5:7	HEB 2:18

Imperative

MAT 15:25	ACT 16:9
MRK 9:22,24	21:28

Active Participle

MRK 16:20	1 CO 16:16
LUK 10:40	2 CO 8:10
ROM 8:26,28	PHL 4:3

1810 ܡܥܕܪܢܐ (m) help, helper

1 CO 12:28	PHL 4:3
2 CO 1:24	1 TH 3:2
6:1	PLM 24
8:23	HEB 13:6
PHL 2:25	3 JN 8

1811 ܡܥܕܪܢܘܬܐ (f) help, aid

2 CO 1:11	COL 1:29

[d]ETHPAAL

Perfect

MRK 5:26	HEB 13:9

Imperfect

MRK 8:36	LUK 9:25

2285 ܥܗܕ (v) remember; (aph) cause to remember

[a]PEAL

Perfect

LUK 1:72	HEB 11:22
HEB 2:6	

Imperfect

JHN 16:4; 2 TM 2:26 | 3 JN 10

Imperative

LUK 24:6; JHN 15:20 | HEB 13:3; 1 PT 5:8

Infinitive

EPH 1:16

Active Participle

MAT 16:9; MRK 8:18; JHN 16:21; ACT 20:31; 1 CO 15:2; GAL 2:10 | EPH 2:11; COL 4:18; 1 TH 1:3; 2:9; 2 TH 2:5; HEB 13:7

2286 ܥܗܝܕܐ (adj) mindful

1 CO 11:2

2293 ܥܘܗܕܢܐ (m) remembrance

PHL 1:3; 1 TH 3:6; 2 TM 1:5 | 2 PT 1:13,15; 3:1

---

cPAEL

Infinitive

ACT 20:35

---

dETHPAAL

Imperfect

2 PT 3:2

---

eAPHEL

Imperfect

JHN 14:26; ROM 15:15 | 1 CO 4:17

Infinitive

JUD 5

Active Participle

1 CO 11:26; 2 TM 1:6; 2:14 | TIT 3:1; 2 PT 1:12

2287 ܥܗܢ (v) be convenient, suitable

aPEAL

Active Participle

ACT 27:12; PHL 1:10 | 2 TM 2:21; 4:11

2254 (ܥܘܒ), ܥܒܐ (m) forest

JAM 3:5,6

2253 (ܥܘܕ), ܥܐܕܐ (m) feast

MAT 27:15; MRK 15:6; JHN 10:22 | JHN 13:1; ACT 18:21; COL 2:16

2282 ܥܕܥܕܐ (m) feast, festival

MAT 26:5; MRK 14:2; LUK 2:41,42; 22:1; 23:17; JHN 2:23; 4:45,45; 5:1 | JHN 6:4; 7:2,8,8,10, 11,14,37; 11:55,56; 12:12,20; 13:29; 1 CO 5:8

2284 (ܥܘܕ), ܥܕܬܐ (f) church, assembly

MAT 16:18; 18:17,17; ACT 2:47; 5:11; 8:1,3; 9:31; 11:22,26; 12:1,5; 13:1; 14:23,27; 15:3,4,22, 41; 16:5; 18:22; 20:17,28; ROM 16:1,4,5, 16,23; 1 CO 1:2; 4:17; 6:4; 7:17; 10:32; 11:16,18, 22; 12:28; 14:4,5,12, | 1 CO 14:19,23, 28,33, 34,35; 15:9; 16:1,19,19; 2 CO 1:1; 8:1,18,19, 23,24; 11:8,28; 12:13; GAL 1:2,13,22; EPH 1:22; 3:10,21; 5:23,24,25, 27,29,32; PHL 3:6; 4:15; COL 1:18,24; 4:15,16; 1 TH 1:1; 2:14; 2 TH 1:1,4; 1 TM 3:5,15; 5:16; PLM 2; HEB 2:12

HEB	12:23	REV	2:1,7,8,11, 12,17,18, 23,29
JAM	5:14		3:1,6,7,13, 14,22
1 PT	5:13		22:16
3 JN	6,9,10,12		
REV	1:4,11,20, 20		

2290 ܥܘܕ (adv-non occ) it is certain

2336 ܥܝܕܐ (m) custom, manner

LUK	1:9	ACT	15:1
	22:7		16:21
	23:17		21:21
JHN	18:39		25:16
	19:40	1 CO	11:16
ACT	6:14	HEB	10:25

2291 (ܥܘܕ) (v-non occ) habituate

[e]APHEL

1809 ܡܥܝܕܐ (adj) accustomed

MAT	27:15	LUK	4:16
MRK	10:1		22:39
	15:6,8	ACT	3:2
LUK	2:42		17:2

2295 ܥܘ̈ܙܝܐ (m) thorns

MAT 27:29

2298 (ܥܘܩ) (v) hinder

[c]PAEL

Perfect

1 TH 2:18

2300 ܥܘܠܐ (m) baby

LUK	1:41,44	LUK	2:12,16

2338 ܥܝܠܐ (m) colt

MAT	21:2,5,7,7	LUK	19:33,35
MRK	11:2,4,5,7	JHN	12:15
LUK	19:30,33,		

2302 ܥܘܠܐ (m) iniquity, unrighteousness

MAT	7:23	1 CO	13:6
	13:41	2 CO	6:14
	23:25,28	2 TH	2:7,10,12
	24:12	2 TM	2:19
LUK	16:8,9,11	TIT	2:14
	18:6	HEB	1:9
JHN	7:18		8:12
ACT	8:23		10:17
ROM	1:18,18	1 PT	2:19
	2:8	2 PT	2:13,13,15
	3:5	1 JN	1:9
	4:7		3:4,4
	6:13,19		5:17
	9:14	REV	18:5
	11:26		

2301 ܥܘܠܐ (adj) unjust, unrighteous

MAT	5:45	1 CO	6:1,9
MRK	15:28	2 TH	2:8
LUK	16:10,10	1 TM	1:9
	22:37	HEB	6:10
ACT	24:15	2 PT	2:9
ROM	3:5	REV	21:8

2303 ܥܘܠܬܐ (f) unrighteousness

ROM 1:29

2299 (ܥܘܠ) (v) (aph) wrong

[e]APHEL

Perfect

2 CO 7:2

Imperfect

REV 22:11[2]

Active Participle

MAT	20:13	REV	22:11[1]

2307 (ܥܘܦ) (v) be tired, faint

[a]PEAL

Imperfect

MAT 15:32

Active Participle

MRK 8:3

2308 (ܥܦܦ)(v) double

cf ܥܦ

[a]PEAL

Imperative

REV 18:6

240 ܐܥܦܝܦܐܝܬ (adv) doubly

2 CO 1:15

2310 (ܥܘܩ)(v) grieve, discourage

[a]PEAL (non occ)

2423 ܥܩܬܐ (f) sorrow, distress

LUK 22:45	1 TH 3:7
ACT 27:22	JAM 4:9
PHL 2:27,27	1 PT 2:19

[c]PAEL (non occ)

2337 ܥܝܩܐ (adj) grieved

MRK 10:22

[e]APHEL

Active Participle

ROM 14:15 | EPH 4:30

Passive Participle

PHL 2:26

[f]ETTAPHAL

Perfect

2 CO 7:11

Imperfect

COL 3:21

Infinitive

MAT 26:37 | MRK 14:33

Participle

MRK 14:19 | 1 PT 1:6

ܥܘܪ see ܥܝܪ

2314 ܥܘܪܐ (adj-non occ) blind

2296 ܥܘܝܪܐ (adj) blind

MAT 12:22	LUK 14:21
23:19,26	ROM 2:19
LUK 4:18	

2297 ܥܘܝܪܘܬܐ (f) blindness

ROM 11:25 | EPH 4:18

2313 (ܥܘܪ) (v) blind

[c]PAEL

Perfect

JHN 12:40 | 2 CO 4:4

[d]ETHPAAL

Perfect

ROM 11:7 | 2 CO 3:14

2321 ܥܫܢ (v) gain force; (ethpa) be touched, groan

[a]PEAL (non occ)

2324 ܥܫܝܢܐ (adj) mighty

ACT 2:2 | JUD 13

2325 ܥܫܝܢܐܝܬ (adv) vehemently

LUK 23:10

[d]ETHPAAL

Perfect

JHN 11:33 | JHN 13:21

Participle

JHN 11:38

2326 ܥܙܠ (v) spin; (ethp) entangle

aPEAL

Active Participle

MAT 6:28 | LUK 12:27

mETHP ܐܬܥܙܠ

Participle

2 PT 2:20

2327 ܥܙܩܬܐ (f) ring

LUK 15:22 | JAM 2:2

2328 (ܥܙܪ), ܥܙܪܘܪܐ (m) swaddling clothes

LUK 2:7,12

2329 ܥܛܐ (v) blot out, hide

aPEAL

Perfect

COL 2:14

Active Participle

JAM 5:20

bETHPEEL

Imperfect

ACT 3:19

2331 ܥܛܠ, ܥܛܠܐ (adj) stubborn, difficult

MAT 19:23
MRK 7:18
10:23,24
LUK 1:37
18:24

2332 ܥܛܡܐ (f) thigh

REV 19:16

2333 ܥܛܦ (v) turn; (pa) clothe

aPEAL

Perfect

REV 1:12

2330 ܥܛܝܦܐ (pp) clothed

MRK 14:51
16:5
REV 4:4
REV 7:13
11:3
12:1

cPAEL

Passive Participle

REV 7:9
10:1
17:4
REV 18:16
19:13

dETHPAAL

Imperfect

REV 19:8

Imperative

ACT 12:8 | 1 PT 5:5

Infinitive

REV 3:18

Participle

REV 3:5

2334 ܥܛܪ (v-non occ) rise up (vapor)

aPEAL

2335 ܥܛܪܐ (m) vapor

ACT 2:19 | REV 8:4

2341 ܥܝܢ, ܥܝܢܐ (f) eye

see also 2339 ܥܝܢ ܟܠܐ

MAT 5:29,38,38
6:22,22,23
7:3,3,4,4,5,
5
9:29,30
13:15,15,
16
MAT 17:8,9
18:9,9,9
20:15,33,
34,34
21:42
26:43
27:24

MRK 2:12
7:22
8:18,23,25
9:2,47,47,47
12:11
14:40
LUK 2:30
4:20
5:25
6:20,41,41,42,42,42,42
8:47
10:23
11:34,34
16:23
18:13
19:42
23:14
24:11,16,31,43
JHN 4:35
6:5
9:6,10,11,14,15,17,21,26,30,32
10:21
11:37,41
12:40,40
15:24
17:1
ACT 1:9
9:8,12,17,18,18,40

ACT 16:37
22:13,13
26:18
28:27,27
ROM 3:18
11:8,10
1 CO 2:9
12:16,17,21
15:52
GAL 2:14
3:1
4:15
EPH 1:18
6:6
COL 3:22
HEB 4:13
1 PT 3:12
2 PT 2:14
1 JN 1:1
2:11,16
REV 1:7,14
2:18
4:6,8
5:6
7:3,17,17
8:10
9:4
13:16
14:1,7,9
16:4
17:5
19:12
20:4
21:4,6
22:4

1813 ܡܒܘܥܐ (f) source, well

MRK 5:29
JHN 4:6,6,14
2 PT 2:17

2343 ܥܝܪ (v) be awake; (aph) wake up; (ettaph) watch

aPEAL (non occ)

2344 ܥܝܪܐ (pp) awake, vigilant

MRK 13:34,37
LUK 12:37
ACT 20:31
COL 4:2
1 TH 5:6,8,10
1 TM 3:2,11
2 TM 4:5
TIT 2:2
REV 3:2
16:15

---

eAPHEL

Perfect

MAT 8:25
LUK 8:24

Imperfect

JHN 11:11
2 TM 1:6
2 PT 1:13

Imperative

1 CO 15:34

Active Participle

ACT 24:5
2 PT 3:1

---

fETTAPHAL

Perfect

LUK 9:32
ACT 16:27

Imperfect

ROM 13:11
REV 3:3

Imperative

MAT 24:42
25:13
26:41
MRK 13:33,35
14:34,38
1 CO 16:13
EPH 5:14
1 PT 1:13
4:7
5:8

Infinitive

MRK 14:37

Participle

MAT 24:43
LUK 12:39

2346 ܥܠ (v) enter; (aph) bring

aPEAL

Perfect

MAT 2:11
8:5,32
9:25
12:4
17:25
21:10,12
22:11,12
24:38
25:10
26:58
27:53
MRK 1:21
2:1,26
3:1
5:13,39,40
6:22,25
7:17,24
9:28,33
MRK 11:11,15
15:43
16:5
LUK 1:9,28,40
4:16,38
6:4,6
7:1,36,44,45
8:33
9:34,46,52
10:38
11:37,52[1]
14:1
17:27
19:1,45
22:3
24:3,29
JHN 4:8,38

JHN	9:21	ACT	21:8,11,18,26,29
	18:1,15,28,33		22:11
	19:9		23:16
	20:5[2],6,8		25:23
ACT	1:13,21		27:2
	3:8		28:8,16
	5:7,10,21	ROM	5:12
	9:12	GAL	2:4
	10:3,24,27	HEB	4:6[2],10
	11:3,8,12,20		6:20
	12:17		7:19
	13:5,14		9:11,12[1],12[2],24[1],24[2]
	14:1,20		11:29,36
	16:29,36,40	JAM	5:4
	17:2	1 PT	3:20
	18:7,19	REV	11:11
	20:18		

Imperfect

MAT	5:20	LUK	14:23
	8:8		16:16
	10:5		18:17,24,25
	12:29		21:21
	18:3,8,9		22:40,46
	19:17,23,24[2]		24:26
	26:41	JHN	3:5
MRK	1:45		10:9[1],9[2]
	3:27	ACT	19:30,31
	5:12		20:29
	8:26	ROM	11:25
	9:25,43,45,47	1 CO	14:23,24
	10:15,23,24,25[1]	HEB	3:11,18
	13:15		4:3[2],5,6[1],11
	14:38	JAM	1:2
LUK	7:6		2:2[1],2[2]
	8:32,41,51	REV	3:20
			22:14

Imperative

MAT	6:6	MAT	25:21,23
	7:13	ACT	9:6

Infinitive

MAT	19:24[1]	JHN	20:5[1]
	23:14[3]	ACT	14:22
MRK	10:25[2]		21:37
LUK	13:24[1],24[2]	HEB	3:19
	15:28		4:1
	17:12	REV	15:8
JHN	3:4		

Active Participle

MAT	7:21	MRK	4:19
	10:11,12		6:10,56
	12:45		7:15,18,19
	15:11,17		11:2
	23:14[1],14[2]		14:14

LUK	8:16	ACT	3:2,3
	9:4		8:3
	10:5,8,10		9:28
	11:26,33,52[2]		10:25
	19:30		17:10
	22:10,11	HEB	4:3[1],12
JHN	10:1,2		6:19
	19:42		9:6,7,25
			10:5

Passive Participle

LUK 8:30

1814 ܡܥܠܢܐ (m) entrance

ROM	5:20	1 TH	2:1
1 TH	1:9	HEB	10:19

1816 ܡܥܠܬܐ (f) entrance

HEB	4:1	2 PT	1:11

2358 ܥܠܠܬܐ (f) harvest, ingathering

LUK	12:16,17	1 CO	9:10

2364 ܥܠܬܐ (f) cause, occasion

MAT	19:3	ACT	19:40
	23:13		22:24
	27:37		23:28,29
MRK	12:40		27:30
	15:26	ROM	7:8,11
LUK	8:47	2 CO	5:12
	20:47		6:3
	23:4,14,22		11:12,12
JHN	15:22	GAL	5:13
	18:38	PHL	1:18
	19:4,6	1 TH	2:5
ACT	4:21	1 TM	5:14
	10:21	HEB	5:9
	13:28		

---

[d]ETHPAAL

Perfect

JHN 13:27

---

[e]APHEL

Perfect

LUK	12:16	ACT	16:24
JHN	18:16		21:28
ACT	7:45[2]		23:18
	9:8	1 TM	6:7,10
	10:23	HEB	2:10

Imperfect

MAT 6:13	ACT 10:22
LUK 5:18,19	22:24
11:4	23:10

Imperative

LUK 14:21

Infinitive

ACT 7:45[1]

Active Participle

LUK 2:27	2 PT 1:5
HEB 1:6	2:1
13:11	

1815 ܡܥܠܢܘܬܐ (f) entrance

JUD 4

2362 (ܥܠ), ܥܠܥܠ (v-non occ) toss, shake

2363 ܥܠܥܠܐ (f) sudden storm, gust

MRK 4:37	ACT 27:14
LUK 8:23	2 PT 2:17

ܥܠܐ see under ܥܠܘܐ

2349 ܥܠܒ (v) take advantage, defraud

[a]PEAL

Perfect

2 CO 7:2

Imperfect

2 CO 2:11

Infinitive

1 TH 4:6

Active Participle

1 CO 6:8

2351 ܥܠܘܒܐ (adj) unjust, covetous

LUK 18:11	1 CO 6:10
1 CO 5:10,11	EPH 5:5

2352 ܥܠܘܒܘܬܐ (f) injustice, covetousness

MRK 7:22	COL 3:5
ROM 1:29	2 PT 2:3,14
EPH 5:3	

---

[d]ETHPAAL

Participle

1 CO 6:7

2350 ܥܠܘܐ (m-non occ) waking state

2347 ܥܠ (prep) on, about, concerning

MAT 2:8,9,18; 3:4,10,16; 4:5,6,6,13,1
5:7,11,14,15,22,23,23,39,44,45,45,45,
45; 6:27,28; 7:24,25,26,28; 8:32; 9:12,
16,18,24,27,32,36; 10:1,13,13,21,27,2
35,35,35; 11:7,10,29; 12:14,18,25,25,
26,28,31,32,32; 13:1,2,4,5,19,20,23;
14:14,19,25,26,28,29; 15:2,3,7,22,29,
32,35; 16:11,13,18; 17:5,6,13,14,15;
18:10,16,19,26,29,29; 19:13,15,28,28;
20:11,24,25,30,30,31,34; 21:1,5,5,7,7,
25,44,44,45; 22:31,42; 23:2,4,15,18,20
22,31,35,35,36; 24:2,3,7,7,30,36,36,45
47; 25:20,21,21,22,23,23,27,31; 26:4,7
7,12,24,39,50,50,55,59,62,64; 27:1,13,
14,19,25,25,27,29,30,37,39,43,45,51,
60; 28:2 MRK 1:10,30,33,40,41;
2:17,21; 3:5,6,10,24,25,26,29; 4:1,1,1,4
5,8,15,16,21,31,38; 5:12,16,19,21,21,
23,27,40; 6:5,7,14,20,25,34,39,47,48,
49; 7:6,17,32; 8:2,6,7,25,27,29,30; 9:7,
12,13,20,22,36,38,39; 10:10,16,16,17,
24,24,41,42,46,47,48; 11:1,4,7,7,25;
12:12,26; 13:2,8,8,12,29,32,32; 14:3,3,
21,35,46,48,48,55,56,57,60,62,65; 15:4
19,19,24,29,33,38,46; 16:18
LUK 1:12,17,20,21,33,35,50,65; 2:8,9,
14,17,17,18,20,25,28,33,33,38,40; 3:2,
9,13,15,19,19,20,22; 4:9,10,11,14,18,
29,37,39,40,43; 5:1,1,2,5,9,12,15,36;
6:20,26,28,29,35,35,48,48,49; 7:2,3,13,
17,24,27; 8:5,6,12,13,16,52,53; 9:1,5,9,
11,11,18,31,34,38,39,43,45,45,49,62;
10:6,6,9,11,30,33,34,34,34,37,41;
11:17,17,18,20,22,33,42,42,44; 12:3,10
10,14,25,26,42,44,52,52,53,53,53,53,
53,53; 13:1,4,13,14; 14:6,7,10,31,32;
15:5,7,7,10,20,20,29; 16:2,24; 17:13,16
18:7,8,9,9,13,31,35,38,39; 19:7,14,17,
19,23,27,29,30,35,35,37,41,44; 20:1,18
18,19,19,26,40,41; 21:5,6,10,10,12,23,
26,34,35,35; 22:19,20,21,25,30,30,32,
37,44,52,52,52,53,64,65; 23:2,4,8,26,
27,28,28,28,30,34,38,39,44,48; 24:4,4,
12,14,19,23,27,38,44,49 JHN 1:7,8,

15,22,30,32,33,45,47,50; 2:7,21,25; 3:23,25,26,31,31,31,36; 4:4,5,6,38; 5:18,31,32,32,33,36,37,39,46; 6:9,18, 19,22,23,41,51,61,71; 7:7,13,23,30,32, 39,44; 8:6,7,8,13,14,18,18,23,26,27,43, 46; 9:6,6,11,15,17,18,23; 10:13,25,36, 41; 11:13,13,18,32,38,41; 12:6,14,15, 16,41; 13:18,18,22,24,25,28; 15:22,26; 16:8,8,8,9,10,11,19,25,26; 17:2,9,9,9, 19,20,20; 18:4,6,10,19,19,22,23,29,34, 37; 19:3,5,11,11,13,19,23,24,24,29,31; 21:1,4,9,20,24 ACT 1:1,3,8,12,16,18, 18,21; 2:3,17,18,18,19,25,25,26,29,30, 31,33; 3:10,10,24; 4:1,2,2,3,9,21,26,26, 27,32,33; 5:4,10,15,18,23,24,28,30,35, 36,42; 6:1,3,3,6,11,11,12,13; 7:10,10, 18,19,23,27,35,52,54,57,58; 8:2,5,15, 16,17,19,24,27,28,34,34,34,35; 9:1,3,4, 6,12,13,17,20,21,21,23,38,40; 10:6,10, 11,17,17,22,28,32,38,39,39,43,44,45; 11:11,15,15,19,20; 12:1,7,11,14,18,20, 20,21; 13:3,11,11,22,29,36,40,46,50,50, 51; 14:3,3,5,10,19,20; 15:3,6,8,10,17, 28; 16:2,13,22,29; 17:1,5,21,23,25,26, 32; 18:12,14,15,15,15,25,28; 19:6,6,8,8, 12,12,13,13,16,16,17,23,40; 20:3,10,19, 21,24,29,36,38; 21:5,5,21,24,24,25,27, 27,32,33,34,40; 22:3,5,6,7,10,12,15,18, 24,25,29,30; 23:2,2,3,6,11,12,14,21,29, 30; 24:1,8,9,10,13,15,21,24,25,25,25; 25:2,5,6,9,10,15,16,17,18,19,19,20,20, 24,26; 26:1,2,2,6,7,7,7,11,13,13,14,16, 21,26; 27:1,4,7,14,18,39,41,44,44; 28:3, 6,8,11,21,21,22,23,23,31,31 ROM 1:3,8,18,27,27; 2:2,4,4,4,15,15, 17,19,23,27; 3:8,9,9,21,22; 4:1,6,9,9; 5:5,14; 6:14; 7:1,16; 8:20,31,32,33,34; 9:1,5,15,18,18,21,22,23,27,28; 10:2,20; 11:2,4,18,21,21,22,22,31,31,32; 12:16, 16,20; 13:6; 14:14; 15:3,5,9,12,14,20, 21,28; 16:24 1 CO 1:4,11,13; 2:9; 3:10,10,12; 4:6,6; 5:10,10,10,10; 6:4,12; 7:1,4,4,25,28,37; 8:1,4,7; 9:9,10,10,12, 16,26; 10:11,30; 11:10,16,24,34; 12:1, 16,22,25; 14:16,25; 15:3,15; 16:1,15 2 CO 1:6,6,7,8,9,9,9,11,11,16,23,23; 2:3,5; 3:1,1,13,14,15; 4:1,4; 5:2,4,15; 7:7,7,7,9,14,15,16; 8:22; 9:1,3,14,15; 10:1,2,7,8; 11:9,9,16,20,20,28,28; 12:5, 5,6,8,9,10,11,13,14,15,16,17,18,21; 13:1 GAL 2:4,18,18; 4:9,15; 5:10,23, 26; 6:16,16 EPH 1:6,16,21,21,22; 2:7, 20; 3:1,13; 4:6,10,26; 5:2,6,20,25,32,32; 6:3,18,19,22,22 PHL 1:3,4,5,6,7,7,14, 27,29,30; 2:17,24,27,27,27,27,30; 3:3,4, 13,14,18 COL 1:3,9,24; 2:18,23; 3:1, 1,2,6,13,19; 4:3,8,8,10,13 1 TH 1:2,8; 2:9,16; 3:2,6,6,7,9; 4:6,9,12,13; 5:1,3,3, 10,25 2 TH 1:3,4,4,5,10,11; 2:1,1,4,4, 10,13; 3:1,4,8 1 TM 1:7,10,16,18; 2:12,14; 3:3; 4:12; 5:5,11,15,16,19,19, 22; 6:2,2,17,17,17 2 TM 2:16; 3:13 TIT 1:2,7,9; 2:5,8; 3:2,6,13,13 PLM 10,18 HEB 1:3,7,8; 2:2,3,4,5, 13,16,16,17; 3:6,18,18; 4:4,7,8; 5:1,3, 11,11,12,12; 6:9,16; 7:8,13,14,14,17,26; 8:8,8,10; 9:5,5,5,13,15,17,19,19,21,21; 10:7,8,12,16,21,28,28,34; 11:1,2,4,4,5, 7,11,12,21,22,29,32,32,32,32,32,32,32, 39; 12:2,2; 13:18 JAM 1:17; 2:6,7,7,9, 11,13,13,21; 3:14,15,17; 4:11,11,11,13; 5:1,1,3,5,7,9,14,16,17 1 PT 1:6,10,10, 13,21; 2:10,10,12,19; 3:12,12,14,15,16, 16,20,22; 4:4,14,14; 5:7,7,9 2 PT 1:5, 5,6,6,6,7,7,10,12,12,12; 2:1,4,5,5,10,11, 22; 3:16 1 JN 2:2,27; 3:3,16; 4:10; 5:9,10,15,16 3 JN 2,3,6,12 JUD 3, 9,15,23 REV 1:7,17,17,20; 2:4,5,14, 16,20,20,24,26; 3:3,3,9,10,10,12,17,20, 21,21; 4:2,4,4,8,9,10; 5:1,1,7,9,10,13; 6:2,4,5,8,8,13,16; 7:1,1,1,1,10,11,15,15, 16; 8:3,3,5,5,6,7,10,10; 9:1,3,5,7,11,14, 17; 10:1,2,2,5,5,8,8,11; 11:8,10,11,11, 11,16,16; 12:1,3,4,9,12,13,17; 13:1,1,1, 7,13,14,14,16,16,17; 14:1,1,1,6,6,6,14, 14,14,15,16,16,17,18,19,20; 15:1,2,2,6, 6; 16:1,2,2,8,9,10,12,14,18,21,21; 17:1, 1,3,4,5,8,9,15,18; 18:6,7,8,9,11,19,20, 24; 19:4,11,12,14,16,16,18,19,21; 20:1, 3,4,4,4,6,9,11; 21:4,5,9,12,14,15,16; 22:2,4,14,18,18

2365 ܥܠܬܐ (f) altar

ACT 17:23

2348 (ܥܠܐ) (v) elevate, exult

cPAEL (non occ)

2354 ܥܠܝܐ (adj) high, upper

LUK 1:32,35,76	GAL 4:26
ACT 19:1	

2357 ܥܠܝܬܐ (f) upper room

MRK 14:15	ACT 9:37,39
LUK 22:12	20:8
ACT 1:13	

---

dETHPAAL

Perfect

ACT 10:16 | 1 PT 3:22

Imperative

LUK 14:10

---

hESHTAPHAL

Perfect

REV 18:7,9

Participle

2 TH 2:4
JAM 2:6,13
JAM 3:5

2353 ܥܠܘܝ, (m) aloe

JHN 19:39

2355 (ܥܠܝܡ), ܥܠܝܡܐ (m) young man, youth

MAT 19:20,22
MRK 14:51; 16:5
LUK 7:14
ACT 5:6,10; 7:58
ACT 20:9,12; 23:17,18, 18,19, 20,22
1 PT 5:5
1 JN 2:13,14

2356 ܥܠܝܡܬܐ (f) young woman

MRK 14:66,69
LUK 22:56
JHN 18:17
ACT 16:16

2359 ܥܠܡܐ (m) age, eternity, world

incl idioms

MAT 4:8; 5:14; 6:13,13; 12:32,32; 13:22,35, 38,39, 40,49; 16:26; 18:7,8; 19:16,28, 29; 21:19; 24:3,14,21; 25:34,41, 46,46; 26:13; 28:20
MRK 3:29,29; 4:19; 8:36; 10:17,30, 30; 11:14; 14:9; 16:15
LUK 1:33,55,70; 2:10; 8:14; 9:25; 10:25; 11:50
LUK 12:30; 16:8,9; 18:18,30, 30; 20:34,35; 21:34
JHN 1:9,10,10, 10,29; 3:15,16,16, 17,17,17, 19,36; 4:14,14,36, 42; 5:24,39,40; 6:14,27,33, 35,40,47, 51,51,54, 58,68; 7:4,7; 8:12,23,23, 26,35,35, 51,52; 9:5,5,32, 39; 10:28,28, 36; 11:9,26,27; 12:19,25, 25,31, 31,34, 46,47,
JHN 12:47,50; 13:1,1,8; 14:16,17, 19,22, 27,30, 31; 15:18,19, 19,19, 19,19; 16:8,11,20, 21,28, 28,33, 33; 17:2,3,5,6, 9,11,11, 12,13, 14,14, 14,15, 16,16, 18,18, 21,23, 24,25; 18:36,36, 37; 20:31; 21:25
ACT 3:21; 8:20; 13:46,48; 15:18; 16:37; 17:24,26
ROM 1:8,20,20, 25,25; 2:7; 3:6,19; 4:13; 5:12,13,21; 6:22,23; 9:5,5; 11:12,15, 36,36; 12:2; 16:24,25, 26,26
1 CO 1:20,20,21, 27,27,28; 2:6,6,7,8, 12; 3:18,19,22; 4:9,13; 5:10,10; 6:2,2,3,4; 7:31,31,33, 34,35; 8:4,13; 10:11; 11:32; 14:10
2 CO 1:12; 4:4,17,17, 18; 5:1,19; 7:10; 9:9
2 CO 11:31,31
GAL 1:4,5,5; 4:3; 6:8,14,14
EPH 1:4,21; 2:2,7,12; 3:9,11,21, 21; 6:12
PHL 2:15; 4:20,20
COL 1:6,26; 2:8,20,20
2 TH 1:9; 2:16
1 TM 1:15,16, 17,17; 3:16; 6:7,12,16, 16,17
2 TM 1:9; 2:4,10; 4:10,18,1
TIT 1:2,2; 2:12,12; 3:7
PLM 15
HEB 1:2,6,8,8; 2:5; 4:3; 5:6,9; 6:2,5,20; 7:3,17,21, 24,25,2; 9:12,14, 26,26; 10:5,12,1; 11:3,7,38; 13:8,20,2 21
JAM 1:27; 2:5; 3:6; 4:4,4
1 PT 1:6,20,23 25; 3:7; 4:11; 5:9,10,10 11,11
2 PT 1:4,11; 2:5,5,20; 3:6,18
1 JN 1:2; 2:2,15,15 16,16, 17,17,2; 3:1,13,15 17; 4:1,3,4,5 5,9,14, 17; 5:4,4,5,1 13,19,2
2 JN 2,7

JUD 7,13,21,25
REV 1:6,6,18,18
4:9,9,10,10
5:13,13
7:12,12
10:6,6
11:15,15,
REV 11:15
13:8
14:6,11,11
15:3,7,7
17:8
19:3,3
20:10,10
22:5,5

2360 ܥܠܡܢܘܬܐ (f) worldliness

EPH 2:2

2361 ܥܠܡܢܝܐ (adj) worldly

HEB 9:1

2366 ܥܡ (prep) with

MAT 1:23; 2:3,11; 4:21; 5:24,25,25,40,41; 8:10,11,23; 9:10,10,11,15,18; 12:3,4,30,30, 41,42,45,46,47; 13:3,10,13,29,34; 14:27; 15:30; 16:5,27; 17:3,17; 18:16; 20:2,12,13; 21:2; 22:16; 23:1,1; 24:30,31,49,51; 25:3,4, 10,27,31; 26:11,18,20,23,29,35,36,38,40,47, 47,51,58,69,71; 27:38,41,44,54,66; 28:12,18, 20 MRK 1:13,20,27,29,36; 2:2,15,15,16, 16,16,19,25,26; 3:6,7,14; 4:10,10,33,34,36; 5:18,24,37,40; 6:22,50; 8:10,11,14,14,16,34, 38; 9:4,8,14,16,34,50; 10:30; 11:11; 12:1; 13:26,26; 14:7,14,17,18,20,31,33,43,54,67; 15:1,1,1,7,27,28,31,32,41; 16:10,19 LUK 1:19,22,28,45,55,55,55,58,66,72; 2:5, 13,15,17,20,36,38,44,51; 4:36; 5:9,19,29,30, 34; 6:3,4,11,17; 7:6,11,12,36; 8:1,7,19,42,45, 51; 9:11,18,26,30,32,49; 11:7,23,23,31,32; 12:13,46,58; 13:1; 14:10,25,31; 15:2,6,9,29, 30,31; 16:26; 18:34; 19:23; 20:1; 21:27; 22:4, 11,14,15,33,37,49,53,56,59; 23:12,20,32,39, 43,49,55; 24:1,5,6,10,14,15,15,17,30,32,33, 36,44 JHN 3:2,22,25,26; 4:9,26,27,27; 5:18; 6:3,22,22,43,52,63,66; 7:33; 8:12,25, 29,40; 9:29,37,40; 10:6; 11:16,31,33,54; 12:2,8,17,29,35; 13:8,18,33; 14:9,16,25,30; 15:3,11,22,27; 16:1,4,4,19,25,25,32; 17:12, 24; 18:1,2,3,5,15,18,20,21,26; 19:10,18,32, 39; 20:7,19,21,24,26,26; 21:3 ACT 1:4,14, 14,14,17,21,22,26; 2:14,28; 3:8,22; 4:13,14, 27,33; 5:1,17,21,26,29; 6:9; 7:6,9,26,38,38, 38,44,45; 8:20,26,31; 9:6,7,27,28,29,39; 10:7,20,23,23,27,32,38,41,45; 11:2,3,12,12, 14,19,19,20,21,26; 12:21,25; 13:15,26,31,42, 50; 14:1,4,20,23,27; 15:2,2,4,22,22,25,27,35, 38,38; 16:3,13,32,32; 17:2,15,17,17,17,18, 34; 18:3,10,18,19; 19:9,25,29,38,38; 20:4,7, 18,29,32,34,36; 21:16,16,18,24,26,29,29,37, 40; 22:2,9,9,10,11,20; 23:9,9,27,30; 24:1,1, 12,18,19,25,26; 25:5,12,18,23,24; 26:13,18, 30,31; 27:1,2,24,25; 28:16 ROM 1:7; 5:10; 6:4,5,6,8,8,8; 8:17,17,32; 9:10; 12:15,15,18; 15:10,26,27,30,32,33; 16:3,7,9,14,15,20,21, 27 1 CO 1:3; 3:1,1,1,9; 4:8; 5:4,4,9,11; 6:1, 6,7,9,17; 7:12,13; 9:5,13,20,20,22; 10:4; 11:5,32; 14:6,6,9,21,21; 15:10; 16:4,11,12, 16,19,23,24 2 CO 1:2,21; 4:14; 5:19; 6:14, 14,15,15,16; 7:13,13,14; 8:18,19,22; 9:4,13, 13; 10:12; 12:18; 13:4,4,11,14 GAL 1:2,3; 2:1,1,3,12,13,20; 4:30; 5:24; 6:18 EPH 1:2; 2:5,6,6,16; 3:18; 4:25,31; 5:19; 6:12,12,12,12,12,16,23,23,24 PHL 1:1,2, 23; 2:17,18,22,22,25; 4:3,3,3,9,21,23 COL 1:2; 2:5,12,12,13,20; 3:1,3,4,9,14; 4:9, 10,18 1 TH 1:1; 2:2,16; 3:13; 4:14,17,17; 5:10,13,28 2 TH 1:2,7,7; 3:14,16,18 1 TM 1:10; 6:21 2 TM 1:8; 2:10,11,11,12, 22; 4:11,11,16,22,22 TIT 3:15,15 PLM 1,2,3,23,25 HEB 1:1,2; 3:14; 4:15; 5:2; 7:2; 11:7,9,25,31; 12:14,19,25,25,25; 13:3,7,23,25 1 PT 3:7,7,8; 4:4; 5:14 2 PT 1:1,18 1 JN 1:3,3,3,6,7; 4:17 2 JN 2,3,13 3 JN 15 JUD 9 REV 1:7, 12; 2:16,22; 3:20,20,21,21; 4:1; 10:8; 11:7, 18; 12:7,9,17; 13:4,7; 14:1,4; 17:1,2,12,14, 14; 18:3,9; 19:5,19,19,20; 20:4,6; 21:3,3,3,9, 15; 22:12,16,21

2367 ܥܡܐ (m) people, nation; (pl) Gentiles

MAT 1:21
2:4,6
4:15,16,23
6:32
10:18
12:18,21
13:15
14:5
15:8
20:19,25
21:23,43
24:7,7,9,14
25:32
26:3,5,47
27:1,15,25,64
28:19
MRK 3:7
7:6
9:25
10:33,42
11:17,18,32
12:12
13:8,8,10
14:2,43
15:8
LUK 1:10,17,21,68,77
2:1,32,32
3:15,18,21
5:15,19
6:17
7:1,5,16,29
8:47
LUK 9:13
12:30
13:17
17:18
18:32,43
19:47,48
20:1,6,9,19,26,45
21:10,10,23,24,24,25,38
22:2,25
23:2,5,13,14,27,35
24:19,47
JHN 5:3
7:12,35,49
8:2
11:48,50,50,51,52
12:20
18:14,20,35
ACT 2:5,6,47
3:9,11,23
4:1,2,8,10,17,21,25,27
5:12,13,20,25,26,34,37
6:5,7,8,12
7:7,17,34,

ACT 7:45, 8:9,14, 9:15, 10:2,22,35,41,42,45, 11:1,17,18,24,26, 12:4,22, 13:15,17,19,24,31,46,47,48, 14:2,5,11,16,18,19,27, 15:3,7,12,14,14,17,19,23,30, 17:8, 18:6,10, 19:4,9,27,33,33, 21:11,19,21,25,27,28,30,35,36,39, 22:21, 23:5,6,7, 24:2,10,17, 25:24, 26:4,17,17,20,23,23, 28:17,19,26,27,28
ROM 1:5,13, 2:14,24, 3:29,29, 4:17,18, 9:24,25,25,26,30, 10:19,19,19,21, 11:1,2,11,12,13,13,25, 15:9,9,10,10,11,12,12,
ROM 15:16,16,18,27, 16:4,25
1 CO 10:7, 14:21
2 CO 6:16, 11:26
GAL 1:16, 2:2,8,9,12,14,15, 3:8,8,14
EPH 2:11, 3:1,6,8, 4:17
COL 1:27
1 TH 2:16, 4:5
1 TM 2:7, 3:16
2 TM 1:11, 4:17
TIT 2:14
HEB 2:17, 3:10, 4:9, 5:3, 7:5,11,27, 8:10, 9:7,19,19, 10:30, 11:25, 13:12
JAM 1:1
1 PT 2:9,10,10
2 PT 2:1
3 JN 7
JUD 1,5
REV 2:26, 5:9, 7:9, 10:11, 11:2,9,18, 12:5, 13:7, 14:6,8, 15:4, 16:19, 17:15, 18:3,4,23, 19:15, 20:3,8, 21:3,24,26, 22:2

2369 ܥܡܕ. (v) be baptized; (aph) baptize

[a]PEAL

Perfect

MAT 3:16
LUK 3:21[1],21[2], 7:29, 11:38
ACT 2:41, 8:13, 9:18, 16:15,33, 19:3,5
ROM 6:3[1],3[2]
1 CO 1:13
1 CO 10:2, 12:13
GAL 3:27

Imperfect

MAT 3:13, 20:22[2],23[2]
MRK 10:38[2],39[2]
LUK 12:50
ACT 1:5[2], 8:36, 10:47,48, 11:16[2]

Imperative

ACT 2:38
ACT 22:16

Infinitive

MAT 3:7
LUK 3:7,12

Active Participle

MAT 3:6, 20:22[1],23[1]
MRK 7:4, 10:38[1],39[1], 16:16
JHN 3:23[2]
ACT 8:12,16, 18:8
1 CO 15:29[1],29

1818 ܡܥܡܘܕܝܬܐ (f) baptism, washing

MAT 20:22,23, 21:25
MRK 1:4, 7:4,8, 10:38,39, 11:30
LUK 3:3, 7:29, 12:50, 20:4
JHN 5:2,4,7, 9:7
ACT 1:22, 10:37, 13:24, 18:25, 19:3,4
ROM 6:4
EPH 4:5
COL 2:12
HEB 6:2,4, 9:10, 10:32
1 PT 3:21

---

[b]ETHPEEL

Perfect

MRK 1:9
LUK 7:30

Imperfect

MAT 3:14

---

[e]APHEL

Perfect

MRK 1:8[1]
ACT 1:5[1], 8:38, 11:16[1]
ACT 19:4
1 CO 1:14,15,16[1],16[2]

Imperfect

MRK 1:8[2]	JHN 1:31,33[1]
LUK 3:16[2]	

Imperative

MAT 28:19

Infinitive

1 CO 1:17

Active Participle

MAT 3:11[1],11[2]	JHN 3:22,23[1], 26
MRK 1:4,5	4:1,2
LUK 3:16[1]	10:40
JHN 1:25,26,28, 33[2]	

1817 ܡܥܡܕܢܐ (m) baptizer

MAT 3:1	MRK 6:14,24,25
11:11,12	8:28
14:2,8	LUK 7:20,28,33
16:14	9:19
17:13	

2370 ܥܡܘܕܐ (m) pillar

GAL 2:9	REV 3:12
1 TM 3:15	10:1

2375 ܥܡܛ (v-non occ) become dark

PEAL

2371 ܥܡܘܛܐ (adj) dark

2 PT 1:19

2376 ܥܡܛܢܐ (m) darkness

ACT 2:20	2 PT 2:4,17
13:11	JUD 6,13

2380 ܥܡܠ (v) toil, labor; (aph) trouble

PEAL

Perfect

PHL 2:16

Imperfect

LUK 7:6	ROM 15:30

Active Participle

ACT 24:16	COL 4:12
COL 1:29	1 TH 2:9

2381 ܥܡܠܐ (m) toil, labor

JHN 4:6,38	1 TH 1:3
1 CO 3:8	3:5
15:58	2 TH 3:8
2 CO 10:15	1 PT 3:1
11:27	REV 2:2
GAL 6:17	14:13

[e]APHEL

Imperfect

LUK 8:49

Active Participle

MRK 5:35

2383 ܥܡܨ (v) shut, close

[c]PAEL

Perfect

MAT 13:15	ACT 28:27

2384 ܥܡܩ (v) be deep; (pa) dig (deeply)

[a]PEAL (non occ)

2304 ܥܘܡܩܐ (m) depth, deep

MAT 13:5	ROM 8:39
18:6	11:33
MRK 4:5	1 CO 2:10
LUK 5:4	2 CO 8:2
ACT 27:41	EPH 3:18

[c]PAEL

Perfect

LUK 6:48

2378 ܥܡܝܩܐ (adj) deep

JHN 4:11	REV 2:24

2379 (ܥܣܒ), ܥܣܒܐ (m) grass

MAT 6:30
LUK 12:28
1 CO 3:12
1 PT 1:24,24

2385 ܥܡܪ (v) dwell

[a]PEAL

Perfect

MAT 2:23
4:13
ACT 7:4[1]
2 TM 1:14
HEB 11:9

Imperfect

ACT 7:2
1 CO 7:12,13
2 CO 6:16
EPH 3:17
COL 3:16
1 TM 2:2

Imperative

1 PT 3:7

Infinitive

COL 1:19

Active Participle

MAT 12:45
23:21
MRK 5:3
LUK 8:27
11:26
13:4
JHN 14:10,17
ACT 1:19
2:5,9,14
7:4[2]
9:22,32,35
11:29
17:26
19:10,17
24:2
28:2
ROM 7:17,18,20
8:9,11[1],
11[2]
1 CO 3:16
6:19
PHL 2:15
COL 2:9
1 TM 6:16
JAM 4:5
1 PT 1:11
2 PT 2:8
3:13
REV 2:13
13:12,14[1],
14[2]
17:8

Passive Participle

ACT 8:9

1819 ܡܥܡܘܪܐ (m) habitation

EPH 2:22
REV 18:2

2305 ܡܥܡܪܐ (m) habitation, manner of life

ACT 17:26
1 TM 2:2
JUD 6

2374 ܥܡܘܪܐ (adj) dweller, inhabitant

ACT 1:20
4:16
13:27
2 CO 5:9
REV 3:10
REV 6:10
8:13
11:10,10
13:8
17:2

2386 ܥܡܪ, ܥܡܪܐ (m) wool

HEB 9:19
REV 1:14

2389 (ܥܢ), ܥܢܐ (f) flock

MAT 26:31
LUK 17:7
JHN 4:12
10:1,2,3,4,
5,7,8,
JHN 10:11,12
12,13
15,16
1 CO 9:7

2393 (ܥܢ), ܥܢܢܐ (f) cloud

MAT 17:5,5
24:30
26:64
MRK 9:7,7
13:26
14:62
LUK 9:34,34,35
12:54
21:27
ACT 1:9
1 CO 10:1,2
1 TH 4:17
HEB 12:1
2 PT 2:17
JUD 12
REV 1:7
4:3
10:1
11:12
14:14,14
15,16

2387 ܥܢܐ (v) answer

[a]PEAL

Perfect

MAT 3:15
4:4
8:8
11:4,25
12:38,39,
48
13:11,37
14:28
15:3,13,15,
16,24
16:2,16,17
17:4,11,17
19:4,27
20:13,22
21:21,24,
27,29,
30
MAT 22:1,29
24:4
25:9,12,
40
26:23,2
33,6
66
27:21,2
28:5
MRK 3:33
7:28
8:29
9:17,19
10:5,20,
29
11:22,3
12:34,3

MRK	14:48,61	JHN	6:26,29,43, 68
	15:2,9		7:16,20,21, 52
LUK	1:19,35,60		8:14,19,39, 48
	3:11,16		9:11,20,25, 30,34,36
	4:4,8,12		10:25
	5:5,22,31		12:23,30
	6:3		13:7,26,36
	7:22,40,43		14:23
	8:21		18:23,30
	9:19,20,41, 49		20:28
	10:27,41	ACT	3:12
	11:45		4:19
	13:2,14,15		5:29
	14:3		8:24
	17:17,20, 37		9:5
	20:3,39		19:2,15
	22:51		21:13
	24:18		22:8,28
JHN	1:26,49		24:10
	2:18,19		25:10
	3:3,5,9,10, 27	2 CO	6:2
	4:10,13	REV	7:13
	5:7,11,19		

Imperfect

MAT 25:44,45 | LUK 13:25
LUK 11:7 | ACT 12:13

2388 ܥܢܐ (v) be occupied

aPEAL

Passive Participle

LUK 10:40 | 2 TM 2:16
1 TH 4:11

bETHPEEL

Imperfect

1 CO 7:5

2390 ܥܢܒܬܐ (c) grapes

MAT 7:16 | REV 14:18
LUK 6:44

2391 ܥܢܕ (v) depart, be absent

aPEAL

Perfect

REV 14:13

Imperfect

2 CO 5:8

Passive Participle

2 CO 5:6

2306 ܥܘܢܕܢܐ (m) departure

2 PT 1:14

2392 ܥܢܘܕܐ (adj) absent, foreigner

2 CO 5:9

2322 (ܥܢܙ), ܥܢܙܐ (f) goat

HEB 11:37

2450 (ܥܢܬ), ܥܢܬܐ (f-non occ) injustice

2451 (ܐܬܥܢܬ) (v-non occ) (ethpa) be crafty

dETHPAAL

2394 ܥܢܬܐ (adj) wicked

2 TH 3:2 | 1 TM 1:9

2395 ܥܣܒ, ܥܣܒܐ (m) green herb, grass

MAT 13:26 | HEB 6:7
MRK 4:28 | JAM 1:10,11
6:39 | REV 8:7
JHN 6:10 | 9:4

2398 ܥܣܩ (v-non occ) be difficult, hard

aPEAL

2397 ܥܣܝܩܐ (pp) hard

2 PT 3:16

2399 ܥܣܩܐ (adj) difficult, perverse

LUK 3:5 | HEB 5:11
PHL 2:15 | 1 PT 2:18

2400 ܥܣܪ (num) ten

see also 269 ܐܪܒܥܣܪ
see also 918 ܚܕܥܣܪ
see also 1035 ܚܡܫܬܥܣܪ
see also 3308 ܫܬܬܥܣܪ
see also 3405 ܬܠܬܬܥܣܪ
see also 3446 ܬܪܥܣܪ

MAT 20:24	JHN 1:39
25:1,28	ACT 25:6
MRK 10:41	REV 2:10
LUK 14:31	11:13
15:8	12:3
17:12,17	13:1,1
19:13,13, 16,17, 24,25	17:3,7,12, 12,16
	21:20

1821 ܡܥܣܪܐ (m) tenth, tithe

HEB 7:2,4,5,6,8,	HEB 7:9

2402 ܥܣܪܝܢ (num) twenty

LUK 14:31	REV 4:4,4,10
JHN 6:19	5:8
ACT 1:15	11:16
27:28	19:4
1 CO 10:8	

2401 (ܥܣܪ) (v) tithe

cPAEL

Active Participle

MAT 23:23	LUK 18:12
LUK 11:42	

dETHPAAL

Perfect

HEB 7:9

2404 ܥܦ (v) fold up

aPEAL

Imperfect

HEB 1:12

2405 ܥܦ (v-non occ) double

cf (ܥܘܦ) and ܐܥܦ

aPEAL

2407 ܥܦܝܦܐ (pp) double

1 TM 5:17

2406 ܥܦܐ (v-non occ) bloom, flourish

aPEAL

2309 ܥܘܦܝܐ (m) springing up, flowe

HEB 12:15	1 PT 1:24,24

2408 ܥܦܩ (v) embrace

cPAEL

Perfect

ACT 20:10,37

2409 ܥܦܪ, ܥܦܪܐ (m) earth, dust

LUK 6:49	REV 18:19
1 CO 15:49	

2410 ܥܦܪܢܐ (adj) earthy, made of dust

1 CO 15:47,48,	1 CO 15:48

2411 ܥܨܐ (v) be obstinate

aPEAL

Active Participle

ROM 2:8

2413 ܥܨܝܘܬܐ (f) stubborn resistance

JUD 11

2414 ܥܨܝܢܐ (m) strife

2 CO 12:20	GAL 5:20

cPAEL

Active Participle

TIT 2:9

2412 ܥܨܒ (v) bandage

aPEAL

Perfect

LUK 10:34

2415 ܥܨܪ (v-non occ) trample, squeeze

aPEAL

1822 ܡܥܨܪܬܐ (f) winepress

MAT 21:33
MRK 12:1
REV 14:19,20,
REV 14:20
19:15

2417 ܥܩܒ, ܥܩܒܐ (f) heel, ankle, footstep

JHN 13:18
ACT 3:7
ROM 4:12
2 CO 12:18
1 PT 2:21

2416 ܥܩܒ (v) trace, track, inquire

cPAEL

Perfect

MAT 2:16
LUK 23:14
1 PT 1:10

Imperfect

LUK 22:23

Imperative

MAT 2:8

Active Participle

ACT 17:27

2311 ܥܘܩܒܐ (m) question

1 CO 10:25,27

dETHPAAL

Participle

ROM 11:33
EPH 3:8

1823 (ܥܩܠ), ܡܥܩܠܐ (adj) perverse

MAT 17:17
LUK 9:41

2418 (ܥܩܡ) (v) turn aside, pervert

cPAEL

Imperfect

ACT 13:8

Infinitive

ACT 13:10

Active Participle

2 PT 3:16

1824 ܡܥܩܡܐ (pp) crooked, perverse

ACT 2:40
20:30
PHL 2:15
TIT 3:11

2312 (ܥܩܣ), ܥܘܩܣܐ (m) sting, goad

ACT 9:4
26:14
1 CO 15:55,56
REV 9:10

2420 ܥܩܪܐ (m) root

MAT 3:10
13:6,21
MRK 4:6,17
11:20
LUK 3:9
8:13
ROM 11:16,17,
18,18
ROM 15:12
EPH 3:17
COL 2:7
1 TM 6:10
HEB 12:15
JUD 12
REV 5:5
22:16

2419 ܥܩܪ (v) uproot

aPEAL

Imperfect

MAT 13:29

2421 ܥܩܪܐ (adj) barren

LUK 1:7,36
23:29
GAL 4:27
HEB 11:11

[b]ETHPEEL

Imperfect

MAT 15:13

Imperative

LUK 17:6

2422 ܥܩܪܒܐ (f) scorpion

LUK 10:19 11:12	REV 9:3,5,10

1827 (ܥܪ), ܡܥܪܬܐ (f) cave, den

MAT 21:13 MRK 11:17 LUK 19:46	JHN 11:38 HEB 11:38 REV 6:15

2433 (ܥܪ), ܥܪܘܪܐ (m) tempest, storm

HEB 12:18

2424 ܥܪܐ (v-non occ) sieze

[a]PEAL

2437 ܥܪܝܐ (m) cold, severe weather

2 CO 11:27

2425 ܥܪܒ (v-non occ) be surity for, pledge

[a]PEAL

2429 ܥܪܒܐ (m) surity, security

ACT 17:9	HEB 7:22

2426 ܥܪܒ (v) sift

[a]PEAL

Imperfect

LUK 22:31

2427 ܥܪܒ (v) set, go down

[a]PEAL

Imperfect

EPH 4:26

1825 ܡܥܪܒܐ (f) setting of sun, west

MAT 8:11 24:27 MRK 1:32 LUK 4:40	LUK 12:54 13:29 REV 21:13

2431 ܥܪܘܒܬܐ (f) eve, day of preparation

MAT 27:62 MRK 15:42	LUK 23:54 JHN 19:14,31

2428 ܥܪܒܐ (m) sheep

MAT 9:36 10:6 12:11,12 15:24 18:12 25:32,33 26:31 MRK 6:34	LUK 15:4,6 JHN 2:14,15 10:3,4,12, 16,26, 27 21:16 1 PT 2:25 REV 18:13

ܥܪܓܠ see under ܥܓܠ

ܥܪܙܠ see under ܥܠ

2434 ܥܪܛܠ (adj) naked

MRK 14:51,52 2 CO 5:3	HEB 4:13 REV 16:15

2435 ܥܪܛܠܝܐ (adj) naked

MAT 25:36,38, 43,44 JHN 21:7 1 CO 4:11	1 CO 15:37 JAM 2:15 REV 3:17 17:16

2436 ܥܪܛܠܝܘܬܐ (f) nakedness

ROM 8:35 2 CO 11:27	REV 3:18

2316 (ܥܪܠ), ܥܘܪܠܐ (adj) uncircumcised

ACT 11:3

2317 ܥܘܪܠܘܬܐ (f) uncircumcision

ROM 2:25,26,26,27	GAL 2:7
3:30	5:6
4:9,10,10,11,11,12	6:15
1 CO 7:18,18,19	EPH 2:11
	COL 2:13
	3:11

2438 ܥܪܡ (v-non occ) gather

ᵃPEAL

2439 ܥܪܡܐ (m) rough place

LUK 3:5

2440 ܥܪܣܐ (f) bed, pallet, bier

MAT 9:2,6	LUK 8:16
MRK 2:4,9,11,12	11:7
4:21	17:34
6:55	JHN 5:8,9,10,11,12
7:4,30	ACT 5:15
LUK 5:18,19,24,25	9:33,34
7:14	HEB 13:4
	REV 2:22

2318 (ܥܪܦ), ܥܘܪܦܐ (m) money (change)

MRK 12:41	JHN 2:15

2441 (ܥܪܦ) (v-non occ) change

ᶜPAEL

1826 ܡܥܪܦܢܐ (m) money changer

MAT 21:12	JHN 2:14,15
MRK 11:15	

2442 ܥܪܦܠܐ (f) mist

HEB 12:18

2443 ܥܪܥ (v) occur, happen

ᵃPEAL

Active Participle

1 PT 5:9

2444 ܥܪܥܐ (m) foreigner, stranger

1 PT 2:11

2445 ܥܪܩ (v) flee

ᵃPEAL

Perfect

MAT 2:14	ACT 7:29
8:33	16:27
26:56	19:16
MRK 5:14	2 PT 2:20
14:50,52	REV 12:6
16:8	16:20
LUK 8:34	20:11

Imperfect

MAT 23:33	ACT 27:42
24:16	ROM 2:3
MRK 13:14	HEB 2:3
LUK 21:21[1],21[2]	REV 9:6

Imperative

MAT 2:13	1 TH 5:22
10:23	1 TM 6:11,20
1 CO 6:18	2 TM 2:22
10:14	

Infinitive

MAT 3:7	LUK 21:36
LUK 3:7	ACT 27:30

Active Participle

JHN 10:5,12,13	2 PT 1:4
JAM 4:7	2:18

2432 ܥܘܪܩܐ (m) flight

MAT 24:20	MRK 13:18

2446 (ܥܪܩ), ܥܪܩܬܐ (f) leather strap

MRK 1:6,7	ACT 13:25
LUK 3:16	21:11,11
JHN 1:27	22:25

2448 ܥܫܢ (v) prevail

[a]PEAL

Perfect

LUK 23:23

2319 ܥܘܫܢܐ (m) power

2 PT	2:11	REV	7:12
REV	5:12		

[c]PAEL (non occ)

2447 ܥܫܝܢܐ (adj) mighty

JAM	3:4	REV	18:10
REV	6:13		19:18

2449 ܥܫܩ (v) accuse

[a]PEAL

Imperfect

LUK 3:14

2452 ܥܬܕ (v) be ready; (pa) prepare

[a]PEAL (non occ)

2453 ܥܬܝܕܐ (pp) (expr fut) shall; ready, prepared

MAT	2:13	JHN	14:22
	11:14		16:13
	12:32		18:32
	16:21,27		20:9
	17:12,22		21:19
	20:17,22	ACT	7:22
	24:6		9:16
	25:34		12:6
MRK	8:31		17:3,31
	10:32		20:3,7,13, 23,38
	13:7,10		
LUK	3:7		23:3,11
	9:22,31,44		24:15,25
	10:1		26:16,22, 23
	17:25		
	19:4,11		27:24
	21:9,26,36	ROM	4:24
	22:23		5:14
	24:7,21,26		8:13,18,38
JHN	3:14		14:10
	6:6,15,71	1 CO	3:22
	7:35,35,39		11:19
	11:51		15:25,37,
	12:4,34		53

2 CO	5:10	HEB	13:14
	9:2,4	JAM	2:12
GAL	3:23		5:3
EPH	1:21	1 PT	1:10,11
COL	2:17		4:5
1 TH	3:4		5:1
1 TM	1:16	2 PT	2:6
	4:8	1 JN	3:2
	6:15,19	REV	1:19
2 TM	4:1		2:10,10
TIT	3:1		3:2,10,16
HEB	1:14		6:11
	2:5		8:13
	3:5		10:7
	6:5		12:4,5
	10:1,27,35		17:8
	11:8,20		

2454 ܥܬܝܕܐܝܬ (adv) readily

ACT	2:41	ACT	10:29

[c]PAEL

Perfect

EPH 3:11

Imperfect

2 CO 9:5

Imperative

ACT 23:23

Active Participle

2 CO	5:5	EPH	6:13

2459 ܥܬܩ (v) grow old; (aph) make old

[a]PEAL

Perfect

HEB $8:13^2$

2455 ܥܬܝܩܐ (adj) old

MAT	13:52	2 CO	5:17
LUK	5:39,39	EPH	4:22
ROM	6:6	COL	3:9
1 CO	5:7,8	1 JN	2:7,7
2 CO	3:14		

2456 ܥܬܝܩܘܬܐ (f) antiquity

ROM 7:6

[e]APHEL

Perfect

HEB 8:13[1]

[e]APHEL

Active Participle

2 CO 6:10

2460 ܥܬܪ (v) grow rich; (aph) make rich

[a]PEAL

Perfect

1 CO 1:5	REV 3:17
4:8	18:3,15,19

Imperfect

2 CO 8:9	1 TM 6:18
9:11	REV 3:18

Infinitive

1 TM 6:9

2320 ܥܘܬܪܐ (m) wealth, riches

MAT 13:22	EPH 3:8,16
MRK 4:19	PHL 4:19
LUK 8:14	COL 1:27
ROM 2:4	2:2
11:12,12, 33	1 TM 6:17
	HEB 11:26
2 CO 8:2	JAM 5:2
EPH 1:7,18	REV 5:12
2:7	18:17

2457 ܥܬܝܪܐ (adj) rich

MAT 19:23,24	ACT 13:50
27:57	15:32
MRK 10:25	ROM 10:12
12:41	2 CO 8:9
LUK 1:53	EPH 2:4
6:24	1 TM 6:17
12:16,21	JAM 1:10,11
14:12	2:5,6
16:1,19,20,	5:1
21,22	REV 2:9
18:23,25	3:17
19:2	6:15
21:1	13:16
ACT 9:36	

2458 ܥܬܝܪܐܝܬ (adv) richly, abundantly

COL 3:16	TIT 3:6
1 TM 6:17	2 PT 1:11

2462 ܦܐܝ (v-non occ) be proper, becoming

aPEAL

2463 ܦܐܝܐ (adj) proper, becoming

2 PT 1:17	3 JN 6

2465 ܦܐܪܐ (m) fruit

MAT 3:8,10 7:16,17,17,18,18,19,20 12:33,33,33 13:8,22,23,26 21:19,34,34,41,43 MRK 4:7,8,19,20,28,29 11:14 12:2 LUK 1:42 3:8,9 6:43,43,44 8:8,14,15 13:6,7,9 20:10 JHN 4:36 12:24 15:2,2,2,4,	JHN 15:5,8,16,16 ACT 2:30 14:17 ROM 6:22 7:4,5 1 CO 9:7 14:14 2 CO 9:10 GAL 5:22 EPH 5:9,11 PHL 1:11,22 4:17 COL 1:6,10 2 TM 2:6 TIT 3:14 PLM 6 HEB 12:11 13:15 JAM 3:17,18 5:7,18 2 PT 1:8 JUD 12 REV 22:2,2

2466 ܦܓܕ (v-non occ) retain

aPEAL

2467 ܦܓܘܕܬܐ (f) bridle

JAM 3:3	REV 14:20

2468 ܦܓܢܐ (m) rue (herb)

LUK 11:42

2469 ܦܓܥ (v) meet

aPEAL

Perfect

MAT 28:9 MRK 5:2 LUK 8:27	LUK 9:37 ACT 16:16

Active Participle

MRK 14:13	LUK 22:10

2470 ܦܓܪ, ܦܓܪܐ (m) body

MAT 5:29,30 6:22,22,23,25,25 10:28,28 19:6 24:28 26:26,41 27:52,58,58,59 MRK 5:29 14:22,38 15:43,45 LUK 11:34,34,34,36 12:4,22,23 17:37 22:19 23:52,55 24:3,23 JHN 2:21 6:51,52,53,54,55,56,63 19:31,38,38,40 20:12 ACT 2:26,31 ROM 1:24 4:19 6:6,12 7:4,24 8:10,11,13,23 12:1,4,5 1 CO 5:3,5 6:13,13,15,16,16,18,18,19,20	1 CO 7:4,4,5,28,34 9:11,27 10:16,17 11:24,27,29 12:12,12,12,13,14,15,15,16,16,17,18,19,20,23,24,25,27 13:3 15:35,37,38,38,39,39,40,40,44,44,44,44 2 CO 1:12 4:10,10,11 5:1,6,8,10,16,16 7:5 12:2,2,3,3 GAL 6:17 EPH 2:16 3:6 4:4,12,16,16 5:23,28,29,30 PHL 1:20,24 3:21,21 COL 1:18,22,24

COL	2:15,17,19, 23	JAM	5:5
	3:15,22	1 PT	2:11,24
1 TH	5:23		3:18,21
1 TM	4:8		4:1,2
HEB	10:5,10,22	2 PT	1:13,14
JAM	2:16,26	1 JN	2:16
	3:2,6	JUD	9
		REV	18:13

2471 ܦܓܪܢܐ (adj) carnal

1 CO 3:1,3,4

2472 ܦܓܪܢܐܝܬ (adv) carnally

JHN 8:15

2473 ܦܓܪܢܝܐ (adj) carnal

HEB 7:16

2474 ܦܕܢܐ (f) plough

LUK 9:62 | LUK 17:7

2475 ܦܗܐ (v) wander, be distracted

[a]PEAL

Imperfect

LUK 12:29

Active Participle

JUD 12

2478 (ܦܘܓ) (v) become cold

[a]PEAL

Imperfect

MAT 24:12

2500 ܦܘܪܬܐ (f-non occ) wrath

2494 (ܦܘܪ) (v) (ethpe) be provoked

[b]ETHPEEL

Perfect

ACT 16:18

Participle

1 CO 13:5

2501 (ܦܘܫ) (v) remain, abide

[a]PEAL

Perfect

LUK 2:43 | 2 TM 4:20
JHN 7:9

Imperative

LUK 24:29

Infinitive

1 TH 3:1

Active Participle

JHN 12:24 | HEB 4:1
PHL 1:25

2506 ܦܚܐ (m) snare

ROM 11:9 | 1 TM 6:9
1 TM 3:7 | 2 TM 2:26

2507 ܦܚܙܐ (adj-non occ) shameless

2508 ܦܚܙܘܬܐ (f) lasciviousness

2 CO 12:21 | EPH 4:19

2509 ܦܚܡ (v) be equal; (pa) make equal, compare

[a]PEAL (non occ)

2510 ܦܚܡܐ (m) equal

PHL 2:6

---

[c]PAEL

Imperfect

2 CO 10:12[1]

Active Participle

LUK 2:19 | 2 CO 10:12[2]
1 CO 2:13

2481 ܦܘܚܡܐ (m) comparison

2 CO 3:10

2511 ܦܚܪܐ (m) potter

MAT 27:7,10
ROM 9:21
2 TM 2:20
REV 2:27

2514 ܦܛܡܐ (m) fattening

LUK 15:23,27,
LUK 15:30

2513 (ܦܛܡ) (v) fatten

cPAEL

Passive Participle

MAT 22:4

2516 ܦܛܪ (v) depart

aPEAL

Infinitive

PHL 1:23

2512 ܦܛܝܪܐ (adj) unleavened; (pl) Feast of Unleavened Bread

MAT 26:17
MRK 14:1,12
LUK 22:1,7
ACT 12:3
20:6
1 CO 5:7

2536 (ܦܝܣ), ܦܝܣܐ (m-non occ) (w/ ܥܒܕ) persuade

2535 ܦܝܣܐ (m) persuasion, assurance

GAL 5:8
COL 2:2,4
1 TH 1:5
TIT 1:16
3:3
HEB 11:1

2534 (ܦܝܣ) (v) persuade, convince

eAPHEL

Perfect

MAT 27:20
ACT 12:20
ACT 19:26

Imperative

1 TM 5:1

Active Participle

MAT 28:14
ACT 7:26
13:43
18:4,13
19:8
26:28
27:33
ACT 28:23
2 CO 5:11
GAL 1:10
1 PT 5:12
1 JN 3:19
2 JN 5
JUD 3

Passive Participle

LUK 1:1
20:6
ACT 26:3,5
ROM 8:38
14:14
15:14
2 CO 5:6
2 TM 1:5,12
HEB 5:13
6:9
1 JN 5:15
JUD 10

1829 ܡܦܝܣܢܘܬܐ (f) persuasion

1 CO 2:4

fETTAPHAL

Perfect

ACT 5:40
18:20
21:14
27:21
ROM 11:31
HEB 3:18
4:6,11
1 PT 3:20

Imperfect

ACT 23:21
ROM 15:21
GAL 5:7

Imperative

HEB 13:17

Infinitive

ACT 5:29

Participle

LUK 1:17
JHN 3:36
ACT 8:6,11
14:2
28:24[1],24[2]
ROM 1:30
2:8[1],8[2]
10:19,21
ROM 11:30
15:31
2 CO 11:4
2 TM 3:2
1 PT 2:7,8
3:1
4:17

1936 ܠܐ ܡܬܛܦܝܣܢܘܬܐ (f)
(w/ ܠܐ) disobedience

ROM 11:30,32	EPH 5:6
EPH 2:2	COL 3:6

2539 ܦܟܐ (m) cheek, jaw

MAT 5:39	JHN 18:22
MRK 14:65	19:3
LUK 6:29	

2540 ܦܟܗ (v) lose flavor, be dull

aPEAL

Imperfect

MAT 5:13	LUK 14:34
MRK 9:50	

cPAEL (non occ)

2541 ܦܟܝܗܐ (adj) foolish; (w/ ܬܬܐ) sycamore

LUK 19:4	1 TM 4:7

2542 ܦܟܝܗܐܝܬ (adv) foolishly

2 CO 11:1

2543 ܦܟܝܗܘܬܐ (f) foolishness

2 CO 11:17

2544 ܦܟܪ (v) bind, entangle

aPEAL

Perfect

ACT 22:29

dETHPAAL

Participle

2 TM 2:4

2545 ܦܠܐܬ, ܦܠܐܬܐ (f)
comparison, parable

MAT 13:3,10,13,	JHN 10:6
34,34	16:25,25,
24:32	29
MRK 13:28	1 CO 13:12
LUK 8:10	GAL 4:24

2546 ܦܠܓ (v) divide, distribute; (ethpe, ethpa) divide, doubt
tr of ܦܠܓ below

aPEAL

Perfect

ROM 12:3	2 CO 10:13
1 CO 7:17	

Imperfect

MAT 10:35	LUK 12:46
24:51	

Active Participle

LUK 12:13	1 CO 9:13

Passive Participle

LUK 12:52	JAM 1:8
ACT 14:4	4:8

2548 ܦܠܓ (v) be in the midst
int of ܦܠܓ (above)

Perfect

JHN 7:14

2549 ܦܠܓܐ (m) half
incl idioms

MAT 25:6	ACT 22:6
MRK 6:23	26:13
13:35	27:27
ACT 16:25	REV 11:9,11
20:7	

2551 ܦܠܓܘܬܐ (f) half
incl idioms

LUK 11:5	REV 8:1
19:8	12:14

2552 ܦܠܓܘܬܐ (f) division, portion

incl idioms

LUK 12:51	1 CO 1:10
15:12	3:3
JHN 7:43	11:18
9:16	12:25
10:19	GAL 5:20
ROM 16:17	JAM 3:17

[b]ETHPEEL

Perfect

ACT 23:7

Imperfect

MAT 21:21*	LUK 12:53

Participle

ACT 2:3*	ROM 14:1*

[c]PAEL

Perfect

MAT 27:35	LUK 23:34
MRK 6:41	JHN 6:11
15:24	19:24
LUK 15:12	

Active Participle

LUK 11:22	1 CO 12:11
ACT 2:45	

1830 ܡܦܠܓܢܐ (adj) divider

LUK 12:14

2483 ܦܘܠܓܐ (m) division, distinction

ACT 11:12	COL 2:16
1 CO 12:4,5,6	HEB 2:4
PHL 2:14	

[d]ETHPAAL

Perfect

MAT 12:26	LUK 11:18
14:31	ROM 4:20
28:17	1 CO 1:13
MRK 3:26	JAM 2:4

Imperfect

MAT 12:25[1],25[2]	MRK 11:23
MRK 3:24,25	LUK 11:17[1]

Participle

LUK 11:17[2]	ROM 14:23
ACT 10:20	JAM 1:6[1],6[2]

2553 ܦܠܚ (v) work, labor; (aph) make serve

[a]PEAL

Perfect

ROM 4:5	HEB 11:33
1 CO 10:7	1 PT 4:3
GAL 4:8	2 JN 8

Imperfect

MAT 4:10	1 CO 9:6
LUK 1:74	2 CO 7:1
4:8	GAL 6:10
13:8	EPH 4:28
JHN 6:27,28	1 TH 1:9
ACT 7:7[1],7[2]	2 TH 3:10
ROM 15:16	1 TM 1:18
1 CO 7:21	

Imperative

MAT 21:28	PHL 2:12

Infinitive

MAT 6:24[1],24[2]	JHN 9:4
LUK 13:14	TIT 3:8
16:13[1],13[2]	

Active Participle

LUK 2:37	1 CO 9:13[1],13[2]
15:29	16:10
ACT 7:42	2 CO 10:3
10:35	GAL 4:25
18:3	PHL 2:22
19:25	3:3
20:19	COL 3:24
24:14	1 TH 4:11
27:23	2 TH 3:8,11,12
ROM 2:9,10	1 TM 5:6
4:4	2 TM 2:4
12:11	TIT 3:14
1 CO 3:9	REV 18:17
4:12	

Passive Participle

JHN 8:33

2554 ܦܠܚܐ (ap) servant, worshipper, soldier

MAT 7:23	1 CO 10:7
LUK 3:14	EPH 5:5
13:27	PHL 2:25
23:11	2 TM 2:3,15
ACT 10:7	PLM 1,2
ROM 16:3,9,21	REV 19:19,19
1 CO 5:10,11	21:8
6:9	22:15

2485 ܦܘܠܚܢܐ (m) service, occupation

ACT 19:25	EPH 4:19
1 CO 3:9	PHL 2:12
10:14	3:20
2 CO 9:12	COL 2:18
GAL 5:20	1 PT 4:3

2556 ܦܠܚܘܬܐ (f) service, warfare

1 CO 9:7	1 TM 1:18
2 CO 10:4	

---

[b]ETHPEEL

Participle

HEB 6:7

---

[c]PAEL (non occ)

2555 ܦܠܚܐ (m) husbandman

MAT 21:33,34, 35,38, 40,41	LUK 13:7,8
	20:9,10,10, 14,16
MRK 12:1,2,7,9	JHN 15:1

---

[e]APHEL

Active Participle

1 CO 9:7

2557 ܦܠܛ (v) escape; (pa) deliver

[c]PAEL

Perfect

ACT 12:11

Imperfect

ACT 23:24

---

[d]ETHPAAL

Perfect

2 CO 11:33

2558 ܦܠܢ (adj) such an one

MAT 26:18

2520 (ܦܠܣܦ), ܦܝܠܣܘܦܐ (m) philosopher

ACT 17:18

2521 ܦܝܠܣܘܦܘܬܐ (f) philosophy

COL 2:8

2559 ܦܠܣ (v-non occ) put aside

[a]PEAL

2560 ܦܠܣܐ (m) occasion, opportunity

MAT 26:16	LUK 22:6
MRK 14:11	

2561 ܦܠܫ (v) break through

[a]PEAL

Active Participle

MAT 6:19,20

---

[b]ETHPEEL

Imperfect

MAT 24:43	LUK 12:39

2486 (ܦܡ), ܦܘܡܐ (m) mouth, edge

MAT 4:4
5:2
12:34
13:35
15:11,11,
17,18
17:27
18:16
21:16
MRK 1:25
14:64
LUK 1:64,70
4:22,35
11:54
19:22
21:15,24
22:71
JHN 19:29
ACT 1:16
3:18,21
4:25
8:32,35
10:34
11:8
15:7
18:14
22:14
23:2
28:25
ROM 3:14,19
10:8,9,10

ROM 15:6
2 CO 6:11
13:1
EPH 4:29
6:19
2 TH 2:8
1 TM 5:19
2 TM 4:17
TIT 1:11
HEB 4:12
10:28
11:33,34,
37
JAM 3:3,10
1 PT 2:15,22
2 JN 12,12
3 JN 14,14
JUD 16
REV 1:16
2:12,16
3:16
9:17,18,19
10:9,10
11:5
12:15,16,
16
13:2,5,6
14:5
16:13,13,
13
19:15,21

2563 ܦܢܐ (v) return; (pa) answer, give back; (aph) cause to turn

[a]PEAL

Perfect

ACT 12:25

Imperfect

MAT 10:13
LUK 12:36

ACT 18:21

---

[b]ETHPEEL

Perfect

MAT 9:22
16:23
MRK 5:30
8:33
LUK 7:9,44
9:55
10:22,23
14:25
22:61

LUK 23:28
JHN 1:38
20:14,16
21:20
ACT 9:35,40
11:21
1 TH 1:9
1 PT 2:25

Imperfect

MAT 13:15
MRK 4:12
LUK 17:4
JHN 12:40
ACT 3:26
14:15

ACT 15:36
26:20
1 CO 7:5
2 CO 3:16
1 TM 2:4

Imperative

LUK 9:38
22:32

ACT 3:19

Participle

ACT 13:46

ACT 15:19

---

[c]PAEL

Perfect

MAT 15:23
27:12

ACT 25:4

Active Participle

MAT 26:62
MRK 12:34
14:60

MRK 15:4
LUK 22:68

2487 ܦܘܢܝܐ (m) conversion, reconciliation

ACT 15:3

ROM 11:15

---

[d]ETHPAAL

Imperfect

HEB 13:19

---

[e]APHEL

Perfect

ACT 17:31

Imperfect

LUK 1:16,17

JAM 5:19

Imperative

MAT 5:39

Active Participle

ACT 1:6

2 CO 7:10

2533 (ܦܝܢ), ܦܝܢܟܐ (m) dish, platter

MAT 14:8,11	LUK 11:39
MRK 6:25,28	

2567 (ܦܢܩ) (v) delight

[c]PAEL (non occ)

2490 ܦܘܢܩܐ (m) luxury

LUK 7:25

---

[d]ETHPAAL

Participle

2 PT 2:13

2568 ܦܢܩܝܬܐ (f) writing tablet

LUK 1:63

2570 ܦܣܐ (f) lot, portion

cf ܦܣܣ

MAT 27:35	ACT 1:17,25,26
MRK 15:24	8:21
LUK 23:34	26:18
JHN 19:24	

2569 (ܦܣܣ) (v) allow, permit

[e]APHEL

Perfect

MAT 19:8	ACT 16:7
MRK 5:13	21:40
10:4	27:3
LUK 8:32[2]	28:16
JHN 19:38	

Imperfect

LUK 8:32[1]

Imperative

MAT 8:21,31	ACT 21:39
LUK 9:59,61	

Active Participle

ACT 21:37	1 TM 2:12
1 CO 16:7	HEB 6:3

Passive Participle

ACT 2:29	ACT 22:25
10:28	26:1
16:21	1 CO 14:34

1831 ܡܦܣܢܘܬܐ (f) permission

ACT 26:12

2573 ܦܣܩ (v) cut off, cut down; (pa) break

[a]PEAL

Perfect

MAT 14:10	ACT 27:32,40
MRK 6:16,27	ROM 3:9
LUK 9:9	9:28
JHN 9:22	1 CO 7:37
18:26	2 CO 1:9
ACT 13:46	EPH 4:19

Imperfect

LUK 6:35	2 CO 11:12
13:9	GAL 5:12[2]

Imperative

MAT 5:30	MRK 9:43,45
18:8	LUK 13:7

Infinitive

GAL 5:12[1]

Active Participle

MAT 21:8	MRK 11:8

Passive Participle

ACT 20:16

2571 ܦܘܣܩܐ (m) section

ACT 8:32

2572 ܦܣܝܩܬܐ (f) (pl w/ ܒ) briefly

ACT 24:4

2574 ܦܣܘܩܐ (m) cutting; (w/ ܒܣܪܐ) mutilation of the flesh

PHL 3:2

[b]ETHPEEL

Perfect

ACT 27:20	REV 20:4

Participle

MAT 3:10 7:19	LUK 3:9

[c]PAEL

Active Participle

MRK 5:4	LUK 8:29

2575 ܦܣܩܝܬܐ (f) bandage

[a]PEAL

JHN 11:44

2576 ܦܨܥ (v) beat, wound

[a]PEAL

Passive Participle

ACT 19:16	REV 13:3

2577 ܦܥܠ (v-non occ) work, labor

[a]PEAL

2578 ܦܥܠܐ (m) laborer, worker

MAT 9:37,38 10:10 20:1,2,8 LUK 10:2,2,7	2 CO 11:13 PHL 3:2 1 TM 5:18 JAM 5:4

2579 ܦܥܪ (v-non occ) open wide

[a]PEAL

2580 ܦܥܪܐ (m) cavern

HEB 11:38

2582 (ܦܨܐ) (v) deliver

[c]PAEL

Perfect

2 TM 3:11	2 PT 2:7

Imperfect

ACT 26:17 ROM 7:24	GAL 1:4 2 TM 4:18

Imperative

MAT 6:13 8:25 27:40	MRK 15:30 LUK 23:39[1],39[2] JHN 12:27

Active Participle

1 TH 1:10

[d]ETHPAAL

Perfect

2 TM 4:17 HEB 11:34	HEB 12:25

Imperfect

ROM 5:9 15:31	2 TH 3:2

Infinitive

HEB 11:35

2583 ܦܨܚ (v-non occ) pass over

[a]PEAL

2585 ܦܨܚܐ (m) Feast of Passover

MAT 26:2,17,18, 19 MRK 14:1,12,12, 14,16 LUK 2:41 22:1,7,8,	LUK 22:11,13, 15 JHN 2:13,23 6:4 11:55 12:1

JHN 13:1, 18:28,39, 19:14 | ACT 12:4 | 1 CO 5:7 | HEB 11:28

2584 ܦܨܚ (v) (pe, ethpe) rejoice

[a]PEAL (non occ)

2586 ܦܨܝܚܘܬܐ (f) cheerfulness, joy

ROM 12:8

[b]ETHPEEL

Imperfect

REV 11:10

Imperative

GAL 4:27
REV 12:12
REV 18:20

Participle

REV 19:7

ܦܨܝ see ܦܨܐ

2464 (ܦܩ), ܦܐܩܐ (adj) stammerer

MRK 7:32

2587 (ܦܩ) (v) stammer

[c]PAEL

Active Participle

MAT 6:7

2588 ܦܩܕ (v) command

[a]PEAL

Perfect

MAT 1:24
8:18
14:9,19
15:35
18:25
21:6
26:19
27:10,58
MRK 6:27,39
8:6
10:49
LUK 5:14[1]
8:55
14:22
18:40
23:24
JHN 11:57
13:29[2]
ACT 4:15
5:28[2],34
7:19
8:38
10:42,48
12:19
13:47
16:22
18:2
ACT 20:13
21:33,34
22:24[1],24[2],
30
23:2,22,35
24:8,23
25:6,17,21,
23,25
27:1,43
1 CO 16:1
1 PT 3:20

Imperfect

LUK 8:31
PLM 8

Imperative

MAT 14:28
MAT 27:64

Infinitive

JHN 13:29[1]
ACT 5:28[1]
2 CO 8:8[1]

Active Participle

MRK 1:27
9:25
LUK 4:36
8:25,29
ACT 16:18
23:3
2 CO 8:8[2]

Passive Participle

LUK 2:27
3:13
17:10
LUK 23:56
ROM 13:1

2493 ܦܘܩܕܢܐ (m) commandment

MAT 5:19
15:3,9
19:17
22:36,38,
40
MRK 7:7,8,9
10:5,19
12:28,29,
30,31
LUK 1:6
2:1
15:29
18:20
JHN 10:18
12:49,50
13:34
14:15,21
15:10,10,
12
ACT 7:53
16:4,24
17:7,26
ROM 2:26
7:8,9,10,
11,12,13
ROM 13:2,9
16:25
1 CO 7:6,19,25
11:2
14:37
GAL 2:18
EPH 2:15
6:2
COL 2:14
1 TH 4:2,16
2 TH 2:15
3:6
1 TM 1:1,5,18
2:14
6:14
TIT 1:3
2:15
HEB 7:5,18
9:19
11:23
2 PT 2:21
3:2
1 JN 2:3,4,7,7,7,
8
3:11,22,23,

1 JN	3:24	REV	12:17
	4:21		14:12
	5:2,3,3		22:14
2 JN	4,5,6,6		

[b]ETHPEEL

Perfect

LUK	17:9	HEB	9:19,20*
ACT	10:33		

Participle

ACT 22:10

[c]PAEL

Perfect

MAT	8:4	JHN	8:5
	10:5		14:31
	16:20	ACT	1:2,4
	17:9		4:18
	19:7		5:40
	28:20		7:44
MRK	1:44		15:24
	5:43		16:23
	6:8		23:30
	8:15	1 CO	9:14
	10:3	1 TH	4:11
	11:6	TIT	1:5
	13:34	HEB	11:22
LUK	5:14[2]	1 JN	3:23

Imperfect

MAT	4:6	1 CO	11:34
LUK	4:10	2 CO	3:1
ACT	15:5	1 TM	1:3

Imperative

1 TM	4:11	1 TM	6:17

Infinitive

MAT 11:1

Active Participle

MRK	9:9	1 CO	11:17
JHN	15:14,17	2 TH	3:4,6,10,
ACT	17:30		12
1 CO	7:10,17	1 TM	5:7

2492 ܦܘܩܕܢܐ (m) commandment

2 CO	3:1	TIT	1:14
EPH	2:15	HEB	7:16
COL	2:22		9:1,10

[d]ETHPAAL

Perfect

ACT	23:31	HEB	12:20
COL	4:10		

2591 ܦܩܚ (v-non occ) blossom

[a]PEAL

2592 ܦܩܚܐ (ap) be profitable

PHL	1:23	HEB	13:17

[c]PAEL

2590 ܦܩܚ (adj) expedient, profitable, better

MAT	5:29,30	JHN	18:14
	18:6	ACT	20:20
	19:10	1 CO	6:12
	26:24		7:8,9,26
MRK	9:42,43,45,		9:15
	47		10:23,33,
	14:21		33
LUK	17:2	2 CO	12:1
JHN	11:50	2 PT	2:21
	16:7		

2593 ܦܩܥ (v-non occ) split

[a]PEAL

2594 ܦܩܥܬܐ (f) plain

LUK	3:4,5	LUK	6:17

[c]PAEL

2589 ܦܩܘܥܐ (m) unripe fig

REV 6:13

2602 (ܦܪܘܓ), ܦܪܘܓܐ (m) chick, young bird

MAT	23:37	LUK	13:34
LUK	2:24		

2596 ܦܪܓܠܐ (m) whip, scourge

MAT 27:26 | JHN 2:15

2598 ܦܪܕ (v-non occ) flee

aPEAL

2600 ܦܪܕܬܐ (f) grain

MAT 13:31	LUK 17:6
17:20	JHN 12:24
MRK 4:31	1 CO 15:37
LUK 13:19	

2599 ܦܪܕܝܣ, ܦܪܕܝܣܐ (m) paradise

LUK 23:43	REV 2:7
2 CO 12:4	

2607 ܦܪܙܠܐ (m) iron

ACT 12:10	REV 12:5
REV 2:27	18:12
9:9	19:15

2608 ܦܪܚ (v) fly; (pa) squander

aPEAL

Imperfect

REV 12:14

Active Participle

REV 4:7	REV 14:6
8:13	

2610 ܦܪܚܬܐ (f) bird

MAT 6:26	LUK 13:19
8:20	ACT 10:12
13:4,32	11:6
MRK 4:4,32	ROM 1:23
LUK 8:5	1 CO 15:39
9:58	JAM 3:7
12:24	REV 19:17,17

fPAEL

Perfect

LUK 15:30

Active Participle

LUK 16:1

2609 ܦܪܚܐܝܬ (adv) wastefully

LUK 15:13

2612 (ܦܪܛܪ), ܦܪܛܘܪ (m-non occ) praetor

2613 ܦܪܛܘܪܝܢ (f) judgement hall, praetorium

MAT 27:27	JHN 19:9
MRK 15:16	ACT 23:35
JHN 18:28,28,33	PHL 1:13

2618 ܦܪܟ (v) rub

aPEAL

Active Participle

LUK 6:1

2538 (ܦܪܡ), ܦܝܪܡܐ (m) censer

REV 8:3,5

2621 ܦܪܢܣ (v-non occ) provide

kP

2495 ܦܘܪܢܣܐ (m) supply

ACT 12:20

2496 (ܦܪܣ), ܦܘܪܣܐ (m) way, means, trick

PHL 1:18

2601 (ܦܪܣ), ܦܪܗܣܝܐ (f) boldness

2 CO 7:4	1 TH 2:2
EPH 3:12	PLM 8
6:20	1 JN 5:14

2622 ܦܪܣ (v-non occ) divide

[a]PEAL

2615 ܦܪܘܣܬܐ (f) bread

ACT 2:46

2624 ܦܪܣܐ (m) portion

LUK 12:42

2623 ܦܪܣ (v) spread

[a]PEAL

Active Participle

LUK 19:36

2625 ܦܪܣܡ (v) expose

[k]P

Perfect

COL 2:15

Imperfect

MAT 1:19

[m]ETHP

Participle

ACT 19:27

2627 ܦܪܥ (v) spring up

[a]PEAL

Perfect

MRK 13:28

Active Participle

MAT 24:32

[e]APHEL

Perfect

HEB 9:4

Active Participle

LUK 21:30

2628 ܦܪܥ (v) recompense

[a]PEAL

Perfect

2 TM 4:14	REV 18:6[2]

Imperfect

MAT 6:4,6,18	1 TH 5:15
16:27	2 TH 1:6
18:25[2],34	1 TM 5:4
LUK 14:14	2 TM 4:8
ROM 2:8	HEB 10:30
12:17	1 PT 3:9
1 CO 7:3	

Imperative

ROM 13:7	REV 18:6[1]
2 CO 6:13	

Infinitive

MAT 18:25[1]	1 TH 3:9
LUK 7:42	

Active Participle

MAT 18:26,29	ROM 2:6
LUK 19:8	PLM 19

2497 ܦܘܪܥܢܐ (m) recompense

LUK 14:12,14	HEB 2:2
ROM 1:27	11:26
11:9	1 PT 1:9
COL 3:24	

2604 ܦܪܘܥܐ (m) rewarder

HEB 11:6

[b]ETHPEEL

Perfect

LUK 23:41

Imperfect

LUK 6:34[1],34[2]	2 TH 1:9
2 CO 5:10	2 JN 8

Participle

EPH 6:8	COL 3:25

2630 ܦܪܩܒ (v) fill (mouth)

cf ܦܪܒ

[m]ETHP

Participle

JUD 12

2632 ܦܪܨܘܦܐ (m) face, countenance, person

MAT	6:16	ACT	2:28
	11:10		3:19
	16:3		6:15,15
	17:2		20:25,38
	18:10	1 CO	4:6
	27:30	2 CO	2:10
MRK	1:2		3:7,7
	12:14		4:6
	14:65		8:24
LUK	1:76		10:7
	2:31	COL	2:1,23
	7:27	2 TH	1:9
	9:51,52,53	HEB	9:24
	10:1	JUD	16
	12:56		

2633 ܦܪܩ (v) depart, deliver, save; (pa) rescue, pursue; (aph) go away

[a]PEAL

Perfect

MAT	26:39	ACT	22:29
LUK	4:13		26:31
	22:41	2 CO	1:10[1]
ACT	1:25	EPH	2:5
	7:10	COL	1:13
	12:10	JUD	5

Imperfect

MAT	27:43	1 TM	4:1
LUK	1:71	2 TM	2:19,26
	24:21	TIT	2:14
ACT	1:4	HEB	3:12
	7:34	2 PT	2:9
	21:21		

Imperative

MAT	9:24	LUK	11:4
	14:30		13:27
LUK	5:8	ACT	5:38

Infinitive

MAT 27:49

Active Participle

LUK	2:37	ACT	19:12
	9:39	2 CO	1:10[2]

Passive Participle

LUK	24:13	COL	2:5
JHN	11:18	1 TH	4:3
ACT	1:12	2 TH	3:6
	15:20	HEB	7:26
PHL	1:27	1 PT	2:9

2498 ܦܘܪܩܢܐ (m) redemption, salvation

MAT	20:28	1 CO	1:30
MRK	10:45	EPH	1:7,14
LUK	1:68,69		4:30
	2:38		6:17
	21:28	COL	1:14
ACT	4:12	1 TM	2:6
	7:25	HEB	9:12,15
	28:28	2 PT	3:15
ROM	3:24	REV	7:10
	8:23		19:1

2605 ܦܪܘܩܐ (m) savior, deliverer

LUK	2:11	2 PT	2:20
ACT	7:35		3:2,18
	13:23	1 JN	4:14
ROM	11:26	JUD	25
2 PT	1:1,11		

[b]ETHPEEL

Perfect

EPH	2:8	1 PT	1:18

Imperfect

LUK 1:74

[c]PAEL

Perfect

ACT 23:27

Imperfect

1 TM 5:13

[d]ETHPAAL

Imperfect

LUK 12:58

Imperative

1 PT 2:11

---

[e]APHEL

Imperfect

2 CO 12:8

Active Participle

1 TM 4:3

2634 ܦܪܩܠܛܐ (m) comforter, advocate

JHN 14:16,26 15:26	JHN 16:7 1 JN 2:1

2635 ܦܪܫ (v) separate, appoint

[a]PEAL

Perfect

LUK 10:1 17:18 ACT 11:29 13:13 15:9,39 17:31 19:9 21:1	ROM 10:12 14:22 1 CO 2:7 11:29 GAL 1:15 2:12 HEB 7:2

Imperfect

MAT 16:3 LUK 12:56[1] ROM 8:35,39	1 CO 3:13 7:10,11, 15[2]

Imperative

ACT 13:2

Infinitive

LUK 9:33	HEB 5:14

Active Participle

LUK 12:56[2] ROM 2:18 12:2 1 CO 7:15[1]	EPH 5:10 PHL 1:10 1 JN 2:20 4:1

Passive Participle

ACT 2:23 1 CO 14:8	GAL 4:1 1 PT 1:20

2616 ܦܪܝܫܐ (pp) Pharisee

MAT 3:7 5:20 7:29 9:11,14,34 12:2,14,24, 38 15:1,12 16:1,6,12 19:3 21:15,45 22:15,34, 41 23:2,13,14, 15,23, 25,26, 27,29 27:41,62 MRK 2:6,16,18, 18,24 3:6 7:1,3,5 8:11,15 10:2 LUK 5:17,21,30, 33 6:2,7 7:30,36,36, 37,39 11:37,38,	LUK 11:39,42, 43,44, 53 12:1 13:31 14:1,3 15:2 16:14 17:20 18:10,11, 14 19:39 JHN 1:24 3:1 4:1 7:32,45,47 48 8:3,13 9:13,15,16 40 11:46,47, 57 12:19,42 18:3 ACT 5:34 15:5 23:6,6,6,7, 8,9 26:5

2499 ܦܘܪܫܢܐ (m) difference

ROM 3:22 1 CO 7:34 12:2	1 CO 14:7 EPH 3:10 HEB 4:12

2606 ܦܪܘܫܘܬܐ (f) discernment

1 CO 12:10

2617 ܦܪܝܫܝܐ (adj) Pharisaic

PHL 3:5

---

[b]ETHPEEL

Perfect

LUK 22:22 24:51 ACT 10:42	ROM 1:1 REV 6:14

Imperfect

2 TH 3:14

Imperative

2 CO 6:17*

Participle

1 JN 3:10*

^cPAEL

Perfect

ACT 17:26

Imperfect

MAT 13:49
19:6
25:32[1]
MRK 10:9
1 CO 14:29

Active Participle

MAT 25:32[2]
LUK 6:22
ACT 17:11
JUD 19

Passive Participle

1 PT 4:10

1835 ܦܪܘܫܢܐ (m) discerner, judge

JAM 2:4

2636 ܦܪܫܐ (m) horseman

ACT 23:23,32 | REV 9:16

2637 ܦܪܬ (v) burst

^bETHPEEL

Perfect

ACT 1:18

^dETHPAAL (non occ)

2640 ܦܪܬܘܬܐ (f) crumb

MAT 15:27
MRK 7:28
LUK 16:21

2644 (ܦܫܓ), ܦܫܝܓܐ (adj) maimed

MAT 15:30,31
18:8
MRK 9:43

2642 ܦܫܚ (v) break off, cut off

^bETHPEEL

Perfect

ROM 11:17,19, | ROM 11:20,24

Imperfect

ROM 11:22

^cPAEL

Imperfect

ACT 23:10

2643 ܦܫܛ (v) (tr) stretch out; (int) be straight

^aPEAL

Perfect

MAT 8:3
12:13[2],49
14:31
MRK 1:41
3:5[2]
LUK 5:13
6:10[2]
ACT 26:1
ROM 10:21

Imperfect

JHN 21:18

Imperative

MAT 12:13[1]
MRK 3:5[1]
LUK 6:10[1]

2645 ܦܫܝܛܐ (pp) simple, upright

MAT 6:22
LUK 11:34
ROM 16:18
COL 3:22
HEB 1:8

2646 ܦܫܝܛܐܝܬ (adv) liberally

JAM 1:5

2647 ܦܫܝܛܘܬܐ (f) simplicity

ROM 12:8 | 2 CO 1:12

2 CO 8:2	2 CO 11:3
9:11,13	EPH 6:5

[b]ETHPEEL

Perfect

LUK 13:13 | JHN 8:7,10

Imperfect

LUK 13:11

2650 ܦܫܟ, ܦܫܟܐ (m-non occ) palm

2502 ܦܘܫܟܐ (m) (w/ ܐܪܥܐ) distress, anxiety

LUK 21:25

2651 ܦܫܩ (v) make plain, easy; (pa) interpret, expound

[a]PEAL (non occ)

2648 ܦܫܝܩܐ (pp) easy

MAT 9:5	LUK 5:23
MRK 2:9	16:17
10:25	ROM 7:18

2649 ܦܫܝܩܐܝܬ (adv) plainly

MRK 7:35	1 TM 4:1
JHN 11:14	

[c]PAEL

Imperfect

1 CO 14:13,27

Imperative

MAT 13:36 | MAT 15:15

Infinitive

HEB 5:11

Active Participle

MRK 4:34	1 CO 12:30
LUK 24:27,32	14:5[1],5[2],
ACT 17:3	28

Passive Participle

1 CO 14:9

2503 ܦܘܫܩܐ (m) interpretation

1 CO 12:10 | 1 CO 14:26

[d]ETHPAAL

Participle

MAT 27:33	HEB 7:2
MRK 15:22	

2652 ܦܫܪ (v-non occ) melt

[a]PEAL

2641 ܦܫܘܪܐ (adj) lukewarm

REV 3:16

2653 ܦܬܐ (v) make broad

[a]PEAL (non occ)

2657 ܦܬܝܐ (pp) broad

MAT 7:13

2658 ܦܬܝܐ (m) breadth

EPH 3:18	REV 21:16,16
REV 20:9	

[e]APHEL

Active Participle

MAT 23:5

2654 ܦܬܓܡܐ (m) word

MAT 12:36	LUK 14:6
15:23	20:26
22:46	22:68
26:62	23:9
27:12,14	JHN 1:22
MRK 12:28,34	18:22
14:60	19:9
15:4,5	ACT 25:4
LUK 2:47	ROM 9:20
4:4	10:8

ROM 14:12	HEB 4:13
COL 4:6	1 PT 4:5

2656 ܦܬܚ (v) open

aPEAL

Perfect

MAT 2:11	ACT 12:14
5:2	14:27
MRK 14:3	16:14
LUK 4:17	REV 6:1,3,7,9, 12
24:45	8:1
ACT 5:19,23	12:16
8:32,35	13:6
9:40	
10:34	

Imperfect

MAT 13:35	COL 4:3
LUK 12:36	REV 3:20
ACT 18:14	5:5

Imperative

MAT 17:27	LUK 13:25
25:11	ACT 22:13[1]

Infinitive

REV 5:2,3,4

Active Participle

LUK 2:23	REV 3:7[1],7[2]
JHN 10:3	

2659 ܦܬܝܚܐ (pp) open

JHN 1:51	2 CO 6:11
ACT 7:56	REV 3:8
9:8	4:1
10:11	10:2
16:27	19:11
ROM 3:13	

1836 ܡܦܬܚ (m) (w/ ܦܘܡܐ)
open mouth

EPH 6:19

bETHPEEL

Perfect

MAT 3:16	2 CO 2:12
LUK 1:64	REV 6:5
3:21	11:19
ACT 12:10	15:5
16:26	20:12[1],12[2]
1 CO 16:9	

Imperfect

MAT 7:7	ACT 9:12*,17*
20:33*	ROM 1:10
LUK 11:9	

Imperative

MRK 7:34*

Participle

MAT 7:8	LUK 11:10

cPAEL

Perfect

JHN 9:14,17,21, 26,30,32	JHN 11:37

Imperfect

ACT 26:18

Infinitive

JHN 10:21

dETHPAAL

Perfect

MAT 9:30	LUK 24:31
20:34	JHN 9:10
27:52	ACT 9:18
MRK 7:35	22:13[2]

2660 ܦܬܟ (v) mingle

aPEAL

Passive Participle

REV 8:7	REV 15:2

2661 ܦܬܟܪܐ (m) idol

incl idioms

ACT 7:41	GAL 5:20
17:16	EPH 5:5
ROM 2:22	COL 3:5
1 CO 5:10,11	1 TH 1:9
6:9	1 JN 5:21
8:1,4,4,7, 10	REV 2:14,20
10:7,14,19, 19	9:20
12:2	21:8
	22:15

2504 ܦܬܩ, ܦܘܬܩܐ (m) inn

LUK 10:34

2505 ܦܘܬܩܝܐ (m) innkeeper

LUK 10:35

2655 (ܦܬܪ), ܦܬܘܪܐ (m) table

MAT	12:4	LUK	19:23
	15:27		22:21,30
	21:12	JHN	2:15
	25:27	ACT	6:2
MRK	2:26		16:34
	7:28	ROM	11:9
	11:15	1 CO	10:21,21
LUK	6:4	HEB	9:2
	16:21		

ܨ

2663 ܨܐܝ (v-non occ) be filthy

[a]PEAL

2662 ܨܐܐ (adj) filthy

JAM 2:2

2664 ܨܐܬܐ (f) filth

1 PT 3:21

2665 ܨܒܐ (v) will, desire

[a]PEAL

Perfect

MAT 1:19; 17:12; 18:23,30; 22:3; 23:37[1],37[2]; 27:34
MRK 3:13; 6:26; 9:13; 15:15
LUK 1:1; 10:24,29; 12:32; 13:34[1],34[2]; 19:27
JHN 1:43; 5:35; 6:11,21
ACT 7:39; 16:3,10; 18:27; 19:13; 22:30; 24:6; 25:26; 27:42; 28:18
ROM 1:13[2]; 9:22; 15:26,27
1 CO 1:21; 12:18
2 CO 8:11[1]
GAL 1:15
EPH 1:11
COL 1:19,27
1 TH 2:18; 3:1
PLM 14
HEB 6:17; 10:5,8; 12:17
JAM 1:18

Imperfect

LUK 4:6; 10:22
JHN 15:7
ACT 18:21
ROM 7:18
2 CO 12:6
COL 2:18
JAM 4:15
REV 11:6

Infinitive

2 CO 8:10,11[2]
PHL 2:13[1]

Active Participle

MAT 2:18; 5:40,42; 7:12; 8:2,3; 11:14,27; 12:7,38; 13:28; 14:5; 15:28,32; 16:24,25; 17:4; 19:17,21; 20:14,15, 21,26, 27,32; 21:29; 23:4; 26:15,17, 39,66; 27:15,17, 21,43
MRK 1:40,41; 6:19,22,48; 7:24; 8:34,35; 9:30,35; 10:35,36, 43,44, 51; 12:38; 14:7,12,38; 15:9,12
LUK 1:62; 5:12,13; 6:31; 8:20; 9:9,23,24, 54; 11:48; 12:49; 13:31; 14:28; 15:28; 16:26; 17:33; 18:4,13,41; 19:3,14; 20:46; 22:9,42; 23:8,20
JHN 3:8; 5:6,21,40; 6:67; 7:1,4,17, 44; 8:44; 9:27[1],27[2]; 12:21; 17:24; 18:39; 19:12; 21:18[1],18[2], 22,23
ACT 5:28; 8:1; 9:26,29; 10:10,33; 13:8; 14:13; 15:37,38; 16:7; 17:18,20; 18:15; 19:30,33; 23:20; 25:9[1],9[2], 22; 26:4,21; 27:12,43; 28:16,22
ROM 1:13[1]; 7:15,16, 19[1],19[2], 20,21; 9:16,18[1], 18[2]; 11:25; 13:3; 16:19
1 CO 4:19,21; 7:7,12,13, 32,36,39; 10:1,20,27; 11:3; 12:1,11; 14:5,19,35; 15:38; 16:7
2 CO 1:8,15; 5:4; 12:10,20[1], 20[2]
GAL 1:7; 3:2; 4:9,17,20, 21

GAL 5:17
6:12,13
PHL 1:12
2:13[2]
COL 2:1
1 TH 4:13
2 TH 3:10
1 TM 2:4,8
5:14
6:9
2 TM 3:12
TIT 3:8
PLM 13
HEB 6:11
10:38
12:6,10
13:18
JAM 2:20
4:4
1 PT 3:10
2 PT 3:5,9
JUD 5
REV 2:21
11:5

2667 ܨܒܘܬܐ (f) thing, matter, affair

MAT 18:19
JHN 3:27
5:19,30
7:17,18,28
8:28,42
11:51
ACT 2:12
5:4
6:3
12:10
18:15
19:27
ROM 16:2
1 CO 7:5,37
1 CO 14:7
16:14
2 CO 7:11
9:3
11:15
PHL 1:24
2:25
1 TH 4:6
5:22
2 TM 2:4
TIT 3:14
HEB 6:18
10:1
JUD 16

2668 ܨܒܝܢܐ (m) will, desire

MAT 6:10
7:21
11:26
12:50
18:14
21:31
26:42
MRK 3:35
6:25
14:36
15:15
LUK 7:30
10:21
11:2
12:47,47
22:42
23:25,51
JHN 1:13,13
4:34
5:30,30
6:38,38,39,
40
7:17
9:31
10:18
ACT 2:23
4:28
13:22,36
15:28
20:27
21:14
22:14,20
ACT 27:13
ROM 1:10
2:18
8:20,27
9:19
10:1
12:2
15:32
1 CO 1:1
7:37
9:17,17
16:12
2 CO 1:1
8:3,5,12,
17
GAL 1:4
EPH 1:1,5,9,11
2:2,3
5:17
6:6
PHL 1:15
COL 1:1,9
4:12
1 TH 4:3
5:18
2 TH 1:11
2 TM 1:1,9
2:26
3:10
PLM 14
HEB 2:4
10:7,9,10,
HEB 10:26,36
13:21
JAM 3:4
1 PT 2:15
3:17
4:2,3,19
5:2
2 PT 1:21
1 JN 2:17
5:14
REV 4:11
17:13,17,
17

[b]ETHPEEL

Perfect

MAT 3:17
12:18
17:5
MRK 1:11
LUK 3:22
1 CO 10:5
2 TH 2:12
2 PT 1:17

2669 ܨܒܥ (v) dip, wash

[a]PEAL

Perfect

JHN 13:26[2]

Imperfect

LUK 16:24

Active Participle

MAT 26:23
MRK 14:20
JHN 13:26[1]

[c]PAEL

Perfect

LUK 7:44

Active Participle

LUK 7:38

2670 ܨܒܥܐ (f) finger

MAT 23:4
MRK 7:33
LUK 11:20,46
LUK 16:24
JHN 20:25,27

2672 ܨܒܬ, ܨܒܬܐ (m) adornment

1 PT 3:3,4

2671 (ܨܒܬ) (v) adorn

[c]PAEL

Imperfect

TIT 2:10

Active Participle

MAT 23:29	1 PT 3:5

Passive Participle

MAT 12:44	LUK 21:5
LUK 11:25	REV 21:2,19

3420 ܬܨܒܝܬܐ (m) adornment

1 TM 2:9

[d]ETHPAAL

Perfect

1 PT 3:4

Imperfect

1 PT 3:3

2673 ܨܕ (v) (w/ ܒ) behold

[e]APHEL

Active Participle

REV 11:12

2674 ܨܕܐ (v) be deserted, desolate

[a]PEAL

Active Participle

GAL 4:27

2675 ܨܗܐ (v) be thirsty

[a]PEAL

Perfect

MAT 25:35,42

Imperfect

JHN 4:13,14,15	REV 7:16
6:35	

2676 ܨܗܝܐ (pp) thirsty

MAT 5:6	ROM 12:20
25:37,44	1 CO 4:11
JHN 7:37	REV 21:6
19:28	22:17

2677 ܨܗܝܐ (m) thirst

2 CO 11:27

2679 (ܨܘܕ) (v) catch, take

cf under ܨܝܕ, ܨܝܕܐ

[a]PEAL

Perfect

LUK 5:9	JHN 21:3[2],10

Imperfect

MAT 22:15	JHN 21:3[1]
MRK 12:13	

Active Participle

LUK 5:10

2682 (ܨܘܡ) (v) fast

[a]PEAL

Perfect

MAT 4:2	ACT 13:3

Imperfect

MAT 9:15[2]	LUK 5:34,35
MRK 2:19,20	

Infinitive

MAT 9:15[1]

Active Participle

MAT 6:16[1],16[2],	LUK 5:33
17,18	18:12
9:14[1],14[2]	ACT 10:30
MRK 2:18[1],18[2],	13:2
18[3]	14:23

2683 ܨܘܡܐ (m) fast

MAT 17:21	1 CO 7:5
MRK 9:29	2 CO 6:5
LUK 2:37	11:27
ACT 27:9	

2701 ܨܝܡܐ (adj) hungry

MAT 15:32	MRK 8:3

2686 (ܨܘܪ) (v-non occ) be dazzled

[a]PEAL

2687 ܨܘܪܐ (m) neck

MAT 18:6 MRK 9:42 LUK 15:20	LUK 17:2 ACT 15:10 ROM 16:4

2689 ܨܘܪܬܐ (f) image

ROM 8:29

2685 (ܨܘܪ) (v) portray, form

[a]PEAL

Infinitive

GAL 3:1

2702 ܨܝܪܐ (pp) portrayed

GAL 3:1

---

[b]ETHPEEL

Imperfect

GAL 4:19

2691 ܨܘܬܐ (f-non occ) voice, sound

2690 (ܨܘܬ) (v) heed, listen to

[a]PEAL

Imperative

ACT 2:14

Active Participle

JHN 3:29	ACT 8:6

2681 (ܨܚܐ), ܨܘܚܬܐ (f) reviling

EPH 5:4 1 TM 5:14	1 PT 3:9,9

2692 (ܨܚܐ) (v) revile

[c]PAEL

Perfect

JHN 9:28	ACT 19:37

Active Participle

MAT 15:4 MRK 7:10 ACT 19:9 23:4	1 CO 4:13 TIT 1:6 1 PT 2:23[2]

---

[d]ETHPAAL

Participle

1 PT 2:23[1]

2693 (ܨܚܐ), ܨܚܘܐ (m) fair weather

MAT 16:2

2694 ܨܚܢ, ܨܚܢܐ (adj-non occ) filthy, impure

2695 ܨܚܢܘܬܐ (f) filthiness

MRK 7:22 GAL 5:19	1 PT 4:3

2696 ܨܝܕ (prep) near, with, at

JHN 13:29 ACT 9:38; 13:42; 17:15; 21:7; 25:11 1 CO 16:10 2 CO 8:17; 11:9 1 TH 3:6 HEB 12:7 1 JN 4:16 REV 1:13; 7:17,17; 20:13; 21:2,10

2697 ܨܝܕ, ܨܝܕܐ (m) catch

LUK 5:4,9

1839 ܡܨܝܕܬܐ (f) net

MAT 4:18,20,21 13:47 MRK 1:16,18,19	LUK 5:2,4,5,6 JHN 21:6,6,8, 11,11

2680 (ܨܘܕ) (v) (ethpe) be captured; (pa) catch

cf root (ܨܘܕ)

[b]ETHPEEL

Perfect

2 TM 2:26	REV 19:20

[c]PAEL (non occ)

2698 ܨܝܕܐ (m) fisherman

MAT 4:18,19 MRK 1:16,17	LUK 5:2

2703 ܨܠ (v) strain

[c]PAEL

Active Participle

MAT 23:24

2704 ܨܠܐ (v) incline toward, heed; (pa) pray

[a]PEAL

Infinitive

LUK 9:12

Passive Participle

ACT 8:10	1 TM 3:8

2706 ܨܠܘܬܐ (f) prayer

MAT 17:21 21:13,22 23:13 MRK 9:29 11:17 12:40 LUK 1:13 2:37 6:12 19:46 20:47 22:45 ACT 1:14 2:42 3:1 6:4 10:4,31	ACT 12:5 16:13,16 26:7 ROM 1:9 12:12 15:30 1 CO 7:5 2 CO 9:14 EPH 1:16 6:18,18 PHL 4:6 COL 4:2,12 1 TH 1:2 1 TM 2:1 4:5 5:5 2 TM 1:3
PLM 4,22 HEB 7:25 JAM 5:15,16 1 PT 3:7	1 PT 4:7 REV 5:8 8:3,4

[b]ETHPEEL

Imperfect

HEB 10:23

[c]PAEL

Perfect

MAT 26:42,44 MRK 14:39 ACT 1:24 6:6 8:15 9:40	ACT 13:3 20:36 21:5 22:17 28:8 JAM 5:17,18

Imperfect

MAT 19:13 26:36 LUK 18:1 ACT 10:9 ROM 8:26[1]	1 CO 11:13 14:13,15[1], 15[2] JAM 5:14

Imperative

MAT 5:44 6:6[2],9 24:20 26:41 MRK 13:18,33 14:38	LUK 6:28 22:40,46 EPH 6:18[1] 1 TH 5:25 2 TH 3:1 HEB 13:18

Infinitive

MAT 6:5[2] 14:23 MRK 6:46 11:25 LUK 6:12	LUK 9:28 11:1[2] 18:10 COL 1:9

Active Participle

MAT 6:5[1],6[1],7 26:39 MRK 1:35 11:24 14:32,35 LUK 1:10 3:21 5:16,33 9:18,29 11:1[1],2 18:11 21:36 22:41,44 ACT 7:59	ACT 9:11 10:30 11:5 12:12 14:23 16:25 27:29 ROM 8:26[2],27 9:3 1 CO 11:4,5 14:14[1],14[2] 2 CO 13:9 EPH 6:18[2] PHL 1:9

COL 1:3	JAM 5:13,16[1],
4:3	16[2]
1 TH 5:17	3 JN 2
2 TH 1:11	JUD 20
1 TM 2:8	

2705 ܨܠܒ (v) crucify

aPEAL

Imperative

JHN 19:6[1],6[2], | JHN 19:15[1],15[2]

Passive Participle

LUK 23:39 | GAL 3:1

2708 ܨܠܝܒܐ (m) cross

MRK 10:21	HEB 12:2
LUK 14:27	1 PT 2:24
ACT 13:29	

bETHPEEL

Perfect

REV 11:8

Imperfect

LUK 24:7

2707 ܨܠܚ (v) prosper

aPEAL

Imperfect

3 JN 2[1]

eAPHEL

Active Participle

3 JN 2[2]

2709 ܨܠܡ, ܨܠܡܐ (m) image

MAT 22:20	REV 13:15
MRK 12:16	14:9,11
LUK 20:24	15:2
ACT 19:35	16:2
ROM 1:23	19:20
HEB 1:3	20:4
REV 13:14,15,	

2710 ܨܠܦ (v) wound

cPAEL

Perfect

MRK 12:4 | LUK 20:12

Active Participle

MRK 5:5

2711 ܨܡܚ (v-non occ) shine

aPEAL

2712 ܨܡܚܐ (m) radiance

HEB 1:3

2714 ܨܢܥܬܐ (f) device, trick

EPH 6:11

2713 (ܨܢܥ) (v) (ethpa) plot, scheme

dETHPAAL

Perfect

ACT 7:19

Participle

EPH 4:14

2715 ܨܥܐ (v) be foul, filthy

aPEAL

Perfect

REV 22:11[1]

mETHP ܐܨܛܥܐ

Imperfect

REV 22:11[2]

2717 ܨܥܪ (v) be despised; (pa) despise

aPEAL (non occ)

2716 ܨܥܝܪܐ (pp) despised

MAT 13:57	MRK 6:4

2718 ܨܥܪܐ (m) shame, dishonor

MRK 12:4	2 CO 6:8
ROM 1:26	11:21
9:21	12:10
1 CO 11:14	2 TM 2:20
15:43	

cPAEL

Perfect

MAT 22:6	HEB 10:29
LUK 20:11	

Imperfect

LUK 18:33	ROM 1:24
ACT 14:5	HEB 6:6

Active Participle

LUK 11:45	ROM 2:23
JHN 8:49	1 CO 4:12

Passive Participle

1 CO 12:23

1841 ܡܨܥܪܢܐ (adj) despiser, reviler

ROM 1:30	1 CO 6:10
1 CO 5:11	1 TM 1:13

dETHPAAL

Perfect

1 TH 2:2

Imperfect

ACT 5:41

Participle

1 CO 4:10

2719 ܨܦܚ (v) fall upon, suprise

aPEAL

Imperfect

LUK 21:35

2720 ܨܦܚܬܐ (f) snare

LUK 21:35

2721 ܨܦܪ, ܨܦܪܐ (m) daybreak, morning

MAT 16:3	JHN 18:28
20:1	20:1
21:18	21:4
27:1	ACT 12:6,18
MRK 1:35	16:35
11:20	20:11
13:35	23:12
15:1	27:33
LUK 4:42	28:23
10:35	REV 2:28
JHN 8:2	22:16

2722 ܨܦܪ, ܨܦܪܐ (f) bird, sparrow

MAT 10:29,31	LUK 12:6,7

2723 ܨܦܝܪܐ (c) goat, kid

HEB 9:12,13	HEB 10:4

2725 ܨܨܐ (m) nail

JHN 20:25

2726 ܨܨܠܐ (m) cymbal

1 CO 13:1

2727 ܨܪܐ (v) rend, burst; (ethpa w/ ܥܠ) despise

aPEAL

Perfect

MRK 14:63

[b]ETHPEEL

Perfect

MAT 27:51[1]	LUK 23:45
MRK 15:38	JHN 21:11*

Participle

MAT 9:17*

[c]PAEL

Perfect

MAT 26:65

Active Participle

MRK 2:22

[d]ETHPAAL

Perfect

MAT 27:51[2]

Participle

LUK 5:6	1 TM 5:11

2728 ܨܪܟ (v) lack

[a]PEAL

Passive Participle

ACT 4:34

ܩ

2733 ܩܒܐ (m) measure

REV 6:6,6

2738 ܩܒܠ (v) appeal to, accuse; (pa, aph) receive, take; (saph, estaph) be present, oppose

[a]PEAL

Perfect

ACT 25:24

Imperfect

ROM 8:33

Active Participle

ROM 11:2

694 ܕܠܘܩܒܠܐ (adj) contrary, on the contrary

2 TH 2:4	1 PT 3:9

1557 ܠܘܩܒܠ (adv) against, near, toward; (w/ ܩܘܡ) resist

MAT	5:39	ACT	4:14
	12:30		5:39
	14:24		6:10,13
	19:8		7:51
	27:61		13:8,45
MRK	6:48		17:7
	9:40		18:5,28
	10:5		19:36
	11:2		20:15
	12:41		21:28,28,28
	13:3		26:9,19
	14:54		27:7,7,15
LUK	8:26		28:17,19,25
	9:50	ROM	7:23
	11:23		8:31
	13:17		9:19
	18:9		13:2,2,2
	19:30	1 CO	13:12
	21:15	2 CO	10:5
JHN	12:18		13:8
		EPH	6:11
		PHL	1:28
			3:14
		2 TM	2:25
			3:8,8
		2 TM	4:15
		TIT	2:8
		HEB	12:4
		JAM	4:7
			5:6
		1 PT	2:11
			5:9

1592 ܠܘܩܒܠܐ (adj) opposite

MAT 21:2

2734 ܩܘܒܠ (m) (w/ ܡܢ) far away

REV 18:10,15

---

[c]PAEL

Perfect

MAT	6:2,5,16	1 CO	6:19
MRK	7:4		11:23
LUK	2:28		15:1,3
	6:24	2 CO	6:1
	8:40		7:15
	9:11,53		8:17
	10:38		11:4
	16:25	GAL	1:9,12
	19:6		4:14
JHN	1:11,12	PHL	4:9,18
	3:33	COL	2:6
	4:45		4:17
	10:18	1 TH	1:6
	17:8		2:13[1],13[2]
ACT	1:9		4:1
	2:41	2 TH	2:10
	7:38,53		3:6
	8:14	1 TM	5:10
	9:19	HEB	2:2
	10:23,47		6:15
	11:1		7:6
	16:24		8:6
	17:15		10:26,32
	19:2		11:17,31,33,39
	20:14,24		12:28
	21:17	JAM	2:25
	22:5[1]	1 PT	1:18
	26:10		4:10
	27:36	1 JN	2:27
	28:7,21		4:21
ROM	1:27		5:15
	5:11		

Imperfect

MAT	18:5[1]	ACT	18:27
	19:29		20:13
	23:13		21:16
MRK	6:11		22:5[2]
	9:37[1]		26:18
	10:15,30		27:33,34
	12:40	ROM	16:2
LUK	1:31	1 CO	3:14
	10:10	2 CO	1:15
	16:4,9		6:17
	18:17,30	GAL	4:5
	20:47	COL	4:10
JHN	5:43[2]	1 TM	5:19
	6:21	HEB	10:29
ACT	1:8,25		11:11
	2:38		13:2
	3:21	1 PT	1:9
	8:15		5:4
	10:43	2 JN	10

Imperative

MAT	11:14	2 CO	11:16
LUK	16:7	PHL	2:29
JHN	20:22	PLM	12,17
ACT	7:59	JAM	1:21

Infinitive

JHN	7:39	1 TM	1:15
	14:17		4:9
ACT	16:21	3 JN	8

Active Participle

MAT	10:14,40[1], 40[2],40[3], 40[4],41[1], 41[2]	JHN	5:43[1],44
			12:48
			13:20[1],20[2], 20[3],20[4]
	13:20	ACT	2:46
	18:5[2]		8:17,19
MRK	4:16,20		18:14
	9:37[2],37[3], 37[4]		22:18
			24:3
LUK	8:13		28:30
	9:5,48[1], 48[2],48[3], 48[4]	1 CO	2:14
			3:8
		COL	3:24
	10:8	HEB	6:7
	15:2		7:5
	17:9	1 JN	5:9
JHN	3:11,32	3 JN	9,10[1],10[2]

Passive Participle

1 PT 2:5

1845 ܡܩܒܠܐ (pp) acceptable

LUK	4:19	2 CO	6:2,2
ACT	10:35	PHL	4:18
	28:22	1 TM	2:3
ROM	12:1,2		5:4
	15:16		

1846 ܡܩܒܠܢܐ (adj) host

ACT	17:7	ROM	16:23

2758 ܩܘܒܠܐ (m) acceptance, reception, feast

LUK	5:29	REV	4:9
	14:13		7:12

[d]ETHPAAL

Perfect

ACT 15:4

Imperfect

ROM 15:31

Participle

LUK	4:24	2 CO	8:12

[e]APHEL

Perfect

LUK 15:27

[i]SAPHEL (non occ)

2230 ܣܩܘܒܠܐ (adj) contrary, adverse

JHN	19:12	COL	2:14
ACT	26:9	1 TH	2:15
	27:4	1 TM	1:10
1 CO	16:9	HEB	12:3
GAL	3:21	1 PT	5:5
	5:17		

[j]ESTAPHAL

Participle

ACT 17:17

2739 ܩܒܥ (v) fix, fasten

[a]PEAL

Perfect

COL	2:14	HEB	8:2

2740 ܩܒܪ (v) bury; (pa) heap up

[a]PEAL

Perfect

MAT 14:12	ACT 8:2
ACT 5:6,10	

Imperfect

MAT 8:21	JHN 19:40
LUK 9:59	

Infinitive

MAT 26:12

Active Participle

MAT 8:22	LUK 9:60

2735 ܩܒܘܪܐ (m) tomb, sepulchre

MAT 8:28	LUK 24:24
23:29	JHN 11:17,38, 38
27:7,52,60, 60	12:7
MRK 5:2,3,5	19:41
6:29	20:1,2,3,4, 6,8
16:2,3,5	
LUK 8:27	ACT 2:29
23:53	13:29
24:1,2,22,	

2736 ܩܒܘܪܐ (m) grave digger

ACT 5:9

2737 ܩܒܘܪܬܐ (f) burial

MRK 14:8

2741 ܩܒܪܐ (m) tomb, sepulchre

MAT 23:27,29	LUK 24:9,12
27:61,64, 66	JHN 5:28
	11:31
28:1,8	12:17
MRK 15:46,46	19:42
16:8	20:1,11,11
LUK 11:44,47, 48	ACT 7:16
	ROM 3:13
23:55	REV 11:9

[b]ETHPEEL

Perfect

LUK 16:22	1 CO 15:4
ACT 2:29	COL 2:12
ROM 6:4	

[c]PAEL

Imperfect

ROM 12:20

2759 (ܩܒܪܢܛ), ܩܘܒܪܢܛܐ (m) shipmaster

ACT 27:11

2730 (ܩܒܬ), ܩܒܘܬܐ (f) ark

HEB 9:4	1 PT 3:20
11:7	REV 11:19

2742 ܩܕ (v) tear, cut off

[a]PEAL

Active Participle

LUK 5:36[1],36[2]

2743 (ܩܕܐ) (v) hold fast

[c]PAEL

Active Participle

1 CO 7:30

2747 ܩܕܠܐ (m) neck

ACT 7:51

2748 ܩܕܡ (v) go before

incl idioms

[a]PEAL

Active Participle

MAT 21:31	MRK 16:7
26:32	1 CO 11:21
28:7	2 PT 3:17
MRK 14:28	

2744 ܩܕܡܝܐ (pp) before; (w/ ܡܢ) before, formerly

MRK	10:32	2 CO	13:2
LUK	1:2	GAL	1:13,23
	23:12		3:17
JHN	6:62,64		4:13
	9:8,13	EPH	2:2,3,10, 11,13
	10:40		
	16:4	COL	1:5,21
	19:39		3:7
ACT	3:26	1 TM	1:13
	11:15	TIT	3:3
	26:9	HEB	1:1
ROM	1:2	1 PT	2:10
	3:25		3:5,20
	7:9	2 PT	2:3
	11:2,30		3:5
	15:4	1 JN	2:24,24
2 CO	1:15		3:11
	9:5		

1558 ܠܘܩܕܡ (adv) before, formerly

MAT	5:24	JHN	18:13
	6:33	ACT	7:12
	7:5	ROM	1:8,16
	8:21		2:9,10
	12:29		3:2
	13:30		8:29
	17:10,11	1 CO	11:18
	23:26		12:28
MRK	3:27		15:3,46
	4:28	2 CO	8:5
	7:27	GAL	1:9
	9:11,12		5:21
	13:10	EPH	4:9
	16:9		5:8
LUK	6:42	1 TH	2:2
	9:59,61		4:16
	10:5	2 TH	2:3
	11:38	1 TM	2:13
	12:1		3:10
	14:28,31		5:4
	17:25	2 TM	1:5
	21:9	HEB	7:27
JHN	1:41	2 PT	1:20
	2:10		3:3
	7:51		

2749 ܩܕܡ (prep) before

MAT 2:9; 5:12,16,24; 6:1,2; 7:6; 8:16, 29; 10:18,32,32,33,33; 11:10,10,26; 13:35; 14:6,22; 17:2; 18:14; 21:9; 23:14; 24:38; 25:32; 26:34,70,75; 27:11,29; 28:14 MRK 1:2; 2:2; 5:33; 6:33,45; 7:25; 11:9; 13:9; 14:30,72; 15:42,44 LUK 1:6,8,15,17,19,74,76; 2:21,22; 4:7; 5:8,18,19; 7:27,27; 8:28,41; 9:23,52; 10:1,21; 11:38; 12:6,8,8,9,9,11; 13:26; 14:2,10; 15:10,18,21; 16:15,15; 17:16; 18:39; 19:24,27,28; 20:26; 21:12,12,36; 22:15,47,61; 24:19,19 JHN 1:15,27, 30; 3:28; 5:7,45; 10:4; 11:55; 12:1,37; 13:1,19; 15:18; 17:5,24; 20:30 ACT 2:47; 3:13,16,19; 4:10,19,37; 5:2, 10,27,36,41; 6:5,6; 7:10,40,45,46; 8:21, 32; 10:4,30,31,33; 13:24; 18:12,17,28; 19:9,19; 20:5; 21:38; 23:1,30,33; 24:13, 16,16,19,20,21; 25:9,26,26; 26:2,26; 27:24,35 ROM 2:13; 3:18,20; 4:17; 11:9; 12:17; 14:10,18,22; 15:23; 16:7 1 CO 1:29; 2:7; 4:5; 6:1,1,6; 10:27; 11:17 2 CO 2:17; 4:2; 5:10; 7:12; 8:21,21; 9:5; 12:2,19 GAL 1:17,20, 23; 3:1 EPH 1:4,4,4; 5:10 PHL 1:12; 3:13; 4:6 COL 1:17,22; 3:20 1 TH 1:3; 2:19; 3:10,13; 4:6 2 TH 1:6 1 TM 2:1,3; 4:15; 5:4,20,21; 6:12,13,13 2 TM 1:9; 2:14,15; 3:9; 4:1,21 TIT 1:2 HEB 4:13,13; 9:24; 11:5; 13:21 JAM 1:27; 2:3; 4:10; 5:9, 12 1 PT 1:17,20; 2:5,12,19; 3:4; 4:8 1 JN 3:19,21,22 3 JN 6 JUD 25 REV 1:4; 2:14; 3:2,4,5,5,8,9; 4:5,6,6,10, 10; 5:8; 6:16; 7:9,9,11,15; 8:2,3,4; 9:13; 11:4,16; 12:4,10,14; 13:6,8,12,13,14; 14:3,3,3,10,10; 15:4; 16:17,19; 19:10, 20; 20:11,12; 22:8,16

2750 ܩܕܡܐ (adj) first

1 TM	1:16	2 TM	2:6

2751 ܩܕܡܝܐ (adj) first

incl idioms

MAT	5:21,33	JHN	19:32
	10:2		20:4,8
	12:45	ACT	1:1
	17:27		12:10
	19:30,30		14:16
	20:8,10,16, 16,27		15:7,21
			20:18
	21:28,31, 36		21:16
			27:41,43
	22:25,38	ROM	10:19
	26:17	1 CO	14:30
	27:64		15:45,47
MRK	9:35	EPH	4:22
	10:31,31, 44		6:2
		PHL	1:5
	12:20,28, 29,30	COL	1:18
		1 TM	1:15,18
	14:12		5:12
LUK	2:2	2 TM	4:16
	9:8,19	HEB	4:6
	11:26		5:12
	13:30,30		7:18
	14:18		8:7,13
	16:5		9:1,2,8,15, 18
	19:16		
	20:29		10:9,32
JHN	1:15,30	1 PT	1:14
	2:11		4:4
	5:4,14	2 PT	1:9
	8:7		2:5,20

3 JN	9	REV	13:12,12
REV	1:17		16:2
	2:4,5,8,19		20:2,5,6
	4:7		21:1,1,19
	8:7		22:13

2752 ܩܕܡܝܬ (adv) first

ACT	11:26	1 JN	4:19
	13:46		

2761 ܩܘܕܡܐ (m) before

ACT 26:20

---

[c]PAEL

Perfect

MAT	17:25	ROM	3:9,25
	24:25		8:28,30
MRK	1:35		9:11,29
	13:23		11:35
	14:8	1 CO	2:7
LUK	19:4	2 CO	7:3
	24:22	GAL	3:8[1],8[2]
JHN	20:4	EPH	1:4,9,11, 12
ACT	1:16		
	2:31	1 TH	3:4
	3:18	HEB	6:20
	4:28		11:40
	7:52	2 PT	3:2
	21:29	JUD	4,17

Imperfect

MRK 13:11

Active Participle

LUK	21:38	2 CO	13:2
ACT	2:25	1 TM	5:24
ROM	12:10		

Passive Participle

1 PT 1:20

1849 ܩܕܡܘܬܐ (f) (w/ ܝܕܥܬܐ) foreknowledge

ACT	2:23	1 PT	1:2

---

[d]ETHPAAL

Imperfect

GAL	6:1	1 TM	5:21

2762 (ܩܕܫ), ܩܘܕܫܐ (m)

holiness

MAT	1:18,20	ACT	11:15,16, 24
	3:11		
	4:1,5		13:2,4,9, 52
	7:6		
	12:32		15:8,28
	28:19		16:6
MRK	1:8		19:2,2,6
	3:29		20:23,28
	12:36		21:11
	13:11		28:25
LUK	1:15,35,41, 67	ROM	1:4
			5:5
	2:25,26		9:1
	3:16,22		14:17
	4:1		15:13,16
	10:21	1 CO	6:19
	11:13		9:13,13
	12:10,12		12:3
JHN	1:33	2 CO	6:6
	14:26		13:14
	20:22	EPH	1:13
ACT	1:2,5,8,16	1 TH	1:5,6
	2:4,33,38	2 TM	1:14
	4:8,25,31	TIT	3:5
	5:3,32	HEB	2:4
	6:5		3:7
	7:51,55		6:4
	8:15,17,18, 19		8:2
			9:1,2,3,3,8
	9:17,31		10:15,19
	10:38,44, 45,47	1 PT	1:12

2754 (ܩܕܫ) (v) sanctify

[c]PAEL

Perfect

JHN	10:36	HEB	2:11[1]

Imperfect

EPH	5:26	HEB	13:12
1 TH	5:23		

Imperative

JHN	17:17	1 PT	3:15
JAM	4:8		

Active Participle

MAT	23:17,19	HEB	9:13
JHN	17:19[1]		

Passive Participle

JHN	17:19[2]	1 CO	1:2
ROM	15:16		7:14[1],14[2]

1850 ܩܘܕܫܐ (m) (w/ ܒܝܬ)

sanctuary, holy place

ROM 2:22
HEB 9:12,24,25
HEB 13:11

2745 ܩܕܝܫܐ (adj) holy, saint

MAT 16:27
24:15
25:31
27:52,53
MRK 1:24
6:20
8:38
LUK 1:35,49,70,72
2:23
4:34
9:26
JHN 17:11
ACT 3:14,21
4:27,30
6:13
7:33
9:13,32,41
10:22
20:32
21:28
26:10,18
ROM 1:2,7
6:22
7:12,12
8:27
11:16,16
12:1,13
15:25,26,31
16:2,15,16
1 CO 1:2
3:17
6:1,2
7:34
14:33
16:1,15,20
2 CO 1:1
8:4
9:1,12
13:12,13
GAL 3:8
EPH 1:1,4,15,18
2:19,21
3:5,8,18
4:12,30
EPH 5:3,27
6:18
PHL 1:1
4:21,22
COL 1:2,4,12,22,26
3:12
1 TH 3:13
4:8
5:26,27
2 TH 1:10
1 TM 5:10
2 TM 1:9
3:15
TIT 2:5
PLM 5,7
HEB 3:1
6:10
9:8
13:24
JAM 1:27
1 PT 1:15,15,16,16,22
2:5,9
3:5
5:14
2 PT 1:18,21,21
2:21
3:2,11
1 JN 2:20
JUD 3,14,20,20
REV 3:7
4:8,8,8
5:8
6:10
8:3,4
11:2,18
13:7,10
14:10,12
16:6
17:6
18:20,24
19:8
20:6,9
21:2,10
22:6,11,19,21

2746 ܩܕܝܫܘܬܐ (f) holiness, sanctification

ACT 24:25
ROM 6:19
1 CO 1:30
5:8
2 CO 7:1
1 TH 3:13
1 TH 4:3,4,7
2 TH 2:13
1 TM 2:15
HEB 12:10,14
1 PT 1:2

---

[d]ETHPAAL

Perfect

1 CO 6:11
HEB 2:11[2]
HEB 10:10,29

Imperfect

MAT 6:9
LUK 11:2
REV 22:11

Participle

1 TM 4:5
HEB 10:14

2764 (ܩܘܐ), ܩܘܝܐ (m-non occ) woven objects

2756 (ܩܘܐ) (v) abide, remain

[c]PAEL

Perfect

MAT 15:32
MRK 8:2
LUK 1:22,56
JHN 1:32
ACT 15:35
17:14
19:22
ACT 20:5,15
21:4
28:12
GAL 1:18
HEB 8:9
JAM 1:25

Imperfect

LUK 24:29
JHN 3:36
12:46
15:4[3],7[1],7[2],10[1],16
21:22,23
ACT 1:4
10:48
14:22
ROM 6:1
9:11
11:22,23
1 CO 3:14
7:8,11,20,24,40
16:6
GAL 2:5
PHL 1:24
COL 1:23
1 TM 1:3
2:15
HEB 7:23
12:27
1 JN 2:24[1],27[1]

Imperative

MAT 26:38
MRK 14:34
LUK 24:49
JHN 15:4[1],9
2 TM 3:14
1 JN 2:27[2],28

Active Participle

JHN 1:33
5:38
6:27,56
8:35[1],35[2]
12:34
15:4[2],5,6,10[2]
ACT 10:24
ACT 17:16
23:21
ROM 8:25
1 CO 11:33
16:8,11
2 CO 3:11
GAL 5:5
PHL 1:25

2 TM 2:13
HEB 7:3
10:13
13:14
1 JN 2:17,24[2],
24[3]
1 JN 3:6,14,15
4:12,13[1],
13[2],15[1],
15[2],16[1],
16[2]
2 JN 2,9[1],9[2]

2825 (ܩܘܠ), ܩܠܐ (m) voice

MAT 2:18
3:3,17
12:19
14:30
17:5
20:30,31
27:46,50
MRK 1:3,11,26
5:7
9:7
15:34,37
LUK 1:42,44
3:4,22
4:33
8:28
9:35,36
11:27
15:25
16:24
17:13,15
18:36
19:37
21:25
23:23,23,
46
JHN 1:23
3:8,29
5:25,28,37
7:28
9:31
10:3,4,5,
16,27
11:43
12:28,30
ACT 2:2,6,14
4:24
7:31,57,60
8:7
9:4,7
10:13,15
11:7,9
12:14,22
14:10,11
ACT 16:28
19:34
22:7,9,14,
22
23:9
26:14,24
ROM 10:16,18
1 CO 12:2
13:1
14:7,8,10,
11
GAL 4:20
1 TH 4:16
1 TM 6:20
HEB 3:7,15
4:7
12:19,19,
26
2 PT 1:17,18
2:16,16
REV 1:10,12,15,
15
3:20
4:1,5
5:2,11,12
6:1,6,7,10
7:2,10
8:5,13
9:9,9,13
10:3,3,4,8
11:12,15,
19
12:10
14:2,2,2,2,
7,9,13,
15,18
16:1,17
18:2,4,22,
23,23
19:1,5,6,6,
6,17
21:3

2770 (ܩܘܡ) (v) rise, stand; (pa) establish; (aph) cause to stand

[a]PEAL

Perfect

MAT 1:24
2:9,14,21
MAT 8:15,26
9:7,9,19,
MAT 9:25
11:11
14:2
20:32
25:7
26:62
27:11,52,
64
28:6,7
MRK 1:35
2:12,14
3:26[1]
4:39
5:42
6:14,16
7:24
9:9,10
10:1,49[1],
50
12:25
14:28,57,
60
16:6,9,14
LUK 1:39
2:38
4:16,29,
39[1],39[2]
5:25,28
6:8[2],17
7:14[1],16,
38
8:24,44,55
9:7,8,19
10:25
15:20
17:12
18:40
19:8
20:1
22:45
23:1
24:4,6,12,
33,34,
36
JHN 2:22
5:9
7:52
11:29,31
12:21
13:4
20:19,26
21:4,14
ACT 1:15
2:14
ACT 3:8
4:1,26
5:6,34,36,
37
6:6,9,12
7:18
8:27
9:8,18,34[2],
39[1],39[2]
10:17,23,
30
11:11,13,
28
12:7[1]
13:16
14:10[2],20
15:5,7,13
17:5,22
19:33[2]
21:40
23:9,27
24:20
25:18
26:19,30
27:18,21,
41
28:17
ROM 1:4
4:25
6:4,9
7:4
8:34
11:20
14:9
1 CO 10:7,12
15:1,4,12,
13,14,
16[2],17,
20
2 CO 5:15
COL 2:12[1]
3:1
1 TH 4:14
2 TM 2:8
3:8[1]
4:17
JAM 5:6
2 PT 3:5
REV 3:20
8:3
11:11
13:1
18:17
20:12

Imperfect

MAT 5:39
10:21
12:25,41,
42
16:21
17:9,23
18:16
20:19
24:7,11,24
MRK 4:27
8:31
9:31
10:34
13:8,9,12,
22
LUK 9:22
11:7,8,18,
31,32

LUK 13:25[1]
15:18
16:31
18:33
21:10,36
24:7,46
ACT 8:38
17:3
20:30
24:19
27:15
ROM 9:19
15:12
16:2
1 CO 15:52
2 CO 13:1
EPH 6:13
COL 4:12
1 TH 4:16
5:3
HEB 7:11
REV 18:15

Imperative

MAT 2:13,20
9:5,6
17:7
26:46
MRK 2:9,11
3:3
5:41
10:49[2]
14:42
LUK 5:23,24
6:8[1]
7:14[2]
8:54
17:19
22:46
JHN 5:8
14:31
ACT 3:6
5:20
8:26
ACT 9:6,11,15,
34[1],40
10:13,20,
26[2]
11:7
12:7[3]
14:10[1]
22:10,16
26:16[1]
1 CO 16:13
GAL 5:1
EPH 5:14
6:14
PHL 4:1
2 TM 4:2
JAM 2:3
4:7
1 PT 5:9
REV 11:1[2]

Infinitive

MAT 6:5
MRK 3:24,25,
26[2]
LUK 21:15
JHN 20:9
ACT 6:10
ACT 27:24
ROM 14:4[3],10
2 CO 5:10
EPH 6:11
REV 6:17

Active Participle

MAT 11:5
12:26,46,
47
13:2
16:28
20:3,6[1],6[2]
24:15
26:32,73
27:47,63
MRK 3:31
4:1
9:1
11:5,25
12:26
13:14
14:47,69,
70
15:35,39
LUK 1:11,19,21
5:1,2
LUK 7:22
8:20
9:27,32
13:17,25[2]
14:9
18:11,13
19:24
20:37
23:10,35,
49
JHN 1:26,35
3:29
6:22
7:37
8:44
11:23,24,
42
12:29
18:5,16,
18[1],18[2],

JHN 18:22,25
19:25,26
20:11,14
ACT 1:10,11
4:10[2],14
5:23,25,39
7:33,51,55,
56
9:7
12:14
13:8,45
16:9
17:7
18:5
19:40
22:20,25
23:2,4
24:21
25:10,20
26:6,22
28:19
ROM 5:2
8:38
12:8
13:2[1],2[2],2[3],
6
14:4[1],4[2],4[4]
1 CO 3:22
11:14
15:16[1],29,
1 CO 15:30,32,
35,42,
43[1],43[2],
44
2 CO 1:24
3:14
13:5
EPH 2:14
PHL 1:27,28
COL 1:17
1 TH 5:12
2 TM 3:8[2]
TIT 2:8
HEB 5:1
7:15
8:3
10:11
JAM 5:9
1 PT 5:12
REV 4:8
5:6
7:1,9,11
8:2
10:5,8
11:1[1],4
12:4
14:1
15:2
18:10
19:17

2771 ܩܘܡܐ (m) fathom

ACT 27:28,28

2772 ܩܘܡܬܐ (f) stature

MAT 6:27
LUK 2:52
12:25
LUK 19:3
EPH 4:13

2806 ܩܘܡܐ (adj) succorer, supporter

ROM 16:2

2812 ܩܝܡܐ (m) covenant, resurrection

LUK 2:34
ACT 23:13
ROM 1:31
9:4
1 CO 4:11
HEB 3:14
9:8

2813 ܩܝܡܬܐ (f) resurrection

MAT 22:28,30,
31
27:53
MRK 12:18,23
LUK 14:14
20:27,33,
LUK 20:35,36
JHN 5:29,29
ACT 1:22
2:31
4:2,33
10:41

ACT	17:18,32	2 TM	2:18
	23:6,8	HEB	6:2
	24:15,21		11:35,35
	26:23	1 PT	1:3
ROM	6:5		3:21
PHL	3:10,11	REV	20:5,6

[c]PAEL

Perfect

ACT	15:32	REV	3:2

Imperfect

1 TH	3:13	2 TH	2:17

Active Participle

ACT 15:41

2765 ܩܘܝܡܐ (m) strengthening

ACT 27:34

2811 ܩܘܝܐ (adj) remaining, abiding

MAT	11:23	2 TM	2:19
LUK	10:30	HEB	1:11
JHN	9:41		4:1,9
1 CO	15:6		7:24
2 CO	9:9	1 PT	1:23,25
1 TM	5:12		

[d]ETHPAAL

Imperfect

1 TH	3:8	1 PT	5:10

Imperative

2 TH 2:15

Participle

ACT	16:5	COL	2:7,19

[e]APHEL

Perfect

MAT	4:5	LUK	9:47
	18:2		12:14
	24:45		22:5
	26:15	JHN	8:3
MRK	1:31		12:1,9,17
	4:38	ACT	1:23
	9:27,36		2:24,32
LUK	1:69		3:7,15,26
	4:9		4:7,10[1]

ACT	5:27,30,31	ACT	23:13,33
	6:13		28:23
	7:10,27,35	ROM	4:24
	9:41		8:11[1],11[2]
	10:26[1],40		9:17
	12:7[2]		10:9
	13:22,23, 30,33, 34,37, 50	1 CO	6:14[1]
			15:15[1],15[2]
		2 CO	4:14[1]
		GAL	1:1
	14:23	EPH	1:20
	15:16[1]		2:6
	17:31[1],31[2]	COL	2:12[2]
	19:33[1]	1 TH	1:10
	20:28	1 PT	1:21
	22:14,30		

Imperfect

MAT	22:24	ACT	7:37,60
	24:47		15:16[2]
	25:21,23, 33		26:16[2]
		ROM	10:3
	26:53		12:1
MRK	7:9		14:4[5]
	12:19	2 CO	4:14[2]
LUK	2:22	EPH	5:27
	12:42,44	COL	1:22,28
	20:28	2 TM	2:15
JHN	6:39,40,44, 54	TIT	1:5
		HEB	10:9
ACT	3:22	JUD	24
	6:3		

Infinitive

MAT	3:9	HEB	11:19
LUK	3:8		

Active Participle

MAT	12:11	1 CO	6:14[2]
JHN	2:19,20	2 CO	1:9
	5:21	HEB	7:28
ACT	18:23	JAM	5:15
	26:8	2 PT	1:8
ROM	3:5,31		

2781 ܩܘܪܝܐ (f) lady

2 JN 1,5

2796 ܩܛܠ (v) kill

[a]PEAL

Perfect

MAT	21:35,39	LUK	20:15
	23:35	ACT	2:23
MRK	12:5[1],8		3:15
LUK	15:27		5:30

ACT 7:24,28[2], 52[1],52[2]
10:39
12:2
ROM 7:11
EPH 2:16
1 TH 2:15
JAM 5:6
1 JN 3:12[1],12[2]

Imperfect

MAT 5:21[1],21[2]
17:23
19:18
21:38
24:9
26:4
MRK 9:31[1]
10:19,34
12:7
14:1
LUK 9:22
11:49
18:20,33
20:14
22:2
JHN 10:10
JHN 11:53
12:10
16:2
ACT 9:23,24
13:28
16:27
23:12,14, 15,21, 27
25:3
ROM 13:9
JAM 2:11[1]
REV 2:23
9:5,15
11:7
19:15

Imperative

LUK 15:23

Infinitive

MAT 10:28[2]
14:5
MRK 6:19
LUK 13:31
JHN 5:16,18
7:1,20[1], 20[2],25
JHN 8:37,40
18:31
ACT 5:33
7:28[1]
9:29
21:31
26:21

Active Participle

MAT 10:28[1]
23:34,37
LUK 12:4,5
13:34
JHN 8:22,44
2 CO 3:6
JAM 2:11[2]
4:2
1 JN 3:15[1],15[2]
REV 13:10[1]

Passive Participle

MAT 22:4
REV 13:8
REV 18:24

2792 ܩܛܘܠܐ (m) murderer

MAT 22:7
ACT 3:14
22:20
28:4
1 TM 1:9
1 PT 4:15
REV 21:8
22:15

2797 ܩܛܠܐ (m) murder

MAT 15:19
MRK 7:21
15:7
LUK 23:19,25
ACT 8:1
9:1

ACT 25:16
ROM 1:29
GAL 5:21
REV 9:21

[b]ETHPEEL

Perfect

MRK 9:31[2]
LUK 11:51
ACT 5:36
REV 2:13
9:20

Imperfect

MAT 16:21
MRK 8:31
LUK 23:32*
REV 13:10[2],15*

Infinitive

REV 11:5

[c]PAEL

Perfect

MAT 2:16
22:6
23:31
MRK 12:5[2]
LUK 11:47,48
13:4
ROM 11:3

Imperfect

ACT 27:42
REV 6:8

Imperative

LUK 19:27

[d]ETHPAAL

Perfect

REV 6:9
9:18
REV 11:13
19:21

Infinitive

REV 6:11

Participle

ACT 26:10

2798 ܩܛܡ, ܩܛܡܐ (m) ash

MAT 11:21
LUK 10:13
HEB 9:13

2799 ܩܛܢ (v-non occ) be narrow

[c]PAEL

2793 ܩܛܝܢܐ (adj) narrow

MAT 7:14

2801 ܩܛܥ (v) cut; (ethpa) be discouraged

[c]PAEL (non occ)

2763 ܩܘܛܥܐ (m) drawing back

HEB 10:39

[d]ETHPAAL

Imperfect

1 TH 3:3	HEB 6:12

Participle

HEB 10:38*

2802 ܩܛܦ (v) pluck, gather

[a]PEAL

Perfect

REV 14:19

Imperative

REV 14:18

Active Participle

LUK 6:44

2803 ܩܛܪ (v) tie together

[a]PEAL (non occ)

2794 ܩܛܝܪܐ (pp) violence, necessity

MAT 5:44	ACT 24:7
11:12	27:41
LUK 6:28	1 CO 9:16
ACT 5:26	2 CO 9:7
7:24	PLM 14
21:35	1 PT 5:2

2795 ܩܛܝܪܢܐ (adj) violent

MAT 11:12

2804 ܩܛܪܐ (m) bond

ACT 8:23

[d]ETHPAAL

Participle

EPH 4:16

2805 ܩܛܓܪ (v) accuse

[k]P

Imperfect

MRK 3:2	ACT 25:5
JHN 8:6	28:19
ACT 24:19	

Active Participle

JHN 5:45[1],45[2]	ACT 24:2,8,13
ACT 18:14	25:11

2790 ܩܛܓܪܢܐ (m) accuser

ACT 23:30,35	ACT 25:18
24:8	

2791 ܩܛܓܪܢܘܬܐ (f) accusation

ACT 22:30	1 TM 5:19

2807 ܩܝܛܐ (m) summer

MAT 24:32	LUK 21:30
MRK 13:28	

2808 ܩܝܛܘܢܐ (m-non occ) bedchamber

2809 ܩܝܛܘܢܝܐ (m) chamberlain

ACT 12:20

2818 (ܩܢ), ܩܝܢܬܐ (f) musical sound

1 CO 14:7

2815 ܩܝܢܝܐ (m) smith

2 TM 4:14

2819 ܩܝܣ, ܩܝܣܐ (m) tree, wood

LUK	23:31	2 TM	2:20
ACT	5:30	JAM	3:4
	10:39	REV	2:7
	27:44		9:20
1 CO	3:12		18:12,12
GAL	3:13		22:2,14,19

2769 (ܩܠ), ܩܘܠܬܐ (f) waterpot

JHN 4:28

2824 ܩܠ (v) lessen; (aph) lighten, make light of

[c]PAEL (non occ)

2831 ܩܠܝܠܐ (adj) little, light, swift

MAT	11:30	ACT	26:28,29
	15:34		27:14,28
	25:21,23	ROM	3:15
	26:39,73		11:25
MRK	1:19		15:15,24
	6:5,31	1 CO	5:6
	8:7		13:9,9,10,12
	14:35,70		
LUK	5:3	2 CO	1:14
	7:47,47		2:5
	10:30		4:17
	15:13		8:15
	16:10,10		11:1,16
	19:17	GAL	5:9
	22:58	PHL	2:28
JHN	2:12	1 TM	5:23
	6:7,7	HEB	2:7,9
	7:33		10:37
	12:35	JAM	4:14
	13:33	1 PT	1:6
	14:18	2 PT	2:18
	16:16,16,17,17,18,19,19	REV	3:4,8
			12:12
			17:10
			20:3
ACT	24:24		

[e]APHEL

Perfect

ACT 27:38

Active Participle

GAL 5:26

2828 (ܩܠܕ), ܩܠܝܕܐ (m) key

MAT	16:19	REV	3:7
LUK	11:52		9:1
REV	1:18		20:1

2766 (ܩܠܢ), ܩܘܠܢܝܐ (f) colony

ACT 16:12

2833 (ܩܠܣ) (v-non occ) laud

[c]PAEL

2767 ܩܘܠܣܐ (m) good report, praise

2 CO	6:8	1 PT	1:7
PHL	4:8		

2834 ܩܠܦ (v-non occ) peel off

[a]PEAL

2835 ܩܠܦܬܐ (f) scales

ACT 9:18

2836 ܩܡܚܐ (m) flour, meal

MAT	13:33	LUK	13:21

2837 ܩܡܛ (v-non occ) shrink

[a]PEAL

2838 ܩܡܛܐ (m) wrinkle

EPH 5:27

2839 ܩܡܨܐ (m) locust

MAT 3:4 | REV 9:3,7
MRK 1:6

2841 ܩܢܐ (m-non occ) nest

2840 ܩܢ (v) (aph) make a nest

[e]APHEL

Perfect

LUK 13:19

Imperfect

MAT 13:32

2842 ܩܢܐ (v) obtain

[a]PEAL

Perfect

ACT 1:18 | ACT 22:28
20:28 | JUD 4

Imperfect

MAT 10:9 | LUK 21:19
16:26 | 1 PT 3:1

Infinitive

1 TH 4:4

Active Participle

LUK 18:12 | 1 TM 3:13

Passive Participle

LUK 21:4 | ACT 4:32,34

2852 ܩܢܝܢܐ (m) possession, goods

MAT 19:21,22 | LUK 15:12,13
25:14 | 16:1
MRK 12:44 | ACT 2:45
LUK 8:3,43 | 8:20
11:21 | 1 TH 5:9
12:33,44 | HEB 10:34
14:33 | 1 JN 3:17

[b]ETHPEEL

Participle

ACT 8:20

[e]APHEL

Active Participle

HEB 10:39 | JAM 1:3

2814 (ܩܢܕܝܢ̈), ܩܢܕܝܢܘܬܐ (f)

peril

ACT 19:40 | 2 CO 11:26,26,
ROM 8:35 | 26,26,
1 CO 15:30 | 26,26
2 CO 11:26,26,

2846 ܩܢܛ (v-non occ) fear, avoid

[a]PEAL

2847 ܩܢܛܐ (m) danger, cause for fear

ACT 27:9,33 | 1 JN 4:18

[c]PAEL

2844 ܩܢܘܛܢܐ (adj) fearful

REV 21:8

2851 ܩܢܘܛܐ (adj) fearful

2 CO 8:20

2848 ܩܢܛܪܘܢܐ (m) centurion

MAT 8:5,8,13 | ACT 23:17,18,
27:54 | 23
MRK 15:39,44 | 24:23
LUK 7:2,6 | 27:1,3,6,
23:47 | 11,31,
ACT 10:1,22 | 43
21:32 | 28:16
22:25,26

2849 ܩܢܝܐ (m) reed

MAT 11:7 | LUK 7:24
12:20 | 3 JN 13
27:29,30, | REV 11:1
48 | 21:15,16
MRK 15:19,36

2773 (ܩܢܡ), ܩܘܢܡܘܢ (m)
cinnamon

REV 18:13

2845 (ܩܢܡ), ܩܢܘܡܐ (m)
individual (self), substance

LUK	11:17	2 CO	12:15
JHN	5:26,26	EPH	2:15
	6:53	COL	2:15
ROM	1:27	1 TH	4:9
	9:3	HEB	1:3
1 CO	6:7		9:28
	9:27		10:1

2855 ܩܣܛܐ (f) pint, pot

MRK	7:4,8	HEB	9:4

2856 (ܩܣܛܢܪ), ܩܣܛܘܢܪܐ (m) guard

MAT	27:65,66	MAT	28:11,12

2860 ܩܥܐ (v) cry aloud; (w/ ܥܠ) appeal to

aPEAL

Perfect

MAT	8:29	JHN	11:43
	14:26		12:44
	27:23,46, 50		18:40
			19:6
MRK	1:23,26	ACT	7:57,60
	5:7		19:34
	6:49		22:22
	9:24,26		23:6
	15:8,13,34, 37,39		24:21
			26:24
LUK	1:42	REV	6:10
	8:28		7:2
	9:38		10:3[1],3[2]
	18:38		14:15,18
	23:18,46		18:2,19
JHN	1:15		19:17

Imperfect

MAT	12:19	ACT	28:19
LUK	19:40		

Infinitive

MRK 10:47

Active Participle

MAT	9:27	JHN	12:13
	11:16		19:12,15
	15:22,23	ACT	8:7
	21:9,15		12:22
MRK	3:11		14:14
	5:5		16:17
	10:48		17:6
	11:9		19:28,32
	15:14		21:34,36
LUK	7:32		22:24
	8:8		25:24
	9:39	JAM	5:4
	18:39	REV	7:10
	23:21		12:2
JHN	7:37		

2862 ܩܥܬܐ (f) cry, clamor

MAT	25:6	ACT	21:34

2861 ܩܥܕ (v) kneel

aPEAL

Perfect

ACT	9:40	ACT	21:5
	20:36		

2864 ܩܦܚ (v) oppress

cPAEL

Active Participle

MAT	26:67	1 CO	8:12
MRK	14:65	2 CO	12:7

dETHPAAL

Participle

1 CO	4:11	2 PT	2:7

2775 (ܩܦܦ), ܩܘܦܝܢܐ (m) basket

MAT	14:20	MRK	8:19
	16:9	LUK	9:17
MRK	6:43	JHN	6:13

2865 ܩܦܣ (v) gather

aPEAL

Perfect

ACT 5:10 | ACT 8:2

2866 ܩܦܣܐ (m) (w/ ܒܝܬ) storehouse

LUK 12:18,24

2867 ܩܨ (v) agree, bargain

aPEAL

Perfect

MAT 20:2,13 | MAT 27:9

2868 ܩܨܐ (v) break (bread)

aPEAL

Perfect

MAT 14:19
15:36
26:26
MRK 6:41
8:6,19
14:22
LUK 9:16
22:19
24:30,35
ACT 20:11
27:35
1 CO 11:24[1]

Imperfect

ACT 20:7

Active Participle

ACT 2:46 | 1 CO 10:16

2869 ܩܨܝܐ (m) fragment

MAT 14:20
15:37
MRK 6:43
MRK 8:8,19,20
LUK 9:17
JHN 6:12,13

2870 ܩܨܝܐ (m) breaking

ACT 2:42

bETHPEEL

Participle

1 CO 11:24[2]

2871 ܩܨܡ (v) divine

aPEAL

Active Participle

ACT 16:16

2872 ܩܨܡܐ (m) divination

ACT 16:16,16

2873 ܩܪ (v-non occ) grow cold

aPEAL

2884 ܩܪܝܪܐ (adj) cold

MAT 10:42 | REV 3:15,15,16

2874 ܩܪܐ (v) call, read; (w/ ܠܘܬ) appeal to

aPEAL

Perfect

MAT 1:25
2:7,15
4:21
10:1,25
12:3,5
15:10,32
18:2,32
19:4
20:25,32
21:16,42
22:31
25:14
26:74
27:47
MRK 1:20
2:25
3:13,23
6:7
7:14
8:1,34
9:35
10:42,49[2]
12:10,26,43
14:68,72[1]
15:16,35,44
LUK 6:3,13
7:19,39
8:54
9:1
13:12
14:9,10,12[1],16
LUK 15:26
16:2,5,24
18:16
19:13
22:60
23:13
JHN 2:9
9:18,24
11:28[1]
12:17
15:15[2]
18:27,33
19:20
ACT 4:18
5:21,40
6:2
9:41
10:7
13:2,7[2]
15:31
16:10,28
20:1
23:17,18,23,34
24:24
25:12
26:32
28:2,17
ROM 8:30[1],30[2]
9:11
1 CO 7:15,17
GAL 1:6,15
5:8
1 TH 2:12

1 TH 4:7
5:24
2 TH 2:14
2 TM 1:9
1 PT 1:15
1 PT 2:9
5:10
2 PT 1:3
1 JN 3:1

Imperfect

MAT 1:21,23
6:2
9:13
22:3
23:9
26:34,75
MRK 2:17
3:31
10:49[1]
14:30,72[2]
LUK 1:13,31
5:32
LUK 14:12[3]
19:15
22:34,61
JHN 1:48
13:38
ACT 2:21,39
ROM 9:25
10:13,14
1 CO 14:8
15:52
HEB 2:11
JAM 5:14

Imperative

MAT 20:8
22:9
LUK 14:13
JHN 4:16
COL 4:16[3]

Infinitive

LUK 4:16

Active Participle

MAT 3:3
19:17
22:43,45
24:15
MRK 1:3
10:18,49[3]
12:37
13:14
15:12
LUK 1:59
3:4
6:46
10:26
14:12[2]
15:6,9
18:7,19
20:44
JHN 1:23
10:3
11:28[2]
JHN 13:13
15:15[1]
ACT 8:28,30[1],30[2],32
9:14,21
10:18[1]
15:21
22:16
25:11
ROM 4:17
8:15
10:12
1 CO 1:2[2]
10:27
GAL 4:6
EPH 3:4
2 TM 2:19,22
1 PT 1:17
3:6
REV 1:3

Passive Participle

MAT 20:16
22:14
LUK 14:17,24
ROM 1:1,6,7
8:28
ROM 9:24
1 CO 1:1,2[1],24
JUD 1
REV 17:14
19:9

1852 ܟܪܘܐ (m) crowing

MRK 13:35

2881 ܩܪܝܐ (m) calling, vocation

ROM 11:29
1 CO 7:20
EPH 1:18
4:1,4
PHL 3:14
2 TH 1:11
1 TM 4:13
2 TM 1:9
HEB 3:1

2888 ܩܪܝܬܐ (f) calling, vocation

1 CO 1:26
2 PT 1:10

---

[b]ETHPEEL

Perfect

MAT 4:18
27:8
LUK 2:21[1],21[2]
JHN 2:2
ACT 1:19
11:26
13:9,15
15:17
24:2
ROM 15:20
1 CO 1:9
7:18[1],18[2],20,21,
1 CO 7:22[1],22[2],24
GAL 5:13
EPH 4:1,4
COL 3:15
4:16[1]
1 TM 6:12
HEB 3:1
9:15
11:8
JAM 2:7,23
1 PT 2:21
3:9

Imperfect

MAT 2:23[2]
5:9,19[1],19[2]
21:13
23:8,10
MRK 11:17
LUK 1:32,35,60,76
2:23
LUK 15:19,21
JHN 1:42
ROM 9:7,26[2]
1 CO 15:9
COL 4:16[2]
1 TH 5:27
HEB 11:16,18,24

Participle

MAT 1:16
2:23[1]
10:2
13:55
23:7
26:3,14,36
27:16,17,22,33
MRK 14:32
15:7
LUK 1:36,61
2:4
6:15
8:2
19:29
21:37
22:1,3,25,47
23:33
JHN 4:5
JHN 5:2
11:54
19:13[1],13[2],17
ACT 1:12,23
3:2,10,11
6:9
7:58
9:11
10:1,5,18[2],32
11:13
13:1,7[1],27
15:22
17:18,19
24:27
27:8,12,14,16
28:1,15
ROM 2:17

ROM 9:26[1]
1 CO 5:11; 8:5
2 CO 3:2,14,15
EPH 2:11[1],11[2]
COL 4:11
2 TH 2:4
HEB 3:13
HEB 5:4; 9:2,3
REV 1:9; 11:8; 12:9; 16:16; 19:11,13

2875 ܩܪܒ (v) draw near, touch, come; (pa) bring near, offer; (aph) war

[a]PEAL

Perfect

MAT 3:2; 4:3,11,17; 5:1; 8:3,5,15, 19,25; 9:14,18,20, 28,29; 10:7; 12:28; 13:10,27, 36; 14:12,15, 36[2]; 15:1,12,23, 30; 16:1; 17:7[2],14, 19,24; 18:1,21; 19:3,16; 20:20,34; 21:1,23,28, 30; 22:23; 24:1,3; 25:20[1],22, 24; 26:7,17,49, 60,69, 73; 27:58; 28:2,9,18
MRK 1:31,41; 5:27,30,31; 6:35
MRK 7:33; 10:2,35; 11:1; 12:28; 14:35,42, 45
LUK 5:13; 7:12,14,39; 8:24,44[2], 45[1],45[2], 46,47; 9:12; 10:9,11; 11:20; 13:31; 15:25; 18:40; 19:37,41; 20:27; 21:8,20,28, 30; 22:47,51; 23:52; 24:28
JHN 6:19; 21:13
ACT 4:3; 21:33; 22:26,27
ROM 13:12
HEB 10:25
JAM 5:8
REV 1:3; 17:8; 22:10

Imperfect

MAT 14:36[1]; 23:4
MRK 6:56[1]; 8:22; 10:13[2]
LUK 18:15[2]
ACT 19:38
COL 2:21
HEB 10:22

Imperative

JAM 4:8[1]

Active Participle

MAT 9:21
MRK 5:28; 6:56[2]
LUK 11:46
LUK 12:33; 23:36[1]
ACT 28:9

2778 ܩܘܪܒܢܐ (m) offering, gift

MAT 2:11; 5:23,24,24; 8:4; 15:5; 23:18,19, 19; 27:6
MRK 1:44; 7:11
LUK 5:14; 21:1,4,5
JHN 16:2
ACT 21:26; 24:17
ROM 15:16
EPH 5:2
HEB 5:1; 8:3,4; 9:9; 10:2,5,8, 10,14, 18; 11:4

2876 ܩܪܒܐ (m) war, battle

MAT 24:6
MRK 13:7
LUK 14:31; 21:9
1 CO 14:8
2 CO 7:5
HEB 11:34
JAM 4:1,2
1 PT 2:11
REV 9:7,9; 11:7; 12:7,17; 13:7; 16:14; 19:19; 20:8

[c]PAEL

Perfect

MAT 2:11; 4:24; 8:16; 9:2,32; 12:22; 14:35; 17:16; 18:24; 19:13; 21:14; 22:19; 25:20[2]
LUK 5:11
LUK 18:15[1]; 23:14
JHN 19:29
ACT 7:42; 8:18; 16:20
ROM 14:3; 15:7[2]
HEB 5:7; 7:27[2]; 9:14,26; 10:12; 11:4,17

Imperfect

MRK 3:9
LUK 21:12
ACT 24:17
2 CO 4:14; 11:2
HEB 5:1,3; 7:27[1]; 8:3[1],3[2]; 9:25
1 PT 3:18

Imperative

MAT 5:24, 8:4
MRK 1:44
LUK 5:14, 6:29, 9:41

Active Participle

MAT 5:23, 10:18
MRK 10:13[1],13[3], 13:11
LUK 9:42, 12:11, 23:36[2]
JHN 16:2
ROM 15:7[1]
1 CO 8:8
2 CO 9:14
1 TM 2:1
HEB 8:4, 9:7,9[2], 10:1[2],11

2777 ܩܘܪܒܐ (m) approach, access

EPH 2:18

2879 ܩܪܝܒܐ (adj) near, neighbor

MAT 5:43, 19:19, 22:39
MRK 1:38, 4:37, 12:31,33, 13:4,29
LUK 1:3, 5:7, 7:2, 8:23,42, 10:27,29, 36, 17:12, 18:35, 19:11, 21:7,31, 22:1, 23:55
JHN 2:13, 4:47, 6:4
JHN 7:2, 11:54,55, 19:20,42
ACT 2:10,10, 10:9, 27:8
ROM 7:21, 10:8, 13:9,10, 15:2
1 CO 5:3,3
2 CO 1:8, 10:11
GAL 5:14
EPH 2:13,17, 4:25
PHL 2:12, 4:5
HEB 6:9, 8:13
JAM 2:8, 4:12

2880 ܩܪܝܒܘܬܐ (f) nearness, access

EPH 3:12

ᵈETHPAAL

Perfect

MAT 17:7[1], 26:50
LUK 8:44[1], 10:34
ACT 7:31, 8:30, 18:2
ACT 21:26, 23:14
ROM 5:2, 13:11
HEB 9:28, 12:18,22

Imperfect

MRK 3:10
JHN 20:17
ACT 5:13
1 CO 7:1
2 CO 6:17
COL 2:2
1 TM 6:16
HEB 4:16, 10:26, 11:28, 12:20
JAM 4:8[2]

Imperative

ACT 8:29

Infinitive

MRK 2:4
LUK 6:19

Participle

LUK 15:1
ACT 12:5, 27:27
1 TM 6:3
HEB 7:19,25
HEB 9:9[1], 10:1[1],8, 11:6
1 PT 2:4
1 JN 5:18

ᵉAPHEL

Perfect

REV 12:7[2]

Imperfect

REV 2:16
REV 17:14

Infinitive

REV 13:4

Active Participle

ROM 7:23
JAM 4:1
REV 12:7[1], 19:11

2780 (ܩܪܛܒ), ܩܘܪܛܒܐ (m) thistle, thornbush

MAT 7:16
HEB 6:8

2887 ܩܪܝ, ܩܪܝܬܐ (f) beam, plank

MAT 7:3,4,5
LUK 6:41,42,42

2886 ܩܪܝܬܐ (f) village, field

MAT 9:35, 10:11,14, 13:24,27,
MAT 13:31,36, 38,44, 44

MAT 14:15,35
19:29
21:2
22:5
24:40
27:8
MRK 1:38
5:14
6:6,36,56
8:23,26,26,27
10:29,30
11:2
15:21
16:12
LUK 5:17
8:1,34
9:6,12,52,56

LUK 10:38
13:22
14:18
15:15,25
17:12
19:30
21:21
23:26
24:13,28
JHN 4:5
7:42
11:1,30,55
ACT 1:18,19,19
4:34,37
5:1,3,8
8:1,25
14:6
26:20
28:7

2889 ܩܪܟܕܢܐ (m) chalcedony

REV 9:17 | REV 21:19

2890 ܩܪܡ (v) overlay

ᵃPEAL

Passive Participle

HEB 9:4

2891 ܩܪܢ, ܩܪܢܐ (f) horn, corner

MAT 6:2
9:20
LUK 1:69
20:17
ACT 4:11
10:11
11:5
1 CO 14:8
15:52

EPH 2:20
1 TH 4:16
HEB 12:19
REV 5:6
9:13
12:3
13:1,1,11
17:3,7,12,16

2732 (ܩܪܣ), ܩܐܪܣܐ (m) time, opportunity, war

MAT 24:6
MRK 13:7

EPH 5:16
COL 4:5

2877 (ܩܪܣܛܠܘܣ), ܩܪܘܣܛܠܘܣ (m) rock, crystal

REV 21:11

2893 ܩܪܨ (v-non occ) sting

ᵃPEAL

2894 ܩܪܨܐ (m) (alw w/ ܐܟܠ) accuse

see also 124 ܐܟܠ ܩܪܨܐ
see also 125 ܐܟܠ ܩܪܨܐ

MAT 12:10
27:12
MRK 15:3
LUK 6:7

LUK 11:54
16:1
23:2,10

2896 ܩܪܩܦܬܐ (f) head, skull

MAT 27:33
MRK 15:22
LUK 23:33
JHN 19:17

ROM 12:20
REV 4:4
9:17,17
13:1,1,3

2895 (ܩܪܩܪ), ܩܪܩܘܪܐ (f) boat

ACT 27:16,30, | ACT 27:32

2897 ܩܪܫ (v-non occ) become chilled

ᵃPEAL

2788 ܩܘܪܫܐ (m) cold

ACT 28:2

2885 ܩܪܝܫܐ (adj) cold

JHN 18:18

2898 ܩܫ (v-non occ) grow old

cPAEL

2903 ܩܫܝܫܐ (adj) elder

MAT	15:2	ACT	15:2,4,6, 22,23
	16:21		16:4
	21:23		18:17
	26:3,47,57, 59		20:17
	27:1,3,12, 20,41		21:18
	28:12		22:5
MRK	7:3,5		23:14
	8:31		24:1
	11:27		25:15
	14:43,53	ROM	9:12
	15:1	PHL	1:1
LUK	2:36	1 TM	3:2
	7:3		5:1,2,17, 19
	9:22	TIT	1:5,7
	15:25		2:2,3
	19:47	HEB	8:11
	20:1		11:2
	22:52,66	JAM	5:14
	24:20	1 PT	5:1,1,5
JHN	7:26	2 JN	1
	8:9	3 JN	1
ACT	2:17	REV	4:4,10
	4:5,8,23		5:5,6,8,11, 14
	5:21		7:11,13
	6:12		11:16
	11:30		14:3
	13:15		19:4
	14:23		

2904 ܩܫܝܫܘܬܐ (f) office of an elder

1 TM	3:1	1 TM	4:14

2900 (ܩܫܐ), ܩܫܝܐ (adj) hard, strong

MAT	14:30	ACT	25:7
	25:24		26:14
MRK	8:17		27:18
LUK	19:21,22	2 TM	3:1
JHN	6:60	JAM	3:4
ACT	7:51	1 PT	2:18
	9:4	JUD	15

2901 ܩܫܝܐܝܬ (adv) sharply, severely

2 CO	13:10	TIT	1:13

2902 ܩܫܝܘܬܐ (f) hardness, difficulty

MAT	19:8	MRK	16:14
MRK	3:5	ROM	2:5
	10:5		11:22,22

2899 (ܩܫܐ) (v) harden

cPAEL

Imperfect

HEB	3:8,15	HEB	4:7

Active Participle

ROM 9:18

dETHPAAL

Imperfect

HEB 3:13

Participle

ACT 19:9

2789 (ܩܘܫܬ), ܩܘܫܬܐ (m) truth

MAT	22:16	EPH	1:13
LUK	12:57		4:21,24,25
	20:21		5:9
JHN	1:14		6:14
	6:32	PHL	1:18
ACT	12:11	COL	1:5,6
ROM	1:18	2 TH	2:10,12
	2:2	1 TM	2:7
	9:1		6:5
1 CO	13:6	JAM	1:18
2 CO	6:7		3:14
	7:14,14		5:19
	13:8,8		

2905 ܩܫܬ, ܩܫܬܐ (f) bow, rainbow

REV	4:3	REV	10:1
	6:2		

2822 (ܩܝܬܪ), ܩܝܬܪܐ (m) stringed instrument

1 CO	14:7	REV	15:2
REV	5:8		18:22
	14:2		

2823 ܩܝܬܪܘܕܐ (m) musician

REV 14:2

ܪ

2907 ܪܒ (v) grow great; (p) multiply

[a]PEAL (non occ)

2908 ܪܒܐ (adj) great, chief; (w/ suff) master

see below 2909 ܪܒ ܒܝܬܐ
see below 2910 ܪܒ ܚܝܠܐ
see below 2911 ܪܒ ܟܗܢܐ
see below 2912 ܪܒ ܟܘܡܪܐ
see below 2913 ܪܒ ܟܢܘܫܬܐ
see below 2924 ܪܒܬ ܒܝܬܘܬܐ

MAT 2:10
4:16
5:19,35
7:27
8:24,26
9:11
10:24,25
11:11,11
12:6,41
13:32
15:28
17:24
18:1,4
20:25,26
22:36,38
23:8,11,17,19
24:21,24,31
26:18
27:60
28:2,8
MRK 4:32,32,37,38,39,41
5:11,42
6:21
9:34
10:42,43
12:31
13:2,26
14:14,15
16:4
LUK 1:15,32,44,49
2:9,10
4:25,36,38
5:29
6:40,40,49
LUK 7:16,28,28
8:24,24,37,45
9:46,48,49
10:17
13:19
14:16
15:14
16:26
17:13
19:2,12
21:11,11,11,23,27
22:11,12,24,26,27
24:52
JHN 1:38,50
3:26,29
4:12,31
5:36
6:18,25
7:37
8:53
9:2
10:29
11:8,28
13:13,14,16,16
14:28
15:13,20
19:11,31
21:11
ACT 2:20
4:33,33
5:5,11,36
8:1,8,9,10,
ACT 8:10,13
10:11
11:28
15:3
16:26,35,36
19:11,20,24,27,28,34,35
20:37
23:9,10
26:22
28:10
ROM 9:2
1 CO 1:26
2:1
9:11
12:31
13:13
14:5
16:9
2 CO 2:4
4:17
11:15
EPH 5:32
PHL 3:21
4:7
1 TH 1:6
2:2
1 TM 2:2
3:16
6:6
2 TM 2:20
TIT 2:13
HEB 4:14
6:13,16,18
7:4
9:11
10:21,31,32
13:20
JAM 5:16
1 PT 5:4
2 PT 1:4
2:11
1 JN 3:20
4:4
5:9
3 JN 4
JUD 6
REV 1:10
2:22
6:4,10,12,15,17
7:10,14
8:8,10
9:2,14
11:8,11,12,13,15,17,18,19
12:1,3,9,10,12,14
13:2,5,13,16
14:2,7,8,9,15,18,18,19
15:1,3
16:1,9,12,14,17,18,18,19,19,21,21
17:5,6,18
18:1,2,2,10,16,18,19,21,21,23
19:1,2,5,17,18
20:1,11,12
21:3,10,12

2909 ܪܒ ܒܝܬܐ (idiom) steward

from 2908 ܪܒܐ (above) and 377 ܒܝܬܐ

MAT 20:8
LUK 8:3
12:42
16:1,2,3,8
ROM 16:23
1 CO 4:1,2
GAL 4:2
TIT 1:7
1 PT 4:10

2910 ܪܒ ܚܝܠܐ (idiom) captain, governor

from 2908 ܪܒܐ (above) and 985 ܚܝܠܐ

LUK 22:4,52	2 CO 11:32

2911 ܪܒ ܟܗܢܐ (idiom) chief priest

from 2908 ܪܒܐ (above) and 1383 ܟܗܢܐ

MAT 2:4	LUK 20:1,19
16:21	22:2,4,50,
20:18	52,54,
21:15,23,	66
45	23:4,10,13,
26:3,3,14,	23
47,51,	24:20
57,58,	JHN 7:32,45
59,62,	11:47,49,
63,65	51,57
27:1,3,6,	12:10
12,20,	18:3,10,13,
41,62	15,16,
28:11	19,22,
MRK 2:26	24,26,
8:31	35
10:33	19:6,15,21
11:18,27	ACT 4:6,6
14:1,10,43,	5:17,21,24,
47,53,	27
53,54,	7:1
55,60,	9:2,14,21
61,63,	19:14
66	22:5,30
15:1,3,10,	24:1
11,31	25:2,15
LUK 9:22	26:10,12
19:47	

2912 ܪܒ ܟܘܡܪܐ (idiom) high priest

from 2908 ܪܒܐ (above) and 1396 ܟܘܡܪܐ

HEB 2:17	HEB 8:1,3
3:1	9:7,11,25
4:14,15	10:11
5:1,5,10	13:11
7:27	

2913 ܪܒ ܟܢܘܫܬܐ (idiom) ruler of the synagogue

from 2908 ܪܒܐ (above) and 1455 ܟܢܘܫܬܐ

MRK 5:22,35,36,	LUK 13:14
38	ACT 18:8
LUK 8:49	

2916 ܪܒܘܬܐ (f) myriad, thousand

MAT 18:24	1 CO 14:19
LUK 12:1	HEB 12:22
ACT 19:19	JUD 14
21:20	REV 5:11,11
1 CO 4:15	9:16,16

2917 ܪܒܘܬܐ (f) greatness; (w/ ܟܘܡܪܘܬܐ) high priesthood

LUK 3:2	EPH 3:19
9:43	PHL 3:8
ROM 13:1	COL 1:11
2 CO 4:7	HEB 1:3
5:19	8:1
8:20	2 PT 1:16,17
EPH 1:19	JUD 25
2:7	

2924 ܪܒܬ ܒܝܬܘܬܐ (idiom) stewardship

incl comp with 2908 ܪܒܐ

LUK 16:2,3,4	1 CO 9:17

---

[k]P (non occ) ܪܒܪܒ

2986 ܪܒܪܒܐܝܬ (adv) greatly

ACT 8:2	2 CO 1:8
20:12	PHL 4:10

---

[m]ETHP

Imperfect

2 CO 10:15	PHL 1:20

2915 ܪܒܘܠܝ (m) master

JHN 20:16

2918 ܪܒܝ (m) rabbi, master

MAT 8:19	MRK 14:45,45
23:7,8	LUK 5:5
26:25,49	7:40
MRK 9:5,38	9:33
10:51	19:39
11:21	JHN 3:2
12:32	

2914 ܪܒܐ (v) grow up, increase; (pa) nourish, cause increase

[a]PEAL

Perfect

MAT 13:32	LUK 13:19
MRK 4:8	

Imperfect

MRK 4:27	COL 1:10
EPH 4:15	

Infinitive

JHN 3:30

Active Participle

MAT 6:28	ACT 12:24
13:30	2 CO 10:15
LUK 1:80	EPH 2:21
2:40,52	COL 1:6
12:27	2:19
ACT 6:7	2 TH 1:3

[c]PAEL

Perfect

ACT 7:21	1 TM 5:10
1 CO 3:6	

Imperfect

2 CO 9:10

Imperative

EPH 6:4

Active Participle

ACT 14:17	1 CO 3:7

Passive Participle

1 CO 11:15

1856 ܡܪܒܝܢܐ (adj) nurse, guardian

ACT 13:1	1 TH 2:7

2920 ܪܒܝܬܐ (f) usury, interest

MAT 25:27	LUK 19:23

3429 ܬܪܒܝܬܐ (f) increase

EPH 4:16	COL 2:19
PHL 1:25	

[d]ETHPAAL

Perfect

LUK 4:16	ACT 22:3
ACT 7:20	

Imperfect

1 PT 2:2

Participle

1 TM 4:6	2 PT 3:18

266 (ܪܒܥ), ܐܪܒܥ (num) four

see below 268 ܐܪܒܥܡܐܐ

see below 269 ܐܪܒܥܣܪ

MAT 15:38	ROM 1:23
16:10	REV 4:4,4,6,7,8,9,10
24:31	5:6,8,8,14
MRK 2:3	6:1,7
8:9,20	7:1,1,1,2,4,11
13:27	8:12
LUK 2:37	9:13,14,15
19:8	11:16
JHN 4:35	14:1,3,3
11:17,39	15:7
19:23	16:8
ACT 10:11,12,30	19:4,4
11:5,6	20:8
21:9,23,38	21:17,19
27:29	

267 ܐܪܒܥܝܢ (num) forty

MAT 4:2,2	ACT 23:13,21
MRK 1:13	2 CO 11:24,24
LUK 4:2	HEB 3:9,17
JHN 2:20	REV 7:4
ACT 1:3	11:2
4:22	13:5
7:23,30,36,42	14:1,3
13:18,21	21:17

268 ܐܪܒܥܡܐܐ (num) four hundred

from 266 ܐܪܒܥ (above) and 1598 ܡܐܐ

ACT 5:36	ACT 13:20
7:6	GAL 3:17

269 ܐܪܒܥܣܪ (num) fourteen

from 266 ܐܪܒܥ (above) and 2400 ܥܣܪ

MAT 1:17,17,17 | 2 CO 12:2
ACT 27:27,33 | GAL 2:1

2923 ܪܒܥܐ (m) measure (liquid)

JHN 2:6

2960 ܪܘܒܥܐ (m) fourth part

REV 6:8

2922 ܪܒܥ (v-non occ) play tambourine; (pa only as pp) square

[a]PEAL

2919 ܪܒܝܥܝܐ (adj) fourth

MAT 14:25 | LUK 3:1,1,1
MRK 6:48

[c]PAEL

1858 ܡܪܒܥܐܝܬ (adv) foursquare

REV 21:16

2921 ܪܒܥ (v-non occ) lie down

[a]PEAL

1857 ܡܪܒܥܐ (m) womb

LUK 2:23 | ROM 4:19

2925 ܪܓ (v) desire, covet, lust

[a]PEAL

Perfect

LUK 22:15 | 1 CO 10:6[2]
ACT 20:33

Imperfect

MAT 5:28 | ROM 13:9
ROM 7:7

Active Participle

1 CO 10:6[1] | GAL 5:17[1],17[2]

1 TM 3:1[1],1[2] | JAM 4:5
HEB 11:16 | 1 PT 1:14

2927 ܪܓܝܓܐ (pp) desirous

PHL 1:23

2928 ܪܓܝܓܘܬܐ (f) lust

MRK 4:19 | TIT 1:8
LUK 8:14 | 2:12
ROM 1:24 | 3:3
6:12 | JAM 4:1,3
13:14 | 1 PT 1:14
GAL 5:24 | 2:11
EPH 2:3 | 4:2
4:22 | 2 PT 1:4
1 TM 6:9 | 2:18
2 TM 2:22 | 3:3
3:4,6 | JUD 16,18
4:3

2938 ܪܓܬܐ (f) desire, lust

LUK 22:15 | 1 TH 4:5
JHN 8:44 | 2 TM 3:3
ROM 1:27 | JAM 1:14,15
7:7,8 | 2 PT 2:10
1 CO 7:5,9 | 1 JN 2:16,16,17
GAL 5:16 | REV 18:14
COL 3:5

[m]ETHP ܐܬܪܓܪܓ

Perfect

MAT 13:17 | 1 TM 6:10

Imperfect

LUK 17:22 | REV 9:6

Imperative

1 PT 2:2

Participle

LUK 15:16 | JAM 4:2
JAM 1:14 | 1 PT 1:12

2926 ܪܓܙ (v) be angry; (aph) provoke

[a]PEAL

Perfect

MAT 18:34 | LUK 15:28
20:24 | REV 11:18
22:7 | 12:17
LUK 14:21

Imperfect

MAT 5:22

Imperative

EPH 4:26

Infinitive

JAM 1:19

Passive Participle

ACT 12:20

2961 ܪܘܓܙܐ (m) anger, wrath

MAT 3:7
LUK 3:7, 21:23
JHN 3:36
ACT 5:33, 26:11
ROM 1:18, 2:5,5,8, 3:5, 4:15, 5:9, 9:22,22,22, 12:19, 13:4,5
2 CO 7:11
EPH 2:3, 4:26,31, 5:6
COL 3:6,8
1 TH 1:10, 2:16, 5:9
1 TM 2:8
HEB 3:11, 4:3
JAM 1:20
REV 6:17, 11:18, 14:10, 16:19, 19:15

[e]APHEL

Perfect

HEB 3:16

Imperfect

ROM 10:19
EPH 6:4
COL 3:21

Infinitive

HEB 3:8,15

2932 ܪܓܠ, ܪܓܠܐ (f) foot

MAT 4:6, 5:35, 7:6, 10:14, 15:30, 18:8,8,29, 22:13,44, 28:9
MRK 1:40, 5:22, 6:11, 7:25, 9:45,45, 12:36
LUK 1:79, 4:11, 5:8, 7:38,38,38, 44,44,45, 46, 8:35,41, 9:5, 10:11,39, 17:16, 20:43, 24:39,40
JHN 11:2,32,44, 12:3,3, 13:5,6,8,9, 10,12, 14,14, 20:12
ACT 2:35, 3:7, 4:35,37, 5:2,9,10, 7:5,33,49, 58, 10:12,25, 11:6, 13:51, 14:8,10, 16:24,29, 21:11, 22:3, 26:16
ROM 1:23, 3:15, 10:15, 16:20
1 CO 12:15,21, 15:25,27
EPH 1:22, 6:15
1 TM 5:10
HEB 1:13, 2:8, 10:13, 12:13
JAM 2:3
REV 1:15,17, 2:18, 3:9, 10:1,2, 11:11, 12:1, 13:2, 19:10, 22:8

2934 ܪܓܠܬܐ (f) brook

JHN 18:1

2931 (ܪܓܠ) (v-non occ) (ethpe) dismount

[b]ETHPEEL

2933 ܪܓܠܐ (m) foot soldier

ACT 23:32

2935 ܪܓܡ (v) stone

[a]PEAL

Perfect

MAT 21:35
MRK 12:4
ACT 14:19

Imperfect

JHN 8:5,59
ACT 5:26, 14:5

Infinitive

JHN 10:31
JHN 11:8

Active Participle

MAT 23:37
LUK 13:34, 20:6
JHN 10:32,33
ACT 7:58,59, 22:20

[b]ETHPEEL

Perfect

2 CO 11:25 | HEB 11:37

Imperfect

HEB 12:20

2936 ܪܓܫ (v) rage, feel; (aph) perceive, know

[a]PEAL

Perfect

ACT 4:25

2930 ܪܓܝܫܐ (pp) aware

ACT 5:2 | HEB 13:2

2937 ܪܓܫܐ (m) sense

HEB 5:14

[e]APHEL

Perfect

MRK 5:29 | ACT 13:27

Active Participle

1 JN 2:3

2939 ܪܕܐ (v) journey, flow, chastise, instruct; (aph) make flow, supply

[a]PEAL

Perfect

MAT 14:34
LUK 8:26
ACT 13:4,13
14:26
15:39
16:11
ACT 18:18,22
20:6,13,15
21:1,2,7
27:4,28
28:11
1 TH 5:14

Imperfect

LUK 2:15
23:16,22
JHN 7:38
ACT 27:2,9,12

Active Participle

MAT 9:20 | MRK 6:48
MRK 10:17
LUK 8:23
10:33,38
13:22
ACT 9:2,31
10:9
15:3,41
27:7,8,13,
17,21,
ACT 27:24,40
COL 3:16
2 TM 2:25
TIT 2:12
HEB 12:6,7,9,
10
1 JN 1:6
REV 3:19

2943 ܪܕܝܐ (pp) instructed

ACT 18:24 | JAM 3:13

1861 ܡܪܕܝܐ (m) journey

LUK 2:44

1862 ܡܪܕܘܬܐ (f) chastisement, instruction

1 CO 10:11
EPH 6:4
2 TM 2:23
2 TM 3:16
HEB 12:5,7,8,
11

1863 ܡܪܕܝܬܐ (f) flow, voyage

MRK 5:25
LUK 8:44
ACT 27:10

2940 ܪܕܘܝܐ (m) instructor

ROM 2:20

[b]ETHPEEL

Perfect

ACT 7:22 | ACT 22:3

Imperfect

1 TM 1:20

Infinitive

1 CO 11:32[1]

Participle

1 CO 11:32[2]
2 CO 6:9
HEB 12:8

2945 ܪܕܦ (v) follow, persecute

[a]PEAL

Perfect

MAT 5:12 | JHN 15:20[1]

ACT 7:52	1 TH 2:15
22:4	REV 12:13
1 CO 15:9	

Imperfect

MAT 23:34	LUK 21:12
LUK 11:49	JHN 15:20[2]

Infinitive

ACT 26:11

Active Participle

MAT 5:11,44	ACT 22:7,8
10:23	26:14,15
JHN 5:16	1 CO 4:12
ACT 8:3	GAL 1:13,23
9:4,5,21	4:29

2941 ܪܕܘܦܐ (m) persecutor

ROM 12:14	1 TM 1:13
PHL 3:6	

2942 ܪܕܘܦܝܐ (m) persecution

MAT 13:21	ACT 13:50
MRK 4:17	ROM 8:35
10:30	2 CO 12:10
ACT 8:1	

2944 ܪܕܘܦܝܘܬܐ (f) persecution

2 TH 1:4	2 TM 3:11,11

---

[b]ETHPEEL

Perfect

MAT 5:10

Imperfect

GAL 6:12

Participle

2 CO 4:9	2 TM 3:12
GAL 5:11	2 PT 2:17

2946 ܪܗܒ (v) agitate; (ethpe, ethpa) be frightened; (saph) hurry

[a]PEAL (non occ)

2955 ܪܗܝܒܐ (pp) troubled

MRK 5:38,39	LUK 10:41

---

[b]ETHPEEL

Perfect

LUK 24:37

---

[d]ETHPAAL

Perfect

LUK 1:29

---

[i]SAPHEL

Passive Participle

ACT 20:16	2 TM 3:4
25:4	JAM 1:19
2 CO 1:17	2 PT 2:1

1804 ܣܘܪܗܒܐܝܬ (adv) hastily

LUK 2:16

2145 ܣܘܪܗܒܐ (m) haste

ACT 19:36

---

[j]ESTAPHAL

Perfect

LUK 19:6

Imperative

LUK 19:5	ACT 22:18

2947 ܪܗܒܘܢܐ (m) earnest, pledge

2 CO 1:22	EPH 1:14
5:5	

2948 ܪܗܘܡܐ (pn) Rome

ACT 2:10	ACT 28:14,16
18:2	ROM 1:7,15
19:21	2 TM 1:17
23:11	

2949 ܪܗܘܡܐܝܬ (adv) in Latin

LUK 23:38	JHN 19:20

2950 ܪܗܘܡܝܐ (adj) Roman

JHN 11:48	ACT 23:10,23,
ACT 16:21,37,	27,27,
38	31
22:25,26,	25:16
27,29	28:17

2951 ܪܗܘܡܝܘܬܐ (f) Roman citizenship

ACT 22:28

2952 ܪܗܛ (v) run

ᵃPEAL

Perfect

MAT 27:48	LUK 24:12
MRK 5:6,13	JHN 20:2,4²
6:33,55	ACT 3:11
9:15	19:29
10:17	21:32
15:36	GAL 2:2¹
LUK 15:20	PHL 2:16
19:4	

Imperfect

ROM 14:19	1 PT 3:11
HEB 12:1	

Imperative

1 CO 9:24³	1 TM 6:11
14:1	2 TM 2:22
1 TH 5:15	HEB 12:14

Active Participle

MAT 28:8	GAL 5:7
MRK 9:25	PHL 3:12,14
JHN 20:4¹	2 TH 3:1
ROM 9:16,30,31	1 TM 3:3
1 CO 9:24¹,24²,	TIT 1:7
25,26	JAM 3:6
GAL 2:2²	REV 9:9

2953 ܪܗܛܐ (m) course

ACT 12:14	2 TM 4:7
20:24	

2956 ܪܘܐ (v) become drunk

ᵃPEAL

Perfect

JHN 2:10	REV 17:2
ACT 2:13	

Infinitive

LUK 12:45

Active Participle

EPH 5:18	1 TH 5:7¹,7²

Passive Participle

ACT 2:15	REV 17:6
1 CO 11:21	

2975 ܪܘܝܐ (adj) drunkard

MAT 24:49	1 CO 6:10
1 CO 5:11	

2976 ܪܘܝܘܬܐ (f) drunkenness

LUK 21:34	GAL 5:21
ROM 13:13	1 PT 4:3

2957 (ܪܘܒ) (v) shout; (aph) cause an uproar

ᵃPEAL (non occ)

2958 ܪܘܒܐ (m) uproar

MAT 27:24	EPH 4:31
ACT 12:18	REV 21:4

ᵉAPHEL

Perfect

ACT 24:9

2964 ܪܘܙ (v) be glad, rejoice

[a]PEAL

Perfect

LUK 10:21
ACT 2:26

Imperfect

1 PT 4:13

Imperative

MAT 5:12
PHL 2:18

Active Participle

ACT 2:46 16:34
PHL 2:17
1 PT 1:8

2965 ܪܘܙܐ (m) gladness

LUK 1:14

2968 ܪܘܚܐ (c) spirit, wind, breath

see also 1625 ܟܪܬ ܪܘܚܐ

MAT 1:18,20 3:11,16 4:1 5:3 7:25,27 8:26,27 10:1,20 11:7 12:18,28,31,32,43,45 14:24,30,32 18:26,29 22:43 24:31 26:41 27:50 28:19
MRK 1:8,10,12,23,26,27 2:8 3:11,29,30 4:37,39,39,41 5:2,8,13 6:7,48,51 7:25 8:12 9:17,20,25,25 12:36 13:11,27 14:38
LUK 1:15,17,35,41,47,67,80 2:25,26,27,40 3:16,22 4:1,1,14,18,33,36 6:18 7:21,24 8:2,23,24,25,29,55 9:39,42,55 10:21 11:13,24,26 12:10,11,12 13:11 18:7 21:14 23:46 24:37,39
JHN 1:32,33,33 3:5,6,6,8,8,34 4:23,24,24 6:18,63,63 7:39,39 11:33 13:21 14:17,26 15:26 16:13 19:30 20:22
ACT 1:2,5,8,16 2:2,4,4,17,18,33,38 4:8,25,31 5:3,9,16,32 6:3,5,10 7:51,55,59 8:7,15,17,18,19,29,39 9:17,31 10:19,38,44,45,47 11:12,15,16,24,28 13:2,4,9,52 15:8,28 16:6,7,16,18 17:16 18:25 19:2,2,6,13,16,33,40 20:22,23,28 21:4,11 22:1 23:8,9 24:10 25:8,16 26:1,2,24 27:4,7,13,15,40 28:13,25
ROM 1:4,9,11,20 2:1,15,29 5:5 7:6,14 8:2,4,5,5,6,9,9,9,10,11,11,13,14,15,15,16,16,23,26,26,27 9:1 11:8 12:11 14:17 15:13,16,19,27,30
1 CO 2:4,10,10,11,11,12,12,13,14 3:16 4:21 5:3,4,5 6:11,17,19,20 7:34,40 9:3,11 10:3,4,4 12:3,3,4,7,8,8,9,9,10,11,13,13 13:4 14:1,2,12,14,15,15,16,32,37 15:44,45 16:18
2 CO 1:22 2:13 3:3,6,6,8,17,17,18 4:13 5:5 6:6,6 7:1,11,13 11:4 12:18,19 13:14
GAL 3:2,3,5,14 4:6,29 5:5,16,17,17,18,22,25,25 6:1,1,8,8,18
EPH 1:3,13,17 2:2,18,22 3:5,16 4:2,3,4,14,23,30 5:18,19 6:12,17,18
PHL 1:7,9,16,19,27 2:1 3:3
COL 1:8,9 2:5 3:12,16
1 TH 1:5,6 4:8 5:14,19,23
2 TH 2:2,8,13
1 TM 3:16 4:1,1
2 TM 1:7,14 2:24 3:10,16 4:16,22
TIT 3:5
PLM 25
HEB 1:7,14 2:4 3:7 4:12 6:4,12,15 9:8,14 10:15,29

HEB 12:9,23
13:22
JAM 1:6
2:26
3:4
4:5
5:7,7,8
1 PT 1:2,11,12
3:4,15,18
4:6,14
2 PT 1:21
3:9
1 JN 3:24
4:1,1,2,2,3,
6,6,13
5:7,7,8
JUD 12,19,20
REV 1:4,10

REV 2:7,11,17,
29
3:1,6,13,
22
4:2,5
5:6
6:13
7:1,1
11:11,11
13:15
14:13
16:13,14
17:3
18:2
19:10
21:10
22:6,17

2969 ܪܘܚܢܐ (adj) spiritual

1 CO 2:13,15
3:1
1 PT 2:2,5,5

2970 ܪܘܚܢܐܝܬ (adv) spiritually

1 PT 5:2
REV 11:8

2971 ܪܘܚܢܝܐ (adj) spiritual

1 CO 2:13,14
12:1
1 CO 15:44,46,
46

2967 ܪܘܚ (v) be ample; (pa) be enlarged; (aph) relieve

[a]PEAL (non occ)

2977 ܪܘܝܚܐ (pp) ample, large

MAT 7:13
2 CO 6:11

2974 ܪܘܚܬܐ (f) relief

2 CO 8:13

---

[c]PAEL

Imperative

2 CO 6:13

---

[e]APHEL

Perfect

1 TM 5:10

ܪܘܙ see ܪܐܙ

2978 (ܪܘܡ)[1] (v) be high; (aph,p) exalt

[a]PEAL (non occ)

1866 ܡܪܘܡܐ (m) height

MAT 21:9
MRK 11:10
LUK 2:14
LUK 19:38
EPH 4:8
HEB 1:3

2979 ܪܘܡܐ (m) height, high place

LUK 1:78
24:49
ROM 8:39
2 CO 10:5
EPH 3:18
REV 21:16

3022 ܪܡܐ (adj) high; (w/ ܩܠܐ) loud voice

MAT 4:8
17:1
27:46,50
MRK 1:26
5:7
9:2
15:34,37
LUK 1:42
4:5,33
6:35
8:28
16:15,24
17:15
19:37
23:23,46
JHN 11:43

ACT 7:57,60
8:7
13:17
14:10
16:28
26:24
27:41
ROM 12:16
2 TM 3:2
JAM 4:6
REV 5:2,12
7:2
10:3
19:17
21:10,12

3026 ܪܡܬܐ (f) hill

LUK 3:5
LUK 23:30

---

[c]PAEL (non occ)

1884 ܡܪܝܡܐ (pp) high, most high

MRK 5:7
LUK 8:28
ACT 7:48
ACT 16:17
HEB 7:1,26

---

[e]APHEL

Perfect

MAT 14:30
17:8
MAT 20:31
MRK 2:4

LUK	1:52	JHN	13:18
	6:20		17:1
	11:27	ACT	2:14
	16:23		4:24
	17:13		5:31
	24:50		13:17
JHN	3:14[1]		14:11
	6:5		22:22
	7:28	REV	10:5
	11:41		

Imperfect

MAT	23:12[1]	JHN	8:28
LUK	14:11[1]	1 PT	5:6
	18:13,14[1]		

Imperative

LUK 21:28 | JHN 4:35

Active Participle

1 CO 4:19 | 1 TM 2:8

[f]ETTAPHAL

Perfect

MAT	11:23	ACT	2:33
LUK	10:15	2 CO	12:7[1],7[2]
JHN	12:32		

Imperfect

MAT	23:12[2]	ROM	11:20
LUK	5:35	1 CO	4:6
	14:11[2]	2 CO	11:7
	18:14[2]	1 TM	3:6
JHN	12:34		6:17

Infinitive

JHN 3:14[2]

Participle

2 CO	10:5	1 TM	6:4
	11:20	1 PT	5:5

[k]P ܪܘܪܡ

Perfect

PHL 2:9

Imperfect

JAM 4:10

2981 ܪܘܪܡܐ (m) exaltation, high estate

JAM 1:9

[m]ETHP

Participle

ACT 19:17

2983 (ܪܘܥ), ܪܘܥܬܐ (f) foam

JUD 13

3046 (ܪܥܬ) (v) foam (at the mouth)

[e]APHEL

Active Participle

MRK 9:18,20 | LUK 9:39

2906 ܪܙܐ, ܪܐܙܐ (m) mystery

also spelled ܐܪܙܐ

MAT	13:11	EPH	3:3,4,9
MRK	4:11		5:32
LUK	8:10		6:19
ROM	11:25	COL	1:26,27
	16:24		2:2
1 CO	2:1,7		4:3
	4:1	2 TH	2:7
	13:2	1 TM	3:9,16
	14:2	REV	1:20
	15:51		10:7
EPH	1:9		17:5,7

2991 ܪܚܝܐ (f) millstone, mill

MAT	18:6	LUK	17:2
	24:41	REV	18:21
MRK	9:42		

2995 ܪܚܡ (v) love, have mercy; (pa, ethpa) have mercy, have compassion

[a]PEAL

Perfect

JHN	12:43	ROM	9:13
	16:27[2]	HEB	1:9

Imperfect

MAT	6:24	ROM	13:9
	22:37,39	EPH	5:33
MRK	12:30,33[1],	1 TM	3:8
	33[2]	TIT	2:4
LUK	10:27	JAM	2:8
	16:13	1 JN	2:15[1]
JHN	14:21[3],23[2]		

Imperative

MAT 5:43

Active Participle

MAT	6:5	JHN	21:15[2],16[1],
	10:37[1],37[2]		16[2],17[1],
	23:6		17[2],17[3],
MRK	12:38		20
LUK	6:32	ROM	12:10,13
	7:5	1 CO	2:9
	11:43		16:22
	16:14	2 CO	9:7
	20:46	1 TM	3:2,3
JHN	5:20	2 TM	3:2[1],2[2],4
	10:17	TIT	1:7,8[1],8[2]
	11:3,36		3:15
	12:25	HEB	12:6
	13:23		13:5
	14:15,21[1],	JAM	1:12
	23[1],24,		2:5
	28,31	1 PT	3:8,10
	15:19		4:9
	16:27[1]	1 JN	2:15[2]
	19:26	3 JN	9
	20:2	REV	3:19
	21:7,15[1],		

2996 ܪܚܡܐ (ap) friend

MAT	11:19	JHN	11:11
LUK	7:6,34		15:13,14,
	11:5,5,6,7		15
	12:4		19:12
	14:10,12	ACT	10:24
	15:6,9,29		19:31
	16:9		27:3
	21:16	JAM	2:23
	23:12		4:4
JHN	3:29	3 JN	15,15

2993 ܪܚܝܡܐ (pp) beloved

ACT	7:20	JUD	1
PHL	4:1,8		

2997 ܪ̈ܚܡܐ (m) bowels, mercy

MAT	5:7	ROM	1:31
LUK	1:78		9:23,23
ACT	2:47		11:31,31
	7:46		12:1
	28:2		15:9
2 CO	1:3	TIT	3:5
	4:1	PLM	7,20
	6:12	HEB	4:16
	7:15		10:28
GAL	6:16	JAM	2:13,13,13
EPH	2:4		3:17
PHL	1:8	1 PT	2:10,10
	2:1	1 JN	3:17
COL	3:12	2 JN	3
1 TM	1:2	JUD	2
2 TM	1:2,16,18		

2998 ܪܚܡܘܬܐ (f) friendship

LUK 11:8

2999 ܪܚܡܬܐ (f) love, friendship

JHN	15:9	JAM	4:4
1 TM	6:10	2 PT	1:7,7
HEB	13:2		

3000 ܪܚܡܬܢܐ (adj) merciful

1 PT 3:8

---

[b]ETHPEEL

Imperfect

JHN 14:21[2]

---

[c]PAEL

Perfect

PHL	2:27	1 TM	1:16

Imperfect

ROM	9:15[1]	ROM	11:32

Active Participle

ROM	9:15[2],18	ROM	12:8

1871 ܡܪܚܡܢܐ (adj) merciful

MAT	5:7	EPH	4:32
LUK	6:36,36	HEB	2:17
ROM	9:16	JAM	5:11

1872 ܡܪܚܡܢܘܬܐ (f) compassion

ACT	27:3	HEB	13:16
TIT	3:4		

[d]ETHPAAL

Perfect

MAT 9:36	MRK 6:34
14:14	LUK 7:13
18:27	10:33,37
20:34	15:20
MRK 1:41	ROM 9:25[1],25[2]
5:19	

Imperative

MAT 9:27	MRK 10:47,48
15:22	LUK 16:24
17:15	17:13
20:30,31	18:38,39
MRK 9:22	JUD 23

Participle

MAT 15:32	MRK 8:2

3001 (ܪܚܡ)(v-non occ) protect

[c]PAEL

1873 ܡܪܚܡܢܐ (adj) tender, compassionate

JAM 5:11

2972 ܪܘܚܡܐ (m) tenderness

PHL 2:1	COL 3:12

3002 ܪܚܩ (v) abstain from, avoid

[a]PEAL (non occ)

2973 ܪܘܚܩܐ (m) far place; (w/ ܡܢ) from afar

MAT 26:58	LUK 17:12
27:55	18:13
MRK 5:6	22:54
8:3	23:49
11:13	ACT 22:21
14:54	HEB 11:13
15:40	REV 18:17
LUK 16:23	

[c]PAEL (non occ)

2994 ܪܚܝܩܐ (adj) far, distant

MAT 14:24	ACT 2:39
15:8	17:27
MRK 7:6	1 CO 5:3
12:34	2 CO 10:1,11
LUK 7:6	13:2,10
14:32	EPH 2:13,17
15:13,20	PHL 2:12
19:12	2 TM 3:5
24:28	HEB 6:8
JHN 21:8	

[d]ETHPAAL

Imperfect

ACT 15:29	ROM 16:17

Imperative

1 TM 6:5

[e]APHEL

Perfect

ACT 19:9

Imperative

MAT 7:23	JAM 1:21

3003 ܪܚܫ (v-non occ) creep

[a]PEAL

3004 ܪܚܫܐ (m) creeping thing

ACT 10:12	ROM 1:23
11:6	JAM 3:7

3005 ܪܛܒ (v) be wet; (pa) moisten

[c]PAEL

Imperfect

LUK 16:24

3006 ܪܛܝܒܐ (adj) moist (green)

LUK 23:31

3007 ܪܛܢ (v) murmur

aPEAL

Perfect

1 CO 10:10[2]

Imperfect

JHN 6:43
1 CO 10:10[1]

Active Participle

MRK 10:41
LUK 5:30
15:2
LUK 19:7
JHN 6:41,61
7:23

3008 ܪܛܢܐ (m) murmuring

JHN 7:12
ROM 1:30
2 CO 12:20
PHL 2:14
1 PT 4:9

cPAEL

Perfect

MAT 20:11
ACT 6:1

eAPHEL

Active Participle

JUD 16

2954 (ܪܛܪ), ܪܗܛܪܐ (m) orator

ACT 24:1

3009 ܪܝܚܐ (m) smell, odor

JHN 12:3
2 CO 2:14,15,16,
16
EPH 5:2
PHL 4:18

2966 (ܪܘܚ) (v) (aph) smell

eAPHEL

Active Participle

1 CO 12:17

3010 ܪܝܫܐ (m) head, beginning; (pl) chiefs

incl idioms

MAT 5:36
6:17
8:20
9:34
10:30
12:24
14:8,10,11
17:24,25
20:25
21:42
22:17,19
23:6,6
24:8,31,31
26:7
27:29,30,
37,39
MRK 1:1
3:22
6:16,21,24,
25,27,27
10:42
12:10,14,
39,39
13:8,19,27,
27
14:3
15:19,29
LUK 3:1,1,1
7:38,46
8:41
9:9,58
11:15,43
12:7,11
14:1,7,8
16:24
18:18
20:17,22,
46,46
21:18,28
22:26
23:2
JHN 2:8,9,9
3:3,7
7:48
12:42
13:9
19:2,30
20:7
ACT 2:29
3:15,17
4:11,21
5:31,37
7:10,27,35,
35
ACT 13:27,50
14:5
15:22
16:12,20
17:6,8
18:18
19:31,35
21:24
22:5,30
23:5,15
24:5
25:2,23
27:34
28:7,17
ROM 4:1
12:8
13:6,7,7
15:12
1 CO 11:3,3,3,4,
4,5,5,5,
7,10,13
12:21
15:24
2 CO 3:1
GAL 4:9,19
EPH 1:10,22
2:2,20
4:15
5:23,23
COL 1:18,18
2:10,16,19
1 TH 4:16
TIT 3:1,5
HEB 2:7,9,10
5:12
6:6,6
7:4
8:1
10:7,29
11:21
12:2
1 PT 1:3,23
2:6
JUD 9,20
REV 1:5,14
6:15
9:7
10:1
12:1,3,3,9
14:14
17:3,7,9
18:19
19:12,18

3011 ܪܝܫܝܐ (adj) best, choicest

MRK 14:3
LUK 15:22
JHN 12:3
ACT 26:5

3012 ܪܫܝܬܐ (f) beginning; (pl) first fruits

MAT 19:4,8	2 TH 2:13
24:21	HEB 1:10
MRK 10:6	3:14
JHN 1:1,2	7:3,4
8:44	JAM 1:18
ACT 26:23	1 JN 1:1
ROM 8:23	2:7,13,14
11:16	3:8
16:5	REV 3:14
1 CO 15:20,23	14:4
16:15	21:6

3013 ܪܫܝܘܬܐ (f) first estate

JUD 6

3014 ܪܟ (v) be soft, tender

aPEAL

Perfect

MRK 13:28

Active Participle

MAT 24:32

cPAEL (non occ)

3017 ܪܟܝܟܐ (adj) soft

MAT 11:8,8	LUK 7:25

3015 ܪܟܒ (v) mount, ride; (pa) construct; (aph) make ride

aPEAL

Perfect

MAT 21:7	LUK 19:30
MRK 11:2,7	

Passive Participle

MAT 21:5	JHN 12:15

1889 ܡܪܟܒܬܐ (f) chariot

ACT 8:28,29,38	REV 18:13
REV 9:9	

3016 ܪܟܒܐ (m) band, fastening

ACT 27:40

dETHPAAL

Participle

EPH 2:21	COL 2:19
4:16	

eAPHEL

Perfect

LUK 19:35

Imperfect

ACT 23:24

3018 ܪܟܢ (v) draw to an end (day); (aph) bow

aPEAL

Perfect

LUK 24:29

eAPHEL

Perfect

JHN 19:30

3019 ܪܟܫ (v-non occ) bind

aPEAL

3020 ܪܟܫܐ (m) horse

JAM 3:3	REV 14:20
REV 9:7,9,17,	18:13
17,19	19:14,18

3021 ܪܡܐ (v) put, place, cast

aPEAL

Active Participle

MAT 4:18	MRK 1:16
9:16,17[1],	2:21,22[1],
17[2]	22[2]
21:8	12:41[1],41[2],

MRK 12:43[1]
LUK 5:5,36,37, 38
9:62
21:1
JHN 15:6
JHN 20:25
1 CO 7:35
2 CO 3:13
JAM 3:3
REV 2:22

Passive Participle

MAT 8:6,14
9:2
MRK 1:30
2:4
5:40
7:30
9:42
LUK 16:20
23:19,25
JHN 5:3,6
13:2
ACT 5:15
9:33
2 CO 3:15

---

[b]ETHPEEL

Perfect

GAL 2:5,13
REV 8:7
12:9[1],9[2],9[3], 10,13
REV 19:20
20:10,14, 15

Imperfect

1 TM 1:4
TIT 1:14

---

[c]PAEL (non occ)

3436 ܬܪܡܝܬܐ (f) foundation

MAT 13:35
25:34
JHN 17:24
ROM 1:20
EPH 1:4
1 PT 1:20
REV 13:8
17:8

---

[e]APHEL

Perfect

MAT 13:48
14:3
15:30
18:30
26:12,50
27:60
MRK 6:17
7:33
9:22
11:7
12:42,43[2], 44[1],44[2]
14:46
15:24
LUK 2:7
9:42
13:19
LUK 19:35
21:2,3,4[1], 4[2]
23:34
JHN 7:30,44
13:5
19:24
21:6[2]
ACT 1:26
4:3
5:18
12:1,4
16:23,37
21:27
26:10
27:28,29
REV 8:5

REV 12:4,15,16
14:16,19[1], 19[2]
REV 18:19,21
20:3

Imperfect

MAT 7:6
10:34[1],34[2]
13:42,50
25:27
27:6
MRK 4:26
7:27
LUK 6:38
12:49,51,
LUK 12:58
20:19
21:12
JHN 5:7
ACT 27:42
GAL 6:17
REV 2:10,14,24
4:10

Imperative

MAT 17:27
LUK 4:9
LUK 5:4
JHN 21:6[1]

Infinitive

MAT 15:26
LUK 12:5
ACT 27:43

Active Participle

HEB 6:1

3023 ܪܡܙ (v) make a sign, beckon

[a]PEAL

Perfect

LUK 1:62
5:7
JHN 13:24
ACT 24:10

Infinitive

LUK 1:22[1]

Active Participle

LUK 1:22[2]

2980 (ܪܡܚ), ܪܘܡܚܐ (f) spear

LUK 2:35

---

288 (ܪܡܠ), ܐܪܡܠܬܐ (f) widow

MAT 23:13
MRK 12:40,42, 43
LUK 2:37
4:25,26
7:12
LUK 18:3,5
20:47
21:2,3
ACT 6:1
9:39,41
1 CO 7:8

1 TM 5:3,3,4,5,9, 11,16,16
JAM 1:27
REV 18:7

3024 ܪܡܫ, ܪܡܫܐ (m) evening

MAT 8:16, 14:15, 16:2, 20:8, 26:20, 27:57, 28:1
MRK 1:32, 4:35
MRK 6:47, 11:11,19, 13:35, 14:17, 15:42
JHN 6:16, 20:19
ACT 4:3, 28:23

3028 ܪܢܐ (v) think, consider

[a]PEAL

Perfect

ACT 4:25

Imperfect

MRK 13:11

Active Participle

MRK 8:17,33
ACT 10:19, 27:39
ROM 14:14
1 CO 7:32,34[1],
1 CO 7:34[2],35
2 CO 5:14, 11:5
EPH 3:20
PHL 3:13

3029 ܪܢܝܐ (m) consideration, care

MAT 13:22
MRK 4:19

3030 ܪܣ (v) sprinkle

[a]PEAL

Perfect

HEB 9:19,21

3032 ܪܣܝܣܐ (pp) sprinkled

HEB 10:22

3033 ܪܣܣܐ (m) sprinkling

HEB 11:28, 12:24
1 PT 1:2

[b]ETHPEEL

Participle

HEB 9:13

3034 ܪܥ (v) break

[a]PEAL (non occ)

3042 ܪܥܝܥܐ (pp) bruised

MAT 12:20

[b]ETHPEEL

Imperfect

MAT 21:44
LUK 20:18

3035 ܪܥܐ (v) feed, tend, rule

[a]PEAL

Imperfect

MAT 2:6
ACT 20:28
REV 7:17, 19:15

Imperative

JHN 21:15,16, 17
1 PT 5:2

Infinitive

LUK 15:15
REV 2:27
REV 12:5

Active Participle

MAT 8:30,33
MRK 5:11,14
LUK 8:32
LUK 17:7
1 CO 9:7
JUD 12

3039 ܪܥܝܐ (ap) shepherd, pastor

MAT 9:36, 25:32, 26:31
MRK 6:34, 14:27
LUK 2:8,15,18, 20, 8:34
JHN 10:2,11,11, 12,14, 16
EPH 4:11
HEB 13:20
1 PT 2:25, 5:4

1892 ܡܪܥܝܬܐ (f) flock

LUK 2:8
ACT 20:28,29
1 CO 9:7
HEB 13:20
1 PT 5:2,3

3040 ܪܥܝܐ (m) pasture

JHN 10:9

3037 (ܪܥܐ)(v) reconcile

^{c}PAEL

Perfect

2 CO	5:18,19	EPH	2:16

Infinitive

COL 1:20

3444 ܬܪܥܘܬܐ (f) reconciliation

ROM	5:10,11	2 CO	5:18,19
	11:15		

^{d}ETHPAAL

Perfect

ROM 5:10

Imperfect

1 CO 7:11

Imperative

MAT	5:24	2 CO	5:20

3041 (ܪܥܐ), ܪܥܝܢܐ (m) mind, conscience; (w/ ܚܣܝܪ) fool

MAT	22:37	1 CO	2:16,16
MRK	12:30,33		7:37,40
LUK	10:27		9:25
	11:40		14:20,20
	12:20,29		15:33
	24:25,45	2 CO	1:12
JHN	7:18		4:2
	16:13		9:2,7
ACT	4:32		11:3,19,21, 23
	10:20		12:11
	19:21		
	26:9	GAL	3:1
ROM	1:30	EPH	4:2,17
	2:20		5:17
	7:21,23,25	PHL	2:2,3
	9:1		4:2
	11:20,25, 34	COL	1:21
			2:18,18
	12:2,16,16		3:12
	15:6	1 TH	5:8
1 CO	1:10	2 TH	2:2
1 TM	3:2,11	TIT	3:3,12
	5:21	HEB	13:5
	6:4,5,17	JAM	1:8
2 TM	3:8	1 PT	4:1
TIT	1:7,10,15		5:5
	2:2	2 PT	3:1

3445 ܬܪܥܝܬܐ (f) mind, thought

LUK	1:51	EPH	2:3
ROM	8:6,6,7,27	PHL	2:2
1 CO	1:10,19		3:19
2 CO	10:5	HEB	4:12
EPH	1:11	1 PT	1:13

3036 ܪܥܐ (v) (ethpa) think

^{d}ETHPAAL

Perfect

MAT	1:19,20	2 CO	1:17^{1},17^{2}
JHN	12:10	HEB	11:19,26

Imperfect

ROM	12:3^{2},16^{2}	2 CO	10:11
1 CO	4:6		12:6
2 CO	3:5	PHL	3:15^{1}

Imperative

PHL	2:5	COL	3:2
	4:8		

Infinitive

PHL 1:7

Participle

MAT	16:7,23	ROM	12:16^{1}
	21:25		14:6^{1},6^{2},6^{3}, 6^{4}
MRK	2:6,8^{1},8^{2}		
LUK	14:31	1 CO	13:5,11
ACT	28:22	2 CO	1:17^{3}
ROM	3:28		10:2
	8:5^{1},5^{2},18	GAL	5:10
	12:3^{1},3^{3},	PHL	3:15^{2}

3043 ܪܥܠ (v) tremble, shake

^{a}PEAL

Active Participle

HEB	12:12	JAM	2:19

3044 ܪܥܡ (v-non occ) thunder

[a]PEAL

3045 ܪܥܡܐ (m) thunder

MRK 3:17	REV 10:3,4,4
JHN 12:29	11:19
REV 4:5	14:2
6:1	16:18
8:5	19:6

[d]ETHPAAL

2982 ܪܘܥܡܐ (m) quarrel, complaint

COL 3:13

3047 ܪܦ (v-non occ) move

[a]PEAL

3051 ܪܦܦܐ (m) movement

1 CO 15:52

3048 ܪܦܐ (v) slacken; (pa) faint; (aph) leave, allow

[a]PEAL (non occ)

3049 ܪܦܝܐ (pp) loose, soft

HEB 12:16

[c]PAEL

Imperfect

HEB 12:5

[d]ETHPAAL

Imperfect

HEB 12:3

[e]APHEL

Perfect

ACT 27:40

Imperfect

1 CO 10:13 | HEB 13:5

3053 ܪܦܫܐ (m) winnowing fan

MAT 3:12 | LUK 3:17

3054 ܪܦܬ (v) (w/ ܒ) swarm with

[a]PEAL

Perfect

ACT 12:23

3056 ܪܨܦ (v-non occ) set closely

[a]PEAL

3055 ܪܨܝܦܬܐ (f) pavement

JHN 19:13

3057 ܪܩ (v) spit

[a]PEAL

Perfect

MAT 26:67	MRK 8:23
27:30	JHN 9:6
MRK 7:33	

Imperfect

MRK 10:34 | LUK 18:32

Active Participle

MRK 14:65 | MRK 15:19

2985 ܪܘܩܐ (m) spittle

JHN 9:6

3058 ܪܩܐ (intrj) fool

MAT 5:22

3059 ܪܩܕ (v) dance; (aph) mourn

[c]PAEL

Perfect

MAT 11:17[1]	MRK 6:22
14:6	LUK 7:32

[e]APHEL

Perfect

MAT 11:17[2]

Imperfect

MAT 24:30	REV 18:9
REV 1:7	

Active Participle

LUK 8:52	LUK 23:27

3060 ܪܩܥ (v) press down

[a]PEAL

Passive Participle

LUK 6:38

68 ܐܘܪܩܥܬܐ (f) piece of cloth

MAT 9:16	LUK 5:36,36
MRK 2:21	ACT 19:12

3061 ܪܫܐ (v) find fault, accuse

[a]PEAL

Active Participle

ACT 23:28,29	HEB 8:8
ROM 9:19	

3063 ܪܫܝܐ (m) accusation, blame; (w/ ܕܠܐ) blameless

ACT 25:7,18	1 TH 3:13
28:18	5:23
1 CO 1:8	1 TM 3:10
PHL 3:6	5:7
COL 1:22	TIT 1:6,7
1 TH 2:10	HEB 8:7

[b]ETHPEEL

Imperfect

ACT 19:40

Participle

ACT 25:16	ACT 26:2,7

[e]APHEL

Active Participle

LUK 23:14

3064 (ܪܫܐ), ܪܫܝܐ (m-non occ) gift

3062 (ܪܫܐ) (v) give, offer

[e]APHEL

Imperfect

ACT 25:9

3066 ܪܫܡ (v) engrave; (w/ ܩܕܡ) foreordain

[a]PEAL

Perfect

ACT 4:28	EPH 1:4,11
ROM 8:29,30	

Passive Participle

REV 5:1	REV 20:15

2987 ܪܘܫܡܐ (m) mark

REV 13:16,17	REV 19:20
14:9,11	20:4
16:2	

[b]ETHPEEL

Perfect

2 CO 3:7

3067 ܪܫܥ (v) act wickedly

[a]PEAL (non occ)

2988 ܪܘܫܥܐ (m) wickedness, ungodliness

ROM 1:18 2 TM 2:16	TIT 2:12 JUD 18

3065 ܪܫܝܥܐ (adj) wicked, ungodly

ACT 2:23 ROM 5:6,7 1 TM 1:9 2 TM 3:2	1 PT 4:18 2 PT 2:5,6 3:7 JUD 4,15

[e]APHEL

Perfect

JUD 15

3068 ܪܬ (v) tremble

[a]PEAL

Active Participle

ACT 16:29

3072 ܪܬܬܐ (c) trembling

MRK 16:8 1 CO 2:3 2 CO 7:15	EPH 6:5 PHL 2:12

3073 ܪܬܬܐ (adj) trembling

MRK 5:33 LUK 8:47	ACT 7:32 HEB 12:21

3069 (ܪܬܐ) (v) admonish, instruct

[e]APHEL

Imperfect

ACT 8:31

Infinitive

ROM 15:14

Active Participle

ACT 20:31 1 CO 4:14	2 TH 3:15 TIT 3:10

1898 ܡܪܬܝܢܘܬܐ (f) instruction

2 TM 1:7

3070 ܪܬܚ (v) boil; (w/ ܪܘܚ) be fervent in spirit

[a]PEAL

Active Participle

ACT 18:25	ROM 12:11

3071 ܪܬܚܐ (m) heat

ACT 28:3

[i]SAPHEL (non occ)

1927 ܡܫܪܬܚܘܬܐ (f) abundance

PHL 4:12

ܫ

3074 ܫܐܕܐ (m) devil

MAT	7:22	LUK	9:1,49
	8:31		10:17,20
	12:24		11:14,14
	15:22		13:32
	17:18	ACT	17:22
MRK	1:39		19:12,13, 15
	5:12,15,16, 18	1 CO	10:20,20, 21,21
	6:13		
	7:26,29,30	2 CO	6:16
	9:26,38	1 TM	4:1
	16:9,17	JAM	2:19
LUK	4:33,35,41		3:15
	7:33	1 PT	4:3
	8:2,29,33, 35,38	REV	16:14
			18:2

3077 ܫܐܠ (v) ask, inquire; (w/ ܫܠܡܐ) salute; (aph) lend

[a]PEAL

Perfect

MAT	17:10	LUK	18:18,40
	22:23,35		20:21,27
	27:11,58		23:3,25,52
MRK	4:10	JHN	1:21,25
	5:9		5:12
	7:5,17		9:2,15
	8:23		12:21
	9:15,28		16:24[1]
	10:10		18:19
	12:14,28	ACT	1:6
	13:3		3:14
	14:60,61		7:1,46
	15:2,4,43, 44		9:2
			12:20
LUK	1:40,63		13:21,28
	8:9,30		18:22
	13:23		28:18
	15:26	HEB	10:6
	17:20	1 JN	5:15[2]

Imperfect

MAT	6:8	MAT	27:20
	7:9,10	MRK	6:23,24
	14:7		10:35
	18:19	LUK	10:4
	21:22		11:11[1],11[2],
LUK	11:12	JHN	16:26
JHN	11:22	ACT	25:13
	14:13,14	JAM	1:5,6
	15:16	1 JN	5:16
	16:23[1],23[2],		

Imperative

MAT	7:7	ROM	16:16[1]
	10:11,12	1 CO	16:20[2]
MRK	6:22	2 CO	13:12
LUK	11:9	PHL	4:21[1]
JHN	16:24[2]	COL	4:15
ROM	16:3,5,6,7,	1 TH	5:26
	8,9,10[1],	TIT	3:15[2]
	10[2],11[1],	HEB	13:24[1]
	11[2],12[1],	1 PT	5:14
	12[2],13,	3 JN	15[2]
	14,15,		

Infinitive

MRK	15:8,18	COL	1:9
JHN	15:7		

Active Participle

MAT	5:42,47	ROM	16:23[2]
	7:8,11	1 CO	1:22
	16:1		16:19[1],19[2], 20[1]
	20:20,22		
MRK	8:11	2 CO	13:13
	10:38	EPH	3:13,20
	11:24	PHL	4:21[2],22
	15:6	COL	4:10,12,14
LUK	6:30	2 TM	4:21
	11:10,13, 16	TIT	3:15[1]
		PLM	23
	22:31	HEB	13:24[2]
	23:23	JAM	4:2,3[1],3[2]
JHN	4:9,10	1 PT	5:13
ACT	3:2,10	1 JN	3:22
	25:3		5:14,15[1]
ROM	16:16[2],21, 22,23[1],	2 JN	13
		3 JN	15[1]

3078 ܫܐܠܬܐ (f) request, petition

LUK	23:24	1 JN	5:15
PHL	4:6		

[b]ETHPEEL

Perfect

ACT	20:27	HEB	12:19,25[2]

Imperfect

HEB 12:25[1],25[3]

Imperative

1 TM	4:7	2 TM	2:16,23
	5:11	TIT	3:9,10

Infinitive

LUK 14:18[1]

Participle

LUK	14:18[2],19	ACT	25:11

[c]PAEL

Perfect

MAT	22:41	JHN	4:52
MRK	8:5		9:19
	9:21		18:7
LUK	9:18	ACT	10:17
	23:6	ROM	10:20

Imperfect

MAT	21:24	LUK	22:68
MRK	9:32	JHN	1:19
	11:29		13:24
	12:34		16:30
LUK	6:9		21:12
	9:45	1 CO	14:35
	20:3		

Imperative

JHN	9:21,23	JHN	18:21[2]

Infinitive

MAT	22:46	JHN	16:19
LUK	20:40		

Active Participle

MAT	2:4	LUK	21:7
	12:10		23:9
	16:13	JHN	8:7
MRK	8:27		16:5
	9:11,16,33		18:21[1]
	10:2,17	ACT	4:7
	12:18		10:18,29
LUK	2:46		19:1
	3:10,14		21:33
	18:36		23:19,34
	19:31		24:8

[d]ETHPAAL

Perfect

ACT 25:26

Imperfect

ACT 22:24

[e]APHEL

Imperative

LUK 11:5

3079 ܫܐܪܝܐ (m) silk

REV 18:12

3080 ܫܒ (v) (tr) let down; (int) decend

[a]PEAL

Perfect

MRK	2:4	ACT	9:25
LUK	5:19	2 CO	11:33

Active Participle

ACT	10:11	ACT	11:5

3082 (ܫܒ), ܫܒܒܐ (adj) neighbor

LUK	1:58,65	LUK	15:6,9
	14:12	JHN	9:8

3100 (ܫܒ), ܫܒܬܐ (f) Sabbath

see also 910 ܚܕ ܒܫܒܐ

MAT	12:1,2,5,8, 10,11, 12	LUK	13:14,15, 16
	24:20		14:1,3,5
	28:1		18:12
MRK	1:21		23:54,56
	2:23,24,27, 27,28	JHN	5:9,10,16, 18
	3:2,4		7:22,23,23
	6:2		9:14,16
	15:42		19:31,31, 42
	16:1	ACT	13:14,27, 42,44
LUK	4:16,31		15:21
	6:1,2,5,6,7, 9		16:13
	13:10,14,		17:2

ACT 18:4
COL 2:16
HEB 4:4

3099 ܫܒܬ (v) rest

eAPHEL

Infinitive

HEB 4:9

3081 ܫܒܐ (v) lead captive

aPEAL

Perfect

EPH 4:8

Active Participle

ROM 7:23
2 CO 10:5
2 TM 3:6

Passive Participle

LUK 4:18
8:29
ROM 16:7
COL 4:10
PLM 23

3087 ܫܒܝܐ (m) captivity

REV 13:10,10

3091 ܫܒܝܬܐ (f) captivity

EPH 4:8

---

bETHPEEL

Imperfect

LUK 21:24

3118 (ܫܒܚ), ܫܘܒܚܐ (m) glory

MAT 4:8
6:29
19:28
24:30
25:31,31
MRK 8:38
10:37
13:26
LUK 2:32
4:6
9:26,32
12:27
18:43
19:38
LUK 21:27
JHN 1:14,14
2:11
5:41,44,44
7:18,18
8:50,54
11:40
12:41,43,
43
17:5,22,24
ROM 16:26
1 CO 2:7
4:5
15:40,41,
1 CO 15:41,41,
41,43
2 CO 3:7,8,9,9,
10,11,11,
18,18
4:4,6,15,
17
6:8
8:19,23
GAL 1:5
5:26
EPH 1:6,14,18
PHL 1:11
2:11
3:21
PHL 4:8,19,20
COL 1:11,27,27
3:4
1 TH 2:6,12
2 TH 1:9
1 TM 3:16
2 TM 2:10
4:18
HEB 1:3
9:5
13:21
1 PT 1:21
5:1,4,10,
11
JUD 25

3088 ܫܒܝܚܐ (adj) praiseworthy

PHL 4:8
REV 18:14

3085 (ܫܒܚ) (v) praise, glorify

cPAEL

Perfect

MAT 9:8
15:31,36
26:30
MRK 14:26
LUK 13:13
16:8
23:47
JHN 12:28[2]
17:4
ACT 3:13
11:18
21:20
27:35
ROM 1:21
8:30
HEB 5:5
REV 18:7

Imperfect

MAT 5:16
MRK 2:12
JHN 16:14
17:1[2]
21:19
ROM 15:6,9
1 CO 11:22[1]
2 CO 10:18[2]
HEB 2:12
1 PT 2:12
4:16
REV 15:4

Imperative

JHN 9:24
12:28[1]
17:1[1],5
ROM 15:11[1],11[2]
REV 19:5

Active Participle

LUK 2:13,20
5:25,26
7:16
17:15
18:43
19:37
24:53
JHN 8:54[1],54[2]
12:28[3]
13:32[2],32[3]
ACT 2:47
3:8,9
ACT 4:21
13:48
16:25
ROM 11:13
1 CO 6:20
11:2,17,
22[2]
2 CO 5:12
9:13
10:18[1]
GAL 1:24
JUD 16

REV 5:9	REV 15:3
14:3	

1900 ܡܫܒܚܐ (pp) praiseworthy, excellent

LUK 7:25	EPH 5:27
JHN 17:10	1 PT 1:8
2 CO 3:10	4:14

3448 ܬܫܒܘܚܬܐ (f) praise, glory

MAT 6:13	EPH 5:19
16:27	PHL 2:3
21:16	3:19
LUK 2:9,14	COL 3:16
9:31	1 TH 2:20
14:10	2 TH 2:14
17:18	1 TM 1:11,17
24:26	TIT 2:13
JHN 11:4	HEB 2:7,9,10
ACT 2:26	3:3
7:2,55	13:15
12:23	JAM 2:1
22:11	1 PT 1:7,11
ROM 1:23,25	2:9,14,20, 20
2:7,10,29	
3:7,23	4:11,13
4:20	2 PT 1:3,17,17
5:2	2:10
6:4	3:18
8:18,21	JUD 8,25
9:4,5,23	REV 1:6
11:36	4:9,11
13:3	5:9,12,13
15:7	7:12
1 CO 2:8	11:13
10:31	14:3,3,7
11:7,7,15	15:3,3,8
2 CO 1:20	16:9
3:7,18	18:1
8:18	19:1,7
EPH 1:12,17	21:11,23, 24,26
3:13,16,21	

dETHPAAL

Perfect

JHN 7:39	JHN 13:32[1]
12:16	2 CO 3:10
13:31[1],31[2],	

Imperfect

MAT 6:2	ROM 8:17
JHN 11:4	EPH 1:6
12:23	2 TH 1:10,12
14:13	1 PT 4:11

Participle

LUK 4:15	1 CO 12:26[1],26[2]
JHN 15:8	2 TH 3:1
1 CO 4:10	

3086 ܫܒܛܐ (m) rod, sceptre, tribe; (w/ ܐܚܕ) magistrate

MAT 10:10	HEB 1:8,8
19:28	9:4
MRK 6:8	REV 2:27
LUK 2:36	5:5
9:3	11:1
22:30	12:5
ACT 16:35,38	19:15
2 CO 11:25	21:12
PHL 3:5	

3089 (ܫܒܠ), ܫܒܝܠܐ (m) path

MAT 3:3	GAL 6:16
MRK 1:3	PHL 3:16
LUK 3:4	HEB 12:13

3092 ܫܒܠ (v) lead

cPAEL

Imperfect

REV 7:17

3093 ܫܒܠܐ (c) blade, ear

MAT 12:1	MRK 4:28,28
MRK 2:23	LUK 6:1

3094 ܫܒܥ (num) seven

MAT 12:45	LUK 20:29,31, 33
15:34,36, 37	JHN 4:52
16:10	ACT 1:12
18:21,22, 22,22	6:3
	13:19
22:25,26, 28	19:14
	20:6
MRK 8:5,6,8,20, 20	21:4,8,27
	28:14
12:20,22, 23	ROM 11:4
	HEB 11:30
16:9	JUD 14
LUK 2:36	REV 1:4,4,11, 12,16,20, 20,20,20, 20,20
8:2	
11:26	
17:4,4	

REV 2:1; 3:1,1; 4:5,5; 5:1,6,6,6; 6:1; 8:1,2,2,6,6; 10:3,4,4,4,7; 11:13,15; 12:3,3
REV 13:1; 15:1,6,6,7,7,8,8; 16:1,1,17; 17:1,1,3,7,9,9,10,11; 21:9,9,9,20

3090 ܫܒܝܥܝܐ (adj) seventh

HEB 4:4

3095 ܫܒܥܝܢ (num) seventy

MAT 18:22
LUK 10:1,17
ACT 7:14; 23:23; 27:37

3096 ܫܒܩ (v) forgive, leave, allow, reserve

[a]PEAL

Perfect

MAT 3:15[2]; 4:11,13,20,22; 6:12[2]; 8:15; 13:36; 16:4; 18:27,32; 19:27; 21:17; 22:22,25; 23:23[1]; 26:44,56; 27:46,50
MRK 1:18,20,31; 4:36; 5:19,37; 7:8; 8:13; 10:28; 11:6; 12:12,19[1],20,21,22; 13:34; 14:50,52; 15:34[1],34[2]
LUK 4:39; 5:11,28; 7:42; 8:51; 10:30,40; 11:4[2]; 18:28; 20:31
JHN 4:3,28,52; 8:29
ACT 7:39; 14:16,17; 15:38; 18:21; 21:3; 24:27; 27:32; 28:4
ROM 1:27; 11:4,27
2 CO 2:10[2],10[3],10[4]
EPH 4:32[2]
COL 2:13; 3:13[2]
2 TM 4:10,13,16,20
TIT 1:5
HEB 2:8; 11:27
1 PT 2:21
2 PT 2:15
JUD 6
REV 2:4,20

Imperfect

MAT 6:14[1],14[2], 18:21,35; 19:5; 23:23[2]
MRK 10:2,7; 11:25[2],26[2]
LUK 5:24; 11:42; 19:44; 23:16,22
JHN 16:32
MAT 6:15[1]
JHN 20:23[1]
ACT 6:2; 28:27
1 CO 7:11,12,13
2 CO 2:7
EPH 5:31
HEB 6:1; 13:5
1 JN 1:9
REV 11:9

Imperative

MAT 3:15[1]; 5:24,40; 6:12[1]; 7:4; 8:22; 13:30; 15:14; 19:14; 27:49
MRK 7:27; 10:14; 11:25[1]; 14:6; 15:36
LUK 4:34; 6:42; 9:60; 11:4[1]; 13:8; 14:18,19; 17:3,4; 18:16; 23:34
JHN 11:44; 12:7; 18:8
ACT 5:38
2 CO 12:13
COL 3:13[3]

Infinitive

MAT 9:6
MRK 2:7,10
LUK 5:21

Active Participle

MAT 6:15[2]; 18:12; 19:9[1],29; 23:14; 24:43
MRK 1:34; 7:12; 10:29; 11:16,26[1]; 12:19[2]
LUK 4:41; 7:49; 12:39; 14:33; 15:4; 18:29
JHN 10:12; 11:48; 14:18,27; 16:28
ACT 2:27; 27:7
2 CO 2:10[1]
EPH 4:32[1]; 6:9
COL 3:13[1]
HEB 10:25

Passive Participle

MAT 5:32; 9:2,5; 19:9[2]
MRK 2:5,9
LUK 5:20,23; 7:47[1],48; 16:18

3119 ܫܘܒܩܢܐ (m) remission, forgiveness, divorce

MAT 19:7; 26:28
MRK 1:4; 3:29; 10:4
LUK 1:77; 3:3; 4:18,18

LUK 24:47
ACT 2:38
5:31
10:43
13:38
ACT 26:18
EPH 1:7
COL 1:14
HEB 9:22
10:18

[b]ETHPEEL

Perfect

LUK 7:43
JHN 8:9
ACT 2:31
ACT 25:14
ROM 4:7
1 JN 2:12

Imperfect

MAT 12:31[1],31[2],
32[1],32[2]
24:2,40
MRK 3:28
4:12
LUK 12:10[1],10[2]
LUK 17:34,35,
36
21:6
JHN 20:23[2]
ACT 8:22

Participle

MAT 23:38
24:41
MRK 13:2
LUK 7:47[2]
LUK 13:35
2 CO 4:9
HEB 7:23
JAM 5:15

3097 ܫܒܪ, ܫܒܪܐ (m) young child

HEB 5:13
1 PT 2:2

3098 ܫܒܘܫܬܐ (f) branch

JHN 15:2,4,5,6

3101 ܫܒܬܐ (f) anise

MAT 23:23

3102 ܫܓܐ (v) go astray

[a]PEAL

Perfect

2 PT 2:15

3105 ܫܓܢ (v-non occ) change

[k]P

3121 ܫܘܓܢܝܐ (m) change

JAM 1:17

3106 ܫܓܪ (v) kindle

[b]ETHPEEL

Participle

REV 9:2

3107 ܫܓܫ (v) stir up, trouble

[a]PEAL

Perfect

LUK 23:5
ACT 6:12
ACT 14:19
24:19

Active Participle

JAM 1:6

Passive Participle

JHN 12:27
ACT 19:32
JAM 1:8

3103 ܫܓܘܫܐ (m) rioter

ACT 19:40

3104 ܫܓܘܫܝܐ (m) riot, uproar

MAT 26:5
MRK 13:8
14:2
LUK 21:9
ACT 15:2
19:23
ACT 20:1
23:10
24:5,18
1 CO 14:33
2 CO 6:5
12:20

[b]ETHPEEL

Perfect

LUK 1:12
ACT 2:6
ACT 19:29,40
21:30

Imperfect

1 PT 3:14

Participle

MAT 9:23, 14:24 | 1 CO 13:4

eAPHEL

Active Participle

LUK 22:41

3108 ܫܕܐ (v) throw, cast

aPEAL

Perfect

MAT 13:48, 27:5
MRK 1:26, 10:50
LUK 4:35
JHN 21:7
ACT 7:45, 27:18,19, 38, 28:5

Imperfect

LUK 4:29 | JHN 8:7

Imperative

MAT 4:6, 5:29,30 | MAT 18:8,9
1 PT 5:7

Active Participle

LUK 14:35
ACT 23:23
1 JN 4:18
REV 6:13

Passive Participle

MRK 9:42 | LUK 17:2

bETHPEEL

Perfect

ACT 7:21 | 1 CO 15:32

Imperfect

MAT 5:13
ACT 27:26
REV 18:21

Participle

MAT 15:17
MRK 7:19
JHN 12:31
JHN 15:6
ACT 7:19

cPAEL

Active Participle

ACT 22:23

3109 ܫܕܠ (v) entice

cPAEL

Active Participle

2 PT 2:14,18

3110 ܫܕܠܐ (adj) enticing

1 TH 2:5

3111 (ܫܕܪ) (v) send

cPAEL

Perfect

MAT 2:8,16, 10:5, 11:2, 14:10,35, 20:2, 21:1,34[1], 36,37, 22:3,4,7, 16, 28:18[1]
MRK 3:31, 6:17,27, 8:26, 9:37, 11:1, 12:2,3,4[1], 4[2],5[1],5[2], 6,13, 14:13
LUK 7:3,6,19, 20, 9:2,48,52, 10:1,17, 14:17, 15:15, 19:14,29, 20:10[1],10[2], 11[1],11[2], 12,20, 22:8,35, 23:7,11,15
JHN 1:19,22,33, 3:17,34, 4:34,38, 5:23,24,30, 33,38, 6:29,38,39, 44,57, 7:16,18,28, 7:29,32,33, 8:16,18,26, 29,42, 9:4, 10:36, 11:3,42, 12:44,45, 49, 13:16,20[2], 14:24, 15:21, 16:5, 17:3,8,18[1], 18[2],21, 23,25, 18:24, 20:21[1]
ACT 3:26, 5:21, 6:11, 7:12,14,35, 8:14, 9:17,30,38, 10:8,20, 29[1],29[2], 33,36, 11:22,30, 12:11, 13:3,24, 15:3,22,25, 27, 16:35,36, 19:22,31, 20:17, 23:17,30, 24:7,24, 28:17
ROM 8:3
1 CO 1:17

1 CO	4:17	COL	4:8
2 CO	8:18,22	1 TH	3:5
	9:3	2 TM	4:12
	12:17,18	TIT	3:12
GAL	4:4,6	PLM	12
EPH	6:22	1 JN	4:9,10,14
PHL	2:28	REV	22:6,16
	4:16,18		

Imperfect

MAT	13:41	ACT	3:20
	21:34[2]		7:34
	24:31		10:22
MRK	3:14		11:29
	5:10		24:25
	6:7		25:3,21
	13:27	1 CO	16:3
LUK	11:49	PHL	2:19,23,25
	16:27	1 TH	3:2
	20:13	2 TH	2:11
	24:49	REV	11:10
JHN	16:7		

Imperative

MRK	5:12	ACT	11:13
LUK	16:24	REV	1:11
ACT	10:5,32		14:15,18

Infinitive

LUK 4:18

Active Participle

MAT	10:16	LUK	14:32
	11:10	JHN	13:20[1]
	21:3		14:26
	23:34		15:26
	28:18[2]		20:21[2]
MRK	1:2	ACT	22:21
	11:3		24:26
LUK	7:27		25:27
	10:3		26:17

Passive Participle

ACT 9:21

[d]ETHPAAL

Perfect

MAT	15:24	ACT	5:22
LUK	4:26,43		10:17
	7:10		11:11
	19:32		13:26
JHN	1:6,24		28:28
	3:2	1 PT	1:12

Imperfect

ACT	25:25	ACT	27:1

Participle

HEB	1:14	REV	5:6
1 PT	2:14		

3112 ܫܗܪ (v) watch

[a]PEAL

Imperfect

MAT 26:40

Imperative

MAT 26:38

Active Participle

LUK	21:36	HEB	13:17
EPH	6:18		

3113 ܫܗܪܐ (m) watching

2 CO	6:5	2 CO	11:27

3114 ܫܘܐ (v) be worthy, equal; (ethpe) agree; (pa) spread, wipe, make a bed; (aph) make equal, smooth

[a]PEAL

Perfect

LUK	7:7	ACT	5:41
	20:35	HEB	13:2

Imperfect

LUK	21:36	2 TH	1:5
2 CO	2:16	1 TM	5:17

Active Participle

MAT	3:8,11	ACT	23:29
	8:8		25:11,25
	10:10,11,		26:20,31
	13[1],13[2],		28:18
	37[1],37[2],	ROM	8:18
	38	1 CO	6:2
	22:8		11:27,29
MRK	1:7		15:9
LUK	3:8,16		16:4
	7:4,6	1 TM	1:15
	10:7		4:9
	12:48		5:18
	15:19,21	HEB	11:38
	23:15,22,	REV	3:4
	41		4:11
JHN	1:27		5:2,4,9,12
ACT	13:25,46		16:6

3135 ܫܘܝܐ (pp) equal, the same

MRK 14:56,59; 1 CO 11:5; 15:39 | 2 PT 1:1; REV 21:16

3136 ܫܘܝܐܝܬ (adv) equally

ACT 11:17 | 1 CO 12:25

3137 ܫܘܝܘܬܐ (f) equality

ROM 15:5; 2 CO 8:14,14 | COL 4:1

---

[b]ETHPEEL

Perfect

ACT 5:9 | 2 PT 1:1

Imperfect

MAT 18:19 | 1 CO 7:5

---

[c]PAEL

Perfect

LUK 7:44; JHN 11:2 | JHN 12:3

Imperative

ACT 9:34

Active Participle

MAT 21:8; MRK 11:8[1],8[2] | LUK 7:38; JHN 13:5

Passive Participle

MRK 14:15 | LUK 22:12

---

[e]APHEL

Perfect

MAT 20:12; 2 CO 3:6 | COL 1:12

Imperfect

1 CO 6:5 | 2 TH 1:11

Imperative

MAT 3:3; MRK 1:3 | JHN 1:23

Active Participle

JHN 5:18

3115 (ܫܘܒ)(v-non occ) wither

[a]PEAL

3116 ܫܘܒܐ (m) heat

REV 7:16

3120 (ܫܘܓ)(v) wash

[a]PEAL (non occ)

1901 ܡܫܓܬܐ (f) basin

JHN 13:5

---

[e]APHEL

Perfect

MAT 27:24; JHN 9:7[2],11[2],15 | JHN 13:12,14[1]; 1 TM 5:10

Imperfect

JHN 13:9,10, | JHN 13:14[2]

Imperative

MAT 6:17 | JHN 9:7[1],11[1]

Infinitive

JHN 13:5

Active Participle

MAT 15:2; MRK 7:3; LUK 5:2 | JHN 13:6,8[1],8[2]; 1 PT 3:21

Passive Participle

MAT 15:20 | MRK 7:2,5

3126 ܫܘܙܒ (v) rescue

[k]P

Imperfect

2 TH 3:3

3124 ܫܘܙܒܐ (m) deliverance

REV 12:10

---

[m]ETHP

Perfect

ACT 27:44 | ACT 28:4

Imperfect

1 CO 3:15

3127 ܫܘܚ (v) spring up

[a]PEAL

Perfect

MAT 13:5

3128 (ܫܘܚ) (v) melt

[a]PEAL

Imperfect

2 PT 3:12

3177 (ܫܘܚ), ܫܘܚܬܐ (f-non occ) boldness

3129 (ܫܘܚ) (v) dare

[e]APHEL

Perfect

PHL 1:14

Imperfect

2 CO 10:2

Active Participle

1 TH 4:6

3134 (ܫܘܛ) (v) despise, treat w/ contempt

[a]PEAL

Perfect

LUK 23:11
GAL 4:14 | JAM 2:6

Imperfect

MAT 6:24
LUK 16:13 | ROM 14:3
1 CO 16:11

Active Participle

ROM 2:22 | ROM 14:10

3178 ܫܛܝܐ (pp) contemptable

2 CO 10:10

---

[b]ETHPEEL

Participle

ACT 19:27

3142 ܫܘܡܬܐ (f) wound

1 PT 2:24

3263 (ܫܥܐ), ܫܥܬܐ (f) hour

see also 447 ܒܪ ܫܥܬܗ

MAT	8:3,13	LUK	24:33
	9:22	JHN	1:39
	10:19		2:4
	15:28		4:6,21,23, 52,53
	17:18		5:25,28,35
	18:1		6:21
	20:3,5,6,9, 12		7:30
	24:36,42, 44,50		8:20
	25:13		11:9
	26:40,45, 55,74		12:23,27, 27
	27:45,45, 46,48		13:1
MRK	1:42		16:2,25,32
	6:25		17:1
	7:35		18:27
	13:11,32		19:14,27
	14:35,37, 41,72	ACT	2:15
	15:25,33, 33,34		3:1,7
LUK	2:38		5:7,10
	7:21		10:3,9,30
	10:21		11:11
	12:12,40, 46		12:23
	13:25		13:11
	19:11		16:18,33
	20:19		19:34
	22:53,59		22:13
	23:44,44		23:23
		ROM	13:11
		1 CO	4:11
			15:30
		2 CO	7:8
		GAL	2:5

1 TH 2:17	REV 11:13
PLM 15	14:7,15
REV 3:3	17:12
8:1	18:10,17,
9:15	19

3144 ܫܘܥܐ (m) rock

MAT 7:24,25	LUK 6:48,48
13:5,20	8:6,13
MRK 4:5,16	ACT 27:29
15:46	REV 6:15,16

3147 (ܫܘܦ) (v-non occ) annoint

aPEAL

3184 ܫܝܦܐ (m) eyesalve

REV 3:18

3273 (ܫܘܩ), ܫܩܐ (f) shin bone, tibia

JHN 19:31,32,	JHN 19:33

3151 ܫܘܩܐ (m) street, marketplace

MAT 6:2,5	LUK 14:21
11:16	20:46
12:19	ACT 5:15
20:3	9:11
23:7	12:10
MRK 6:56	16:19
7:4	17:5,17
11:4	20:20
12:38	28:15
LUK 7:32	REV 11:8
10:10	21:21
11:43	22:2
13:26	

3153 ܫܘܪ (v) leap

aPEAL

Perfect

ACT 3:8[1]	ACT 16:29
14:10,14	19:16

cPAEL

Active Participle

ACT 3:8[2]

3154 ܫܘܪܐ (m) wall

ACT 9:25	REV 21:12,14,
2 CO 11:33	15,17,
HEB 11:30	18,19

3158 ܫܘܫܢܬܐ (f) lily

MAT 6:28	LUK 12:27

3160 ܫܘܬܦܐ (adj) partaker

MAT 23:30	EPH 3:6
LUK 5:10	5:7
ROM 11:17	PHL 1:7
1 CO 9:23	PLM 17
10:18,20	1 PT 5:1
2 CO 1:7,7	2 PT 1:4
8:23	REV 1:9

3161 ܫܘܬܦܘܬܐ (f) partnership, fellowship

ROM 9:10	GAL 2:9
15:26	PHL 1:5
1 CO 1:9	2:1
10:16,16	PLM 6
2 CO 6:14	HEB 13:16
13:14	1 JN 1:3,3,6,7

3159 ܫܘܬܦ (v) be partaker

kP

Active Participle

ACT 8:1

Passive Participle

2 JN 11

mETHP

Perfect

ACT 26:10	PHL 4:14,15
ROM 15:27	HEB 2:14[1],14[2]
2 CO 9:13	10:33

Imperfect

MAT 1:18 | 1 TM 5:22
1 CO 10:21 | HEB 12:10
2 CO 8:4 | 1 PT 1:14
GAL 6:6 | REV 18:4
PHL 3:10

Infinitive

1 TM 6:18

Participle

ACT 2:42 | EPH 5:11
ROM 1:32 | 1 PT 4:13
12:13

3162 ܫܚܕ (v-non occ) bribe

[a]PEAL

3130 ܫܘܚܕܐ (m) bribe

ACT 24:26

3164 ܫܚܦܐ (m-non occ) name of an illness

3163 (ܫܚܦ) (v-non occ) consume, corrupt

[c]PAEL

1907 ܡܫܚܦܢܐ (m) corruptor

ACT 24:5

3165 ܫܚܢ (v) warm

[a]PEAL

Imperfect

JHN 18:18[1] | ACT 28:2

Imperative

JAM 2:16

Active Participle

MRK 14:54,67 | JHN 18:18[2],25

3132 ܫܘܚܢܐ (m) sore

LUK 16:20,21 | REV 16:2,11

3166 ܫܚܩ (v) break, harass

[a]PEAL

Perfect

MRK 9:26 | LUK 9:39

Imperfect

ROM 16:20 | REV 2:27

Active Participle

ACT 15:19 | ACT 21:13

3167 ܫܘܚܩܐ (m) harassment

ROM 3:16 | 1 TM 6:5

3168 ܫܚܪ (v) fear; (pa) compel

[c]PAEL

Perfect

MAT 27:32 | MRK 15:21

Active Participle

MAT 5:41

3169 (ܫܚܪ) (v) (ethpe) to be left, remain

cf eshtaphal under ܐܚܪ

[b]ETHPEEL

Perfect

ROM 11:3,5

Participle

1 TH 4:15,17

3170 ܫܚܬ (v) rust, tarnish

[a]PEAL (non occ)

3133 ܫܘܚܬܐ (m) rust, tarnish

JAM 5:3

[e]APHEL

Perfect

JAM 5:3

3171 ܫܛܐ (v) become foolish; (aph) make foolish

[a]PEAL

Perfect

ROM 1:22

Active Participle

1 CO 4:10	2 CO 12:6
2 CO 5:13	

3172 ܫܛܝܘܬܐ (f) foolishness

MRK 7:22	EPH 5:4
1 CO 1:18,21,23, 25	2 TM 3:9
2:14	2 PT 2:16

[e]APHEL

Perfect

1 CO 1:20

3174 ܫܛܦ (v-non occ) cleave (cut), open

[a]PEAL

3173 ܫܛܝܦܬܐ (f) alabaster box

MAT 26:7	LUK 7:37
MRK 14:3	JHN 12:3

3175 ܫܛܪܐ (m) bill, handwriting

COL 2:14

3176 ܫܝܘܠ (f) sheol, hell

MAT 11:23	ROM 10:7
16:18	1 CO 15:55
LUK 10:15	1 PT 3:19
16:23	REV 1:18
ACT 2:24,24,27, 31	6:8
	20:13,14

3183 ܫܝܢܐ (m) peace, peace treaty

MAT 10:34,34	ROM 1:31
MRK 9:50	2 CO 13:11
LUK 11:21	EPH 2:14,15
12:51	1 TH 5:3
ACT 10:36	JAM 3:18
12:20	REV 1:4
24:2	

3182 ܫܝܢ (v) make peace, reconcile

[c]PAEL

Perfect

COL 1:20,21

[d]ETHPAAL

Imperfect

ACT 7:26

Imperative

1 TH 5:13

3186 ܫܝܫܐ (m) marble

REV 18:12

3187 ܫܝܫܠܬܐ (f) chain

MRK 5:3,4,4	EPH 6:20
LUK 8:29	2 TM 1:16
ACT 12:6,7	2 PT 2:4
21:33	REV 20:1
28:20	

3189 ܫܟܒ (v) sleep, lie down

[a]PEAL

Perfect

JHN 11:11	ACT 13:36
ACT 7:60	2 PT 3:4

Active Participle

1 CO 6:9	1 TM 1:10

Passive Participle

MAT 27:52

3190 ܐܫܟܚ (v) find, happen, be able

Peal may be Aphel

[a]PEAL

Perfect

MAT 2:8; 8:10; 10:39[1]; 13:44,46; 17:16,19; 18:28; 20:6; 21:19; 22:10,46; 26:40[1],40[2],43,60; 27:32

MRK 1:37; 2:2,4; 7:24,30; 9:18,28; 11:4,13[2]; 14:16,37[1],37[2],40,55

LUK 1:30; 2:16,45,46; 4:17; 5:19; 6:48; 7:9,10; 8:35,43; 9:40; 11:24,25; 13:6; 14:6,30; 15:5,6,9[1],9[2]; 19:32; 20:26; 22:13,45; 23:2,14,22; 24:2,3,23,24,33

JHN 1:41,43,45[1],45[2]; 2:14; 5:14; 6:25; 9:35; 11:17; 12:14; 21:6[2]

ACT 4:21; 5:10,22,23[1],23[2]; 7:21,46[1]; 9:33; 10:27; 11:26; 12:19; 13:6,22,28,39; 15:10; 17:6,23; 18:2; 19:1; 21:2,4; 23:29; 24:5,12,18,20; 25:18,26; 27:6,15,16,28[1],28[2]; 28:14,18

ROM 4:1; 7:8,11; 11:7[1],7[2]

1 CO 3:1

2 CO 2:13

PHL 3:11

2 TM 1:17

HEB 3:19; 9:12; 10:1; 12:17

JAM 3:8

2 JN 4

REV 2:2; 3:2

Imperfect

MAT 7:7; 8:28; 10:39[2]; 16:25; 17:27; 18:13; 24:46

MRK 1:45; 3:20; 4:32; 11:13[1]; 13:36

LUK 1:20; 6:7; 9:12; 11:9,54; 12:37,38,43; 13:24; 14:29; 15:4,8; 16:26; 18:8; 21:15

JHN 7:34[1],36[1]; 8:12; 10:9

ACT 7:46[2]; 9:2

ROM 8:39

1 CO 6:5; 10:13

2 CO 1:4

2 CO 3:7; 9:4; 12:20[1]

EPH 3:18; 6:11,13

2 TM 1:18; 2:10

TIT 1:9; 2:8

HEB 4:16

REV 9:6; 18:15,21

Active Participle

MAT 3:9; 5:14,36; 6:24[1],24[2],27; 7:8,14,18; 8:2; 9:15,28; 10:28[1],28[2]; 11:29; 12:29,34,43,44; 19:12,25,26[1],26[2]; 20:22[1],22[2]; 21:2; 22:9; 24:24; 26:9,39,42,53,61; 27:42

MRK 1:40; 2:7,19; 3:23,24,25,26,27; 4:33; 5:3,4; 6:5,19; 7:15,18; 8:4; 9:3,22,23[1],23[2],29,39; 10:26,27[1],27[2],38,39; 11:2; 13:22; 14:5,7,35,36; 15:31

LUK 1:22; 2:12; 3:8; 5:12,21,34; 6:39,42; 8:19; 11:7,10; 12:25,26; 13:7,11,33; 14:20,26,27,31,33; 16:2,3,13[1],13[2]; 17:1; 18:26,27[1],27[2]; 19:3,30,48; 20:36; 23:4

JHN 1:46; 3:2,3,4[1],4[2],5,9,27; 5:19,30,44; 6:44,52,60,65; 7:7,34[2],35,36[2]; 8:21,22,43; 9:4,16,33; 10:21,29,35; 11:37; 12:39; 13:33,36,37; 14:5,17; 15:4,5; 16:12; 18:38; 19:4,6; 21:6[1]

ACT 2:24; 4:14,16,20; 6:10; 8:31; 10:47; 15:1; 17:19,27; 18:10; 19:36,40; 20:16,32; 21:34; 23:9; 24:8,11; 25:7; 26:32; 27:12,31,39,43

ROM 1:30

ROM 4:21
7:18,21
8:7,8
11:23
12:18
15:14
16:24
1 CO 2:14
3:2[1],2[2],11
7:21
10:21[1],21[2]
12:3,21[1],
21[2]
14:31
15:50
2 CO 13:8
GAL 3:17,21
4:15
EPH 3:4
1 TH 2:6
3:9
1 TM 3:5
1 TM 5:25
6:7,16
2 TM 2:13
3:7,15
HEB 2:18
5:2,7
6:4,18
7:25
9:9
10:4,11
11:6
12:20
JAM 1:21
2:14
3:2,11,12[1],
12[2]
4:12
1 JN 3:9,15
4:20
JUD 24
REV 6:17
13:4

3191 ܫܟܝܚܐ (pp) found

2 PT 1:8,9

[b]ETHPEEL

Perfect

MAT 1:18
LUK 9:36
15:24,32
16:12
19:17
ACT 1:10
8:40
ROM 7:10
10:20
2 CO 7:14
GAL 2:17
PHL 2:7
HEB 11:5
1 PT 2:22
REV 5:4
12:8
14:5
16:20
18:24
20:11,15

Imperfect

ACT 5:39
27:29
1 CO 4:2
2 CO 5:3
11:12
2 CO 12:20[2]
PHL 3:9
HEB 4:1
12:15,16
2 PT 3:10,14

Participle

1 CO 15:15
PHL 1:19
1 TM 3:2
1 PT 4:18

3194 ܫܟܢ (v) lodge

[a]PEAL

Imperfect

MRK 4:32

1912 ܡܫܟܢܐ (m) tabernacle, habitation

ACT 7:43,44,45,
46
15:16
HEB 8:2,5
9:2,3,6,7,8,
HEB 9:11,21
11:9
13:10
REV 15:5

3193 (ܫܟܪ), ܫܟܝܪܐ (adj-non occ) shameful

3196 (ܫܟܪ) (v-non occ) make hideous

[c]PAEL

1913 ܡܫܟܪܐ (pp) shameful

1 CO 11:6

3197 ܫܟܪ, ܫܟܪܐ (m) strong drink

LUK 1:15

3220 (ܫܠ), ܫܠܬܐ (m) drop (of blood)

LUK 22:44

3198 ܫܠܐ (v) cease, be quiet; (pa) quiet, stop

[a]PEAL

Perfect

MAT 14:32
MRK 4:39[2]
6:51
LUK 7:45
23:56
ACT 11:18
17:13
20:1,31
1 PT 4:1

Imperative

MRK 4:39[1]

Active Participle

ACT 5:42
6:13
13:10
ROM 9:2
COL 1:9

Passive Participle

ACT 19:36
1 TH 4:11
1 TM 2:2

3202 ܫܠܘܐ (m) (w/ ܕܠܐ) w/o ceasing

ROM 1:9	1 TH 5:17

3209 ܫܠܝܐ (m) calm, silence; (w/ ܡܢ) suddenly

MAT 8:26	ACT 9:3
MRK 9:8	16:26
13:36	22:6
LUK 2:13	1 TH 5:3
8:24	2 TH 3:12
9:39	1 TM 2:11,12
21:34	2 PT 3:10
ACT 2:2	REV 4:8

[c]PAEL

Perfect

ACT 19:35

[d]ETHPAAL

Participle

EPH 1:16

3199 ܫܠܕܐ (f) corpse

MAT 14:12	ACT 9:40
MRK 6:29	REV 11:8,9,9

ܫܠܗܒ see (ܠܗܒ)

3205 ܫܠܚ (v) send

[a]PEAL

Perfect

MAT 10:40	ACT 13:15
27:19	23:10
LUK 4:18	1 CO 1:11
10:16	REV 1:1
JHN 5:36,37	

Passive Participle

MAT 23:37	LUK 13:34

3210 ܫܠܝܚܐ (pp) apostle, sent one

MAT 10:2	LUK 6:13
MRK 6:30	9:6,10

LUK 11:49	1 CO 9:1,2,5
17:5	12:28,29
22:14	15:7,9,9
24:10	2 CO 1:1
JHN 3:28	8:23
13:16	11:5,13,13
ACT 1:2,26	12:11,12
2:14,37,42, 43	GAL 1:1,17,19
4:33,35,36, 37	EPH 1:1
5:2,12,18, 21,29,34, 40	2:20
6:2,6	3:5
8:1,14,18	4:11
9:27	PHL 2:25
11:1	COL 1:1
14:4	1 TH 2:6
15:2,4,6, 22,23, 33	1 TM 1:1
16:4	2:7
ROM 1:1	2 TM 1:1,11
11:13	TIT 1:1
16:7	HEB 3:1
1 CO 1:1	1 PT 1:1
4:9	2 PT 1:1
	3:2
	JUD 17
	REV 2:2
	18:20
	21:14

3211 ܫܠܝܚܘܬܐ (f) apostleship

ACT 1:25	1 CO 9:2
ROM 1:5	GAL 2:8,8

[b]ETHPEEL

Perfect

LUK 1:19,26	ACT 15:30
ACT 13:4	

Imperfect

ACT 15:20	ROM 10:15

3206 ܫܠܚ (v) strip (oneself); (pa, aph) strip, plunder

[a]PEAL

Imperative

COL 3:9

Infinitive

2 CO 5:4

Passive Participle

ACT 19:16

3207 ܫܠܚܐ (m) putting off

COL 2:11,15

cPAEL

Perfect

LUK 10:30

eAPHEL

Perfect

MAT 27:28,31	MRK 15:20

3208 ܫܠܛ (v) (pe, ethpa) have power, have authority; (aph) give authority

aPEAL (non occ)

3138 ܫܘܠܛܢܐ (m) power, authority

MAT 8:9 9:6,8 10:1 21:23,23, 24,27 28:18 MRK 1:27 6:7 11:28,28, 29,33 13:34 LUK 4:6,36 7:8 9:1 10:19 20:2,2,8, 20 22:53 23:7 JHN 1:12 17:2 19:11 ACT 1:7 3:12 8:19 9:14 26:10,12, 18 ROM 8:38	ROM 13:1,1,1,2, 3 1 CO 8:9 9:6,12,12, 18 11:10 15:24 2 CO 10:8 13:10 EPH 1:21 2:2 3:10 COL 1:13,16 2:10 1 TM 6:16 HEB 2:14 1 PT 2:13 REV 2:26 6:8 9:3,10,19 11:6,6 13:2,4,5,7, 12 14:18 16:9 17:12,13 18:1 20:6 22:14

cPAEL (non occ)

1914 ܡܫܠܛܐ (adj) having authority

MAT 7:29 MRK 1:22	LUK 4:32

3212 ܫܠܝܛܐ (adj) lawful, permitted; (pl) magistrates, rulers

MAT 12:2,4,10, 12 14:4 19:3 20:15,25 22:17 27:6 MRK 2:10,24,26 3:4,15 6:18 10:2,42 12:14 LUK 5:24 6:2,4,9 12:5,11 14:3 19:17,19 20:22 22:25 JHN 5:10	JHN 10:18,18 18:31 19:10,10 ACT 4:26 5:4 8:27,27 ROM 7:1 9:21 1 CO 2:6,8 6:12,12 7:4,4,37 9:4,5 10:23,23 2 CO 12:4 EPH 6:12 COL 2:15 2 TH 3:9 TIT 3:1 HEB 13:10 1 PT 3:22

dETHPAAL

Imperfect

1 CO 6:12

Participle

ROM 6:9,14

eAPHEL

Perfect

JHN 5:27	HEB 2:7

Passive Participle

HEB 2:16[1],16[2]

3216 ܫܠܡ (v) be fulfilled, die; (w/ ܠ) obey, agree, follow; (ethpe) be delivered up; (pa) fulfill, complete; (aph) deliver, betray

[a]PEAL

Perfect

MRK 1:15
15:28,37,
39
LUK 2:43
LUK 23:46
JHN 7:8
19:24
JAM 2:23

Imperfect

MRK 14:49
LUK 21:22,24
22:16
JHN 13:18
JHN 18:9,32
GAL 5:25
PHL 3:16

Active Participle

MAT 13:14
LUK 5:36
23:51
ACT 15:15
21:24
22:20
ACT 28:25
ROM 4:12
7:21
GAL 4:25
6:16

3217 ܫܠܡܐ (adj) whole; (w/ ܝܩܕܐ) burnt offering

HEB 10:6,8

3218 ܫܠܡܐ (m) peace; (w/ ܫܐܠ) salute

MAT 5:9,47
10:12,13,
13
23:7
26:49
27:29
28:9
MRK 5:34
9:15
12:38
15:18,18
LUK 1:28,29,40,
41,44,79
2:14,29
7:50
8:48
10:4,5,6,6
11:43
14:32
19:38,42
20:46
24:36
JHN 14:27,27
16:33
19:3
JHN 20:19,21,
26
ACT 9:31
10:36
15:23,33
16:36
18:18,22
21:7,19
23:26
25:13
ROM 1:7
2:10
3:17
5:1
8:6
10:15
12:18
14:17,19
15:13,33
16:3,5,5,6,
7,8,9,
10,10,
11,11,
12,12,
13,14,
ROM 16:15,16,
16,20,
21,22,
23,23
1 CO 1:3
7:15
14:33
16:11,19,
19,20,
20,21
2 CO 1:2
13:12,13,
14
GAL 1:3
5:22
6:16
EPH 1:2
2:17
4:3
6:15,23
PHL 1:2
4:7,9,21,
21,22
COL 1:2
3:15
4:10,12,14,
15,18
1 TH 1:1
1 TH 5:3,23,26
2 TH 1:2
3:16,16,17
1 TM 1:2
2 TM 1:2
2:22
4:19,21
TIT 1:4
3:15,15
PLM 3,23
HEB 7:2
11:31
12:11,14
13:20,24,
24
JAM 1:1
2:16
3:17,18
1 PT 1:2
3:11
5:13,14,14
2 PT 1:2
3:14
2 JN 3,13
3 JN 15,15,15
JUD 2
REV 6:4

3219 ܫܠܡܘܬܐ (f) peace, agreement

2 CO 6:15
2 CO 13:11

---

[b]ETHPEEL

Perfect

MAT 4:12
11:27
MRK 1:14
LUK 10:22
ACT 28:17
ROM 4:25
ROM 6:17
2 CO 12:7
HEB 11:36
2 PT 2:21
JUD 3

Imperfect

MAT 17:22
LUK 9:44
18:32
LUK 24:7
JHN 18:36

Participle

MAT 20:18
26:2,24,45
MRK 9:31
10:33[1]
MRK 14:21,41
LUK 22:22
1 CO 11:23[2]
2 CO 4:11

---

[c]PAEL

Perfect

MAT 7:28
MAT 11:1

MAT 13:53
19:1
26:1
LUK 2:39
4:2,13
7:1
LUK 11:1
JHN 17:4
ACT 12:25
13:27,29
14:26
2 TM 4:7

Imperfect

MAT 5:33
10:23
17:11
LUK 9:61
JHN 4:34
JHN 5:36
ACT 20:24
2 CO 8:6,11[2]
EPH 4:10
PHL 1:6

Imperative

2 CO 8:11[1]
PHL 2:2
2 TM 4:5

Infinitive

LUK 14:28,29,30
1 TH 2:16

Active Participle

ACT 13:25
GAL 3:3
HEB 9:6
JAM 2:8

Passive Participle

JHN 19:30[1]
1 JN 2:5

1915 ܡܫܠܡܐ (adj) perfect, complete

2 TM 3:17
HEB 9:11
JAM 1:4,25
2 JN 8

3139 ܫܘܠܡܐ (m) end

MAT 13:39,40,49
24:3,6,14
28:20
LUK 1:45
2 CO 3:13
GAL 4:4
HEB 6:16
7:3
13:7
1 PT 3:8
REV 21:6
22:13

---

[d]ETHPAAL

Perfect

LUK 4:21
22:37
JHN 19:28
ACT 19:21
REV 10:7
20:7

Imperfect

LUK 9:31
24:44
EPH 4:16
2 TM 4:17

Infinitive

MRK 13:4

Participle

LUK 18:31
ROM 13:9
1 JN 4:17

---

[e]APHEL

Perfect

MAT 10:4
18:34
25:14
27:2,4,18,26
MRK 3:19
7:13
15:1,10,15
LUK 1:2
23:25
24:20
JHN 18:35
19:11,16,30[2]
ACT 2:23
3:13
ACT 6:14
7:42,52
12:4[1]
15:26
27:1
ROM 1:24,26,28
8:32
1 CO 11:2,23[1]
13:3
15:3
2 CO 8:5
EPH 4:19
5:2,25
1 TM 1:20
2 PT 2:4

Imperfect

MAT 5:25[1],25[2]
10:19,21
20:19
24:9,10
26:16,23
MRK 10:33[2]
13:9,11,12
14:10,11,18
LUK 12:58
LUK 20:20
21:12,16
22:4,6
JHN 6:71
12:4
13:2,21
ACT 12:4[2],6
17:5
21:11
1 CO 5:5

Active Participle

MAT 10:17
26:15,21,46
MRK 14:42,44
LUK 22:48
JHN 6:64
13:11
JHN 18:30
21:20
ACT 8:3
22:4,19
1 CO 15:24
1 PT 2:23

Passive Participle

LUK 4:6
1 PT 5:2

1916 ܡܫܠܡܢܐ (m) betrayer

MAT 26:25,47,48
27:3
MRK 14:44
LUK 6:16
22:21
JHN 18:2,5
2 TM 3:4

1917 ܡܫܠܡܢܘܬܐ (f) tradition

MAT 15:2,3,6
MRK 7:3,5,8,9,
MRK 7:13

3222 ܫܡ, ܫܡܐ (m) name

MAT 1:21,23,25
6:9
7:22,22,22
9:9
10:2,22,41,
41,42
12:21
18:5,20
19:29
21:9
23:39
24:5,9
27:32,57
28:19
MRK 3:16,17
5:9,9,22
6:14
9:37,38,39,
41
11:9
13:6,13
16:17
LUK 1:5,5,13,
26,27,27,
31,49,59,
61,63
2:21,25
5:27
6:22
7:11
8:30,41
9:48,49
10:17,20,
38,39
11:2
13:35
16:20
19:2,38
21:8,12,17
23:6,50
24:13,18,
47
JHN 1:6,12
3:1,18
5:43,43
9:11
10:3,25
11:49
12:13,28
14:13,14,
26
15:16,21
16:23,24,
26
17:6,11,12,
26
JHN 18:10
20:31
ACT 2:21,38
3:6,16
4:7,10,12,
17,18,30
5:1,1,28,
34,40,41
8:9,12,16
9:10,12,14,
15,16,21,
27,29,33,
36
10:1,22,43,
48
11:28
12:13
13:6,8
14:10
15:14,17,
26
16:1,14,18
17:34
18:2,7,15,
24
19:5,9,13,
13,14,
17,24,
33
20:9
21:10,13,
16
22:16
26:9,11
27:1,8
28:7
ROM 1:5
2:24
9:17
10:13
15:9,20
1 CO 1:2,10,13,
15
5:4
6:11
EPH 1:21
5:20
PHL 2:9,9,10
4:3
COL 3:17
2 TH 1:12
3:6
1 TM 6:1
2 TM 2:19
HEB 1:4
2:12
HEB 6:10
7:2
13:15
JAM 2:7
5:10,14
1 PT 4:14,16
1 JN 2:12
3:23
5:13
3 JN 7,15
REV 2:3,13,17
3:1,4,5,5,8,
12,12,12
6:8
REV 8:11
9:11,11
11:13,18
13:1,6,17,
17
14:1,1,11
15:2,4
16:9,11
17:3,8
19:5,12,13,
16
21:12,12,
14
22:4

3223 (ܫܡܗ) (v) name, call

[c]PAEL

Perfect

MRK 3:16
LUK 6:13,14
ACT 14:12

Imperfect

LUK 1:62

---

[d]ETHPAAL

Perfect

ACT 1:23
HEB 5:10

Imperfect

EPH 5:3[2]

Infinitive

EPH 5:3[1]

Participle

1 CO 5:1
EPH 1:21
EPH 3:15

3227 ܫܡܛ (v) draw (a sword)

[a]PEAL

Perfect

MAT 26:51
MRK 14:47
JHN 18:10

3228 ܫܡܝܐ (c) heaven

MAT 3:2,16,17
4:17
5:3,10,12,
MAT 5:16,18,19,
19,20,34,
45,48

MAT 6:1,9,10,14,20,26,26,32
7:11,21,21
8:11,20
10:7,32,33
11:11,12,23,25
12:50
13:11,24,31,32,33,44,45,47,52
14:19
15:13
16:1,2,3,3,17,19,19,19
18:1,3,4,10,10,14,18,18,19,23,35
19:12,14,21,23
20:1
21:25,25
22:2,30
23:9,14,22
24:29,29,30,30,31,35,36
25:1
26:64
28:2,18

MRK 1:10,11
4:30
6:41
7:34
8:11
10:21
11:25,30,31
12:25
13:25,25,27,31,32
14:62
16:19

LUK 2:13,15
3:21,22
4:25
6:23
9:16,54,58
10:15,18,20,21
11:2,2,13,16
12:33,56
13:19
15:7,18,21
16:17
17:24,24,29
18:13,16,22
19:38
20:4,5
21:11,26,33
22:43
24:51

JHN 1:32,51
3:12,13,13,13,27,31
6:31,32,32,33,38,41,42,50,51,58
12:28
17:1

ACT 1:10,11,11,11
2:2,5,19,34
3:21
4:12,24
7:42,49,55,56
9:3
10:11,11,12,16
11:5,6,9,10
14:15,17
17:24
19:35
22:6,23
26:13

ROM 1:18
10:6

1 CO 8:5
15:47,48,49,50

2 CO 5:1,2
12:2

GAL 1:8

EPH 1:3,10,20
2:6
3:10,15
4:10
6:9,12

PHL 2:10
3:20

COL 1:5,16,20,23
4:1

1 TH 1:10
4:16

2 TH 1:7

2 TM 4:18

HEB 1:10
3:1
4:14
6:4
7:26
8:1,5
9:24
10:34
11:12,16
12:22,23,25,26

JAM 5:12,18

1 PT 1:4,12
3:22

2 PT 1:18
3:5,7,10,12,13

REV 4:1,2
5:3,13
6:13,14
8:1,10,13
9:1
10:1,1,4,5,6,8
11:6,12,12,13,15,19
12:1,3,4,7,8,10,12
13:6,13
14:2,6,7,13,17
15:1,5
16:11,21
18:1,4,5,20
19:1,11,14,17
20:1,9,11
21:1,1,2,3,10

3229 ܫܡܝܢܐ (adj) heavenly

ACT 26:19
1 CO 15:40,40,48
HEB 9:23,23

3225 (ܫܡܢ), ܫܡܘܢܐ (m) small coin

MAT 5:26
MRK 12:42
LUK 12:59
21:2

3231 ܫܡܢ (v) be fat, ripe

aPEAL

Perfect

MRK 4:29

3141 ܫܘܡܢܐ (m) fatness

ROM 11:17

---

cPAEL (non occ)

3230 ܫܡܝܢܐ (adj) ripe, rich

REV 18:14

3232 ܫܡܥ (v) hear, obey; (aph) cause to hear

aPEAL

Perfect

MAT 2:3,9,22
4:12
5:21,27,33,38,43

MAT 8:10; 9:12; 11:2; 12:24; 13:15[1],17[3]; 14:1,13[1],13[2]; 15:12; 17:6; 18:15,16; 19:22,25; 20:24,30; 21:45; 22:7,22,33,34; 26:65; 27:47
MRK 2:1,17; 3:8,21; 4:15,16,18; 5:27,36; 6:2,14,16,29; 7:25; 10:41,47; 11:14,18; 12:28; 13:7; 14:11,58,64; 15:35; 16:8,11
LUK 1:41,58,66; 2:18,20; 4:23,28; 7:3,9,22[1],29; 8:13,18,50; 9:7; 10:24[3]; 11:28; 14:15; 15:25; 16:14; 18:22,23,26,36; 20:16; 22:71; 23:6
JHN 1:37,40; 3:32; 4:1,42,47; 5:37; 6:60[1]; 7:32,40; 8:9,26,40; 9:27[1],35,40; 10:8; 11:6,20,29,41; 12:9,12,18,29,34; 14:28; 15:15; 18:21; 19:8,13; 21:7
ACT 1:4; 2:37; 4:4,13,20,24; 5:5[1],5[2],11,24,33; 6:11,14; 7:12,34,54; 8:14,30; 9:4,13,38; 11:7,18; 14:9,14; 16:36,38; 17:8,32[1]; 18:26; 19:5,10,28; 21:12,20; 22:2,7,9,15,22,26; 23:16; 24:24; 26:14; 28:15
ROM 10:14[1],18; 15:21
1 CO 2:9
2 CO 7:7; 12:4
GAL 1:13
EPH 1:13,15; 3:2; 4:21
PHL 2:26; 4:9
COL 1:4,5,6,9,23
2 TM 1:13; 2:2
PLM 5
HEB 2:1,2,3; 3:16; 4:2[1],2[2]; 12:19
JAM 5:11
2 PT 1:18
1 JN 1:1,3,5; 2:7,18,24[1],24[2]; 3:11; 4:3
2 JN 6
REV 1:10; 3:3; 4:1; 5:11,13; 6:1,2,3,5,6,7; 7:4; 8:13; 9:13,16; 10:4,8; 11:12; 12:10; 14:2[1],2[2],13; 16:1,5,7; 18:4; 19:1,6; 21:3; 22:8[1],8[2]

Imperfect

MAT 11:15[1],15[2]; 12:19,42; 13:9[1],9[2],14,15[2],43[1],43[2]; 18:17[1],17[2]
MRK 4:9[1],9[2],12[2],23[1],23[2]; 6:11; 7:16[1],16[2],37
LUK 6:18; 8:8[1],8[2]; 11:31; 14:35[1],35[2]; 15:1; 16:29
JHN 5:25[1],28; 7:51; 10:16; 16:13
ACT 3:23; 4:19; 7:37; 10:22,33; 13:7; 15:7; 22:14; 24:4; 25:22[1]; 26:3; 28:22,26,27
ROM 10:14[2]; 11:8
1 CO 14:21
PHL 1:27
2 TM 4:17
HEB 3:7,15; 4:7
3 JN 4
REV 2:7,11,17,29; 3:6,13,22; 13:9

Imperative

MAT 13:18; 15:10; 17:5; 21:33
MRK 4:3; 7:14; 9:7; 12:29
LUK 9:35; 18:6
ACT 2:22; 3:22; 4:8; 7:2; 13:16; 15:13; 22:1
JAM 2:5

Infinitive

MAT 13:17[1]; 24:6
MRK 4:33
LUK 5:1,15; 10:24[1]; 19:48; 21:38
JHN 6:60[2]; 9:27[2]
ACT 13:44; 17:21
JAM 1:19
1 PT 3:12
REV 9:20

Active Participle

MAT 7:24,26; 10:14,27; 11:4,5; 13:13[1],13[2],16,17[2],19,20,22,23; 21:16; 27:13
MRK 4:12[1],20,24[1],24[2]; 6:20[1],20[2],55; 8:18; 12:37
LUK 2:46,47; 6:27,47,49; 7:22[2]; 8:10,12,14,15,21

LUK	9:9	ACT	17:11,32[2]
	10:16[1],16[2], 24[2],39		18:8
	16:2,31		19:26
	19:11		20:9
	20:45		23:35
	21:9		24:22
	23:8		25:22[2]
JHN	3:8		26:29
	5:24,25[2], 30		27:11
	6:45		28:28
	8:43,47[1], 47[2]	1 CO	11:18
	9:31[1],31[2]		14:2
	10:3,20,27	2 CO	12:6
	11:42	GAL	1:23
	12:47		4:21
	14:24		6:6[1]
	18:37	EPH	4:29
ACT	2:6,8,11, 33	PHL	1:30
	8:6	2 TH	3:11
	9:7,21	1 TM	4:16
	10:44,46	2 TM	2:14
	13:48	PLM	21
	15:12	1 JN	4:5,6[1],6[2]
	16:14,25		5:14,15
		REV	1:3
			3:20
			22:17,18

Passive Participle

ACT 15:24 | ACT 19:2

1919 ܡܫܡܥܐ (m) hearing, obedience

ROM 6:16; 10:17,17 | ROM 15:18; 16:25

1920 ܡܫܡܥܬܐ (f) hearing, obedience

LUK	7:1	2 CO	10:5
ACT	7:51	2 TM	4:3
	17:20	HEB	5:11
	28:27	1 PT	1:2
1 CO	12:17,17		

3226 ܫܡܘܥܐ (m) hearer

ROM 2:13 | JAM 1:22,23,25

3233 ܫܡܥܐ (m) hearing, report

MAT	13:14	ACT	28:26
	14:1	GAL	3:2,5
	24:6	JAM	1:25
JHN	12:38	2 PT	2:8

[b]ETHPEEL

Perfect

MAT	2:18	ROM	1:8
	4:24		6:17
	28:14		10:16
LUK	1:13	2 CO	9:5
JHN	9:32	PHL	2:8,12
	12:28	1 TH	1:8[1],8[2]
ACT	10:31	HEB	5:7
	11:1,22		11:8,31
	21:31		

Imperfect

LUK	12:3	2 TM	4:3
ROM	1:5	TIT	3:1
	6:12,16[1]	REV	18:22,23

Imperative

EPH	6:1,5	HEB	13:17
COL	3:20,22		

Infinitive

2 CO 11:19

Participle

MAT	6:7	ROM	6:16[2]
	8:27	1 CO	5:1
MRK	1:27		16:16
	4:41	2 CO	2:9
LUK	8:25		10:6
	17:6	2 TH	3:14
ACT	6:7	HEB	5:9
	21:22		

1930 ܡܫܬܡܥܢܐ (adj) obedient

JAM 3:17 | 1 PT 1:14

1931 ܡܫܬܡܥܢܘܬܐ (f) obedience

ROM	5:19,19	2 CO	10:6
	16:19	HEB	5:8
2 CO	7:15	1 PT	1:22

[e]APHEL

Active Participle

GAL 6:6[2]

3249 (ܫܡܫ)(v) minister, serve

[c]PAEL

Perfect

MAT 25:44 | ACT 13:36

ACT 20:34
ROM 1:25
15:8
1 TM 3:13
2 TM 1:18
HEB 6:10[1]
7:13

Imperfect

MAT 20:28[2]
MRK 10:45[2]
LUK 12:37
ACT 6:2
ROM 6:6
7:6
15:25,27
1 TM 3:10
6:2
HEB 9:14
12:28
1 PT 4:10
REV 22:3

Imperative

LUK 17:8
EPH 6:7

Infinitive

LUK 10:40

Active Participle

MAT 4:11
8:15
27:55
MRK 1:13,31
15:41
LUK 4:39
8:3
22:27[1],27[2]
JHN 12:2,26[1],
26[2]
ACT 13:5
19:22
24:23
ROM 1:9
14:18
16:18
2 TM 1:3
PLM 13
HEB 6:10[2]
8:5
10:11
13:10
JAM 1:26
1 PT 4:11
REV 7:15

1921 ܡܫܡܫܢܐ (adj) minister, servant

MAT 20:26
22:13
23:11
MRK 9:35
10:43
14:54
LUK 1:2
4:20
22:26
JHN 2:5,9
12:26
18:36
ACT 26:16
ROM 13:4,4,6
15:16
16:1
1 CO 3:5
1 CO 4:1
2 CO 3:6
6:4
11:15,15,
23
GAL 2:17
EPH 3:7
6:21
PHL 1:1
2:25
COL 1:7,23,25
4:7
1 TH 3:2
1 TM 3:8,12
4:6
HEB 1:7
8:2

3449 ܬܫܡܫܬܐ (f) ministry, office

LUK 1:5,8,23
10:40
LUK 12:42
ACT 1:17,20,25

ACT 6:1,4
11:29
12:25
13:25
20:24
21:19
ROM 9:4
11:13
12:1,7,7
15:31
1 CO 12:5
16:15
2 CO 3:7,8,9,9
4:1
5:18
2 CO 6:3
8:4
9:1,12,13
11:8
EPH 4:12
PHL 2:17,30
COL 4:17
1 TM 1:12
6:2
2 TM 4:5,11
HEB 1:14,14
8:6
9:1,6,21
JAM 1:26,27
REV 2:19

[d]ETHPAAL

Perfect

2 CO 3:3

Imperfect

MAT 20:28[1]
MRK 10:45[1]

Participle

ACT 17:25
2 CO 8:19,20

3250 ܫܡܫ, ܫܡܫܐ (c) sun

MAT 5:45
13:6,43
17:2
24:29
MRK 1:32
4:6
13:24
16:2
LUK 4:40
21:25
23:45
ACT 2:20
13:11
26:13
27:20
1 CO 15:41
EPH 4:26
JAM 1:11
2 PT 1:19
REV 1:16
6:12
7:2,16
8:12
9:2
10:1
12:1
16:8,12
19:17
21:23
22:5

3252 ܫܢܐ (f) tooth, ivory

MAT 5:38,38
8:12
13:42,50
22:13
24:51
25:30
MRK 9:18
LUK 9:39
13:28
ACT 7:54
REV 9:8
18:12

3253 ܫܢܐ (v) be mad; (pa) depart, remove

[a]PEAL

Perfect

JHN 10:20[2]	1 CO 14:23
ACT 26:24[1],25	

Imperfect

ACT 26:24[2]

Infinitive

JHN 10:20[1]

Active Participle

LUK 24:11

3256 ܫܢܝܐ (m) madness

REV 18:3

[c]PAEL

Perfect

MAT 4:12	JHN 5:24
11:1	6:15
12:9,15	ACT 7:4
13:53	14:6
14:13	PLM 15
15:29	HEB 11:5[2]
27:5	1 JN 3:14

Imperfect

MAT 8:34	ACT 7:43
17:20[2]	16:39
LUK 10:7	1 CO 13:2
JHN 13:1	HEB 11:5[3]

Imperative

MAT 17:20[1]	JHN 7:3

Active Participle

LUK 5:16

[d]ETHPAAL

Perfect

ACT 7:16	HEB 11:5[1]

Participle

EPH 4:14

3259 ܫܢܐ, ܫܢܬܐ (f) year

MAT 2:16	ACT 18:11
9:20	19:10
MRK 5:25,42	20:31
LUK 2:36,37,41, 42	24:10,17, 27
3:1,23	28:30
4:19,25	ROM 4:19
8:42,43	15:23
12:19	2 CO 12:2
13:7,8,11, 16	GAL 1:14,18
15:29	2:1
JHN 2:20	3:17
5:5	4:10
8:57	1 TM 5:9
9:21,23	HEB 1:12
11:49,51	3:9,17
18:13	9:7,25
ACT 4:22	10:1,3
7:6,23,30, 36,42	11:11
9:33	JAM 4:13
11:26	5:17
13:18,20, 21	2 PT 3:8,8
	REV 9:15
	20:2,4,6,7

3260 (ܫܢܐ), ܫܢܬܐ (f) sleep

MAT 1:24	ACT 20:9,9
LUK 9:32	ROM 13:11
JHN 11:13	

3255 ܫܘܢܕܐ (m) torture

HEB 11:35

3254 (ܫܢܕ) (v) (pa) torture

[d]ETHPAAL

Participle

ACT 26:11

3258 ܫܢܘܩܐ (m-non occ) lingering disease

3257 (ܫܢܩ) (v) torment

[c]PAEL

Perfect

REV 11:10

Imperfect

MAT 8:29	LUK 8:28
MRK 5:7	

Active Participle

2 PT 2:8

3143 ܫܘܢܩܐ (m) torment

2 PT 2:4	REV 18:7,15

3450 ܬܫܢܝܩܐ (m) torment

MAT 4:24	REV 9:5,5
25:46	14:11
LUK 16:28	18:10

---

dETHPAAL

Imperfect

REV 9:5	REV 20:10
14:10	

Participle

MAT 8:6	ACT 20:38
MRK 6:48	2 PT 2:9
LUK 16:23,24,	REV 12:2
25	

3261 ܫܥܐ (v) (ethpe) play; (ethpa) narrate

aPEAL (non occ)

3146 ܫܘܥܝܬܐ (f) fable, story

1 CO 15:33	2 TM 4:4
1 TM 1:4	TIT 1:14
4:7	

3262 ܫܥܝܐ (m) jesting

EPH 5:4

---

bETHPEEL

Infinitive

1 CO 10:7

---

cPAEL (non occ)

3453 ܬܫܥܝܬܐ (f) narrative, account

LUK 1:1	TIT 3:9
1 TM 1:4	

---

dETHPAAL

Perfect

MRK 5:16	ACT 9:27
LUK 7:18	10:8
8:34,36	11:13
9:10	12:17[1]
24:35	15:4,14
JHN 1:18	25:14
ACT 4:23	

Imperfect

ACT 8:33	HEB 11:32
28:20	

Imperative

MAT 11:4	LUK 8:39
MRK 5:19	ACT 12:17[2]

Participle

ACT 13:41	ACT 19:18
14:27	21:19
15:3,12	1 TH 1:9

3264 ܫܦܐ (v-non occ) become clear

aPEAL

3265 ܫܦܝܐ (pp) straight, honest, pure

LUK 3:5	2 PT 3:1
8:15	

3266 ܫܦܝܐ (m) thorn, hindrance

2 CO 12:7

3269 ܫܦܠ (v) be low; (pa) humble, weaken

cPAEL

Perfect

ACT 19:16

3148 (ܫܦܢ), ܫܘܦܢܝܢܐ

(m) turtledove

LUK 2:24

3270 ܫܦܥ (v) pour

[c]PAEL (non occ)

1922 ܡܫܦܥܐ (pp) abundant

LUK 6:38 | ROM 5:5

3149 ܫܘܦܥܐ (m) pouring, shedding

HEB 9:22

[d]ETHPAAL

Perfect

ACT 10:45 | 1 PT 2:10

[e]APHEL

Perfect

MAT 26:7
MRK 14:3 | ROM 9:23
EPH 1:6

3185 (ܫܦܪ), ܫܝܦܘܪܐ (m)

trumpet

MAT 24:31
REV 1:10
4:1 | REV 8:2,6,13
9:14
18:22

3271 ܫܦܪ (v) please

[a]PEAL

Perfect

MAT 14:6
MRK 6:22
ACT 6:5
12:3 | ROM 15:3
EPH 1:5
HEB 11:5

Imperfect

ROM 15:1,2
1 CO 7:32,33,34
GAL 1:10[1]
COL 1:10
1 TH 2:4 | 1 TH 4:1
2 TM 2:4
HEB 11:6
12:28

Infinitive

ROM 8:8

Active Participle

JHN 8:29
ROM 14:18
1 CO 10:33
2 CO 5:9
GAL 1:10[2] | EPH 6:6
PHL 4:18
COL 3:22
1 TH 2:15
HEB 13:16

3150 ܫܘܦܪܐ (m) beauty

JAM 1:11

3268 ܫܦܝܪܐ (adj) beautiful, good,

well

MAT 5:44
7:17
12:12,33,
33
15:7,26
17:4
23:27
26:10
MRK 7:6,9,27,
37
9:5,50
12:28,32
14:6,7
LUK 6:26,27
8:8
9:33
14:34
20:39
21:5
JHN 4:17
8:48
10:32,33
13:13
18:23
ACT 3:2,10
4:9
6:2
10:33
15:29
27:8
28:25
ROM 7:16
11:20
14:21
15:31
1 CO 5:6
7:1,26,35, | 1 CO 7:37,38,38
14:17
2 CO 8:21
11:4
GAL 4:17,18,18
5:7
EPH 4:29
5:10
6:3,8
PHL 4:14
COL 3:20
1 TH 5:21
2 TH 3:13
1 TM 1:8,18
2:3,9
3:4,5,7,12,
13
4:4
5:10,17
6:13,18
2 TM 4:7
TIT 2:3,5
3:13
HEB 6:9
11:23
13:9,18,21
JAM 2:2,3,3,8,
19
3:13
1 PT 2:12,12,15,
19,20
3:1,16
4:19
5:3
2 PT 1:19
1 JN 3:22
3 JN 6

3272 ܫܦܪܐ (m) daybreak, dawn

MRK 16:2,9
LUK 24:1 | ACT 5:21

[d]ETHPAAL

Imperfect

TIT 2:9

3275 ܫܩܝܐ, ܫܩܘܝܐ (m-non occ)

cup-bearer

3274 (ܫܩܐ) (v) water, give to drink

[e]APHEL

Perfect

MAT 25:35,37, 42	1 CO 3:2,6
	REV 14:8

Imperfect

MRK 9:41	MRK 15:36

Imperative

ROM 12:20

Active Participle

MAT 10:42	LUK 13:15
27:48	1 CO 3:7,8

3277 ܫܩܠ (v) take up, bear

[a]PEAL

Perfect

MAT 2:14	JHN 8:59
13:33	10:31
14:12,19, 20	11:41
15:36,37	12:3,13
16:8,9,10	13:4,12
19:1	18:10
20:10[2],11, 12	19:23,30, 38[2],40
22:25	20:2,13, 15[1]
24:39	21:13
26:26,27, 51	ACT 5:2
27:6,24,30, 48,59	7:43
MRK 2:12	20:14
6:29,43	21:11
8:8,19,20	27:17,38
9:36	28:3
10:16	ROM 4:11
14:47	2 CO 8:15[1],15[2]
LUK 5:25	COL 2:14
9:17	HEB 7:6
11:52	1 PT 2:24
JHN 5:9	REV 5:8
6:11	14:9,11
	18:21

Imperfect

MAT 4:6	LUK 9:3,23
5:40	10:4
16:24	17:31
27:32	JHN 5:10
MRK 6:8	17:15
8:34	19:38[1]
13:16	20:15[2]
15:21	ACT 9:15
16:18	ROM 15:1
LUK 4:11	GAL 6:5

Imperative

MAT 9:6	JHN 5:8,11,12
11:29	11:39
MRK 2:9,11	19:15[1],15[2]
LUK 5:24	ACT 21:36
23:18	1 CO 5:13
JHN 2:16	2 TM 1:8

Infinitive

MAT 3:11	MRK 13:15

Active Participle

MAT 5:32	LUK 16:3
10:38	19:21,22
20:10[1]	JHN 1:29
MRK 4:15	10:18
LUK 6:29,30	11:48
8:12	15:2
11:22	ACT 16:35,38
14:27	REV 17:12
15:5	

Passive Participle

MAT 11:28	JHN 19:17
22:16	20:1
MRK 2:3	ACT 3:2
6:55	ROM 11:18[1],18[2]
12:14	2 CO 4:10
14:13	GAL 6:17
LUK 7:14	HEB 13:13
22:10	REV 12:15

3278 ܫܩܠ ܐܝܕܐ (idiom) diligence

from 3279 ܫܩܠܐ (above) and 1200 ܐܝܕܐ

ACT 24:2	2 PT 1:5

3279 ܫܩܠܐ (m) taking away

see below 3278 ܫܩܠ ܐܝܕܐ

[b]ETHPEEL

Perfect

MRK	2:20	ACT	20:9
LUK	24:31		

Imperfect

MAT	9:15	LUK	8:18
	13:13	ACT	22:22
	21:43	1 CO	5:2
	25:29	EPH	4:31
MRK	4:25	2 TH	2:7

Imperative

MAT	21:21	MRK	11:23

Participle

ACT	8:33	2 CO	3:16

[c]PAEL (non occ)

1923 ܡܫܩܠܐ (pp) proud

2 PT 2:10

3276 (ܫܩܦ), ܫܩܝܦܐ (m) steep place

MAT	8:32	LUK	4:29
MRK	5:13		8:33

3152 (ܫܩܪ), ܫܘܩܪܐ (m) lie

MAT	15:19	LUK	13:27
	19:18		18:20
	26:60	2 TH	2:11
MRK	14:57		

3280 ܫܪ (v) be strong; (pa) establish; (aph) strengthen, believe

[a]PEAL

Perfect

ACT 3:7

3299 ܫܪܪܐ (m) truth

MRK	5:33	LUK	4:25
	12:14,32		9:27
LUK	1:4		16:11
LUK	21:3	GAL	4:16
JHN	1:9,17		5:7
	3:21	PHL	1:7
	4:23,24,37	2 TH	2:13
	5:33	1 TM	2:4,7
	8:32,32,44,44,45,46		3:15
			4:3
	14:6,17		5:3,16
	15:1,26	2 TM	2:15,18,25
	16:7,13,13		3:7,8
	17:3,17,17,19		4:4
		TIT	1:1,14
	18:37,37,38		2:10
		HEB	8:2
	19:35		10:26
ACT	10:34	1 PT	1:22
	26:25	2 PT	1:12
ROM	1:25		2:2
	2:8,20	1 JN	1:6,8
	3:7		2:4,21,21
	15:8		3:18,19
2 CO	2:17		4:6
	4:2		5:7
	8:8	2 JN	1,1,2,3,4
	11:10	3 JN	1,3,3,4,8,12
	12:6		
GAL	2:5,14		

[c]PAEL

Perfect

HEB 7:20

Imperfect

ROM	16:24	1 TH	3:2
1 CO	1:8	HEB	13:9
2 CO	2:8		

Imperative

LUK	22:32	JAM	5:8
HEB	12:12		

Active Participle

ACT	14:22	COL	2:7
1 CO	15:58	TIT	3:8
2 CO	1:21	1 PT	5:9

Passive Participle

2 PT 1:10

3291 ܫܪܝܪܐ (adj) true, steadfast

MAT	22:16	JHN	8:17,26,40
MRK	12:14		10:41
JHN	3:33		19:35
	4:23		21:24
	5:31,32	ACT	12:9
	7:18,28		15:29
	8:13,14,16,		21:34

ROM 3:4	HEB 6:16
4:16	9:24
2 CO 1:7	10:22
6:8	1 PT 5:12
EPH 3:17	2 PT 1:19
4:15	2:22
PHL 4:3,8	1 JN 2:8,8,27
COL 1:23	5:20,20,20
1 TH 1:5,9	3 JN 12
1 TM 1:2,5	REV 3:7,14
6:19	6:10
2 TM 1:5	15:3
2:19	16:7
TIT 1:2,4	19:2,9,11
HEB 3:14	21:5
5:12,14	22:6

3292 ܫܪܝܪܐܝܬ (adv) truly

MAT 14:33	ACT 2:36
26:73	4:27
27:54	16:15
MRK 11:32	22:30
14:70	23:15
15:39	ROM 8:9
LUK 12:44	1 CO 7:37
22:59	14:25
23:47	GAL 3:21
24:34	EPH 4:21
JHN 1:47	1 TH 2:13
4:18,42	5:2
6:14,55,55	1 TM 3:16
7:26,40	5:5
8:31,36	TIT 1:13
17:8	1 JN 2:5

3293 ܫܪܝܪܘܬܐ (f) steadfastness

COL 2:5

---

[d]ETHPAAL

Perfect

1 CO 1:6	HEB 2:2,3
GAL 3:15,17	9:18
2 TM 3:14	

Imperfect

ROM 1:11	EPH 3:16
14:5	1 PT 5:10

Participle

1 CO 8:10	HEB 9:17

---

[e]APHEL

Perfect

ACT 3:16	HEB 11:11
ROM 4:21	

Imperfect

ROM 15:8

Active Participle

MRK 16:20

3281 ܫܪܐ (v) loosen, lodge; (pa) begin; (ethpa) loose, dine

[a]PEAL

Perfect

MAT 14:23	ACT 5:40
15:39	7:48
18:27	15:33
27:26	17:9,10,14
MRK 6:46	18:3
8:10	19:41
15:15	21:7,8
LUK 1:53	22:30
8:38	23:22,32
14:4	27:40
19:7	2 CO 2:13
23:25	EPH 2:14
ACT 2:24	2 TM 1:5
4:21	

Imperfect

MAT 1:19	LUK 9:12[3]
5:17[1],17[2],	23:17,20
19	JHN 1:27
15:32	18:39[1],39[2]
16:19[1]	19:10,12[1]
18:18[1]	ACT 3:13
19:3,7,8	6:14
26:61	13:25
27:15,17,	28:16,18
21	ROM 14:20
MRK 1:7	HEB 2:15
10:4,11,12	12:1
15:9,11	1 JN 3:8
LUK 3:16	

Imperative

MAT 14:15	LUK 19:30
15:23	23:18
21:2	JHN 11:44
MRK 6:36	ACT 7:33
11:2	16:15,35
LUK 6:37[1]	REV 9:14
9:12[1]	

Infinitive

MRK 15:6	REV 20:3
REV 5:2,3,4,5,9	

Active Participle

MAT	5:31,32	LUK	19:33[2]
	14:22		22:68
MRK	6:45	JHN	5:18
	8:3		19:12[2]
	11:4,5	ACT	17:24
	14:58	1 JN	3:24[1],24[2]
	15:29	REV	1:5
LUK	13:15		9:11
	16:18		21:3
	19:31,33[1],		

Passive Participle

MAT	9:36	ACT	11:11
	16:19[2]		14:13
	18:18[2]		28:23
LUK	2:7,8	1 CO	7:27
	13:12	2 CO	5:6
ACT	9:43	1 JN	2:14
	10:6,17,18, 23,32	REV	12:12
			13:6

1924 ܡܫܪܝܐ (m) lodging

MRK	14:14	REV	13:6
LUK	22:11		21:3
PLM	22		

1926 ܡܫܪܝܬܐ (f) military encampment

ACT	21:34,37	HEB	11:34
	22:24		13:11,13
	23:10,16, 32	REV	20:9

3285 ܫܪܘܬܐ (f) meal

MAT	22:4	LUK	14:12
LUK	11:38		

3287 ܫܪܝܐ (m) release

1 CO	7:27	2 PT	1:20

---

[b]ETHPEEL

Perfect

ACT	4:23	ACT	28:25
	13:43	HEB	13:23
	16:26	REV	9:15
	27:41		

Imperfect

LUK	6:37[2]	ACT	26:32
	13:16	2 CO	5:1
JHN	7:23	2 TM	4:6
	10:35	2 PT	3:10,12
ACT	16:36	REV	20:7

Participle

ACT	5:38	HEB	7:16
	19:39	2 PT	3:11

---

[c]PAEL

Perfect

MAT	4:17	LUK	9:12[2],33
	11:7,20		11:29,53
	12:1		12:1
	14:30		14:18,30
	16:21,22		15:14,24
	18:24		19:37,45
	26:22,37, 74		20:9
			21:28
MRK	1:45		22:23
	4:1		23:2,5
	5:17,20		24:27
	6:2,7,34, 55	JHN	8:9,25
			13:5
	8:11,31,32	ACT	1:1
	10:28,32, 41,47		8:35
			9:3
	11:15		15:14
	12:1		18:26
	13:5		22:6
	14:19,33, 65,69, 71,72	2 CO	8:6,10
		GAL	3:3
		PHL	1:6
	15:8,18	2 TH	2:7
LUK	4:21	1 TM	5:15
	5:21	HEB	2:3
	7:15,24,38, 49	1 JN	2:8

Imperfect

MAT	24:49	LUK	13:25,26
LUK	3:8		23:30
	12:45[1],45[2]	1 PT	4:17[1]

Imperative

MAT	20:8	LUK	2:29

Active Participle

ACT	14:12	1 PT	4:17[2]
2 CO	3:1		

1925 ܡܫܪܝܐ (pp) sick, paralytic

MAT	4:24	LUK	5:18,20,24
	8:6	ACT	8:7
	9:2,2,6		9:33
MRK	2:3,4,5,9, 10	HEB	12:12

3155 ܫܘܪܝܐ (m) beginning

LUK	24:47	JHN	15:27

ACT 26:4
PHL 4:15
HEB 4:3
6:1
9:26
2 PT 3:4
2 JN 5,6
JUD 4
REV 22:13

dETHPAAL

Perfect

MRK 7:35 | JHN 21:15

Imperfect

LUK 11:37

Imperative

JHN 21:12

3282 (ܫܪܒ), ܫܪܒܬܐ

(f) generation, tribe

MAT 1:17,17,17,
17
11:16
12:39,41,
42,45
16:4
17:17
23:36
24:30,34
MRK 8:12,12,38
9:19
13:30
LUK 1:48,50,61
2:4
7:31
9:41
11:29,30,
31,32,
50,51
16:8
17:25
21:32
ACT 2:40
3:25
ACT 4:6
7:24
10:28
13:21,26,
36
26:7
ROM 11:1
1 TH 2:14
1 TM 1:4
TIT 3:9
HEB 7:3,6,13,
14
JAM 1:1
3:6
1 PT 2:9
REV 1:7
5:9
7:4,5,5,5,6,
6,6,7,7,7,
8,8,8,9
11:9
13:7
14:6
22:16

3283 ܫܪܓܐ (m) light, lamp

MAT 5:15
6:22
12:20
MRK 4:21
LUK 8:16
11:33,34,
36
12:35
LUK 15:8
JHN 5:35
ACT 16:29
2 PT 1:19
REV 18:23
21:23
22:5

3284 ܫܪܓܪܓ (v) imagine

mETHP

Participle

JUD 8

3288 (ܫܪܚ), ܫܪܝܚܐ (adj-non occ) lascivious

3286 (ܫܪܚ) (v) (pa) burn with passion

dETHPAAL

Perfect

ROM 1:27 | JUD 11

Participle

1 PT 4:4

3289 ܫܪܝܐ (m) joint

COL 2:19

3290 ܫܪܝܐ (m) breastplate

EPH 6:14
1 TH 5:8
REV 9:9,9,17

3294 ܫܪܝܬܐ (f) joint

EPH 4:16 | HEB 4:12

3295 ܫܪܟ (v-non occ) be left

aPEAL

3296 ܫܪܟܐ (m) residue, rest

MAT 22:6
27:49
MRK 4:19
16:13
LUK 8:10
12:26
18:11
24:9,10
ACT 2:37
15:17
27:44
28:9
ROM 1:13
ROM 11:7
1 CO 7:12
9:5
11:34
14:29
15:37
2 CO 2:17
13:2
GAL 2:13
EPH 2:3
4:17
PHL 1:13
4:3

COL	2:1	REV	2:24
1 TH	4:5,13		3:2
	5:6		9:20
1 TM	5:20		11:13
HEB	11:32		12:17
2 PT	3:16		19:21

3297 ܫܪܟܐ (m) remnant

ROM	9:27	ROM	11:5

3298 ܫܪܥ (v) (pe, ethpe) offend, stumble

[a]PEAL

Active Participle

JAM	2:10	JAM	3:2[2]

3156 ܫܘܪܥܬܐ (f) stumbling, offense

ROM	5:15,15	JUD	24

[b]ETHPEEL

Participle

JAM	3:2[1]	2 PT	1:10

302 ܫܬ, ܐܫܬܐ (f) foundation

see below 3302 ܫܬܐܣܬܐ

3302 ܫܬܐܣܬܐ (f) foundation

from 302 ܐܫܬܐ (above) and 238 ܐܣܬܐ

MAT	7:25	1 TM	3:15
LUK	6:48,48,49		6:19
	14:29	2 TM	2:19
ACT	16:26	HEB	1:10
ROM	15:20		6:1
1 CO	3:10,11,12		11:10
EPH	2:20	REV	21:14,19, 19
	3:17		
COL	1:23		

3300 ܫܬ (num) six

see below 3305 ܫܬܡܐܐ

see below 3308 ܫܬܬܥܣܪ

MAT	17:1	MAT	27:45
	20:5	MRK	9:2
MRK	15:33	ACT	18:11
LUK	1:26,36		27:37
	4:25	JAM	5:17
	13:14	REV	4:8
	23:44		6:12
JHN	2:6,20		9:13
	4:6		13:18
	12:1		16:12
	19:14		21:20
ACT	11:12		

3303 ܫܬܝܢ (num) sixty

MAT	13:8,23	REV	11:3
MRK	4:8,20		12:6
LUK	24:13		13:18
1 TM	5:9		

3304 ܫܬܝܬܝܐ (adj) sixth

REV	9:14

3305 ܫܬܡܐܐ (num) six hundred

from 3300 ܫܬ (above) and 1598 ܡܐܐ

REV	13:18

3308 ܫܬܬܥܣܪ (num) sixteen

from 3300 ܫܬ (above) and 2400 ܥܣܪ

ACT	12:4

3301 ܫܬܐ (v) drink

[a]PEAL

Perfect

MAT	26:42	ACT	9:9
MRK	14:23		10:41
LUK	13:26	1 CO	10:4[1]
JHN	4:12		12:13
ACT	2:13	HEB	6:7

Imperfect

MAT	6:25,31	JHN	4:14
	20:23		6:53
	26:29[1],29[2]		7:37
	27:34[1]		18:11
MRK	10:38[1],39[2]	ACT	23:12,21
	14:25[1],25[2]	ROM	14:21
	16:18	1 CO	10:21
LUK	1:15		11:22
	12:29		15:32
	17:8[1],8[2]	1 TM	5:23[1]
	22:30	REV	14:10
JHN	4:7,10,13,		

Imperative

MAT 26:27
LUK 12:19

Infinitive

MAT 20:22[1],22[2]
27:34[2]
MRK 15:23
LUK 12:45
JHN 4:9
1 CO 9:4
10:7
REV 16:6

Active Participle

MAT 11:18,19[1],
19[2]
24:38,49
MRK 2:16
10:38[2],39[1]
LUK 5:30,33,39
7:33,34[1],
34[2]
10:7
LUK 17:27,28
JHN 6:54,56
1 CO 10:4[2],31
11:20,25,
26,27,
28,29[1],
29[2]
1 TM 5:23[2]

1928 ܡܫܬܘܬܐ (f) wedding feast

MAT 22:2,3,4,8,
9,10,11,
12
LUK 12:36
LUK 14:8
JHN 2:1,2
REV 19:7,9

1929 ܡܫܬܝܐ (m) drink

JHN 6:55
ROM 14:17
1 CO 10:4
COL 2:16
HEB 9:10

303 (ܫܬܦ), ܐܫܬܘܦ (intrj)

(w/ ܕܝܢ) oh that

1 CO 4:8
2 CO 11:1
GAL 3:4
5:12

3306 ܫܬܩ (v) keep silent, be still; (pa) silence

[a]PEAL

Perfect

LUK 5:4
9:36
14:4
LUK 20:26
ACT 15:12,13

Imperfect

MAT 20:31
MRK 10:48
LUK 18:39
19:40
ACT 12:17
18:9
1 CO 14:28,30

Passive Participle

MAT 26:63
MRK 3:4
9:34
14:61
LUK 1:20
ACT 8:32
1 CO 14:34

3307 ܫܬܩܐ (m) silence

REV 8:1

[c]PAEL

Perfect

MAT 22:34

[d]ETHPAAL

Perfect

MAT 22:12

Imperfect

1 CO 13:8

ܬ

3313 ܬܐܛܪܘܢ (f) theater

ACT 19:29,30,31,32	1 CO 4:9

3314 ܬܐܡܐ (m) twin

JHN 11:16	JHN 21:2
20:24	ACT 28:11

3316 (ܬܐܢ), ܬܐܬܐ (f) fig, fig tree

MAT 7:16	LUK 6:44
21:19,19,20,21	13:6,7
24:32	19:4
MRK 11:13,13,20,21	21:29
13:28	JHN 1:48,50
	JAM 3:12,12
	REV 6:13

3315 ܬܐܪܬܐ (f) conscience

ACT 23:1	1 TM 3:9
24:16	4:2
ROM 2:15	2 TM 1:3
13:5	TIT 1:15
1 CO 8:7,7,10,12	HEB 9:9,14
10:25,27,28,29,29	10:2,22
1 TM 1:5,19	13:18
	1 PT 2:19
	3:16,21

3318 ܬܒܝܠ (f) habitable earth

ROM 10:18	REV 16:14
REV 3:10	

3320 ܬܒܢܐ (m) chaff, straw

MAT 3:12	LUK 3:17

3321 ܬܒܥ (v) avenge, require

[a]PEAL

Perfect

ACT 7:24	REV 19:2

Imperfect

LUK 3:13[1]	LUK 12:48[2]
6:30	18:5

Imperative

LUK 18:3

Infinitive

LUK 3:13[2]

Active Participle

MAT 25:27	ROM 12:19
LUK 12:20	1 PT 3:15
19:23	REV 6:10

3317 ܬܒܘܥܐ (m) avenger

ROM 13:4	1 TH 4:6

3322 ܬܒܥܬܐ (f) vengeance

LUK 18:7,8	2 TH 1:8
21:22	HEB 10:30
2 CO 7:11	1 PT 2:14
10:6	

[b]ETHPEEL

Imperfect

LUK 11:50	LUK 12:48[1]

Participle

LUK 11:51

3323 ܬܒܪ (v) break

[a]PEAL

Imperfect

MAT 12:20

3319 ܬܒܝܪܐ (pp) broken

LUK 4:18,18

[b]ETHPEEL

Imperfect

JHN 19:36

[c]PAEL

Perfect

JHN 19:32,33

Imperfect

JHN 19:31

Active Participle

MRK 5:4

3324 ܬܓܐ (m) crown

REV 12:3 13:1	REV 19:12

3326 ܬܓܪܐ (m) merchant

MAT 13:45 REV 18:3,11,15,	REV 18:23

3309 ܬܐܓܘܪܬܐ (f) merchandise, barter

MAT 22:5 LUK 12:58 JHN 2:16 ACT 16:16,19	ACT 19:25 ROM 6:23 1 TM 6:5,6

3325 (ܬܓܪ) (v) make gain, trade

[d]ETHPAAL

Perfect

MAT 25:16,17, 20,22	LUK 19:15

Imperfect

2 PT 2:3

Imperative

LUK 19:13

Participle

JAM 4:13

3327 ܬܕܐ (m) breast

LUK 11:27 23:29	REV 1:13

3331 (ܬܗܐ) (v) delay

[c]PAEL

Perfect

ACT 24:22

3343 ܬܘܗܝܐ (m) delay

ACT 25:17

3332 ܬܗܘܡܐ (c) abyss

LUK 8:31 ROM 10:7	REV 9:1,11 20:1,3

3334 ܬܗܪ (v) marvel, be amazed

[a]PEAL

Perfect

MAT 21:20 ACT 4:13	ACT 10:45

Imperfect

MAT 13:54

3333 ܬܗܝܪܐ (pp) amazed

MAT 7:28 19:25 MRK 6:51	ACT 2:7 3:11

3335 ܬܗܪܐ (m) amazement

MRK 16:8

3336 ܬܘ (f) the letter tau

REV 1:8
21:6
REV 22:13

3337 ܬܘܐ (v) (pe, ethpe) repent

[a]PEAL

Active Participle

2 CO 7:8[1],8[2]

3360 ܬܘܬܐ (f) repentance

2 CO 7:10

[b]ETHPEEL

Perfect

MAT 21:29,32
MAT 27:3

Imperfect

REV 2:22

Participle

JUD 23

3338 (ܬܘܒ) (v) return, repent; (aph) answer, vomit

[a]PEAL

Perfect

MAT 11:20,21
12:41
LUK 10:13
11:32
2 CO 12:21
REV 9:20,21
16:9,11

Imperfect

MRK 6:12
LUK 13:3,5
ACT 3:26
17:30
ACT 26:20
28:27
REV 2:5

Imperative

MAT 3:2
4:17
MRK 1:15
ACT 2:38
ACT 3:19
8:22
REV 2:16
3:3,19

Infinitive

REV 2:21

Active Participle

LUK 15:7,10
16:30
LUK 17:3,4
ROM 2:5

3339 ܬܘܒ (adv) again, furthermore

MAT 4:7,8; 5:33; 13:44,45,47; 18:19; 19:24; 20:5; 21:19,36; 22:1,4,46; 26:42, 43,44,72; 27:50 MRK 2:1,13; 3:1,20; 4:1; 5:21; 7:31; 8:25; 9:25; 10:1,10,24; 11:27; 12:4,5,34; 14:25,39,40,61,69,70, 70; 15:4,13 LUK 2:45; 13:20; 14:22; 15:11; 17:28; 20:31,36,40; 22:71; 23:20 JHN 1:21; 3:4; 4:3,13,15,46,54; 5:14; 7:33; 8:2,8,11,12,21,28; 9:15,17,26,27; 10:7,17,18,19,31,39; 11:7,8; 12:28,39; 14:3; 16:10,12,16,17,19,22,28; 18:7,27, 38; 19:4,9,37; 20:10,21,26; 21:1,16 ACT 4:17; 5:4; 8:39; 10:15; 11:9; 12:8; 13:34,35; 17:6; 18:21; 20:15,25,38; 25:24; 27:28 ROM 1:27; 6:2,6,9; 8:15; 11:9,23; 15:10,11,12 1 CO 1:16; 3:20; 6:6; 7:5; 12:31 2 CO 1:10,16; 2:1; 3:1; 5:12; 11:16; 12:19; 13:2,2 GAL 1:9,17; 2:1,18; 4:9; 5:1,3 PHL 1:9,26; 2:28; 4:4 HEB 1:5,6,10; 2:13,13; 4:5,7; 5:12; 6:1,6; 7:2,15; 8:12; 10:30; 11:15,32; 12:26 JAM 5:18 1 PT 1:14 2 PT 2:20 1 JN 2:8 REV 3:12; 9:12; 10:6,8,11; 13:17; 18:11,14,21,22,23,23; 20:3; 21:1,4; 22:11,11,11,11

3374 ܬܝܒܘܬܐ (f) repentance

MAT 3:8,11
MRK 1:4
LUK 3:3,8
5:32
15:7
24:47
ACT 5:31
11:18
13:24
19:4
ACT 20:21
26:20
ROM 2:4
2 CO 7:9
2 TM 2:25
HEB 6:1,6
12:17
1 PT 3:20
2 PT 3:9
REV 2:21

[e]APHEL

Perfect

MRK 12:28
LUK 23:9

Infinitive

COL 4:6
REV 3:16

3375 ܬܝܘܒܐ (m) vomit

2 PT 2:22

3342 ܬܘܗ (v) be troubled, amazed

[a]PEAL

Perfect

MRK 9:15

Imperfect

2 TH 2:2

3344 ܬܘܗܬܐ (f) amazement

LUK 21:25

3351 ܬܘܢܐ (m) small room

MAT 6:6	LUK 12:3,24
24:26	

3354 ܬܘܪ (v-non occ) be amazed

[c]PAEL

3346 ܬܘܝܪܐ (adj) amazed

ACT 2:12	ACT 5:24

3355 ܬܘܪ, ܬܘܪܐ (m) ox, steer

MAT 22:4	JHN 2:14,15
LUK 13:15	ACT 14:13
14:5,19	1 CO 9:9,9
15:23,27, 30	1 TM 5:18
	HEB 10:4

3359 ܬܘܬܐ (m) mulberry (sycamine) tree

LUK 17:6

3365 ܬܚܘܡܐ (m) boundary, coast

MAT 2:16	MRK 5:17
4:13	7:24,31,31
8:34	10:1
15:21,22, 39	ACT 13:50
	17:26
19:1	2 CO 10:13

3366 ܬܚܝܬ (adv, prep) under

MAT 2:16; 4:6; 5:15,35; 8:8,9,9; 22:44; 23:37; 27:51 MRK 4:21,21; 7:28; 12:36; 14:66; 15:38 LUK 4:9; 7:6,8,8; 8:16; 11:33; 13:34; 17:24; 20:43; 23:7 JHN 1:48,50; 8:6,23 ACT 2:5; 4:12; 7:49; 9:3; 22:6 ROM 3:9,13; 6:14,14,15,15; 16:20 1 CO 9:20,20,20; 10:1; 15:25,27 GAL 3:10,22,25; 4:2,3,4,5,21; 5:18 EPH 1:22; 6:12 PHL 2:10 COL 1:23 1 TM 6:1 HEB 1:13; 2:8; 10:13 JAM 5:12 1 PT 5:6 JUD 6,7 REV 5:3,13; 6:9; 12:1

3372 ܬܚܬܝܐ (adj) low

MRK 6:11	2 PT 2:4
EPH 4:9	

3371 ܬܚܬܝ (v) bring low

[m]ETHP

Imperfect

MAT 11:23	LUK 10:15

3377 ܬܟܒ (v) urge, insist

[a]PEAL

Active Participle

LUK 23:23

3378 ܬܟܒܐܝܬ (adv) earnestly

LUK 22:44

3381 ܬܟܠ (v) (pe, ethpe) trust, be confident

[a]PEAL (non occ)

3379 ܬܟܝܠܐ (pp) confident

MAT 27:43	GAL 5:10
MRK 10:24	PHL 1:6
LUK 11:22	2:24
18:9	3:3
ACT 16:15	2 TH 3:4
2 CO 1:13	PLM 21
2:3	HEB 2:13
5:8	13:18
7:16	1 JN 5:15
10:1,7	

3347 ܬܘܟܠܢܐ (m) trust, confidence

2 CO 1:9,15	EPH 3:12
3:4	PHL 3:4,4
8:22	1 TM 6:17
10:2	HEB 10:22

3380 ܬܘܟܠܢܐܝܬ (adv) confidently

PHL 1:25	HEB 13:6

[b]ETHPEEL

Perfect

ROM 2:19	PHL 1:14

Imperfect

1 TM 6:17

3382 (ܬܟܠ), ܬܟܠܬܐ (f) fringe, border

MAT 23:5

3383 ܬܟܣ (v) hinder

[c]PAEL

Imperfect

1 CO 9:12

Active Participle

LUK 11:53

[d]ETHPAAL

Perfect

ROM 15:22

Participle

JAM 3:8

3394 (ܬܠ), ܬܠܠܐ (m-non occ) dampness

3387 (ܬܠ) (v-non occ) soil

[c]PAEL

3390 ܬܠܝܠܘܬܐ (f) moisture

LUK 8:6

3388 ܬܠܐ (v) hang up

[a]PEAL

Perfect

ACT 5:30	ACT 27:40
10:39	

Active Participle

ACT 28:4

Passive Participle

MAT 18:6	LUK 17:2
22:40	19:48

[b]ETHPEEL

Participle

GAL 3:13

3389 ܬܠܓܐ (m) snow

MAT 28:3	REV 1:14
MRK 9:3	

3349 (ܬܠܥ), ܬܘܠܥܐ (f) worm

MRK 9:44,46,48	ACT 12:23

3393 ܬܠܬ (num) three

see below 3396 ܬܠܬܝܐ

MAT 12:40,40, 40,40	MAT 20:3,19
13:33	22:26
15:32	26:34,44, 61,75
16:21	27:40,63, 64
17:4,23	MRK 8:2,31
18:16,20	

MRK 9:5,31
10:34
12:21
14:30,41,
58,72
15:25,29
LUK 1:56
2:46
4:25
9:22,33
10:36
11:5
12:38,52,
52
13:7,21,32
18:33
20:12,31
22:34,61
23:22
24:7,21,46
JHN 2:1,6,19,
20
13:38
21:11,14,
17,17
ACT 2:15,41
5:7
7:20
9:9
10:16,19,
40
11:10,11

ACT 17:2
19:8
20:3,9,31
23:23
25:1
27:19
28:7,11,12,
15,17
1 CO 10:8
13:13
14:27,29
15:4
2 CO 11:25,25
12:2,8,14
13:1,1
GAL 1:18
1 TM 5:19
HEB 10:28
11:23
JAM 5:17
1 JN 5:8,8
REV 4:7
6:5,5,6
8:10,13
9:18
11:9,11,14
14:9
16:4,13,19
21:13,13,
13,13,
19

3350 ܬܠܝܬܝܐ (adj) third

REV 8:7,7,8,9,9,
10,11,12,
12,12,12,

REV 8:12
9:15,18
12:4

3395 ܬܠܬܝܢ (num) thirty

MAT 13:8,23
26:15
27:3,9
MRK 4:8,20

LUK 3:23
JHN 5:5
6:19
GAL 3:17

3396 ܬܠܬܡܐܐ (num) three hundred

from 3393 ܬܠܬ (above) and 1598 ܡܐܐ

MRK 14:5 | JHN 12:5

3400 (ܬܡܡ), ܬܡܝܡܐ (adj) harmless, simple

MAT 10:16
ROM 16:19

PHL 2:15

3397 ܬܡܗ (v) (pe, ethpa) be astonished; (aph) astonish

[a]PEAL

Perfect

MRK 12:17
15:44
16:5
LUK 2:48

LUK 8:56
ACT 10:45
12:16

Imperfect

ACT 13:41

Active Participle

ACT 8:13

3399 ܬܡܝܗܐ (pp) astonished

MRK 1:22
5:20
10:32
11:18
LUK 1:21
2:33,47

LUK 4:32
13:17
24:4
ACT 9:7,21
GAL 4:20
REV 15:1,3

3398 ܬܡܗܐ (m) amazement

LUK 4:36
5:9,26

ACT 3:10
10:10

[d]ETHPAAL

Participle

MAT 22:33 | LUK 24:41

[e]APHEL

Perfect

LUK 24:22 | ACT 8:11

309 (ܬܡܠ), ܐܬܡܠ (adv) yesterday

JHN 4:52
ACT 7:28

HEB 13:8

3402 ܬܡܢ (adv) there

see also 792 ܗܪܬܡܢ

MAT 2:13,15,22; 4:21; 5:23,24,26; 6:21; 8:12; 9:9,27; 10:11; 11:1; 12:9,10,15; 13:42,

50,53,58; 14:13,23; 15:17,21,29,29; 18:20; 19:2,15; 21:17; 22:11,13; 24:28,51; 25:30; 26:71; 27:36,47,55,61; 28:7,10 MRK 1:13, 35,38; 2:6; 3:1; 5:11; 6:1,5,10,10,11,33; 7:24; 9:30; 10:1,1; 14:15; 16:7 LUK 2:5,6,8; 6:6, 12; 8:32; 9:4,4; 10:6; 11:26; 12:18,34,59; 13:11,28; 14:7,8; 15:13; 16:26; 17:37; 22:12; 23:33; 24:23 JHN 2:1,6,12; 3:1,22,23; 4:6, 43; 5:2,5; 6:3,22,24; 10:40; 11:8,15,15,54,54; 12:2,9,26; 18:2,3; 19:42; 20:24 ACT 1:15; 5:23; 7:4,15,30; 8:6,9,40; 9:6,23,30; 10:18, 27; 11:15,23,27,30; 12:12; 13:4; 14:3,7,19, 20,26,26,28; 15:33; 16:1,7,11,12,13,13,40; 17:5,6,6,10,11,13,21; 18:2,7,18,23; 19:1,21, 24,33; 20:3,6,8,13,15,16; 21:1,2,3,3,4,7,10; 22:5,10,12; 23:4; 25:6,9,20; 26:31; 27:4,6,9, 12; 28:10,12,13,14,15,30 ROM 5:20; 9:26; 15:24 PHL 3:20 TIT 3:12 JAM 3:16; 4:13 REV 2:14; 12:6,14; 21:25,27; 22:3,5

3403 ܬܡܢܝܐ (num) eight

see below 3405 ܬܡܢܬܥܣܪ

LUK 1:59, 2:21, 9:28 | JHN 5:5, 20:26 | ACT 9:33 | ACT 25:6 | PHL 3:5 | 1 PT 3:20 | 2 PT 2:5 | REV 17:11, 21:20

3401 ܬܡܝܢܝܐ (adj) eighth

ACT 7:8

3404 ܬܡܢܝܢ (num) eighty

LUK 2:37 | LUK 16:7

3405 ܬܡܢܬܥܣܪ (num) eighteen

from 3403 ܬܡܢܐ (above) and 2400 ܥܣܪ

LUK 13:4,11,16

3410 (ܬܢ), ܬܢܝܢܐ (m) dragon

REV 12:3,4,7,7,9,13,16,17; 13:2,4,11 | REV 16:13, 17:11, 20:2

3413 (ܬܢ), ܬܡܢ (adv) here

MAT 12:41; 14:17; 16:28; 17:4,4; 28:6 MRK 6:3; 9:1; 16:6 LUK 24:6,41 JHN 6:9; 11:21,32

3414 (ܬܢ), ܬܢܢܐ (m) smoke

ACT 2:19 | REV 9:2,2,2,3,17,18; 14:11 | REV 15:8, 18:9,18, 19:3

3407 ܬܢܐ (v-non occ) repeat

aPEAL

3411 ܬܢܝܢܐ (adj) second

REV 2:11, 20:6,14 | REV 21:8

3412 ܬܢܝܢܘܬܐ (f) (as adv) twice

JUD 12

3408 ܬܢܘܪܐ (m) oven

MAT 6:30 | LUK 12:28

3418 ܬܥܠ, ܬܥܠܐ (m) fox

MAT 8:20 | LUK 9:58 | LUK 13:32

3419 ܬܦ̈ܠܐ (m) phylacteries

MAT 23:5

3423 ܬܩܠ (v) stumble, hinder

aPEAL

Imperfect

MAT 4:6 | LUK 4:11

3352 ܬܘܩܠܬܐ (f) offense, stumbling block

MAT 16:23 | ROM 9:32,33, 11:9,11,12, 14:13,20 | 1 CO 1:23 | 1 CO 8:9, 10:32 | 2 CO 6:3 | PHL 1:10 | 1 PT 2:8

ᵇETHPEEL

Perfect

ROM 9:32 | ROM 11:11

Participle

JHN 11:9,10
ROM 14:21
GAL 2:11*
1 PT 2:8*
3:7*

3424 ܬܩܢ (v) be restored; (pa, aph) restore, prepare

ᵃPEAL

Perfect

MAT 12:13
MRK 3:5
MRK 8:25
LUK 6:10

3425 ܬܩܝܢܐ (adj) honest, good

ACT 24:2 | 2 CO 5:13

3426 ܬܩܝܢܘܬܐ (f) honesty

ACT 26:25

ᶜPAEL

Perfect

MAT 21:16 | MAT 25:7

Imperative

MRK 14:15

Active Participle

MAT 4:21 | MRK 1:19

ᵈETHPAAL

Perfect

HEB 11:3

ᵉAPHEL

Perfect

LUK 9:51

Imperfect

MAT 11:10
MRK 1:2
9:12
LUK 7:27
9:52
TIT 1:5

Imperative

GAL 6:1

Active Participle

ACT 10:10 | ACT 27:17

Passive Participle

2 CO 10:16 | HEB 9:5

3427 ܬܩܦ (v) prevail

ᵃPEAL

Perfect

ACT 7:17

Active Participle

ACT 19:20

3353 ܬܘܩܦܐ (m) power

EPH 1:19 | EPH 6:10

ᶜPAEL (non occ)

3421 ܬܩܝܦܐ (adj) strong, mighty

LUK 1:52
ACT 20:29
1 PT 5:6

3422 ܬܩܝܦܐܝܬ (adv) mightily

ACT 18:28

3428 ܬܪܐܐ (m) instructor

1 CO 4:15 | GAL 3:24,25

3430 ܬܪܓܡ (v) interpret

ᵏP (non occ)

3356 ܬܘܪܓܡܐ (m) interpretation

ACT 1:19

ᵐETHP

Participle

MAT 1:23
ACT 4:36
ACT 13:8

3433 ܬܪܝܢ (num) two

see below 3446 ܬܪܥܣܪ

MAT 2:16, 4:18,21, 5:41, 6:24, 8:28, 9:17,27, 10:10,29, 13:30, 14:17,19, 15:14, 17:24,24,24, 18:8,8,9,16,16,19,20, 19:5,6, 20:21,24,30, 21:1,28,31, 22:26,39,40, 24:40,41, 25:15,17,17,22,22,22, 26:2,37,42,60, 27:21,38,51
MRK 5:13, 6:7,7,9,38,41,41, 9:43,45,47, 10:8,8, 11:1, 12:21,31,42, 14:1,13,30,72,72, 15:27,38, 16:12
LUK 1:6,7, 2:24, 3:11, 5:2,7,38, 6:39, 7:19,41,42, 9:3,13,16,30,32, 10:1,1,35, 12:6,38,52,52, 15:11, 16:13, 17:34,35,36, 18:10,12, 19:18,29, 20:30, 21:2, 22:38, 23:32, 24:4,13
JHN 1:35,37, 2:6,6, 3:4, 4:40,43,54, 6:9, 8:17, 9:24, 11:3,6, 19:18, 20:4,12, 21:2,16
ACT 1:10,23,24, 7:13,29, 8:38, 9:38, 10:7,15, 12:6,6,10, 13:33, 19:10,22,34, 21:33, 23:23, 24:27, 27:41, 28:13,30
1 CO 6:13,16, 7:5, 14:27,29, 15:47
2 CO 13:1,2
GAL 4:22,24, 5:17
EPH 2:14,15,16,18, 5:31
PHL 1:23, 4:16
1 TH 2:18
1 TM 3:8, 5:19
TIT 3:10
HEB 4:12, 6:18, 8:7, 9:3,28, 10:9,28
2 PT 3:1
JUD 5
REV 2:12, 4:7, 6:3,3, 8:8, 9:12,16, 11:2,3,4,4,10,14, 12:14, 13:5,11, 14:8, 16:3, 19:3,20, 21:19

3446 ܬܪܥܣܪ (num) twelve

from 3433 ܬܪܝܢ (above) and 2400 ܥܣܪ

MAT 9:20, 10:1,2,5, 11:1, 14:20, 19:28,28, 20:17, 26:14,20,47,53
MRK 3:14, 4:10, 5:25,42, 6:7,43, 8:19, 9:35, 10:32, 11:11, 14:10,17,20,43
LUK 2:42, 6:13, 8:1,42,43, 9:1,17, 18:31, 22:3,14,30,47
JHN 6:13,67,70,71, 11:9, 20:24
ACT 6:2, 7:8, 19:7, 24:11, 26:7
1 CO 15:5
JAM 1:1
REV 7:5,5,5,6,6,6,7,7,7,8,8,8, 12:1, 21:12,12,12,14,14,16,20,21,21, 22:2

3437 ܬܪܡܠܐ (f) bag, wallet

MAT 10:10
MRK 6:8
LUK 9:3, 10:4, 22:35,36

3439 ܬܪܢܓܠܐ (m) cock

MAT 26:34,74,75
MRK 13:35, 14:30,68,72,72
LUK 22:34,60,61
JHN 13:38, 18:27

3438 ܬܪܢܓܘܠܬܐ (f) hen

MAT 23:37
LUK 13:34

3431 (ܬܪܢܣ), ܬܪܘܢܘܣ(m)
throne

MAT 19:28	MAT 25:31

3440 ܬܪܣ(v) nourish, support

ᵏP

Perfect

MAT 25:37	JAM 5:5
ACT 13:18	

Imperfect

1 TM 5:16	REV 12:6
JAM 4:3	

Active Participle

MAT 6:26	EPH 5:29
LUK 12:24	

3357 ܬܘܪܣܝܐ (m) nourishment

ACT 14:17	ACT 27:36

ᵐETHP

Infinitive

REV 12:14

3441 ܬܪܥ(v) flow, open

ᵃPEAL

Passive Participle

LUK 8:43

3442 ܬܪܥܐ (m) door, gate

MAT 6:6	LUK 13:25
7:13,13,14	16:20
16:18	23:45
24:33	JHN 10:1,2,3,3,
25:10	7,9
27:51,60	11:38
28:2	18:16,16,
MRK 1:33	17
2:2	20:19,26
11:4	ACT 3:2,10
13:29	5:9,19,23
15:38,46	9:24
16:3	10:17
LUK 7:12	11:11
11:7	12:6,10,13,
13:24,25,	14,14,

ACT 12:16	HEB 10:20
14:13,27	JAM 5:9
16:13,26,	REV 3:8,20,20
27	4:1
21:30	21:12,12,
1 CO 16:9	13,13,
2 CO 2:12	13,13,
COL 4:3	21,21,
HEB 6:19	25
9:3	22:14

3443 ܬܪܥܐ (m) doorkeeper

MRK 13:34

3447 ܬܪܨ(v) (tr) direct, make straight;
(int) rush

ᵃPEAL

Perfect

MAT 8:32	ACT 16:11
LUK 8:33	

Imperfect

LUK 1:79	2 TH 3:5
1 TH 3:11	

Imperative

LUK 3:4

3434 ܬܪܝܨܐ (pp) straight, upright

ACT 8:21	2 PT 2:15
9:11	REV 15:4
13:10	19:8
HEB 12:13	

3435 ܬܪܝܨܐܝܬ (adv) rightly,
uprightly

LUK 7:43	ACT 27:7
10:28	GAL 2:14
20:21	2 TM 2:15
ACT 21:1	

ᶜPAEL (non occ)

3358 ܬܘܪܨܐ (m) correction

2 TM 3:16	HEB 9:10

3451 ܬܫܥ (num) nine

MAT	18:12,13	LUK	17:17
	20:5		23:44
	27:45,46	ACT	3:1
MRK	15:33,34		10:3,9,30
LUK	15:4,7	REV	21:20

3452 ܬܫܥܝܢ (num) ninety

MAT	18:12,13	LUK	15:4,7

Proper Nouns

8 ܐܒܝܐ Abia (Abijam)

MAT 1:7,7

9 ܐܒܝܐ Abia (course of)

LUK 1:5

11 ܐܒܝܘܕ Abiud

MAT 1:13,13

13 ܐܒܝܠܝܢܐ Abilene

LUK 3:1

14 ܐܒܝܬܪ Abiathar

MRK 2:26

18 ܐܒܪܗܡ Abraham (Abram)

MAT 1:1,2,17
3:9,9
8:11
22:32
MRK 12:26
LUK 1:55,73
3:8,8,34
13:16,28
16:22,23,
24,25,
29,30,
31
19:9
20:37
JHN 8:33,37,39,
39,39,40,
52,53,56,
57,58
ACT 3:13,25

ACT 7:2,4,16,
17,32
13:26
ROM 4:1,2,3,9,
12,13,16
9:7
11:1
2 CO 11:22
GAL 3:6,7,8,9,
14,16,18,
29
4:22
HEB 2:16
6:13
7:1,2,4,5,6,
9
11:8,17
JAM 2:21,23
1 PT 3:6

19 ܐܓܒܘܣ Agabus

ACT 11:28
ACT 21:10

21 ܐܓܘܣܛܘܣ (Caesar) Augustus

see also (pn) Caesar, ܩܣܪ

LUK 2:1

28 ܐܓܪܝܦܘܣ Agrippa

surname of Herod Agrippa I

see also (pn) Herod, ܗܪܘܕܣ

ACT 12:1
25:13,22,
23,24,
26

ACT 26:1,2,7,
19,26,
27,28,
32

30 ܐܕܘܡ Idumaea

MRK 3:8

31 ܐܕܝ Addi

LUK 3:28

32 ܐܕܡ Adam

LUK 3:38
ROM 5:14,14
1 CO 15:22,45,

1 CO 15:45
1 TM 2:13,14
JUD 14

35 ܐܕܪܡܛܘܣ Adramyttium

ACT 27:2

37 ܐܗܪܘܢ Aaron

LUK 1:5
ACT 7:40

HEB 5:4
7:11
HEB 9:4

41 ܐܘܒܘܠܘܣ Eubulus

2 TM 4:21

42 ܐܘܗܕܝܐ Euodias

PHL 4:2

44 ܐܘܛܘܟܘܣ Eutychus

ACT 20:9

55 ܐܘܢܝܩܐ Eunice

2 TM 1:5

58 ܐܘܪܒܢܘܣ Urbane

ROM 16:9

60 ܐܘܪܘܣ (non occ) Euros, East wind

67 ܐܘܪܩܠܝܕܘܢ Euroclydon, Northeast wind

ACT 27:14

62 ܐܘܪܝܐ Urias (Uriah)

MAT 1:6

69 ܐܘܪܫܠܡ Jerusalem

MAT 2:1,3
3:5
4:25
5:35
15:1
16:21
20:17,18
21:1,10
23:37,37
MRK 1:5
3:8,22
MRK 7:1
10:32,33
11:1,11,14, 27
15:41
LUK 2:22,25,38, 41,43,45
4:9
5:17
6:17
9:31,51,53
LUK 10:30
13:4,22,33, 34,34
17:11
18:31
19:11,28
21:20,24
23:7,28
24:13,18, 33,47, 49,52
JHN 1:19
2:13,23
4:20,21,45
5:1,2
7:25
10:22
11:18,55
12:12
ACT 1:4,8,12, 12,19
2:5,14,43
4:6,16
5:16,28
6:7
8:1,14,25, 26,27
9:2,13,21, 26,28
10:39
ACT 11:2,22,27
12:25
13:13,27, 31
15:2,4
16:4
18:21
19:21
20:16,22
21:4,11,12, 13,15, 17
22:5,17,18
23:11
24:11
25:1,3,7,9, 15,20, 24
26:4,10,20
28:17,21
ROM 15:19,25, 26,31
1 CO 16:3
GAL 1:17,18
2:1
4:25,26
HEB 12:22
REV 3:12
21:2,10

71 ܐܙܘܛܘܣ Azotus (Ashdod)

ACT 8:40

76 ܐܚܙ Achaz (Ahaz)

MAT 1:9,9

85 ܐܝܘܒ Job

JAM 5:11

87 ܐܝܛܘܪܝܐ Ituraea

LUK 3:1

88 ܐܛܠܝܐ Attalia

ACT 14:25

89 ܐܝܛܠܝܐ Italy

ACT 18:2; 27:1,6 | ACT 28:13 | HEB 13:24

90 ܐܝܛܠܝܩܝܐ (adj) Italian

ACT 10:1

94 ܐܝܠ God

MAT 27:46,46 | MRK 15:34,34

101 ܐܝܣܘܢ Jason

ACT 17:5,6,7,9 | ROM 16:21

102 ܐܝܣܚܩ Isaac

MAT 1:2,2
8:11
22:32
MRK 12:26
LUK 3:34
13:28
20:37
ACT 3:13
7:8,8,32
ROM 9:7,10
GAL 4:28
HEB 11:9,17,18, 20
JAM 2:21

103 ܐܝܣܟܪ Issachar

REV 7:7

104 ܐܝܣܪܝܠ Israel

MAT 2:6,20,21
8:10
9:33
10:6,23
15:24,31
19:28
27:9,42
MRK 12:29
15:32
LUK 1:16,54,68, 80
2:25,32,34
4:25,27
7:9
22:30
24:21
JHN 1:31,47,49
3:10
12:13
ACT 1:6
2:22,36
ACT 3:12
4:8,10,27
5:21,31,35
7:23,25,37, 42
9:15
10:36
13:16,23, 24
21:28
28:20
ROM 9:4,6,6,27, 27,31
10:19,21
11:1,2,7, 25,26
1 CO 10:18
2 CO 3:7,13
GAL 6:16
EPH 2:12
PHL 3:5
HEB 8:8,10
11:22
REV 2:14
REV 7:4
21:12

105 ܐܝܣܪܝܠܝܐ (adj) Israelite

2 CO 11:22

107 ܐܝܩܘܢ Iconium

ACT 13:51
14:19,21
ACT 16:2
2 TM 3:11

109 ܐܝܪܦܘܠܝܣ Hierapolis

COL 4:13

110 ܐܝܪܝܚܘ Jericho

MAT 20:29
MRK 10:46,46
LUK 10:30
LUK 18:35
19:1
HEB 11:30

111 ܐܝܫܝ Jesse

MAT 1:5,6
LUK 3:32
ACT 13:22
ROM 15:12

114 ܐܟܐܝܐ Achaia

ACT 18:12,27
19:21
ROM 15:26
16:5
1 CO 16:15
2 CO 1:1
9:2
11:10
1 TH 1:7,8

115 ܐܟܐܝܩܘܣ Achaicus

1 CO 16:17

121 ܐܟܝܡ Achim

MAT 1:14,14

ܐܟܠ ܩܪܨܐ Devil, see main body under ܐܟܠ

140 ܐܠܘܡܐܘܣ Elymas

ACT 13:8

141 ܐܠܘܡܦܐ Olympas

ROM 16:15

143 ܐܠܘܪܝܩܘܢ Illyricum

ROM 15:19

145 ܐܠܝܐ Elias (Elijah)

MAT 11:14
16:14
17:3,4,10,
11,12
27:47,49
MRK 6:15
8:28
9:4,5,11,
12,13
MRK 15:35,36
LUK 1:17
4:25,26
9:8,19,30,
33,34,54
JHN 1:21,25
ROM 11:2
JAM 5:17

146 ܐܠܝܘܕ Eliud

MAT 1:14,15

147 ܐܠܝܥܙܪ Eleazar

MAT 1:15,15

148 ܐܠܝܥܙܪ Eliezer

LUK 3:29

150 ܐܠܝܩܝܡ Eliakim

MAT 1:13,13 | LUK 3:30

151 ܐܠܝܫܒܥ Elisabeth

LUK 1:5,7,13,
24,36,40,
LUK 1:41,41,56,
57

152 ܐܠܝܫܥ Eliseus (Elisha)

LUK 4:27

153 ܐܠܟܣܢܕܪܘܣ Alexander

may refer to more than one person

MRK 15:21
ACT 4:6
19:33
1 TM 1:20
2 TM 4:14

154 ܐܠܟܣܢܕܪܝܐ Alexandria

ACT 18:24 | ACT 27:6

155 ܐܠܟܣܢܕܪܝܐ (adj) Alexandrian

ACT 6:9 | ACT 28:11

156 ܐܠܡܘܕܕ Elmodam

LUK 3:28

157 ܐܠܡܝܐ (adj) Elamites

ACT 2:9

164 ܐܡܘܢ Amon

MAT 1:10,10

170 ܐܡܦܝܦܘܠܝܣ Amphipolis

ACT 17:1

171 ܐܡܦܠܝܐܘܣ Amplias

ROM 16:8

179 ܐܢܣܝܦܘܪܘܣ Onesiphorus

2 TM 1:16 | 2 TM 4:19

181 ܐܢܕܪܐܘܣ Andrew

MAT 4:18; 10:2
MRK 1:16,29; 3:18; 13:3
LUK 6:14
JHN 1:40,44; 6:8; 12:22,22
ACT 1:13

182 ܐܢܕܪܘܢܝܩܘܣ Andronicus

ROM 16:7

184 ܐܢܘܫ Enos

LUK 3:38

186 ܐܢܛܝܘܟܝ Antioch of Syria

ACT 11:19,20, 22,26, 26; 12:25; 13:1
ACT 14:26; 15:22,23, 30,35; 18:22
GAL 2:11

188 ܐܢܛܝܘܟܝܐ (adj) Antiochene

ACT 6:5

187 ܐܢܛܝܘܟܝ Antioch of Pisidia

ACT 13:14; 14:19,21
2 TM 3:11

190 ܐܢܛܝܦܛܪܝܣ Antipatris

ACT 23:31

191 ܐܝܢܐ Aeneas

ACT 9:33,34

194 ܐܢܣܝܡܘܣ Onesimus

COL 4:9
PLM 10

200 ܐܣܐ Asa

MAT 1:7,8

205 ܐܣܘܢܩܪܝܛܘܣ Asyncritus

ROM 16:14

210 ܐܣܛܘܐܝܩܐ (adj) Stoic

ACT 17:18

213 ܐܣܛܟܘܣ Stachys

ROM 16:9

216 ܐܣܛܦܢܐ Stephanas

1 CO 1:16
1 CO 16:15,17

217 ܐܣܛܦܢܘܣ Stephen

ACT 6:5,8,9; 7:59; 8:2
ACT 11:19; 22:20

222 ܐܣܝܐ Asia

ACT 2:9; 6:9; 16:6; 19:10,22, 26,27, 31; 20:4,4,16, 18
ACT 21:27; 24:19; 27:2
1 CO 16:19
2 CO 1:8
2 TM 1:15
1 PT 1:1
REV 1:4

232 ܐܣܦܢܝܐ Spain

ROM 15:24,28

246 ܐܦܘܠܘܢܝܐ Apollonia

ACT 17:1

247 ܐܦܝܐ Apphia

PLM 2

248 ܐܦܝܘܣ ܦܘܪܘܣ Appii Forum

ACT 28:15

251 ܐܦܝܩܘܪܘܣ Epicurus; (ܕܡܢ ܝܘܠܦܢܗ) Epicureans

ACT 17:18

252 ܐܦܠܐ Apelles

ROM 16:10

253 ܐܦܠܘ Apollos

ACT 18:24; 19:1 | 1 CO 1:12; 3:4,5,6,22 | 1 CO 4:6; 16:12 | TIT 3:13

255 ܐܦܝܢܛܘܣ Epaenetus

ROM 16:5

257 ܐܦܣܘܣ Ephesus

ACT 18:19,21, 24; 19:1,17,26; 20:16,17 | 1 CO 15:32; 16:8 | EPH 1:1 | 1 TM 1:3 | 2 TM 1:18; 4:12 | REV 1:11; 2:1

258 ܐܦܣܝܐ (adj) Ephesian

ACT 19:28,34, 35,35 | ACT 21:29

260 ܐܦܦܪܐ Epaphras

COL 1:7; 4:12 | PLM 23

261 ܐܦܦܪܘܕܝܛܘܣ Epaphroditus

PHL 2:25 | PHL 4:18

262 ܐܦܪܝܡ Ephraim

JHN 11:54

264 ܐܩܘܠܐܘܣ Aquila

ACT 18:2,18,21, 26 | ROM 16:3 | 1 CO 16:19 | 2 TM 4:19

265 ܐܪܒܝܐ Arabia

GAL 1:17 | GAL 4:25

2430 ܥܪܒܝܐ (adj) Arabian

ACT 2:11

272 ܐܪܛܐܣ Aretas

2 CO 11:32

273 ܐܪܛܡܐܐ Artemas

TIT 3:12

274 ܐܪܛܡܝܣ Diana (Artemis)

ACT 19:24,27, 28,34, | ACT 19:35

276 ܐܪܝܘܣ ܦܓܘܣ Areopagus

ACT 17:19,22, | ACT 17:34

281 ܐܪܟܝܦܘܣ Archippus

COL 4:17 | PLM 2

282 ܐܪܟܠܐܘܣ Archelaus

MAT 2:22

283 ܐܪܡ Aram

MAT 1:3,4 | LUK 3:33

ܐܪܡ Syria and deriv, see main body

287 ܐܪܡܝܐ Jeremiah

MAT 2:17 | MAT 16:14

290 ܐܪܣܛܒܘܠܘܣ Aristobulus

ROM 16:10

291 ܐܪܣܛܘܣ Erastus

may refer to more than one person

ACT 19:22
ROM 16:23
2 TM 4:20

292 ܐܪܣܛܪܟܘܣ Aristarchus

ACT 19:29
20:4
27:2
COL 4:10
PLM 24

295 ܐܪܥܘ Ragau (Reu)

LUK 3:35

297 ܐܪܦܟܫܕ Arphaxad

LUK 3:36

299 ܐܫܝܪ Aser (Asher)

LUK 2:36 | REV 7:6

300 ܐܫܥܝܐ Esaias (Isaiah)

MAT 3:3
4:14
8:17
12:17
13:14
15:7
MRK 1:2
7:6
LUK 3:4
LUK 4:17
JHN 1:23
12:38,39,
41
ACT 8:28,30
28:25
ROM 9:27,29
10:16,20
15:12

311 ܐܬܢܘܣ Athens

ACT 17:15,16
18:1
1 TH 3:1

312 ܐܬܢܝܐ (adj) Athenian

ACT 17:21,22

317 ܒܒܠ Babylon

MAT 1:11,12,17,
17
ACT 7:43
1 PT 5:13
REV 14:8
16:19
17:5
18:2,10,21

371 ܒܝܬ ܚܣܕܐ Bethesda

JHN 5:2

372 ܒܝܬ ܠܚܡ Bethlehem

MAT 2:1,5,6,8,
16
LUK 2:4,15
JHN 7:42

373 ܒܝܬ ܢܗܪܝܢ

Mesopotamia

ACT 2:9 | ACT 7:2

374 ܒܝܬ ܥܢܝܐ Bethany

MAT 21:17
26:6
MRK 11:1,11,12
14:3
LUK 19:29
LUK 24:50
JHN 1:28
11:1,17,18
12:1

375 ܒܝܬ ܦܓܐ Bethphage

MAT 21:1
MRK 11:1
LUK 19:29

376 ܒܝܬ ܨܝܕܐ Bethsaida

may refer to more than one place

MAT 11:21
MRK 6:45
8:22
LUK 9:10
LUK 10:13
JHN 1:44
12:21

389 ܒܠܣܛܘܣ Blastus

ACT 12:20

392 ܒܠܥܡ Balaam

2 PT 2:15
JUD 11
REV 2:14

394 ܒܠܩ Balac (Balak)

REV 2:14

396 ܒܢܝ ܪܓܫ Boanerges

MRK 3:17

398 ܒܢܝܡܝܢ Benjamin (the tribe)

ACT 13:21
ROM 11:1
PHL 3:5
REV 7:8

413 ܒܘܣܪ Bosor (Beor)

2 PT 2:15

415 ܒܥܙ Booz (Boaz)

MAT 1:5,5
LUK 3:32

421 ܒܥܠܐ Baal

ROM 11:4

425 ܒܥܠܙܒܘܒ Beelzebub

MAT 10:25
12:24,27
MRK 3:22
LUK 11:15,18,
19

438 ܒܪ ܐܒܐ Barabbas

MAT 27:16,17,
20,21,
26
MRK 15:7,11,15
LUK 23:18
JHN 18:40,40

442 ܒܪ ܛܝܡܝ Bartimaeus, son of Timaeus

surname of Timaeus, ܛܝܡܝ

MRK 10:46

443 ܒܪ ܝܘܢܐ Bar-jona, son of Jonas

surname of Simon Peter, ܫܡܥܘܢ

MAT 16:17
JHN 1:42
JHN 21:15,16,
17

444 ܒܪ ܫܒܐ (Joseph) Barsabas

ACT 1:23

445 ܒܪ ܫܒܐ (Judas) Barsabas

ACT 15:22

446 ܒܪ ܫܘܡܐ Barjesus (Barshuma)

ACT 13:6,8

448 ܒܪ ܬܘܠܡܝ Bartholomew

MAT 10:3
MRK 3:18
LUK 6:14
ACT 1:13

454 ܒܪܘܐ Berea

ACT 17:10,13
ACT 20:4

464 ܒܪܟܝܐ Barachias

MAT 23:35

466 ܒܪܢܒܐ Barnabas

ACT 4:36 9:27 11:22,30 12:25 13:1,2,7, 13,46, 50 14:12,14,	ACT 14:20 15:2,2,12, 22,25, 35,36, 37,39 1 CO 9:6 GAL 2:1,9,13 COL 4:10

467 ܒܪܢܝܩܐ Bernice

ACT 25:13,23	ACT 26:30

468 ܒܪܩ Barak

HEB 11:32

475 ܒܝܬܘܢܝܐ Bithynia

ACT 16:7	1 PT 1:1

480 ܓܐܝܘܣ Gaius

may refer to more than one person

ACT 19:29 20:4 ROM 16:23	1 CO 1:14 3 JN 1

481 ܓܐܠܝܘܢ Gallio

ACT 18:12,14,	ACT 18:17

495 ܓܒܪܝܠ Gabriel

LUK 1:19,26

496 ܓܓܘܠܬܐ Golgotha

MAT 27:33 MRK 15:22	JHN 19:17

498 ܓܕ Gad (the tribe)

REV 7:5

504 ܓܕܣܡܢ Gethsemane

MAT 26:36	MRK 14:32

505 ܓܕܥܘܢ Gedeon (Gideon)

HEB 11:32

507 ܓܕܪܝܐ (adj) Gadarene

MAT 8:28 MRK 5:1	LUK 8:26,37

510 ܓܗܢܐ hell (Gehenna)

MAT 5:22,29,30 10:28 18:9	MAT 23:15,33 MRK 9:43,45,47 LUK 12:5

512 ܓܘܓ Gog

REV 20:8

532 ܓܙܐ Gaza

ACT 8:26

556 ܓܠܛܝܐ Galatia

ACT 16:6 18:23 GAL 1:2	2 TM 4:10 1 PT 1:1

557 ܓܠܛܝܐ (adj) Galatian

1 CO 16:1	GAL 3:1

562 ܓܠܝܠܐ Galilee

MAT 2:22 3:13 4:12,15,18, 23,25 15:29	MAT 17:22 19:1 21:11 26:32 27:55

MAT 28:7,10,16
MRK 1:9,14,16, 28,39
3:7
6:21
7:31
9:30
14:28
15:41
16:7
LUK 1:26
2:4,39
3:1
4:14,31,44
5:17
8:26
LUK 17:11
23:5,6,49, 55
24:6
JHN 1:43
2:1,11
4:3,43,45, 46,47,54
6:1
7:1,9,41, 52,52
12:21
21:2
ACT 9:31
10:37
13:31

563 ܓܠܝܠܝܐ (adj) Galilean

MRK 14:70
LUK 13:1,2,2
22:59
23:6
JHN 4:45
ACT 1:11
2:7
5:37

572 ܓܡܠܝܐܝܠ Gamaliel

ACT 5:34 | ACT 22:3

588 ܓܢܣܪ Gennesaret

MAT 14:34
MRK 6:53
LUK 5:1

596 ܓܦܝܦܬܐ Gabbatha

JHN 19:13

614 ܕܝܡܐܣ Demas

COL 4:14
2 TM 4:10
PLM 24

637 ܕܘܝܕ David

MAT 1:1,6,6,17, 17,20
9:27
12:3,23
15:22
20:30,31
21:9,15
22:42,43, 45
MRK 2:25
MRK 10:47,48
11:10
12:35,36, 37
LUK 1:27,32,69
2:4,4,11
3:31
6:3
18:38,39
20:41,42,
LUK 20:44
JHN 7:42,42
ACT 1:16
2:25,29,34
4:25
7:45
13:22,22, 34,36
15:16
ROM 1:3
ROM 4:6
11:9
2 TM 2:8
HEB 4:7
7:21
11:32
REV 3:7
5:5
22:16

666 ܕܝܘܛܪܦܣ Diotrephes

3 JN 9

673 ܕܝܘܢܘܣܝܘܣ Dionysius

ACT 17:34

690 ܕܠܡܛܝܐ Dalmatia

2 TM 4:10

691 ܕܠܡܢܘܬܐ Dalmanutha

MRK 8:10

699 ܕܡܛܪܝܘܣ Demetrius

ACT 19:24,38 | 3 JN 12

705 ܕܡܪܝܣ Damaris

ACT 17:34

709 ܕܢܝܐܝܠ Daniel

MAT 24:15 | MRK 13:14

720 ܕܪܒܐ Derbe

ACT 14:6,20
16:1
ACT 20:4

723 ܕܪܘܣܝܠܐ Drusilla

ACT 24:24

727 ܕܪܡܣܘܩ Damascus

ACT 9:2,3,8,10, 19,22,27 22:5,6,10, 11	ACT 26:12,20 2 CO 11:32 GAL 1:17

728 ܕܪܡܣܘܩܝܐ (adj) Damascene

2 CO 11:32

736 ܗܒܝܠ Abel

MAT 23:35 LUK 11:51	HEB 11:4 12:24

742 ܗܓܪ Agar (Hagar)

GAL 4:24,25

746 ܗܕܪܝܘܣ Adria; (w/ ܝܡܐ) Adriatic Sea

ACT 27:27

750 ܗܘܡܢܐܘܣ Hymenaeus

1 TM 1:20	2 TM 2:17

755 ܗܘܫܥ Osee (Hosea)

ROM 9:25

764 ܗܠܝ Heli

LUK 3:23

768 ܗܠܣ Greece

ACT 20:2

779 ܗܪܘܕܝܐ Herodias

MAT 14:3,6 MRK 6:17,19,22	LUK 3:19

780 ܗܪܘܕܝܘܢ Herodion

ROM 16:11

781 ܗܪܘܕܣ Herod the Great

see below 370 ܒܝܬ ܗܪܘܕܣ

MAT 2:1,3,7,12, 13,15,16,	MAT 2:19,22 LUK 1:5

370 ܒܝܬ ܗܪܘܕܣ (idiom) Herodians

from 377 ܒܝܬܐ and 781 ܗܪܘܕܣ (above)

MAT 22:16 MRK 3:6	MRK 12:13

782 ܗܪܘܕܣ Herod Antipas

MAT 14:1,3,6,6 MRK 6:14,16,17, 18,20,21, 22 8:15 LUK 3:1,19 8:3	LUK 9:7,9 13:31 23:7,7,8, 11,12, 15 ACT 4:27 13:1

783 ܗܪܘܕܣ Herod Agrippa I

ACT 12:1,11,19, 20,21	ACT 23:35

786 ܗܪܡܐ Hermas

ROM 16:14

787 ܗܪܡܐ Hermes

ROM 16:14

788 ܗܪܡܓܢܣ Hermogenes

2 TM 1:15

789 ܗܪܡܝܣ Mercurius (Hermes)

ACT 14:12

798 ܙܐܢܐ Zenas

TIT 3:13

799 ܙܒܕܝ Zebedee

MAT 4:21,21; 10:2; 20:20; 26:37; 27:56
MRK 1:19,20; 3:17; 10:35
LUK 5:10
JHN 21:2

800 ܙܒܘܠܘܢ Zabulun (Zebulun)

MAT 4:13,15
REV 7:8

809 ܙܕܘܩ Sadoc

MAT 1:14,14

810 ܙܕܘܩܝܐ (adj) Sadducee

MAT 3:7; 16:1,6,11,12; 22:23,34
MRK 12:18
LUK 20:27
ACT 4:1; 5:17; 23:6,7,8

838 ܙܘܪܒܒܠ Zorobabel (Zerubbabel)

MAT 1:12,13
LUK 3:27

846 ܙܟܝ Zacchaeus

LUK 19:2,3,5,8

848 ܙܟܪܝܐ Zacharias (John's father)

LUK 1:5,11,12,13,18,21,22,40,59,67; 3:2

849 ܙܟܪܝܐ Zacharias (Barachias' son)

MAT 23:35
LUK 11:51

877 ܙܪܚ Zara

MAT 1:3

925 ܚܘܐ Eve

2 CO 11:3
1 TM 2:13

967 ܚܙܩܝܐ Ezekias (Hezekiah)

MAT 1:9,10

1015 ܚܠܦܝ Alphaeus

MAT 10:3
MRK 2:14; 3:18
LUK 6:15
ACT 1:13

1023 ܚܡܘܪ Emmor (Hamor)

ACT 7:16

1041 ܚܢܐ Anna

LUK 2:36

1043 ܚܢܘܟ Enoch

LUK 3:37
HEB 11:5
JUD 14

1046 ܚܢܢ Annas

LUK 3:2
JHN 18:13,24
ACT 4:6

1048 ܚܢܢܝܐ Ananias (Sapphira's husband)

ACT 5:1,3,5

1049 ܚܢܢܝܐ Ananias

ACT 9:10,10,12, 13,17 | ACT 22:12

1050 ܚܢܢܝܐ Ananias (high priest)

ACT 23:2 | ACT 24:1

1063 ܚܫܠܝ Esli

LUK 3:25

1083 ܚܨܪܘܢ Esrom

MAT 1:3,3 | LUK 3:33

1100 ܚܪܢ Charran (Haran)

ACT 7:2,4

1137 ܛܒܝܬܐ Tabitha

ACT 9:36,39,40

1140 ܛܒܪܝܘܣ Tiberias (city)

JHN 6:1,23 | JHN 21:1

1141 ܛܒܪܝܘܣ Tiberias (Caesar)

cf (pn) Caesar, ܩܣܪ

LUK 3:1

1150 ܛܘܟܝܩܘܣ Tychicus

ACT 20:4
EPH 6:21
COL 4:7
2 TM 4:12
TIT 3:12

ܛܘܪܐ ܕܙܝܬܐ Mt of Olives, see main body ܙܝܬܐ

1159 ܛܘܪܢܘܣ Tyrannus

ACT 19:9

1163 ܛܛܘܣ Titus

ACT 18:7
2 CO 2:13
7:6,13,14
8:6,16,23
2 CO 12:18,18
GAL 2:1,3
2 TM 4:10
TIT 1:4

1167 ܛܝܡܘܢ Timon

ACT 6:5

1168 ܛܝܡܝ Timaeus

MRK 10:46

1169 ܛܝܡܬܐܘܣ Timotheus, Timothy

ACT 16:1
17:14,15
18:5
19:22
20:4
ROM 16:21
1 CO 4:17
16:10
2 CO 1:1,19
PHL 1:1
PHL 2:19
COL 1:1
1 TH 1:1
3:2,6
2 TH 1:1
1 TM 1:2,18
6:20
2 TM 1:2
PLM 1
HEB 13:23

1206 ܛܪܘܐܣ Troas

ACT 16:8,11
20:5,6
2 CO 2:12
2 TM 4:13

1207 ܛܪܘܓܘܠܝܘܢ Trogyllium

ACT 20:15

1208 ܛܪܘܦܝܡܘܣ Trophimus

ACT 20:4
21:29
2 TM 4:20

1209 ܛܪܘܦܢܐ Tryphena

ROM 16:12

1210 ܛܪܘܦܣܐ Tryphosa

ROM 16:12

1211 ܛܪܛܝܘܣ Tertius

ROM 16:22

1212 ܛܪܛܠܘܣ Tertullus

ACT 24:1,2

1213 ܛܪܟܘܢܐ Trachonitis

LUK 3:1

1214 ܛܪܣܘܣ Tarsus

ACT 9:11,30; 11:25 | ACT 21:39; 22:3

1222 ܝܢܐ Janna

LUK 3:24

ܝܗܘܕ Judea and deriv, see main body

1236 ܝܗܘܕܐ Judas Iscariot

MAT 10:4; 26:14,25,47,48; 27:3; MRK 3:19; 14:10,43; LUK 6:16 | LUK 22:3,47,48; JHN 6:71; 12:4; 13:2,26,29,30; 18:2,3,5; ACT 1:16,25

1237 ܝܗܘܕܐ Judas (Jesus' brother)

MAT 13:55 | MRK 6:3

1238 ܝܗܘܕܐ Jude

LUK 6:16; ACT 1:13 | JUD 1

1239 ܝܗܘܕܐ Judas (an apostle)

JHN 14:22

1240 ܝܗܘܕܐ Judas (the Galilean)

ACT 5:37

1241 ܝܗܘܕܐ Judas (the Damascene)

ACT 9:11

1242 ܝܗܘܕܐ Judas (Barsabas)

ACT 15:22,27, | ACT 15:32

1243 ܝܗܘܕܐ Judas (Judah)

MAT 1:2,3 | LUK 3:26,30,33

1244 ܝܗܘܕܐ Judah (the tribe)

HEB 7:14; 8:8 | REV 5:5; 7:5

1248 ܝܗܘܫܦܛ Josaphat (Jehoshaphat)

MAT 1:8,8

1249 ܝܘܐܝܠ Joel

ACT 2:16

1250 ܝܐܝܪܘܣ Jairus

MRK 5:22 | LUK 8:41

1253 ܝܘܚܢ Joanna

LUK 8:3 | LUK 24:10

1254 ܝܘܚܢܢ John the Baptist

MAT 3:1,4,13, 14
4:12
9:14
11:2,4,7, 11,12, 13,18
14:2,3,4,8, 10
16:14
17:13
21:25,26, 32
MRK 1:4,6,9,14
2:18,18
6:14,16,17, 18,20,24, 25,27,27
8:28
11:30,32
LUK 1:13,60,63
3:2,15,16, 19,20
LUK 5:33
7:18,19,20, 22,24,24, 28,29,33
9:7,9,19
11:1
16:16
20:4,6
JHN 1:6,15,19, 26,28,29, 32,35,40
3:23,24,25, 26,27
4:1
5:33,36
10:40,41, 41
ACT 1:5,22
10:37
11:16
13:24,25
18:25
19:3,4

1255 ܝܘܚܢܢ John

ACT 4:6

1256 ܝܘܚܢܢ John Mark

see also Mark, ܡܪܩܘܣ

ACT 12:12,25
13:5,13
ACT 15:37

1257 ܝܘܚܢܢ John (the disciple)

MAT 4:21
10:2
17:1
MRK 1:19,29
3:17
5:37
9:2,38
10:35,41
13:3
14:33
LUK 5:10
6:14
LUK 8:51
9:28,49,54
22:8
ACT 1:13
3:1,3,4,11
4:13,19
8:14,25
12:2
GAL 2:9
REV 1:1,4,9
22:8

1258 ܝܘܚܢܢ Joanna

LUK 3:27

1259 ܝܘܟܢܝܐ Jechonias

MAT 1:11,12

1260 ܝܘܠܝܐ Julia

ROM 16:15

1261 ܝܘܠܝܘܣ Julius

ACT 27:1

ܝܘ Greece and deriv, see main body

1268 ܝܘܢܝܐ Junia

ROM 16:7

1270 ܝܘܢܡ Jonan (Jonam)

LUK 3:30

1271 ܝܘܢܢ Jonas (Jonah)

MAT 12:39,40, 41,41
16:4
LUK 11:29,30, 32,32

1272 ܝܘܣܐ Jose

LUK 3:29

1273 ܝܘܣܐ Joses

MAT 13:55
27:56
MRK 6:3
15:40,47

1274 ܝܘܣܛܘܣ Justus (Jesus)

surname of a Jesus, ܝܫܘܥ

COL 4:11

1275 ܝܘܣܛܘܣ Justus

surname of Joseph called Barsabas

ACT 1:23

1276 ܝܘܣܦ Joseph (Mary's husband)

MAT 1:18,19,20,24; 2:13,14,19,21
MRK 15:45,46
LUK 1:27; 2:4,16,33,43; 3:23
LUK 4:22
JHN 1:45; 4:5; 6:42
ACT 7:9,13,13,14,18
HEB 11:21,22
REV 7:8

1277 ܝܘܣܦ Joseph (Mary's father)

MAT 1:16

1278 ܝܘܣܦ Joseph of Arimathea

MAT 27:57,59
MRK 15:43
LUK 23:50
JHN 19:38

1279 ܝܘܣܦ Joseph (Mattathias' son)

LUK 3:24

1280 ܝܘܣܦ Joseph (Juda's son)

LUK 3:26

1281 ܝܘܣܦ Joseph (Jonan's son)

LUK 3:30

1282 ܝܘܣܦ Joseph (Barsabas)

ACT 1:23

1283 ܝܘܣܦ Joseph (Barnabas)

ACT 4:36

1284 ܝܘܦܐ Joppa

ACT 9:36,38,43; 10:5,8,23,
ACT 10:32; 11:5,13

1286 ܝܘܪܕܢܢ Jordan

MAT 3:5,6,13; 4:15,25; 19:1
MRK 1:5,9; 3:8; 10:1
LUK 3:3; 4:1
JHN 1:28; 3:26; 10:40

1287 ܝܘܪܡ Joram

MAT 1:8,8

1288 ܝܘܪܡ Jorim

LUK 3:29

1291 ܝܘܫܝܐ Josias (Josiah)

MAT 1:10,11

1292 ܝܘܬܡ Joatham

MAT 1:9,9

1294 ܐܝܙܒܠ Jezebel

REV 2:20

1309 ܝܡܐ ܕܣܘܦ Red Sea, sea of reeds

ACT 7:36
HEB 11:29

1310 ܝܡܒܪܣ Jambres

2 TM 3:8

1314 ܝܢܝܣ Jannes

2 TM 3:8

ܝܣܪܝܠ see ܐܝܣܪܝܠ

1321 ܝܥܩܘܒ Jacob

MAT 1:2,2	JHN 4:5,6,12
8:11	ACT 3:13
22:32	7:8,8,12, 14,15,32, 46
MRK 12:26	ROM 9:13
LUK 1:33	11:26
3:34	HEB 11:9,20,21
13:28	
20:37	

1322 ܝܥܩܘܒ Jacob (Mary's grandfather)

MAT 1:15,16

1323 ܝܥܩܘܒ James (John's brother)

MAT 4:21	MRK 13:3
10:2	14:33
17:1	LUK 5:10
MRK 1:19,29	6:14
3:17,17	8:51
5:37,37	9:28,54
9:2	ACT 1:13
10:35,41	12:2

1324 ܝܥܩܘܒ James (Alpheus' son)

MAT 10:3	LUK 6:15
MRK 3:18	ACT 1:13

1325 ܝܥܩܘܒ James (Jesus' brother)

MAT 13:55	1 CO 15:7
MRK 6:3	GAL 1:19
ACT 12:17	2:9,12
15:13	JAM 1:1
21:18	

1326 ܝܥܩܘܒ James (Mary's son)

MAT 27:56	MRK 16:1
MRK 15:40	LUK 24:10

1327 ܝܥܩܘܒ James (Jude's brother)

LUK 6:16	JUD 1
ACT 1:13	

1341 ܝܪܕ Jared

LUK 3:37

1347 ܝܫܘܥ Jesus

MAT 1:1,16,18,21,25; 2:1; 3:13,15,16; 4:1,7, 10,12,17,19,23; 5:1; 7:28; 8:3,4,5,7,10,13,14, 18,20,22,23,24,26,28,29,32,34; 9:2,4,9,10, 12,15,19,22,23,27,28,30,32,35,36; 10:5; 11:1,4,7,20,25; 12:1,9,15,25; 13:1,34,36,51, 53,57; 14:1,12,13,14,18,25,27,29,29; 15:1,3, 21,28,29,30,32,34; 16:8,13,17,21,24; 17:1,2, 4,7,8,9,11,17,18,19,20,22,25,26; 18:1,2,22; 19:1,14,18,21,23,26,28; 20:17,22,25,29,30, 32,34; 21:1,6,7,11,12,16,21,23,24,27,31,42; 22:1,18,20,29,37,41; 23:1; 24:1,3,4; 26:1,4,6, 7,10,17,19,25,26,31,34,36,49,50,50,51,52, 55,57,59,63,64,69,71,75; 27:1,3,11,11,17,20, 22,26,27,37,46,50,54,55,57,58; 28:5,9,10,16, 18 MRK 1:1,9,14,17,24,25,41,45; 2:1,4,5, 8,15,17,19,23,25; 3:1,7,23; 4:11,33,38; 5:6,7, 15,20,21,24,27,30,36,40; 6:1,4,14,30,34,48; 7:14,17,24,27,29,31; 8:17,27,29,34; 9:2,4,8, 19,21,23,25,27,28,35,39; 10:5,14,18,21,23, 24,27,29,32,39,42,46,47,49,50,51,52; 11:6,7, 7,11,15,22,29,33; 12:17,24,29,34,35,41,43; 13:1,2,3,5; 14:3,6,10,18,22,27,30,48,53,55, 60,61,62,67,72; 15:1,5,15,34,37,43; 16:6,19 LUK 1:31; 2:21,27,43,52; 3:21,23; 4:1,4,8, 12,14,17,23,34,35,38,43; 5:3,8,10,12,12,13, 17,19,20,22,27,31; 6:1,3,8,9,11,12,17; 7:1,3, 4,6,9,13,19,20,22,40,40,43,50; 8:1,22,23,28, 28,29,30,35,35,37,38,39,40,41,42,45,48,50, 51,52; 9:1,10,13,14,16,28,33,36,41,42,43,47, 50,58,60,62; 10:1,21,26,28,30,37,41; 11:2, 17,39; 12:1,14,42; 13:2,10,12,14,15,18,20, 24,32; 14:3,16; 15:3,11; 16:15; 17:1,11,13, 16,17,20; 18:16,19,22,24,27,29,31,37,38,39, 40,42; 19:1,3,4,5,8,9,28,35,35; 20:3,8,25,34; 21:1,5; 22:8,14,25,31,34,47,48,51,52,61,63, 70; 23:8,9,20,25,26,28,34,42,43,46,49,52; 24:3,15,19,25,36,38 JHN 1:17,29,36,37, 38,40,42,42,43,45,47,48,50; 2:1,2,3,4,7,11, 13,19,22,23,24; 3:2,3,5,10,22; 4:1,2,6,7,10, 13,16,17,21,26,34,43,44,46,47,48,50,50,53, 54; 5:1,6,8,13,14,15,16,17,19; 6:1,3,5,10,11, 14,15,17,19,20,22,23,24,24,26,29,32,35,42, 43,53,61,64,67,70; 7:1,3,5,6,14,16,21,28,33, 37,39,50; 8:1,6,10,11,12,14,19,21,25,28,31, 34,39,42,49,54,58,59; 9:3,11,14,35,37,39,41; 10:6,7,23,25,32,34; 11:2,3,4,5,9,11,13,14,17, 20,21,23,25,30,32,33,35,38,39,40,41,44,45, 46,51,54,56; 12:1,1,3,7,9,9,11,12,14,16,21, 22,23,30,35,36,44; 13:1,3,7,8,10,11,21,23, 25,26,26,27,31,36,38; 14:6,9,23; 16:19,31;

17:1,3; 18:1,2,4,5,5,6,7,7,8,11,12,15,15,19, 20,22,22,23,24,28,32,33,34,36,37; 19:1,5,9, 9,11,13,16,18,19,20,23,25,26,28,30,33,38, 38,38,39,40,41,42; 20:2,12,14,14,15,16,17, 19,21,24,26,29,30,31; 21:1,4,4,5,7,7,10,12, 13,14,15,15,16,17,20,20,21,22,23,25 ACT 1:1,11,14,16,21; 2:22,32,36,38; 3:6,13, 20; 4:10,13,18,27,30,33; 5:30,40,42; 6:14; 7:55,59; 8:12,16,35; 9:5,17,20,27,29,34; 10:36,38,48; 11:17,20; 13:23,33; 14:10; 15:11,26; 16:7,18,31; 17:3,7,18; 18:5,25,28; 19:4,5,13,13,15,17; 20:21,24,35; 21:13; 22:8; 25:19; 26:9,11,15; 28:23,31 ROM 1:1,4,6, 7,8; 2:16; 3:22,24,26; 4:24; 5:1,11,15,17,21; 6:3,4,11,23; 7:25; 8:1,2,11,11,17,39; 10:9; 13:14; 14:14; 15:5,6,8,16,17,30; 16:3,18,20, 24,26,27 1 CO 1:1,2,2,3,4,7,8,9,10,30; 2:2; 3:11; 4:15; 5:4,4,5; 6:11; 8:6; 9:1; 11:23; 12:3,3; 15:31,57; 16:22,23,24 2 CO 1:1,2, 3,14,19; 4:5,5,6,10,10,11,11,14,14; 8:9; 11:4, 31; 13:5,14 GAL 1:1,3,12; 2:4,16,16,17; 3:1,14,22,26,28; 4:14; 5:6; 6:14,17,18 EPH 1:1,1,2,3,5,15,17; 2:6,7,10,13,20; 3:1, 11,14,21; 4:21; 5:20; 6:23,24 PHL 1:1,1,2, 6,8,11,19,26; 2:5,10,11,19,21; 3:3,8,10,12, 14,20; 4:7,19,21,23 COL 1:1,2,3,4,28; 2:6; 3:17 1 TH 1:1,3,10; 2:14,15,19; 3:11,13; 4:1,2,14,14; 5:9,18,23,28 2 TH 1:1,2,7,8, 12,12; 2:1,8,14,16; 3:6,12,18 1 TM 1:1,1, 2,12,14,15,16; 2:5; 3:13; 4:6; 5:21; 6:3,13,14 2 TM 1:1,1,2,9,10,13; 2:1,3,8,10; 3:12,15; 4:1,22 TIT 1:1,4; 2:13; 3:6 PLM 1,3,5, 6,9,23,25 HEB 2:9; 3:1; 4:14; 6:20; 7:22; 8:6; 10:10,19; 12:2,24; 13:8,12,20,21 JAM 1:1; 2:1 1 PT 1:1,2,3,3,7,13; 2:5; 3:21; 4:11; 5:10 2 PT 1:1,1,2,8,11,14,16; 2:20; 3:18 1 JN 1:3,7; 2:1,22; 3:23; 4:2,3, 15; 5:1,5,6,20 2 JN 3,7 JUD 1,1,4,17, 21,25 REV 1:1,2,5,9,9; 6:9; 12:17; 14:12; 17:6; 19:10,10; 20:4; 22:16,20,21

1348 ܝܫܘܥ Joshua

ACT 7:45 | HEB 4:8

1349 ܝܫܘܥ Jesus (called Justus)

COL 4:11

1367 ܟܐܦܐ Cephas

see also (pn) Peter, ܦܛܪܘܣ

see also (pn) Simon, ܫܡܥܘܢ

MAT 4:18, 10:2, 14:28,29, 15:15, 16:16,18, 16:22,23, 17:1,4,24,25, 18:21, 19:27, 26:33,35,37,40,58,69,73,75
MRK 3:16, 5:37, 8:29,32, 9:2,5, 10:28, 13:3, 14:29,33,37,70, 16:7
LUK 5:3,8, 6:14, 8:45, 12:41, 18:28, 22:8,58,60,61
JHN 1:42, 6:8,68, 13:6,8,9,24,36, 13:37, 18:10,11,15,25, 20:2, 21:2,3,7,11,15,17,20,21
ACT 1:15, 2:14, 3:1, 4:8,19, 8:14,20, 10:5,18,32, 11:13, 12:3
1 CO 1:12, 3:22, 9:5, 15:5
GAL 1:18, 2:7,8,9,11,14

1391 ܟܘܙܐ Chuza

LUK 8:3

1404 ܟܘܪܙܝܢ Chorazin

MAT 11:21 | LUK 10:13

1406 ܟܘܫ Ethiopia (Cush)

ACT 8:27

1407 ܟܘܫܝܐ (adj) Ethiopian

ACT 8:27

1416 ܟܝܘܣ Chios

ACT 20:15

1434 ܟܠܘܐ Chloe

1 CO 1:11

1436 ܟܠܕܝܐ (adj) Chaldaean

ACT 7:4

1456 ܟܢܥܢ Chanaan (Canaan)

ACT 7:11 | ACT 13:19

1457 ܟܢܥܢܝܐ (adj) Canaanite

MAT 15:22

1477 ܟܦܪܢܚܘܡ Capernaum

MAT 4:13 8:5 11:23 17:24 MRK 1:21 2:1 9:33	LUK 4:23,31 7:1 10:15 JHN 2:12 4:46 6:17,24,59

1497 ܟܪܣܛܝܢܐ (adj) Christian

ACT 11:26, 26:28 | 1 PT 4:16

1514 ܠܐܣܐܐ Lasea

ACT 27:8

1519 ܠܒܝ Lebbaeus

MAT 10:3

1521 ܠܒܢܝܐ (adj) Lebanese

REV 1:15 | REV 2:18

1569 (ܠܒܪܛܝ), ܠܒܪܛܝܢܘ (adj) Libertine

ACT 6:9

1530 ܠܕܝܩܝܐ Laodicea

COL 2:1, 4:13,15,16, 16 | REV 1:11, 3:14

1535 ܠܘܐܝܣ Lois

2 TM 1:5

1536 ܠܘܒܐ Libya

ACT 2:10

1538 ܠܘܕ Lydda

ACT 9:32,35,38

1539 ܠܘܕܝܐ Lydia

ACT 16:14,40

1542 ܠܘܛ Lot

LUK 17:28,29, 32 | 2 PT 2:7

1545 ܠܘܝ Levi (the tribe)

HEB 7:5,9 | REV 7:7

1549 ܠܘܝܐ (adj) Levite

LUK 10:32, JHN 1:19 | ACT 4:36, HEB 7:11

1546 ܠܘܝ Levi

see also (pn) Matthew, ܡܬܝ

MRK 2:14 | LUK 5:27,29

1547 ܠܘܝ Levi (Melchi's son)

LUK 3:24

1548 ܠܘܝ Levi (Simeon's son)

LUK 3:29

1553 ܠܘܣܛܪܐ Lystra

ACT 14:6,8,21; 16:1,2 | ACT 20:4; 2 TM 3:11

1554 ܠܘܣܝܘܣ (Claudius) Lysias

ACT 23:26 | ACT 24:7

1555 ܠܘܣܢܝܐ Lysanias

LUK 3:1

1556 ܠܘܩܐ Luke

COL 4:14; 2 TM 4:11 | PLM 24

1559 ܠܘܩܝܐ Lycia

ACT 27:5

1560 ܠܘܩܝܘܣ Lucius

may refer to more than one person

ACT 13:1 | ROM 16:21

1561 ܠܘܩܢܝܐ Lycaonia

ACT 14:6

1571 ܠܝܢܘܣ Linus

2 TM 4:21

1583 ܠܡܟ Lamech

LUK 3:36

1589 ܠܥܙܪ Lazarus (parable)

LUK 16:20,23, | LUK 16:24,25

1590 ܠܥܙܪ Lazarus (of Bethany)

JHN 11:1,2,5, 11,14, 43 | JHN 12:1,2,9, 10,17

1604 ܡܐܢܢ Menan

LUK 3:31

1606 ܡܐܬ Maath

LUK 3:26

1614 ܡܓܕܘ Magdala

MAT 15:39

1615 ܡܓܕܘ Armageddon

REV 16:16

1617 ܡܓܕܠܝܬܐ (adj) Magdelene

MAT 27:56,61; 28:1; MRK 15:40,47; 16:1,9 | LUK 8:2; 24:10; JHN 19:25; 20:1,18

1619 ܡܓܘܓ Magog

REV 20:8

1632 ܡܕܝܐ (adj) Mede

ACT 2:9

1633 ܡܕܝܢ Madian (Midian)

ACT 7:29

1648 ܡܗܠܠܐܝܠ Maleleel (Mahalaleel)

LUK 3:37

1658 ܡܘܣܝܐ Mysia

ACT 16:7,8

1661 ܡܘܪܐ Myra

ACT 27:5

1664 ܡܘܫܐ Moses

MAT 8:4
17:3,4
19:7,8
22:24
23:2
MRK 1:44
7:10
9:4,5
10:3,4
12:19,26
LUK 2:22
5:14
9:30,33,34
16:29,31
20:28,37
24:27,44
JHN 1:17,45
3:14
5:45,46,46
6:32
7:19,22,22,23
8:5
9:28,29
ACT 3:22
ACT 6:11,14
7:20,22,29,31,32,35,37,40,44
13:39
15:5,21
21:21
26:22
28:23
ROM 5:14
9:15
10:5,19
1 CO 9:9
10:2
2 CO 3:7,13,15
2 TM 3:8
HEB 3:2,3,5,16
7:14
8:5
9:19,19
10:28
11:23,24
12:21
JUD 9
REV 15:3

1703 ܡܛܬ Mattathias

LUK 3:26

1704 ܡܛܬܐ Mattatha

LUK 3:31

1705 ܡܛܬܬ Matthat

LUK 3:24

1708 ܡܝܛܘܠܝܢܐ Mitylene

ACT 20:14

1710 ܡܝܟܐܝܠ Michael

JUD 9 | REV 12:7

1712 ܡܠܝܛܐ Melita

ACT 28:1

1713 ܡܝܠܝܛܘܣ Miletus

ACT 20:15,17 | 2 TM 4:20

1743 ܡܠܝܐ Melea

LUK 3:31

1749 ܡܠܟܘ Malchus

JHN 18:10

1753 ܡܠܟܘܡ Moloch

ACT 7:43

1755 ܡܠܟܝ Melchi (Janna's son)

LUK 3:24

1756 ܡܠܟܝ Melchi (Addi's son)

LUK 3:28

1757 ܡܠܟܝܙܕܩ Melchisedec

HEB 5:6,10,11
6:20
HEB 7:1,10,11,15,17,21

1773 ܡܢܐܝܠ Manaen

ACT 13:1

1780 ܡܢܣܘܢ Mnason

ACT 21:16

1784 ܡܢܫܐ Manasses (Manasseh)

MAT 1:10,10

1785 ܡܢܫܐ Manasses (the tribe)

REV 7:6

1844 ܡܨܪܝܢ Egypt

MAT 2:13,14,15, 19
ACT 2:10
7:9,10,10, 11,12,15, 17,18,34, 34,36,39,
ACT 7:40
13:17
HEB 3:16
8:9
11:26,27
JUD 5
REV 11:8

1843 ܡܨܪܝܐ (adj) Egyptian

ACT 7:22,24,28
21:38
HEB 11:29

1847 ܡܩܕܘܢܝܐ Macedonia

ACT 16:9,10,12
18:5
19:21,22
20:1,3,6
27:2
ROM 15:26
1 CO 16:5
2 CO 1:16
11:9
PHL 4:15
1 TH 1:7,8
4:10
1 TM 1:3

1848 ܡܩܕܘܢܝܐ (adj) Macedonian

ACT 16:9
19:29
1 CO 16:5
2 CO 1:16
2 CO 2:13
7:5
8:1
9:2,4

1877 ܡܪܝܡ Mary (Jesus' mother)

MAT 1:16,18,20
2:11
13:55
MRK 6:3
LUK 1:27,30,34,
LUK 1:38,39,41, 42,46,56
2:5,16,19, 34
ACT 1:14

1878 ܡܪܝܡ Mary Magdalene

MAT 27:56,61
28:1
MRK 15:40,47
16:1,9
LUK 8:2
LUK 24:10
JHN 19:25
20:1,11,16, 18

1879 ܡܪܝܡ Mary (James and Joses' mother)

MAT 27:56,61
28:1
MRK 15:40,47
MRK 16:1
LUK 24:10

1880 ܡܪܝܡ Mary (Cleophas' wife)

JHN 19:25

1881 ܡܪܝܡ Mary (Lazarus' sister)

LUK 10:39,42
JHN 11:1,2,5, 19,20, 28,29,
JHN 11:31,32, 45
12:3

1882 ܡܪܝܡ Mary (John Mark's mother)

ACT 12:12

1883 ܡܪܝܡ Mary (Roman believer)

ROM 16:6

1893 ܡܪܩܘܣ Mark

surname of John, ܝܘܚܢܢ

ACT 12:12,25
15:37,39
COL 4:10
2 TM 4:11
PLM 24
1 PT 5:13

1896 ܡܪܬܐ Martha

LUK 10:38,40, 41,41
JHN 11:1,5,19, 20,21,
JHN 11:24,30, 39
12:2

ܡܫܝܚܐ Messiah, Christ, see main body under ܡܫܚ

1933 ܡܬܘܫܠܚ Mathuselah (Methuselah)
LUK 3:37

1937 ܡܬܝ Matthew
see also (pn) Levi, ܠܘܝ
MAT 9:9; 10:3 | MRK 3:18 | LUK 6:15 | ACT 1:13

1938 ܡܬܝܐ Matthias
ACT 1:23,26

1939 ܡܬܬܐ Matthat
LUK 3:29

1943 ܡܬܢ Matthan
MAT 1:15,15

1946 ܡܬܬܐ Mattathias
LUK 3:25

1947 ܢܐܝܢ Nain
LUK 7:11

1948 ܢܐܦܘܠܝܣ Neapolis
ACT 16:11

1949 ܢܩܘܠܐܝܛܐ (adj) Nicolatian
REV 2:6,15

1950 ܢܐܪܘܣ Nereus
ROM 16:15

1960 ܢܓܝ Nagge
LUK 3:25

1980 ܢܘܚ Noe (Noah)
MAT 24:37,38 | LUK 3:36; 17:26,27 | HEB 11:7 | 1 PT 3:20 | 2 PT 2:5

1988 ܢܘܡܦܐ Nymphas
COL 4:15

1989 ܢܘܢ Nun
HEB 4:8

1995 ܢܚܘܡ Naum (Nahum)
LUK 3:25

1996 ܢܚܘܪ Nachor (Nahor)
LUK 3:34

2001 ܢܚܫܘܢ Naasson (Nahshon)
MAT 1:4,4 | LUK 3:32

2007 ܢܓܪ Niger
surname of Simeon, ܫܡܥܘܢ
ACT 13:1

2012 ܢܝܢܘܝܐ (adj) Ninevite
MAT 12:41 | LUK 11:30,32

2013 ܢܝܩܕܡܘܣ Nicodemus
JHN 3:1,4,9; 7:50 | JHN 19:39

2014 ܢܝܩܠܐܘܣ Nicolas

ACT 6:5

2015 ܢܝܩܢܘܪ Nicanor

ACT 6:5

2016 ܢܝܩܦܘܠܝܣ Nicopolis

TIT 3:12

2043 ܢܥܡܢ Naaman

LUK 4:27

2055 ܢܦܬܚ Jephthah

HEB 11:32

2056 ܢܦܬܠܝ Nephthalim (Naphtali)

MAT 4:13,15 | REV 7:6

2065 ܢܨܪܬ Nazareth

MAT 2:23	LUK 2:4,39,51
4:13	4:16
21:11	24:19
MRK 1:9	JHN 1:45,46
LUK 1:26	ACT 10:38

2064 ܢܨܪܝܐ (adj) Nazarene

MAT 2:23	JHN 19:19
26:69,71	ACT 2:22
MRK 1:24	3:6
10:47	4:10
14:67	6:14
16:6	9:5
LUK 4:34	22:8
18:37	24:5
JHN 18:5,7	26:9,15

2078 ܢܪܝ Neri

LUK 3:27

2079 ܢܪܩܝܣܘܣ Narcissus

ROM 16:11

2083 ܢܬܢ Nathan

LUK 3:31

2084 ܢܬܢܐܝܠ Nathanael

JHN 1:45,46,47,48,49 | JHN 21:2

2089 ܣܐܪܘܢܐ Saron

ACT 9:35

2093 ܣܒܣܛܐ (adj) Augustan

ACT 27:1

2110 ܣܕܘܡ Sodom

MAT 10:15	ROM 9:29
11:23,24	2 PT 2:6
MRK 6:11	JUD 7
LUK 10:12	REV 11:8
17:29	

2134 ܣܘܢܛܝܟܐ Syntyche

PHL 4:2

2137 ܣܘܣܝܦܛܪܘܣ Sosipater

ROM 16:21

2138 ܣܘܣܬܢܝܣ Sosthenes

may refer to more than one person

ACT 18:17 | 1 CO 1:1

2143 ܣܘܦܛܪܘܣ Sopater

ACT 20:4

2146 ܣܘܪܝܐ Syria

cf main body Syria, ܐܪܡ

MAT 4:24
MRK 7:26
LUK 2:2
ACT 15:23,41
ACT 18:18
20:3
21:3
GAL 1:21

ܣܛܢܐ Satan, see main body

2161 ܫܡܥܘܢ Simon (the sorcerer)

ACT 8:9,13,18, | ACT 8:24

2165 ܣܝܢܝ Sinai (Sina)

ACT 7:30,38 | GAL 4:24,25

2177 ܣܟܪܝܘܛܐ Iscariot

see also (pn) Judas Iscariot, ܝܗܘܕܐ

MAT 10:4
26:14
MRK 3:19
14:10,43
LUK 6:16
LUK 22:3
JHN 6:71
13:2,26
14:22

2179 ܣܠܘܢܘܣ Silvanus (Silas)

see also (pn) Silas, ܫܝܠܐ

2 CO 1:19
1 TH 1:1
2 TH 1:1

2180 ܣܠܘܢܘܣ Silvanus

1 PT 5:12

2181 ܣܠܘܩܝܐ Seleucia

ACT 13:4

2182 ܣܠܡܘܢ Salmon

MAT 1:4,5 | LUK 3:32

2183 ܣܠܡܘܢܐ Salmone

ACT 27:7

2184 ܣܠܡܝܢܐ Salamis

ACT 13:5

2187 ܣܡܘܣ Samos

ACT 20:15

2188 ܣܡܘܪܢܐ Smyrna

REV 1:11 | REV 2:8

2189 ܣܡܘܬܪܐܩܝ Samothracia

ACT 16:11

2229 ܣܩܘܐ Sceva

ACT 19:14

2231 ܣܩܘܢܕܘܣ Secundus

ACT 20:4

2232 ܣܪܐ Sarah

ROM 4:19
9:9
HEB 11:11
1 PT 3:6

2235 ܣܪܓܝܘܣ ܦܘܠܘܣ

Sergius Paulus

ACT 13:7

2238 ܣܪܕܝܣ Sardis

REV 1:11 | REV 3:1,4

2239 ܣܪܘܓ Saruch (Serug)
LUK 3:35

2249 ܣܘܪܩܘܣܐ Syracuse
ACT 28:12

2258 ܥܒܕܘ Abaddon
REV 9:11

2263 ܥܒܪ Heber
LUK 3:35

ܥܒܪܝܐ Hebrew and deriv, see main body

2289 ܥܘܒܝܕ Obed
MAT 1:5,5 | LUK 3:32

2294 ܥܘܙܝܐ Ozias (Uzziah)
MAT 1:8,9

2323 ܥܙܘܪ Azor
MAT 1:13,14

2340 ܥܝܢ ܝܘܢ Aenon
JHN 3:23

2342 ܥܝܪ Er
LUK 3:28

2345 ܥܟܘ Ptolemais (Accho)
ACT 21:7

2368 ܥܡܐܘܣ Emmaus
LUK 24:13

2372 ܥܡܘܨ Amos
LUK 3:25

2373 ܥܡܘܪܐ Gomorrah
MAT 10:15, MRK 6:11, ROM 9:29 | 2 PT 2:6, JUD 7

2377 ܥܡܝܢܕܒ Aminadab
MAT 1:4,4 | LUK 3:33

2382 ܥܡܢܘܐܝܠ Emmanuel
MAT 1:23

2396 ܥܣܘ Esau
ROM 9:13, HEB 11:20 | HEB 12:16

2403 ܥܣܪܬ ܡܕܝܢ̈ܬܐ Decapolis
MAT 4:25, MRK 5:20 | MRK 7:31

ܥܪܒܝܐ Arabian, see under (pn) ܐܪܒܝܐ

2461 ܦܛܪܐ Patara
ACT 21:1

2476 ܦܗܣܛܘܣ (Porcius) Festus
ACT 24:27, 25:1,4,9,12,13,14,22, | ACT 25:23,24, 26:24,25,32, 27:1

2477 ܦܘܒܐ Phebe

ROM 16:1

2479 ܦܘܓܠܘܣ Phygellus

2 TM 1:15

2480 ܦܘܕܣ Pudens

2 TM 4:21

2482 ܦܘܛܝܐܠܘܣ Puteoli

ACT 28:13

2484 ܦܘܠܘܣ Paul

see also Saul, ܫܐܘܠ

ACT 13:9,13,16, 45,46, 50
14:9,9,11, 12,14, 19
15:2,2,12, 22,25, 35,36, 38,40
16:3,9,10, 14,17, 18,19, 25,28, 29,36, 37
17:2,4,10, 13,14, 15,16, 22,33
18:1,5,9, 12,14, 18,19
19:1,4,6,8, 9,11,13, 15,21, 26,29, 30
20:1,7,9, 10,13, 16
21:4,11,13, 18,19, 26,29, 30,32, 35,37, 39,40
ACT 22:22,25, 28,30
23:1,2,3,5, 6,10,11, 12,14, 16,16, 17,18, 20,24, 31,33
24:1,10,10, 23,24, 26,27
25:2,4,6,8, 9,10,14, 19,20, 23
26:1,1,24, 24,25, 29
27:1,3,9, 11,21, 24,31, 33,43
28:3,5,8, 15,16, 17,25, 30
ROM 1:1
1 CO 1:1,12,13, 13
3:4,5,22
16:21
2 CO 1:1
10:1
GAL 1:1
5:2
EPH 1:1
3:1
PHL 1:1
COL 1:1,23
4:18
1 TH 1:1
2:18
2 TH 1:1
2 TH 3:17
1 TM 1:1
2 TM 1:1
TIT 1:1
PLM 1,9,19
2 PT 3:15

2488 ܦܘܢܝܩܐ Phenicia

MRK 7:26
ACT 11:19
ACT 15:3
21:2

2489 ܦܘܢܝܩܣ Phenice

ACT 27:12

2491 ܦܘܦܠܝܘܣ Publius

ACT 28:7,8

ܦܛܝܪܐ Feast of Unleavened Bread see under ܦܛܝܪ

2515 ܦܛܡܘܣ Patmos

REV 1:9

2517 ܦܛܪܒܐ Patrobas

ROM 16:14

2518 ܦܛܪܘܣ Peter

see also (pn) Cephas, ܟܐܦܐ
see also (pn) Simon, ܫܡܥܘܢ

ACT 1:13
1 PT 1:1
2 PT 1:1

2519 ܦܝܠܕܠܦܝܐ Philadelphia

REV 1:11
REV 3:7

2522 ܦܝܠܛܘܣ (Pontius) Pilate

MAT 27:2,13,17,18,22,24,58,58,62,65
MRK 15:1,2,4,5,9,10,12,14,15,43,44
LUK 3:1
13:1
23:1,3,4,6,11,12,13,20,
LUK 23:24,52
JHN 18:29,31,33,35,37,38
19:1,4,5,6,8,10,12,13,15,19,21,22,31,38,38
ACT 3:13
4:27
13:28
1 TM 6:13

2523 ܦܝܠܝܛܘܣ Philetus

2 TM 2:17

2524 ܦܝܠܝܡܘܢ Philemon

PLM 1

2525 ܦܝܠܝܦܘܣ Philip (the apostle)

MAT 10:3
MRK 3:18
LUK 6:14
JHN 1:43,44,45,46,48
JHN 6:5,7
12:21,22,22
14:8,9
ACT 1:13

2526 ܦܝܠܝܦܘܣ Philip (Herod's son)

MAT 14:3
MRK 6:17
LUK 3:19

2527 ܦܝܠܝܦܘܣ Philip (the tetrarch)

LUK 3:1

2528 ܦܝܠܝܦܘܣ Philip (one of the seven)

ACT 6:5
8:5,12,13,26,29,31,
ACT 8:34,35,38,39,40
21:8

2529 ܦܝܠܝܦܘܣ Philippi

ACT 16:12
20:6
PHL 1:1
1 TH 2:2

2530 ܦܝܠܝܦܣܝܐ (adj) Philippian

PHL 4:15

2531 ܦܝܠܟܣ Felix

ACT 23:24,26
24:3,22,24,
ACT 24:25,27
25:14

2532 ܦܝܠܠܓܘܣ Philologus

ROM 16:15

2537 ܦܝܣܝܕܝܐ Pisidia

ACT 13:14
ACT 14:24

2547 ܦܠܓ Phalec (Peleg)

LUK 3:35

2550 ܦܠܓܘܢ Phlegon

ROM 16:14

2562 ܦܡܦܘܠܝܐ Pamphylia

ACT 2:10
13:13
14:24
ACT 15:38
27:5

2564 ܦܢܘܐܝܠ Phanuel

LUK 2:36

2565 ܦܢܛܘܣ Pontus

ACT 2:9
18:2
1 PT 1:1

2566 ܦܢܛܩܘܣܛܐ Pentecost

ACT 2:1; 20:16 | 1 CO 16:8

2581 ܦܦܘܣ Paphos

ACT 13:6,13

ܦܨܚܐ Feast of Passover, see main body under ܦܨܚ

2595 ܦܪܓܐ Perga

ACT 13:13,14 | ACT 14:25

2597 ܦܪܓܡܘܣ Pergamos

REV 1:11 | REV 2:12

2603 ܦܪܘܓܝܐ Phrygia

ACT 2:10; 16:6 | ACT 18:23

2611 ܦܪܛܘܢܛܘܣ Fortunatus

1 CO 16:17

2614 ܦܪܝܣܩܠܐ Priscilla

ACT 18:2,18,21,26; ROM 16:3 | 1 CO 16:19; 2 TM 4:19

ܦܪܝܫܐ Pharisee, see main body under ܦܪܫ

2619 ܦܪܟܪܘܣ Prochorus

ACT 6:5

2620 ܦܪܡܢܐ Parmenas

ACT 6:5

2626 ܦܪܣܣ Persis

ROM 16:12

2629 ܦܪܥܘܢ Pharaoh

ACT 7:10,13,21; ROM 9:17 | HEB 11:24

2631 ܦܪܨ Phares

MAT 1:3,3 | LUK 3:33

2638 ܦܪܬ Euphrates

REV 9:14 | REV 16:12

2639 ܦܪܬܘܝܐ (adj) Parthian

ACT 2:9

2666 ܨܒܐܘܬ (w/ ܡܪܝܐ) Lord of hosts

ROM 9:29 | JAM 5:4

2678 ܨܗܝܘܢ Sion (Zion)

MAT 21:5; JHN 12:15; ROM 9:33; 11:26 | HEB 12:22; 1 PT 2:6; REV 14:1

2684 ܨܘܪ Tyre

MAT 11:21,22; 15:21; MRK 3:8; 7:24,31 | LUK 6:17; 10:13,14; ACT 21:3,7

2688 ܨܘܪܝܐ (adj) man of Tyre

ACT 12:20

2699 ܨܝܕܢ Sidon

MAT	11:21,22	LUK	4:26
	15:21		6:17
MRK	3:8		10:13,14
	7:24,31	ACT	27:3

2700 ܨܝܕܢܝܐ (adj) man of Sidon

ACT 12:20

2729 ܨܪܦܬ Sarepta

LUK 4:26

2731 ܩܐܝܢ Cain

HEB	11:4	JUD	11
1 JN	3:12		

2753 ܩܕܪܘܢ Cedron (Kidron)

JHN 18:1

2755 ܩܘ Coos

ACT 21:1

2757 ܩܘܐܪܛܘܣ Quartus

ROM 16:23

2760 ܩܠܘܕܐ Clauda

ACT 27:16

2768 ܩܘܠܘܣܣ Colosse

COL 1:2

2774 ܩܘܣܡ Cosam

LUK 3:28

2776 ܩܘܦܪܘܣ Cyprus

ACT	4:36	ACT	15:39
	11:19,20		21:3,16
	13:4		27:4

2779 ܩܘܪܚ Core

JUD 11

2782 ܩܘܪܝܢܐ Cyrene

ACT	2:10,10	ACT	13:1
	11:20		

2784 ܩܘܪܝܢܝܐ (adj) Cyrenian

MAT	27:32	LUK	23:26
MRK	15:21	ACT	6:9

2783 ܩܘܪܝܢܘܣ Cyrenius, Quirinius

LUK 2:2

2785 ܩܘܪܢܬܘܣ Corinth

ACT	18:1,11	2 CO	1:1,23
	19:1	2 TM	4:20
1 CO	1:2		

2786 ܩܘܪܢܬܝܐ (adj) Corinthian

ACT	18:8	2 CO	6:11

2787 ܩܘܪܢܠܝܘܣ Cornelius

ACT	10:1,3,17,	ACT	10:31
	22,24,		11:11
	25,30,		

2800 ܩܛܢܐ Cana

JHN	2:1,11	JHN	21:2
	4:46		

2810 ܩܝܠܝܩܝܐ Cilicia

ACT	6:9	ACT	21:39
	15:23,41		22:3

ACT 23:34, 27:5 | GAL 1:21

2816 ܩܝܢܢ Cainan (Enos' son)

LUK 3:37

2817 ܩܝܢܢ Cainan (Arphaxad's son)

LUK 3:36

2820 ܩܝܦܐ Caiaphas

MAT 26:3,57
MRK 14:53
LUK 3:2
JHN 11:49
JHN 18:13,14, 24,28
ACT 4:6

2821 ܩܝܫ Cis (Kish)

ACT 13:21

2826 ܩܠܘܕܝܐ Claudia

2 TM 4:21

2827 ܩܠܘܕܝܘܣ Claudius (emperor)

ACT 11:28 | ACT 18:2

2829 ܩܠܝܘܦܐ Cleopas

LUK 24:18

2830 ܩܠܝܘܦܐ Cleophas

JHN 19:25

2832 ܩܠܝܡܝܣ Clement

PHL 4:3

2843 ܩܢܕܩ Candace

ACT 8:27

2850 ܩܢܝܕܘܣ Cnidus

ACT 27:7

2853 ܩܢܟܪܐܘܣ Cenchrea

ACT 18:18 | ROM 16:1

2854 ܩܢܢܝܐ (adj) Canaanite

MAT 10:4 | MRK 3:18

2857 ܩܣܪ Caesar

MAT 22:17,21, 21,21
MRK 12:14,16, 17,17
LUK 2:1
3:1
20:22,24, 25,25
23:2
JHN 19:12,12, 15
ACT 11:28
17:7
18:2
25:8,10,11, 12,12, 21,21, 25,26
26:32
27:1,24
28:19
PHL 4:22

2858 ܩܣܪܝܐ Caesarea

ACT 8:40
9:30
10:1,24
11:11
12:19
ACT 18:22
21:8,16
23:23,33
25:1,4,6, 13

2859 ܩܣܪܝܐ ܕܦܝܠܝܦܘܣ

Caesarea Philippi

MAT 16:13 | MRK 8:27

2863 ܩܦܕܘܩܝܐ Cappadocia

ACT 2:9 | 1 PT 1:1

2878 ܩܪܛܐ Crete

ACT 2:11, 27:7,12,13, | ACT 27:21 | TIT 1:5,12

2882 ܩܪܝܣܦܘܣ Crispus

ACT 18:8 | 1 CO 1:14

2883 ܩܪܝܣܩܘܣ Crescens

2 TM 4:10

2892 ܩܪܦܘܣ Carpus

2 TM 4:13

2929 ܪܓܝܘܢ Rhegium

ACT 28:13

ܪܗܘܡܐ Rome and deriv see main body

2959 ܪܘܒܝܠ Reuben (the tribe)

REV 7:5

2962 ܪܘܕܐ Rhoda

ACT 12:13

2963 ܪܘܕܘܣ Rhodes

ACT 21:1

2984 ܪܘܦܘܣ Rufus

may refer to more than one person

MRK 15:21 | ROM 16:13

2989 ܪܚܒ Rahab

MAT 1:5 | HEB 11:31 | JAM 2:25

2990 ܪܚܒܥܡ Roboam (Rehoboam)

MAT 1:7,7

2992 ܪܚܝܠ Rachel

MAT 2:18

3025 ܪܡܬܐ Arimathaea

MAT 27:57 | MRK 15:43 | LUK 23:50 | JHN 19:38

3027 ܪܡܬܐ Rama (Ramah)

MAT 2:18

3031 ܪܝܣܐ Rhesa

LUK 3:27

3038 ܪܥܘܬ Ruth

MAT 1:5

3050 ܪܦܢ Remphan (Rephan)

ACT 7:43

3052 ܪܦܩܐ Rebecca (Rebekah)

ROM 9:10

3075 ܫܐܘܠ Saul

see also (pn) Paul, ܦܘܠܘܣ

ACT 7:58, 8:1,3, 9:1,4,4,8, 11,17,22, 24 | ACT 11:25,30, 12:25, 13:1,2,7,9, 22:7,7,13, 26:14,14

3076 ܫܐܘܠ Saul (son of Kish)

ACT 13:21

ܫܒܬܐ Sabbath, see main body (ܫܒ), ܫܒܬܐ

3157 ܫܘܫܢ Susanna

LUK 8:3

ܫܝܘܠ sheol, hell, see main body

3179 ܫܝܠܐ Silas

see also (pn) Silvanus, ܣܠܘܢܘܣ

ACT 15:22,27, 32,40
16:19,25, 29
ACT 17:4,10,14, 15
18:5

3180 ܫܝܠܘܚܐ Siloam

LUK 13:4 | JHN 9:7,11

3181 ܫܝܡ Sem (Shem)

LUK 3:36

3188 ܫܝܬ Seth

LUK 3:38

3192 ܫܟܝܡ Sychem

ACT 7:16

3195 ܫܟܪ Sychar

JHN 4:5

3203 ܫܠܘܡ Salome

MRK 15:40 | MRK 16:1

3204 ܫܠܚ Sala

LUK 3:35

3213 ܫܠܝܡ Salem

HEB 7:1,2

3214 ܫܠܝܡ Salim

JHN 3:23

3215 ܫܠܝܡܘܢ Solomon

MAT 1:6,7
6:29
12:42,42
LUK 11:31,31
12:27
JHN 10:23
ACT 3:11
5:12
7:47

3221 ܫܠܬܐܝܠ Salathiel

MAT 1:12,12 | LUK 3:27

3224 ܫܡܘܐܝܠ Samuel

ACT 3:24
13:20
HEB 11:32

3234 ܫܡܥܘܢ Simon (Peter)

see also (pn) Cephas, ܟܐܦܐ

see also (pn) Peter, ܦܛܪܘܣ

MAT 4:18
8:14
10:2
15:15
16:16,17
17:25,26
26:58
MRK 1:16,29,30, 36
3:16
5:37
8:29,33
11:21
MRK 14:37,54, 66,72
LUK 4:38,38
5:3,4,5,8, 10,10
6:14
8:45,51
9:20,28,32, 33
12:41
18:28
22:31,31, 33,34,

LUK 22:54,55,61,62; 24:12,34
JHN 1:40,41,42,44; 6:8,68; 13:6,6,8,9,24,36,37; 18:10,15,16,16,17,18,25,26,27; 20:2,3,4,6; 21:2,3,7,11,15,15,16,17,20
ACT 1:15; 2:14,37,38; 3:1,3,4,6,11,12; 4:8,13,19; 5:3,8,9,15,29; 8:14,20,25; 9:32,34,38,39,40,40; 10:5,9,13,14,17,18,19,21,23,25,26,32,34,44,46; 11:2,4,7,13; 12:3,5,6,11,14,14,16,18; 15:7,14
2 PT 1:1

3235 ܫܡܥܘܢ Simon (Zelotes)

MAT 10:4 | MRK 3:18 | LUK 6:15 | ACT 1:13

3236 ܫܡܥܘܢ Simon (Jesus' brother)

MAT 13:55 | MRK 6:3

3237 ܫܡܥܘܢ Simon (the leper)

MAT 26:6 | MRK 14:3

3238 ܫܡܥܘܢ Simon (the Cyrenian)

MAT 27:32 | MRK 15:21 | LUK 23:26

3239 ܫܡܥܘܢ Simon (the Pharisee)

LUK 7:40,43,44

3240 ܫܡܥܘܢ Simon (J. Iscariot's father)

JHN 6:71 | JHN 13:2,26

3241 ܫܡܥܘܢ Simon (the tanner)

ACT 9:43 | ACT 10:6,17,32

3242 ܫܡܥܘܢ Simeon

LUK 2:25,34

3243 ܫܡܥܘܢ Simeon (the tribe)

REV 7:7

3244 ܫܡܥܘܢ Simeon (Juda's son)

LUK 3:30

3245 ܫܡܥܘܢ Simeon (called Niger)

ACT 13:1

3246 ܫܡܥܝ Semei

LUK 3:26

3248 ܫܡܪܝܢ Samaria

JHN 4:7 | ACT 9:31

3247 ܫܡܪܝܐ (adj) Samaritan

MAT 10:5
LUK 9:52; 10:33; 17:11,16
JHN 4:4,5,9,9,9,39,40; 8:48
ACT 1:8; 8:1,5,9,14,25; 15:3

3251 ܫܡܫܘܢ Samson

HEB 11:32

3267 ܫܦܝܪܐ Sapphira

ACT 5:1

3310 ܬܐܘܛܝܪܐ Thyatira

ACT 16:14
REV 1:11
REV 2:18,24

3311 ܬܐܘܡܐ Thomas

MAT 10:3
MRK 3:18
LUK 6:15
JHN 11:16
14:5
JHN 20:24,26,
27,28
21:2
ACT 1:13

3312 ܬܐܘܦܝܠܐ Theophilus

LUK 1:3
ACT 1:1

3328 ܬܕܝ Thaddaeus

surname of Lebbaeus, ܠܒܝ

MAT 10:3
MRK 3:18

3340 ܬܘܕܐ Theudas

ACT 5:36

3406 ܬܡܪ Thamar (Tamar)

MAT 1:3

3415 ܬܣܘܣ Assos

ACT 20:13,14

3416 ܬܣܠܘܢܝܩܐ Thessalonica

ACT 17:1,11,13
27:2
PHL 4:16
2 TM 4:10

3417 ܬܣܠܘܢܝܩܝܐ (adj)
Thessalonian

ACT 20:4
1 TH 1:1
2 TH 1:1

3432 ܬܪܚ Thara (Terah)

LUK 3:34

Index

Pg/Col	Pronunciation	Word	No	Pg/Col	Pronunciation	Word	No
17a	'ulṣānā	ܐܘܠܨܢܐ	48	6a	'aḥā	ܐܚܐ	73
18a	'umānā	ܐܘܡܢܐ	49	7a	'eḥad	ܐܚܕ	74
18a	'umānuṯā	ܐܘܡܢܘܬܐ	50	7a	'aḥuṯā	ܐܚܘܬܐ	75
17b	'umṯā	ܐܘܡܬܐ	51	394b	'āḥāz	ܐܚܙ	76
4b	'on	ܐܘܢ	52	8a	'aḥīḏ 'kul	ܐܚܝܕ ܟܠ	77
4b	'awānā	ܐܘܢܐ	53	7a	(')ḥəyānā	ܐܚܝܢܐ	78
4b	'ewangelīwān	ܐܘܢܓܠܝܘܢ	54	9a	'auḥar (aph)	ܐܚܪ	79
				8b	(')ḥərāyā	ܐܚܪܝܐ	80
394a	'eunīqī	ܐܘܢܝܩܐ	55	8b	(')ḥərınā	ܐܚܪܝܢܐ	81
31a	'auṣrā	ܐܘܨܪܐ	56	9a	(')ḥərānya'īṯ	ܐܚܪܢܝܐܝܬ	82
4b	'euqīnā	ܐܘܩܝܢܐ	57	146a	'īḏā	ܐܝܕܐ	83
394a	'urbanāus	ܐܘܪܒܢܘܣ	58	9b	'ıyu	ܐܝܘ	84
31b	'urdə'ā	ܐܘܪܕܥܐ	59	394b	'ıyauḇ	ܐܝܘܒ	85
394a	'ēurus	ܐܘܪܘܣ	60	5a	'īzgadā	ܐܝܙܓܕܐ	86
31b	'urḥā	ܐܘܪܚܐ	61	394b	'īṭuriya	ܐܝܛܘܪܝܐ	87
394a	'urıyā	ܐܘܪܝܐ	62	394b	'īṭalıya	ܐܝܛܠܝܐ	88
32a	'uryā	ܐܘܪܝܐ	63	395a	'īṭalıya	ܐܝܛܠܝܐ	89
32a	'uraıṯā	ܐܘܪܝܬܐ	64	395a	'īṭalīqī	ܐܝܛܠܝܩܐ	90
32a	'urkā	ܐܘܪܟܐ	65	9b	'aıḵ	ܐܝܟ	91
32b	'ur'ā	ܐܘܪܥܐ	66	10a	'aıkā	ܐܝܟܐ	92
394a	'eurāqlīdāun	ܐܘܪܩܠܝܕܘܢ	67	10b	'aıkanā	ܐܝܟܢܐ	93
				395a	'īl	ܐܝܠ	94
346a	'urqa'ṯā	ܐܘܪܩܥܬܐ	68	10b	'aılā	ܐܝܠܐ	95
394a	'urıšlem	ܐܘܪܫܠܡ	69	10b	'īlānā	ܐܝܠܢܐ	96
33b	'uša'nā	ܐܘܫܥܢܐ	70	11a	'aımekā	ܐܝܡܟܐ	97
394b	'azāuṭāus	ܐܙܘܛܘܣ	71	157a	'īmāmā	ܐܝܡܡܐ	98
5a	'ezal	ܐܙܠ	72	11a	'īn	ܐܝܢ	99

Pg/Col	Pronunciation	Word	No
11a	'aınā	ܐܝܢܐ	100
395a	'yasāun	ܐܝܣܘܢ	101
395a	'īsḥāq	ܐܝܣܚܩ	102
395a	'īsākār	ܐܝܣܟܪ	103
395a	'īsrā'eil	ܐܝܣܪܐܝܠ	104
395b	'īsrālāyā	ܐܝܣܪܠܝܐ	105
11b	'īqī	ܐܝܩܝܐ	106
395b	'īqanāun	ܐܝܩܢܘܢ	107
160a	'īqārā	ܐܝܩܪܐ	108
395b	'īrāupāulīs	ܐܝܪܘܦܘܠܝܣ	109
395b	'īrīḥu	ܐܝܪܝܚܘ	110
395b	'īšaı	ܐܝܫܝ	111
11b	'īṯ	ܐܝܬ	112
12b	'īṯuṯā	ܐܝܬܘܬܐ	113
395b	'aḵa'ya	ܐܟܐܝܐ	114
395b	'aḵa'yıqāus	ܐܟܐܝܩܘܣ	115
12b	'āḵeḏnā	ܐܟܕܢܐ	116
13b	'āḵulā	ܐܟܘܠܐ	117
12b	'aḵwāṯ	ܐܟܘܬ	118
12b	'aḵzᵊnā	ܐܟܙܢܐ	119
13a	'aḵḥᵊḏā	ܐܟܚܕܐ	120
395b	'aḵīn	ܐܟܝܢ	121
14b	'aḵīpa'īṯ	ܐܟܝܦܐܝܬ	122
13a	'eḵal	ܐܟܠ	123
13b	'āḵel qarṣā	ܐܟܠ ܩܪܨܐ	124
13b	'āḵel qarṣā	ܐܟܠ ܩܪܨܐ	125
14a	'āḵlā	ܐܟܠܐ	126
14a	'āḵlāus	ܐܟܠܘܣ	127
14b	'eḵam	ܐܟܡ	128
175b	'aḵsᵊnāyā	ܐܟܣܢܝܐ	129
14b	'eḵap̄	ܐܟܦ	130
14b	'aḵārā	ܐܟܪܐ	131
12b	'aḵṯā	ܐܟܬܐ	132
14b	'elā	ܐܠܐ	133
15a	'elā	ܐܠܐ	134
15a	'alāhā	ܐܠܗܐ	135
16a	'alāhuṯā	ܐܠܗܘܬܐ	136
16a	'alāhāyā	ܐܠܗܝܐ	137
16a	'alāhṯā	ܐܠܗܬܐ	138
16a	'elu	ܐܠܘ	139
396a	'elumāus	ܐܠܘܡܘܣ	140
396a	'ālumpa	ܐܠܘܡܦܐ	141
17a	'āluṣā	ܐܠܘܨܐ	142
396a	'elurīqāun	ܐܠܘܪܝܩܘܢ	143
15a	'elıyā	ܐܠܝܐ	144
396a	'elyā	ܐܠܝܐ	145
396a	'elīyuḏ	ܐܠܝܘܕ	146
396a	'elī'āzar	ܐܠܝܥܙܪ	147
396a	'elī'āzār	ܐܠܝܥܙܪ	148
17a	'alīṣā	ܐܠܝܨܐ	149
396a	'elıyāqīm	ܐܠܝܩܝܡ	150
396a	'elīšᵊḇa'	ܐܠܝܫܒܥ	151
396b	'elıša'	ܐܠܝܫܥ	152

Pg/Col	Pronunciation	Word	No
396b	'aleksandrāus	ܐܠܟܣܢܕܪܘܣ	153
396b	'aleksandrıya	ܐܠܟܣܢܕܪܝܐ	154
396b	'aleksandrıya	ܐܠܟܣܢܕܪܝܐ	155
396b	'elmuḏāḏ	ܐܠܡܘܕܕ	156
396b	'alanāyē	ܐܠܢܝܐ	157
16b	'ālap̄	ܐܠܦ	158
16b	'alp̄ā	ܐܠܦܐ	159
16b	'elp̄ā	ܐܠܦܐ	160
16b	'elp̄ārā	ܐܠܦܪܐ	161
16b	'elaṣ	ܐܠܨ	162
17b	'emā	ܐܡܐ	163
396b	'amun	ܐܡܘܢ	164
22b	'amuṯısṭāus	ܐܡܘܬܣܛܘܣ	165
18a	'amīn	ܐܡܝܢ	166
18a	'amīnā	ܐܡܝܢܐ	167
18a	'amīnā'īṯ	ܐܡܝܢܐܝܬ	168
18a	'eṯe'men (ethpe)	ܐܡܢ	169
396b	'emp̄īpwālīs	ܐܡܦܝܦܘܠܝܣ	170
396b	'ampēlāus	ܐܡܦܠܐܘܣ	171
20a	'emar	ܐܡܪ	172
22b	'emrā	ܐܡܪܐ	173
17b	'amṯā	ܐܡܬܐ	174
17b	'amṯā	ܐܡܬܐ	175
22b	'emaṯı	ܐܡܬܝ	176
22b	'en	ܐܢ	177
23a	'enā	ܐܢܐ	178
396b	ānīsīp̄ārāus	ܐܢܝܣܝܦܪܐܘܣ	179
23a	'endein	ܐܢܕܝܢ	180
397a	'andrēwās	ܐܢܕܪܐܘܣ	181
397a	'andrāunīqāus	ܐܢܕܪܘܢܝܩܘܣ	182
24b	'anusıya	ܐܢܘܣܝܐ	183
397a	'ānuš	ܐܢܘܫ	184
24b	'enaḥ	ܐܢܚ	185
397a	'anṭiyāukī	ܐܢܛܝܘܟܝ	186
397a	'anṭıyāukī	ܐܢܛܝܘܟܝ	187
397a	'anṭᵊyukāyā	ܐܢܛܝܘܟܝܐ	188
24b	'anṭīkrīsṭāus	ܐܢܛܝܟܪܝܣܛܘܣ	189
397a	'anṭīpaṭrāus	ܐܢܛܝܦܛܪܘܣ	190
397a	'anīyas	ܐܢܝܣ	191
24b	'ananqī	ܐܢܢܩܐ	192
24b	'enas	ܐܢܣ	193
397a	'ānisīmāus	ܐܢܝܣܝܡܘܣ	194
25a	(')nāšā	ܐܢܫܐ	195
25a	(')nāšuṯā	ܐܢܫܘܬܐ	196
25b	'a(n)t	ܐܢܬ	197

Pg/Col	Pronunciation	Word	No
26b	'anṯupaṭāus	ܐܢܬܘܦܛܘܣ	198
26a	'a(n)ttā	ܐܢܬܬܐ	199
397a	'āsā	ܐܣܐ	200
27a	'asī (pa)	ܐܣܐ	201
27b	'esāḏē	ܐܣܕ̈ܐ	202
27b	'āsoṭā	ܐܣܘܛܐ	203
27b	'āsuṭuṯā	ܐܣܘܛܘܬܐ	204
397b	'āsunqriṭāus	ܐܣܘܢܩܪܝܛܘܣ	205
29a	'asurā	ܐܣܘܪܐ	206
29b	'asuryā	ܐܣܘܪܝܐ	207
27b	'esṭᵊdā	ܐܣܛܕܐ	208
27b	'esṭᵊwā	ܐܣܛܘܐ	209
397b	'esṭāu'īqu	ܐܣܛܘܐܝܩܘ	210
27b	'esṭuksā	ܐܣܛܘܟܣܐ	211
28a	'esṭumkā	ܐܣܛܘܡܟܐ	212
397b	'esṭaḵāus	ܐܣܛܟܘܣ	213
28a	'esṭᵊlā	ܐܣܛܠܐ	214
28a	'esṭasīs	ܐܣܛܣܝܣ	215
397b	'esṭep̄anā	ܐܣܛܦܢܐ	216
397b	'esṭap̄anāus	ܐܣܛܦܢܘܣ	217
28a	'esṭraṭıya	ܐܣܛܪܛܝܐ	218
28a	'esṭraṭīgā	ܐܣܛܪܛܝܓܐ	219
28a	'esṭraṭıyuṭā	ܐܣܛܪܛܝܘܛܐ	220
28a	'esṭranıya	ܐܣܛܪܢܝܐ	221
397b	'asıya	ܐܣܝܐ	222
26b	'āsyā	ܐܣܝܐ	223
27a	'āsyuṯā	ܐܣܝܘܬܐ	224
29a	'asīrā	ܐܣܝܪܐ	225
28a	'eskulī	ܐܣܟܘܠܐ	226
28a	'eskīmā	ܐܣܟܝܡܐ	227
28b	'esan	ܐܣܢ	228
28b	'esp̄ugā	ܐܣܦܘܓܐ	229
28b	'espuqlāṭᵊrā	ܐܣܦܘܩܠܛܪܐ	230
28b	'espīrā	ܐܣܦܝܪܐ	231
397b	'aspanıya	ܐܣܦܢܝܐ	232
28b	'espes	ܐܣܦܣ	233
28b	'espᵊrīḏā	ܐܣܦܪܝܕܐ	234
28b	'esar	ܐܣܪ	235
29b	'asārā	ܐܣܪܐ	236
29b	'esārā	ܐܣܪܐ	237
27b	'esṯā	ܐܣܬܐ	238
29b	'estīrā	ܐܣܬܝܪܐ	239
262a	'a'īpā'īṯ	ܐܥܝܦܐܝܬ	240
29b	'e'ap̄	ܐܥܦ	241
29b	'ạ'p̄ā	ܐܥܦܐ	242
29b	'āp̄	ܐܦ	243
30b	'apē (pl)	ܐܦ̈ܐ	244
31a	'ap̄uḏā	ܐܦܘܕܐ	245
397b	'apāulāunıya	ܐܦܘܠܘܢܝܐ	246
397b	'apıya	ܐܦܝܐ	247

Pg/Col	Pronunciation	Word	No
		ܐܦܝܘܣ ܦܘܪܘܣ	248
398a	'apıyāus p̄āurāus		
31a	'epīṭrupā	ܐܦܝܛܪܘܦܐ	249
31a	'epīsqupā	ܐܦܝܣܩܘܦܐ	250
398a	'epīqurāus	ܐܦܝܩܘܪܘܣ	251
398a	'apelī	ܐܦܠܐ	252
398a	'apālu	ܐܦܠܘ	253
30b	'āp̄en	ܐܦܢ	254
398a	'epeneṭāus	ܐܦܢܛܘܣ	255
31a	'ap̄suntā	ܐܦܣܘܢܬܐ	256
398a	'ep̄esāus	ܐܦܣܘܣ	257
398a	'ep̄esāyā	ܐܦܣܝܐ	258
31a	'apsentıyāun	ܐܦܣܢܬܝܘܢ	259
398a	'epap̄ra	ܐܦܦܪܐ	260
398b	'epap̄rāudīṭāus	ܐܦܦܪܘܕܝܛܘܣ	261
398b	'āp̄reim	ܐܦܪܝܡ	262
31a	'āparsānā	ܐܦܪܣܢܐ	263
398b	'aqulas	ܐܩܘܠܣ	264
398b	'arabıya	ܐܪܒܝܐ	265
329b	'arba'	ܐܪܒܥ	266
329b	'arbᵊ'īn	ܐܪܒܥܝܢ	267
329b	'arba'mā	ܐܪܒܥܡܐ	268
329b	'arba'sar	ܐܪܒܥܣܪ	269
31b	'argᵊwānā	ܐܪܓܘܢܐ	270
31b	'ardıklā	ܐܪܕܝܟܠܐ	271

Pg/Col	Pronunciation	Word	No
398b	'areṭāus	ܐܪܛܘܣ	272
398b	'arṭema	ܐܪܛܡܐ	273
398b	'arṭemīs	ܐܪܛܡܝܣ	274
32a	'aryā	ܐܪܝܐ	275
		ܐܪܝܘܣ ܦܓܘܣ	276
398b	'arıyāus pağāus		
32a	'arīḵ	ܐܪܝܟ	277
32a	'eraḵ	ܐܪܟ	278
32a	'arkā	ܐܪܟܐ	279
32a	'arkonā	ܐܪܟܘܢܐ	280
398b	'arkīpwās	ܐܪܟܝܦܘܣ	281
399a	'arḵela'āus	ܐܪܟܠܐܘܣ	282
399a	'ārām	ܐܪܡ	283
32a	'ārām	ܐܪܡ	284
32b	'armā'īṯ	ܐܪܡܐܝܬ	285
32b	'armāyā	ܐܪܡܝܐ	286
399a	'eramya	ܐܪܡܝܐ	287
342b	'armaltā	ܐܪܡܠܬܐ	288
32b	'armenāun	ܐܪܡܢܘܢ	289
399a	'arisṭāḇwālāus	ܐܪܣܛܒܘܠܘܣ	290
399a	'erastāus	ܐܪܣܛܘܣ	291
399a	'arisṭarḵāus	ܐܪܣܛܪܟܘܣ	292
32b	'era'	ܐܪܥ	293
32b	'ar'ā	ܐܪܥܐ	294
399a	'ar'u	ܐܪܥܘ	295

Pg/Col	Pronunciation	Word	No
33b	'ar'ānāyā	ܐܪܥܢܝܐ	296
399a	'arp̄aksar	ܐܪܦܟܫܪ	297
33b	'ešaḏ	ܐܫܕ	298
399a	'ašīr	ܐܫܝܪ	299
399b	'eša'ya	ܐܫܥܝܐ	300
33b	'ešāṯā	ܐܫܬܐ	301
380a	'eštā	ܐܫܬܐ	302
381a	'eštup̄	ܐܫܬܘܦ	303
34a	'eštᵊqaḏ(ı)	ܐܫܬܘܩܕ	304
34a	'āṯā	ܐܬܐ	305
34a	'eṯā	ܐܬܐ	306
35b	'aṯunā	ܐܬܘܢܐ	307
34a	'āṯuṯā	ܐܬܘܬܐ	308
387b	'eṯmāl(ı)	ܐܬܡܠ	309
35b	'aṯānā	ܐܬܢܐ	310
399b	'aṯıneus	ܐܬܝܢܣ	311
399b	'aṯınāyā	ܐܬܝܢܝܐ	312
35b	'aṯrā	ܐܬܪܐ	313
		ܒ	314
	not included in concordance		
37a	bīrā	ܒܐܪܐ	315
37a	bēš	ܒܐܫ	316
399b	bāḇel	ܒܒܠ	317
59a	bᵊgau	ܒܓܘ	318
62a	bᵊgleyā	ܒܓܠܝܐ	319
38a	bagen (pa)	ܒܓܢ	320
38a	bᵊgen	ܒܓܢ	321
38a	bᵊḏā	ܒܕܐ	322
38a	beḏyā	ܒܕܝܐ	323
38a	bᵊḏaq	ܒܕܩ	324
38b	bᵊḏar	ܒܕܪ	325
38b	bᵊhel	ܒܗܠ	326
38b	šaḇhar (shaph)	ܒܗܪ	327
38b	bahrā	ܒܗܪܐ	328
39a	bᵊheṯ	ܒܗܬ	329
39b	behtᵊṯā	ܒܗܬܬܐ	330
40b	buḥrānā	ܒܘܚܪܢܐ	331
42a	buyā'ā	ܒܘܝܐܐ	332
44a	buḵrā	ܒܘܟܪܐ	333
44b	buḵruṯā	ܒܘܟܪܘܬܐ	334
39b	bulē	ܒܘܠܐ	335
39b	buleuṭī	ܒܘܠܘܛܐ	336
46b	busāmā	ܒܘܣܡܐ	337
39b	buṣā	ܒܘܨܐ	338
50b	buqyā	ܒܘܩܝܐ	339
39b	bār (pe 3sm)	ܒܘܪ	340
39b	burā	ܒܘܪܐ	341
54a	burkā	ܒܘܪܟܐ	342
54a	burkᵊṯā	ܒܘܪܟܬܐ	343
55a	bursāyā	ܒܘܪܣܝܐ	344
43b	baṯ (pe 3sm)	ܒܘܬ	345
40a	baz	ܒܙ	346
40a	bazaḥ (pa)	ܒܙܚ	347
40a	bezḥā	ܒܙܚܐ	348

Pg/Col	Pronunciation	Word	No
40a	bᵊza‘	ܒܙܥ	349
40a	bez‘ā	ܒܙܥܐ	350
40a	bezṯā	ܒܙܬܐ	351
40b	bᵊhar	ܒܗܪ	352
144a	bᵊṭušyā	ܒܛܘܫܝܐ	353
41a	baṭīlā	ܒܛܝܠܐ	354
41a	bᵊṭīlā’īṯ	ܒܛܝܠܐܝܬ	355
41a	bᵊṭīluṯā	ܒܛܝܠܘܬܐ	356
40b	bᵊṭel	ܒܛܠ	357
41a	baṭālā	ܒܛܠܐ	358
41b	baṭālā’īṯ	ܒܛܠܐܝܬ	359
41b	bᵊṭen	ܒܛܢ	360
41b	baṭnā	ܒܛܢܐ	361
41b	baṭnᵊṯā	ܒܛܢܬܐ	362
42a	baya (pa)	ܒܝܐ	363
42b	bīm	ܒܝܡ	364
42b	bainai	ܒܝܢܝ	365
37a	bīšā	ܒܝܫܐ	366
37b	bīšā’īṯ	ܒܝܫܐܝܬ	367
37b	bīšuṯā	ܒܝܫܘܬܐ	368
43b	beiṯ ’asīre	ܒܝܬ ܐܣܝܪܐ	369
403b	beiṯ herāudes	ܒܝܬ ܗܪܘܕܣ	370
399b	beiṯ ḥesdā	ܒܝܬ ܚܣܕܐ	371
399b	beiṯ lᵊḥem	ܒܝܬ ܠܚܡ	372
399b	beiṯ nahrīn	ܒܝܬ ܢܗܪܝܢ	373
399b	beiṯ ‘nyā	ܒܝܬ ܥܢܝܐ	374
400a	beiṯ pāgē	ܒܝܬ ܦܓܐ	375
400a	beiṯ ṣayāḏā	ܒܝܬ ܨܝܕܐ	376
42b	baitā	ܒܝܬܐ	377
44a	bᵊḵā	ܒܟܐ	378
44a	beḵyā	ܒܟܝܐ	379
44b	bᵊkīrāyā	ܒܟܝܪܝܐ	380
175a	bᵊḵesyā	ܒܟܣܝܐ	381
44a	bᵊḵar	ܒܟܪ	382
44a	bᵊḵātā	ܒܟܬܐ	383
44b	bᵊlā	ܒܠܐ	384
44b	balu‘ā	ܒܠܘܥܐ	385
112b	balhuḏ	ܒܠܚܘܕ	386
44b	bᵊlāyā	ܒܠܝܐ	387
44b	bᵊlam	ܒܠܡ	388
400a	bᵊlestāus	ܒܠܣܛܘܣ	389
44b	bᵊla‘	ܒܠܥ	390
45a	bel‘āḏ	ܒܠܥܕ	391
400a	bel‘am	ܒܠܥܡ	392
45a	bᵊlaṣ	ܒܠܨ	393
400a	bālāq	ܒܠܩ	394
45a	bᵊnā	ܒܢܐ	395
400a	bᵊnai regš(i)	ܒܢܝ ܪܓܫ	396
45b	banāyā	ܒܢܝܐ	397
400a	benyāmīn	ܒܢܝܡܝܢ	398
45b	benyānā	ܒܢܝܢܐ	399
45b	bᵊsā	ܒܣܐ	400
46a	besāḏyā	ܒܣܕܝܐ	401

Pg/Col	Pronunciation	Word	No
46b	basīmā	ܒܣܝܡܐ	402
46b	basīmā'īṯ	ܒܣܝܡܐܝܬ	403
46b	basīmuṯā	ܒܣܝܡܘܬܐ	404
46a	bᵊsem	ܒܣܡ	405
46a	besmā	ܒܣܡܐ	406
46b	bᵊsar	ܒܣܪ	407
47a	besrā	ܒܣܪܐ	408
47a	bestar	ܒܣܬܪ	409
47b	bestᵊrā	ܒܣܬܪܐ	410
47b	bᵊ'ā	ܒܥܐ	411
48b	'aḇ'eḏ (aph)	ܒܥܕ	412
400a	bᵊ'ur	ܒܥܘܪ	413
48b	bā'uṯā	ܒܥܘܬܐ	414
400a	bā'āz	ܒܥܙ	415
48b	bᵊ'aṭ	ܒܥܛ	416
49a	bᵊ'īltā	ܒܥܝܠܬܐ	417
49b	bᵊ'īrā	ܒܥܝܪܐ	418
49a	bᵊ'al	ܒܥܠ	419
48b	ba'lā	ܒܥܠܐ	420
400a	ba'lā	ܒܥܠܐ	421
49a	bᵊ'eldᵊḇaḇā	ܒܥܠܕܒܒܐ	422
		ܒܥܠܕܒܒܘܬܐ	423
49a	bᵊ'eldᵊḇāḇuṯā		
49a	bᵊ'eldīnā	ܒܥܠܕܝܢܐ	424
400b	bᵊ'elzᵊḇuḇ	ܒܥܠܙܒܘܒ	425
49a	bᵊ'aq	ܒܥܩ	426
49b	ba'rīrāyā	ܒܥܪܝܪܝܐ	427
48b	bᵊ'āṯā	ܒܥܬܐ	428
49b	bᵊṣā	ܒܨܐ	429
49b	bᵊṣīrā	ܒܨܝܪܐ	430
49b	bᵊṣīrā'īṯ	ܒܨܝܪܐܝܬ	431
49b	bᵊṣīruṯā	ܒܨܝܪܘܬܐ	432
49b	bᵊṣar	ܒܨܪ	433
50a	bāqā	ܒܩܐ	434
50a	bᵊqā	ܒܩܐ	435
50b	bᵊqār	ܒܩܪ	436
50b	baqrā	ܒܩܪܐ	437
400b	bar 'abā	ܒܪ ܐܒܐ	438
52a	bar 'egārā	ܒܪ ܐܓܪܐ	439
52b	bar (')nāšā	ܒܪ ܐܢܫܐ	440
53a	bar ḥīrā	ܒܪ ܚܐܪܐ	441
400b	bar ṭīmai	ܒܪ ܛܝܡܝ	442
400b	bar yāuna	ܒܪ ܝܘܢܐ	443
400b	bar šabā	ܒܪ ܫܒܐ	444
400b	bar šabā	ܒܪ ܫܒܐ	445
400b	bar šumā	ܒܪ ܫܘܡܐ	446
53a	bar šā'ṯeh	ܒܪ ܫܥܬܗ	447
400b	bar tulmai	ܒܪ ܬܘܠܡܝ	448
50b	barā	ܒܪܐ	449
51a	bᵊrā	ܒܪܐ	450
53b	bᵊrā	ܒܪܐ	451
54a	barbᵊrāyā	ܒܪܒܪܝܐ	452
54a	barᵊḏā	ܒܪܕܐ	453
400b	berwā'a	ܒܪܘܐܐ	454

Pg/Col	Pronunciation	Word	No
54a	bāruyā	ܒܪܘܝܐ	455
55a	berulā	ܒܪܘܠܐ	456
50b	barāyā	ܒܪܝܐ	457
53b	bārᵊyā	ܒܪܝܐ	458
54b	bᵊrīḵā	ܒܪܝܟܐ	459
53b	bᵊrīruṯā	ܒܪܝܪܘܬܐ	460
53b	bıryāṯā	ܒܪܝܬܐ	461
54a	bᵊrīṯā	ܒܪܝܬܐ	462
54b	bᵊreḵ	ܒܪܟ	463
401a	bᵊraḵyā	ܒܪܟܝܐ	464
55a	bᵊram	ܒܪܡ	465
401a	barnaḇa	ܒܪܢܒܐ	466
401a	barnīqī	ܒܪܢܝܩܐ	467
401a	bārāq	ܒܪܩ	468
55a	bᵊraq	ܒܪܩ	469
55a	barqā	ܒܪܩܐ	470
53b	barṯā	ܒܪܬܐ	471
55a	bᵊṯulā	ܒܬܘܠܐ	472
55b	bᵊṯuluṯā	ܒܬܘܠܘܬܐ	473
55b	bᵊṯultā	ܒܬܘܠܬܐ	474
401a	bıṯunıya	ܒܬܘܢܝܐ	475
36a	bāṯar	ܒܬܪ	476
36b	bāṯarken	ܒܬܪܟܢ	477
56a	ga'yā	ܓܐܝܐ	478
56a	ga'yā'īṯ	ܓܐܝܐܝܬ	479
401a	ga'yıwās	ܓܐܝܘܣ	480
401a	ga'lıyun	ܓܐܠܝܘܢ	481
56a	ge'rā	ܓܐܪܐ	482
65a	gabā	ܓܒܐ	483
56a	gᵊḇā	ܓܒܐ	484
57a	gabāyā	ܓܒܝܐ	485
56b	gaḇyā	ܓܒܝܐ	486
56b	gaḇyuṯā	ܓܒܝܘܬܐ	487
57a	gᵊḇīltā	ܓܒܝܠܬܐ	488
57a	gᵊḇīnā	ܓܒܝܢܐ	489
56b	gᵊḇīṯā	ܓܒܝܬܐ	490
57a	gᵊḇal	ܓܒܠ	491
58a	gᵊḇar	ܓܒܪ	492
57a	gaḇrā	ܓܒܪܐ	493
58a	gaḇruṯā	ܓܒܪܘܬܐ	494
401a	gaḇrī'eıl	ܓܒܪܝܐܝܠ	495
401a	gāgultā	ܓܓܘܠܬܐ	496
58a	gağrāṯā	ܓܓܪܬܐ	497
401b	gaḏ	ܓܕ	498
58a	gaḏ	ܓܕ	499
58a	gaduḏā	ܓܕܘܕܐ	500
58a	gᵊḏulā	ܓܕܘܠܐ	501
58a	gaḏyā	ܓܕܝܐ	502
58a	gᵊḏal	ܓܕܠ	503
401b	gadsımān	ܓܕܣܡܢ	504
401b	geḏ'un	ܓܕܥܘܢ	505
58b	gᵊḏap̄	ܓܕܦ	506
401b	geḏrāya	ܓܕܪܝܐ	507
58b	gᵊḏaš	ܓܕܫ	508

Pg/Col	Pronunciation	Word	No
59a	gəhen	ܓܗܢ	509
401b	gıhanā	ܓܗܢܐ	510
59a	gawā	ܓܘܐ	511
401b	gāug	ܓܘܓ	512
58b	gudāpā	ܓܘܕܦܐ	513
59b	gāz (pe 3sm)	ܓܘܙ	514
60a	gauzel	ܓܘܙܠ	515
60a	gauzālā	ܓܘܙܠܐ	516
61a	guḥkā	ܓܘܚܟܐ	517
59a	gawāyā	ܓܘܝܐ	518
59a	gəwāyā	ܓܘܝܐ	519
63b	gumāṣā	ܓܘܡܨܐ	520
65b	gunḥā	ܓܘܢܚܐ	521
64b	gunāyā	ܓܘܢܝܐ	522
59b	'etgawas (ethpa)	ܓܘܣ	523
59b	gausā	ܓܘܣܐ	524
65b	gu'lānā	ܓܘܥܠܢܐ	525
59b	gār (pe 3sm)	ܓܘܪ	526
59b	gaurā	ܓܘܪܐ	527
66b	gurāğā	ܓܘܪܓܐ	528
67b	gušmā	ܓܘܫܡܐ	529
67b	gušmānā'īt	ܓܘܫܡܢܐܝܬ	530
60a	gaz	ܓܙ	531
401b	gaza	ܓܙܐ	532
60a	gazā	ܓܙܐ	533
60a	gāzuzā	ܓܙܘܙܐ	534
60b	gəzurtā	ܓܙܘܪܬܐ	535
60a	gəzam	ܓܙܡ	536
60a	gəzāmā	ܓܙܡܐ	537
60b	gəzar	ܓܙܪ	538
60b	gəzārā	ܓܙܪܐ	539
60b	gāzartā	ܓܙܪܬܐ	540
61a	gəḥek	ܓܚܟ	541
58a	gīğlā	ܓܝܓܠܐ	542
60a	gıyurā	ܓܝܘܪܐ	543
61a	gayāsā	ܓܝܣܐ	544
61a	geir	ܓܝܪ	545
59b	gayārā	ܓܝܪܐ	546
62a	galā	ܓܠܐ	547
62a	galā	ܓܠܐ	548
62a	gelā	ܓܠܐ	549
62a	galā	ܓܠܐ	550
62a	gəlā	ܓܠܐ	551
63a	geldā	ܓܠܕܐ	552
63b	gəlusqəmā	ܓܠܘܣܩܡܐ	553
62b	gālutā	ܓܠܘܬܐ	554
63a	gəlaz	ܓܠܙ	555
401b	galaṭıya	ܓܠܛܝܐ	556
401b	galaṭāyā	ܓܠܛܝܐ	557
62a	galyā	ܓܠܝܐ	558
62b	galyā'īt	ܓܠܝܐܝܬ	559
63a	gəlīdā	ܓܠܝܕܐ	560
62b	galyutā	ܓܠܝܘܬܐ	561
401b	gəlīlā	ܓܠܝܠܐ	562

Pg/Col	Pronunciation	Word	No	Pg/Col	Pronunciation	Word	No
402a	gəlīlāyā	ܓܠܝܠܝܐ	563	65b	gəsar	ܓܣܪ	590
62b	gelyānā	ܓܠܝܢܐ	564	65b	gəʿā	ܓܥܐ	591
63b	gəlap̄	ܓܠܦ	565	66a	’etgəʿel (ethpe)	ܓܥܠ	592
64a	gāmurā	ܓܡܘܪܐ	566	66a	gəʿar	ܓܥܪ	593
64a	gəmurṯā	ܓܡܘܪܬܐ	567	65b	gəʿāṯā	ܓܥܬܐ	594
64a	gəmīrā	ܓܡܝܪܐ	568	66a	gep̄ā	ܓܦܐ	595
64a	gəmīrā’īṯ	ܓܡܝܪܐܝܬ	569	402a	gəp̄īp̄tā	ܓܦܝܦܬܐ	596
64a	gəmīruṯā	ܓܡܝܪܘܬܐ	570	66a	gəp̄etā	ܓܦܬܐ	597
63b	gamlā	ܓܡܠܐ	571	66a	gar	ܓܪ	598
402a	gamalī’eil	ܓܡܠܝܐܝܠ	572	66b	gərā	ܓܪܐ	599
63b	gəmar	ܓܡܪ	573	66b	gəreḇ	ܓܪܒ	600
64a	gəmārā	ܓܡܪܐ	574	66b	gərāḇā	ܓܪܒܐ	601
64b	’aḡen (aph)	ܓܢ	575	66b	garbā	ܓܪܒܐ	602
64b	gənā	ܓܢܐ	576	66b	garḇā	ܓܪܒܐ	603
64b	ganī (pa)	ܓܢܐ	577	66b	garbəyā	ܓܪܒܝܐ	604
64b	gənaḇ	ܓܢܒ	578	66b	gareḡ (pa)	ܓܪܓ	605
65a	ge(n)ḇ	ܓܢܒ	579	67a	gərīṣtā	ܓܪܝܨܬܐ	606
65a	ganāḇā	ܓܢܒܐ	580	67a	gəram	ܓܪܡ	607
65a	ganāḇuṯā	ܓܢܒܘܬܐ	581	67a	garmā	ܓܪܡܐ	608
64b	gənunā	ܓܢܘܢܐ	582	67a	gəraʿ	ܓܪܥ	609
65b	gənaḥ	ܓܢܚ	583	67a	gəraš	ܓܪܫ	610
65a	gənīzā	ܓܢܝܙܐ	584	67a	gaš	ܓܫ	611
65b	gənīḥṯā	ܓܢܝܚܬܐ	585	67b	gāšušā	ܓܫܘܫܐ	612
64b	ganānā	ܓܢܢܐ	586	68a	dīḇā	ܕܐܒܐ	613
65b	gensā	ܓܢܣܐ	587	402a	dēmā	ܕܐܡܐ	614
402a	genesar	ܓܢܣܪ	588	68a	debā	ܕܒܐ	615
64b	ganṯā	ܓܢܬܐ	589	68a	dəḇaḥ	ܕܒܚ	616

Pg/Col	Pronunciation	Word	No
68a	debḥā	ܕܒܚܐ	617
68a	debḥətā	ܕܒܚܬܐ	618
68a	dəbīḥutā	ܕܒܝܚܘܬܐ	619
68b	dəbīḥā	ܕܒܝܚܐ	620
68b	dəbeq	ܕܒܩ	621
68b	dəbar	ܕܒܪ	622
69a	dabrā	ܕܒܪܐ	623
70a	debšā	ܕܒܫܐ	624
70a	dagel (pa)	ܕܓܠ	625
70a	dagālā	ܕܓܠܐ	626
70a	dagālutā	ܕܓܠܘܬܐ	627
70b	dādā	ܕܕܐ	628
70b	'adheb (aph)	ܕܗܒ	629
70a	dahbā	ܕܗܒܐ	630
70b	dəwā	ܕܘܐ	631
69b	dubārā	ܕܘܒܪܐ	632
70b	dawed (pa)	ܕܘܕ	633
70b	dəwādā	ܕܘܕܐ	634
70b	duwānā	ܕܘܘܢܐ	635
70b	dāuyā	ܕܘܝܐ	636
402a	dawīd	ܕܘܝܕ	637
76b	duk	ܕܘܟ	638
77a	dukayā	ܕܘܟܝܐ	639
77b	dukrānā	ܕܘܟܪܢܐ	640
76b	duktā	ܕܘܟܬܐ	641
71a	daulā	ܕܘܠܐ	642
78a	dulālā	ܕܘܠܠܐ	643
79a	dumyā	ܕܘܡܝܐ	644
80a	dumsā	ܕܘܡܣܐ	645
80a	dumārā	ܕܘܡܪܐ	646
71a	dān (pe 3sm)	ܕܘܢ	647
80b	dunbā	ܕܘܢܒܐ	648
81b	du'ətā	ܕܘܥܬܐ	649
72b	dāṣ (pe 3sm)	ܕܘܨ	650
72b	dāq (pe 3sm)	ܕܘܩ	651
73a	dār (pe 3sm)	ܕܘܪ	652
82a	durkətā	ܕܘܪܟܬܐ	653
82b	durāšā	ܕܘܪܫܐ	654
73a	dāš (pe 3sm)	ܕܘܫ	655
73b	dəḥā	ܕܚܐ	656
74b	daḥultānā	ܕܚܘܠܬܢܐ	657
74a	dəḥīlā	ܕܚܝܠܐ	658
74b	daḥīlā	ܕܚܝܠܐ	659
73b	dəḥel	ܕܚܠ	660
74a	deḥlā	ܕܚܠܐ	661
74a	deḥlətā	ܕܚܠܬܐ	662
74b	dəḥaq	ܕܚܩ	663
74b	daḥšā	ܕܚܫܐ	664
74b	daıwā	ܕܝܘܐ	665
402b	dıyāuṭərepīs	ܕܝܘܛܪܦܝܣ	666
74b	daıwānā	ܕܝܘܢܐ	667
76a	dəyutā	ܕܝܘܬܐ	668
74b	dīl	ܕܝܠ	669
75a	dein	ܕܝܢ	670

Pg/Col	Pronunciation	Word	No
71a	dīnā	ܕܝܢܐ	671
71b	dayānā	ܕܝܢܐ	672
402b	dıyānāusıyāus	ܕܝܢܘܣܝܘܣ	673
81a	dīnārā	ܕܝܢܪܐ	674
73a	daırā	ܕܝܪܐ	675
76a	dıyaṯīqī	ܕܝܬܝܩܐ	676
76b	dəḵā	ܕܟܐ	677
76b	daḵyā	ܕܟܝܐ	678
76b	daḵya'īṯ	ܕܟܝܐܝܬ	679
77a	daḵyuṯā	ܕܟܝܘܬܐ	680
77b	dəḵīr	ܕܟܝܪ	681
77b	'eṯdəḵar (ethpe)	ܕܟܪ	682
78a	deḵrā	ܕܟܪܐ	683
78b	dalel (pa)	ܕܠ	684
78a	dəlā	ܕܠܐ	685
78a	dəluḥyā	ܕܠܘܚܝܐ	686
78a	dəlaḥ	ܕܠܚ	687
78a	dəlīlā	ܕܠܝܠܐ	688
193a	dalmā	ܕܠܡܐ	689
402b	dalmaṭıya	ܕܠܡܛܝܐ	690
402b	dalmānuṯā	ܕܠܡܢܘܬܐ	691
78b	dəlaq	ܕܠܩ	692
78b	dalqā	ܕܠܩܐ	693
307a	dalquḇlā	ܕܠܩܘܒܠܐ	694
78b	dam	ܕܡ	695
78b	dəmā	ܕܡܐ	696
79a	dəmā	ܕܡܐ	697
79a	dəmuṯā	ܕܡܘܬܐ	698
402b	dımṭrıyāus	ܕܡܛܪܝܘܣ	699
79a	dāmyā	ܕܡܝܐ	700
79b	dəmayā	ܕܡܝܐ	701
79b	dəmeḵ	ܕܡܟ	702
80a	dem'əṯā	ܕܡܥܬܐ	703
80a	'eṯdamar (ethpa)	ܕܡܪ	704
402b	damarīs	ܕܡܪܝܣ	705
80b	dənā	ܕܢܐ	706
81a	dənaḥ	ܕܢܚ	707
81a	denḥā	ܕܢܚܐ	708
402b	dānī'eıl	ܕܢܝܐܝܠ	709
81a	də'eḵ	ܕܥܟ	710
81b	də'ar	ܕܥܪ	711
81b	dapā	ܕܦܐ	712
81b	dap̄nā	ܕܦܢܐ	713
81b	daq	ܕܩ	714
81b	daqdəqā	ܕܩܕܩܐ	715
82a	deqlā	ܕܩܠܐ	716
82a	dəqar	ܕܩܪ	717
72b	dārā	ܕܪܐ	718
82a	dərā	ܕܪܐ	719
402b	derbī	ܕܪܒܐ	720
82a	dargā	ܕܪܓܐ	721
82a	dardərē	ܕܪܕܪܐ	722
403a	dursıla	ܕܪܘܣܝܠܐ	723
82b	dārušā	ܕܪܘܫܐ	724

Pg/Col	Pronunciation	Word	No
82a	dərakḵ	ܕܪܟ	725
82a	dərāḵtā	ܕܪܟܬܐ	726
403a	darməsuq	ܕܪܡܣܘܩ	727
403a	darməsuqāyā	ܕܪܡܣܘܩܝܐ	728
82b	dərā'ā	ܕܪܥܐ	729
82b	dəraš	ܕܪܫ	730
82b	dərāšā	ܕܪܫܐ	731
73a	dārtā	ܕܪܬܐ	732
83a	hā	ܗܐ	733
83a	hab	ܗܒ	734
83a	habāḇā	ܗܒܒܐ	735
403a	hāḇeıl	ܗܒܝܠ	736
83a	habṯā	ܗܒܬܐ	737
83a	həḡā	ܗܓܐ	738
83b	həḡam	ܗܓܡ	739
83b	heḡmonā	ܗܓܡܘܢܐ	740
83b	hıḡmānutā	ܗܓܡܢܘܬܐ	741
403a	hāḡār	ܗܓܪ	742
83b	heḏyoṭā	ܗܕܝܘܛܐ	743
83b	hadāmā	ܗܕܡܐ	744
83b	heḏrā	ܗܕܪܐ	745
403a	heḏrıyāus	ܗܕܪܝܘܣ	746
84a	hu	ܗܘ	747
85a	hau	ܗܘ	748
86a	həwā	ܗܘܐ	749
403a	humenēwās	ܗܘܡܢܐܘܣ	750
89a	hawen (pa)	ܗܘܢ	751
89a	haunā	ܗܘܢܐ	752
93a	hup̄āḵā	ܗܘܦܟܐ	753
93b	heuparkıyā	ܗܘܦܪܟܝܐ	754
403a	hušā'	ܗܘܫܥ	755
86a	hauṯā	ܗܘܬܐ	756
89a	hāıdeın	ܗܝܕܝܢ	757
89a	haıklā	ܗܝܟܠܐ	758
19b	haımānuṯā	ܗܝܡܢܘܬܐ	759
89b	hāḵwāṯ	ܗܟܘܬ	760
89b	haḵīl	ܗܟܝܠ	761
90a	hāḵanā	ܗܟܢܐ	762
90a	halel (pa)	ܗܠܠ	763
403a	helī	ܗܠܝ	764
90b	həlaḵ	ܗܠܟ	765
90b	həlakṯā	ܗܠܟܬܐ	766
90a	haleluya	ܗܠܠܘܝܐ	767
403a	hales	ܗܠܣ	768
91a	'ahmī (aph)	ܗܡܐ	769
91a	hānā	ܗܢܐ	770
92a	hənā	ܗܢܐ	771
92a	hanī'uṯā	ܗܢܝܘܬܐ	772
92a	henyānā	ܗܢܝܢܐ	773
92b	həp̄uḵyā	ܗܦܘܟܝܐ	774
92b	həp̄aḵ	ܗܦܟ	775
92b	həp̄āḵṯā	ܗܦܟܬܐ	776
93b	hep̄arkā	ܗܦܪܟܐ	777

Pg/Col	Pronunciation	Word	No
93b	har	ܗܪ	778
403b	herāudıya	ܗܪܘܕܝܐ	779
403b	herāudıyāun	ܗܪܘܕܝܢ	780
403b	herāuḏes	ܗܪܘܕܣ	781
403b	herāuḏes	ܗܪܘܕܣ	782
403b	herāuḏes	ܗܪܘܕܣ	783
93b	heromā	ܗܪ̈ܘܡܐ	784
93b	hārkā	ܗܪܟܐ	785
403b	herma	ܗܪܡܐ	786
403b	hermī	ܗܪܡܐ	787
403b	harmāğenīs	ܗܪܡܓܢܝܣ	788
404a	hermīs	ܗܪܡܝܣ	789
94a	heresyuṭā	ܗܪܣܝܘܛܐ	790
93b	heresīs	ܗܪܣܝܣ	791
94a	hārtamān	ܗܪܬܡܢ	792
94a	hāšā	ܗܫܐ	793
95a	wāı	ܘܝ	794
95a	wālē (ap)	ܘܠܐ	795
95b	wa'eḏ	ܘܥܕ	796
95a	wa'dā	ܘܥܕܐ	797
404a	zīna	ܙܐܢܐ	798
404a	zaḇᵊḏaı	ܙܒܕܝ	799
404a	zᵊḇāulāun	ܙܒܘܠܘܢ	800
97b	zāḇurā	ܙܒܘܪܐ	801
96a	zabel (pa)	ܙܒܠ	802
96a	zeḇlā	ܙܒܠܐ	803
96a	zᵊḇan	ܙܒܢ	804

Pg/Col	Pronunciation	Word	No
97a	zaḇnā	ܙܒܢܐ	805
97b	zᵊğuğā	ܙܓܘܓܐ	806
97b	zᵊğuğīṯā	ܙܓܘܓܝܬܐ	807
97b	zᵊğar	ܙܓܪ	808
404a	zāḏuq	ܙܕܘܩ	809
404a	zaḏuqāyā	ܙܕܘܩܝܐ	810
98a	zaḏīqā	ܙܕܝܩܐ	811
98a	zaḏīqā'īṯ	ܙܕܝܩܐܝܬ	812
98a	zaḏīquṯā	ܙܕܝܩܘܬܐ	813
98a	zadeq (pa)	ܙܕܩ	814
97b	zāḏqā	ܙܕܩܐ	815
97b	zeḏqā	ܙܕܩܐ	816
98a	zeḏqᵊṯā	ܙܕܩܬܐ	817
98b	zᵊhī	ܙܗܝ	818
98b	zahyā'īṯ	ܙܗܝܐܝܬ	819
98b	zᵊhīrā	ܙܗܝܪܐ	820
99a	zᵊhīrā'īṯ	ܙܗܝܪܐܝܬ	821
98b	zᵊhar	ܙܗܪ	822
99a	'ezdᵊhar (ethpe)	ܙܗܪ	823
98b	zᵊhārā	ܙܗܪܐ	824
99b	zaweğ (pa)	ܙܘܓ	825
99b	zaugā	ܙܘܓܐ	826
99b	zaweḏ (pa)	ܙܘܕ	827
99b	zᵊwāḏā	ܙܘܕܐ	828
99b	zuwāğā	ܙܘܘܓܐ	829
99b	zuzā	ܙܘܙܐ	830
99b	zāḥ (pe 3sm)	ܙܘܚ	831

Pg/Col	Pronunciation	Word	No
99b	zauḥā	ܙܘܚܐ	832
99a	zāwīṯā	ܙܘܝܬܐ	833
100b	zayen (pa)	ܙܘܢ	834
100a	zā‘ (pe 3sm)	ܙܘܥ	835
100a	zau‘ā	ܙܘܥܐ	836
100b	zupā	ܙܘܦܐ	837
404a	zurbāḇel	ܙܘܪܒܒܠ	838
100b	zəḥurīṯā	ܙܚܘܪܝܬܐ	839
100b	ziṭıma	ܙܝܛܡܐ	840
100b	zīzānā	ܙܝܙܢܐ	841
100b	zaınā	ܙܝܢܐ	842
101a	zaıtā	ܙܝܬܐ	843
101a	zəḵā	ܙܟܐ	844
101a	zāḵuṯā	ܙܟܘܬܐ	845
404a	zakaı	ܙܟܝ	846
101b	zakāyā	ܙܟܝܐ	847
404a	zəkaryā	ܙܟܪܝܐ	848
404b	zəkaryā	ܙܟܪܝܐ	849
101b	’azleğ (aph)	ܙܠܓ	850
101b	zelgā	ܙܠܓܐ	851
101b	zalhez	ܙܠܗܙ	852
101b	zəla‘	ܙܠܥ	853
101b	zam	ܙܡ	854
102a	zəmīnā	ܙܡܝܢܐ	855
102a	zəmīrtā·	ܙܡܝܪܬܐ	856
102a	zamen (pa)	ܙܡܢ	857
102a	zəmar	ܙܡܪ	858

Pg/Col	Pronunciation	Word	No
102a	zəmārā	ܙܡܪܐ	859
102b	zamārā	ܙܡܪܐ	860
102b	zəmargəḏā	ܙܡܪܓܕܐ	861
102b	zənā	ܙܢܐ	862
102b	zənā	ܙܢܐ	863
103a	zanāyā	ܙܢܝܐ	864
102b	zānyuṯā	ܙܢܝܘܬܐ	865
102b	zānīṯā	ܙܢܝܬܐ	866
103a	zə‘urā	ܙܥܘܪܐ	867
103b	zə‘uruṯā	ܙܥܘܪܘܬܐ	868
103a	zə‘ap̄	ܙܥܦ	869
103a	zə‘aq	ܙܥܩ	870
103a	zə‘ar	ܙܥܪ	871
103b	zeqā	ܙܩܐ	872
104a	zəqīp̄ā	ܙܩܝܦܐ	873
103b	zəqap̄	ܙܩܦ	874
104a	zəqar	ܙܩܪ	875
104b	zāru‘ā	ܙܪܘܥܐ	876
404b	zārāh	ܙܪܚ	877
104a	zəra‘	ܙܪܥ	878
104b	zar‘ā	ܙܪܥܐ	879
104b	zar‘unā	ܙܪܥܘܢܐ	880
105a	ḥīp̄ā	ܚܐܦܐ	881
130b	ḥīrā	ܚܐܪܐ	882
130b	ḥīruṯā	ܚܐܪܘܬܐ	883
105a	ḥaḇ	ܚܒ	884
105a	ḥabuḇā	ܚܒܘܒܐ	885

Pg/Col	Pronunciation	Word	No
108a	ḥəḇušyā	ܚܒܘܫܝܐ	886
106a	ḥəḇaṭ	ܚܒܛ	887
105a	ḥabīḇā	ܚܒܝܒܐ	888
107b	ḥaḇīrā	ܚܒܝܪܐ	889
106b	ḥəḇal	ܚܒܠ	890
107a	ḥəḇal	ܚܒܠ	891
106b	ḥəḇālā	ܚܒܠܐ	892
107a	ḥaḇlā	ܚܒܠܐ	893
107a	ḥeḇlē	ܚܒ̈ܠܐ	894
107a	’eṯḥaban (ethpa)	ܚܒܢ	895
107a	ḥaḇnā	ܚܒܢܐ	896
107a	ḥəḇanānā	ܚܒܢܢܐ	897
107a	ḥəḇanānuṯā	ܚܒܢܢܘܬܐ	898
107b	ḥəḇaṣ	ܚܒܨ	899
107b	ḥeḇṣā	ܚܒܨܐ	900
107b	ḥabārā	ܚܒܪܐ	901
107b	ḥaḇrā	ܚܒܪܐ	902
107b	ḥəḇartā	ܚܒܪܬܐ	903
107b	ḥəḇaš	ܚܒܫ	904
105a	ḥabṯā	ܚܒܬܐ	905
108a	ḥəḡīsā	ܚܓܝܣܐ	906
108a	ḥəḡīrā	ܚܓܝܪܐ	907
108a	ḥəḡar	ܚܓܪ	908
108a	ḥaḏ	ܚܕ	909
109a	ḥaḏ bəšabā	ܚܕ ܒܫܒܐ	910
109a	ḥəḏāḏē	ܚ̈ܕܕܐ	911
110b	ḥāḏurā	ܚܕܘܪܐ	912
109b	ḥaḏuṯā	ܚܕܘܬܐ	913
109b	ḥəḏı	ܚܕܝ	914
110a	ḥaḏyā	ܚܕܝܐ	915
110a	ḥadāyā	ܚܕܝܐ	916
110a	ḥāḏyā’īṯ	ܚܕܝܐܝܬ	917
109a	ḥəḏa‘sar	ܚܕܥܣܪ	918
110a	ḥəḏar	ܚܕܪ	919
110b	ḥəḏārā	ܚܕܪܐ	920
110b	ḥəḏeṯ	ܚܕܬ	921
110b	ḥa(d)ṯā	ܚܕܬܐ	922
111a	ḥa(d)tā’īṯ	ܚܕܬܐܝܬ	923
111a	ḥa(d)ṯuṯā	ܚܕܬܘܬܐ	924
404b	ḥawā	ܚܘܐ	925
111a	ḥawī (pa)	ܚܘܐ	926
111b	ḥāḇ	ܚܘܒ	927
111b	ḥaubā	ܚܘܒܐ	928
105a	ḥubā	ܚܘܒܐ	929
107a	ḥuḇlā	ܚܘܒܠܐ	930
112a	ḥaubṯā	ܚܘܒܬܐ	931
110b	ḥuḏrānā’īṯ	ܚܘܕܪܢܐܝܬ	932
111a	ḥuḏāṯā	ܚܘܕܬܐ	933
113a	ḥāṭ (pe 3sm)	ܚܘܛ	934
113a	ḥuṭā	ܚܘܛܐ	935
118b	ḥuṭrā	ܚܘܛܪܐ	936
113a	ḥeuyā	ܚܘܝܐ	937
112a	ḥuyāḇā	ܚܘܝܒܐ	938
122a	ḥulā	ܚܘܠܐ	939

Pg/Col	Pronunciation	Word	No
122b	ḥulṭānā	ܚܘܠܛܢܐ	940
124b	ḥumā	ܚܘܡܐ	941
127a	ḥunṭəṯā	ܚܘܢܛܬܐ	942
113a	ḥās	ܚܘܣ	943
127b	ḥusāyā	ܚܘܣܝܐ	944
113a	ḥausānā	ܚܘܣܢܐ	945
128b	ḥusrānā	ܚܘܣܪܢܐ	946
113b	ḥāṣ (pe 3sm)	ܚܘܨ	947
113b	ḥār (pe 3sm)	ܚܘܪ	948
114a	ḥəwar	ܚܘܪ	949
114a	ḥewārā	ܚܘܪܐ	950
114a	ḥaurā	ܚܘܪܐ	951
130b	ḥorā	ܚܘܪܐ	952
131a	ḥurbā	ܚܘܪܒܐ	953
132a	ḥurāqā	ܚܘܪܩܐ	954
133b	ḥušāḇā	ܚܘܫܒܐ	955
133a	ḥušbānā	ܚܘܫܒܢܐ	956
133b	ḥušāḥā	ܚܘܫܚܐ	957
135a	ḥuṯḥāṯā	ܚܘܬܚܬܐ	958
114b	ḥəzā	ܚܙܐ	959
116a	ḥezwā	ܚܙܘܐ	960
116a	ḥazāyā	ܚܙܝܐ	961
116a	ḥəzāyā	ܚܙܝܐ	962
117a	ḥəzīrā	ܚܙܝܪܐ	963
117a	ḥəzīrtā	ܚܙܝܪܬܐ	964
116b	ḥəzaq	ܚܙܩ	965
117a	ḥəzāqā	ܚܙܩܐ	966
404b	ḥezaqyā	ܚܙܩܝܐ	967
116a	ḥəzāṯā	ܚܙܬܐ	968
117a	ḥaṭ	ܚܛ	969
117a	ḥəṭā	ܚܛܐ	970
117b	ḥəṭāhā	ܚܛܗܐ	971
118a	ḥāṭupā	ܚܛܘܦܐ	972
118b	ḥəṭupyā	ܚܛܘܦܝܐ	973
117b	ḥaṭāyā	ܚܛܝܐ	974
118a	ḥəṭīṯā	ܚܛܝܬܐ	975
118a	ḥəṭap	ܚܛܦ	976
117a	ḥeṭṯā	ܚܛܬܐ	977
118b	ḥəyā	ܚܝܐ	978
119a	ḥayā	ܚܝܐ	979
119b	ḥayē	ܚܝ̈ܐ	980
112a	ḥayāḇā	ܚܝܒܐ	981
112b	ḥayāḇuṯā	ܚܝܒܘܬܐ	982
120a	ḥayuṯā	ܚܝܘܬܐ	983
121a	ḥayel (pa)	ܚܝܠ	984
120b	ḥailā	ܚܝܠܐ	985
121a	ḥailəṯānā	ܚܝܠܬܢܐ	986
113b	ḥəyāṣā	ܚܝܨܐ	987
113b	ḥīṣā'īṯ	ܚܝܨܐܝܬ	988
120a	ḥaiṯā	ܚܝܬܐ	989
121b	ḥaḵīmā	ܚܟܝܡܐ	990
121b	ḥaḵīma'īṯ	ܚܟܝܡܐܝܬ	991
121b	ḥəkam	ܚܟܡ	992
121b	ḥeḵməṯā	ܚܟܡܬܐ	993

Pg/Col	Pronunciation	Word	No
122a	ḥalel (pa)	ܚܠ	994
122a	ḥal	ܚܠ	995
113a	ḥālā	ܚܠܐ	996
122a	ḥalā	ܚܠܐ	997
122a	ḥelā	ܚܠܐ	998
122a	ḥalᵊḇā	ܚܠܒܐ	999
122b	ḥᵊlaḏ	ܚܠܕ	1000
122b	ḥalāḏīṯā	ܚܠܕܝܬܐ	1001
122a	ḥᵊlulā	ܚܠܘܠܐ	1002
122b	ḥᵊlaṭ	ܚܠܛ	1003
122b	ḥelṭā	ܚܠܛܐ	1004
122b	ḥᵊlī	ܚܠܝ	1005
122b	ḥalyā	ܚܠܝܐ	1006
123a	ḥᵊlīmā	ܚܠܝܡܐ	1007
123a	ḥᵊlīmuṯā	ܚܠܝܡܘܬܐ	1008
124a	ḥᵊlīṣā	ܚܠܝܨܐ	1009
123a	'eṯḥᵊlem (ethpe)	ܚܠܡ	1010
123a	ḥᵊlam	ܚܠܡ	1011
123a	ḥelmā	ܚܠܡܐ	1012
123b	ḥᵊlap̄	ܚܠܦ	1013
123b	ḥᵊlāp̄	ܚܠܦ	1014
404b	ḥalp̄aı	ܚܠܦܝ	1015
124a	ḥᵊlaṣ	ܚܠܨ	1016
124a	ḥalāšā	ܚܠܫܐ	1017
122a	ḥelṯā	ܚܠܬܐ	1018
124b	ḥam	ܚܡ	1019
124b	ḥam	ܚܡ	1020
124b	ḥᵊmā	ܚܡܐ	1021
125a	ḥᵊmā	ܚܡܐ	1022
404b	ḥᵊmur	ܚܡܘܪ	1023
124b	ḥamīmā	ܚܡܝܡܐ	1024
125b	ḥᵊmīrā	ܚܡܝܪܐ	1025
125a	ḥᵊmal	ܚܡܠ	1026
125a	ḥamsen	ܚܡܣܢ	1027
125a	ḥᵊmaʻ	ܚܡܥ	1028
125b	ḥameṣ (pa)	ܚܡܨ	1029
125b	ḥᵊmārā	ܚܡܪܐ	1030
125b	ḥamrā	ܚܡܪܐ	1031
125b	ḥameš	ܚܡܫ	1032
126a	ḥamšīn	ܚܡܫܝܢ	1033
126a	ḥamešmā'	ܚܡܫܡܐܐ	1034
126a	ḥamšaʻsar	ܚܡܫܥܣܪ	1035
126a	ḥᵊmaṯ	ܚܡܬ	1036
124b	ḥᵊmāṯā	ܚܡܬܐ	1037
126a	ḥemṯā	ܚܡܬܐ	1038
126a	ḥemṯānā	ܚܡܬܢܐ	1039
126b	ḥan	ܚܢ	1040
404b	ḥanā	ܚܢܐ	1041
126b	ḥᵊnā	ܚܢܐ	1042
404b	ḥᵊnuḵ	ܚܢܘܟ	1043
126b	ḥānuṯā	ܚܢܘܬܐ	1044
127a	ḥᵊnaṭ	ܚܢܛ	1045
404b	ḥanān	ܚܢܢ	1046
126b	ḥᵊnānā	ܚܢܢܐ	1047

Pg/Col	Pronunciation	Word	No
404b	ḥananyā	ܚܢܢܝܐ	1048
405a	ḥananyā	ܚܢܢܝܐ	1049
405a	ḥananyā	ܚܢܢܝܐ	1050
127a	ḥanp̄ā	ܚܢܦܐ	1051
127a	ḥᵊnaq	ܚܢܩ	1052
113b	ḥās	ܚܣ	1053
127b	ḥasī (pa)	ܚܣܐ	1054
127b	ḥaseḏ (pa)	ܚܣܕ	1055
127a	ḥesdā	ܚܣܕܐ	1056
127b	ḥasyā	ܚܣܝܐ	1057
127b	ḥasyuṯā	ܚܣܝܘܬܐ	1058
128b	ḥasīnā	ܚܣܝܢܐ	1059
128b	ḥasīrā	ܚܣܝܪܐ	1060
128b	ḥasīruṯā	ܚܣܝܪܘܬܐ	1061
128a	ḥᵊsaḵ	ܚܣܟ	1062
405a	ḥeslī	ܚܣܠܝ	1063
128a	ḥᵊsam	ܚܣܡ	1064
128a	ḥᵊsāmā	ܚܣܡܐ	1065
128a	ḥᵊsan	ܚܣܢ	1066
128a	ḥesnā	ܚܣܢܐ	1067
128b	ḥᵊsar	ܚܣܪ	1068
129a	ḥᵊp̄ā	ܚܦܐ	1069
129a	ḥᵊp̄aṭ	ܚܦܛ	1070
129a	ḥᵊp̄īṭā	ܚܦܝܛܐ	1071
129a	ḥᵊp̄īṭā'īṯ	ܚܦܝܛܐܝܬ	1072
129a	ḥᵊp̄īṭuṯā	ܚܦܝܛܘܬܐ	1073
129b	ḥᵊp̄ar	ܚܦܪ	1074
129b	ḥaṣā	ܚܨܐ	1075
129b	ḥᵊṣā	ܚܨܐ	1076
129b	ḥᵊṣaḏ	ܚܨܕ	1077
130a	ḥᵊṣāḏā	ܚܨܕܐ	1078
130a	ḥāṣuḏā	ܚܨܘܕܐ	1079
130a	ḥaṣīp̄uṯā	ܚܨܝܦܘܬܐ	1080
130a	ḥᵊṣap̄	ܚܨܦ	1081
130a	ḥeṣpā	ܚܨܦܐ	1082
405a	ḥeṣrun	ܚܨܪܘܢ	1083
130a	ḥaqlā	ܚܩܠܐ	1084
130b	ḥarar (pa)	ܚܪ	1085
131a	'eṯḥᵊrī (ethpe)	ܚܪܐ	1086
131a	ḥᵊreḇ	ܚܪܒ	1087
131a	ḥᵊraḇ	ܚܪܒ	1088
131b	ḥarbā	ܚܪܒܐ	1089
131b	ḥarbā	ܚܪܒܐ	1090
131b	ḥardᵊlā	ܚܪܕܠܐ	1091
131b	ḥaruḇā	ܚܪܘܒܐ	1092
130b	ḥᵊrurā	ܚܪܘܪܐ	1093
130b	ḥᵊrurē	ܚܪ̈ܘܪܐ	1094
131a	ḥeryānā	ܚܪܝܢܐ	1095
132a	ḥarīp̄ā	ܚܪܝܦܐ	1096
132a	ḥarīp̄ā'īṯ	ܚܪܝܦܐܝܬ	1097
131b	ḥᵊrem	ܚܪܡ	1098
131b	ḥermā	ܚܪܡܐ	1099
405a	ḥārān	ܚܪܢ	1100
132a	ḥar'ā	ܚܪܥܐ	1101

Pg/Col	Pronunciation	Word	No
132a	ḥar'uṯā	ܚܪܥܘܬܐ	1102
132a	ḥ°rep̄	ܚܪܦ	1103
132a	ḥ°raq	ܚܪܩ	1104
132a	ḥ°reš	ܚܪܫ	1105
132a	ḥaršā	ܚܪܫܐ	1106
132b	ḥarāšā	ܚܪܫܐ	1107
132b	ḥaršē	ܚܪ̈ܫܐ	1108
132b	ḥarāšuṯā	ܚܪܫܘܬܐ	1109
8a	ḥarṯā	ܚܪܬܐ	1110
132b	ḥaš	ܚܫ	1111
132b	ḥašā	ܚܫܐ	1112
133a	ḥ°šaḇ	ܚܫܒ	1113
134a	ḥešuḵā	ܚܫܘܟܐ	1114
133a	ḥāšušā	ܚܫܘܫܐ	1115
133b	ḥ°šaḥ	ܚܫܚ	1116
134a	ḥāšḥuṯā	ܚܫܚܘܬܐ	1117
134a	ḥ°šaḥṯā	ܚܫܚܬܐ	1118
134a	ḥ°šeḵ	ܚܫܟ	1119
134b	ḥ°šal	ܚܫܠ	1120
134b	ḥešl°ṯā	ܚܫܠܬܐ	1121
134b	'aḥšem (aph)	ܚܫܡ	1122
134b	ḥ°šāmīṯā	ܚܫܡܝܬܐ	1123
7a	ḥāṯā	ܚܬܐ	1124
135a	ḥatḥet	ܚܬܚܬ	1125
135b	ḥ°ṯīrā	ܚܬܝܪܐ	1126
135b	ḥ°ṯīruṯā	ܚܬܝܪܘܬܐ	1127
135a	ḥ°ṯam	ܚܬܡ	1128

Pg/Col	Pronunciation	Word	No
135a	ḥāṯmā	ܚܬܡܐ	1129
135a	ḥaṯnā	ܚܬܢܐ	1130
135b	ḥ°ṯar	ܚܬܪ	1131
136a	ṭēḇ	ܛܐܒ	1132
136a	ṭaḇ	ܛܒ	1133
136a	ṭebā	ܛܒܐ	1134
136b	ṭāḇa	ܛܒܐ	1135
137b	ṭāḇuṯā	ܛܒܘܬܐ	1136
405a	ṭ°ḇīṯā	ܛܒܝܬܐ	1137
136a	ṭ°ḇa'	ܛܒܥ	1138
136a	ṭaḇ'ā	ܛܒܥܐ	1139
405a	ṭiḇeriyāus	ܛܒܪܝܘܣ	1140
405a	ṭiḇeriyāus	ܛܒܪܝܘܣ	1141
136b	'eṯṯagar (ethpa)	ܛܓܪ	1142
138a	ṭayeḇ (pa)	ܛܝܒ	1143
137a	ṭuḇā	ܛܘܒܐ	1144
137b	ṭubānā	ܛܘܒܢܐ	1145
137b	ṭuḇṯānā	ܛܘܒܬܢܐ	1146
136b	ṭohmā	ܛܘܗܡܐ	1147
136b	ṭauyā	ܛܘܝܐ	1148
138b	ṭuyāḇā	ܛܘܝܒܐ	1149
405a	ṭuḵīqāus	ܛܘܟܝܩܘܣ	1150
140b	ṭulšā	ܛܘܠܫܐ	1151
142a	ṭu'yai	ܛܘܥܝܝ	1152
138b	ṭāp̄	ܛܘܦ	1153
143a	ṭupaḏiyāun	ܛܘܦܐܕܝܘܢ	1154

Pg/Col	Pronunciation	Word	No
143b	ṭupāuniqāus	ܛܘܦܐܘܢܝܩܐܘܣ	1155
138b	ṭaupānā	ܛܘܦܢܐ	1156
143b	ṭupsā	ܛܘܦܣܐ	1157
138b	ṭurā	ܛܘܪܐ	1158
405b	ṭuranāus	ܛܘܪܢܘܣ	1159
144a	ṭurāpā	ܛܘܪܦܐ	1160
139a	ṭaš (pe 3sm)	ܛܘܫ	1161
139a	ṭəḥen	ܛܚܢ	1162
405b	ṭiṭāus	ܛܝܛܘܣ	1163
139a	ṭeṭrarca	ܛܛܪܪܟܐ	1164
137b	ṭaibuṯā	ܛܝܒܘܬܐ	1165
139a	ṭīmā	ܛܝܡܐ	1166
405b	ṭīmāun	ܛܝܡܘܢ	1167
405b	ṭīmai	ܛܝܡܝ	1168
405b	ṭīmāṯe'aus	ܛܝܡܬܐܘܣ	1169
139a	ṭīnā	ܛܝܢܐ	1170
138b	ṭəyārā	ܛܝܪܐ	1171
139a	ṭairā	ܛܝܪܐ	1172
139b	ṭāḵ	ܛܟ	1173
139b	ṭakes	ܛܟܣ	1174
139b	ṭeḵsā	ܛܟܣܐ	1175
139b	ṭalel (pa)	ܛܠܠ	1176
140a	ṭalyā	ܛܠܝܐ	1177
140a	ṭalyuṯā	ܛܠܝܘܬܐ	1178
140a	ṭəlīṯā	ܛܠܝܬܐ	1179
139b	ṭelālā	ܛܠܠܐ	1180
140a	ṭəlam	ܛܠܡ	1181
139b	ṭelānīṯā	ܛܠܢܝܬܐ	1182
140b	ṭəleq	ܛܠܩ	1183
140b	ṭelārē	ܛܠܪ̈ܐ	1184
140b	ṭəlaš	ܛܠܫ	1185
140b	ṭama (pa)	ܛܡܐ	1186
140b	ṭamā'	ܛܡܐܐ	1187
140b	ṭam'uṯā	ܛܡܐܘܬܐ	1188
141a	ṭəmar	ܛܡܪ	1189
141a	ṭan	ܛܢ	1190
141a	ṭənānā	ܛܢܢܐ	1191
141a	ṭanānā	ܛܢܢܐ	1192
141b	ṭənep̄	ܛܢܦ	1193
141b	ṭanp̄ā	ܛܢܦܐ	1194
141b	ṭanpuṯā	ܛܢܦܘܬܐ	1195
141b	ṭə'ā	ܛܥܐ	1196
142a	ṭā'yuṯā	ܛܥܝܘܬܐ	1197
142b	ṭə'em	ܛܥܡ	1198
143a	ṭə'en	ܛܥܢ	1199
143a	ṭa'nā	ܛܥܢܐ	1200
143a	ṭə'eš	ܛܥܫ	1201
143b	ṭap̄ṭep̄	ܛܦܛܦ	1202
143b	ṭep̄rā	ܛܦܪܐ	1203
143b	ṭərā	ܛܪܐ	1204
143b	ṭəraḏ	ܛܪܕ	1205
405b	ṭrāu'aus	ܛܪܘܐܘܣ	1206
405b	ṭrāugaliyun	ܛܪܘܓܠܝܘܢ	1207

Pg/Col	Pronunciation	Word	No
405b	ṭrāup̄īmāus	ܛܪܘܦܝܡܘܣ	1208
406a	ṭrup̄āna	ܛܪܘܦܢܐ	1209
406a	ṭrup̄āsa	ܛܪܘܦܣܐ	1210
406a	ṭerṭıyaus	ܛܪܛܝܘܣ	1211
406a	ṭarṭelāus	ܛܪܛܠܘܣ	1212
406a	ṭrak̲āunā	ܛܪܟܘܢܐ	1213
406a	ṭarsāus	ܛܪܣܘܣ	1214
144a	ṭᵊrap̄	ܛܪܦ	1215
144a	ṭarep̄	ܛܪܦ	1216
144a	ṭarp̄ā	ܛܪܦܐ	1217
144a	ṭᵊšā	ܛܫܐ	1218
145a	yı'eb̲	ܝܐܒ	1219
145a	yāyā	ܝܐܝܐ	1220
145a	yāyut̲ā	ܝܐܝܘܬܐ	1221
406a	ya'nī	ܝܐܢܝ	1222
146a	yabīšā	ܝܒܝܫܐ	1223
145a	yabel (pa)	ܝܒܠ	1224
145b	yıb̲eš	ܝܒܫ	1225
145b	yab̲šā	ܝܒܫܐ	1226
147a	'audı (aph)	ܝܕܐ	1227
149a	yād̲u'ā	ܝܕܘܥܐ	1228
149a	yıd̲ī'ā	ܝܕܝܥܐ	1229
149b	yıd̲ı'ut̲ā	ܝܕܝܥܘܬܐ	1230
147b	yıd̲a'	ܝܕܥ	1231
149b	yıd̲a't̲ā	ܝܕܥܬܐ	1232
150b	ya(h)b̲	ܝܗܒ	1233
152a	yāhub̲ā	ܝܗܘܒܐ	1234
152b	yıhud̲	ܝܗܘܕ	1235
406a	yıhud̲ā	ܝܗܘܕܐ	1236
406a	yıhud̲ā	ܝܗܘܕܐ	1237
406b	yıhud̲ā	ܝܗܘܕܐ	1238
406b	yıhud̲ā	ܝܗܘܕܐ	1239
406b	yıhud̲ā	ܝܗܘܕܐ	1240
406b	yıhud̲ā	ܝܗܘܕܐ	1241
406b	yıhud̲ā	ܝܗܘܕܐ	1242
406b	yıhud̲ā	ܝܗܘܕܐ	1243
406b	yıhud̲ā	ܝܗܘܕܐ	1244
152b	yıhud̲ā'īt̲	ܝܗܘܕܐܝܬ	1245
152b	yıhud̲āyā	ܝܗܘܕܝܐ	1246
153a	yıhud̲āyut̲ā	ܝܗܘܕܝܘܬܐ	1247
406b	yāhušāp̄āṭ	ܝܗܘܫܦܛ	1248
406b	yu'eıl	ܝܘܐܝܠ	1249
406b	yu'ārāš	ܝܘܐܪܫ	1250
145a	yub̲ālā	ܝܘܒܠܐ	1251
153a	yud̲	ܝܘܕ	1252
407a	yuḥan	ܝܘܚܢ	1253
407a	yuḥanān	ܝܘܚܢܢ	1254
407a	yuḥanān	ܝܘܚܢܢ	1255
407a	yuḥanān	ܝܘܚܢܢ	1256
407a	yuḥanān	ܝܘܚܢܢ	1257
407b	yuḥanān	ܝܘܚܢܢ	1258
407b	yuk̲anyā	ܝܘܟܢܝܐ	1259
407b	yulyā	ܝܘܠܝܐ	1260
407b	yulıyāus	ܝܘܠܝܘܣ	1261

Pg/Col	Pronunciation	Word	No
156a	yulp̄ānā	ܝܘܠܦܢܐ	1262
153a	yaumā	ܝܘܡܐ	1263
154a	yaumnā	ܝܘܡܢܐ	1264
154a	yawān	ܝܘܢ	1265
154b	yaunā	ܝܘܢܐ	1266
154a	yaunā'īṯ	ܝܘܢܐܝܬ	1267
407b	yāunya	ܝܘܢܝܐ	1268
154a	yaunāyā	ܝܘܢܝܐ	1269
407b	yunām	ܝܘܢܡ	1270
407b	yaunān	ܝܘܢ	1271
407b	yusī	ܝܘܣܐ	1272
407b	yāusī	ܝܘܣܐ	1273
408a	yusṭāus	ܝܘܣܛܘܣ	1274
408a	yusṭāus	ܝܘܣܛܘܣ	1275
408a	yausep̄	ܝܘܣܦ	1276
408a	yausep̄	ܝܘܣܦ	1277
408a	yausep̄	ܝܘܣܦ	1278
408a	yausep̄	ܝܘܣܦ	1279
408a	yausep̄	ܝܘܣܦ	1280
408a	yausep̄	ܝܘܣܦ	1281
408a	yausep̄	ܝܘܣܦ	1282
408b	yausep̄	ܝܘܣܦ	1283
408b	yupī	ܝܘܦܐ	1284
160b	yuqrā	ܝܘܩܪܐ	1285
408b	yurdənān	ܝܘܪܕܢܢ	1286
408b	yurām	ܝܘܪܡ	1287
408b	yuram	ܝܘܪܡ	1288
161b	yurāqā	ܝܘܪܩܐ	1289
161b	yurṯānā	ܝܘܪܬܢܐ	1290
408b	yušıyā	ܝܘܫܝܐ	1291
408b	yuṯām	ܝܘܬܡ	1292
163b	yuṯrānā	ܝܘܬܪܢܐ	1293
408b	yezaḇıl	ܝܙܒܠ	1294
154b	yızep̄	ܝܙܦ	1295
154b	šauḥeḏ (shaph)	ܝܚܕ	1296
154b	yaḥṭā	ܝܚܛܐ	1297
154b	yıḥıḏāyā	ܝܚܝܕܝܐ	1298
155a	'ailel (aph)	ܝܠ	1299
155a	yıleḏ	ܝܠܕ	1300
155a	yaldā	ܝܠܕܐ	1301
155b	yaluḏā	ܝܠܘܕܐ	1302
155a	yāluḏā	ܝܠܘܕܐ	1303
155b	yılıḏuṯā	ܝܠܝܕܘܬܐ	1304
155a	yıleltā	ܝܠܠܬܐ	1305
156a	yılep̄	ܝܠܦ	1306
157b	yımā	ܝܡܐ	1307
157b	yamā	ܝܡܐ	1308
408b	yamā ḏəsup̄	ܝܡܐ ܕܣܘܦ	1309
408b	yambris	ܝܡܒܪܝܣ	1310
158a	yamīnā	ܝܡܝܢܐ	1311
158b	yamen (pa)	ܝܡܢ	1312
158a	yamṯā	ܝܡܬܐ	1313
409a	yānis	ܝܢܣ	1314
158b	yıneq	ܝܢܩ	1315

Pg/Col	Pronunciation	Word	No
158b	'ausep̄ (aph)	ܝܣܦ	1316
159a	yı'ā	ܝܥܐ	1317
159a	'etya'an (ethpa)	ܝܥܢ	1318
159a	ya'nā	ܝܥܢܐ	1319
159a	ya'nuṯā	ܝܥܢܘܬܐ	1320
409a	ya'qub̠	ܝܥܩܘܒ	1321
409a	ya'qub̠	ܝܥܩܘܒ	1322
409a	ya'qub̠	ܝܥܩܘܒ	1323
409a	ya'qub̠	ܝܥܩܘܒ	1324
409a	ya'qub̠	ܝܥܩܘܒ	1325
409a	ya'qub̠	ܝܥܩܘܒ	1326
409b	ya'qub̠	ܝܥܩܘܒ	1327
159a	'aup̄ī (aph)	ܝܦܐ	1328
159b	yaṣīp̄ā	ܝܨܝܦܐ	1329
159b	yaṣīp̄ā'īṯ	ܝܨܝܦܐܝܬ	1330
159b	yaṣīp̄uṯā	ܝܨܝܦܘܬܐ	1331
159a	yıṣep̄	ܝܨܦ	1332
159b	yıqaḏ	ܝܩܕ	1333
160a	yaqdā	ܝܩܕܐ	1334
160a	yaqdānā	ܝܩܕܢܐ	1335
160a	yaqundā	ܝܩܘܢܕܐ	1336
160b	yaqīrā	ܝܩܝܪܐ	1337
161a	yaqīrā'īṯ	ܝܩܝܪܐܝܬ	1338
160a	yıqar	ܝܩܪ	1339
161a	yıreb̠	ܝܪܒ	1340
409b	yareḏ	ܝܪܕ	1341
161a	yarḥā	ܝܪܚܐ	1342
161b	nı'rak̠ (pe imperf 3sm)	ܝܪܟ	1343
161b	yarqā	ܝܪܩܐ	1344
161b	yıreṯ	ܝܪܬ	1345
162a	yartuṯā	ܝܪܬܘܬܐ	1346
409b	yešu'	ܝܫܘܥ	1347
410a	yešu'	ܝܫܘܥ	1348
410a	yešu'	ܝܫܘܥ	1349
162a	'aušeṭ (aph)	ܝܫܛ	1350
162a	yašpeh	ܝܫܦܗ	1351
162a	yıṯeb̠	ܝܬܒ	1352
163b	yatīrā	ܝܬܝܪܐ	1353
164a	yatīrā'īṯ	ܝܬܝܪܐܝܬ	1354
164a	yatīruṯā	ܝܬܝܪܘܬܐ	1355
163a	yaṯmā	ܝܬܡܐ	1356
163a	yıṯar	ܝܬܪ	1357
165a	kā	ܟܐ	1358
165a	kā'	ܟܐܐ	1359
165a	kēb̠	ܟܐܒ	1360
165b	kīb̠ā	ܟܐܒܐ	1361
165b	kīb̠ānā	ܟܐܒܢܐ	1362
168a	kīnā	ܟܐܢܐ	1363
168a	kīnā'īṯ	ܟܐܢܐܝܬ	1364
168a	kīnuṯā	ܟܐܢܘܬܐ	1365
165b	kīp̄ā	ܟܐܦܐ	1366
410a	kīp̄ā	ܟܐܦܐ	1367
166a	ka'ar (pa)	ܟܐܪ	1368
165a	kāṯā	ܟܐܬܐ	1369

Pg/Col	Pronunciation	Word	No
166a	kaḇdā	ܟܒܕܐ	1370
166a	kaḇlā	ܟܒܠܐ	1371
166a	kᵊḇar	ܟܒܪ	1372
166a	kᵊḇar	ܟܒܪ	1373
166a	keḇrīṯā	ܟܒܪܝܬܐ	1374
166a	kᵊḇaš	ܟܒܫ	1375
166b	kaḏ	ܟܕ	1376
167a	kadeḇ (pa)	ܟܕܒ	1377
167a	kadāḇā	ܟܕܒܐ	1378
167b	kadāḇuṯā	ܟܕܒܘܬܐ	1379
167b	kadu	ܟܕܘ	1380
167b	kᵊḏan	ܟܕܢ	1381
167b	kahen (pa)	ܟܗܢ	1382
167b	kāhnā	ܟܗܢܐ	1383
167b	kāhnuṯā	ܟܗܢܘܬܐ	1384
167b	kāhnāyā	ܟܗܢܝܐ	1385
168a	kᵊwā	ܟܘܐ	1386
166a	ku'ārā	ܟܘܐܪܐ	1387
166a	kubā	ܟܘܒܐ	1388
166b	kuḇšā	ܟܘܒܫܐ	1389
168b	kuwānā	ܟܘܘܢܐ	1390
410b	kuza	ܟܘܙܐ	1391
168a	keweılā	ܟܘܝܠܐ	1392
168a	kaukḇā	ܟܘܟܒܐ	1393
169b	'aḵīl (aph)	ܟܘܠ	1394
172a	kulīṯā	ܟܘܠܝܬܐ	1395
172b	kumrā	ܟܘܡܪܐ	1396
173a	kumruṯā	ܟܘܡܪܘܬܐ	1397
173a	kumrᵊṯā	ܟܘܡܪܬܐ	1398
168a	kān (pe 3sm)	ܟܘܢ	1399
176b	kupārā	ܟܘܦܪܐ	1400
177a	korā	ܟܘܪܐ	1401
169a	ḵorā	ܟܘܪܐ	1402
178a	kurhānā	ܟܘܪܗܢܐ	1403
410b	kāurazīn	ܟܘܪܙܝܢ	1404
179b	kursᵊyā	ܟܘܪܣܝܐ	1405
410b	kuš	ܟܘܫ	1406
410b	kušāyā	ܟܘܫܝܐ	1407
180b	kušᵊp̄ā	ܟܘܫܦܐ	1408
168a	kauṯā	ܟܘܬܐ	1409
182a	kutīnā	ܟܘܬܝܢܐ	1410
182a	kuṯmᵊṯā	ܟܘܬܡܬܐ	1411
169a	kᵊḥeḏ	ܟܚܕ	1412
169a	kᵊḥal	ܟܚܠ	1413
169a	keḥlā	ܟܚܠܐ	1414
169a	kaı	ܟܝ	1415
410b	kıyāus	ܟܝܘܣ	1416
169b	kaılā	ܟܝܠܐ	1417
169b	kᵊyāltā	ܟܝܠܬܐ	1418
172b	kīmonā	ܟܝܡܘܢܐ	1419
168b	kᵊyānā	ܟܝܢܐ	1420
168b	kᵊyānā'īṯ	ܟܝܢܐܝܬ	1421
169b	kīsā	ܟܝܣܐ	1422
169b	kakᵊrā	ܟܟܪܐ	1423

Pg/Col	Pronunciation	Word	No	Pg/Col	Pronunciation	Word	No
169b	kakārīṯā	ܟܟܪܝܬܐ	1424	173a	kᵊmar	ܟܡܪ	1451
169b	kul	ܟܠ	1425	173a	ken	ܟܢ	1452
171b	kalel (pa)	ܟܠ	1426	173a	kanī (pa)	ܟܢܝ	1453
170b	kul (')nāš	ܟܠ ܐܢܫ	1427	173b	kᵊnušyā	ܟܢܘܫܝܐ	1454
171a	kul zᵊḇan	ܟܠ ܙܒܢ	1428	173b	kᵊnuštā	ܟܢܘܫܬܐ	1455
171a	kul ḥaḏ	ܟܠ ܚܕ	1429	411a	kᵊnaʿan	ܟܢܥܢ	1456
171a	kul yom	ܟܠ ܝܘܡ	1430	411a	kᵊnaʿnāyā	ܟܢܥܢܝܐ	1457
171a	kul medem	ܟܠ ܡܕܡ	1431	173b	kenp̄ā	ܟܢܦܐ	1458
171b	kul ʿedān	ܟܠ ܥܕܢ	1432	173b	kᵊnaš	ܟܢܫ	1459
171b	kᵊlā	ܟܠܐ	1433	174a	kenšā	ܟܢܫܐ	1460
410b	kᵊlā'ē	ܟܠܐܐ	1434	173a	kᵊnāṯā	ܟܢܬܐ	1461
172a	kalbā	ܟܠܒܐ	1435	175a	'eṯkᵊses (ethpe)	ܟܣ	1462
410b	kalᵊḏāyā	ܟܠܕܝܐ	1436	169a	kāsā	ܟܣܐ	1463
171b	kᵊlīlā	ܟܠܝܠܐ	1437	175a	kᵊsā	ܟܣܐ	1464
172a	kelyānā	ܟܠܝܢܐ	1438	175b	kasyā'īṯ	ܟܣܝܐܝܬ	1465
172a	kīlıyarḵā	ܟܠܝܪܟܐ	1439	175a	kᵊsāsā	ܟܣܣܐ	1466
172a	kālīṯā	ܟܠܝܬܐ	1440	176a	kespā	ܟܣܦܐ	1467
172a	klamīs	ܟܠܡܝܣ	1441	176a	kap̄	ܟܦ	1468
172b	'aḵleš (aph)	ܟܠܫ	1442	176b	kāp̄urā	ܟܦܘܪܐ	1469
172b	kelšā	ܟܠܫܐ	1443	176a	kᵊp̄īp̄ā	ܟܦܝܦܐ	1470
171b	kalṯā	ܟܠܬܐ	1444	176a	kᵊp̄en	ܟܦܢ	1471
172b	kᵊmā	ܟܡܐ	1445	176a	kap̄nā	ܟܦܢܐ	1472
172b	kᵊmīnā	ܟܡܐܝܢܐ	1446	176b	kap̄nā	ܟܦܢܐ	1473
172b	kamunā	ܟܡܘܢܐ	1447	176b	kᵊp̄ar	ܟܦܪ	1474
173a	kᵊmīrā	ܟܡܝܪܐ	1448	177a	kap̄rā	ܟܦܪܐ	1475
173a	kᵊmīrā'īṯ	ܟܡܝܪܐܝܬ	1449	177a	kap̄runē	ܟܦܪ̈ܘܢܐ	1476
172b	kᵊmen	ܟܡܢ	1450	411a	kᵊp̄arnaḥum	ܟܦܪܢܚܘܡ	1477

Pg/Col	Pronunciation	Word	No
177a	kar	ܟܪ	1478
177a	kᵊrā	ܟܪܐ	1479
177b	kᵊrab̲	ܟܪܒ	1480
177b	kᵊrah	ܟܪܗ	1481
177b	kᵊrub̲ā	ܟܪܘܒܐ	1482
177b	kārub̲ā	ܟܪܘܒܐ	1483
178a	kāruzā	ܟܪܘܙܐ	1484
178a	kāruzut̲ā	ܟܪܘܙܘܬܐ	1485
180a	kᵊruspᵊrasā	ܟܪܘܣܦܪܣܐ	1486
178b	kᵊraz	ܟܪܙ	1487
179a	karṭīsā	ܟܪܛܝܣܐ	1488
177b	kᵊrīhā	ܟܪܝܗܐ	1489
178a	kᵊrīhut̲ā	ܟܪܝܗܘܬܐ	1490
177a	karyut̲ā	ܟܪܝܘܬܐ	1491
179a	kᵊrak̲	ܟܪܟ	1492
179a	kerkā	ܟܪܟܐ	1493
179a	kark̲ā	ܟܪܟܐ	1494
179b	karmā	ܟܪܡܐ	1495
179b	karsā	ܟܪܣܐ	1496
411a	krisṭᵊyana	ܟܪܣܛܝܢܐ	1497
180a	'et̲kᵊšel (ethpe)	ܟܫܠ	1498
180a	kešlā	ܟܫܠܐ	1499
180b	'et̲kašap̄ (ethpa)	ܟܫܦ	1500
180b	kᵊt̲ab̲	ܟܬܒ	1501
181a	kᵊt̲āb̲ā	ܟܬܒܐ	1502
181b	kᵊt̲āb̲unā	ܟܬܒܘܢܐ	1503
181b	kᵊt̲āb̲tā	ܟܬܒܬܐ	1504
182a	kᵊt̲am	ܟܬܡ	1505
182a	ketānā	ܟܬܢܐ	1506
182a	kat̲pā	ܟܬܦܐ	1507
182b	katar (pa)	ܟܬܪ	1508
182b	kᵊt̲aš	ܟܬܫ	1509
	not included in concordance	ܠ	1510
183a	lā	ܠܐ	1511
185a	lᵊ'ā	ܠܐܐ	1512
185a	le'ut̲ā	ܠܐܘܬܐ	1513
411a	lası'a	ܠܐܣܝܐ	1514
186a	labeb̲ (pa)	ܠܒ	1515
185b	lebā	ܠܒܐ	1516
186b	lᵊb̲untā	ܠܒܘܢܬܐ	1517
186b	lᵊb̲ušā	ܠܒܘܫܐ	1518
411a	labī	ܠܒܝ	1519
186b	lᵊb̲ak̲	ܠܒܟ	1520
411a	leb̲nāyā	ܠܒܢܝܐ	1521
50b	lᵊb̲ar	ܠܒܪ	1522
186b	lᵊb̲eš	ܠܒܫ	1523
187a	lᵊb̲āšā	ܠܒܫܐ	1524
59a	lᵊḡau	ܠܓܘ	1525
187a	leḡyonā	ܠܓܝܘܢܐ	1526
62b	leḡlᵊyā	ܠܓܠܝܐ	1527
64a	laḡmār	ܠܓܡܪ	1528
187a	laḡt̲ā	ܠܓܬܐ	1529
411a	lad̲īqıya	ܠܕܝܩܝܐ	1530
187a	lahgā	ܠܗܓܐ	1531

Pg/Col	Pronunciation	Word	No
90b	lᵊhal	ܠܗܠ	1532
187b	lau	ܠܘ	1533
187b	lᵊwā	ܠܘܐ	1534
411b	lāu'īs	ܠܘܐܝܣ	1535
411b	luḇī	ܠܘܒܝ	1536
186a	lubābā	ܠܘܒܒܐ	1537
411b	luḏ	ܠܘܕ	1538
411b	luḏıya	ܠܘܕܝܐ	1539
187b	luḥā	ܠܘܚܐ	1540
189a	luḥāmā	ܠܘܚܡܐ	1541
411b	luṭ	ܠܘܛ	1542
187b	lāṭ (pe 3sm)	ܠܘܛ	1543
188a	lauṭṯā	ܠܘܛܬܐ	1544
411b	lewī	ܠܘܝ	1545
411b	lewī	ܠܘܝ	1546
411b	lewī	ܠܘܝ	1547
411b	lewī	ܠܘܝ	1548
411b	lewāyā	ܠܘܝܐ	1549
187b	lᵊwīṯā	ܠܘܝܬܐ	1550
188a	lukāıṯā	ܠܘܟܝܬܐ	1551
188a	laulārā	ܠܘܠܪܐ	1552
412a	lusṭᵊra	ܠܘܣܛܪܐ	1553
412a	lusıyāus	ܠܘܣܝܘܣ	1554
412a	lusanıya	ܠܘܣܢܝܐ	1555
412a	luqā	ܠܘܩܐ	1556
307a	luqᵊḇal	ܠܘܩܒܠ	1557
310a	luqᵊḏam	ܠܘܩܕܡ	1558
412a	luqıya	ܠܘܩܝܐ	1559
412a	luqıyāus	ܠܘܩܝܘܣ	1560
412a	luqanıya	ܠܘܩܢܝܐ	1561
188a	lᵊwāṯ	ܠܘܬ	1562
188b	lᵊḥā	ܠܚܐ	1563
112b	lᵊḥuḏ	ܠܚܘܕ	1564
188b	lᵊḥaḵ	ܠܚܟ	1565
188b	lᵊḥem	ܠܚܡ	1566
189a	laḥmā	ܠܚܡܐ	1567
189a	lᵊḥeš	ܠܚܫ	1568
411a	līḇerṭīnu	ܠܝܒܪܛܝܢܘ	1569
189b	līṭrā	ܠܝܛܪܐ	1570
412a	līnāus	ܠܝܢܘܣ	1571
189b	laıṯ	ܠܝܬ	1572
190a	lᵊḵā	ܠܟܐ	1573
190a	lal	ܠܠ	1574
190a	lelā	ܠܠܐ	1575
190a	leluṯā	ܠܠܘܬܐ	1576
189b	lılyā	ܠܠܝܐ	1577
190a	lam	ܠܡ	1578
193b	lᵊmā	ܠܡܐ	1579
191a	lᵊmīnā	ܠܡܝܢܐ	1580
190a	lᵊmaḏ	ܠܡܕ	1581
128a	lᵊmaḥsen	ܠܡܚܣܢ	1582
412a	lameḵ	ܠܡܟ	1583
208b	lᵊmānā	ܠܡܢܐ	1584
191a	lampīḏā	ܠܡܦܝܕܐ	1585

Pg/Col	Pronunciation	Word	No
191a	lesṭā	ܠܣܛܐ	1586
191a	'etla'ab (ethpa)	ܠܥܒ	1587
191a	la'bā	ܠܥܒܐ	1588
412a	lā'āzar	ܠܥܙܪ	1589
412b	lā'āzar	ܠܥܙܪ	1590
191a	lə'es	ܠܥܣ	1591
307b	ləqublā	ܠܩܘܒܠܐ	1592
191b	ləqaṭ	ܠܩܛ	1593
191b	ləqīšāyā	ܠܩܝܫܝܐ	1594
191b	leqšā	ܠܩܫܐ	1595
191b	lešānā	ܠܫܢܐ	1596
193a	mā	ܡܐ	1597
193b	mā'	ܡܐܐ	1598
14a	mēkultā	ܡܐܟܘܠܬܐ	1599
14a	mēkal qarṣā	ܡܐܟܠ ܩܪܨܐ	1600
14a	mēklā	ܡܐܟܠܐ	1601
193b	mēn	ܡܐܢ	1602
194a	mānā	ܡܐܢܐ	1603
412b	manī	ܡܐܢܝ	1604
29b	mēsārtā	ܡܐܣܪܬܐ	1605
412b	mā'at	ܡܐܬ	1606
35a	mētyā	ܡܐܬܝܐ	1607
193b	matein	ܡܐܬܝܢ	1608
35a	mētītā	ܡܐܬܝܬܐ	1609
216a	mabu'ā	ܡܒܘܥܐ	1610
40a	məbazḥānā	ܡܒܙܚܢܐ	1611
42a	məbayānā	ܡܒܝܢܐ	1612
47a	məbasrānā	ܡܒܣܪܢܐ	1613
412b	mağdu	ܡܓܕܘ	1614
412b	mağdu	ܡܓܕܘ	1615
58a	mağdəlā	ܡܓܕܠܐ	1616
412b	mağdəlāitā	ܡܓܕܠܝܬܐ	1617
58b	məgadəpānā	ܡܓܕܦܢܐ	1618
412b	māğuğ	ܡܓܘܓ	1619
194a	məğušē	ܡܓܘܫܐ	1620
62b	mağlē	ܡܓܠܐ	1621
216b	maglā	ܡܓܠܐ	1622
62a	məğaltā	ܡܓܠܬܐ	1623
194a	mağān	ܡܓܢ	1624
217a	mağrat ruḥā	ܡܓܪܬ ܪܘܚܐ	1625
194b	mad	ܡܕ	1626
68b	madbəḥā	ܡܕܒܚܐ	1627
69a	madbərā	ܡܕܒܪܐ	1628
69a	madbərāyā	ܡܕܒܪܝܐ	1629
69b	mədabrānā	ܡܕܒܪܢܐ	1630
69b	mədabərānutā	ܡܕܒܪܢܘܬܐ	1631
412b	mādāyā	ܡܕܝܐ	1632
412b	medyan	ܡܕܝܢ	1633
195a	mādein	ܡܕܝܢ	1634
71b	mədī(n)tā	ܡܕܝܢܬܐ	1635
73a	medyārā	ܡܕܝܪܐ	1636

Pg/Col	Pronunciation	Word	No
194b	madeḵ (pa)	ܡܕܟ	1637
194b	madᵊḵā	ܡܕܟܐ	1638
194b	medem	ܡܕܡ	1639
80a	maḏmᵊkā	ܡܕܡܟܐ	1640
81a	maḏnᵊḥā	ܡܕܢܚܐ	1641
149b	mad‘ā	ܡܕܥܐ	1642
81b	mᵊḏa‘rānā	ܡܕܥܪܢܐ	1643
72b	mᵊḏāq	ܡܕܩ	1644
195a	meḏrā	ܡܕܪܐ	1645
19b	mᵊhaimnā	ܡܗܝܡܢܐ	1646
19a	mᵊhaimnā	ܡܗܝܡܢܐ	1647
412b	mahlālā’eil	ܡܗܠܠܐܝܠ	1648
145b	maublā	ܡܘܒܠܐ	1649
152a	mauhaḇtā	ܡܘܗܒܬܐ	1650
197a	muḥā	ܡܘܚܐ	1651
199b	mukākā	ܡܘܟܟܐ	1652
155b	maulāḏā	ܡܘܠܕܐ	1653
203b	mulāyā	ܡܘܠܝܐ	1654
205a	mulkānā	ܡܘܠܟܢܐ	1655
195a	mumā	ܡܘܡܐ	1656
157b	mumāṯā	ܡܘܡܬܐ	1657
413a	musiya	ܡܘܣܝܐ	1658
195a	mayeq (pa)	ܡܘܩ	1659
210b	murā	ܡܘܪܐ	1660
413a	murā	ܡܘܪܐ	1661
195a	murun	ܡܘܪܘܢ	1662
195a	māš (pe 3sm)	ܡܘܫ	1663
413a	mušē	ܡܘܫܐ	1664
195b	māṯ (pe 3sm)	ܡܘܬ	1665
196a	mautā	ܡܘܬܐ	1666
163a	mautᵊḇā	ܡܘܬܒܐ	1667
196b	mautānā	ܡܘܬܢܐ	1668
164b	mautᵊrānā	ܡܘܬܪܢܐ	1669
197a	mᵊzaḡ	ܡܙܓ	1670
102a	mazmurā	ܡܙܡܘܪܐ	1671
103a	maz‘uqē	ܡܙܥܘܩܐ	1672
197a	mᵊḥā	ܡܚܐ	1673
106b	mᵊḥablānā	ܡܚܒܠܢܐ	1674
108a	mᵊḥaḡrā	ܡܚܓܪܐ	1675
109a	meḥḏā	ܡܚܕܐ	1676
197b	mᵊḥuṯā	ܡܚܘܬܐ	1677
116a	maḥzē	ܡܚܙܐ	1678
116a	maḥzīṯā	ܡܚܙܝܬܐ	1679
117a	mᵊḥaṭā	ܡܚܛܐ	1680
197b	mᵊḥīlā	ܡܚܝܠܐ	1681
197b	mᵊḥīluṯā	ܡܚܝܠܘܬܐ	1682
120b	maḥyānā	ܡܚܝܢܐ	1683
197b	mᵊḥel	ܡܚܠ	1684
125a	mᵊḥamsᵊnānuṯā	ܡܚܡܣܢܢܘܬܐ	1685
127a	maḥnuqīṯā	ܡܚܢܘܩܝܬܐ	1686
127b	mᵊḥasᵊḏānā	ܡܚܣܕܢܐ	1687
197b	mᵊḥār	ܡܚܪ	1688
133a	maḥšaḇtā	ܡܚܫܒܬܐ	1689

Pg/Col	Pronunciation	Word	No
134b	maḥšulā	ܡܚܫܘܠܐ	1690
221a	maḥatᵊtā	ܡܚܬܬܐ	1691
197b	mᵊṭā	ܡܛܐ	1692
139b	mᵊṭakᵊsutā	ܡܛܟܣܘܬܐ	1693
198a	metul	ܡܛܠ	1694
139b	maṭ(l)lā	ܡܛܠܠܐ	1695
139b	mᵊṭaltā	ܡܛܠܬܐ	1696
142b	maṭ'ᵊyānā	ܡܛܥܝܢܐ	1697
142b	maṭ'ᵊyānutā	ܡܛܥܝܢܘܬܐ	1698
199a	mᵊṭar	ܡܛܪ	1699
199a	meṭrā	ܡܛܪܐ	1700
221b	maṭartā	ܡܛܪܬܐ	1701
144b	maṭšᵊyā'īt	ܡܛܫܝܐܝܬ	1702
413a	maṭat	ܡܛܬ	1703
413a	maṭᵊtā	ܡܛܬܐ	1704
413a	maṭᵊtat	ܡܛܬܬ	1705
199a	mayā	ܡܝܐ	1706
196b	māyututā	ܡܝܘܬܘܬܐ	1707
413a	mīṭulīnī	ܡܝܛܘܠܝܢܝ	1708
196b	mayītā	ܡܝܝܬܐ	1709
413b	mīkā'eil	ܡܝܟܐܝܠ	1710
199a	mīlā	ܡܝܠܐ	1711
413b	mīlīṭī	ܡܝܠܝܛܐ	1712
413b	mīlīṭāus	ܡܝܠܝܛܐܘܣ	1713
160b	mᵊyaqarā	ܡܝܩܪܐ	1714
196a	mītā	ܡܝܬܐ	1715
196b	mītutā	ܡܝܬܘܬܐ	1716
163b	mᵊyatrā	ܡܝܬܪܐ	1717
164a	mᵊyatᵊrutā	ܡܝܬܪܘܬܐ	1718
199a	mak	ܡܟ	1719
200a	mekā	ܡܟܐ	1720
165b	makēbā	ܡܟܐܒܐ	1721
199b	makīkā	ܡܟܝܟܐ	1722
199b	makīkuta	ܡܟܝܟܘܬܐ	1723
200a	mekīl	ܡܟܝܠ	1724
200b	mᵊkīrā	ܡܟܝܪܐ	1725
169a	mᵊkānā	ܡܟܢܐ	1726
200a	mākᵊsā	ܡܟܣܐ	1727
200a	maksā	ܡܟܣܐ	1728
175a	maksānutā	ܡܟܣܢܘܬܐ	1729
200a	mᵊkar	ܡܟܪ	1730
179a	makrᵊzānā	ܡܟܪܙܢܐ	1731
180a	makšulā	ܡܟܫܘܠܐ	1732
182a	maktᵊbānutā	ܡܟܬܒܢܘܬܐ	1733
201b	malel (pa)	ܡܠܠ	1734
202b	mᵊlā	ܡܠܐ	1735
203a	mᵊlā'ā	ܡܠܐܐ	1736
185a	malakā	ܡܠܐܟܐ	1737
204b	mᵊlag	ܡܠܓ	1738
204b	mᵊlaḥ	ܡܠܚ	1739
204b	malāḥā	ܡܠܚܐ	1740
204b	melḥā	ܡܠܚܐ	1741

Pg/Col	Pronunciation	Word	No	Pg/Col	Pronunciation	Word	No
203a	melyā	ܡܠܝܐ	1742	206a	man	ܡܢ	1768
413b	malyā	ܡܠܝܐ	1743	206a	man	ܡܢ	1769
203a	malyā’īṯ	ܡܠܝܐܝܬ	1744	206b	men	ܡܢ	1770
203a	malyuṯā	ܡܠܝܘܬܐ	1745	208a	mānā	ܡܢܐ	1771
204b	malīḥā	ܡܠܝܚܐ	1746	208b	mᵊnā	ܡܢܐ	1772
201a	mᵊlīlā	ܡܠܝܠܐ	1747	413b	mana’eıl	ܡܢܐܝܠ	1773
203a	mᵊlīṯā	ܡܠܝܬܐ	1748	216b	mᵊnaḡᵊḏānā	ܡܢܓܕܢܐ	1774
413b	mālek̠	ܡܠܟ	1749	209a	manḥaı	ܡܢܚܝ	1775
204b	mᵊlak̠	ܡܠܟ	1750	208b	manyā	ܡܢܝܐ	1776
205a	malkā	ܡܠܟܐ	1751	209a	menyānā	ܡܢܝܢܐ	1777
205a	melkā	ܡܠܟܐ	1752	223a	mᵊnak̠ap̄	ܡܢܟܦ	1778
413b	malkum	ܡܠܟܘܡ	1753	209a	ma(n)nā	ܡܢܢܐ	1779
205b	malkuṯā	ܡܠܟܘܬܐ	1754	413b	mᵊnasāun	ܡܢܣܘܢ	1780
413b	malkī	ܡܠܟܝ	1755	225b	mᵊnasyānā	ܡܢܣܝܢܐ	1781
413b	malkī	ܡܠܟܝ	1756	209a	mᵊna‘	ܡܢܥ	1782
413b	malkīzᵊḏeq	ܡܠܟܝܙܕܩ	1757	220a	mᵊnārtā	ܡܢܪܬܐ	1783
205b	malkᵊṯā	ܡܠܟܬܐ	1758	414a	mᵊnašē	ܡܢܫܐ	1784
157a	malp̄ānā	ܡܠܦܢܐ	1759	414a	mᵊnašē	ܡܢܫܐ	1785
157a	malp̄ānuṯā	ܡܠܦܢܘܬܐ	1760	208b	menṯā	ܡܢܬܐ	1786
200b	melṯā	ܡܠܬܐ	1761	209a	mᵊnāṯā	ܡܢܬܐ	1787
206a	māmonā	ܡܡܘܢܐ	1762	209b	mᵊsā	ܡܣܐ	1788
203a	mamlē	ܡܡܠܐ	1763	209b	masaṯā	ܡܣܐܬܐ	1789
201a	mam(l)lā	ܡܡܠܠܐ	1764	225a	masbā	ܡܣܒܐ	1790
211b	mᵊmaryānā	ܡܡܪܝܢܐ	1765	235b	mᵊsabᵊrānā	ܡܣܒܪܢܐ	1791
		ܡܡܪܡܪܢܐ	1766			ܡܣܒܪܢܘܬܐ	1792
210b	mᵊmarmᵊrānā			235a	mᵊsabᵊrānuṯā		
214a	memṯum	ܡܡܬܘܡ	1767	209b	māsurā	ܡܣܘܪܐ	1793

Pg/Col	Pronunciation	Word	No
242a	masṭəyānuṯā	ܡܣܛܝܢܘܬܐ	1794
240a	məsaibuṯā	ܡܣܝܒܘܬܐ	1795
236a	məsaibərānuṯa	ܡܣܝܒܪܢܘܬܐ	1796
245a	maskəlānā	ܡܣܟܠܢܐ	1797
245b	masken	ܡܣܟܢ	1798
245a	meskınā	ܡܣܟܝܢܐ	1799
245a	meskınuṯā	ܡܣܟܝܢܘܬܐ	1800
246a	masləya	ܡܣܠܝܐ	1801
233a	məsānā	ܡܣܢܐ	1802
209b	məsar	ܡܣܪ	1803
333b	məsarhəḇā'īṯ	ܡܣܪܗܒܐܝܬ	1804
209b	mesṯā	ܡܣܬܐ	1805
246a	mestalyānuṯā	ܡܣܬܠܝܢܘܬܐ	1806
256a	ma'bəḏānā	ܡܥܒܕܢܐ	1807
256a	ma'bəḏānuṯā	ܡܥܒܕܢܘܬܐ	1808
261a	mə'āḏā	ܡܥܕܐ	1809
259b	mə'adərānā	ܡܥܕܪܢܐ	1810
259b	mə'adərānuṯā	ܡܥܕܪܢܘܬܐ	1811
209b	mə'ayā	ܡܥܝܐ	1812
264a	mə'īnā	ܡܥܝܢܐ	1813
265b	ma'lānā	ܡܥܠܢܐ	1814
266a	ma'lānuṯā	ܡܥܠܢܘܬܐ	1815
265b	ma'altā	ܡܥܠܬܐ	1816
271a	ma'məḏānā	ܡܥܡܕܢܐ	1817
270b	ma'muḏīṯā	ܡܥܡܘܕܝܬܐ	1818
272a	ma'mərā	ܡܥܡܪܐ	1819
209b	mə'as	ܡܥܣ	1820
274a	ma'sarē	ܡܥܣܪܐ	1821
275a	ma'ṣartā	ܡܥܨܪܬܐ	1822
275b	mə'aqlā	ܡܥܩܠܐ	1823
275b	mə'aqmā	ܡܥܩܡܐ	1824
276b	ma'rəḇā	ܡܥܪܒܐ	1825
277a	mə'arəp̄anā	ܡܥܪܦܢܐ	1826
276a	mə'arṯā	ܡܥܪܬܐ	1827
226b	mapultā	ܡܦܘܠܬܐ	1828
282b	məpīsānuṯā	ܡܦܝܣܢܘܬܐ	1829
284a	məp̄algānā	ܡܦܠܓܢܐ	1830
287b	mapsānuṯā	ܡܦܣܢܘܬܐ	1831
228a	mapqā	ܡܦܩܐ	1832
228a	mapqānā	ܡܦܩܢܐ	1833
228a	mapaqtā	ܡܦܩܬܐ	1834
295a	məp̄aršānā	ܡܦܪܫܢܐ	1835
297a	map̄taḥ	ܡܦܬܚ	1836
210a	məṣā	ܡܨܐ	1837
230a	maṣuṯā	ܡܨܘܬܐ	1838
302b	məṣīḏtā	ܡܨܝܕܬܐ	1839
210a	meṣ'āyā	ܡܨܥܝܐ	1840

Pg/Col	Pronunciation	Word	No	Pg/Col	Pronunciation	Word	No
305a	mᵊṣaʿrānā	ܡܨܥܪܢܐ	1841	212a	ʾamraḥ (aph)	ܡܪܚ	1868
210a	mᵊṣaʿṯā	ܡܨܥܬܐ	1842	211b	marāḥā	ܡܪܚܐ	1869
414a	meṣrāyā	ܡܨܪܝܐ	1843	211b	marāḥāʾīṯ	ܡܪܚܐܝܬ	1870
414a	meṣrein	ܡܨܪܝܢ	1844	338b	mᵊraḥmānā	ܡܪܚܡܢܐ	1871
308a	mᵊqabᵊlā	ܡܩܒܠܐ	1845			ܡܪܚܡܢܘܬܐ	1872
308b	mᵊqabᵊlānā	ܡܩܒܠܢܐ	1846	338b	mᵊraḥmānuṯā		
414a	maqeḏunya	ܡܩܕܘܢܝܐ	1847	339a	mᵊraḥᵊpānā	ܡܪܚܦܢܐ	1873
414a	maqeḏunāyā	ܡܩܕܘܢܝܐ	1848	212a	mᵊraṭ	ܡܪܛ	1874
311a	mᵊqadᵊmuṯā	ܡܩܕܡܘܬܐ	1849	212a	marṭuṭā	ܡܪܛܘܛܐ	1875
312a	maqdᵊšā	ܡܩܕܫܐ	1850	211b	mᵊrīḏā	ܡܪܝܕܐ	1876
210a	maqelun	ܡܩܠܘܢ	1851	414a	maryam	ܡܪܝܡ	1877
322a	maqrā	ܡܩܪܐ	1852	414a	maryam	ܡܪܝܡ	1878
210a	mar	ܡܪ	1853	414b	maryam	ܡܪܝܡ	1879
211a	mārē	ܡܪܐ	1854	414b	maryam	ܡܪܝܡ	1880
211b	marī (pa)	ܡܪܐ	1855	414b	maryam	ܡܪܝܡ	1881
329a	mᵊrabᵊyānā	ܡܪܒܝܢܐ	1856	414b	maryam	ܡܪܝܡ	1882
330a	marbᵊʿā	ܡܪܒܥܐ	1857	414b	maryam	ܡܪܝܡ	1883
330a	mᵊrabᵊʿāʾīṯ	ܡܪܒܥܐܝܬ	1858	336b	mᵊraimā	ܡܪܝܡܐ	1884
211b	margānīṯā	ܡܪܓܢܝܬܐ	1859	210b	marīrā	ܡܪܝܪܐ	1885
211b	mᵊraḏ	ܡܪܕ	1860	210b	marīrāʾīṯ	ܡܪܝܪܐܝܬ	1886
332b	mardē	ܡܪܕܐ	1861	210b	marīruṯā	ܡܪܝܪܘܬܐ	1887
332b	marduṯā	ܡܪܕܘܬܐ	1862	212a	merīṯā	ܡܪܝܬܐ	1888
332b	mardīṯā	ܡܪܕܝܬܐ	1863	341a	markaḇṯā	ܡܪܟܒܬܐ	1889
211b	māruḏā	ܡܪܘܕܐ	1864	212a	mᵊraʿ	ܡܪܥ	1890
211b	māruḏuṯā	ܡܪܘܕܘܬܐ	1865	212a	marʿā	ܡܪܥܐ	1891
336b	mᵊraumā	ܡܪܘܡܐ	1866	343b	marʿīṯā	ܡܪܥܝܬܐ	1892
211b	māruṯā	ܡܪܘܬܐ	1867	414b	marqāus	ܡܪܩܘܣ	1893

Pg/Col	Pronunciation	Word	No
210b	mərārā	ܡܪܪܐ	1894
210b	mərārtā	ܡܪܪܬܐ	1895
414b	mārtā	ܡܪܬܐ	1896
210b	merṯā	ܡܪܬܐ	1897
347b	martəyanuṯā	ܡܪܬܝܢܘܬܐ	1898
232a	mašəḇā	ܡܫܒܐ	1899
351a	məšabḥā	ܡܫܒܚܐ	1900
356b	məšāḡtā	ܡܫܓܬܐ	1901
154b	məšauḥadta	ܡܫܘܚܕܬܐ	1902
213a	məšuḥṯā	ܡܫܘܚܬܐ	1903
212a	məšaḥ	ܡܫܚ	1904
213a	məšaḥ	ܡܫܚ	1905
213a	mešḥā	ܡܫܚܐ	1906
359a	məšaḥṭānā	ܡܫܚܛܢܐ	1907
124a	məšaḥləp̄ā	ܡܫܚܠܦܐ	1908
212b	məšīḥā	ܡܫܝܚܐ	1909
213a	məšīḥuṯā	ܡܫܝܚܘܬܐ	1910
213a	meškā	ܡܫܟܐ	1911
362b	maškənā	ܡܫܟܢܐ	1912
362b	məšaḵrā	ܡܫܟܪܐ	1913
364b	məšalṭā	ܡܫܠܛܐ	1914
366a	məšalmānā	ܡܫܠܡܢܐ	1915
366b	mašləmānā	ܡܫܠܡܢܐ	1916
367a	mašləmānuṯa	ܡܫܠܡܢܘܬܐ	1917
204a	məšamləyā	ܡܫܡܠܝܐ	1918

Pg/Col	Pronunciation	Word	No
370a	mašməʿā	ܡܫܡܥܐ	1919
370a	mašmaʿṯā	ܡܫܡܥܬܐ	1920
371a	məšamšānā	ܡܫܡܫܢܐ	1921
374a	məšapaʿ	ܡܫܦܥ	1922
376a	məšaqlā	ܡܫܩܠܐ	1923
378a	mašrəyā	ܡܫܪܝܐ	1924
378b	məšaryā	ܡܫܪܝܐ	1925
378a	mašrīṯā	ܡܫܪܝܬܐ	1926
347b	məšartəḥuṯā	ܡܫܪܬܚܘܬܐ	1927
381a	meštuṯā	ܡܫܬܘܬܐ	1928
381a	maštəyā	ܡܫܬܝܐ	1929
370b	meštamʿānā	ܡܫܬܡܥܢܐ	1930
370b	meštamʿānuṯā	ܡܫܬܡܥܢܘܬܐ	1931
213b	məṯum	ܡܬܘܡ	1932
415a	maṯušəlaḥ	ܡܬܘܫܠܚ	1933
213b	məṯaḥ	ܡܬܚ	1934
107a	meṯḥablānuṯā	ܡܬܚܒܠܢܘܬܐ	1935
283a	mettəpīsānuṯā	ܡܬܬܦܝܣܢܘܬܐ	1936
415a	matai	ܡܬܝ	1937
415a	matiya	ܡܬܝܐ	1938
415a	maṯīṯā	ܡܬܝܬܐ	1939
213b	məṯal	ܡܬܠ	1940
213b	maṯlā	ܡܬܠܐ	1941

Pg/Col	Pronunciation	Word	No
152a	matlā	ܡܬܠܐ	1942
415a	māṯān	ܡܬܢ	1943
257b	meṯ‘aḇrānuṯā	ܡܬܥܒܪܢܘܬܐ	1944
214a	maṯrᵊyān	ܡܬܪ̈ܝܢ	1945
415a	matta	ܡܬܬܐ	1946
415a	na'īn	ܢܐܝܢ	1947
415a	nı'apwālīs	ܢܐܦܘܠܝܣ	1948
415a	nīqulīṯā	ܢܝܩܘܠܝܬܐ	1949
415a	nīrāus	ܢܝܪܘܣ	1950
215b	nabī (pa)	ܢܒܐ	1951
215a	nᵊḇıyā	ܢܒܝܐ	1952
215b	nᵊḇıyuṯā	ܢܒܝܘܬܐ	1953
215b	nᵊḇīṯā	ܢܒܝܬܐ	1954
215b	nᵊḇa	ܢܒܒ	1955
216a	nᵊḡaḏ	ܢܓܕ	1956
216a	neḡdā	ܢܓܕܐ	1957
216b	nᵊḡah	ܢܓܗ	1958
216a	nāḡuḏā	ܢܓܘܕܐ	1959
415b	nagī	ܢܓܐ	1960
217a	naḡīrā	ܢܓܝܪܐ	1961
217a	naḡīruṯā	ܢܓܝܪܘܬܐ	1962
217a	nᵊḡar	ܢܓܪ	1963
217b	naḡārā	ܢܓܪܐ	1964
217b	nad	ܢܕ	1965
217b	nᵊḏīḏā	ܢܕܝܕܐ	1966
217b	nᵊḏar	ܢܕܪ	1967
217b	neḏrā	ܢܕܪܐ	1968
218a	nahīrā	ܢܗܝܪܐ	1969
218a	nahīrā'īṯ	ܢܗܝܪܐܝܬ	1970
217b	nᵊham	ܢܗܡ	1971
217b	nᵊhar	ܢܗܪ	1972
218b	nahrā	ܢܗܪܐ	1973
218b	naweḡ (pa)	ܢܘܓ	1974
217a	nuḡrā	ܢܘܓܪܐ	1975
218b	nāḏ (pe 3sm)	ܢܘܕ	1976
218b	naudā	ܢܘܕܐ	1977
217b	nuhrā	ܢܘܗܪܐ	1978
218b	nuwāḡā	ܢܘܘܓܐ	1979
415b	nuḥ	ܢܘܚ	1980
218b	nāḥ (pe 3sm)	ܢܘܚ	1981
219a	nauḥā	ܢܘܚܐ	1982
220a	nuḥāmā	ܢܘܚܡܐ	1983
223a	nuḵāpā	ܢܘܟܦܐ	1984
223b	nuḵrāyā	ܢܘܟܪܝܐ	1985
219b	nām (pe 3sm)	ܢܘܡ	1986
219b	nāumī	ܢܘܡܐ	1987
415b	numpī	ܢܘܡܦܐ	1988
415b	nun	ܢܘܢ	1989
219b	nunā	ܢܘܢܐ	1990
219b	nausā	ܢܘܣܐ	1991
219b	nāp (pe 3sm)	ܢܘܦ	1992
220a	nurā	ܢܘܪܐ	1993
232a	nušaqtā	ܢܘܫܩܬܐ	1994

Pg/Col	Pronunciation	Word	No
415b	naḥum	ܢܚܘܡ	1995
415b	nāḥur	ܢܚܘܪ	1996
220a	naḥlā	ܢܚܠܐ	1997
220a	naḥem (pa)	ܢܚܡ	1998
220a	nᵊḥāmtā	ܢܚܡܬܐ	1999
220a	nᵊḥāšā	ܢܚܫܐ	2000
415b	naḥšun	ܢܚܫܘܢ	2001
220b	nᵊḥet	ܢܚܬ	2002
221a	naḥtā	ܢܚܬܐ	2003
221b	nāṭurā	ܢܛܘܪܐ	2004
221b	nᵊṭurtā	ܢܛܘܪܬܐ	2005
221a	nᵊṭar	ܢܛܪ	2006
415b	nīger	ܢܝܓܪ	2007
219a	nᵊyāḥā	ܢܝܚܐ	2008
218b	nīḥā	ܢܝܚܐ	2009
219a	nīḥutā	ܢܝܚܘܬܐ	2010
219a	nᵊyāḥtā	ܢܝܚܬܐ	2011
415b	nīnwāyā	ܢܝܢܘܝܐ	2012
415b	nīqādımus	ܢܝܩܕܝܡܘܣ	2013
416a	nīqāla'āus	ܢܝܩܠܐܘܣ	2014
416a	nīqanāur	ܢܝܩܢܘܪ	2015
416a	nīqāpāulīs	ܢܝܩܦܘܠܝܣ	2016
222a	nīrā	ܢܝܪܐ	2017
222a	nīšā	ܢܝܫܐ	2018
222a	nᵊkā	ܢܟܐ	2019
222b	nakultānā	ܢܟܘܠܬܢܐ	2020
222b	nᵊkīlā	ܢܟܝܠܐ	2021
222b	nᵊkīlutā	ܢܟܝܠܘܬܐ	2022
222a	nᵊkal	ܢܟܠ	2023
222b	neklā	ܢܟܠܐ	2024
222b	nᵊkas	ܢܟܣ	2025
222b	neksā	ܢܟܣܐ	2026
222b	neksᵊtā	ܢܟܣܬܐ	2027
223a	nᵊkep	ܢܟܦ	2028
223a	nakpā	ܢܟܦܐ	2029
223a	nakputā	ܢܟܦܘܬܐ	2030
223b	nakar (pa)	ܢܟܪ	2031
223b	nᵊkat	ܢܟܬ	2032
223b	nāmosā	ܢܡܘܣܐ	2033
224a	nemrā	ܢܡܪܐ	2034
224a	nānʻā	ܢܢܥܐ	2035
225b	nasī (pa)	ܢܣܐ	2036
224a	nᵊsab	ܢܣܒ	2037
225a	nᵊsāyā	ܢܣܝܐ	2038
225a	nesyunā	ܢܣܝܘܢܐ	2039
225a	nesyānā	ܢܣܝܢܐ	2040
226a	nᵊsar	ܢܣܪ	2041
226a	naʻbā	ܢܥܒܐ	2042
416a	naʻᵊmān	ܢܥܡܢ	2043
229b	nᵊpīšā	ܢܦܐܫܐ	2044
226a	nᵊpaḥ	ܢܦܚ	2045
226a	napṭīrā	ܢܦܛܝܪܐ	2046
226a	nᵊpal	ܢܦܠ	2047
226b	nᵊpas	ܢܦܣ	2048

Pg/Col	Pronunciation	Word	No
227a	nəp̄aṣ	ܢܦܨ	2049
227a	nəp̄aq	ܢܦܩ	2050
228a	nep̄qəṯā	ܢܦܩܬܐ	2051
228b	nap̄šā	ܢܦܫܐ	2052
229b	nap̄šānāyā	ܢܦܫܢܝܐ	2053
226a	nəp̄āṯā	ܢܦܬܐ	2054
416a	nap̄taḥ	ܢܦܬܚ	2055
416a	nap̄talī	ܢܦܬܠܝ	2056
229b	nəṣā	ܢܨܐ	2057
230a	nəṣaḇ	ܢܨܒ	2058
230a	neṣbəṯā	ܢܨܒܬܐ	2059
230a	nəṣaḥ	ܢܨܚ	2060
230a	naṣāyā	ܢܨܝܐ	2061
230a	naṣīḥā	ܢܨܝܚܐ	2062
230b	nəṣal	ܢܨܠ	2063
416a	nāṣrāyā	ܢܨܪܝܐ	2064
416a	nāṣraṯ	ܢܨܪܬ	2065
230b	nəqā	ܢܩܐ	2066
230b	nəqaḇ	ܢܩܒ	2067
230b	neqbəṯā	ܢܩܒܬܐ	2068
230b	naqdā	ܢܩܕܐ	2069
230b	neqyā	ܢܩܝܐ	2070
231a	naqīp̄ā	ܢܩܝܦܐ	2071
230b	neq'ā	ܢܩܥܐ	2072
230b	nəqep̄	ܢܩܦ	2073
231a	nəqar	ܢܩܪ	2074
231a	nəqaš	ܢܩܫ	2075
231b	nārgā	ܢܪܓܐ	2076
231b	nardīn	ܢܪܕܝܢ	2077
416a	nırī	ܢܪܝ	2078
416b	narqısāus	ܢܪܩܣܘܣ	2079
231b	nəšaḇ	ܢܫܒ	2080
232a	nəšaq	ܢܫܩ	2081
232a	nešrā	ܢܫܪܐ	2082
416b	nāṯān	ܢܬܢ	2083
416b	naṯana'īl	ܢܬܢܐܝܠ	2084
232a	nəṯap̄	ܢܬܦ	2085
233a	sēḇ	ܣܐܒ	2086
233a	sīmā	ܣܐܡܐ	2087
233a	sēn	ܣܐܢ	2088
416b	sarāuna	ܣܐܪܘܢܐ	2089
233a	saṯā	ܣܐܬܐ	2090
242b	sāḇā	ܣܒܐ	2091
233b	səḇal	ܣܒܠ	2092
416b	seḇasṭī	ܣܒܣܛܝܐ	2093
233b	səḇa'	ܣܒܥ	2094
234a	sab'ā	ܣܒܥܐ	2095
234a	saḇ'ā	ܣܒܥܐ	2096
234a	səḇar	ܣܒܪ	2097
235b	sabar (pa)	ܣܒܪ	2098
234b	saḇrā	ܣܒܪܐ	2099
235a	səḇarṯā	ܣܒܪܬܐ	2100
236b	səḡā	ܣܓܐ	2101
238a	səḡeḏ	ܣܓܕ	2102

Pg/Col	Pronunciation	Word	No
238a	sāgudā	ܣܓܘܕܐ	2103
238a	sᵊgulā	ܣܓܘܠܐ	2104
236b	sagıyā'	ܣܓܝܐܐ	2105
237b	sagī'utā	ܣܓܝܐܘܬܐ	2106
238b	sᵊgīpā	ܣܓܝܦܐ	2107
238b	sᵊgap	ܣܓܦ	2108
238b	sadā	ܣܕܐ	2109
416b	sᵊdum	ܣܕܘܡ	2110
238b	sedunā	ܣܕܘܢܐ	2111
238b	sᵊdeq	ܣܕܩ	2112
238b	sedqā	ܣܕܩܐ	2113
239a	sᵊhed	ܣܗܕ	2114
239a	sāhdā	ܣܗܕܐ	2115
239a	sāhdutā	ܣܗܕܘܬܐ	2116
240a	sahrā	ܣܗܪܐ	2117
240a	sᵊwe (pp)	ܣܘܐ	2118
240a	sayeb (pa)	ܣܘܒ	2119
240b	sāg (pe 3sm)	ܣܘܓ	2120
236b	sugā'	ܣܘܓܐܐ	2121
238b	sudārā	ܣܘܕܪܐ	2122
240b	suwāḥā	ܣܘܘܚܐ	2123
240b	sᵊwah	ܣܘܚ	2124
242a	suḥāpā	ܣܘܚܦܐ	2125
242a	suṭmā	ܣܘܛܡܐ	2126
240a	suyābā	ܣܘܒܐ	2127
240b	sāk (pe 3sm)	ܣܘܟ	2128
241a	saukā	ܣܘܟܐ	2129
244a	sukālā	ܣܘܟܠܐ	2130
241a	saukānā	ܣܘܟܢܐ	2131
246b	sulāqā	ܣܘܠܩܐ	2132
248a	sumāqā	ܣܘܡܩܐ	2133
416b	sunṭīka	ܣܘܢܛܝܟܐ	2134
249a	sunqānā	ܣܘܢܩܢܐ	2135
241a	susyā	ܣܘܣܝܐ	2136
416b	susīpaṭrāus	ܣܘܣܝܦܛܪܘܣ	2137
416b	sustenīs	ܣܘܣܬܢܝܣ	2138
244a	saya' (pa)	ܣܘܥ	2139
249b	su'rānā	ܣܘܥܪܢܐ	2140
241a	sāp	ܣܘܦ	2141
241a	saupā	ܣܘܦܐ	2142
416b	supaṭrāus	ܣܘܦܛܪܘܣ	2143
251b	surādā	ܣܘܪܕܐ	2144
333b	surhābā	ܣܘܪܗܒܐ	2145
417a	surıya	ܣܘܪܝܐ	2146
241b	sᵊḥā	ܣܚܐ	2147
241b	saḥwā	ܣܚܘܐ	2148
241b	sᵊḥāyā	ܣܚܝܐ	2149
241b	sᵊḥap	ܣܚܦ	2150
241b	sᵊḥātā	ܣܚܬܐ	2151
242a	sᵊṭā	ܣܛܐ	2152
242a	sᵊṭam	ܣܛܡ	2153
242a	sāṭānā	ܣܛܢܐ	2154
242b	seṭrā	ܣܛܪܐ	2155

Pg/Col	Pronunciation	Word	No
242b	saib̲ut̲ā	ܣܝܒܘܬܐ	2156
236a	saibart̲ā	ܣܝܒܪܬܐ	2157
240b	sᵊyāgā	ܣܝܓܐ	2158
242b	sām (pe 3sm)	ܣܝܡ	2159
243b	sᵊyāmā	ܣܝܡܐ	2160
417a	sīmun	ܣܝܡܘܢ	2161
243b	sīmt̲ā	ܣܝܡܬܐ	2162
		ܣܝܡܬ ܒܢܝܐ	2163
243b	sīmat̲ bᵊnāyā		
244a	sᵊyānā	ܣܝܢܐ	2164
417a	sīnai	ܣܝܢܝ	2165
244a	sīʿᵊt̲ā	ܣܝܥܬܐ	2166
244a	saip̄ā	ܣܝܦܐ	2167
244a	sakī (pa)	ܣܟܐ	2168
240b	sākā	ܣܟܐ	2169
244b	sakult̲ānā	ܣܟܘܠܬܢܐ	2170
244a	sakel (pa)	ܣܟܠ	2171
245a	’askel (aph)	ܣܟܠ	2172
244b	sak̲lā	ܣܟܠܐ	2173
244b	sak̲lut̲ā	ܣܟܠܘܬܐ	2174
245b	sᵊkar	ܣܟܪ	2175
245b	sakra	ܣܟܪܐ	2176
417a	sᵊkaryuṭā	ܣܟܪܝܘܛܐ	2177
245b	sᵊlā	ܣܠܐ	2178
417a	silwanāus	ܣܠܘܢܘܣ	2179
417a	silwanāus	ܣܠܘܢܘܣ	2180
417a	selāuqiya	ܣܠܘܩܝܐ	2181
417a	salmun	ܣܠܡܘܢ	2182
417b	salamāuna	ܣܠܡܘܢܐ	2183
417b	salamina	ܣܠܡܝܢܐ	2184
246a	sᵊleq	ܣܠܩ	2185
247a	samā	ܣܡܐ	2186
417b	samāus	ܣܡܘܣ	2187
417b	sᵊmurna	ܣܡܘܪܢܐ	2188
417b	samuṭra’qī	ܣܡܘܛܪܐܩܝ	2189
247a	sᵊmī	ܣܡܝ	2190
247a	samyā	ܣܡܝܐ	2191
247a	sᵊmīd̲ā	ܣܡܝܕܐ	2192
247b	sᵊmīk̲ā	ܣܡܝܟܐ	2193
247b	sᵊmak̲	ܣܡܟ	2194
247b	sāmk̲ā	ܣܡܟܐ	2195
247b	sᵊmāk̲ā	ܣܡܟܐ	2196
248a	semālā	ܣܡܠܐ	2197
248a	sᵊmaq	ܣܡܩ	2198
248a	san	ܣܢ	2199
248a	sᵊnā	ܣܢܐ	2200
248b	sᵊnē (pp)	ܣܢܐ	2201
248b	sānā’	ܣܢܐܐ	2202
249a	sanwart̲ā	ܣܢܘܪܬܐ	2203
248b	sanyā	ܣܢܝܐ	2204
248b	sᵊniyā’	ܣܢܝܐܐ	2205
248a	sᵊnīnā	ܣܢܝܢܐ	2206
249a	sᵊnīqut̲ā	ܣܢܝܩܘܬܐ	2207
248b	sᵊnaq	ܣܢܩ	2208
249a	sāsā	ܣܣܐ	2209

Pg/Col	Pronunciation	Word	No
249a	sᵊʻā	ܣܥܐ	2210
249b	sāʻurā	ܣܥܘܪܐ	2211
249a	sᵊʻar	ܣܥܪ	2212
250a	saʻrā	ܣܥܪܐ	2213
250a	sᵊʻārtā	ܣܥܪܬܐ	2214
250a	sepā	ܣܦܐ	2215
250a	sapīlā	ܣܦܝܠܐ	2216
250a	sᵊpī(n)tā	ܣܦܝܢܬܐ	2217
250b	sᵊp̄īqā	ܣܦܝܩܐ	2218
250b	sᵊp̄īqā'īṯ	ܣܦܝܩܐܝܬ	2219
250a	sapānā	ܣܦܢܐ	2220
250a	sap̄sīrā	ܣܦܣܝܪܐ	2221
250b	sᵊp̄aq	ܣܦܩ	2222
250b	sapar (pa)	ܣܦܪ	2223
250b	sep̄rā	ܣܦܪܐ	2224
251a	sāp̄rā	ܣܦܪܐ	2225
251a	sᵊp̄ārā	ܣܦܪܐ	2226
250a	sep̄ṯā	ܣܦܬܐ	2227
251a	saqā	ܣܩܐ	2228
417b	sqewa	ܣܩܘܐ	2229
308b	saquḇlā	ܣܩܘܒܠܐ	2230
417b	saqundāus	ܣܩܘܢܕܘܣ	2231
417b	sarā	ܣܪܐ	2232
251a	sᵊrā	ܣܪܐ	2233
251a	sᵊraḡ	ܣܪܓ	2234
417b	sergᵊyāus paulāus	ܣܪܓܝܘܣ ܦܘܠܘܣ	2235
251b	sᵊraḏ	ܣܪܕ	2236
251b	sārdun	ܣܪܕܘܢ	2237
417b	sardīs	ܣܪܕܝܣ	2238
418a	sāruḡ	ܣܪܘܓ	2239
251b	sᵊraḥ	ܣܪܚ	2240
251b	sᵊraṭ	ܣܪܛ	2241
251b	serṭā	ܣܪܛܐ	2242
251a	sᵊrīḡtā	ܣܪܝܓܬܐ	2243
251b	sᵊrīḏā	ܣܪܝܕܐ	2244
251b	sᵊrīqā	ܣܪܝܩܐ	2245
252a	sᵊrīqā'īṯ	ܣܪܝܩܐܝܬ	2246
252a	sᵊrīquṯā	ܣܪܝܩܘܬܐ	2247
251b	sᵊraq	ܣܪܩ	2248
418a	saraqāusa	ܣܪܩܘܣܐ	2249
252a	'astī (aph)	ܣܬܐ	2250
252a	saṯwā	ܣܬܘܐ	2251
252b	sᵊṯar	ܣܬܪ	2252
260b	ʻīḏā	ܥܐܕܐ	2253
260b	ʻāḇā	ܥܒܐ	2254
253a	ʻᵊḇaḏ	ܥܒܕ	2255
255a	ʻaḇdā	ܥܒܕܐ	2256
255a	ʻᵊḇāḏā	ܥܒܕܐ	2257
418a	ʻaḇadu	ܥܒܕܘ	2258
255b	ʻaḇdutā	ܥܒܕܘܬܐ	2259
256a	ʻāḇuḏā	ܥܒܘܕܐ	2260
257a	ʻᵊḇurā	ܥܒܘܪܐ	2261
256b	ʻᵊḇī	ܥܒܝ	2262

Pg/Col	*Pronunciation*	*Word*	*No*	*Pg/Col*	*Pronunciation*	*Word*	*No*
418a	‘əḇar	ܥܒܪ	2263	261a	‘uḏ	ܥܘܕ	2290
257a	‘āḇār	ܥܒܪ	2264	261a	’a‘īḏ (aph)	ܥܘܕ	2291
257b	‘əḇārā	ܥܒܪܐ	2265	259b	‘uḏrānā	ܥܘܕܪܢܐ	2292
257b	‘eḇrā	ܥܒܪܐ	2266	260a	‘uhdānā	ܥܘܗܕܢܐ	2293
257b	‘eḇrā’īṯ	ܥܒܪܐܝܬ	2267	418a	‘uzıyā	ܥܘܙܝܐ	2294
257b	‘eḇrāyā	ܥܒܪܝܐ	2268	261a	‘auznāyē	ܥܘܙܢܝܐ	2295
258a	‘agel (pa)	ܥܓܠ	2269	262b	‘əwīrā	ܥܘܝܪܐ	2296
258a	‘əḡal	ܥܓܠ	2270	262b	‘əwīruṯā	ܥܘܝܪܘܬܐ	2297
258a	‘eḡlā	ܥܓܠܐ	2271	261a	‘aweḵ	ܥܘܟ	2298
258a	‘əḡeltā	ܥܓܠܬܐ	2272	261b	’a‘wel (aph)	ܥܘܠ	2299
258a	‘əḡen	ܥܓܢ	2273	261a	‘ulā	ܥܘܠܐ	2300
258a	‘aḏ	ܥܕ	2274	261b	‘awālā	ܥܘܠܐ	2301
258b	‘əḏā	ܥܕܐ	2275	261b	‘aulā	ܥܘܠܐ	2302
258b	‘əḏaḵīl	ܥܕܟܝܠ	2276	261b	‘auluṯā	ܥܘܠܘܬܐ	2303
258b	‘əḏal	ܥܕܠ	2277	271b	‘umqā	ܥܘܡܩܐ	2304
258b	‘aḏlā	ܥܕܠܐ	2278	272a	‘umrā	ܥܘܡܪܐ	2305
258b	‘eḏlāyā	ܥܕܠܝܐ	2279	273b	‘undānā	ܥܘܢܕܢܐ	2306
259a	‘əḏamā	ܥܕܡܐ	2280	261b	‘āp̄ (pe 3sm)	ܥܘܦ	2307
259a	‘edānā	ܥܕܢܐ	2281	262a	‘āp̄ (pe 3sm)	ܥܘܦ	2308
260b	‘aḏ‘ıḏā	ܥܕܥܕܐ	2282	274b	‘up̄yā	ܥܘܦܝܐ	2309
259a	‘əḏar	ܥܕܪ	2283	262a	‘āq (pe 3sm)	ܥܘܩ	2310
260b	‘ı(d)tā	ܥܕܬܐ	2284	275a	‘uqāḇā	ܥܘܩܒܐ	2311
259b	‘ehaḏ	ܥܗܕ	2285	275b	‘uqəsā	ܥܘܩܣܐ	2312
260a	‘ahīḏā	ܥܗܝܕܐ	2286	262b	‘əwar	ܥܘܪ	2313
260b	‘əhen	ܥܗܢ	2287	262b	‘əwārā	ܥܘܪܐ	2314
253a	‘ubā	ܥܘܒܐ	2288	258a	‘urgālā	ܥܘܪܓܠܐ	2315
418a	‘uḇīḏ	ܥܘܒܝܕ	2289	277a	‘urlā	ܥܘܪܠܐ	2316

Pg/Col	Pronunciation	Word	No
277a	‘urluṯā	ܥܘܪܠܘܬܐ	2317
277a	‘urp̄ānā	ܥܘܪܦܢܐ	2318
278a	‘ušnā	ܥܘܫܢܐ	2319
279a	‘uṯrā	ܥܘܬܪܐ	2320
262b	‘az	ܥܙ	2321
273b	‘ezā	ܥܙܐ	2322
418a	‘āzur	ܥܙܘܪ	2323
262b	‘azīzā	ܥܙܝܙܐ	2324
262b	‘azīzā’īṯ	ܥܙܝܙܐܝܬ	2325
263a	‘əzal	ܥܙܠ	2326
263a	‘ezeqṯā	ܥܙܩܬܐ	2327
263a	‘azrurā	ܥܙܪܘܪܐ	2328
263a	‘əṭā	ܥܛܐ	2329
263b	‘əṭīp̄ā	ܥܛܝܦܐ	2330
263a	‘aṭlā	ܥܛܠܐ	2331
263a	‘aṭmā	ܥܛܡܐ	2332
263b	‘əṭap̄	ܥܛܦ	2333
263b	‘əṭar	ܥܛܪ	2334
263b	‘eṭrā	ܥܛܪܐ	2335
261a	‘əyāḏā	ܥܝܕܐ	2336
262a	‘ayīqā	ܥܝܩܐ	2337
261a	‘īlā	ܥܝܠܐ	2338
62b	‘īn baḡlē	ܥܝܢ ܥܓܠܐ	2339
418a	‘īn yāun	ܥܝܢ ܝܘܢ	2340
263b	‘aınā	ܥܝܢܐ	2341
418a	‘īr	ܥܝܪ	2342
264a	‘ār (pe 3sm)	ܥܝܪ	2343
264a	‘īrā	ܥܝܪܐ	2344
418a	‘aḵu	ܥܟܘ	2345
264b	‘al	ܥܠ	2346
266b	‘al	ܥܠ	2347
267b	‘alī (pa)	ܥܠܐ	2348
266a	‘əlaḇ	ܥܠܒ	2349
266b	‘əlāwā	ܥܠܘܐ	2350
266a	‘āluḇā	ܥܠܘܒܐ	2351
266b	‘āluḇuṯā	ܥܠܘܒܘܬܐ	2352
268a	‘alwaı	ܥܠܘܝ	2353
267b	‘elāyā	ܥܠܝܐ	2354
268a	‘əlaımā	ܥܠܝܡܐ	2355
268a	‘əlaımṯā	ܥܠܝܡܬܐ	2356
267b	‘elīṯā	ܥܠܝܬܐ	2357
265b	‘əlalṯā	ܥܠܠܬܐ	2358
268a	‘ālmā	ܥܠܡܐ	2359
269a	‘ālmāyuṯā	ܥܠܡܝܘܬܐ	2360
269a	‘almānāyā	ܥܠܡܢܝܐ	2361
266a	‘al‘el	ܥܠܥܠ	2362
266a	‘al‘ālā	ܥܠܥܠܐ	2363
265b	‘elṯā	ܥܠܬܐ	2364
267b	‘əlāṯā	ܥܠܬܐ	2365
269a	‘am	ܥܡ	2366
269b	‘amā	ܥܡܐ	2367
418b	‘ema’us	ܥܡܐܘܣ	2368
270a	‘əmaḏ	ܥܡܕ	2369
271a	‘amuḏā	ܥܡܘܕܐ	2370

Pg/Col	*Pronunciation*	*Word*	*No*	*Pg/Col*	*Pronunciation*	*Word*	*No*
271a	ʿamuṭā	ܥܡܘܛܐ	2371	273b	ʿəsaq	ܥܣܩ	2398
418b	ʿamuṣ	ܥܡܘܨ	2372	273b	ʿasqā	ܥܣܩܐ	2399
418b	ʿamurā	ܥܡܘܪܐ	2373	274a	ʿəsar	ܥܣܪ	2400
272b	ʿāmurā	ܥܡܘܪܐ	2374	274a	ʿasar (pa)	ܥܣܪ	2401
271a	ʿəmaṭ	ܥܡܛ	2375	274a	ʿesrīn	ܥܣܪܝܢ	2402
271a	ʿamṭānā	ܥܡܛܢܐ	2376			ܥܣܪܬ ܡܕ̈ܝܢܬܐ	2403
418b	ʿamīnāḏāḇ	ܥܡܝܢܕܒ	2377	418b	ʿesraṯ mədīnāṯā		
271b	ʿamīqā	ܥܡܝܩܐ	2378	274a	ʿap̄	ܥܦ	2404
272a	ʿəmīrā	ܥܡܝܪܐ	2379	274a	ʿap̄	ܥܦ	2405
271a	ʿəmal	ܥܡܠ	2380	274b	ʿəp̄ā	ܥܦܐ	2406
271b	ʿamlā	ܥܡܠܐ	2381	274b	ʿəp̄īp̄ā	ܥܦܝܦܐ	2407
418b	ʿamanuʾīl	ܥܡܢܘܐܝܠ	2382	274b	ʿəp̄aq	ܥܦܩ	2408
271b	ʿəmaṣ	ܥܡܨ	2383	274b	ʿap̄rā	ܥܦܪܐ	2409
271b	ʿəmaq	ܥܡܩ	2384	274b	ʿap̄rānā	ܥܦܪܢܐ	2410
272a	ʿəmar	ܥܡܪ	2385	274b	ʿəṣā	ܥܨܐ	2411
272b	ʿamrā	ܥܡܪܐ	2386	275a	ʿəṣaḇ	ܥܨܒ	2412
272b	ʿənā	ܥܢܐ	2387	274b	ʿeṣyayuṯā	ܥܨܝܝܘܬܐ	2413
273a	ʿənā	ܥܢܐ	2388	274b	ʿeṣyānā	ܥܨܝܢܐ	2414
272b	ʿānā	ܥܢ̈ܐ	2389	275a	ʿəṣar	ܥܨܪ	2415
273a	ʿenbəṯā	ܥܢܒܬܐ	2390	275a	ʿəqaḇ	ܥܩܒ	2416
273a	ʿənaḏ	ܥܢܕ	2391	275a	ʿeqḇā	ܥܩܒܐ	2417
273b	ʿānuḏā	ܥܢܘܕܐ	2392	275b	ʿaqem (pa)	ܥܩܡ	2418
272b	ʿənānā	ܥܢܢܐ	2393	275b	ʿəqar	ܥܩܪ	2419
273b	ʿanāṯā	ܥܢܬܐ	2394	275b	ʿeqārā	ܥܩܪܐ	2420
273b	ʿesbā	ܥܣܒܐ	2395	275b	ʿaqrā	ܥܩܪܐ	2421
418b	ʿısu	ܥܣܘ	2396	276a	ʿeqarəḇā	ܥܩܪܒܐ	2422
273b	ʿəsīqā	ܥܣܝܩܐ	2397	262a	ʿaqṯā	ܥܩܬܐ	2423

Pg/Col	Pronunciation	Word	No	Pg/Col	Pronunciation	Word	No
276a	‘ᵊrā	ܥܪܐ	2424	273b	‘atī (pa)	ܥܬܐ	2451
276a	‘ᵊrab̲	ܥܪܒ	2425	278a	‘ᵊṯed	ܥܬܕ	2452
276a	‘ᵊrab̲	ܥܪܒ	2426	278a	‘ᵊṯīḏā	ܥܬܝܕܐ	2453
276b	‘ᵊrab̲	ܥܪܒ	2427	278b	‘ᵊṯīḏā’īṯ	ܥܬܝܕܐܝܬ	2454
276b	‘erbā	ܥܪܒܐ	2428	278b	‘atīqā	ܥܬܝܩܐ	2455
276a	‘arāḇā	ܥܪܒܐ	2429	278b	‘atīquṯā	ܥܬܝܩܘܬܐ	2456
398b	‘arḇāyā	ܥܪܒܝܐ	2430	279a	‘atīrā	ܥܬܝܪܐ	2457
276b	‘ᵊrub̲tā	ܥܪܘܒܬܐ	2431	279a	‘atīrā’īṯ	ܥܬܝܪܐܝܬ	2458
277b	‘ᵊruqyā	ܥܪܘܩܝܐ	2432	278b	‘ᵊṯeq	ܥܬܩ	2459
276a	‘ᵊrurā	ܥܪܘܪܐ	2433	279a	‘ᵊṯar	ܥܬܪ	2460
276b	‘arṭel	ܥܪܛܠ	2434	418b	pa’ṭara	ܦܐܛܪܐ	2461
276b	‘arṭelāyā	ܥܪܛܠܝܐ	2435	280a	pē’	ܦܐ,	2462
276b	‘arṭelāyuṯā	ܥܪܛܠܝܘܬܐ	2436	280a	pa’yā	ܦܐܝܐ	2463
276a	‘aryā	ܥܪܝܐ	2437	289a	pīqā	ܦܐܩܐ	2464
277a	‘ᵊram	ܥܪܡ	2438	280a	pīrā	ܦܐܪܐ	2465
277a	‘armā	ܥܪܡܐ	2439	280a	pᵊgaḏ	ܦܓܕ	2466
277a	‘arsā	ܥܪܣܐ	2440	280a	pᵊguḏtā	ܦܓܘܕܬܐ	2467
277a	‘arep̄ (pa)	ܥܪܦ	2441	280a	pıḡana	ܦܓܢܐ	2468
277a	‘arpelā	ܥܪܦܠܐ	2442	280b	pᵊga‘	ܦܓܥ	2469
277b	‘ᵊraṣ	ܥܪܨ	2443	280b	paḡrā	ܦܓܪܐ	2470
277b	‘ārṣā	ܥܪܨܐ	2444	281a	paḡrānā	ܦܓܪܢܐ	2471
277b	‘ᵊraq	ܥܪܩ	2445	281a	paḡrānā’īṯ	ܦܓܪܢܐܝܬ	2472
277b	‘eraqṯā	ܥܪܩܬܐ	2446	281a	paḡrānāyā	ܦܓܪܢܝܐ	2473
278a	‘ašīnā	ܥܫܝܢܐ	2447	281a	padānā	ܦܕܢܐ	2474
278a	‘ᵊšen	ܥܫܢ	2448	281a	pᵊhā	ܦܗܐ	2475
278a	‘ᵊšaq	ܥܫܩ	2449	418b	p̄ehsṭāus	ܦܗܣܛܘܣ	2476
273b	‘etā	ܥܬܐ	2450	419a	p̄ub̲ī	ܦܘܒܐ	2477

Pg/Col	Pronunciation	Word	No
281a	pāg̱ (pe 3sm)	ܦܓ	2478
419a	p̄ug̱elāus	ܦܘܓܠܘܣ	2479
419a	puḏıs	ܦܘܕܣ	2480
282a	puḥāmā	ܦܘܚܡܐ	2481
419a	puṭıya'lāus	ܦܘܛܝܐܠܘܣ	2482
284a	pulāg̱ā	ܦܘܠܓܐ	2483
419a	paulāus	ܦܘܠܘܣ	2484
285a	pulḥānā	ܦܘܠܚܢܐ	2485
286a	pumā	ܦܘܡܐ	2486
286b	punāyā	ܦܘܢܝܐ	2487
419b	p̄unīqī	ܦܘܢܝܩܐ	2488
419b	pānīks	ܦܘܢܟܣ	2489
287a	punāqā	ܦܘܢܩܐ	2490
419b	pāuplıyāus	ܦܘܦܠܝܘܣ	2491
290a	puqāḏā	ܦܘܩܕܐ	2492
289b	puqdānā	ܦܘܩܕܢܐ	2493
281a	'ettᵊp̄īr (ethpe)	ܦܘܪ	2494
291b	purnāsā	ܦܘܪܢܣܐ	2495
291b	pursā	ܦܘܪܣܐ	2496
292b	pur'ānā	ܦܘܪܥܢܐ	2497
293b	purqānā	ܦܘܪܩܢܐ	2498
294b	puršānā	ܦܘܪܫܢܐ	2499
281a	purṯā	ܦܘܪܬܐ	2500
281b	pāš	ܦܘܫ	2501
296a	pušāḵā	ܦܘܫܟܐ	2502
296b	pušāqā	ܦܘܫܩܐ	2503
298a	putᵊqā	ܦܘܬܩܐ	2504
298a	putᵊqāyā	ܦܘܬܩܝܐ	2505
281b	paḥā	ܦܚܐ	2506
281b	paḥzā	ܦܚܙܐ	2507
281b	paḥzuṯā	ܦܚܙܘܬܐ	2508
281b	pᵊḥam	ܦܚܡ	2509
281b	peḥmā	ܦܚܡܐ	2510
282a	paḥārā	ܦܚܪܐ	2511
282a	paṭīrā	ܦܛܝܪܐ	2512
282a	paṭem (pa)	ܦܛܡ	2513
282a	peṭmā	ܦܛܡܐ	2514
419b	paṭmāus	ܦܛܡܘܣ	2515
282a	pᵊṭar	ܦܛܪ	2516
419b	patrāḇa	ܦܛܪܒܐ	2517
419b	peṭrāus	ܦܛܪܘܣ	2518
419b	pīlaḏelp̄ıya	ܦܝܠܕܠܦܝܐ	2519
285b	pīlāusup̄ā	ܦܝܠܘܣܘܦܐ	2520
285b	pīlāusāup̄uṯā	ܦܝܠܘܣܘܦܘܬܐ	2521
420a	pīlaṭāus	ܦܝܠܛܘܣ	2522
420a	pīlīṭāus	ܦܝܠܝܛܘܣ	2523
420a	pīlīmāun	ܦܝܠܝܡܘܢ	2524
420a	pīlīpāus	ܦܝܠܝܦܘܣ	2525
420a	pīlīpāus	ܦܝܠܝܦܘܣ	2526
420a	pīlīpāus	ܦܝܠܝܦܘܣ	2527
420a	pīlīpāus	ܦܝܠܝܦܘܣ	2528
420b	pīlīpāus	ܦܝܠܝܦܘܣ	2529
420b	pīlīpısāyā	ܦܝܠܝܦܣܝܐ	2530

Pg/Col	Pronunciation	Word	No	Pg/Col	Pronunciation	Word	No
420b	pīlīks	ܦܝܠܝܟܣ	2531	285b	pəlan	ܦܠܢ	2558
420b	pīlālāgāus	ܦܝܠܠܓܘܣ	2532	285b	pəla'	ܦܠܥ	2559
287a	pīnkā	ܦܝܢܟܐ	2533	285b	pel'ā	ܦܠܥܐ	2560
282a	'apīs (aph)	ܦܝܣ	2534	285b	pəlaš	ܦܠܫ	2561
282a	pəyāsā	ܦܝܣܐ	2535	420b	pampūliya	ܦܡܦܘܠܝܐ	2562
282a	pīsē	ܦܝܣܐ	2536	286a	pənā	ܦܢܐ	2563
420b	pīsīdiya	ܦܝܣܝܕܝܐ	2537	420b	pənu'īl	ܦܢܘܐܝܠ	2564
291b	pīrmā	ܦܝܪܡܐ	2538	420b	pānṭāus	ܦܢܛܘܣ	2565
283a	pakā	ܦܟܐ	2539			ܦܢܛܩܘܣܛܐ	2566
283a	pəkah	ܦܟܗ	2540	421a	penṭiqāusṭī		
283a	pakīhā	ܦܟܝܗܐ	2541	287a	paneq (pa)	ܦܢܩ	2567
283a	pakīha'īt	ܦܟܝܗܐܝܬ	2542	287a	penqītā	ܦܢܩܝܬܐ	2568
283a	pakīhutā	ܦܟܝܗܘܬܐ	2543	287a	'apes (aph)	ܦܣ	2569
283a	pəkar	ܦܟܪ	2544	287a	pesā	ܦܣܐ	2570
283b	pelētā	ܦܠܐܬܐ	2545	287b	pāsuqā	ܦܣܘܩܐ	2571
283b	pəlag	ܦܠܓ	2546	287b	pāsīqtā	ܦܣܝܩܬܐ	2572
420b	pālāg	ܦܠܓ	2547	287b	pəsaq	ܦܣܩ	2573
283b	pəleg	ܦܠܓ	2548	288a	pəsāqā	ܦܣܩܐ	2574
283b	pelgā	ܦܠܓܐ	2549	288a	pesqītā	ܦܣܩܝܬܐ	2575
420b	pəlegāun	ܦܠܓܘܢ	2550	288a	pa'	ܦܥ	2576
283b	pelgutā	ܦܠܓܘܬܐ	2551	288a	pə'al	ܦܥܠ	2577
284a	pālgutā	ܦܠܓܘܬܐ	2552	288a	pā'lā	ܦܥܠܐ	2578
284b	pəlaḥ	ܦܠܚ	2553	288b	pə'ar	ܦܥܪ	2579
285a	pālḥā	ܦܠܚܐ	2554	288b	pe'rā	ܦܥܪܐ	2580
285a	palāḥā	ܦܠܚܐ	2555	421a	papāus	ܦܦܘܣ	2581
285a	pālḥutā	ܦܠܚܘܬܐ	2556	288b	paṣī (pa)	ܦܨܐ	2582
285a	pəlaṭ	ܦܠܛ	2557	288b	pəṣaḥ	ܦܨܚ	2583

Pg/Col	Pronunciation	Word	No
289a	pᵊṣaḥ	ܦܨܚ	2584
288b	peṣḥā	ܦܨܚܐ	2585
289a	pᵊṣīḥuṯā	ܦܨܝܚܘܬܐ	2586
289a	paqeq (pa)	ܦܩ	2587
289a	pᵊqaḏ	ܦܩܕ	2588
290b	paqu'ā	ܦܩܘܥܐ	2589
290b	paqāḥ	ܦܩܚ	2590
290b	pᵊqaḥ	ܦܩܚ	2591
290b	pāqḥā	ܦܩܚܐ	2592
290b	pᵊqa'	ܦܩܥ	2593
290b	pᵊqa'tā	ܦܩܥܬܐ	2594
421a	pargī	ܦܪܓܐ	2595
291a	pᵊrāḡelā	ܦܪܓܠܐ	2596
421a	pergamāus	ܦܪܓܡܘܣ	2597
291a	pᵊraḏ	ܦܪܕ	2598
291a	pardaısā	ܦܪܕܝܣܐ	2599
291a	pᵊredtā	ܦܪܕܬܐ	2600
291b	pare(h)sıya	ܦܪܗܣܝܐ	2601
290b	parugā	ܦܪܘܓܐ	2602
421a	p̄ᵊrugya	ܦܪܘܓܝܐ	2603
292b	pāru'ā	ܦܪܘܥܐ	2604
293b	pāruqā	ܦܪܘܩܐ	2605
294b	pārušuṯā	ܦܪܘܫܘܬܐ	2606
291a	parzᵊlā	ܦܪܙܠܐ	2607
291a	pᵊraḥ	ܦܪܚ	2608
291b	parāḥā'īṯ	ܦܪܚܐܝܬ	2609
291a	pāraḥtā	ܦܪܚܬܐ	2610
421a	pārṭunatāus	ܦܪܛܘܢܛܘܣ	2611
291b	pᵊreṭur	ܦܪܛܘܪ	2612
291b	pᵊreṭāurīn	ܦܪܛܘܪܝܢ	2613
421a	prīsqıla	ܦܪܝܣܩܠܐ	2614
292a	pᵊrīstā	ܦܪܝܣܬܐ	2615
294b	pᵊrīšā	ܦܪܝܫܐ	2616
294b	pᵊrīšāyā	ܦܪܝܫܝܐ	2617
291b	pᵊraḵ	ܦܪܟ	2618
421a	pᵊrāḵārāus	ܦܪܟܪܘܣ	2619
421b	parmina	ܦܪܡܢܐ	2620
291b	parnes	ܦܪܢܣ	2621
292a	pᵊras	ܦܪܣ	2622
292a	pᵊras	ܦܪܣ	2623
292a	pᵊrāsā	ܦܪܣܐ	2624
292a	parsī	ܦܪܣܝ	2625
421b	parsıs	ܦܪܣܣ	2626
292a	pᵊra'	ܦܪܥ	2627
292b	pᵊra'	ܦܪܥ	2628
421b	p̄er'un	ܦܪܥܘܢ	2629
293a	parpa'	ܦܪܦܥ	2630
421b	parṣ	ܦܪܨ	2631
293a	parṣapā	ܦܪܨܘܦܐ	2632
293a	pᵊraq	ܦܪܩ	2633
294a	paraqlīṭā	ܦܪܩܠܝܛܐ	2634
294a	pᵊraš	ܦܪܫ	2635
295a	parāšā	ܦܪܫܐ	2636
295a	pᵊraṯ	ܦܪܬ	2637

Pg/Col	Pronunciation	Word	No
421b	p̄ərāṯ	ܦܪܬ	2638
421b	parṯwāyā	ܦܪܬܘܝܐ	2639
295a	partuṯā	ܦܪܬܘܬܐ	2640
296b	pāšurā	ܦܫܘܪܐ	2641
295b	pəšaḥ	ܦܫܚ	2642
295b	pəšaṭ	ܦܫܛ	2643
295b	pəšīġā	ܦܫܝܓܐ	2644
295b	pəšīṭā	ܦܫܝܛܐ	2645
295b	pəšīṭā'īṯ	ܦܫܝܛܐܝܬ	2646
295b	pəšīṭuṯā	ܦܫܝܛܘܬܐ	2647
296a	pəšīqā	ܦܫܝܩܐ	2648
296a	pəšīqā'īṯ	ܦܫܝܩܐܝܬ	2649
296a	peškā	ܦܫܟܐ	2650
296a	pašeq (pa)	ܦܫܩ	2651
296b	pəšar	ܦܫܪ	2652
296b	pəṯā	ܦܬܐ	2653
296b	peṯgāmā	ܦܬܓܡܐ	2654
298a	pāṯurā	ܦܬܘܪܐ	2655
297a	pəṯaḥ	ܦܬܚ	2656
296b	paṯyā	ܦܬܝܐ	2657
296b	pəṯāyā	ܦܬܝܐ	2658
297a	pəṯīḥā	ܦܬܝܚܐ	2659
297b	pəṯaḵ	ܦܬܟ	2660
297b	pəṯaḵrā	ܦܬܟܪܐ	2661
299a	ṣā'ā	ܨܐܐ	2662
299a	ṣī(1)	ܨܐܝ	2663
299a	ṣāṯā	ܨܐܬܐ	2664
299a	ṣəḇā	ܨܒܐ	2665
421b	ṣəḇa'uṯ	ܨܒܐܘܬ	2666
300a	ṣəḇuṯā	ܨܒܘܬܐ	2667
300a	ṣeḇyānā	ܨܒܝܢܐ	2668
300b	ṣəḇa'	ܨܒܥ	2669
300b	ṣeḇ'ā	ܨܒܥܐ	2670
301a	ṣabeṯ	ܨܒܬ	2671
300b	ṣeḇtā	ܨܒܬܐ	2672
301a	ṣaḏ	ܨܕ	2673
301a	ṣəḏā	ܨܕܐ	2674
301a	ṣəhā	ܨܗܐ	2675
301b	ṣahyā	ܨܗܝܐ	2676
301b	ṣahyā	ܨܗܝܐ	2677
421b	ṣehyun	ܨܗܝܘܢ	2678
301b	ṣāḏ (pe 3sm)	ܨܘܕ	2679
303a	'ettəṣīḏ (ethpe)	ܨܘܕ	2680
302a	ṣuḥīṯā	ܨܘܚܝܬܐ	2681
301b	ṣām (pe 3sm)	ܨܘܡ	2682
301b	ṣaumā	ܨܘܡܐ	2683
421b	ṣur	ܨܘܪ	2684
302a	ṣār (pe 3sm)	ܨܘܪ	2685
302a	ṣār (pe 3sm)	ܨܘܪ	2686
302a	ṣaurā	ܨܘܪܐ	2687
421b	ṣurāyā	ܨܘܪܝܐ	2688
302a	ṣurtā	ܨܘܪܬܐ	2689
302a	ṣāṯ (pe 3sm)	ܨܘܬ	2690
302a	ṣautā	ܨܘܬܐ	2691

Pg/Col	Pronunciation	Word	No	Pg/Col	Pronunciation	Word	No
302b	ṣaḥī (pa)	ܨܚܐ	2692	305b	ṣᵊp̄aḥ	ܨܦܚ	2719
302b	ṣaḥwā	ܨܚܘܐ	2693	305b	ṣāp̄aḥṯā	ܨܦܚܬܐ	2720
302b	ṣaḥnā	ܨܚܢܐ	2694	305b	ṣap̄rā	ܨܦܪܐ	2721
302b	ṣaḥnuṯā	ܨܚܢܘܬܐ	2695	305b	ṣep̄rā	ܨܦܪܐ	2722
302b	ṣeıḏ	ܨܝܕ	2696	305b	ṣıp̄rāyā	ܨܦܪܝܐ	2723
302b	ṣaıdā	ܨܝܕܐ	2697	159b	ṣep̄ṯā	ܨܦܬܐ	2724
303a	ṣayāḏā	ܨܝܕܐ	2698	305b	ṣeṣā	ܨܨܐ	2725
422a	ṣaıdān	ܨܝܕܢ	2699	305b	ṣıṣlā	ܨܨܠܐ	2726
422a	ṣaıdānāyā	ܨܝܕܢܝܐ	2700	305b	ṣᵊrā	ܨܪܐ	2727
302a	ṣayāmā	ܨܝܡܐ	2701	306a	ṣᵊraḵ	ܨܪܟ	2728
302a	ṣīrā	ܨܝܪܐ	2702	422a	ṣarpaṯ	ܨܪܦܬ	2729
303a	ṣalel (pa)	ܨܠ	2703	309b	qıḇuṯā	ܩܐܒܘܬܐ	2730
303a	ṣᵊlā	ܨܠܐ	2704	422a	qā'eın	ܩܐܡ	2731
304a	ṣᵊlaḇ	ܨܠܒ	2705	325a	qīrsā	ܩܐܪܣܐ	2732
303a	ṣᵊluṯā	ܨܠܘܬܐ	2706	307a	qabā	ܩܒܐ	2733
304a	ṣᵊlaḥ	ܨܠܚ	2707	307b	qᵊḇul	ܩܒܘܠ	2734
304a	ṣᵊlīḇā	ܨܠܝܒܐ	2708	309a	qᵊḇurā	ܩܒܘܪܐ	2735
304a	ṣalmā	ܨܠܡܐ	2709	309a	qāḇurā	ܩܒܘܪܐ	2736
304b	ṣᵊlap̄	ܨܠܦ	2710	309a	qᵊḇurtā	ܩܒܘܪܬܐ	2737
304b	ṣᵊmaḥ	ܨܡܚ	2711	307a	qᵊḇal	ܩܒܠ	2738
304b	ṣemḥā	ܨܡܚܐ	2712	308b	qᵊḇa'	ܩܒܥ	2739
304b	ṣana' (pa)	ܨܢܥ	2713	309a	qᵊḇar	ܩܒܪ	2740
304b	ṣen'ᵊṯā	ܨܢܥܬܐ	2714	309a	qaḇrā	ܩܒܪܐ	2741
304b	ṣa'	ܨܥ	2715	309b	qaḏ	ܩܕ	2742
305a	ṣᵊ'īrā	ܨܥܝܪܐ	2716	309b	qadī (pa)	ܩܕܐ	2743
305a	ṣᵊ'ar	ܨܥܪ	2717	310a	qᵊdīmā	ܩܕܝܡܐ	2744
305a	ṣa'rā	ܨܥܪܐ	2718	312a	qadīšā	ܩܕܝܫܐ	2745

Pg/Col	Pronunciation	Word	No
312a	qadīšuṯā	ܩܕܝܫܘܬܐ	2746
309b	qᵊḏālā	ܩܕܠܐ	2747
309b	qᵊḏam	ܩܕܡ	2748
310a	qᵊḏām	ܩܕܡ	2749
310b	qaḏmā	ܩܕܡܐ	2750
310b	qaḏmāyā	ܩܕܡܝܐ	2751
311a	qaḏmāyaṯ	ܩܕܡܝܬ	2752
422a	qeḏrun	ܩܕܪܘܢ	2753
311b	qadeš	ܩܕܫ	2754
422a	qāu	ܩܘ	2755
312b	qawī (pa)	ܩܘܐ	2756
422a	qāwarṭāus	ܩܐܪܛܘܣ	2757
308b	qubālā	ܩܘܒܠܐ	2758
309b	quḇernīṭī	ܩܘܒܪܢܝܛܐ	2759
422a	quḏa	ܩܘܕܐ	2760
311a	quḏmā	ܩܘܕܡܐ	2761
311b	quḏšā	ܩܘܕܫܐ	2762
317a	quṭā'ā	ܩܘܛܥܐ	2763
312b	qᵊwayā	ܩܘܝܐ	2764
315a	quyāmā	ܩܘܝܡܐ	2765
318b	quluniya	ܩܘܠܘܢܝܐ	2766
318b	qulāsā	ܩܘܠܣܐ	2767
422a	qulasāus	ܩܘܠܣܘܣ	2768
318a	qulṯā	ܩܘܠܬܐ	2769
313a	qām (pe 3sm)	ܩܐܡ	2770
314b	qaumā	ܩܘܡܐ	2771
314b	qaumṯā	ܩܘܡܬܐ	2772
320a	qunāumāun	ܩܘܢܘܡܘܢ	2773
422a	qusam	ܩܘܣܡ	2774
320b	qup̄īnā	ܩܘܦܝܢܐ	2775
420b	quprāus	ܩܘܦܪܘܣ	2776
324a	qurāḇā	ܩܘܪܒܐ	2777
323b	qurbānā	ܩܘܪܒܢܐ	2778
422b	qurāḥ	ܩܘܪܚ	2779
324b	qurṭbā	ܩܘܪܛܒܐ	2780
315b	quriya	ܩܘܪܝܐ	2781
422b	qurīnī	ܩܘܪܝܢܐ	2782
422b	qurīnāus	ܩܘܪܝܢܘܣ	2783
422b	qurīnāyā	ܩܘܪܝܢܝܐ	2784
422b	qurīnṯāus	ܩܘܪܝܢܬܘܣ	2785
422b	qurīnṯāyā	ܩܘܪܝܢܬܝܐ	2786
422b	qurnīliyāus	ܩܘܪܢܝܠܝܘܣ	2787
325b	quršā	ܩܘܪܫܐ	2788
326b	quštā	ܩܘܫܬܐ	2789
317b	qᵊṭiḡrānā	ܩܛܓܪܢܐ	2790
317b	qᵊṭiḡrānuṯā	ܩܛܓܪܢܘܬܐ	2791
316a	qāṭulā	ܩܛܘܠܐ	2792
317a	qaṭīna	ܩܛܝܢܐ	2793
317a	qᵊṭīrā	ܩܛܝܪܐ	2794
317b	qᵊṭīrānā	ܩܛܝܪܢܐ	2795
315b	qᵊṭal	ܩܛܠ	2796
316a	qeṭlā	ܩܛܠܐ	2797
316b	qeṭmā	ܩܛܡܐ	2798
317a	qᵊṭan	ܩܛܢ	2799

Pg/Col	Pronunciation	Word	No
422b	qāṭnē	ܩܛܢܐ	2800
317a	qᵊṭaʿ	ܩܛܥ	2801
317a	qᵊṭap̄	ܩܛܦ	2802
317a	qᵊṭar	ܩܛܪ	2803
317b	qeṭrā	ܩܛܪܐ	2804
317b	qaṭreḡ	ܩܛܪܓ	2805
314b	qāyumā	ܩܝܘܡܐ	2806
317b	qaıṭā	ܩܝܛܐ	2807
317b	qaıṭunā	ܩܝܛܘܢܐ	2808
317b	qaıṭunqānā	ܩܝܛܘܢܩܢܐ	2809
422b	qīlīqiya	ܩܝܠܝܩܝܐ	2810
315a	qayāmā	ܩܝܡܐ	2811
314b	qᵊyāmā	ܩܝܡܐ	2812
314b	qᵊyamtā	ܩܝܡܬܐ	2813
319b	qīnḏunāus	ܩܝܢܕܘܢܘܣ	2814
318a	qaınāyā	ܩܝܢܝܐ	2815
423a	qaınan	ܩܝܢܢ	2816
423a	qaınan	ܩܝܢܢ	2817
318a	qıntā	ܩܝܢܬܐ	2818
318a	qaısā	ܩܝܣܐ	2819
423a	qayāp̄ā	ܩܝܦܐ	2820
423a	qīš	ܩܝܫ	2821
326b	qīṯārā	ܩܝܬܪܐ	2822
326b	qīṯāruḏā	ܩܝܬܪܘܕܐ	2823
318a	qal	ܩܠ	2824
313a	qālā	ܩܠܐ	2825
423a	qᵊlauḏıya	ܩܠܘܕܝܐ	2826
423a	qᵊlauḏıyāus	ܩܠܘܕܝܘܣ	2827
318b	qᵊlīḏā	ܩܠܝܕܐ	2828
423a	qᵊleyāupa	ܩܠܝܘܦܐ	2829
423a	qᵊleyāupa	ܩܠܝܘܦܐ	2830
318a	qalīla	ܩܠܝܠܐ	2831
423a	qᵊlımīs	ܩܠܡܝܣ	2832
318b	qales (pa)	ܩܠܣ	2833
318b	qᵊlap̄	ܩܠܦ	2834
318b	qᵊlāp̄ṯa	ܩܠܦܬܐ	2835
318b	qamḥā	ܩܡܚܐ	2836
318b	qᵊmaṭ	ܩܡܛ	2837
318b	qemṭā	ܩܡܛܐ	2838
319a	qamṣā	ܩܡܨܐ	2839
319a	qan	ܩܢ	2840
319a	qenā	ܩܢܐ	2841
319a	qᵊnā	ܩܢܐ	2842
423b	qanḏaq	ܩܢܕܩ	2843
319b	qanuṭᵊṯānā	ܩܢܘܛܬܢܐ	2844
320a	qᵊnumā	ܩܢܘܡܐ	2845
319b	qᵊnaṭ	ܩܢܛ	2846
319b	qenṭā	ܩܢܛܐ	2847
319b	qentrunā	ܩܢܛܪܘܢܐ	2848
319b	qanyā	ܩܢܝܐ	2849
423b	qᵊnıḏāus	ܩܢܝܕܘܣ	2850
319b	qanīṭā	ܩܢܝܛܐ	2851
319a	qenyānā	ܩܢܝܢܐ	2852
423b	qankre'us	ܩܢܩܪܐܘܣ	2853

Pg/Col	*Pronunciation*	*Word*	*No*
423b	qᵊnānāyā	ܩܢܢܝܐ	2854
320a	qesṭā	ܩܣܛܐ	2855
320a	qesṭunārā	ܩܣܛܘܢܪܐ	2856
423b	qesar	ܩܣܪ	2857
423b	qesarya	ܩܣܪܝܐ	2858
423b	qesarıya dᵊpīlīpāus	ܩܣܪܝܐ ܕܦܝܠܝܦܘܣ	2859
320a	qᵊʻā	ܩܥܐ	2860
320b	qᵊʻaḏ	ܩܥܕ	2861
320b	qᵊʻāṯā	ܩܥܬܐ	2862
423b	qapaḏuqıya	ܩܦܕܘܩܝܐ	2863
320b	qᵊp̄aḥ	ܩܦܚ	2864
321a	qᵊp̄as	ܩܦܣ	2865
321a	qᵊp̄āsā	ܩܦܣܐ	2866
321a	qaṣ	ܩܨ	2867
321a	qᵊṣā	ܩܨܐ	2868
321a	qaṣyā	ܩܨܝܐ	2869
321a	qᵊṣāyā	ܩܨܝܐ	2870
321b	qᵊṣam	ܩܨܡ	2871
321b	qeṣmā	ܩܨܡܐ	2872
321b	qar	ܩܪ	2873
321b	qᵊrā	ܩܪܐ	2874
323a	qᵊreḇ	ܩܪܒ	2875
323b	qᵊrāḇā	ܩܪܒܐ	2876
325b	qrusṭalāus	ܩܪܘܣܛܠܠܘܣ	2877
424a	qrıṭī	ܩܪܛܐ	2878
324a	qarīḇā	ܩܪܝܒܐ	2879

Pg/Col	*Pronunciation*	*Word*	*No*
324a	qarīḇuṯā	ܩܪܝܒܘܬܐ	2880
322b	qeryānā	ܩܪܝܢܐ	2881
424a	qrīspāus	ܩܪܝܣܦܘܣ	2882
424a	qrīsqus	ܩܪܝܣܩܘܣ	2883
321b	qarīrā	ܩܪܝܪܐ	2884
325b	qarīša	ܩܪܝܫܐ	2885
324b	qᵊrīṯā	ܩܪܝܬܐ	2886
324b	qārīṯā	ܩܪܝܬܐ	2887
322b	qᵊrāıṯā	ܩܪܝܬܐ	2888
325a	qarkeḏnā	ܩܪܟܕܢܐ	2889
325a	qᵊram	ܩܪܡ	2890
325a	qarnā	ܩܪܢܐ	2891
424a	qarpāus	ܩܪܦܘܣ	2892
325b	qᵊraṣ	ܩܪܨ	2893
325b	qarṣā	ܩܪܨܐ	2894
325b	qarqurā	ܩܪܩܘܪܐ	2895
325b	qarqap̄tā	ܩܪܩܦܬܐ	2896
325b	qᵊraš	ܩܪܫ	2897
326a	qaš	ܩܫ	2898
326b	qašī (pa)	ܩܫܐ	2899
326a	qašyā	ܩܫܝܐ	2900
326a	qašyā'īṯ	ܩܫܝܐܝܬ	2901
326a	qašyuṯā	ܩܫܝܘܬܐ	2902
326a	qašīšā	ܩܫܝܫܐ	2903
326a	qašīšuṯā	ܩܫܝܫܘܬܐ	2904
326b	qeštā	ܩܫܬܐ	2905
337b	rāzā	ܪܐܙܐ	2906

Pg/Col	Pronunciation	Word	No
327a	rab̲	ܪܒ	2907
327a	rabā	ܪܒܐ	2908
327b	rab̲ baıtā	ܪܒ ܒܝܬܐ	2909
328a	rab̲ ḥailā	ܪܒ ܚܝܠܐ	2910
328a	rab̲ kāhnā	ܪܒ ܟܗܢܐ	2911
328a	rab̲ kumrā	ܪܒ ܟܘܡܪܐ	2912
		ܪܒ ܟܢܘܫܬܐ	2913
328a	rab̲ kᵊnuštā		
329a	rᵊb̲ā	ܪܒܐ	2914
328b	rabulī	ܪܒܘܠܝ	2915
328b	rebwāṯā	ܪܒܘܬܐ	2916
328b	rabuṯā	ܪܒܘܬܐ	2917
328b	rabī	ܪܒܝ	2918
330a	rᵊb̲ī'āyā	ܪܒܝܥܝܐ	2919
329a	reb̲īṯā	ܪܒܝܬܐ	2920
330a	rᵊb̲a'	ܪܒܥ	2921
330a	rᵊb̲a'	ܪܒܥ	2922
330a	reb̲'ā	ܪܒܥܐ	2923
		ܪܒܬ ܒܝܬܘܬܐ	2924
328b	rabaṯ baıtuṯā		
330a	rağ	ܪܓ	2925
330b	rᵊğez	ܪܓܙ	2926
330b	rᵊğīğā	ܪܓܝܓܐ	2927
330b	rᵊğīğāṯā	ܪܓܝܓܬܐ	2928
424a	reğyun	ܪܓܝܘܢ	2929
332a	rᵊğīšā	ܪܓܝܫܐ	2930
331b	'eṯrᵊğel (ethpe)	ܪܓܠ	2931

Pg/Col	Pronunciation	Word	No
331a	reğlā	ܪܓܠܐ	2932
331b	rağālā	ܪܓܠܐ	2933
331b	rᵊgeltā	ܪܓܠܬܐ	2934
331b	rᵊğam	ܪܓܡ	2935
332a	rᵊğaš	ܪܓܫ	2936
332a	reğšā	ܪܓܫܐ	2937
330b	reğṯā	ܪܓܬܐ	2938
332a	rᵊḏā	ܪܕܐ	2939
332b	rāḏuyā	ܪܕܘܝܐ	2940
333a	rāḏupā	ܪܕܘܦܐ	2941
333a	rᵊḏup̄yā	ܪܕܘܦܝܐ	2942
332b	rāḏyā	ܪܕܝܐ	2943
333a	rᵊḏīp̄uṯā	ܪܕܝܦܘܬܐ	2944
332b	rᵊḏap̄	ܪܕܦ	2945
333b	rᵊheb̲	ܪܗܒ	2946
333b	rahᵊb̲unā	ܪܗܒܘܢܐ	2947
334a	r(h)omī	ܪܗܘܡܝܐ	2948
334a	r(h)omā'īṯ	ܪܗܘܡܐܝܬ	2949
334a	r(h)omāyā	ܪܗܘܡܝܐ	2950
		ܪܗܘܡܝܘܬܐ	2951
334a	r(h)omāyuṯā		
334a	rᵊheṭ	ܪܗܛ	2952
334b	rehṭā	ܪܗܛܐ	2953
340a	rehṭrā	ܪܗܛܪܐ	2954
333b	rᵊhīb̲ā	ܪܗܝܒܐ	2955
334b	rᵊwā	ܪܘܐ	2956
334b	rāb̲	ܪܘܒ	2957

Pg/Col	Pronunciation	Word	No
334b	raubā	ܪܘܒܐ	2958
424a	rubeıl	ܪܘܒܝܠ	2959
330a	ruḇʻā	ܪܘܒܥܐ	2960
331a	rugzā	ܪܘܓܙܐ	2961
424a	rāudē	ܪܘܕܐ	2962
424a	rāudāus	ܪܘܕܘܣ	2963
335a	rᵊwaz	ܪܘܙ	2964
335a	rᵊwāzā	ܪܘܙܐ	2965
340a	rᵊwaḥ	ܪܘܚ	2966
336a	’arīḥ (aph)	ܪܘܚ	2967
335a	ruḥā	ܪܘܚܐ	2968
336a	ruḥānā	ܪܘܚܢܐ	2969
336a	ruḥānā’īt	ܪܘܚܢܐܝܬ	2970
336a	ruḥānāyā	ܪܘܚܢܝܐ	2971
339a	ruḥāpā	ܪܘܚܦܐ	2972
339a	ruḥqā	ܪܘܚܩܐ	2973
336a	rᵊwāḥtā	ܪܘܚܬܐ	2974
334b	rawāyā	ܪܘܝܐ	2975
334b	rawayutā	ܪܘܝܘܬܐ	2976
336a	rᵊwīḥā	ܪܘܝܚܐ	2977
336b	rām (pe 3sm)	ܪܘܡ	2978
336b	raumā	ܪܘܡܐ	2979
342b	rumḥā	ܪܘܡܚܐ	2980
337b	rumrāmā	ܪܘܡܪܡܐ	2981
345a	ruʻāmā	ܪܘܥܡܐ	2982
337b	ruʻᵊtā	ܪܘܥܬܐ	2983
424a	rupāus	ܪܘܦܘܣ	2984
345b	ruqā	ܪܘܩܐ	2985
328b	raurᵊbā’ıt	ܪܘܪܒܐܝܬ	2986
346b	rušmā	ܪܘܫܡܐ	2987
347a	rušʻā	ܪܘܫܥܐ	2988
424b	rāḥāb	ܪܚܒ	2989
424b	rᵊḥabʻam	ܪܚܒܥܡ	2990
337b	raḥyā	ܪܚܝܐ	2991
424b	rāḥeıl	ܪܚܝܠ	2992
338a	rᵊḥīma	ܪܚܝܡܐ	2993
339b	raḥīqā	ܪܚܝܩܐ	2994
337b	rᵊḥem	ܪܚܡ	2995
338a	rāḥmā	ܪܚܡܐ	2996
338a	raḥmē	ܪ̈ܚܡܐ	2997
338b	rāḥmutā	ܪܚܡܘܬܐ	2998
338b	reḥmᵊtā	ܪܚܡܬܐ	2999
338b	raḥmᵊtānā	ܪܚܡܬܢܐ	3000
339a	raḥep	ܪܚܦ	3001
339a	rᵊḥeq	ܪܚܩ	3002
339b	rᵊḥeš	ܪܚܫ	3003
339b	raḥšā	ܪܚܫܐ	3004
339b	rᵊṭeb	ܪܛܒ	3005
339b	raṭībā	ܪܛܝܒܐ	3006
340a	rᵊṭen	ܪܛܢ	3007
340a	reṭnā	ܪܛܢܐ	3008
340a	rīḥā	ܪܝܚܐ	3009
340b	rīšā	ܪܝܫܐ	3010
340b	rīšāyā	ܪܝܫܝܐ	3011

Pg/Col	Pronunciation	Word	No
341a	rīšītā	ܪܝܫܝܬܐ	3012
341a	rīšānuṯā	ܪܝܫܢܘܬܐ	3013
341a	raḵ	ܪܟ	3014
341a	rᵊḵeḇ	ܪܟܒ	3015
341b	rāḵbā	ܪܟܒܐ	3016
341a	raḵīḵā	ܪܟܝܟܐ	3017
341b	rᵊḵen	ܪܟܢ	3018
341b	rᵊḵaš	ܪܟܫ	3019
341b	raḵšā	ܪܟܫܐ	3020
341b	rᵊmā	ܪܡܐ	3021
336b	rāmā	ܪܡܐ	3022
342b	rᵊmaz	ܪܡܙ	3023
343a	ramšā	ܪܡܫܐ	3024
424b	rāmṯā	ܪܡܬܐ	3025
336b	rāmṯā	ܪܡܬܐ	3026
424b	rāmṯā	ܪܡܬܐ	3027
343a	rᵊnā	ܪܢܐ	3028
343a	renyā	ܪܢܝܐ	3029
343a	ras	ܪܣ	3030
424b	rāsā	ܪܣܐ	3031
343a	rᵊsīsā	ܪܣܝܣܐ	3032
343a	rᵊsāsā	ܪܣܣܐ	3033
343b	ra‘	ܪܥ	3034
343b	rᵊ‘ā	ܪܥܐ	3035
344b	’eṯra‘ī (ethpa)	ܪܥܐ	3036
344a	ra‘ī (pa)	ܪܥܐ	3037
424b	rᵊ‘uṯ	ܪܥܘܬ	3038
343b	rā‘yā	ܪܥܝܐ	3039
344a	re‘yā	ܪܥܝܐ	3040
344a	re‘yānā	ܪܥܝܢܐ	3041
343b	rᵊ‘ī‘ā	ܪܥܝܥܐ	3042
344b	rᵊ‘el	ܪܥܠ	3043
345a	rᵊ‘em	ܪܥܡ	3044
345a	ra‘mā	ܪܥܡܐ	3045
337b	’ar‘eṯ	ܪܥܬ	3046
345a	rap̄	ܪܦ	3047
345a	rᵊp̄ā	ܪܦܐ	3048
345a	rap̄yā	ܪܦܝܐ	3049
424b	rᵊp̄ān	ܪܦܢ	3050
345a	rᵊp̄āp̄ā	ܪܦܦܐ	3051
424b	rap̄qā	ܪܦܩܐ	3052
345b	rap̄šā	ܪܦܫܐ	3053
345b	rᵊp̄aṯ	ܪܦܬ	3054
345b	rᵊṣīp̄tā	ܪܨܝܦܬܐ	3055
345b	rᵊṣap̄	ܪܨܦ	3056
345b	raq	ܪܩ	3057
345b	raqa	ܪܩܐ	3058
346a	rᵊqaḏ	ܪܩܕ	3059
346a	rᵊqa‘	ܪܩܥ	3060
346a	rᵊšā	ܪܫܐ	3061
346b	’aršī (aph)	ܪܫܐ	3062
346a	rešyānā	ܪܫܝܢܐ	3063
346b	rešyānā	ܪܫܝܢܐ	3064
347a	rašī‘ā	ܪܫܝܥܐ	3065

Pg/Col	Pronunciation	Word	No	Pg/Col	Pronunciation	Word	No
346b	rᵊšam	ܪܫܡ	3066	351b	šᵊḇal	ܫܒܠ	3092
347a	rᵊšaʻ	ܪܫܥ	3067	351b	šebᵊlā	ܫܒܠܐ	3093
347a	raṯ	ܪܬ	3068	351b	šᵊḇa	ܫܒܥ	3094
347a	’artī (aph)	ܪܬܐ	3069	352a	šaḇʻīn	ܫܒܥܝܢ	3095
347b	rᵊṯaḥ	ܪܬܚ	3070	352a	šᵊḇaq	ܫܒܩ	3096
347b	raṯḥā	ܪܬܚܐ	3071	353a	šaḇrā	ܫܒܪܐ	3097
347a	rᵊṯīṯā	ܪܬܝܬܐ	3072	353a	šᵊḇıštā	ܫܒܫܬܐ	3098
347a	raṯīṯā	ܪܬܝܬܐ	3073	350a	šᵊḇaṯ	ܫܒܬ	3099
348a	šīḏā	ܫܐܕܐ	3074	349b	šabᵊṯā	ܫܒܬܐ	3100
424b	šā’ul	ܫܐܘܠ	3075	353a	šᵊḇetā	ܫܒܬܐ	3101
425a	šā’ul	ܫܐܘܠ	3076	353a	šᵊḡā	ܫܓܐ	3102
348a	šēl	ܫܐܠ	3077	353b	šāḡušā	ܫܓܘܫܐ	3103
348b	šēlṯā	ܫܐܠܬܐ	3078	353b	šᵊḡušyā	ܫܓܘܫܝܐ	3104
349b	šīrāyā	ܫܐܪܝܐ	3079	353b	šaḡnī	ܫܓܢ	3105
349b	saḇ	ܫܒ	3080	353b	šᵊḡar	ܫܓܪ	3106
350a	šᵊḇā	ܫܒܐ	3081	353b	šᵊḡaš	ܫܓܫ	3107
349b	šᵊḇāḇā	ܫܒܒܐ	3082	354a	šᵊḏā	ܫܕܐ	3108
38b	šaḇhᵊrānā	ܫܒܗܪܢܐ	3083	354b	šᵊḏal	ܫܕܠ	3109
		ܫܒܗܪܢܘܬܐ	3084	354b	šadālā	ܫܕܠܐ	3110
38b	šaḇhᵊrānuṯā			354b	sadar	ܫܕܪ	3111
350b	šᵊḇaḥ	ܫܒܚ	3085	355b	šᵊhar	ܫܗܪ	3112
351b	šaḇṭā	ܫܒܛܐ	3086	355b	šahrā	ܫܗܪܐ	3113
350a	šeḇyā	ܫܒܝܐ	3087	355b	šᵊwā	ܫܘܐ	3114
350b	šᵊḇīḥā	ܫܒܝܚܐ	3088	356b	šāḇ (pe 3sm)	ܫܘܒ	3115
351b	šᵊḇīlā	ܫܒܝܠܐ	3089	356b	šaubā	ܫܘܒܐ	3116
352a	šᵊḇīʻāyā	ܫܒܝܥܝܐ	3090	39a	šuḇhārā	ܫܘܒܗܪܐ	3117
350a	šᵊḇīṯā	ܫܒܝܬܐ	3091	350a	šuḇḥā	ܫܘܒܚܐ	3118

Pg/Col	*Pronunciation*	*Word*	*No*
352b	šuḇqānā	ܫܘܒܩܢܐ	**3119**
356b	šāḡ (pe 3sm)	ܫܘܓ	**3120**
353b	šuḡnāyā	ܫܘܓܢܝܐ	**3121**
147b	šu(w)dāyā	ܫܘܘܕܝܐ	**3122**
150a	šu(w)dā'ā	ܫܘܘܕܥܐ	**3123**
357a	šu(w)zāḇā	ܫܘܘܙܒܐ	**3124**
9b	šu(w)ḥārā	ܫܘܘܚܪܐ	**3125**
356b	šauzeḇ	ܫܘܙܒ	**3126**
357a	šᵊwaḥ	ܫܘܚ	**3127**
357a	šāḥ (pe 3sm)	ܫܘܚ	**3128**
357a	'ašīḥ (aph)	ܫܘܚ	**3129**
359a	šuḥdā	ܫܘܚܕܐ	**3130**
124a	šuḥlāpā	ܫܘܚܠܦܐ	**3131**
359a	šuḥnā	ܫܘܚܢܐ	**3132**
359b	šuḥtā	ܫܘܚܬܐ	**3133**
357a	šāṭ (pe 3sm)	ܫܘܛ	**3134**
356a	šauyā	ܫܘܝܐ	**3135**
356a	šauya'īṯ	ܫܘܝܐܝܬ	**3136**
356a	šauyuṯā	ܫܘܝܘܬܐ	**3137**
364a	šulṭānā	ܫܘܠܛܢܐ	**3138**
366a	šulāmā	ܫܘܠܡܐ	**3139**
204a	šumlāyā	ܫܘܡܠܝܐ	**3140**
368b	šumnā	ܫܘܡܢܐ	**3141**
357b	šumṯā	ܫܘܡܬܐ	**3142**
373a	šunāqā	ܫܘܢܩܐ	**3143**
358a	šu'ā	ܫܘܥܐ	**3144**
256b	šu'bāḏā	ܫܘܥܒܕܐ	**3145**
373a	šu'īṯā	ܫܘܥܝܬܐ	**3146**
358a	šāp̄ (pe 3sm)	ܫܘܦ	**3147**
374a	šup̄nīnā	ܫܘܦܢܝܢܐ	**3148**
374a	šupā'ā	ܫܘܦܥܐ	**3149**
374b	šup̄rā	ܫܘܦܪܐ	**3150**
358a	šuqā	ܫܘܩܐ	**3151**
376a	šuqrā	ܫܘܩܪܐ	**3152**
358a	šᵊwar	ܫܘܪ	**3153**
358b	šurā	ܫܘܪܐ	**3154**
378b	šurāyā	ܫܘܪܝܐ	**3155**
380a	šura'ṯā	ܫܘܪܥܬܐ	**3156**
425a	šušan	ܫܘܫܢ	**3157**
358b	šušanṯā	ܫܘܫܢܬܐ	**3158**
358b	šautep̄	ܫܘܬܦ	**3159**
358b	šautāpā	ܫܘܬܦܐ	**3160**
358b	šautāp̄uṯā	ܫܘܬܦܘܬܐ	**3161**
359a	šᵊḥaḏ	ܫܚܕ	**3162**
359a	šaḥeṭ (pa)	ܫܚܛ	**3163**
359a	šᵊḥāṭā	ܫܚܛܐ	**3164**
359a	šᵊḥen	ܫܚܢ	**3165**
359b	šᵊḥaq	ܫܚܩ	**3166**
359b	šᵊḥāqā	ܫܚܩܐ	**3167**
359b	šᵊḥar	ܫܚܪ	**3168**
359b	'ešṭᵊḥar (ethpe)	ܫܚܪ	**3169**
359b	šᵊḥeṯ	ܫܚܬ	**3170**
360a	šᵊṭā	ܫܛܐ	**3171**
360a	šāṭyuṯā	ܫܛܝܘܬܐ	**3172**

Pg/Col	Pronunciation	Word	No
360a	šāṭīptā	ܫܛܝܦܬܐ	3173
360a	šᵊṭap	ܫܛܦ	3174
360a	šᵊṭārā	ܫܛܪܐ	3175
360a	šᵊyul	ܫܝܘܠ	3176
357a	šīḥuṯā	ܫܝܚܘܬܐ	3177
357b	šīṭā	ܫܝܛܐ	3178
425a	šīlā	ܫܝܠܐ	3179
425a	šīluḥā	ܫܝܠܘܚܐ	3180
425a	šīm	ܫܝܡ	3181
360b	šayen (pa)	ܫܝܢ	3182
360b	šaınā	ܫܝܢܐ	3183
358a	šᵊyāpā	ܫܝܦܐ	3184
374a	šīpurā	ܫܝܦܘܪܐ	3185
360b	šīšā	ܫܝܫܐ	3186
360b	šīšaltā	ܫܝܫܠܬܐ	3187
425a	šīṯ	ܫܝܬ	3188
360b	šᵊḵeḇ	ܫܟܒ	3189
361a	'eškaḥ	ܫܟܚ	3190
362a	šᵊḵıḥā	ܫܟܝܚܐ	3191
425a	šᵊḵīm	ܫܟܝܡ	3192
362b	šᵊḵīrā	ܫܟܝܪܐ	3193
362a	šᵊḵen	ܫܟܢ	3194
425a	šākar	ܫܟܪ	3195
362b	šakar (pa)	ܫܟܪ	3196
362b	šaḵrā	ܫܟܪܐ	3197
362b	šᵊlā	ܫܠܐ	3198
363a	šᵊladā	ܫܠܕܐ	3199
187a	šalheḇ	ܫܠܗܒ	3200
187a	šalheḇīṯā	ܫܠܗܒܝܬܐ	3201
363a	šalwā	ܫܠܘܐ	3202
425b	šālum	ܫܠܘܡ	3203
425b	šᵊlaḥ	ܫܠܚ	3204
363a	šᵊlaḥ	ܫܠܚ	3205
363b	šālāḥ	ܫܠܚ	3206
364a	šᵊlāḥā	ܫܠܚܐ	3207
364a	šᵊlaṭ	ܫܠܛ	3208
363a	šelyā	ܫܠܝܐ	3209
363a	šᵊlīḥā	ܫܠܝܚܐ	3210
363b	šᵊlīḥuṯā	ܫܠܝܚܘܬܐ	3211
364b	šalīṭā	ܫܠܝܛܐ	3212
425b	šālīm	ܫܠܝܡ	3213
425b	šālīm	ܫܠܝܡ	3214
425b	šᵊleımun	ܫܠܝܡܘܢ	3215
365a	šᵊlem	ܫܠܡ	3216
365a	šalmā	ܫܠܡܐ	3217
365a	šᵊlāmā	ܫܠܡܐ	3218
365b	šalmuṯā	ܫܠܡܘܬܐ	3219
362b	šelṯā	ܫܠܬܐ	3220
425b	šelaṯı'ıl	ܫܠܬܐܝܠ	3221
367a	šᵊmā	ܫܡܐ	3222
367b	šamah (pa)	ܫܡܗ	3223
425b	šᵊmu'eıl	ܫܡܘܐܝܠ	3224
368b	šāmunā	ܫܡܘܢܐ	3225
370a	šamu'ā	ܫܡܘܥܐ	3226

Pg/Col	Pronunciation	Word	No
367b	šəmaṭ	ܫܡܛ	3227
367b	šəmayā	ܫܡܝܐ	3228
368b	šəmayānā	ܫܡܝܢܐ	3229
368b	šamīnā	ܫܡܝܢܐ	3230
368b	šəmen	ܫܡܢ	3231
368b	šəma‘	ܫܡܥ	3232
370a	šem‘ā	ܫܡܥܐ	3233
425b	šem‘un	ܫܡܥܘܢ	3234
426a	šem‘un	ܫܡܥܘܢ	3235
426a	šem‘un	ܫܡܥܘܢ	3236
426a	šem‘un	ܫܡܥܘܢ	3237
426a	šem‘un	ܫܡܥܘܢ	3238
426a	šem‘un	ܫܡܥܘܢ	3239
426a	šem‘un	ܫܡܥܘܢ	3240
426b	šem‘un	ܫܡܥܘܢ	3241
426b	šem‘un	ܫܡܥܘܢ	3242
426b	šem‘un	ܫܡܥܘܢ	3243
426b	šem‘un	ܫܡܥܘܢ	3244
426b	šem‘un	ܫܡܥܘܢ	3245
426b	šam‘ī	ܫܡܥܝ	3246
426b	šāmrāyā	ܫܡܪܝܐ	3247
426b	šāmrīn	ܫܡܪܝܢ	3248
370b	šameš (pa)	ܫܡܫ	3249
371b	šemšā	ܫܡܫܐ	3250
426b	šemšun	ܫܡܫܘܢ	3251
371b	šenā	ܫܢܐ	3252
372a	šənā	ܫܢܐ	3253
372b	šaneḏ (pa)	ܫܢܕ	3254
372b	šendā	ܫܢܕܐ	3255
372a	šənāyā	ܫܢܝܐ	3256
372b	šaneq (pa)	ܫܢܩ	3257
372b	šənāqā	ܫܢܩܐ	3258
372b	ša(n)tā	ܫܢܬܐ	3259
372b	šenṯā	ܫܢܬܐ	3260
373a	šə‘ā	ܫܥܐ	3261
373a	še‘yā	ܫܥܝܐ	3262
357b	šā‘ṯā	ܫܥܬܐ	3263
373b	šəp̄ā	ܫܦܐ	3264
373b	šap̄yā	ܫܦܝܐ	3265
373b	šəp̄āyā	ܫܦܝܐ	3266
426b	šapīra	ܫܦܝܪܐ	3267
374b	šapīra	ܫܦܝܪܐ	3268
373b	šəp̄el	ܫܦܠ	3269
374a	šəpa‘	ܫܦܥ	3270
374a	šəp̄ar	ܫܦܪ	3271
374b	šap̄rā	ܫܦܪܐ	3272
358a	’ašqī (aph)	ܫܩܐ	3273
375a	šāqā	ܫܩܐ	3274
375a	šāqyā	ܫܩܝܐ	3275
376a	šəqīp̄ā	ܫܩܝܦܐ	3276
375a	šəqal	ܫܩܠ	3277
375b	šəqal ṭa‘nā	ܫܩܠ ܛܥܢܐ	3278
375b	šəqālā	ܫܩܠܐ	3279
376a	šar	ܫܪ	3280

Pg/Col	Pronunciation	Word	No
377b	šərā	ܫܪܐ	3281
379a	šarbəṯā	ܫܪܒܬܐ	3282
379a	šərāḡā	ܫܪܓܐ	3283
379b	šəraḡreḡ	ܫܪܓܪܓ	3284
378a	šāruṯā	ܫܪܘܬܐ	3285
379b	šaraḥ (pa)	ܫܪܚ	3286
378a	šərāyā	ܫܪܝܐ	3287
379b	šərīḥā	ܫܪܝܚܐ	3288
379b	šeryānā	ܫܪܝܢܐ	3289
379b	šeryānā	ܫܪܝܢܐ	3290
376b	šarīrā	ܫܪܝܪܐ	3291
377a	šarīrā'īṯ	ܫܪܝܪܐܝܬ	3292
377a	šarīruṯā	ܫܪܝܪܘܬܐ	3293
379b	šārīṯā	ܫܪܝܬܐ	3294
379b	šərek	ܫܪܟ	3295
379b	šarkā	ܫܪܟܐ	3296
380a	šarkānā	ܫܪܟܢܐ	3297
380a	šəra'	ܫܪܥ	3298
376a	šərārā	ܫܪܪܐ	3299
380a	šeṯ	ܫܬ	3300
380b	šəṯā	ܫܬܐ	3301
380a	šeṯēstā	ܫܬܐܣܬܐ	3302
380b	šəṯīn	ܫܬܝܢ	3303
380b	šəṯīṯāyā	ܫܬܝܬܝܐ	3304
380b	šeṯmā'	ܫܬܡܐܐ	3305
381a	šəṯeq	ܫܬܩ	3306
381b	šeṯqā	ܫܬܩܐ	3307
380b	šəṯāta'sar	ܫܬܬܥܣܪ	3308
383a	tēḡurtā	ܬܐܓܘܪܬܐ	3309
427a	ṯēwaṭīra	ܬܐܘܛܝܪܐ	3310
427a	tāmā	ܬܐܘܡܐ	3311
427a	ṯe'aupīlē	ܬܐܘܦܝܠܐ	3312
382a	ṯe'aṭrāun	ܬܐܛܪܘܢ	3313
382a	tāmā	ܬܐܡܐ	3314
382a	tīrtā	ܬܐܪܬܐ	3315
382a	tītā	ܬܐܬܐ	3316
382b	tāḇu'ā	ܬܒܘܥܐ	3317
382a	tıḇeıl	ܬܒܝܠ	3318
383a	təḇīrā	ܬܒܝܪܐ	3319
382a	teḇnā	ܬܒܢܐ	3320
382b	təḇa'	ܬܒܥ	3321
382b	təḇa'ṯā	ܬܒܥܬܐ	3322
383a	təḇar	ܬܒܪ	3323
383a	tāḡā	ܬܓܐ	3324
383a	'ettagar	ܬܓܪ	3325
383a	tagārā	ܬܓܪܐ	3326
383b	təḏā	ܬܕܐ	3327
427a	ṯadaı	ܬܕܝ	3328
77a	taḏkīṯā	ܬܕܟܝܬܐ	3329
80b	teḏmurtā	ܬܕܡܘܪܬܐ	3330
383b	tahī (pa)	ܬܗܐ	3331
383b	təhumā	ܬܗܘܡܐ	3332
383b	tahīrā	ܬܗܝܪܐ	3333
383b	təhar	ܬܗܪ	3334

Pg/Col	Pronunciation	Word	No	Pg/Col	Pronunciation	Word	No
383b	tehrā	ܬܗܪܐ	3335	163a	tautāḇuṯā	ܬܘܬܒܘܬܐ	3362
384a	tau	ܬܘ	3336	163b	tautārā	ܬܘܬܪܐ	3363
384a	tᵊwā	ܬܘܐ	3337	111b	taḥwīṯā	ܬܚܘܝܬܐ	3364
384a	tāḇ (pe 3sm)	ܬܘܒ	3338	385a	tᵊḥumā	ܬܚܘܡܐ	3365
384b	tuḇ	ܬܘܒ	3339	385b	tᵊḥeıt	ܬܚܝܬ	3366
427a	ṯauḏa	ܬܘܕܐ	3340	123b	taḥlupā	ܬܚܠܘܦܐ	3367
147a	taudīṯā	ܬܘܕܝܬܐ	3341	125b	taḥmeṣtā	ܬܚܡܨܬܐ	3368
385a	tᵊwah	ܬܘܗ	3342	126b	taḥnantā	ܬܚܢܢܬܐ	3369
383b	tuhāyā	ܬܘܗܝܐ	3343	129a	taḥpīṯā	ܬܚܦܝܬܐ	3370
385a	tauhṯā	ܬܘܗܬܐ	3344	385b	taḥtī	ܬܚܬܝ	3371
9b	tauḥārtā	ܬܘܚܪܬܐ	3345	385b	taḥtāyā	ܬܚܬܝܐ	3372
385a	tawīrā	ܬܘܝܪܐ	3346	139b	taṭlīlā	ܬܛܠܝܠܐ	3373
386a	tuḵlānā	ܬܘܟܠܢܐ	3347	384b	tᵊyābuṯā	ܬܝܒܘܬܐ	3374
191a	tulmāḏā	ܬܘܠܡܕܐ	3348	384b	tᵊyuḇā	ܬܝܘܒܐ	3375
386b	taulʻā	ܬܘܠܥܐ	3349	158b	taımnā	ܬܝܡܢܐ	3376
387a	tulṯā	ܬܘܠܬܐ	3350	385b	tᵊkaḇ	ܬܟܒ	3377
385a	tawānā	ܬܘܢܐ	3351	385b	tᵊkībāʼīṯ	ܬܟܝܒܐܝܬ	3378
388b	tuqalṯā	ܬܘܩܠܬܐ	3352	385b	tᵊkīlā	ܬܟܝܠܐ	3379
389b	tuqp̄ā	ܬܘܩܦܐ	3353	386a	tᵊkīlāʼīṯ	ܬܟܝܠܐܝܬ	3380
385a	tᵊwar	ܬܘܪ	3354	385b	tᵊkel	ܬܟܠ	3381
385a	taurā	ܬܘܪܐ	3355	386a	teklᵊṯā	ܬܟܠܬܐ	3382
389b	turgāmā	ܬܘܪܓܡܐ	3356	386a	tᵊkas	ܬܟܣ	3383
391a	tursāyā	ܬܘܪܣܝܐ	3357	175b	taḵsıṯā	ܬܟܣܝܬܐ	3384
391b	turāṣā	ܬܘܪܨܐ	3358	180b	taḵšep̄tā	ܬܟܫܦܬܐ	3385
385a	tuṯā	ܬܘܬܐ	3359	182b	taḵtušā	ܬܟܬܘܫܐ	3386
384a	tᵊwāṯā	ܬܘܬܐ	3360	386b	talel (pa)	ܬܠܠ	3387
163a	tautāḇā	ܬܘܬܒܐ	3361	386b	tᵊlā	ܬܠܐ	3388

Pg/Col	Pronunciation	Word	No
386b	talgā	ܬܠܓܐ	3389
386b	talīluṯā	ܬܠܝܠܘܬܐ	3390
190b	talmeḏ	ܬܠܡܕ	3391
190a	talmīḏā	ܬܠܡܝܕܐ	3392
386b	tᵊlāṯ	ܬܠܬ	3393
386b	teltā	ܬܠܬܐ	3394
387a	tᵊlāṯīn	ܬܠܬܝܢ	3395
387a	tᵊlāṯmā’	ܬܠܬܡܐܐ	3396
387b	tᵊmah	ܬܡܗ	3397
387b	temhā	ܬܡܗܐ	3398
387b	tamīhā	ܬܡܝܗܐ	3399
387a	tamīmā	ܬܡܝܡܐ	3400
388a	tᵊmīnāyā	ܬܡܝܢܝܐ	3401
387b	tamān	ܬܡܢ	3402
388a	tᵊmānē	ܬܡܢܐ	3403
388a	tᵊmānīn	ܬܡܢܐܝܢ	3404
388a	tᵊmānta‘sar	ܬܡܢܬܥܣܪ	3405
427a	tāmār	ܬܡܪ	3406
388b	tᵊnā	ܬܢܐ	3407
388b	tanurā	ܬܢܘܪܐ	3408
24b	tenḥāṯā	ܬܢܚܬܐ	3409
388a	tanīnā	ܬܢܝܢܐ	3410
388b	tenyānā	ܬܢܝܢܐ	3411
388b	tenyānuṯā	ܬܢܝܢܘܬܐ	3412
388a	tᵊnān	ܬܢܢ	3413
388b	tenānā	ܬܢܢܐ	3414
427a	ṯesāus	ܬܣܘܣ	3415
427a	ṯesalāunīqī	ܬܣܠܘܢܝܩܝܐ	3416
		ܬܣܠܘܢܝܩܝܐ	3417
427a	ṯesalāunıqaya		
388b	ta‘lā	ܬܥܠܐ	3418
388b	tep̄lē	ܬܦܠܐ	3419
301a	taṣbīṯā	ܬܨܒܝܬܐ	3420
389b	taqīp̄ā	ܬܩܝܦܐ	3421
389b	taqīp̄ā’īṯ	ܬܩܝܦܐܝܬ	3422
388b	tᵊqal	ܬܩܠ	3423
389a	tᵊqen	ܬܩܢ	3424
389a	taqnā	ܬܩܢܐ	3425
389a	taqnuṯā	ܬܩܢܘܬܐ	3426
389b	tᵊqep̄	ܬܩܦ	3427
389b	tārā’	ܬܪܐܐ	3428
329b	tarbīṯā	ܬܪܒܝܬܐ	3429
389b	targem	ܬܪܓܡ	3430
391a	ṯrāunāus	ܬܪܘܢܘܣ	3431
427b	taraḥ	ܬܪܚ	3432
390a	tᵊreın	ܬܪܝܢ	3433
391b	tᵊrīṣā	ܬܪܝܨܐ	3434
391b	tᵊrīṣā’īṯ	ܬܪܝܨܐܝܬ	3435
342a	tarmīṯā	ܬܪܡܝܬܐ	3436
390b	tarmālā	ܬܪܡܠܐ	3437
390b	tarnāgultā	ܬܪܢܓܘܠܬܐ	3438
390b	tarnaḡlā	ܬܪܢܓܠܐ	3439
391a	tarsī	ܬܪܣܝ	3440
391a	tᵊra‘	ܬܪܥ	3441

Pg/Col	*Pronunciation*	*Word*	*No*
391a	tar'ā	ܬܪܥܐ	3442
391b	tarā'ā	ܬܪܥܐ	3443
344a	tar'uṯā	ܬܪܥܘܬܐ	3444
344b	tar'īṯā	ܬܪܥܝܬܐ	3445
390b	tᵊre'sar	ܬܪܥܣܪ	3446
391b	tᵊraṣ	ܬܪܨ	3447
351a	tešbuḥtā	ܬܫܒܘܚܬܐ	3448
371a	tešmeštā	ܬܫܡܫܬܐ	3449
373a	tašnīqā	ܬܫܢܝܩܐ	3450
392a	tᵊša'	ܬܫܥ	3451
392a	teš'īn	ܬܫܥܝܢ	3452
373b	taš'īṯā	ܬܫܥܝܬܐ	3453